Europea
Airlines

John K Morton

MIDLAND
An imprint of
Ian Allan Publishing

European Airlines
© 2005 John K Morton

ISBN 1 85780 210 1

Published by Midland Publishing
4 Watling Drive, Hinckley, LE10 3EY, England
Tel: 01455 254 490   Fax: 01455 254 495
E-mail: midlandbooks@compuserve.com

Midland Publishing is an imprint of
Ian Allan Publishing Ltd

Worldwide distribution (except North America):
Midland Counties Publications
4 Watling Drive, Hinckley, LE10 3EY, England
Telephone: 01455 254 450   Fax: 01455 233 737
E-mail: midlandbooks@compuserve.com
www.midlandcountiessuperstore.com

North American trade distribution:
Specialty Press Publishers & Wholesalers Inc.
39966 Grand Avenue, North Branch, MN 55056
Tel: 651 277 1400   Fax: 651 277 1203
Toll free telephone: 800 895 4585
www.specialtypress.com

Design concept and layout
© 2005 Midland Publishing

Printed in England
by Ian Allan Printing Ltd
Riverdene Business Park, Molesey Road,
Hersham, Surrey, KT12 4RG

Photographs on the opposite page:

**Yugoslav Airlines Boeing 727 YU-AKG
photographed in July 1998 as it came in to
land at London Heathrow.**

**Aeroflot Ilyushin IL-86 RA-86067 was putting
in an appearance at Majorca's Palma Airport
wheh photographed in September 1997.**

Contents

Introduction

It is almost impossible to put a figure on the number of airlines currently operating in Europe, new carriers are appearing regularly whilst existing ones are disappearing, either as a result of a take-over or due to financial difficulties. Within the pages of European Airlines I have attempted to portray, through the use of over 180 of my photographs, a collection of over 100 basically passenger-carrying *European airlines* from 33 countries. I appreciate that several airlines are not included within these pages, due to space restrictions it was a difficult task deciding what should be included and what should be omitted. I trust however that my final choice meets with your approval and now invite you to feast your eyes upon the aircraft and colour schemes which some of the European carriers have to offer.

Many of the photographs reproduced in this title could not have been obtained without the help and co-operation of staff employed at certain of the airports I visited. To all these kind individuals, especially at Palma, Helsinki, Sharjah, Rhodes, Geneva and Frankfurt/Main, I wish to render my heartfelt thanks.

Dedication

This book is dedicated to my dear and beloved wife Margaret, who sadly passed away whilst the book was in its final stages of production.

Margaret was equally as interested in travel and visiting new places as I, and was regularly with me when many of the photographs in my collection, including those reproduced in this title, were shot.

She will be greatly missed both by myself and by the many friends we have made in the various countries we have visited over the past 45 years.

John K Morton, April 2005

Ireland

The island of Ireland lies off the west coast of the United Kingdom. Southern Ireland, officially known as the Republic of Ireland or Eire, occupies around 85% of the land area.

The capital of the Republic is Dublin, the base of both the state airline Aer Lingus, whose recent troubles seem to be behind them, and the expanding low-cost carrier Ryanair.

Aer Arann

Aer Arann, founded in 1969 and Dublin-based, has a fleet of ten ATR 42 and 72 aircraft. Services originally began from Galway, providing an island-hopping air service from the mainland to each of the Aran Islands. The airline was purchased by its present owner in 1994 and has become the world's fastest-growing regional airline, now carrying as many passengers in one week as it did during the entire year of 1998. One of four new routes launched in the spring of 2003 was between Galway and Manchester and it was at the latter destination that ATR 72 EI-BYO was photographed in June 2004.

Aer Lingus

Aer Lingus has been in operation since 1936 and is the national airline of Eire, providing scheduled and charter, passenger and cargo services to domestic and international destinations. With its modern fleet of Airbus and Boeing airliners the carrier operates to a number of European cities, besides scheduled services to North American points operated by their Airbus A330 aircraft. Their Airbus A321, EI-CPE, is seen on final approach to London-Heathrow in July 1999.

The Aer Lingus Boeing 737 fleet is made up of both 400 and 500 series models, all having been delivered to the carrier during the early 1990s. Two examples of each series aircraft carry the special 'dot.com' colour scheme and one of the four, 737-548 EI-CDB, was photographed in April 2003 upon arrival at Dublin.

CityJet

CityJet is another Dublin-based airline and was founded in 1993. The CityJet fleet consists of BAe 146 airliners which operate the company's scheduled services. In this March 1997 photograph, BAe 146 EI-CMY is seen as it prepares to land at Manchester. Most of CityJet's aircraft now operate services for new owners Air France and the aircraft seen in this photograph has since acquired their titles and colours.

Ryanair

Ryanair is a major Dublin-based low-fare carrier and has been in business since 1985, currently operating to more than 70 destinations between Ireland, the UK and Europe. The Ryanair fleet is made up entirely of Boeing 737s, the majority being recently delivered 800 series models. Series 200 EI-CKQ illustrates the regular livery carried on the company airliners and was photographed in April 1997 on final approach to Manchester.

Around six of the company's 737-200s were painted in special advertising liveries and EI-CNY, photographed about to depart Manchester in July 2001, has been given 'Kilkenny – The Cream of Irish Beer' titles and colours. Other advertisement schemes were for major companies such as Hertz, Jaguar and Vodafone.

Skynet

Skynet Airlines was formed with assistance from the Russian airline Aeroflot, commencing flying six days per week in June 2001 between Shannon, Amsterdam and Moscow. Two Boeing 737-400s were leased to operate these services and were based at the company's headquarters at Shannon. It was hoped to expand services to include Warsaw, Vienna and Brussels but, at the time of writing, the airline had ceased operations and was hoping to restart flights with the co-operation of another Russian airline. EI-CZK was operating a charter flight when photographed in May 2003, transporting football spectators from Ireland for a match at Manchester United's ground.

United Kingdom

The United Kingdom of Great Britain and Northern Ireland also includes the nations of England, Scotland and Wales. British Airways, the country's flag carrier, competes with other scheduled carriers such as Virgin Atlantic and bmi International, while a variety of operators serve the extensive inclusive-tour and low-cost markets.

Air Scandic

Manchester is the main base of charter airline Air Scandic, a company with offices in the Channel Islands which started in May 1998. Flights to European resorts, mainly from Manchester and Glasgow, are performed for a number of UK tour operators Two recently retired Airbus A300s configured for 317 passengers carried the Air Scandic livery, one being G-TTMC which was photographed at Manchester in February 2001.

Astraeus

The mythological character Astraeus was the name chosen by the directors of this airline, founded in 2001 to operate Boeing 737 aircraft on inclusive tour and contract charter flights. Aircraft were based at Gatwick and Manchester Airports with services commencing in late March 2002 to the Spanish and Greek Islands. Astraeus is one of the UK's fastest-growing independent charter airlines and has built up a reputation for on-board service. The carrier's call sign is 'Flystar' and the star theme continues within the company with some Boeing 737s named after bright stars or constellations. Boeing 737-76N G-STRF was about to depart Manchester in July 2004, just a few months after being delivered to the airline.

Aurigny Air Services

Aurigny Air Services has served the Channel Islands since 1968 operating passenger flights between Guernsey, Jersey and Alderney and to destinations in the UK and continental Europe. The airline is based in Guernsey and operates a fleet of fourteen Britten-Norman Trislander, Shorts, Saab and ATR aircraft. G-RUNG is one of the two Saab 340 33-seat airliners in service and was photographed in May 2003, almost ready for departure as it positioned on to Manchester's 24L runway.

bmi - british midland

Formerly British Midland and now known as bmi, this airline is the UK's second largest scheduled service operator, mainly providing flights within the UK and Europe. Upon the introduction of Airbus A330s to the fleet, transatlantic services commenced in May 2001 with Manchester to Washington flights. Airbus aircraft are used on a number of services within Europe and on flights within the United Kingdom. Photographed on approach to London-Heathrow in July 2001 was A320 G-MIDT which shows the new colours introduced upon the unveiling of the carrier's new name.

bmi is a member of Star Alliance and Boeing 737-3Q8 G-BYZJ was given the livery applied to aircraft which are members of the group. Shortly after receiving the scheme, the airliner was photographed as it exited the Manchester Airport runway in May 2000.

A total of three A330 twin-jets are now operated by bmi and services now fly to three North American cities, Chicago and Las Vegas having been added to the original destination of Washington DC. During the summer of 2004 the carrier provided a daily service to Toronto. Two of the A330s carry the new bmi scheme, as seen on G-WWBM about to commence its take off roll at Manchester in August 2003, whilst the third aircraft carries the Star Alliance scheme.

bmibaby

bmibaby is essentially a no-frills offshoot of bmi – british midland, operating from its main base at Nottingham East Midlands Airport, as well as Birmingham, Cardiff, Manchester and Durham Tees Valley, to European cities using a fleet of Boeing 737-300s and -500s leased from the parent company. As one would expect from a no-frills carrier, there is no in-flight entertainment, neither is free food or drink served. Boeing 737-5Q8 G-BVZG was photographed in April 2003 whilst taxiing for departure from East Midlands Airport.

British Airways

British Airways provides services to more than two hundred destinations in almost a hundred countries with its vast fleet of Boeing and Airbus airliners of various types. The airline is repainting the fleet to show a modernised version of the Union Flag colours. Boeing 767 G-BNWH illustrates this scheme, photographed about to depart Manchester in July 2002 on the carrier's daily flight to New York-JFK.

The controversial tail colours applied to a number of BA aircraft since the June 1997 face-lift have gradually been replaced, re-emerging with the new scheme applied to the Boeing 767 shown. Boeing 757 G-BIKC was given the 'Ndebele Emmly' tail colours and, when operating a London-Heathrow to Manchester shuttle flight in September 1999, it was photographed as it taxied to a gate at the north of England city.

The tail of Boeing 747-236B G-BDXO was given a very delicate design known as 'Paithani', and the aircraft was photographed at the conclusion of a long-haul flight as it came in to land at London-Heathrow in July 1999.

Channel Express

Channel Express (Air Services) Ltd is a Bournemouth-based passenger charter and freight operator. The company has been flying for more than 25 years, originally with up to fourteen Dart Heralds. The company fleet now consists of Fokker F27s, Boeing 737s and Airbus A300s, the latter type all being configured for cargo-carrying. The Boeing 737s provide seating for 148 passengers and see service on various holidaymaker flights throughout the season. TF-ELP, a 737-330QC, was operating a flight on behalf of a tour company when photographed upon arrival at Manchester in May 2002.

Eastern Airways

The Eastern Airways fleet is made up of British Aerospace and Saab turboprops and Embraer regional jets. This airline, founded in 1997, is based at Humberside Airport in Yorkshire and operates a comprehensive service to many of the United Kingdom's smaller airports. A three times per weekday service operates from Inverness to Manchester and it was at the latter airport where Jetstream 32 G-OEST was photographed in July 2002. Whilst this particular aircraft is configured to carry 19 passengers, it is also fitted with a cargo pod.

easyJet

easyJet is a Luton-based, low-cost, no-frills airline which started operating in the UK in 1995, on two routes from London-Luton to Glasgow and Edinburgh. In subsequent years the carrier commenced providing additional services from Stansted, Gatwick and Liverpool to an increasing number of destinations in Spain, Greece, Holland, Switzerland and Eastern Europe. Airbus A319 G-EZAM was photographed at Palma whilst operating a flight from London-Gatwick in September 2004.

European

European Air Charter is the full name of this Bournemouth-based company which commenced operations in 1994 providing ad hoc passenger charters from European mainland and United Kingdom airports. Boeing 737 G-CEAD is one of a number of the type currently in service. As a dedicated charter airline, EAC is able to offer its services to tour operators, and the Boeing illustrated here upon arrival at Manchester in May 2002 had returned from sunnier climes with homecoming holidaymakers.

Excel Airways

Known as Sabre Airways when founded in 1994, the company changed its name to Excel Airways and has now become a major UK carrier, currently operating a fleet of Boeing 737s, 757s and 767s, all fitted with leather seating. Excel Airways, which prides itself on its in-flight service, is based at London-Gatwick, from where it flies to major tourist destinations along with similar services from other United Kingdom airports. Boeing 767 G-BNYS is an extended-range model fitted with 290 economy-class seats and, whilst it carries full Excel colours and titles, it is in fact leased from Air Atlanta. When photographed in June 2004 the airliner was about to enter the departure runway at Manchester.

Jet2

Jet2 is a division of Channel Express, a subsidiary of Dart Group plc, and started operations as a scheduled passenger airline in February 2003 with flights from Leeds-Bradford International Airport. Boeing 737-300s operate to many European destinations. One of the Boeings leased to the carrier by the holding company is G-CELV, photographed in April 2003 as it prepared to depart Leeds-Bradford.

MyTravelLite

MyTravelLite started flying in 2002 from Birmingham Airport to selected destinations. The airline was an offshoot of the charter airline MyTravel (originally known as Airtours), and operated scheduled flights mainly to Spain and Portugal with Airbus A320s leased from the parent company until the brand was absorbed back into it. A320 G-JOEM made an appearance at Manchester in May 2004 and was photographed as it prepared to depart.

ScotAirways

Formerly known as Suckling Airways, this company changed its name to Scot Airways in October 1999 following a re-launch. Originally established in 1984, the company's main base remains in the city of Cambridge from where it offers scheduled flights to Amsterdam. It is at this Dutch destination that Dornier 328 G-BYTY was photographed about to touch down on one of Schiphol's several runways in June 2000.

Sky-Trek

When photographed in September 1999, Britten-Norman Trislander G-BEDP was carrying Sky-Trek titles and colours. Le Touquet Airport is the location the 16-seat aircraft was preparing to depart from on the short flight across the English Channel to Lydd Airport in Kent. At that time the carrier was due to suspend services pending re-organisation. The airline re-emerged in January 2002 as Lydd Air along with new colours and titles although its services are pretty much the same as before. Passengers aboard flights over the Channel are rewarded with superb views as each seat offers a window from which to view the busy shipping lanes below.

Titan Airways

Titan Airways has become a prestigious charter airline specialising in corporate and VIP travel and has established itself as one of Europe's leading airlines. Established in 1988, Titan operates a small fleet of ATR, BAe and Boeing airliners from its base at Stansted. The fleet also includes a Beechcraft King Air B200C aircraft registered G-ZAPT which doubles as an 8-passenger or freighter aircraft. This was captured by the author's camera as it prepared to take off from Manchester in July 2003.

Virgin Atlantic

Virgin Atlantic is the United Kingdom's second largest long-haul carrier with services to a number of the world's major cities operating from both Heathrow and Gatwick Airports using a mix of Boeing 747s and Airbus A340s. The airline commenced services in 1984, initially with London-Gatwick to New York-Newark flights, later it added other routes bringing the number of destinations served to almost twenty. Airbus A340 G-VFLY was photographed when on final approach to London-Heathrow in August 2000.

The airline introduced its 'Silver Dream Machine' livery in the summer of 1999, here seen on Boeing 747-219B G-VSSS photographed after pushback at London-Gatwick in September 2000. A comprehensive daily service of Virgin flights operates from this airport and two more of the company's 747s can be seen at their gates being prepared for departure.

Upon the delivery to the airline of the Boeing 747-400s, some of the original -200 series Jumbos were taken out of service. At the time of writing over a dozen of the stretched upper deck variety now operate Virgin's services. The new silver colours had been applied to 747-443 G-VGAL, photographed as it was about to put down at Miami Airport in January 2003 following a flight from London-Heathrow. All Virgin aircraft carry names – this one is called *Jersey Girl.*

Belgium

Shockwaves went through the airline industry when Sabena, the country's flag carrier, the largest Belgian passenger airline and one of the longest-established airlines in the world succumbed to market forces in November 2001. The changes that resulted were to have implications beyond the confines of this relatively small country.

SN Brussels Airlines

SN Brussels Airlines is the new Belgian full-service airline which started operations in February 2002. The airline has emerged from DAT (Delta Air Transport), the regional airline which was re-organised to fill the vacuum left by the demise of Sabena. The carrier's fleet has been enlarged and now includes Airbus A319s and A330s together with a substantial number of BAe 146 aircraft. A regular service between Brussels and Manchester is operated by the latter type, and in September 2003 OO-DJN was photographed at Manchester as it was about to return to Brussels.

Virgin Express

In 1996, the UK-based Virgin Group acquired the Belgium company EuroBelgian Airlines: that company having been formed in 1992 as a charter airline. Upon the takeover, the airline became known as Virgin Express, operating out of Brussels with Belgian-registered Boeing 737s. The aircraft received the familiar Virgin colours and provided charter flights to holiday destinations alongside scheduled services to selected European cities. Boeing 737-36N OO-VEG was photographed whilst performing a charter flight to Rhodes in August 1998.

VLM Airlines

Antwerp-based VLM Airlines commenced flying in 1992 and currently operates a fleet of a dozen Fokker 50 twin-prop 50-seat aircraft. As well as providing flights from Antwerp to London-City, the company aircraft also perform a comprehensive weekday service between London-City and Manchester. It is at the latter airport where OO-VLM was photographed lining up for departure to London in October 2002.

The Netherlands

The Kingdom of the Netherlands has a population of almost 16 million with the majority of the inhabitants residing in Amsterdam. The country's flag carrier, KLM Royal Dutch Airlines, has contributed to the emergence of Schiphol Airport as a global hub, thanks to its strategic alliances with Northwest Airlines and Air France.

DutchBird

DutchBird was a Schiphol-based airline which was in operation from 2000 until late 2004 providing transportation for holidaymakers on inclusive tours to the sunspots in the Mediterranean and Canary Islands. Two types of aircraft were in service, consisting of two Airbus A320s and three Boeing 757s which inaugurated flights in 2000. Photographed at Amsterdam-Schiphol in June 2003 was Airbus A320 PH-BMC which had just left its gate at the terminal and was negotiating its way to the departure runway.

KLM

KLM (Koninklijke Luchtvaart Maatschappij) is the largest of the Dutch airlines, and the oldest in the world still operating under its original name. Scheduled domestic and international passenger and cargo services operate to 75 countries around the world utilising a very comprehensive fleet of modern jetliners. Boeing 737s are used exclusively on the carrier's European routes and this manufacturer's -300, -400, -800 and -900 models can be regularly observed at airports throughout Europe. PH-BXA is a Boeing 737-8K2 and was photographed at Schiphol in June 2000. This aircraft was one of five of the type to be wearing Euro 2000 football tournament stickers at that time.

A large number of Boeing 747-400s make up the KLM long-haul fleet, several having a side cargo door to facilitate the loading and unloading of freight on pallets carried in the rear fuselage. PH-BFH is one such model, a 747-406SCD with KLM Asia titles, and used primarily on the carrier's Taiwan/Hong Kong services. The airliner carries the name *City of Hong Kong*, and was photographed during pushback at Schiphol in August 1997.

In 1989, KLM acquired a 20% stake in the North American carrier Northwest Airlines and now operates services on a code-share basis with it. An aircraft once flew in a dual colour scheme carrying both the KLM and Northwest liveries, the designs being reversed on each side of the fuselage. McDonnell Douglas DC-10 N237NW was the aircraft so treated, here seen about to touch down at Osaka-Kansai in May 1999.

The KLM Jumbo fleet is now mainly made up of the latest -400 series, three of which are pure freighters whilst the remaining two-thirds are configured for both passenger and cargo transportation. At one time a small number of the -300 series operated the company's long-haul services but these were withdrawn during 2003. In September 2003 PH-BUU, one of the 747-300s, was photographed about to depart the island of St Maarten on its twice-weekly one-stop flight to Amsterdam. The subsequent departure certainly left a good few ripples in the Caribbean!

KLM Cityhopper

KLM Cityhopper is a regional subsidiary of KLM and has operated since 1991 linking Amsterdam with a number of cities in Europe. Only Fokker 50s, 70s and 100s are included in the carrier's fleet, which performs scheduled international flights to more than two dozen destinations. Fokker 100 PH-OFA was about to depart Manchester to Amsterdam when photographed in May 2004, a service also operated by Boeing 737s.

Martinair

Martinair was founded in 1958 by Dutch Air Force pilot J Martin Schroder as Martin's Air Charter, an airline flying passengers to holiday destinations by day and transporting flowers by night. In 1966 the airline changed its name to Martinair by which time the company had grown from local charter airline to international carrier. Airbus, Boeing and McDonnell Douglas airliners are included in a fleet of over 20 aircraft, the majority being configured for passenger use whilst some are pure freighters. Boeing 767 PH-MCL when photographed departing Amsterdam in June 2003 had a 'Fox Kids' livery applied and the aircraft was at the time making regular flights carrying holidaymakers between Amsterdam and Orlando, Florida.

Martinair use both the Boeing 747 and McDonnell Douglas MD-11 for transporting cargo. Whilst some examples are configured for both passengers and cargo, the MD-11 shown here is purely a freighter. PH-MCU had a special roses scheme applied in May 2003 on the occasion of a naming ceremony performed by Princess Maxima. The aircraft now carries her name. The trijet was photographed as it came into land at Miami in January 2004.

Transavia

KLM hold a majority shareholding in Transavia, the largest Dutch holiday carrier with a 40% share of the market. The operator provides flights to destinations in and around the Mediterranean from Rotterdam and Amsterdam, with charters in winter months to sports destinations in France, Austria and Switzerland. The airline is an independent organisation within KLM operating a fleet made up entirely of Boeing 737-700s and -800s. One of their new-generation jets, 737-8K2 PH-HZB, was photographed at Rhodes in August 1999.

In the spring of 2000, Transavia's Boeing 737-8K2 PH-HZE emerged into traffic bearing the company's website address. It was photographed in that condition in May of that year on final approach to Schiphol.

France

The French Republic covers a vast area of Western Europe from the English Channel in the north to the Mediterranean in the south. National airline Air France is one of the world's leading airlines having been in operation since 1933. Charter airlines serve a variety of holiday destinations, some of which are in very distant parts of 'France Outremer'.

Air France

Examples from both of the main aircraft manufacturers are included in the very comprehensive fleet operated by Air France. F-GRHH is one of the A319s to be put into service on the carrier's European services, and was photographed about to depart Berlin-Tegel in February 2000.

During the latter months of 1990, Air France began to put the Airbus A340 into long-haul passenger service. One route connects Paris with the French Antilles with a six-times per week flight to the island of St Maarten. F-GLZS was operating this flight when the author photographed it as it was about to return to Paris on a very hot and sunny late August 2003 afternoon.

The majority of the Boeing 737-300s and -500s were delivered to the airline during the 1990s and used mainly for short-haul services linking Paris with other European cities. F-GJNE is a 737-528, delivered new to the airline in 1992 and seen here at Düsseldorf in October 2003 about to return on the 257-mile journey to Paris.

Air Mediterranée

Tarbes-based Air Mediterranée's speciality is providing transportation for Catholics visiting the shrine at Lourdes and the airline arranges charter flights for this purpose. A chartered Boeing 737-200, F-GCJL, was photographed in August 1999 as it taxied to the departure runway at Manchester at the commencement of such a flight.

Blue Line

One of France's latest airlines is Blue Line, founded in 2002 and currently operating charter services with two Fokker 100s and one McDonnell Douglas MD-83. F-GNLH, one of the Fokker 100s, was photographed in October 2002 upon its arrival at Malta.

CCM Airlines

CCM Airlines was created in 1989 with the aim of providing better services to Corsica and, thanks to an improved partnership with Air France, the airline has now expanded its routes. Some of the aircraft operated by CCM fly in Air France colours with additional titles placed on the forward fuselage as shown on Fokker 100 F-GNLJ, photographed upon arrival at Lille in July 2001.

Corsair

Paris-based Corsair's main activity is providing regular worldwide charter services to Asia, the Americas and Europe. Usually their Boeing 747s and Airbus A330s are employed on long-haul routes and Boeing 737s on flights within Europe. There are however instances where short flights require larger aircraft, as was the case when Boeing 747 F-GSUN was put into service transporting football supporters into Manchester in July 1999.

Since its creation in 1981, Corsair has carried out flights for several major tour operators and recently-delivered Airbus A330s, configured for over 350 passengers, play a very important part on some routes. A charter flight from Paris operated by F-HBIL had just arrived at Malta when photographed in October 2002.

Crossair Europe

Crossair Europe was established as a subsidiary of Swiss Air Lines, operating from a Basle-Mulhouse base with a small fleet of Saab aircraft, all of which carry a French registration. Düsseldorf is one of a handful of European cities from which local services operate and Saab 340 F-GPKM, a 33-seater, was photographed about to depart there in June 2003.

Air Horizons

Founded in 2000 as Horizon, the charter arm of Euralair, this airline underwent a change of name to Air Horizons in January 2004. This Paris-Le Bourget-based carrier provides contract charter operations to Spanish destinations on behalf of tour companies. A large proportion of business comes from the tour operator Voyages FRAM and Boeing 737-800 F-GRNA shows the original colour scheme of the airline together with the additional titles of the tour company. Tenerife South is the location for this March 2001 picture.

Regional

Regional is a 100% owned subsidiary of Air France and was created in March 2001 through a merger with three other French airlines. Regional's network serves most of France and several major European cities and is operated by a fleet of turboprop and jet aircraft. Operating a service into Amsterdam-Schiphol in May 2000 was Saab 2000 F-GTSL. At that time the airline was known as Regional Airlines, one of the three companies that merged to create the present carrier.

Star Airlines

Star Airlines is a privately owned company dedicated to providing transportation for passengers on charters to medium-haul destinations in Spain and to long-haul destinations in the Middle East and Africa. Founded in 1995 as Star Europe, the present name was announced in October 1997. The airline is based at Paris-CDG from which its fleet of Airbus A320s operates to a variety of tourist hot-spots. A320 F-GRSG had earlier brought in a plane-load of holidaymakers to the island of Majorca when photographed in September 1998 and is seen turning onto the runway at Palma prior to returning to France.

Germany

After Russia, the Republic of Germany is the most populous country in Europe with coastlines on both the Baltic and North Seas. Following the reunification of East and West in 1990, the two Germanys were reunited after a period of 45 years of separation, and Berlin is again the capital city. The country's flag carrier is Lufthansa, the world's sixth largest airline.

Air-Berlin

Following the end of World War Two, only aircraft from the Allied Powers were allowed to operate into Berlin and, for this reason, Air-Berlin was founded. The airline was started in 1978 and established in Oregon flying a Boeing 707 carrying Air-Berlin USA titles. The airline is now based in Berlin and flies regularly to major holiday destinations favoured by the German people. These include Palma, where daily flights from twelve German airports add up to a total of almost 200 services a week. Prior to three Fokker 100s being delivered to the carrier at the beginning of 2004 only Boeing 737s were in service by the airline, each configured to carry up to 184 economy-class passengers. Photographed in February 2000 at Berlin-Tegel was Boeing 737-86J D-ABAO which has since been fitted with winglets.

Augsburg Airways

Originally known as Interot Airways, this German regional and domestic passenger airline changed its name in 1996 to Augsburg Airways following its involvement in operating scheduled services on behalf of Lufthansa. At this time only de Havilland Dash 8s are operated by Augsburg. One is D-BIRT which made an appearance at Manchester in June 1998 on the occasion of a football match.

Avanti Air

Siegerland-based Avanti Air was established in 1994 as a regional carrier operating a small fleet of Beechcraft and ATR aircraft. The airline also provided services tailored to suit their customers' requirements. Beechcraft 1900D D-CBIG was operating on behalf of Air Wales when photographed in April 2003 and was about to depart Cork for Cardiff.

Condor

Condor commenced operations in 1956 as a scheduled international and charter carrier in what was then Western Germany. There are now two divisions of the airline. Condor Berlin, started in 1997 and based at that city's Schönefeld Airport, flies a fleet of Airbus A320s while Condor Flugdienst is based at Frankfurt with a fleet of Boeing 757s and 767s. Both divisions are now part of the Thomas Cook Group and, where Thomas Cook titles appear, additional stickers applied to the fuselage indicate 'powered by Condor'. Some aircraft still remain in the original Condor colours whilst others have had Thomas Cook colours and titles applied. Boeing 757 D-ABOK, photographed at Düsseldorf in October 2003, still had the Condor yellow colours but with the Thomas Cook tail logo.

dba

Formerly known as Deutsche BA, and 100% owned by British Airways, this Munich-based airline is now called DBA Luftfahrtgesellschaft and is under German ownership. When under British Airways control, the tails of its aircraft carried the controversial designs now slowly being phased out in favour of the new Union Flag design. Upon the airline's change of ownership a new scheme was introduced and applied to its fleet of Boeing 737-300s. This new livery is shown on Boeing 737 D-ADBV, photographed upon arrival at Malta in October 2002.

Eurowings

Eurowings is a partner of Lufthansa and operates as Lufthansa Regional. Operating from bases at Nuremberg and Dortmund, its fleet of ATR, Bombardier and BAe aircraft can be observed at the majority of German regional airports. One domestic route takes the Eurowings colours to Düsseldorf, where ATR 72 D-ANFA was photographed about to depart in June 2000.

Germania

Germania is one of Germany's major holiday charter airlines and has been operational since 1978, originally under the SAT name – changed to its present title in the summer of 1986. The airline began replacing its entire fleet in 1998 and now flies a modern fleet of Boeing 737-700 aircraft, some of which had advertising schemes of various German companies applied, and recently delivered Fokker 100s. D-AGEU is one of the 737-700s bearing advertisements, in this case for Siemens mobile telephones, and is here seen about to depart Lanzarote in November 2001. Now using the marketing name Germania Express, the company merged with dba in 2005.

germanwings

Germanwings, formed in 1996, is a wholly owned subsidiary of Eurowings and operates from bases at Köln-Bonn and Stuttgart with a fleet of Airbus A319s and A320s. Services at attractive economy prices operate to 22 European destinations. Airbus A319 D-AKNI was photographed in June 2003 upon its arrival at Köln-Bonn.

One of Germanwings' A320s was given a special colour scheme to promote Köln-Bonn Airport. D-AIPH proudly displays this scheme as it prepared to depart there in June 2003. The aircraft also carries the name *Spirit of Cologne Bonn*.

Hapag-Lloyd Express

Hapag-Lloyd Express commenced operations in 2002 and now flies from Cologne, Hannover and Stuttgart airports. The airline is wholly owned by TUI, the world's largest travel and tourism company and operates a fleet of Boeing 737-500s and -700s. A very distinctive colour scheme is applied to the carrier's fleet, illustrated here on Boeing 737-75B D-AGEN which was photographed as it approached its allocated gate at Cologne Airport in June 2003.

Hapag-Lloyd

Hapag-Lloyd is a long established German scheduled charter and international airline, formed in 1972 as the air charter subsidiary of the Hapag-Lloyd shipping group. The airline started its charter operations in 1973 with three Boeing 727s which have since been withdrawn and replaced with what is now a modern fleet of Boeing 737s and Airbus A310s. The Hapag-Lloyd colours have been familiar at most of the European holiday airports, and Airbus A310 D-AHLX was making one of its visits to Palma Airport when photographed while about to take off in September 1998.

Hapag-Lloyd are now part of the TUI airline management and aircraft in the fleet are being painted in the TUI colours, as are planes of the other carriers who are part of the organisation. Boeing 737-8K5 D-AHFR, a 184-seat aircraft, was operating into Düsseldorf when photographed in October 2003. All aircraft in the fleet, with the exception of two Airbus A310s, are fitted with winglets.

LTU

LTU was founded in Frankfurt in 1955 bearing the name Lufttransport-Union. Today, LTU is one of Germany's largest holiday airlines flying to more than seventy airports worldwide with its Airbus fleet. The A330 entered LTU service in 1995 and examples of the type continued to be delivered until the end of 2002. D-AERF was photographed at Lanazrote in November 2001 making its way over the coastline to put down on the airport's runway 03.

Airbus A330 D-AERF is configured with all-economy seating for 387 passengers, and is again featured in this LTU spread, this time at Rhodes in August 1998.

The other Airbus types in LTU service are A320s and A321s. During 2001 a revised scheme was introduced but, due to its being unpopular, was not proceeded with and the original colours were retained. A320 D-ALTC carried the revised scheme for a period and was photographed in that condition when visiting Lanzarote in November 2001.

Lufthansa

Following World War Two it was not until 1953 that the first signs of a new German national airline appeared, but Lufthansa is now again one of the world's major airlines employing a staff of 25,000. One of the services provided by the carrier is a comprehensive programme of international flights to various holiday destinations and, in the summer of 1996, the airline put into service the first of what was to become a total of twenty Airbus A319s to operate these flights. One example is D-AILI, which was photographed in September being pushed back at Palma prior to departure for a German destination.

43

OLT

OLT (Ostfriesische Lufttransport) operate regional services out of bases at Emden and Bremen to points within Germany, Belgium and Denmark as well as London-City Airport. The airline was established in 1958 and currently flies a fleet of various types of aircraft, ranging from a Cessna with seating for six passengers to a Saab with a capacity for fifty. Erfurt is one of the German destinations served by OLT and is where Saab 340 D-COLE was photographed in June 2003 being prepared for a midday flight to Munich.

Star Alliance

Lufthansa is a member of Star Alliance and certain aircraft in the fleet carry stickers to that effect together with smaller Lufthansa titles. In March 2003, the airline took delivery of two Boeing 767s, the only examples of this type to enter the Lufthansa fleet. Each aircraft was put into revenue-earning service in different styles of livery: one had a black tail whilst the other had a white tail. Both of these styles are illustrated here. D-ABUV was photographed in January 2004 on final approach to Miami following a flight from Munich and D-ABUW was at Frankfurt-Main about to depart to Atlanta in June 2003.

Lufthansa Cargo

Lufthansa Cargo is an independent logistics company within the Lufthansa group and was founded in November 1994. Whilst a large number of McDonnell Douglas MD-11s and Boeing 747s carry the Lufthansa Cargo titles and perform the carrier's daily airport to airport services, the company also carries freight in Lufthansa passenger aircraft. Boeing 747 D-ABZC had just arrived at Sharjah when photographed in May 2002.

PrivatAir

PrivatAir (on behalf of Lufthansa) is a subsidiary of PrivatAir SA, a company based in Switzerland. As part of the PrivatAir Group, the airline has been designed to meet the high expectations of its business passengers who require luxurious transportation. From a base at Düsseldorf the airline performs flights with a fleet of four Airbus A319s: two are configured for 126 economy-class passengers whilst the other two are fitted out for 48 business passengers. The latter two aircraft are scheduled to operate the carrier's daily flights to New York-Newark and Chicago. The Newark service was being flown by A319 D-APAC when it was photographed departing Düsseldorf in June 2003.

Austria

Austria lies in the heart of Europe and is dominated by the Alps, making the country attractive to tourists who flock to see the magnificent scenery. The capital city is Vienna where Austrian Airlines, the country's major airline is based. Both Lauda Air and Tyrolean are in process of being absorbed, with Austrian Arrows branding being applied.

Austrian Airlines

Austrian Airlines has been flying since 1958 and presently provides services to well over 100 worldwide destinations. A wide range of aircraft types, from Fokker 70s configured for 75 passengers through to Airbus A340s with seating for 307, caters for all the carrier's needs. European services are mainly in the hands of Airbus A320 and A321 twin-jets, and OE-LBO, one of the A320s, was photographed upon the completion of a scheduled flight from Vienna as it came into land at Athens in June 1998.

The 75-seat Fokker 70s, of which there are three examples in the Austrian Airlines fleet, operate the carrier's European services. One of the trio is OE-LFQ which had just arrived at Düsseldorf when photographed in June 2003.

Lauda Air

Austria's second major airline is Lauda Air, founded by the Formula 1 motor racing champion Niki Lauda, and now a subsidiary of Austrian Airlines. Flights commenced in 1985 and now include more than thirty worldwide destinations. Long-haul flights are performed by Boeing 767 and 777 aircraft laid out in a two-class configuration, and for the European services the airline has a fleet of Boeing 737s of various models. Photographed at Geneva in August 2000 whilst waiting for passengers to board was Boeing 737 OE-LNH, one of two -400 series machines to carry the Lauda colours.

Styrian Spirit

Styrian Spirit is a regional airline founded in 2002 and based in Graz. Flights are tailored to local needs covering business travel between Austria and Germany and are performed by a small fleet of Bombardier CRJ200s. Three German cities are served by the carrier including Frankfurt-Main where CRJ200 OE-LSD was photographed in June 2003 as it taxied to the departure runway prior to returning to Graz.

Tyrolean Airways

Tyrolean Airways commenced flying in 1980 offering regional and charter services from its base in Innsbruck. The airline was acquired by Austrian Airlines in 1998. The main activity of the airline is providing regional flights within Austria, with other services connecting Innsbruck to cities in Europe performed by a mix of propeller-driven and small jet aircraft. De Havilland Dash 8s have now been joined by Canadair Regional Jets and Fokker 70s and 100s. OE-LCN is one of sixteen CRJs in service with Tyrolean and was photographed when operating a scheduled flight out of Düsseldorf in June 2001. The aircraft are gradually acquiring Austrian Arrows branding.

Austrian Arrows

Some of Austrian Airlines services are operated by Austrian Arrows. These flights are flown on their behalf by group member Tyrolean Airlines with Fokker 70 and Bombardier CRJ aircraft. This London-Heathrow arrival was Fokker 70 OE-LFJ, photographed on an August 2004 morning. This aircraft is one of several in the Tyrolean Airways fleet now carrying Austrian Arrows titles and colours.

Switzerland

Tourism plays a very important part in the country's economy, with the Alps drawing visitors both winter and summer. Emerging after the demise of Swissair, Swiss International, the country's major airline, has recently been acquired by Lufthansa.

Belair

Belair is a charter airline, founded in 2001 and a member of the Hotelplan Group, operating flights on their behalf: the majority flying from Zürich to holiday destinations in Spain and the Mediterranean. Three aircraft make up the carrier's fleet, two Boeing 757s and a Boeing 767, and each aircraft has the company titles presented in different colours on either side of the fuselage. Boeing 757 HB-IHR's colours are yellow and green whilst the colours of the other two aircraft are blue/yellow and orange/green. The aircraft illustrated carries the name *Solemar* and was photographed whilst turning onto the departure runway at Lanzarote in October 2001.

Helvetic Airways

Helvetic Airways, formed in 2001, is the first Swiss budget airline and connects Zürich with important European cities. The carrier's fleet is basically 100-seat Fokker 100s with six of the type currently in service and others due to be leased later. The airline was formerly known as Odette Airways and a McDonnell Douglas MD-83 operates under this marketing name on charter flights. Helvetic Airways works closely with a major tour company and operates holiday flights to destinations in the Mediterranean. Fokker 100 HB-JVF was photographed in September 2004 as it arrived at Palma following its daily flight from Zürich.

Edelweiss Air

Edelweiss Air was established in 1995 and commenced flying in 1996 as a charter airline providing flights for tour companies to the sun-spots of the Mediterranean. Initial services were performed by a small fleet of McDonnell Douglas MD-83s. These remained in the Edelweiss fleet for only a short period of time, being replaced in 1999 by Airbus A320s offering additional capacity. The second of the type to be delivered to the airline was HB-IHY, here seen about to land at Tenerife South in March 2001 bringing tourists from Zürich to the island. In 2001 and 2002 Edelweiss Air received the Golden Travelstar Award for its excellent achievements.

PrivatAir

PrivatAir is a leading international business aviation group with headquarters in Geneva. The airline also operates from Düsseldorf (see page 45). The group's main activity is providing private charters for VIPs and executives and it was the first operator of the Boeing Business Jet. HB-IIO was the first BBJ to be delivered to the airline and is configured for 28 first-class passengers, here seen at Düsseldorf in June 2003 about to depart on a VIP flight.

Swiss International

Switzerland's new carrier, Swiss International, was formed in 2002 by the renaming of the existing Swiss carrier Crossair. The company headquarters remain in Basle. Services operate from Zürich and Geneva to several European cities together with long-haul international flights. As well as a new name, the airline introduced a revised livery retaining the Swiss flag on the tail which had been a feature on Swissair aircraft for the past 75 years. McDonnell Douglas MD-11 HB-IWE was the last of the type in the fleet and was photographed in December 2002 as it brought its passengers from Zürich into Miami.

For services within the UK and Europe, Swiss use a mix of Embraer, Saab and BAe aircraft. Operating a flight to Basle in September 2003 was Embraer EMB-145 HB-JAD, photographed at Manchester as it positioned for take-off.

Some aircraft within the Swiss fleet still retain the Crossair livery. Embraer EMB-145 HB-JAK showed its original identity when photographed in July 2001 about to depart Manchester on a Basle service.

Another Crossair aircraft still in evidence several months after the launch of Swiss was Saab 2000 HB-IZZ taken at Düsseldorf in October 2003. The aircraft displays the old Crossair colour scheme together with its '25th Concordino' stickers.

Luxembourg

The Grand Duchy of Luxembourg is a very small European country, sharing its borders with Germany, France and Belgium. Luxair is the only major passenger airline operating in the country, but Cargolux, the well-known freight carrier, operate their modern fleet far beyond the confines of their small and land-locked home country.

Cargolux Airlines

Cargolux Airlines is a major cargo carrier with a fleet of a dozen relatively new Boeing 747-400 freighters. Founded by Luxair in 1970, the carrier's first flights were performed by a CL-44 swing-tail freighter. Their Jumbo freighters now fly worldwide to destinations in the USA, South America, the Far East and Australia. Boeing 747-400 LX-MCV was operating a cargo flight into Manchester when photographed in May 2003.

Luxair

As the national airline of Luxembourg, Luxair operates a network of scheduled services within Europe as well as charter flights to holiday destinations. All the aircraft in its fleet are economy-class configured, allowing the carrier to utilise its aircraft on any type of service. Boeing 737-500 LX-LGP was performing a flight from Tenerife South when photographed in March 2001.

Embraer EMB-145 Eurojets operate Luxair's scheduled services from Luxembourg to Manchester, and it was at this North of England airport where LX-LGU was photographed upon arrival in August 1999.

Romania

Romania lies off the Black Sea coast with the River Danube at its southern border. Only one major passenger airline carries the Romanian flag.

Tarom

Tarom is Romania's national flag carrier and has been in operation since 1946. Both regional and international services are provided by the carrier with its fleet of twenty or so aircraft. The airline's main base is in Bucharest, the country's capital city, from where flights mostly to Europe and the Middle East are made. A daily service operates from Bucharest to London and it is at that city's Heathrow Airport that Boeing 737-300 YR-BGC was about to land in September 1999.

Balkan Holidays Airlines

Holidaymakers from the United Kingdom booked on inclusive tours to Bulgaria are likely to be transported to their destination by an airliner sporting the colours of Balkan Holidays Airlines, a subsidiary of Balkan Holidays International. Formed in 2001, this company specialises in charter traffic with its Airbus A320 and Tupolev Tu-154 aircraft. Tupolev Tu-154 LZ-HMI, photographed about to depart Manchester for Bulgaria, shows off the company colours.

Bulgaria Air

Following the demise of Balkan Bulgarian Airlines, a new national airline called Bulgaria Air emerged in November 2002 with its first passenger flight operating on 4th December on the Sofia-London-Paris route. The airline now flies throughout Europe with a fleet of five Boeing 737s. Boeing 737-530 LZ-BOI, photographed at Frankfurt-Main in June 2003, was operating a three times per week flight from Sofia. The schedule allowed for a one-hour turnround before the twin-jet returned to Sofia, a journey of 867 miles.

Bulgarian Air Charter

Bulgarian Air Charter is a Sofia-based private airline currently operating international charter flights for both summer and winter tourist traffic using only the Tupolev Tu-154 aircraft. Flights commenced in 2000 and the carrier has since built up an established charter operation which take their aircraft to many of Europe's holiday airports. Tu-154 LZ-LCA, a 1996-built machine and the second of the type to enter BAC service, was photographed whilst taxying at Düsseldorf in October 2003.

Bulgaria

Bulgaria is located in South-Eastern Europe, a country separated from Romania by the River Danube. The capital city is Sofia, where the majority of the country's airlines are based.

Although still operating some Soviet-built airliners, the carriers that serve the country's tourist industry sport a variety of decidedly non-Soviet colour schemes.

Hemus Air

Hemus Air is a Sofia-based regional aviation company formed in 1991. This carrier is also involved in the transport of holidaymakers to Bulgaria's Black Sea resorts, specialising in charter flights from Scandinavia, Central and Eastern Europe and the UK in the tourist season, and also providing scheduled and domestic flights at other times. The majority of the airline's fleet is Russian-built, including, of course, the Tupolev Tu-154 favoured by other of the country's airlines. LZ-HMS, one of four carrying Hemus Air colours, was about to depart to Bulgaria when photographed at Manchester in July 2001.

Air VIA

Air VIA Bulgarian Airlines was founded in 1990 by a group of investors as a holiday charter airline providing flights for tour companies. Five Tupolev Tu-154s operate these services, all configured for 157 economy-class passengers. During the holiday season Air VIA aircraft make regular appearances at United Kingdom airports transporting vacationers to and from the Bulgarian resorts, and LZ-MIK was photographed on arrival at Manchester Airport in April 1998.

Hungary

Budapest is the capital of the Republic of Hungary, a landlocked country lying in the heart of Central Europe. The capital stands on the banks of the River Danube, one side is called Buda and the other side is called Pest. Hungary's national airline, Malev, has largely replaced its Soviet-built fleet with more modern Western equipment.

Malev

Malev commenced operations in 1947, has alliances with a number of other airlines, and operates a wide variety of international scheduled services to most European destinations with a fleet of Boeing and Fokker aircraft. Domestic flights are also made to a small number of airports by Fokker 70s. The airline has a very modern and constantly updated fleet. Boeing 737-300 HA-LEJ, which was operating a flight to Budapest when photographed departing Amsterdam in June 2003, has since been replaced by new-generation 737s.

Malev Express

Malev Express is a subsidiary of Malev Hungarian Airlines and operates flights on behalf of the parent company. Services commenced in 2002 and operate to regional destinations with a small fleet of Bombardier CRJ200s. One example is HA-LNC, the third to be delivered in April 2003. It was captured by the author's camera as it taxied for departure from Düsseldorf in June 2003.

Italy

Alitalia is the country's national airline, founded in 1947 as Aerolinee Italiane Internazionali. It currently operates domestic and international services from a base in Rome having thus far resisted the icy winds of change that have affected other traditional European flag carriers so badly. A number of regional airlines operate an extensive network of domestic routes.

Air Dolomiti

Northern Italy's main regional airline is Trieste-based Air Dolomiti which performs flights across the Alps to neighbouring countries. These services have operated since 1991 and are currently flown by a fleet of ATR 42 and ATR 72 aircraft. ATR 42 I-ADLG was operating an international flight into Barcelona when photographed in June 1996.

Air Dolomiti's ATR 42 I-ADLI, photographed on one of the taxiways at Frankfurt-Main in August 1997, had been given the colours of the designer label FENDI. The airline also operates feeder flights to hub airports allowing passengers to connect with flights operated by other carriers. These flights are centred on Munich, Frankfurt-Main and Vienna, timed to connect with flights operated primarily by Lufthansa and other Star Alliance members. Air Dolomiti has been under the control of Lufthansa since April 2003.

Air Europe

Air Europe is a Milan-based airline founded in 1989. The company is involved in operating charter flights with Airbus A320s, A321s and A330s originally leased from the parent company Volare. Airbus A320 I-PEKI carries the full Air Europe colours, and was photographed on a very wet and dismal rainy day in June 2001 as it prepared to depart Düsseldorf.

Air One

Air One is an independent airline which commenced operations in November 1995 providing charter and domestic passenger services from two of Italy's main airports. Boeing 737s of -200, -300 and -400 series operate flights from most of the country's airports to selected destinations. Charter flights also operate to holiday destinations and Boeing 737-300 EI-CLZ was photographed as it was about to turn onto the runway at Rhodes in August 1998.

Alitalia

Alitalia is the largest of the many airlines operating in Italy, with a workforce in excess of 22,000 staff. A very modern fleet is operated including examples from all the major aircraft builders, flying more than 22 million Alitalia passengers a year on 8000 flights a day to more than 500 world-wide destinations. The carrier put the Boeing 777 into service on their long-haul flights during 2002 and one route took the type to Miami. I-DISE was photographed at this Southern Florida city as it came into land in December 2004.

The carrier's internal and European routes are flown by a comparably large number of Airbus A319s, A320s and A321s, together with McDonnell Douglas MD-82s. Düsseldorf is served by Alitalia with flights to Milan and Rome. A319 I-BIMA was in charge of the Milan flight when photographed about to depart Düsseldorf in June 2003.

Alitalia Express

Alitalia Express is a subsidiary of the Alitalia Group and operates on behalf of, and in conjunction with, its parent company. The airline has its own dedicated fleet comprising ATR and Embraer economy-configured aircraft, one of the more recent types to be delivered being the Embraer EMB-145. I-EXMH, one of fourteen in service, was photographed at Düsseldorf in June 2003.

Alpi Eagles

Alpi Eagles is a Venice-based scheduled and charter passenger carrier, originally formed in 1979. Only Fokker 100 aircraft feature in the fleet, eight examples of which are currently in use. Photographed about to land at Athens in June 1998 was I-ALPI, one of the first to be delivered to the airline in 1996.

At the turn of the century the airline introduced its new colour scheme, seen here applied to Fokker 100 I-ALPK. Papa-Kilo was being pushed back from its gate at Berlin-Tegel in February 2000 at the commencement of a return flight to Venice.

Blue Panorama

Blue Panorama is one of the more recent Italian airlines to take to the skies, having commenced flying in December 1998. It offers international charter services from its base in Rome on behalf of its parent company Astra Travel. Boeing 737-400s and 767s currently make up the carrier's fleet. One of the 737s is EI-CUD, seen about to put down onto the Geneva runway in August 2000.

Eurofly

Eurofly is an affiliate of Alitalia formed in 1989 as a passenger charter airline to operate inclusive tours to Europe, Africa and the Middle East. The carrier's main base is in Milan. It is quite common for the airline to lease aircraft from Alitalia when circumstances dictate. Airbus A320 I-BIKD, seen in this photograph at Lanzarote in November 2001, carries the Alitalia tail colours as well as Eurofly titles.

Meridiana

Meridiana was formerly known as Alisarda. Now, as a subsidiary of Interprogramme, this scheduled carrier operates flights from bases in Olbia and Florence with a fleet of Airbus A319s and McDonnell Douglas MD-80s to several Italian cities together with other selected European destinations. MD-83 EI-CRJ was operating a flight into Geneva when photographed in August 2000.

Volare

Volare was created in 1997 by a group of Italian businessmen and foreign investors to operate scheduled domestic flights from the carrier's main base located in Verona. The Airbus A320 was selected as the ideal equipment, and, at its peak, some eighteen of the type were flying in the colours of this now defunct carrier. One of the first to be put into service was French-registered F-GJVX which, when photographed in August 1998, was operating a flight to the Greek island of Rhodes.

In 2001 the company leased two 209-seat Airbus A321s which flew in Volare colours for around two years. The author was fortunate to obtain a photograph of one at Lanzarote in November 2001. I-PEKM had just lifted off the runway into a rather steeper climb than previous departures.

Spain

Madrid is the capital of Spain, the South-western European country famous for tourism, sunshine and beaches. The country's major flag carrier is Iberia which operates an international network of scheduled passenger and cargo services. Several of Spain's other airlines specialise in the transport of holidaymakers from various European cities to the many resorts the country has to offer, on a scale rarely seen elsewhere.

AeBal

AeBal – Aerolineas Baleares is a Palma-based airline formed in 2000. Its fleet of Boeing 717s operates on domestic flights from hubs at Madrid and Barcelona, mostly on behalf of Spanair. The airline is also involved in charter flights to European destinations. Flights flown on behalf of Spanair operate as Spanair Link, and Boeing 717 EC-HNZ was in use as such when photographed in September 2004 arriving at Palma.

Air Europa

Palma-based Air Europa specialises in inclusive tour services between Europe and the Spanish holiday resorts with an all-Boeing fleet of 737s and 767s. The current livery was introduced in 1999 upon the introduction of Boeing's new-generation 737-800s to the company fleet, here applied to EC-HGP seen about to depart Geneva in August 2000.

Air Nostrum

Spain's leading regional airline is Air Nostrum, established in 1994 with its headquarters in Valencia. Flights are operated under a franchise agreement with Iberia as Iberia Regional using a fleet of four types of aircraft: Dash 8, Fokker 50, ATR 72 and Bombardier CRJ200s, all configured for 50 passengers. EC-HEJ, one of the carrier's ATR 72s, was photographed at Madrid in May 2003 as is made its way towards a gate at the terminal.

Air Plus Comet

Air Plus Comet began flying in 1980 providing services from Europe to the Caribbean and America. Boeing 737s and 747s, together with Airbus A310s, currently make up the fleet of the Madrid-based airline. EC-GOT, one of the A310s, was photographed in September 1997 as it moved slowly away from a remote stand at Palma Airport.

Binter Canarias

Binter Canarias was founded in February 1988 by Grupo Iberia as a subsidiary to provide passenger and cargo transportation in the archipelago. The company's first flights linked the islands of Grand Canaria, Tenerife and Fuerteventura, and the airline has since grown in size allowing it to make daily links to every one of the Canary Islands airports. The carrier's ATR 72 fleet makes around 140 daily flights, one of them was an arrival at Lanzarote operated by EC-EUJ in November 2001.

Cygnus Air

Cygnus Air is a purely cargo-carrying airline, with a fleet of three McDonnell Douglas DC-8s, which was established in 1994. The company is based in Madrid which is the location of the photograph of EC-IGZ, shot in May 2003 as it made its way to the runway soon after departing the freight terminal.

Futura

Futura is another of Spain's charter airlines to be based on the island of Majorca. This company started operations in 1990 providing inclusive-tour charter flights to European destinations. Similar operations are also performed from Tenerife where the airline has a second base. A fleet of Boeing 737s carry the recently revised Futura colour scheme, here illustrated on 737-800 EC-HJJ photographed about to depart Lanzarote in November 2001.

Hola Airlines

Also with a base in Palma, Majorca is Hola Airlines, formed in 2002. Three Boeing 737s transport holidaymakers from towns and cities in Europe to the Spanish sunshine islands and resorts. 737-33A EC-IEZ carried the rather plain livery of the airline as it arrived at Palma in September 2004.

Iberia

Iberia's all-jet fleet of McDonnell Douglas, Boeing and Airbus airliners operates from Spanish mainland and island airports to many domestic and international destinations, including regular services to the main European cities. Airbus A320s feature prominently on these flights. EC-HDN was photographed about to depart Geneva at the commencement of a flight to Barcelona in August 2000.

Four of Iberia's A319s were based in Miami for a time to provide 'same airline' onward connections to Hispanic countries. Shortly after the arrival of Iberia's Boeing 747 flight from Madrid, all four A319s would depart to Guatemala City, Managua, San José and San Pedro. An early afternoon arrival from one of these cities by EC-HGR was about to touch down at Miami in January 2003 just ahead of the 747 arrival from Madrid.

Iberworld Airlines

Iberworld Airlines is part of the Iberostar Group, a company with years of experience in the leisure and tourism industry. The airline was formed in 1998 and has ten aircraft in its fleet, a mix of Airbus A320s and A330s, all configured for economy class travel. Flights operate mainly within Europe and the Spanish resorts. Airbus A320 EC-GUR was photographed at Lanzarote in November 2001 about to commence its take-off roll.

Spanair

Spanair began operations with European charter flights in 1988, continuing these services until the introduction of international long-haul flights in 1991, followed in 1994 by scheduled domestic flights. The carrier's main base is at Palma from which the majority of the company's domestic and charter services operate, normally flown by McDonnell Douglas MD-80s and Airbus A320s and A321s. A320 EC-IAZ, a 2001-built aircraft, was photographed at Manchester in October 2002 as it prepared to take off with a tour company's charter to a Spanish destination.

Portugal

With its long Atlantic coastline, Portugal lies on the western side of the Iberian Peninsula joining Spain as a country attracting tourists to its many resorts, a popular destination being the Algarve, a region which is predominantly dry and sunny. The national airline is TAP Air Portugal which operates from Lisbon, the country's capital.

Air Luxor

Air Luxor is a private Portuguese airline with a modern Airbus fleet which includes A320s for short-haul flights and A330s for the carrier's long-haul services. The company was established in 1988 and operates from Lisbon for international travel and tour operators, some routes being seasonal whilst others operate year-round. One seasonal route brings the Air Luxor colours to Bournemouth where Airbus A320 EC-TMW was photographed as it taxied to the terminal buildings in September 2002.

EuroAtlantic Airways

EuroAtlantic Airways was founded in Lisbon in 1997 as Air Madeira, later to become known as Air Zarco. The present name was adopted in 2000. The airline is involved in charter flights from Europe to Africa and Central and South America together with the leasing of its aircraft to other carriers in peak periods or in cases of non-availability of a company's aircraft. EuroAtlantic's only Lockheed L-1011 TriStar was leased on several occasions to British West Indies Airways during the summer of 2003 to cover for the unavailability of their own aircraft. Registered CS-TED, it made regular visits to Manchester during the leasing period, and was photographed in August of that year about to touch down following a flight from Port of Spain.

PGA Portugalia Airlines

PGA Portugalia Airlines was set up as a Portuguese regional carrier and commenced flying in 1990 from its main base in Lisbon. Domestic flights operate to Faro and Oporto, whilst the carrier's international services take the Portugalia colours to several destinations within Europe. A small fleet of Embraer EMB-145s and Fokker 100s make up the fourteen aircraft currently in service. Operating a flight from Geneva in August 2000 was Fokker 100 CS-TPF.

SATA International

SATA International is a subsidiary of SATA Air Açores and provides scheduled passenger services in the Azores Archipelago. Based in Lisbon and Ponta Delgada, the airline operates international services to Europe's major cities including Paris, Vienna and Rome, and charter services between Funchal, Faro, Lisbon and Porto with a small fleet of Boeing 737s and Airbus A310s. Boeing 737-36N CS-TGQ was operating a charter flight to Manchester when photographed in May 2000.

TAP

TAP (Transportes Aereos Portugueses) has been flying since 1946 and currently provides a regular service of scheduled, charter, international and domestic passenger flights with an all-Airbus fleet of jetliners. The TAP colours can be observed at many of the world's airports including some in North and South America. Airbus A310 CS-TEW which carries the name *Vasco da Gama*, commemorating the adventurous Portuguese explorer, had been put into service on a flight to London when photographed about to land at Heathrow in July 1998.

Iceland

Situated in the North Atlantic just south of the Arctic Circle, the country's flag carrier, Icelandair, serves fourteen countries on both sides of the Atlantic from its base in the capital city Reykjavik. The extensive leasing activities of Air Atlanta ensure that the country's TF-registration prefix is to be seen right around the globe.

Air Atlanta

Air Atlanta Icelandic leases aircraft to airlines requiring extra capacity and, depending on requirements, can offer a choice of Boeing 747s, 757s or 767s. Air Atlanta Europe is a UK company partially owned by the Icelandic company and is primarily involved in supplying aircraft for charter operations in addition to operating charter flights under its own flight numbers. Boeing 747 TF-ARG was operating a flight to Orlando when photographed about to depart Manchester in July 2004. This Jumbo previously flew in a three-class 380-seat configuration for British Airways but now carries 472 economy-class passengers.

Icelandair

Icelandair is the largest private company in Iceland employing over 2000 staff. Its young and modern fleet of Boeing aircraft provides both scheduled passenger and cargo services from Iceland to most European destinations. Boeing 757 TF-FID illustrates the colour scheme introduced in 1999 as it lands at Amsterdam-Schiphol in May 2000.

Charter flights operated on behalf of tour companies are also performed by Icelandair and Boeing 757 TF-FIW was photographed at Manchester in July 2001 with additional stickers applied to the fuselage.

Islandsflug

Islandsflug is another Reykjavik-based airline, formed in 1991 to operate a mix of scheduled passenger and cargo flights. In the summer of 1999 the company introduced the operating name Icebird Airlines, under which international leasing operations are performed. One Boeing 737-300 operated those services, usually configured for 142 passengers but also being able to be used as a pure freighter. The aircraft in question, TF-ELN, was making one of several visits to Manchester when photographed in May 2000.

Finland

Finland is a low-lying country of forests and over 60,000 lakes. Occupying a strategic position, bordered by Norway and Sweden in the northwest and by Russia in the east. The country's national airline, Finnair, has always looked to the West for its equipment.

Finnair

Finnair is by far the largest airline is Finland and has been in operation since 1924. All types of passenger and cargo services are offered and a large fleet of aircraft, ranging from 66-seat ATR 72s to 317-seat Airbus A300s, is available for both domestic and international flights. In winter months a series of charter flights operate from Finland to the sunnier and warmer climes of Southern Florida, and Boeing 757 OH-LBT, suitably adorned with illustrations of Santa and his sleigh, was photographed in December 1998 about to depart Fort Lauderdale prior to a return journey to Finland of almost 5,000 miles.

A fleet of Airbus A319s, A320s and A321s operate on Finnair's longer European routes. Recently delivered A319 OH-LVE was photographed at Manchester Airport in September 2003 about to take off for Helsinki, a journey of 1,125 miles.

Taken on the Helsinki Airport ramp in July 2000 was this shot of McDonnell Douglas MD-82 OH-LPA, the first aircraft in the Finnair fleet to be given the airline's newly revised colour scheme. The MD-82 had just arrived at the terminal and is seen approaching its gate.

Poland

Strategically placed between Western and Eastern Europe, bordering Russia to the East and Germany to the West, Poland was treated as a captive customer for the Soviet aviation industry during the days of the Warsaw Pact. National carrier LOT's fleet has undergone a complete makeover with Western equipment in the years leading up to EU membership.

EuroLOT

ATR 72 SP-LFF is a member of the fleet of the airline EuroLOT, a carrier formed by LOT Polish Airlines in 1997 to provide domestic and regional services for its parent company. The 64-seater twin-prop was photographed at Frankfurt-Main in June 2003 as it made its way to the departure runway.

LOT Polish Airlines

LOT Polish Airlines was formed by the Polish government in 1929 and currently flies both passenger and cargo scheduled flights to cities in Europe and the United States. Boeing 767 extended range models perform services to North America, whilst Boeing 737s are put to use on the carrier's European flights. Diagrammed to perform one of the airline's services to London in June 1998 was Boeing 737-36N SP-LMD, photographed on approach to Heathrow Airport at the conclusion of its outward journey.

Included in the LOT fleet are a number of Embraer regional jets which perform local services in and around the surrounding areas. A daily service operates between Warsaw and Estonia flown by this type. SP-LGA, a 48-seat EMB-145, was photographed at Estonia's capital Tallinn in September 2002 as it was about to return to its homeland.

Russia

Although certain regions of Russia are located within Europe it would be impossible to include all of the carriers that fall into this category within the pages of this book. Here is a small selection covering a few of the more well-known airlines in this vast country.

Aeroflot

Aeroflot is Russia's major airline, operating international and domestic services to more than 100 destinations. In 1994 the carrier was renamed Aeroflot – Russian International Airlines and, following reorganisation, its mainly Soviet-built fleet began receiving Western-built equipment from both the Boeing and Airbus plants. Ilyushin aircraft still feature prominently in the fleet. RA-86075, one of this manufacturer's IL-86 passenger airliners, was photographed arriving at London-Heathrow on a scheduled service in July 1999.

Boeing 737s, 767s and 777s, together with Airbus A319s, A320s and A321s are the Western-built airliners chosen by Aeroflot. The two 737s are 400 series models and operate from Moscow to points in Western Europe. One destination is Geneva where VP-BAL was photographed as it prepared to return to Moscow in August 2000.

Pulkovo Aviation

Pulkovo Aviation is a St Petersburg passenger airline based at that city's Pulkovo Airport and previously part of the massive Aeroflot airline. The Pulkovo fleet currently consists of Soviet-built Tupolev and Ilyushin aircraft constructed between 1976 and 1997 and used on services linking St Petersburg with cities in both east and west. Tupolev Tu-154 RA-85785 was photographed in June 2001 at Düsseldorf about to return to St Petersburg on a midday flight.

Sibir Airlines

Sibir Airlines (Siberian Airlines) is one of Russia's leading domestic carriers and the country's second largest airline. Formed in 1992 with branches in five locations, the airline's primary base and largest hub is at Moscow's Domodedovo Airport. The carrier's fleet consists of Tupolev and Ilyushin jets, all configured for passenger use. International services operate from Moscow to the Far East, Europe and the United Arab Emirates, and it is at Sharjah that IL-86 RA-86105 was photographed in April 1998.

At the turn of the century Sibir Airlines put the Tupolev Tu-204 into passenger service with their fleet. Tu-204 RA-64011 was photographed in June 2003 at Frankfurt-Main as it was making its way to runway 18 at the start of a late evening service to Novosibirsk, a non-stop flight of almost 3,000 miles.

Transaero Airlines

Transaero Airlines was born in 1991, commencing with scheduled flights from its Moscow base to international destinations within Europe. Whilst some Soviet-built airliners are included, the majority of aircraft in the carrier's fleet are Boeings. The airline eventually commenced flying from Moscow to London-Gatwick. A switch was made to London-Heathrow, where Boeing 737 RA-73001 was photographed arriving in August 2000, but flights have since returned to Gatwick.

Denmark

Denmark is the most southerly country in Scandinavia, occupying the Jutland Peninsula together with over 400 islands. Copenhagen is Denmark's capital city and the base of the country's three major airlines. These operate alongside multi-national SAS – Scandanavian Airlines System, whose aircraft are also registered in Norway and Sweden.

Cimber Air

Danish airline Cimber Air operates scheduled domestic flights out of Sonderborg Airport with a small fleet of ATR 42s and 72s and Bombardier Regional Jets. The airline was formed in 1950 and currently provides services to a number of regional destinations, along with flights to cities in Germany, France and Belgium. Airborne at Berlin-Tegel in February 2000 was OY-CIN, one of the first ATR 72s to enter service with the airline.

In April 1989, Cimber Air joined 'Team Lufthansa Partner' and later began operating German domestic services between Kiel and Munich. ATR42 OY-CIB shows the livery applied to some of the carrier's aircraft, photographed at Berlin's Tegel Airport in February 2000.

Maersk Air

Maersk Air commenced operations in 1970 and from its Copenhagen base flies both scheduled and charter services to destinations throughout Europe. With an all-jet fleet of Bombardier CRJ200s and Boeing 737s, its aircraft are some of the youngest in the country. Boeing 737-7L9 OY-MRG, photographed in November 2001, was bringing holidaymakers to the island of Lanzarote.

Sterling European

Sterling European is one of Denmark's major charter airlines, formed in 1994 from the assets of the failed Sterling Airways. Sterling European has a fleet of Boeing 737 -800s which it uses to transport holidaymakers from Denmark to Mediterranean resorts. Boeing 737-85H OY-SEI was operating a charter flight into Tenerife South when photographed in March 2001. The company's 737s are turned out in five different colours.

Sun-Air

Sun-Air of Scandinavia is a regional airline with a main base in Copenhagen, initially operating as an air taxi service and subsequently becoming a regional airline. In 1996 the carrier became a British Airways franchisee and operated flights in the colours of BA, their BAe ATP aircraft being used on scheduled flights between Copenhagen and Manchester. It was at the north of England city's airport where ATP OY-SVU was photographed in May 2000 as it prepared to depart on a return flight to Denmark. As well as operating in the British Airways 'Wings' colours, small Sun-Air titles are to be seen beneath the flightdeck window.

Also photographed at Manchester was BAe Jetstream 31 OY-MUE, which was operating a Copenhagen flight on an August morning in 2001. The nine-seat aircraft had just departed the terminal and was positioning for take-off.

Sweden

Sweden is situated on the Scandinavian Peninsula between Norway and Finland. Stockholm is the country's capital and the base of a number of airlines, including Scandinavian Airlines, the multi-national carrier also serving Norway and Denmark.

City Airline

City Airline is a regional airline and operates from its base at Gothenburg to destinations in the UK and parts of Europe. Three Embraer regional jets currently fly passengers to a number of cities, one destination is Manchester where EMB-145 SE-RAC was photographed in October 2002 about to depart on the early morning weekday service to Gothenburg.

Golden Air

Regional airline Golden Air is based in Trollhattan and commenced operations in 1993 with scheduled domestic passenger flights to destinations within Scandinavia and Finland using a fleet of Saab aircraft. The carrier's aircraft are regular visitors to Helsinki where Saab 340 OH-FAE was photographed in July 2000, about to receive attention prior to being put back into service performing one of many short hops.

Novair

Novair is one of Sweden's international passenger charter airlines, established in 1997 to operate from Stockholm to the Mediterranean resorts on behalf of its owner, a major travel group. A small number of Airbus A330s have recently been added to the fleet enabling the airline to provide long-haul services to the West Indies and the Far East. Most services to destinations closer to Sweden are performed by Airbus A321s delivered to the airline at the turn of the century. SE-DVU is now the carrier's only Boeing 737 and was photographed about to land at Lanzarote in November 2001.

Scandinavian Airlines

Scandinavian Airlines was established in 1946 and currently serves 100 destinations, operating around 1000 flights a day with a very comprehensive fleet of jetliners from the Boeing and Airbus plants. LN-RPB is one of the Boeing 737-600s in the SAS fleet and was photographed at Manchester in September 1999.

SAS is the multi-national state carrier of Denmark, Norway and Sweden and aircraft in its fleet carry three prefix registrations – LN (Norway), OY (Denmark) and SE (Sweden). Examples of the Airbus A321 began to be delivered to the carrier in 2001 and Danish registered OY-KBB was observed operating a flight out of Frankfurt-Main in June 2003.

Aircraft operating feeder and commuter flights within the SAS organisation carry 'Commuter' titling, the marketing name used by the carrier. Fokker 50 and Bombardier Dash 8s are employed on these services, and LN-RDT, one of two dozen Dash 8s assigned to the Commuter division, was photographed taxying away from its Tallinn stand in September 2002.

Skyways Express

Skyways Express operate a fleet of Saab, Embraer and Fokker passenger aircraft flying to most destinations in Sweden. The airline has had an alliance with SAS since 1997 and is now a full member of the group, quoting 'Well Connected with SAS' alongside its own titles on its aircraft. Embraer EMB-145 SE-DZB was photographed in October 2002 as it positioned for take-off at Manchester.

Norway

Norway occupies the western part of Scandinavia bordering Sweden, Finland and Russia. Oslo is the country's capital. The lengthy independence of Braathens recently came to an end, with its absorption into SAS, but Widerøe still operate on routes that go way north of the Arctic Circle into some of Europe's most inhospitable terrain.

Yugoslavia

The 'new' Federal Republic of Yugoslavia comprises the Republic of Serbia and Montenegro, bordered by seven other countries and the Adriatic Sea. Belgrade is the capital city and the base of JAT Airways, the country's national carrier, which has been considerably downsized since the break-up of the former Yugoslavian Federation.

Braathens

Braathens, Norway's largest airline, has been operational since 1946 and provides scheduled and charter, regional and international services to domestic and other destinations within Europe. Until 1998 the airline was known as Braathens SAFE, and it is now a member of the SAS group. The carrier's fleet consists of Boeing 737-400s, -500s and -700s, all configured for economy class travel on more than two dozen routes. Boeing 737 LN-BRP was a 737-405 which left the fleet in 2003. It was photographed approaching a gate at Amsterdam-Schiphol in June 2000.

Widerøe

Widerøe started out in 1934 as a flying boat airline flying to Norway's small and remote locations. The carrier is now a regional airline and the largest European user of the Dash 8 aircraft of which some thirty examples take the Widerøe colours to around thirty-five Norwegian destinations. For a time, services linked Bergen with Manchester and it is at the latter city's airport that Dash 8 LN-WDC was photographed in July 2004 as it prepared to return to Norway.

JAT Airways

JAT Airways, which changed its name in January 2003, set about re-establishing the former network, and has re-commenced the international flights to European Union countries which had been suspended due to civil unrest in the country. The midday flight from Belgrade is here seen arriving at Heathrow Airport in July 2001 in the hands of Boeing 727 YU-AKI. The airline was originally called Jugoslovenski Aero-Transport and had been flying as such since 1947. In February 2005, the airline was placed in financial administration in a bid to stave off bankruptcy.

JAT Airways

JAT Airways was expecting to replace its ageing fleet. First to go would be the Boeing 727s, most of which are currently in store, being replaced with newer Boeing 737-300s and -400s. Boeing 737-3H9 YU-AND was photographed in June 2003 whilst operating a flight out of Düsseldorf.

Montenegro Airlines

Montenegro Airlines is that country's only airline. It started operations in the spring of 1997 providing regular and charter flights to destinations in central and Eastern Europe. The airline's main base is at Podgorica from where flights are made to seven European destinations along with charter flights to various other towns and cities. Fokker 100 YU-AOL, one of four in the Montenegro Airlines fleet, was photographed at Frankfurt-Main in June 2003 as it prepared to depart on the mid-afternoon service to Podgorica.

Macedonia

The former Yugoslav Republic of Macedonia, one of Europe's youngest countries, borders Serbia and Montenegro to the north, and Greece to the south. Skopje is the capital city and the base of Macedonian Airlines, the national carrier.

MAT - Macedonian Airlines

MAT's main activity is directed at providing both passenger and cargo transport in the domestic and international traffic market, along with scheduled and non-scheduled charter flights. The company is based in Skopje and operated its first flight in June 1994. Two Boeing 737-300s currently make up the carrier's fleet and additional aircraft are leased from JAT as and when required. Both Boeings in the company fleet are illustrated in this spread. Z3-ARF looked decidedly in need of a face lift when arriving at Berlin-Schönefeld in March 2000 following a flight from Skopje, whilst sister ship Z3-AAA looked resplendent in the carrier's latest colour scheme departing from Düsseldorf in June 2003.

Slovenia

Slovenia is a former Republic of Yugoslavia and gained independence in 1991 prior to the actual break-up of Yugoslavia. Ljubljana is its capital city. Adria Airways, now the country's national airline, operating scheduled services, was a holiday airline in its previous existence.

Adria Airways

Established as Adria Aviopromet in 1961, Adria Airways relies on a small fleet of Canadair Regional Jets and Airbus A320s to operate its scheduled and charter services to more than a dozen European countries. The latter type of aircraft have served the carrier since 1989 and make regular appearances at the main European airports, S5-AAB being photographed at Frankfurt-Main in June 2001 upon arrival from Ljubljana. The 'Sloveniia' stickers applied to the fuselage are recent additions to the livery.

Air Adriatic

With its headquarters in the Croatian city of Rijeka, Air Adriatic was established as the country's first private airline and currently flies charter services on routes to Russia, Israel, North Africa and within Europe with a fleet of two McDonnell Douglas MD-82s, each configured for 158 one-class passengers. Tourism is one of the country's main industries and Air Adriatic is contracted to several tour companies to provide transportation for visitors. One MD-82, registered 9A-CBC, was photographed in June 2002 as it prepared to depart Düsseldorf at the start of a flight to Croatia.

Croatia Airlines

The flag carrier of the Republic is Croatia Airlines which has been flying since its formation in 1991, linking Zagreb with cities in Europe. Domestic operations performed by ATR 42s and international services operated by Airbus equipment are included in the carrier's schedules, taking their aircraft to the majority of the main European airports. Photographed upon arrival at Manchester in September 1999 was Airbus A320 9A-CTF, its simple yet quite attractive colours catching the last rays of the evening sunshine.

Croatia

Located to the south of Slovenia, Croatia was another part of the former Yugoslavia to have gained its independence, and is now known as the Republic of Croatia, with Zagreb as its capital.

Czech Republic

Previously part of Czechoslovakia, Prague remains capital city of the Czech Republic and has more airlines than its neighbour Slovakia, the other independent state formed following the elections held in 1990. The relative prosperity of this Eastern European country can be deduced from the airlines which exist to transport Czechs to sunnier climes.

CSA Czech Airlines

CSA Czech Airlines is the Czech Republic's national airline operating a comprehensive service of domestic, international and cargo flights from its base at Prague's Ruzyne Airport. ATR 42s and 72s perform the carrier's domestic routes, with Boeing 737s being available for international European flights and Airbus A310s for their long-haul services. London-Heathrow is one of the European cities served. Boeing 737-45S OK-DGM was photographed there in September 1999.

One of CSA's ATR 42s was visiting Geneva when photographed in August 2000. OK-AFE, the first of the type to appear in the company colours, had just arrived at the airport and was taxying to its gate using the power of just one of its two engines.

Fischer Air

Prague-based Fischer Air started operations in 1997 operating solely for the Czech tour operator of the same name, providing transport for its clients to a number of European destinations. Three Boeing 737s currently carry the Fischer titles and colours and OK-FUN, a 737-33A, was photographed at Rhodes in 1998.

Travel Service

Travel Service is the largest private airline company in the Czech Republic, established in 1997 as a major charter carrier. The airline is based at Prague's Ruzyne Airport from which its fleet of Boeing 737s operate to many of the tourist hot-spots within Europe and the Mediterranean. The carrier is a subsidiary of Canaria Travel and stickers to that effect are positioned on the engine cowlings of their aircraft. Boeing 737-86N OK-TVA illustrates the airline's colours as it prepares to land at Lanzarote in November 2001.

Slovakia

Slovakia is the less developed half of the
former Czechoslovakia, bordering Austria,
Poland, the Ukraine and Hungary. Bratislava
is the country's capital.

Estonia

The Republic of Estonia is the most Western-oriented of the Baltic States, bordered on the east by the Russian Federation. The country officially gained its independence in 1991 after previously being a province of Russia. Tallinn is the capital city and base of the country's airline Estonian Air.

Slovak Airlines

Although Slovak Airlines, the flag carrier of the Slovak Republic, was established in 1995, it was not until 1998 that their services commenced. The airline currently operates a programme of scheduled, charter and domestic passenger and cargo flights to mainly Eastern European destinations. Only two Fokker 100s and a Boeing 737 are now in service although, when photographed in August 1998, the carrier had Tupolev Tu-154s in their fleet. One of the type was OM-AAB which had been put into service on a charter flight to Rhodes where it was photographed taxying for departure.

Slovak Government Flying Service

The Slovak Government Flying Service is a division of the Ministry of the Interior, a non-commercial organisation involved in providing aircraft for patrols and VIP flights. OM-BYR, a Tupolev Tu-154 is one of the fleet and was photographed in April 2002 as it rested on the Larnaca airport ramp after providing transportation for a VIP visiting Cyprus.

Aero Airlines

Aero Airlines is a new 2001 start-up airline based in Tallinn. Whilst having an association with Finnair, the airline is now becoming a major short-haul carrier within the Baltic region alongside its six times a day ATR 72 flights between Tallinn and Helsinki. ATR 72 OH-KRK, photographed in September 2002 on the Tallinn Airport ramp, had just received instructions to start engines and was preparing for departure.

Airest

Airest is a small, Tallinn-based passenger and cargo airline operating Czech-built LET L-410 aircraft, of which there are two in the fleet. ES-LLB is a 1991-constructed example, photographed at Tallinn in September 2002.

Enimex

The majority of services operated by Tallinn-based Enimex are cargo flights. This carrier was established in 1994 and commenced operations with an Antonov An-72 aircraft. Further examples of the type have since been added to the company fleet and at the time of writing, seven or eight are in service. Cargo flights operate to many European destinations and An-72 ES-NOB had flown into Bournemouth when photographed in September 2002.

Estonian Air

Estonian Air, the country's national airline, was established in 1991 following the re-establishment of the country's independence. The carrier has a fleet of five Boeing 737s which perform services to twelve destinations around Europe. ES-ABD is one, here seen taxying away from the terminal at Tallinn at the commencement of a late afternoon flight to London-Gatwick in September 2002.

Lithuania

Lying on the coast of the Baltic Sea, Lithuania achieved its independence from the former USSR in 1991. The capital city is Vilnius, the base of the country's national airline.

Lithuanian Airlines

As the national carrier of the Republic of Lithuania, Lithuanian Airlines offers both domestic and international scheduled services to a number of cities in Western and Eastern Europe. Originally established in 1938, the airline was re-established as a state-owned enterprise in 1991, around the same time as the granting of independence. Two types of aircraft are in use, Saab 2000s and Boeing 737s. Operating a flight into London-Heathrow in August 1997 was Boeing 737-2T4 LY-BSD, photographed as it prepared to touch down on the airport's northern runway.

Latvia

Latvia is situated on the eastern coast of the Baltic Sea lying between Estonia and Lithuania. Its eastern border is with the Russian Federation, from whom it gained its independence in 1991. Riga is both the country's capital city and the main tourist destination.

Air Baltic

Air Baltic is the national airline of Latvia, it is a very young airline having been established in 1995. The carrier is 'Well Connected to SAS' through its affiliation with SAS Scandinavian Airlines who own shares in the company. Fokker 50s are included in the carrier's fleet which also include BAe 146 and Boeing 737 types, the former being used on services linking Riga, the airline's base, with destinations in Finland, Russia and Estonia. Three daily weekday flights operate between Riga and Estonia and Fokker 50 YL-BAR had just arrived at Tallinn with the afternoon flight when photographed in September 2002.

Greece

The Hellenic Republic is the southernmost nation of the Balkans, surrounded by the Aegean, Ionian and Cretan Seas. Included in its territory are two thousand islands, some being the destination for holidaymakers from most parts of Europe. Athens is the capital city.

Aegean Airlines

Established in 1999, Aegean Airlines is an Athens-based carrier involved in transporting holidaymakers to Greece, together with providing aircraft for special charter traffic. The airline's fleet is made up of Lear Jets used for executive private flights, and BAe 146 and Boeing 737s which operate their other services. The Aegean colours are often seen at Düsseldorf where Boeing 737-3Y0 SX-BGK was photographed in charge of a departing flight in June 2003.

Hellas Jet

Hellas Jet is a Greek international airline established in 2002 with a base in Athens from which it operates to destinations like Brussels, Zürich, Paris, London and Manchester. Three brand new Airbus A320 airliners, each given names from Greek mythology and fitted out in two classes, currently make up the Hellas Jet fleet. Airbus A320 SX-BVC carries the name *Orion* and is one of the three twinjets delivered to the airline in May 2003. It was photographed in June 2004 at Manchester upon its arrival on the twice-weekly flight from Athens.

Olympic Airlines

Olympic Airways was the national airline of Greece, founded by Aristotle Onassis in April 1957. In December 2003 the airline ended operations following 47 years of operations due to financial difficulties, shortly afterwards to be restructured by the government and re-named Olympic Airlines. Boeing 737-484 SX-BKC photographed at Rhodes in August 1998 is still flying with the re-modelled carrier.

Macedonian Airways

Prior to the reconstruction of Olympic Airways, Macedonian Airways was another of Greece's airlines operating from Athens Airport. Following the 2003 reconstruction, Macedonian became part of the Olympic Group of Companies and its three Boeing 737-400s were taken into the Olympic fleet. SX-BMA, with Macedonian titles and colours and also carrying 'Subsidiary of Olympic Airways' stickers, is here seen departing Düsseldorf in October 2003.

We hope you enjoyed this book . . .

Midland Publishing offers an extensive range of outstanding aviation titles, of which a small selection are shown here.

We always welcome ideas from authors or readers for books they would like to see published.

In addition, our associate, Midland Counties Publications, offers an exceptionally wide range of aviation, military, naval and transport books and videos for sale by mail-order worldwide.

For a copy of the appropriate catalogue, or to order further copies of this book, and any other Midland Publishing titles, please write, telephone, fax or e-mail to:

Midland Counties Publications
4 Watling Drive, Hinckley,
Leics, LE10 3EY, England
Tel: (+44) 01455 254 450
Fax: (+44) 01455 233 737
E-mail: midlandbooks@compuserve.com
www.midlandcountiessuperstore.com

US distribution by Specialty Press –
see page 2.

RUSSIAN AIRLINES AND THEIR AIRCRAFT

Dmitriy Komissarov & Yefim Gordon

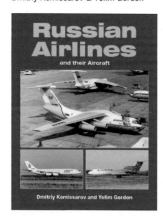

Following the ending of Aeroflot's monopoly in 1992 and the break-up of the Soviet Union, the Russian civil air transport scene has been considerably transformed.

This full-colour album covers the major airlines operating in Russia today, illustrating the types operated by each carrier, their equipment and the various colour schemes worn by them. A brief history and fleet information are provided for each airline, as are detailed photo captions.

Softback, 280 x 215 mm, 160 pages
449 full colour photographs
1 85780 176 8 **£19.99**

ARRIVALS & DEPARTURES
North American Airlines 1990-2000

John K Morton

This is a photographic record, with extended captions, of new and departed North American airlines during the last decade of the 20th century. It is divided into three sections: 'Arrivals' contains 32 airlines which began operations during the period and were still operational at the end of it; 'Arrivals and Departures' features 24 carriers which came and went, and 'Departures' covers 29 airlines which went out of business in the 1990s. Included here are famous names such as PanAm, Eastern and Tower Air.

Softback, 280 x 215 mm, 112 pages
168 full colour photographs
1 85780 200 4 **£14.99**

1000 CIVIL AIRCRAFT IN COLOUR

Gerry Manning

From Air Alfa to Zoom Airlines, here are photographs of civil airliners and other transport types, both large and small. Captured worldwide in recent years, they display a multiplicity of markings as they go about tasks ranging from international schedules to obscure freight operations. Extended captions detail type, individual aircraft, operator and location. Additional features include BA's fast-disappearing 'World Images' colours and aircraft in eye-catching special or promotional colour schemes.

Softback, 280 x 215 mm, 160 pages
over 1,000 full colour photographs
1 85780 208 X **£18.99**

AIRLINERS WORLDWIDE
Over 100 Current Airliners Described and Illustrated in Colour (2nd edition)

Tom Singfield

The coverage in this new edition of this valuable guidebook is markedly different, up-to-the-minute and indispensable. The text for each type has been revised and updated. Each type has an historical narrative and description of model variants and type of operations plus principal technical details and a listing of current operators. The photographic selection is all new and types new to this edition include the Embraer 170 and 195, the Antonov An-140, Airbus A318 and A380.

Softback, 240 x 170 mm, 128 pages
136 colour photographs
1 85780 189 X **£13.99**

AIRLINES WORLDWIDE
Over 360 Airlines Described and Illustrated in Colour (4th edition)

B I Hengi

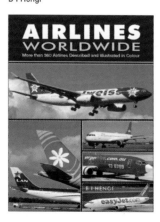

Airlines Worldwide, first published in 1994, has established itself as a trusted and sought-after reference work. It aims to give an overview and illustrate the world's leading or more interesting airlines, including smaller national operators, with their history, routes, aircraft fleet and operations.

This latest edition is more than ever revised and updated, notably in the light of the turbulent events and rapid changes in the airline industry over the past couple of years.

Softback, 240 x 170 mm, 384 pages
c360 colour photographs
1 85780 155 5 **£18.99**

AIRLINES REMEMBERED
Over 200 Airlines of the Past, Described and Illustrated in Colour

B I Hengi

In the same format as the enormously popular *Airlines Worldwide* and *Airliners Worldwide*, this companion reviews the histories and operations of over 200 airlines from the last thirty years which are no longer with us, each illustrated with a full colour photograph showing at least one of their aircraft in the colour scheme of that era. Operators such as BEA, CP Air, Eastern, Invicta, Jet 24, Laker and Fred Olsen are examples of the extensive and varied coverage.

Softback, 240 x 170 mm, 224 pages
c200 colour photographs
1 85780 091 5 **£14.95**

AIRLINES WORLDWIDE
76 Older Types, Worldwide, Described and Illustrated in Colour

Tom Singfield

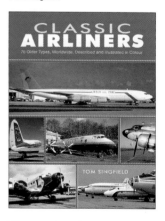

This companion volume reviews the histories, operations and specifications of 76 airliner types which have been familiar during the last fifty years, and includes over 200 outstanding colour photos showing the airliners both in service and preserved. Included are less well-known yet significant types, for instance the Dassault Mercure, Breguet Deux Ponts, Saab Scandia, and VFW-614. Of course, all the appropriate Boeing, Douglas, Antonov, Lockheed, Ilyushin, and Tupolev types appear.

Softback, 240 x 170 mm, 160 pages
over 200 colour photographs
1 85780 098 2 **£13.95**

HISTORIC HOUSES
CASTLES & GARDENS

THE ORIGINAL GUIDE TO THE TREASURES OF GREAT BRITAIN & IRELAND

Mellerstain House, Borders, Scotland (*top*) *&* **Iford Manor Gardens, Wiltshire**
Joint Winners of Christie's / HHA Garden of the Year Award presented in 1999

a
JOHANSENS
p u b l i c a t i o n

www.historichouses.co.uk

THE GARDENS AT
HATFIELD HOUSE
Hertfordshire

The gardens at Hatfield House date from the early 17th century when Robert Cecil, 1st Earl of Salisbury, employed John Tradescant the Elder to plant and lay them out around his new home. Tradescant was sent to Europe where he found and brought back trees, bulbs, plants and fruit trees, which had never previously been grown in England. These beautifully designed gardens included orchards, elaborate fountains, scented plants, water parterres, terraces, herb gardens and a foot maze. Following the fashion for landscape gardening and some neglect in the 18th century, restoration of these gardens started in earnest in Victorian times. Today, the present Marchioness continues to re-create and maintain the grounds entirely organically in a style that reflects their Jacobean history. The gardens to the west of the house, which include the Herb, Knot and Wilderness areas, can be seen when the house is open. However, all 42 acres, including the Kitchen Garden and the formal parterres to the East of the house leading down to the lake, are open specially for connoisseurs on Fridays.

FOR DETAILS SEE HERTFORDSHIRE SECTION

Contents

Stourhead, Wiltshire

Castle Howard, Yorks

Château de Cheverny, Loire Valley

HIGHCLERE CASTLE
Ardington House and Newbury Manor

Although Highclere Castle is considered to be the finest Victorian Home still in existence it is from Georgian era that the partnership between the Castle, Ardington House and Newbury Manor seems totally appropriate. Both Ardington House and Newbury Manor were built in 1720 and until 1842, when the 3rd Earl of Carnarvon decided his Georgian house was not grand enough, they would have represented a unique combination of architectural styles that reflect the glory of this period.

Newbury Manor

Ardington House

Foreword by Alan Titchmarsh

Wanting to be a gardener seemed the most natural thing in the world to me. I can't remember a time when I didn't love being outdoors - either in the woods or on the moors or down by the river where I grew up in Yorkshire. My interest in growing things was ignited on my grandfather's allotment when I was a toddler, fuelled by my mother's encouragement in our tiny back garden, and then blossomed when I got my first job - as an apprentice gardener in the nursery of our local parks department.

Why was I so ensnared by things that grow? It must be in the blood. It wasn't until I was much older that my father - a plumber by trade - confessed that both his father and grandfather had been gardeners - he had been made to weed and decided there and then that the spade held no thrill for him. I couldn't wait to pick it up.

In my mother's garden I grew lobelia and dwarf double daisies, alyssum and nasturtiums. I built a small greenhouse out of polythene when I was twelve, inside which I grew geraniums and spider plants given to me by our next-door neighbour. Life was blissful. But school? Only art and drama gave me any pleasure - maths and physics were not at all my cup of tea.

And so, with one 'O' level in art under my belt, I left school at 15 to take up the apprenticeship at the nursery. I loved it. Being paid to grow plants! And in a proper wooden greenhouse! Over the next five years I learned my trade - everything from washing pots and stoking boilers to taking 15,000 geranium cuttings a year.

After the nursery came a year full-time at horticultural college in Hertfordshire and then I was taken on as a student gardener at the Royal Botanic Gardens, Kew. If the nursery had been a thrill, Kew was like

heaven – here I looked after plants that had been brought to Britain by Captain Cook and other intrepid explorers and I started to get to know some of our other great gardens - Wisley and Sissinghurst, Hidcote and Wakehurst Place.

Growing plants was no longer enough. I wanted to tell people about the pleasure that gardening gave me, so after teaching at Kew for a couple of years as Supervisor of Staff Training, I took up the pen, first as a gardening books editor, then as Deputy Editor of Amateur Gardening magazine and finally as a freelance writer with the likes of The Express and Radio Times.

Thanks to an invasion of greenfly in Margate, my television break came twenty years ago on Nationwide and now I can earn my living doing what I love best - showing gardening techniques and great gardens on BBC's Gardeners' World and transforming patches of wasteland into tiny oases on Ground Force.

The success of Ground Force has increased the popularity of gardening tremendously. Today, folk are not only keen to make a difference in their own back gardens, but also to visit great gardens from which they can draw inspiration.Historic Houses, Castles and Gardens plays a vital role in fostering this interest, whether you like looking at stately and majestic plots, or smaller, more intimate slices of horticulture.

My own garden at Barleywood - one and a third acres on a chalky, flinty Hampshire hillside - has been created over the last eighteen years, and it is by visiting other people's gardens that I've found ideas to incorporate on my own patch of inhospitable soil.

Historic Houses, Castles and Gardens is a great companion for outings, whatever the season. Sample the grandeur of Chatsworth in Derbyshire where Capability Brown's landscapes are now at their spectacular best. Marvel, as I did, at the views from Lanhydrock House in Cornwall and enjoy the rich diversity of planting at Great Dixter in East Sussex - home of Christopher Lloyd, one of our greatest gardeners.

After a few days in my own garden, or tucked away in my shed writing novels like Mr MacGregor or The Last Lighthouse Keeper, I'm glad to get out and stretch my legs and my imagination in other people's gardens. I hope this guide will help you to do the same.

L'art de vivre
at every
Johansens
Recommended
Hotel

How to use this guide

If you want to identify a historic house, castle or garden, whose name you already know, look for it in the Index of all properties from page 347.

If you want to find a historic house, castle or garden in a particular county or area you can:
• Turn to the maps at the back of the book
• Look through the guide for the county you require, they are sorted in alphabetical order. The properties are then listed alphabetically wherever possible. The maps cover the counties of England, Ireland, Scotland and Wales. Each historic house, castle and garden is clearly named and marked on these maps. Properties in Belgium, France, Germany and The Netherlands have their approximate positions labelled on the illustrated maps in each country introduction.

Starting from page 297 there are a number of properties listed in certain categories: supplementary list by appointment only, Cambridge and Oxford Universities, film locations, garden specialists, plants for sale, art collections, weddings, "top teas", open all year, conference facilities and accommodation.

To find somewhere local to stay, a full listing of Johansens recommended hotels, country houses and inns are included in county order on page 323.

Publishing Manager:	Phoebe Hobby
Editorial Manager:	Yasmin Razak
Sales Executive:	Juliette Cutting
European Contributor:	Stéphanie Court
Production Director:	Daniel Barnett
Production Controller:	Kevin Bradbrook
Senior Designer:	Michael Tompsett
Designer:	Sue Dixon
Special Promotions Editor:	Fiona Patrick
Sales & Marketing Manager:	Laurent Martinez
Marketing Executive:	Stephen Hoskin
Sales Administrator:	Susan Butterworth
Map Illustrations:	Linda Clark
Publishing Director:	Peter Hancock
Managing Director:	Andrew Warren

Johansens Ltd, Therese House, Glasshouse Yard, London EC1A 4JN
Tel: 020 7566 9700 Fax: 020 7490 2538

Find Johansens on the Internet at: www.historichouses.co.uk

Copyright © 1999 Johansens Ltd.
a subsidiary of the Daily Mail and General Trust plc
ISBN 1 860 177166
Printed in England by St Ives plc
Colour origination by Catalyst Creative Imaging
Distributed in the UK and Europe by Johnsons International Media Services Ltd, London (direct sales) & ABS, Kent (bookstores). In North America by Hunter Publishing, New Jersey (bookstores). In Australia and New Zealand by Bookwise International, Findon, South Australia

Key to Symbols

- The National Trust
- The National Trust for Scotland
- Historic Scotland
- English Heritage
- CADW
- Historic Houses Association
- HITHA
- Park
- Garden
- Refreshments
- Children's Playground
- Accommodation Available
- Meals Available
- Picnic Area
- Wedding Licence
- Disabled Access
- Guided Tours
- Gift Shop
- Nurseries – Plants for Sale
- Live Entertainment
- House by Appointment Only
- Haunted
- Conference Facilities
- Used for Filming
- Special Group Rates

HONDA

First man, then machine

The Honda Accord has won critical acclaim from both the public and press alike.

What Car? Magazine voted it best in class in their 1999 Car of the Year Awards.

Now there's the choice of a 5 door model within the range, offering increased versatility.

Like all Accords, the 5 door is one of the quietest and most refined in its class.

It's powered by Honda's Formula One bred VTEC engine, which combines high power with high economy (147ps and 32.8mpg* from the 2.0i).

With multi-link double-wishbone suspension- which keeps the wheels as vertical as possible, thereby maximising road grip-plus ABS and air conditioning, it's a pleasure to drive.

Call 0345 159 159 or visit www.honda.co.uk

Same story, different ending.

The Honda Accord.

*COMBINED FIGURE FOR THE 2.0i MANUAL

A portrait of the man as an artist

Lord Bath discusses property, paintings and polygyny

The Thynn family portrait

Built in the 16th century and widely regarded as the finest example of Elizabethan architecture in Great Britain, Longleat has housed fourteen generations of the Thynn (or Thynne) family for over 450 years. Standing impressively in 'Capability' Brown landscaped grounds comprising enchanting labyrinths, a safari park and the world's longest hedge maze, the house first opened to the public in 1949.

As he reminisced about the early years, Alexander Thynn stated "My father's greatest achievement was opening Longleat to the public. The government set up a system whereby you received a tax benefit if you opened to the public. He was the first person to take advantage of it and was soon copied by other stately homes. I have many recollections of the opening day. My father liked the idea that every member of the family would be doing something and my role, along with that of my brothers, was to help people into the car park. There were different car parks and there was intense rivalry as to who was getting the most tips! As for the year itself, I would have been at school largely. I just remember that it was something that was much written about and I knew that my father was succeeding. I was aware of this as the newspapers told me so!"

Although his childhood was spent in a house on the fringes of the estate, Lord Bath moved into Longleat in 1953 at the age of 21. He began running the estate, with the exception of the park and its tourist attractions which were firmly under his father's control, a mere three years later. "I certainly relished the challenge of taking over but I had never thought of my life

An idyllic view of Longleat

differently – right from the earliest memories I recall hearing that I was going to live at Longleat and bring up the next generation there. It was an idea I never questioned as I was born into the expectation of inheriting the estate."

As he discussed the early 1950s and his residence in the house, the differences between the current Marquess and his father are evident. "I think he always took a line that I felt was wrong and that was that 'Alexander doesn't love the place, he is just thinking about himself and his paintings.' To me, that was always a false line as thinking about the paintings was actually with regards to the décor of the place and I do love Longleat. I just felt he hadn't got his own position worked out and chose to voice opinions in that manner for reasons of not being able to voice them in more personal ways." He then stated that he had the "tendency to become a recluse" yet he did not feel that the public's presence at his family home exacerbated the situation. "Other things exaggerated the situation, I wasn't getting on so well with my father and therefore, I was in his house and withdrawn into a corner of it and not really able to walk around the place with a great feeling of belonging, but I didn't resent the people. The public were going around the house before I moved in so I was adjusting to a situation and

9

supposing that they might have a bit of difficulty adjusting to the fact that a corner was now occupied."

Whilst the importance afforded to his relationship with his father is evident, Lord Bath's interest in familial matters is steeped in his penchant for polygyny. The initial public statement which aroused the interest in his personal inclinations was the announcement of his

Above: A life in pictures - The Autobiography Mural. Below: Emerging Extroverts in The Disco Mural

'anti–marriage' in 1966. "I was living with a young girl and the tabloid press had been badgering me as to whether she was to be my future bride and in an exasperated moment I declared that we were getting anti–married. I suppose it was a statement of the 60s where there was irreverence for the fundamental concepts of religion, politics and marriage. It cohered with the period and that type of revolution. Subsequently, when she announced that she was leaving me, the press declared it an anti–divorce!" He believes that European culture is gradually moving over from being a monogamous society to a polymorphous society and, citing the increasing media statistics and interest in the subject, he explained that "I feel that the fact that

women are getting married at a later stage in life and that many people are rejecting the traditional convention of marriage points to what I believe. I feel that social history is pinpointing these new directions all the time. I believe it is becoming more and more

acceptable and the question is, how long will it be before the majority start to think along these lines and change? I would have thought we are experiencing so much insecurity from the way monogamy does end in tumbles, I mean ruptures, that looking into other forms is certainly the way forward. States must assist and provide what is needed like psychological clinics which people are encouraged to visit. There should be marriage clinics for single partners and group partners where you can discuss your problems. These will become more common and the counsellors certainly won't be saying "come back when you are monogamous". I do believe that society will eventually change and when it becomes common practice, the government will take steps. I don't think the government will be forced to do this, I just think that the forward–thinking politician looks for legislation that will help what is happening."

Lord Bath entered a state of marriage with Anna Gael, an actress and journalist, after drawing up a written list of points and receiving a verbal agreement. "Of course I had spoken to Anna about my views regarding the sort of family I could contribute well towards. She accepted my polygynous intents provided that I would leave her to decide in her own time and way, whether she might wish to participate within whatever practices I might successfully bring to fruition."

As he then acquired his circle of lady friends, choosing a term to describe them was most important. "People wrote phrases such as 'mistresses' and it wasn't said too nicely. I have tried to use a term which is affectionate, humourous and not offensive. I mean, the term 'anti–wives' was offensive to my wife Anna, so I tried to coin a term which I didn't invent. The word had been used to mean 'little wife' in previous centuries and I thought that was a nice word."

The subject of the 'wifelets' has been the source of immense public interest, particularly from those within the locality, and rumours abound regarding their status, the property they may own and the manorial rights they may or may not be entitled to. However, the most discussed subject is the number of 'wifelets' and as Lord Bath explained, "Journalists do love to paint a picture of the number of relationships I've had in my life as all grouped together in one house and that's not the case. At any given time there's likely to be around five and also you would have to see if I am actually seeing the fourth and fifth as often as the second and third. It's not really a question of numbers."

It was with much pleasure that he revealed that his polygynous endeavours can finally be regarded as fruitful. "I do have one other child by one of my wifelets. There have been quite a few others who have been pregnant and lost it, not by intention. So when I heard people say that 'he can't have any, he's infertile', it's always so irritating because that was never the case. The aforementioned child is a girl, more than a year old now. I am surprised that the birth had remained a secret from the press for so long. I was often being asked if it occurred to me that maybe I couldn't have any more children but I already knew that I could and that I had!"

Whilst the controversy surrounding the 'wifelets' and his fascination with polgyny has gained him a degree of infamy, Lord Bath would like to be known for his artistic and literary talents.

His flair for painting was identified at an early age and has escalated throughout his life. "I was praised by art teachers as a boy of ten or so but my talent lay dormant until my last year at Eton. Then, after taking School Certificate, you could take a special subject and I took art. I found myself praised by the brother of Sir Anthony Blunt, Wilfred Blunt. He was encouraging me to become an artist. He was suggesting it was something I could think about and I thought about this and other subjects. It had been an early thought and it became stronger."

Inside Longleat, the walls are adorned with captivating murals which serve as a testament to the laborious toil of the artist. He was inspired to paint them when sitting in a room which had been prepared for artists and featured rococo panels. "No—one ever got around to commissioning an artist to fill them. Sitting there as a painter, it would have been peculiar if I hadn't! Calling them murals is technically incorrect because I have lined the panels with something like canvas and chipboard so effectively you could lift them off the walls."

"There are several ways in which these murals can be assessed. Some of them I describe as cocoons – the idea of me being like a caterpillar who views all his own handiwork while looking up from the inside, with a feeling perhaps that this constitutes his vision of the universe. It is difficult for me to choose a favourite mural, I have several which I am fondly attached to but if I was to just briefly cover a few then: the first one that I did which was The Ages of Man, then The Disco Mural and finally The Kama Sutra Mural. The latter two fall into the category of mural which I describe as therapies. By painting The Disco Mural I was urging myself to emerge from introversion towards extroversion whereas The Kama Sutra Mural relates to the expulsion of my sexual inhibitions."

"The Paranoia Mural is one of the therapies and it took a subject that I feel I needed psychological evolution, in as much that I was paranoid and I felt the world was plotting against me. I felt other people would think my paranoia was absurd so that somehow that whole vision of life became something one can laugh at and dismiss. The mural was illustrating what I was trying to do; I was trying to tell myself that paranoia is ridiculous."

The nursery suite is a magnificent orgy of colour and it is here that another category of murals are displayed. The fantasies were painted for Lord Bath's two children, Lenka and Ceawlin, and comprise four magical works. Featuring a multi–racial youth and the animal kingdom, the Marquess explained that "I was really trying to prompt certain values in my children's hearts by making them feel that they belong to a world with other races and other beasts and animals."

Lord Bath candidly discussed the idea of exhibiting his murals, stating that "You must remember that most of the murals take up the whole of a wall and I can't see many places taking up the expense of transporting and displaying them particularly because I wouldn't be offering them for sale. Of course, I am interested in knowing their value and I am using the internet as a medium to find out. I've put up one 'erotic apple' – I am not especially trying to sell it but I have put up a respectable price of £10,000 if anyone wants to buy it! If it sells then I know that they can sell at that price!"

With regards to literature, Lord Bath admits that he rarely finds the time to read, "In the morning, reading the newspapers is a lazy occupation of mine whilst eating my breakfast. The Independent and The Mail are my two papers. There was a period when I was reading extensively after I had just come down from Oxford as I was feeling that I wasn't really acquainted much with English Literature so I read extensively until I felt I had got the feel of what English Literature was about and then I decided to write a journal on what I felt I could contribute."

"In relation to the autobiography, I have kept a journal since 1954 and so what I am really doing now is I am going through the books and revising them. There are entries in longhand so I am now transforming the journal into autobiography. Then there is another process of taking it, editing it, omitting certain paragraphs and compiling the internet edition. They are just notebooks but I've kept the writing up consistently, sticking in press cuttings. It averages out at about once a week that I write in them."

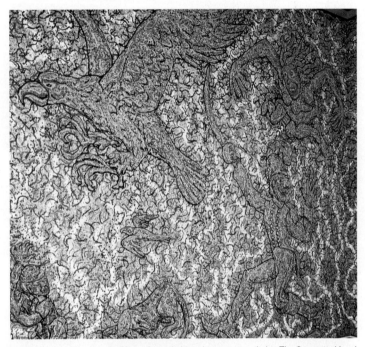

Above: A psychological past is revealed in The Paranoia Mural

Looking towards the future, the 7th Marquess of Bath was hesitant to reveal any of the forthcoming plans for Longleat, "I couldn't really say much in detail as I try to always maintain the element of surprise. I do have some ideas, nothing too sensational, but the business of owning a stately home involves always having something that is a novelty."

On a more personal level, his ambitions are inexorably linked with his artistic aspirations. "To complete the murals in the private apartments and to complete the autobiography would be two very significant work efforts and I'd be happy enough if I did that!"

Finally from a familial perspective, it is clear that he has not fully sated his desires. "There have been gradual movements on all fronts throughout my life and I'm content with that, but I can't rejoice in it being as fast or as far as I would have liked. I never did have as many children as I would have liked – but there still is time!"

Yasmin Razak

ERCOL

THE CLOSER YOU LOOK
THE MORE YOU DISCOVER

PREFERRED FURNITURE

Loch, Scot & Two Smoking Barrels

A proud and bloody heritage is preserved within the walls of Scotland's great castles.

Floors Castle at dusk

Scotland is the land of the brave and it is through its many castles and historic houses, that the modern visitor can learn more about the history of the people and the country. Many castles in Scotland display collections of armour reflecting the bloody history of this great land, particularly those at Blair Castle in Strath Garry with its armour from the infamous Battle of Culloden and Inverary Castle with its magnificent hall. It is the variety offered by Scottish castles that brings visitors back again and again – landscaped gardens are combined with breathtaking architecture and glorious ornate chambers, filled with art treasures from around the world and relics of a Scotland past. Several castles feature collections of artworks and furniture that can be found nowhere else in the world; Blair Castle in Perthshire houses the famous Mortlake tapestries, once belonging to Charles I of England. After Oliver Cromwell ordered the tapestries to be sold, the 1st Duke of Atholl was lucky enough to purchase them. The Scots are a proud and noble race and are justifiably proud of their heritage. The castles which are situated throughout the country, often dating back hundreds of years or more, help to retain the legacy of the past, so that future generations can enjoy these historic vestiges.

Of all Scotland's great houses, Dunrobin Castle in Sutherland is the most northerly and is the largest in the Northern Highlands. For thirty years now it has welcomed visitors to look around the magnificent property, dating in part from the early 1300s. In addition to the house, there is a museum, displaying a collection of hunting trophies and other ephemera in a summerhouse built by William, Earl of Sutherland, and beautiful landscaped grounds,

inspired by the formal gardens of Versailles. These date back to 1850 and were conceived by the architect, Sir Charles Barry, who was responsible for the Victorian extension to the Castle and who, more famously, designed the Houses of Parliament. Inside, a visitor to the Castle is met by a myriad of magnificent, stately rooms. A light and spacious drawing room, replete with beautiful Louis XV furniture commands amazing views of the gardens while a world renowned collection of Wemyss Ware china is found in the Queens Corridor. The Green and Gold Room in the Castle is rather famous for being the room where Queen Victoria slept when she visited in 1872 and in the adjoining Ladies Sitting Room are some magnificent tapestries, commissioned especially for the royal visit, with a picture of Dunrobin woven into the centre of two of them.

Legend has it that Dunrobin has a ghost; in the 15th century, the wicked Earl of Sutherland is said to have captured a beautiful young girl from the Mackay clan after a battle and locked her up in the room, next to the night nursery. He wanted to marry her, but she refused him and one night, when he came to her room, he found her trying to escape down a rope of sheets. In his anger, he drew his sword and cut the rope, causing her to fall to her death at the foot of the tower and it is said that she is supposed to be heard wailing and weeping. On the floor below the fated room, in Duchess Clare's bedroom, an unearthly set of footsteps has also been heard and on one occasion twenty five years ago, a male figure was seen walking along the landing and through a closed door!

Left: Blair Castle on a cold autumnal morning. Right: The Castle's impressive collection of china.

The Atholl family first made their home in Blair Castle more than 700 years ago, when it was a defensive stronghold in the Grampians. Blair Castle no longer has to defend the mountain passes and now welcomes more visitors than any other private house in Scotland. As a draughty medieval castle, a stately Georgian mansion or a comfortable Victorian family home, Blair Castle has drawn visitors for hundreds of years. One or two must have been turned away with a bucket of boiling oil or musket fire, but most have been warmly welcomed, as visitors are today. The castle and surrounding estate was placed into trust in 1995 so that the building and its contents would be preserved for future generations to enjoy. The grand entrance hall also doubles as an armoury, housing targes and muskets used at the famous Battle of Culloden of 1746, which saw the hopes of Bonnie Prince Charlie crushed and the end of the Jacobite rising. The young Duke's courage at this battle has passed into Scottish legend and the armoury collection helps bring this history to life.

For lovers of grand tradition, Blair Castle has its own elegant tearoom, with huge Chippendale and Sheraton cabinets containing a marvellous display of Sevres china. Although visitors cannot take tea in this grand setting, there is a restaurant where beverages are served. The castle also has its own impressive china room, with over 1700 pieces of china in a specially converted room, including a magnificent Coalport set painted by Amelia, daughter of the 4th Duke.

Drumlanrig Castle is the Ancient Douglas stronghold and Dumfriesshire home of the Duke of Buccleuch and Queensberry. Almost 700 years ago, the Douglasses were among the foremost

Bonnie Prince Charlie's elegant bedroom in Drumlanrig Castle

supporters of Robert the Bruce, King of Scotland. The present castle was built between 1679 and 1691 upon the 14th century Douglas stronghold, traces of which are still discernible. The castle is made of local pink sandstone, and enjoys magnificent views across the Queensberry Estate. Distinguished guests ranging from James VI to Bonnie Prince Charlie, to our present Queen and Prince Philip, and even Neil Armstrong, have all left their mark at Drumlanrig. It was here that the young Prince stayed in 1745, on his retreat northwards with a force of 200 highlanders. Some personal relics of the 'young pretender' can be viewed in Bonnie Prince Charlie's bedroom. A more whimsical feel is to be found in the Staircase Gallery, which houses a magnificent silver chandelier (c.1670) with 16 branches in the form of dolphins and mermaids. This was purchased by the 5th Duke of Buccleuch in 1835 and weighs an astonishing 120 pounds!

Bowhill is a great family home, with a unique art collection ranging from works by Van Dyck to Sir Henry Raeburn and 18th century Italian Masters. The house dates from 1812 and the Scott Clan who live there were originally given part of the forest in which the building stands, way back in 1550. Bowhill has an interesting connection to the Scottish writer, Sir Walter Scott (1771-1832). During the 19th century, many additions were made to Bowhill and much of this was completed under the watchful eye of Sir Walter Scott, a kinsman and frequent visitor, who christened it "Sweet Bowhill" in his famous poem "Lay of the Last Minstrel." The Sir Walter Scott Room displays portraits

Raeburn's portrait of Sir Walter Scott

and relics of the man and the showcase contains many manuscripts and proof editions. Scott was deeply patriotic and his writing is often credited with having rekindled the embers of Scottish nationalism and sentiment.

Other interesting features to peruse at Bowhill, are the 'Italian room,' filled with beautiful paintings by Italian Masters and the Drawing room with its hand-painted Chinese wallpaper. A gift from the British envoy to China in 1790, the wallpaper has been beautifully preserved to this day.

Inverary Castle is still home to the 12th Duke of Argyll and was built in the 18th century on a site inhabited by the Campbell's since the 15th century and whose origins can be traced back 900 years. Inside the Castle there is a 'Clan' room which contains a fascinating family tree showing the related branches and septs of Clan Campbell and methods for worldwide members to join in their own countries. One of the most striking aspects in the Castle is the 95ft high Armoury Hall, where arms are displayed in decorative patterns, as ordered by the 5th Duke in 1783. This makes for a stunning display when combined with the soaring height of the Hall.

Inverary Castle's Royal Connection can be seen in the 'Victorian Room,' which contains a beautiful Maplewood desk that Queen Victoria gave to her daughter as a wedding present, when in 1871 Princess Louise, married the Marquess of Lorne, who later become the 9th Duke of Argyll. The State Dining Room at Inverary is of worldwide significance with the only surviving work of the French artists Girard and Guinard, in some spectacular wall panels. The ornamental painting in this room is quite simply stunning and any visit to the Castle is incomplete without an appreciation of this splendid, lavish chamber.

Floors Castle in Roxburghshire was built for the 1st Duke of Roxburghe in 1721 and what the modern visitor sees today is an evolving house with vestiges left by succeeding generations. Perhaps the most obvious change to the house occurred between 1837 and

The Armoury Hall at Inveraray Castle

1847 when the 6th Duke invited the celebrated Edinburgh architect, William Playfair, to remodel the Castle. The finished result was as Playfair had wanted - a romantic fairytale castle with a roofscape of turrets, pinnacles and cupolas. In addition, there are beautiful formal gardens including a walled kitchen garden that became a flourishing garden centre in 1978 and still supplies the castle with fresh flowers and plants.

In 1903, the 8th Duke had followed contemporary fashion by taking on an American bride, Duchess May. The Castle today is filled with the French art and furniture that May had inherited from her family and many rooms have her special 'touch' on them. The Needle Room, with its crimson silk wall hangings, contains many priceless works of art including two by Henri Matisse. Duchess May's collection can also be viewed in the Ballroom where many of her larger works of art are displayed to wonderful effect, in particular, the 17th century Gobelins tapestries. The Drawing room also contains many fine tapestries and even a Royal commode from the Bedchamber of Comtesse d'Artas at the Palace of Versailles!

Whilst the castles and dukedoms throughout Scotland are diverse in their architecture and varied in their surrounds, all offer a rich history and tradition that is synonymous with the country's proud heritage.

Gemma Slade

The National Gardens Scheme

What precisely is the National Gardens Scheme? To put it at its simplest, it's a very British way of having your cake and eating it – of having a good time while also doing good.

The scheme began back in 1927 when Miss Elsie Wagg of the Queen's Nursing Institute had the bright idea of raising funds for that charity by persuading people to open their private gardens to the public for the grand sum of 'a shilling a head.' From those modest beginnings – with only a few, mostly large-scale gardens opening for the benefit of a single charity – it's grown to become nothing less than a national institution, with almost three and a half thousand gardens, of every possible size and style, raising over a million pounds a year for nearly a dozen charities. From woodland gardens awash in bluebells in spring through to flaming vistas in autumn and mellow winter scenes whitewashed with snowdrops, there is almost always a garden you can visit through the National Gardens Scheme. If no dates are listed in the diary section of a particular county, visitors can browse for gardens that open by appointment.

Do you need to be a devoted gardener to be interested in all of this? No, you don't. The gardens which open for the National Gardens Scheme certainly include some of the most outstanding in the country – many of them offering plants for sale, frequently with rare plants at remarkably low prices – but you don't need to be expert, or even interested in the details of the plants or planting to enjoy a National Gardens Scheme garden visit simply as a beautiful and relaxing way to spend an afternoon. Many visitors delight in particular gardens as much for the delicious home-made teas which are often on offer, as for the gardens themselves!

And always, at the back of your mind when you visit a garden open for the National Gardens Scheme, is the pleasant knowledge that your money (usually around £1.50 nowadays, rather than 5p or 'a shilling') is going to help a whole range of good causes: providing Macmillan and Marie Curie nurses to those suffering from cancer, awards for innovations in nursing practice, help for nurses when they are in need, support for hospices, much-needed relief for carers, and training for a new generation of gardeners to maintain this country's tradition of gardening excellence.

For thousands of people the arrival of each year's Yellow Book, listing the gardens open for the Scheme in England and Wales, has come to be as much a sign of spring as the arrival of the first swallow. And while one swallow may not make a summer, one Yellow Book certainly does! And now there's the website: www.ngs.org.uk

While intrepid garden visitors won't set off without a copy of the Yellow Book, visit planning is even easier now, with GardenFinder™, the unique search and mapping facility found on the NGS website. GardenFinder™ enables visitors to search for gardens by county, date, garden name or feature - so whether you are looking for white gardens in Devon in June, or plant sales in Yorkshire in September, GardenFinder™ will help you to locate the information, and provide you with a range of maps to help you find your way there.

Other website features include useful Bulletins, which give up-to-date garden opening information - last minute openings or closings can be easily checked before setting out on a garden visit. News Updates includes articles about the Scheme and general gardening topics, including features by Garden Owners. The Events pages list major gardening and horticultural activities in the UK and Europe as well as selected information on garden-related activities in other parts of the world. Site visitors can send the NGS their own events information for inclusion. The extensive Links pages are an invaluable resource for keen gardeners, and visitors are encouraged to add their own links.

Gardens of England and Wales 2000 will be available in bookstores throughout the country from the end of February 2000 for £4.50. The book may also be ordered from the Scheme's website through Amazon.com or by post for £5.75 including p&p from The National Gardens Scheme, Hatchlands Park, East Clandon, Guildford, Surrey GU4 7RT. ISSN No. ISSN 1365-0572. ISBN No. ISBN 0-900558-32-6. EAN No. 9 780900 558320

Top left: Tulips - 69 Albert Road, Berkshire. Top right: Parterre with box hedging - Brookwell, Surrey. Middle left: Water Garden - Ashover, West Midlands. Middle right: Lake - Swan Oast, Kent. Bottom left: Hostas - Flat 1 Oval Road, London. Bottom middle: Border & lawn - Bishops Manor, Notts. Bottom right: Porch & pots - Eastgrove Cottage Garden, Worcs.

About Johansens

Established in 1982, Johansens is a publishing company owned by the Daily Mail & General Trust Plc. The range of titles includes the popular Johansens hotel guides and Historic Houses, Castles & Gardens.

Annual visits by a team of 12 regional inspectors to hotels and inns in the British Isles ensure that Johansens' unashamedly subjective quality standards are maintained. Over half of the properties inspected each year fail to achieve Johansens Recommendation and therefore do not appear in our guides.

For those who require help in finding the right venue for a holiday, luxury break or business meeting please refer to the display of Johansens titles depicted on the outside back cover. These include guides to recommended hotels in Europe, North America and Southern Africa.

All of the properties featured in these guides, including those found within this title, are represented in full colour on our fully-illustrated website which can be viewed at www.johansens.com or alternatively www.historichouses.co.uk
The site offers searching by location, facilities, price or 'key word' and displays availability of accommodation at many hotels, inns and houses on given dates.

Johansens Recommended Hotels
Europe & The Mediterranean

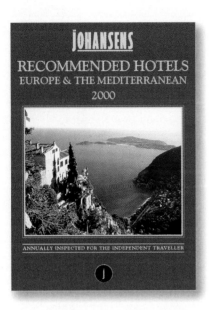

For those using the European section of "Historic Houses, Castles & Gardens," which includes properties in Belgium, France, Germany and The Netherlands, we hope that "Johansens Recommended Hotels – Europe & The Mediterranean" will be an invaluable source of information about where to stay when going on a trip to see the wonderful historic jewels that stud these lands.

It probably won't come as a surprise to you that there is a crossover between the two guides. Many hotels reside in buildings of great historic significance and it can be a real treat to ask a keen (and preferably well-informed) member of the hotel staff to tell you any stories. Why not ask Countess Strasoldo at the "Landhaus Hubertushof" about her illustrious and well-connected family or ask the von Gernerth's

to show you their quaint castle just outside Salzburg? Feast your eyes on the "Hotel im Palais Schwarzenberg" in central Vienna or stay in the former summer residence of Prince Johann-Friedrich von Hohenlohe-Oehringen near Friedrichsruhe. Stay in countless historical Chateaux and Schlosses in France and Germany, many still inhabited by the families who built them. Then consult your "Historic Houses, Castles & Gardens" and visit the neighbouring places of interest.

Europe is truly one of the treasure houses of the world. We hope you will enjoy exploring it.

Your guide to holiday relaxation.

Recognising quality educational access at historic properties

The Sandford Awards for Heritage Education

For two decades, The Heritage Education Trust has recognised and promoted the excellence of educational services offered in 'Historic Houses, Castles and Gardens' and 'Museums & Galleries', through the granting of Sandford Awards for Heritage Education

Recipients of the Sandford Awards for Heritage Education in 1999 stretch from the Combes of Somerset to the Clyde Valley in Scotland, from former industrial sites in Yorkshire to the wilds of Pembrokeshire. They encompass a range of historical settings, which reflect the diversity of the wealth of heritage educational experiences available throughout Great Britain, Iron Age Forts, remains of Roman Baths, Viking Sites, Stately Homes, former Industrial Sites and a restored Hospital Workhouse. The richness of the educational experiences available includes handling archaeological pieces, dressing up in period costume, costumed interpretation, recognising quality and excellence. There is no stipulation for entry on the size of the property, or the extent of the educational services provided.

Some educational services can be provided on an extensive budget, whilst others are exceedingly modestly financed, running alongside the public openings of properties and manned by volunteer staff. Ownership of Award Holding sites reflects the diversity of the range of historic properties from private titled owners to National Parks from The National Trusts to Borough Councils..

Any historic property, artefact and historic landscape is eligible. As an illustration, previous Sandford Award winners include Blenheim Palace, Canterbury Cathedral, Flagship Portsmouth and The Manchester Jewish Museum

The Trust has also refined and clarified the criteria, which are used to assess the education service of a historic property.

Criteria for the 2000 'Sandford Award for Heritage Education'. In future judges will look for:

- The awareness of and adherence to the statutory requirements of the national curricula
- An interpretation of the property that contributes to raising the awareness of the understanding of the local and national heritage. For example – Use of the historical and geographical position of the site; its connection with great historical periods or events, links with well known historical characters.
- Evidence of good liaison between the property and appropriate educational establishments. For example – Teachers, advisors, inspectors, professional bodies, Educational Business Partnerships, Universities, Colleges of Education
- How well the educational potential of the property is being developed. For example – Context of property and its environment, archival evidence, oral history, use of costume, use of artefacts, leisure and tourism courses
- Provision of relevant educational resources. Quality of content and ease of use – rather than design presentation, ability to be updated or amended to fulfil changing needs, cross section of material for differing ability levels and foreign languages
- Attention to good management and administration concerning all aspects of the visit. To include – Facilities for previsits and processes for making visits meet the stated requirements of individual groups, booking system, greeting, orientation, evaluation, evidence of good on–site liaison and cooperation
- Availability of the necessary domestic facilities. To include – Health and Safety Policy, Risk Assessments, toilets, bag storage, refreshment areas, a recognition of the needs of all visitors
- Provision of additional facilities that enhance the quality of the students' visit. May include – use of modern technology, interactive features, dedicated education officer, outreach programme

The Sandford Award should be regarded as a independently judged Quality Assured Assessment of Heritage Education in historic properties.

The Heritage Education Trust is an independent educational charity under the Chairmanship of The Countess of Dalkeith. It is supported by donations from charitable Trusts, including the National Trust and commercial sponsorship.

The Heritage Education Trust is pleased to offer advice to potential applicants and provides a consultative service to all properties, as recommended by The Historic Houses Association

The Trust can be contacted through Gareth Fitzpatrick, Chief Executive, The Heritage Education Trust, Boughton House, Kettering, Northamptonshire, NN14 1BJ, telephone 01536 515731.

Sandford Award Winners 1999

Full Award: Cannon Hall Museum & Country Park, Castell Henllys, Iron Age Fort, Duncombe Park, Elsecar Heritage Centre, Fishbourne Roman Palace, Margam Country Park, New Lanark, Thackray Medical Museum

Quinquennial Review Awards: Chiltern Open Air Museum, Chirk Castle, Combe Sydenham Country Park, Croxteth Hall and Country Park, Culzean Castle and Country Park, Llancaiach Fawr Living History Museum, Moseley Old Hall, Roman Baths and Pump Room, Wimpole Hall and Home Farm

Continued Listing for 1 year of Quinquennial Properties: Coldharbour Mill, Dunham Massey Hall, Harewood House

TOP: Chirk Castle - "The 'Hands On' Education Programme - Using Tudor Costumes in the Long Gallery. BOTTOM: Culzean Castle - "Exploring Rock Pools below the Culzean Castle's Cliffs - Shoreline Excursions are always the most popular and the lava platforms on the Culzean Country Park Coastline are a precious resource.

Heritage Education Trust

Sandford Award Holders

The following properties received Sandford Awards in the years in brackets after their names in recognition of the excellence of their educational services and facilities and their outstanding contribution to Heritage Education. Two or more dates indicate that the property has been reviewed and received further recognition under the system of quinquennial review introduced by the Heritage Education Trust in 1986.

The Argory, Co. Tyrone, Northern Ireland (1995)
Aston Hall, Birmingham (1993, 1998)
Avoncroft Museum of Buildings, Bromsgrove, Worcs. (1988,1993,1998)
Bass Museum Visitor Centre and Shire Horse Stables, Burton upon Trent,Staffs. (1990, 1995)
Beaulieu Abbey, Near Lyndhurst, Hampshire. (1978, 1986, 1991)
Bede Monastery Museum, Jarrow, Tyne and Wear, (1988)
Belton House, Grantham, Lincolnshire, (1979)
Bedford Museum and The Cecil Higgins Art Gallery, (1993, 1998)
Bewdley Museum, Worcestershire (1992,1997)
Bickleigh Castle, Near Tiverton, Devon (1983, 1988)
Blakesley Hall Museum, Birmingham (1993, 1998)
Blenheim Palace, Woodstock, Oxfordshire (1982, 1987, 1992, 1997)
Boat Museum, Ellesmere Port South Wirral (1986)
Bolling Hall, Bradford, West Yorkshire (1978, 1987)
Bodiam Castle, East Sussex (1995)
Boughton House, Kettering, Northamptonshire (1988, 1993, 1998)
Bowhill House & Country Park, Bowhill, Near Selkirk, Borders, Scotland (1993, 1998)
Bronte Parsonage Museum, Haworth, Near Keighley, West Yorks (1993)
Buckfast Abbey, Buckfastleigh, Devon (1985, 1990, 1995)
Buckland Abbey, Yelvedon, Devon (1995, 1996)
Cannock Chase Heritage Centre, (1998)
Cannon Hall Museum and Country Park, Barnsley (1999)
Canterbury Cathedral Canterbury, Kent (1988, 1993, 1998)
Castell Henllys Iron Age Fort, Pembrokeshire (1999)
Castle Museum, York, North Yorkshire (1987, 1993, 1998)
Castle Ward, County Down, Northern Ireland (1980, 1987, 1994)
Cathedral & Abbey Church of St. Alhan, St Albans, Hertfordshires (1986,1991,1996)
Chester Cathedral, (1998)
Chiltern Open Air Museum, Chalfont St Giles, Buckinghamshire (1994,1999)
Chirk Castle, Chirk, Clwyd, Wales (1994,1999)
Clive House Museum, Shrewsbury, Shropshire (1992,1997)
Clipper Ship Cutty Sark, Greenwich (1998)
Coldharbour Mill, Working Wood Museum, Cullompton, Devon (1989,1994)
Combe Sydenham, Near Taunton, Somerset (1984, 1989, 1994,1999)
Corfe Castle, Dorset (1998)
Crathes Castle and Gardens, Kincardineshire, Scotland (1992, 1997)
Croxteth Hall and Country Park, Liverpool, Merseyside (1980, 1989,1994,1999)
Culzean Castle and Country Park, Ayrshire, Scotland (1984, 1989, 1994,1999)
Doddington Hall, Doddington, Lincolnshire, (1978, 1986)
Dove Cottage and the Wordsworth Museum, Grasmere, Cumbria (1 990, 1995)
Drumlanrig Castle and Country Park, Dumfriesshire, Scotland (1989)
Dulwich Picture Gallery, London (1990,1995)
Duncombe Park, Ryedale, North Yorkshire (1999)
Dunham Massey, Altrincham, Cheshire (1994)
Elscar Heritage Centre, Barnsley, Yorkshire (1999)
Erddig Hall, Near Wrexham, Clwyd, Wales (1991, 1996)
Exeter Cathedral, Devon (1995)
Fishbourne Roman Palace, West Sussex (1999)
Flagship Portsmouth, Portsmouth (1996)
Ford Green Hall, Stoke-on-Trent (1996)
Florence Courthouse, Co Fermanagh, Northern Ireland (1995)
Gainsborough Old Hall Gainsborough, Lincs (1988, 1993)
Georgian House, Edinburgh & Lothian, Scotland (1978)
Gladstone's Land, Edinburgh, Scotland (1995)

Godolphin, Helston, Cornwall (1 993)
Goodwood Estate, Goodwood, West Sussex (1998)
Glamis Castle, Angus, Scotland (1997)
Hagley Hall, West Midlands (1981)
The Heritage Centre – Macclesfield, (1998)
Harewood House, Leeds, West Yorks (1979,1989,1994)
Sir Harold Hillier Gardens and Arboretum, Ampfield, Nr Romsey, Hants (1993, 1998)
Holdenby House, Northampton, Northamptonshire (1985, 1990, 1995)
Holker Hall, Cark–in–Cartnell, Cumbria, (1982,1988)
Hopetoun House, South Queensferry, Lothian, Scotland (1983, 1991)
Hornsea Museum, North Humberside, (1987)
lxworth Abbey, Near Bury St Edmunds, Suffolk (1982)
Jewellery Quarter Discovery Centre, Birmingham (1996)
Kingston Lacy House, Wimbome, Dorset (1990, 1995)
Lamport Hall, Northampton, (1985)
Laundry Cottage, Normandby Hall Country Park, South Humberside (1994)
Leighton Hall, Carnforth, Lancashire (1982)
Lichfield Cathedral and Visitors' Study Centre, Lichfield, Staffordshire (1991, 1996)
Llancaiach Fawr Living History Museum, Nelson, Mid Glamorgan (1994, 1999)
Manchester Jewish Museum, (1998)
Macclesfield Museums, Macclesfield, Cheshire (1988, 1993)
Margam Country Park, Near Port Talbort, West Glamorgan (1981, 1986, 1999)
Moseley Old Hall, Wolverhampton, West Midlands (1983,1989,1994)
Museum of Kent Life, Cobtree, Kent (1995)
National Waterways Museum, Gloucester, (1991, 1996)
New Lanark, Scotland (1999)
Norton Priory, Cheshire (1992, 1997)
Oakwell Hall Country Park, Birstall, West Yorkshire (1988, 1993, 1998)
Penhow Castle, Near Newport, Gwent, Wales (1980, 1986, 1991)
The Priest's House Museum, Wimbome Minster, Dorset (1993)
Quarry Bank Mill, Styal, Cheshire (1987, 1992, 1997)
The Queen's House, Greenwich (1995)
Ranger's House, Blackheath, London (1979, 1987)
Rockingham Castle, Near Corby, Northamptonshire (1980, 1987, 1992, 1998)
Roman Baths and Pump Room, Bath, Avon, (1994, 1999)
Rowley's House Museum, Shrewsbury, Shropshire (1993, 1998)
Ryedale Folk Museum, (1993, 1998)
Sheldon Manor, Wiltshire, (1985)
The Shugborough Estate, Stafford, Staffordshire (1987, 1992, 1997)
South Shields Museum and Art Gallery, (Arbeia Roman Fort), Arbeia (1996)
Spring Hill, (1995)
St. Peter's Village Tour, Kent (1998)
Sudbury Hall, Near Derby, Derbyshire (1978)
Sutton House, Hackney (1996)
Tatton Park, Knutsford, Cheshire (1 979, 1986, 1991, 1996)
Tenement House, Glasgow (1996)
The Old School, Bognor Regis (1996)
Tower of London, Tower Bridge, London (1978, 1986, 1991, 1996)
Weald and Downland Open Air Museum, Chichester (1996)
Wigan Pier, Lancashire (1987, 1992, 1997)
Wightwick Manor, Wolverhampton, West Midlands (1986, 1991, 1996)
Wilberforce House and Georgian Houses, Hull, Humberside (1990)
Wimpole Hall and Home, Near Cambridge, Cambridgeshire (1988, 1993, 1999)
York Minster, York (1984, 1989)
York Castle Museum (1998)

Hildon Ltd., Broughton, Hampshire SO20 8DG, ☎ 01794 - 301 747

Bedfordshire

There is something gracious about the landscape of Bedfordshire, a quality which is apparent in all its four types of scenery – in the chalk hills in the south, in the green sand hills of the centre, in the broad basin of the Ouse and in the gently undulating countryside of the north.

Contrasts in the landscape of this home county, are in turn echoed to some extent in its town architecture. Bedfordshire plays host to two very different towns. Steeped in history, Bedford itself is a town of Anglo-Saxon origins and has a long standing association with John Bunyan, the rebellious and unconventional author of Pilgrim's Progress. Milton Keynes, the largest example of a new town in England, is almost beyond comparison due to its recent development.

Bedfordshire's gentle landscapes are easily accessed. A vast network of motorways leads out from the urban sprawl of London to this county of contrasts.

CECIL HIGGINS ART GALLERY

Castle Close, Castle Lane, Bedford
Tel: 01234 211222 Fax: 01234 327149

An unusual combination of recreated Victorian Mansion (originally the home of the Higgins family, wealthy Bedford brewers) and adjoining modern gallery housing an internationally renowned collection of watercolours, prints and drawings, ceramics, glass and lace. Room settings include many items from the Handley–Read Collection and furniture by Victorian architect William Burges. Situated in pleasant gardens near the river embankment. **Location:** Centre of Bedford, just off The Embankment, east of High Street. **Open:** Tues–Sat 11–5pm, Sun & Bank Holiday Mons 2–5pm (last admission 4.45pm). **Admission:** From Jan 2000: Adult £2, concessions free. Disabled access. **NB:** Watercolour collection not on permanent display. Visitors are advised to telephone beforehand.

map 4 E2

SWISS GARDEN

Old Warden, Biggleswade, Bedfordshire
Tel: 01767 627666 (Bedfordshire County Council)

9 acre landscaped garden, set out in the 1830s, alongside a further 10 acres of native woodland with lakeside picnic area. Garden includes many tiny buildings, footbridges, ironwork features and intertwining ponds. Romantic landscape design highlighted by daffodils, rhododendrons and old rambling roses in season. **Location:** Signposted from A1 and A600. 2 miles W of Biggleswade, next door to the Shuttleworth Collection. **Open:** Please phone for opening times and prices. **Admission:** Charges apply. (Share to 'Friends of the Swiss Garden®'). Disabled access. Plants available for sale. No dogs except guide dogs.

WOBURN ABBEY

Woburn, Bedfordshire,
Tel: 01525 290666 Fax: 01525 290271
(The Marquess of Tavistock and the Trustees of the Bedford Estates)

Woburn Abbey is the home to the Marquess and Marchioness of Tavistock and their family. The art collection, one of the most important in the country, includes paintings by Van Dyck, Gainsborough and Reynolds. In the Venetian Room there are 21 views of Venice by Canaletto. There is also French and English 18th century furniture, silver and gold and exquisite porcelain. There are 9 species of deer in 3,000 acre deer park including the Pere David deer, saved from extinction here at Woburn. The Flying Duchess Pavilion serves lunches, snacks and teas and there are gift shops and an Antiques Centre. Woburn Abbey and Safari Park has been named as the 1998 Good Guide to Britain Family Attraction of the Year. **E-mail:** woburnabey@aol.com

map 4 E2

WREST PARK GARDENS

Silsoe, Bedfordshire MK45 4HS
Tel: 01525 860152 (English Heritage)

Take a fascinating journey through a century and a half of gardening styles. Enjoy a leisurely stroll by the Long Water, canals and Leg O'Mutton Lake and explore a charming range of garden buildings, including the baroque Archer Pavilion, Orangery and classical Bath House. Discover bridges and ponds, temples and altars, fountains and statues in over 90 acres of carefully landscaped gardens, laid out before a fabulous French-style Victorian Mansion. There is an informative audio-tour available. **Location:** 10 miles south of Bedford. **Open:** 1 Apr–31 Oct: 10–6pm (5pm in Oct), weekends and Bank Holidays only. Last admission one hour before closing time. **Admission:** Adult £3.40, concs £2.60, child £1.70. (15% discount for groups of 11 or more).

map 4 E2

Berkshire

Berkshire is an unassuming county. Quiet and unpretentious – little concerned with outside approbation and making no effort to popularise its charms or to advertise its beauty and serenity. Whilst it is host to arguably the most famous castle in the kingdom and is graced with some of the most charming and unspoilt villages in the Thames Valley, it is reticent about its attractions. To the east of the county is Windsor, which is undoubtedly Berkshire's jewel. The town is dwarfed by the enormous castle on the hill above, which is surrounded by narrow streets, brimming with shops and old buildings.

Crossing over the Thames lies Eton and its famous public school which is presently educating the future king of England. It was founded by Henry VI in 1440.

To the west of Berkshire lies Newbury, once a centre for the wool trade. Across the rolling Berkshire Downs is the Ridgeway, which was a vital trade route during the Bronze Ages and now offers wonderful walks across some of the highest points in the county.

The Savill Garden

BASILDON PARK

Lower Basildon, Reading RG8 9NR
Tel: 0118 984 3040 Infoline: 01494 755558 Fax: 0118 984 1267 (The National Trust)

Elegant classical 18th century house designed by Carr of York. Overlooking the River Thames is the Octagon drawing room containing fine furniture and pictures. The grounds include formal and terrace gardens, pleasure grounds and woodland walks. **Open:** 1 Apr–31 Oct, Wed–Sun & BH Mon 1–5.30pm. (Closed Good Friday). Park, garden & woodland walks as house. Note: House & grounds close at 5pm on 11–12 August. **Admission:** House, park & garden: Adult £4.20, child £2.10, family ticket £10.50. Park & garden only: Adult £1.80, child 90p, family ticket £4.50. **E-mail:** www.tbdgen@smtp. ntrust.org.uk

map 4
C4

ETON COLLEGE

Windsor, Berkshire SL4 6DW, UK
Tel: 01753 671177 Fax: 01753 671265

Founded in 1440 by Henry VI, Eton College is one of the oldest schools in the country. Visitors are invited to experience and share the beauty and traditions of the College. **Open:** Times are governed by both the dates for term and holidays on the school calendar, but the College will be open to visitors from the end of March until the beginning of October. Guided Tours during the season are available for individuals at 2.15 and 3.15pm daily. Guided Tours for groups by prior arrangement with the Visits Manager, Mrs Hunkin.

map 4
C4

DORNEY COURT

Dorney, Nr Windsor, Berkshire SL4 6QP
Tel: 01628 604638 Fax: 01628 665772 (Mrs Peregrine Palmer)

'One of the finest Tudor Manor Houses in England' – Country Life. Built about 1440 and lived in by the present family for over 450 years. The rooms are full of the atmosphere of history: early 15th and 16th century oak, 17th century lacquer furniture, 18th and 19th century tables, 400 years of portraits, stained glass and needlework. The 14th century church of St. James is a lovely, cool, cheerful and very English Church. **Location:** 2 miles W of Eton & Windsor in village of Dorney on B3026. From M4 use exit 7. **Open:** May: Bank Hol Mons & preceding Sun. July & Aug: Mon, Tues, Wed & Thurs, 1–4.30pm, Last adm. 4pm. **Admission:** Adults £5, children over 9 £3. **Refreshments:** Teas at the Plant Centre. PYO fruit from June–Sept. **E-mail:** palmer@dorneycourt. freeserve.co.uk **Internet:** www.dorneycourt.co.uk

map 4
E4

THE SAVILL GARDEN

Windsor Great Park
Tel: 01753 847518

World renowned woodland garden of 35 acres, situated in the tranquil surroundings of Windsor Great Park. The garden contains a fine range of rhododendrons, azaleas, camellias and magnolias; with adjoining rose gardens and herbaceous borders. Autumn provides a great feast of colour and the whole garden offers much of great interest and beauty at all seasons. Queen Elizabeth Temperate House. **Location:** To be approached from A30 via Wick Road and Wick Lane, Englefield Green. **Station(s):** Egham (3 m). **Open:** Daily 10–6pm Mar–Oct, 10–4pm Nov–Feb (closed Dec 25/26). **Admission:** Adults: Apr–May £5, June–Oct £4, Nov–Mar £3. Concessions for Senior Citizens and Groups. **Refreshments:** Licensed self-service restaurant. Well stocked plant centre/gift shop. Ample parking.

map 4 E4

ENGLEFIELD HOUSE

Englefield, Theale, Reading RG7 5EN
Tel: 01189 302221 Fax: 01189 303226 (Sir William Benyon)

A seven acre garden, herbaceous and rose borders, fountain, stone balustrades and staircases, woodland and water garden, set in Deer Park **Location:** 4m West of Reading off A4 11/4m of A4 at Theale. **Open:** Mondays throughout the year 10–6pm. 1st Apr–1 Oct, Mon–Thur, 10–6pm. **Admission:** Adults £2, children free.

SWALLOWFIELD PARK

Swallowfield, Berkshire RG7 1TG
Tel: 0118 9883815 Fax: 0118 9883930 (Country Houses Association)

Built by the Second Earl of Clarendon in 1678. **Location:** In the village of Swallowfield, 6 miles SE of Reading. **Open:** May–Sept, Wed– Thurs 2–5pm. Last entry 4pm. **Admission:** Adults £2.50, children £1. Free car park. No dogs admitted. Groups by arrangement.

TAPLOW COURT

Berry Hill, Taplow, Nr Maidenhead, Berks SL6 0ER
Tel: 01628 591215 Fax: 01628 773055 (SGI–UK)

Set high above the Thames affording spectacular views. A pre-Domesday manor. Remodelled mid-19th century by William Burn, retaining earlier neo-Norman Hall. 18th century home of Earls and Countesses of Orkney and more recently of Lord and Lady Desborough who entertained "The Souls" here. Tranquil gardens and grounds with Cedar Walk. Anglo-Saxon burial mound. Permanent and temporary exhibitions. Arts Festivals. **Location:** OS Ref. SU907 822. M4/J7 off Bath Road towards Maidenhead. 6m off M40/J2. **Open:** House and grounds: Easter Sunday and every Sunday and Bank Holiday Monday until the end of July, 2–6pm. Please ring to confirm opening. **Admission:** No charge. Free parking.

map 4 D4

ST GEORGE'S CHAPEL WINDSOR

Windsor, Berks SL4 1NJ
Tel: 01753 865538 Fax: 01753 620165 (The Dean & Canons of Windsor)

A fine example of perpendicular architecture. Begun in 1475 by Edward IV and it was completed in the reign of Henry VIII. Choir stalls dedicated to the order of the Knights of the Garter, founded by Edward III. **Location:** OS Ref: SU968 770. In Windsor town, just off the M4. **Open:** As Windsor Castle. Opening times are subject to change at short notice. Please call visitors office for further details. **Admission:** Free admission on payment of charge into Windsor Castle.

WELFORD PARK

Welford, Newbury RG20 8HU
Tel: 01488 608203 (J.H.L. Puxley)

Queen Anne house with later additions. Attractive gardens and grounds. **Location:** 6 miles NW of Newbury and 1 mile N of Wickham village off B4000. **Station:** Newbury. **Open:** Late spring and August Bank Holidays and 1–26 June inclusive from 2.30–5pm. **Admission:** Adults £3.50, OAPs and under 16s £2. Interior by prior appointment only.

map 4 C4

HIGHCLERE CASTLE

Nr Newbury, RG20 9RN
Tel: 01635 253210 Fax: 01635 255315

Designed by Charles Barry in the 1830s at the same time as he was building the Houses of Parliament. This soaring pinnacled mansion provided a perfect setting for the 3rd Earl of Carnarvon, one of the great hosts of Queen Victoria's reign. Old master paintings mix with portraits by Van Dyck and 18th century painters. Napoleon's desk and chair rescued from St. Helena sits with other 18th century furniture. The 5th Earl of Carnarvon, discovered the Tomb of Tutankhamun with Howard Carter. The castle houses a unique exhibition of some of his discoveries which were only rediscovered in the castle in 1988. The current Earl is the Queen's Horseracing Manager. In 1993 to celebrate his 50th year as a leading owner and breeder 'The Lord Carnarvon Racing Exhibition' was opened and offers a fascinating insight into a racing history that dates back three generations. The magnificent parkland, with its massive cedars, was designed by Capability Brown. The Secret Garden has a romance of its own with a beautiful curving lawn surrounded by densely planted herbaceous gardens. A place for poets and romantics. Guided tours are often provided, free of charge, to visitors. **Location:** 4.4 miles S of Newbury on A34, Jct 13 of M4 about 2 miles from Newbury. **Open:** 1 July–3 Sept 2000, 7 days a week 11–5pm, last adm. 4pm, Sat last adm. 2.30pm. **Refreshments:** Lunches, teas, ices, soft drinks. **Conferences:** Business conferences, management training courses, film and photographic location. Licensed for civil weddings. Ample car park and picnic area adjacent to Castle. Suitable for disabled persons on ground floor only. Visitors can buy original items in Castle Gift Shop. No dogs are permitted in the house or gardens except guide dogs. No photography in the house. Occasionally subject to closure. **E-mail:** theoffice@highclerecastle. co.uk **Internet:** www.highclerecastle.co.uk

map 4
C5

Windsor Castle the Long Walk   The Royal Collection © 1999, H. M. Queen Elizabeth II

WINDSOR CASTLE

Windsor, Berkshire SL4 1NJ

Tel: Visitor Office 01753 869898 Information Line (24 hours): 01753 831118 Fax: 01753 832290

Windsor Castle, Buckingham Palace, and the Palace of Holyroodhouse are the Official residences of the Sovereign and are used by The Queen as both home and office. The Queen's personal standard flies when Her Majesty is in residence. Furnished with works of art from the Royal Collection, these buildings are used extensively by The Queen for State ceremonies and Official entertaining. They are opened to the public as much as these commitments allow. A significant proportion of Windsor Castle is opened to visitors on a regular basis including the Upper and Lower Wards, the North Terrace with its famous view towards Eton, Queen Mary's Dolls' House, the State Apartments including St. George's Hall, the Crimson Drawing Room and other newly restored rooms. <u>Open:</u> Everyday except Good Friday, 16 Feb, 23 May, 19 June, Christmas Day and Boxing Day and during any State visits. Nov–Feb 9.45–4.15pm (last admission 3pm) Mar–Oct 9.45–5.15pm (last admission 4pm). St. George's Chapel is closed to visitors on Sundays as services are held throughout the day. Worshippers are welcome. <u>**Admission:**</u> Adult £10.50, children (under 17) £5, senior citizens (over 60) £8. Family ticket (2 adult and 2 under 17) £25.50.

The King's Bedchamber
The Royal Collection © 1999, H. M. Queen Elizabeth II/John Freeman

The King's Dining Room
The Royal Collection © 1999, H. M. Queen Elizabeth II/John Freeman

map 4
E4

The Green Drawing Room   The Royal Collection © 1999, H. M. Queen Elizabeth II/Mark Fiennes

St. George's Hall   The Royal Collection © 1999, H. M. Queen Elizabeth II/Mark Fiennes

Buckinghamshire

Hughenden Manor

Henley on Thames officially rests in Buckinghamshire although three counties – Oxfordshire, Berkshire and Buckinghamshire meet there. Its historic buildings, including one of Britain's oldest theatres, are a fitting backdrop to the annual Royal Regatta week in July. Marlow is far less pretentious, set between the banks of the river Thames and the beautiful Chiltern Hills, but has as much character as its big cousin.

Buckingham, set in the northern part of the county, is home to the country's only private university. The town houses lots of lively small pubs and a market. Locally, there are many stately homes and gardens, including Stowe, which are all worth a visit.

CHILTERN OPEN AIR MUSEUM

Newland Park, Gorelands Lane, Chalfont St. Giles, Buckinghamshire, HP8 4AD. Tel: Information Line: 01494 872163 Office 01494 871117 (Chiltern Open Air Museum Ltd)

Museum of historic buildings, rescued from demolition and re-erected in a beautiful parkland setting, reflecting the vernacular heritage of the Chilterns. You can explore barns, granaries, cartsheds and stables, a blacksmiths forge, a toll house, a 1940's prefab and more. Demonstrations and displays of traditional skills such as the pole-lathe, spinning and dyeing, spoon making and rag rug making. Hands-on activities for children in half terms and holidays. **Open:** 1 Apr–31 Oct: Daily 10–5pm. **Admission:** Adults £5.50, concessions £4.50, children (5–16) £3, family (2 Adults & 2 children) £15. Under 5's Free. **Refreshments:** Tearooms, shop, playground, nature/seat trail.

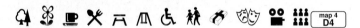

CLAYDON HOUSE

Middle Claydon, Nr Buckingham, Bucks MK18 2EY
Tel: 01296 730349 (The National Trust)

One of England's most extraordinary houses. In continuous occupation by the Verney family for over 350 years. Claydon was originally a Jacobean manor house, but was remodelled in the 1750s at a time when the craze for Chinoiserie was at its height. The result was the remarkable series of rooms we see today, lavishly decorated in intricately-carved white woodwork covered with motifs based on Oriental birds, pagodas and summer-houses. **Open:** 1 Apr–31 Oct: daily except Thur & Fri, 1–5pm. **Admission:** £4.20, family ticket £10.50. Tearoom: open 2–5pm (open at 1pm on Sun & Bank Hol Mon). **E-mail:** tcdgen@smtp.ntrust.org.uk

CLIVEDEN

Taplow, Maidenhead, SL6 0JA, Bucks
Tel: 01628 605069 Fax: 01628 669461 (The National Trust)

On cliffs above the Thames, this estate has magnificent views over the river. The great 19th century mansion (now let as a hotel) was once the home of Nancy, Lady Astor. There are a series of gardens, each with its own character and featuring roses, topiary, water gardens, statuary, and formal parterre. **Open:** Entire Estate: 15 Mar–31 Oct: daily 11–6pm. 1 Nov–31 Dec: daily 11–4pm. House (three rooms open): Apr–Oct: Thurs & Sun 3–5.30pm. Entry by timed ticket from information kiosk. **Admission:** Woodland Car Park only £3, family ticket £7.50. Grounds: £5, family ticket £12.50. House £1 extra. Licensed conservatory restaurant and shop. **E-mail:** www.tclest@smtp.ntrust.org.uk

COWPER & NEWTON MUSEUM

Orchard Side, Market Place, Olney, MK46 4AJ
Tel: 01234 711 516 E-mail: museum@olney.co.uk

Once the home of the 18th century poet and letter writer William Cowper and now containing furniture, paintings and belongings of both Cowper and his ex-slave trader friend, Rev. John Newton (author of "Amazing Grace"). Attractions include re-creations of a Victorian country kitchen and wash-house, two peaceful gardens and Cowper's restored summerhouse, costume gallery, important collections of dinosaur bones and bobbin lace and local history displays. **Location:** 6 miles N of Newport Pagnell via A509. (Leave M1 at junction 14). **Station(s):** Milton Keynes or Bedford. **Open:** 1 Mar–23 Dec, Tue–Sat & Bank Hol Mons, 10am–1pm & 2–5pm. Sundays in June, July & Aug 2–5pm. Closed Good Friday. **Admission:** Adults £2, children/students (with cards) £1, concs £1.50, family £5. **Internet:** www.olio.demon.co.uk/cnmhome.html

HUGHENDEN MANOR

High Wycombe, Bucks HP14 4LA
Tel: 01494 755573 Infoline: 01494 755565 (The National Trust)

The home of Queen Victoria's favourite Prime Minister, Benjamin Disraeli. Much of his furniture, pictures and books remain and there are beautiful walks through the surrounding park and woodland. The garden is a recreation of the colourful designs of his wife, Mary Anne. **Open:** House: 1–30 Mar, Sat & Sun only, 1 Apr–31 Oct, daily except Mon & Tues (closed Good Fri, but open Bank Hol Mon) 1–5pm. Garden: same days as house 12–5pm. Park & Woodland: open all year. **Admission:** House & garden: £4.20, family ticket £10.50. Garden only £1.50, children 75p. Park & Woodland free. Tearoom and shop available.

NETHER WINCHENDON HOUSE

Aylesbury HP18 0DY
Tel: 01844 290199
(Robert Spencer Bernard Esq.)

Medieval and Tudor manor house with 18th century Strawberry Hill Gothic additions. Home of Sir Francis Bernard, Governor of New Jersey and Massachusetts, 1760. **Location:** 1 mile N of A418 Aylesbury/Thame Road, in village of Lower Winchendon, 6 miles SW Aylesbury. **Stations:** Aylesbury (7 miles). Haddenham and Thame Parkway (2 miles). **Open:** 1–29 May and 27–28 Aug, 2.30–5.30pm. Last party each day at 4.45pm. Parties at any time of year by written appointment. **Admission:** Adults £4, children (under 12) and OAPs £2 (not weekends or bank holidays). HHA members free. **Refreshments:** By arrangement. Correspondence to Robert Spencer Bernard Esq.

map 4 D3

STOWE LANDSCAPE GARDENS

Buckingham, Bucks MK18 5EH
Tel: 01280 822850. Fax: 01280 822437 (The National Trust)

One of the first and finest landscape gardens in Europe. Adorned with buildings by Vanbrugh, Gibbs and Kent, including arches, temples, a Palladian bridge and other monuments, the sheer scale of the garden must make it Britain's largest work of art. **Open:** 29 Mar–2 July (closed Sat 27 May) & 10 Sept–29 Oct: daily except Mon & Tues; 4 Jul–10 Sept: daily except Mon. 2–23 Dec: daily except Mon & Tues. Open all BH Mons. Times: Mar–Oct 10–5.30pm, last admission 4pm. Dec 10–4pm, last admission 3pm. **Admission:** Gardens £4.60. Family £11.50. Licensed tearoom. **E-mail:** tstmca@smtp.ntrust.org.uk

map 4 D2

STOWE (STOWE SCHOOL)

Stowe, MK18 5EH
Tel: 01280 813650

Formerly the home of the Dukes of Buckingham it is a house adorned with the traditions of aristocracy and learning. For over one and a half centuries up to the great sale of 1848, the Temples and Grenvilles almost continuously rebuilt and refurbished it in an attempt to match their ever growing ambitions with the latest fashions. Around the mansion is one of Britain's most magnificent landscape gardens now in the ownership of the National Trust. **Location:** 4 miles north of Buckingham town. **Stations:** Milton Keynes. **Open:** 29 Mar–23 Apr, 3 July–10 Sept, daily 2–5pm. Sun 12–5pm. The house is closed, at times, for private functions. Please telephone first to check. **Admission:** Adults £2 children £1. Guide books and souvenirs available from Stowe Bookshop situated in the Menagerie on the South Front – open Mon–Fri, 10–12noon and 1–4.30pm.

 map 4 D2

WINSLOW HALL

Winslow, Buckinghamshire, MK18 3HL
Tel: 01296 712 323 (Sir Edward & Lady Tomkins)

Built 1698–1702. Almost certainly designed by Sir Christopher Wren. Has survived without any major structural alteration and retains most of its original features. Modernised and redecorated by the present owners. Good 18th century furniture, mostly English. Some fine pictures, clocks and carpets. Several examples of Chinese art, notably of the Tang period. Beautiful gardens with many unusual trees and shrubs. **Location:** At entrance to Winslow on A413, the Aylesbury road. **Station(s):** Milton Keynes or Aylesbury (both 10 miles). **Open:** All Bank Hol weekends (except Christmas), 2–5pm. July–Aug, Wed & Thur, 2.30–5.30pm or by appointment throughout the year. **Admission:** Adults £5.00, children free. **Refreshments:** Catering by arrangement.

map 4 D2

WYCOMBE MUSEUM

Priory Avenue, High Wycombe, Bucks
Tel: 01494 421895 Fax: 01494 421897

Set in Castle Hill House and surrounded by spacious lawns and shrubberies, the newly refurbished Wycombe Museum explores the fascinating history of the area, with interactive displays, changing exhibitions and children's activities. Discover the renowned collection of Windsor chairs and traditional chairmaking in the Chilterns. With gift shop, drinks machine, baby changing facilities, fully accessible ground floor and disabled toilet. Picnicking encouraged. Service dogs only. Admission free. Guided tours by arrangement. Call for details of special events. **Open:** Mon–Sat 10–5pm, Sun 2–5pm. (Additional specialist British Regional Furniture Study Centre - behind Museum - open 10–4pm Mon and Fri only).

map 4 D3

WADDESDON MANOR

Nr. Aylesbury, Buckinghamshire, HP18 0JW
Tel: 01296 653211 Fax: 01296 653208

Waddesdon Manor was built at the end of the last century for Baron Ferdinand de Rothschild to entertain his guests and display his vast collection of art treasures. It has won many awards including Museum of the Year, Best National Trust Property 1997 and the England for Excellence Silver Award 1998. The French Renaissance-style château houses one of the finest collection of French 18th century decorative arts in the world and an important collection of English portraits. The garden is famous for its landscape of specimen trees and seasonal bedding displays and the Rococo-style aviary houses a splendid collection of exotic birds. Thousands of bottles of vintage Rothschild wines are found in the wine cellars. There are gift and wine shops and a licensed restaurant. Many events are organised throughout the year including Collection study days, floodlit openings, wine tastings and garden workshops. **Location:** A41 between Aylesbury & Bicester. **Open: Grounds, aviary, restaurant and shops:** 1 Mar–24 Dec, Wed–Sun & Bank Hol Mons, 10–5pm. **House (including wine cellars):** 30 Mar–29 Oct, Thurs–Sun, Bank Hol Mons and Weds in Jul & Aug. 11–4pm. (Recommended last admission 2.30pm) Bachelors' Wing open Thurs & Fri & Weds in Jul & Aug. **Admission: House & grounds:** Adults £10, child £7.50. **Grounds only:** Adults £3, child £1.50. Bachelors' Wing £1. National Trust Members free. Timed tickets to the House can be purchased on site or reserved in advance by phoning 01296 653226, Mon–Fri 10–4pm. Advance booking fee: £3 per transaction. During 2000 we will be making some essential repairs to one section of the Manor's roof. Unfortunately this means that part of the house will be covered with scaffolding.

map 4D3

Cambridgeshire

Wansford

In Cambridge and Ely, this county has two of the most historic cities in England. Cambridge is an idyllic and irresistibly charming city, home to one of the oldest universities in the world. Some of the most ancient of Cambridge's thirty colleges adorn the timeless velvety green banks of the River Cam. Others, such as the ancient college of Gonville & Caius, one of Cambridge's oldest, lie grouped around squares known as courts and line the ancient streets of this busy market city. The bustling student community and their bicycles, create a wonderfully lively atmosphere in this collegiate city.

The ancient city of Ely is dominated by its wonderful cathedral, which overlooks the flat fens that surround it. Indeed, the city is reputed to take its name from the Saxon word "elig", meaning "Eel Island" and was once an island. Today, the drained fens form some of the most fertile agricultural land in England. It is also home, at Wicken Fen, to the oldest nature reserve in Britain.

ELTON HALL
Elton, Peterborough PE8 6SH
Tel: 01832 280468 Fax: 01832 280584 (Mr & Mrs William Proby)

This romantic house has been the home of the Proby family for over 350 years. Excellent furniture and outstanding paintings by Gainsborough, Reynolds, Constable and other fine artists. There are over 12,000 books, including Henry VIII's prayer book. Wonderful gardens, including restored Rose Garden, knot and sunken gardens and recently planted Arboretum. Stunning new Gothic Orangery. Bressingham Plant Centre is in the walled Kitchen Garden. **Location:**

On A605, 8 miles W of Peterborough. **Open:** 2–5pm last Bank Hol in May (Sun/Mon 28/29 May) Weds in June, Weds, Thurs and Suns in July and Aug and Bank Hol Mon (28). **Admission:** Adults £5, accompanied children free. Garden only: Adults £2.50, accompanied children free. Private parties by appointment with Administrator. **Refreshments:** Home-made teas, lunches by arrangement.

map 9 7F

ISLAND HALL

Post Street, Godmanchester PE18 8BA
Tel: 0171 491 3724 (Mr Christopher & The Hon Mrs Vane Percy)

A mid 18th C mansion of great charm, owned and restored by an award winning Interior Designer. This family home has lovely Georgian rooms with fine period detail and possessions relating to the owners' ancestors since their first occupation of the house in 1800. A riverside setting with formal gardens and ornamental island forming part of the grounds in an area of Best Landscape. Octavia Hill wrote "This is the loveliest, dearest old house, I never was in such a one before". **Open:** Island Hall will be open on the following Suns in the year 2000: July 2nd/9th/16th/23rd/30th 2.30–5pm. Last admittance 4.30pm. **Admission:** Adults £3.50. Grounds only: Adults £2. Child 13–16 £2. Accompanied child under 13, grounds only £1. Group rate (by appt): May–Sept (except Aug) £3 per head (when over 40 persons). Under 15 persons min charge £52.50 per group. Home-made teas.

KIMBOLTON CASTLE

Kimbolton, Cambs
Tel: 01480 860505 Fax: 01480 861763 (Governors of Kimbolton School)

Tudor manor house associated with Katherine of Aragon, completely remodelled by Vanbrugh (1708–20); courtyard c.1694. Fine murals by Pellegrini in chapel, boudoir and on staircase. Gatehouse by Robert Adam. Parkland. **Location:** 8 miles NW of St Neots on B645; 14 miles N of Bedford. **Station(s):** St Neots (9 miles) **Open:** Easter Sun & Mon, Spring Bank Hol Sun & Mon, Summer Bank Hol Sun & Mon, also Sun 30 July, 6, 13, 20, & 27 Aug 2–6pm **Admission:** Adults £2.50, children & OAPs £1.50. **Conferences:** By negotiation. Guided tours for groups of 20 or more by arrangement on days other than advertised.

KING'S COLLEGE

King's Parade, Cambridge CB2 1ST
Tel: 01223 331212

Visitors are very welcome, but remember that this is a working College. Please respect the privacy of those who work, live and study here at all times. Recorded messages for services, concerts and visiting times: 01223 331155. **Open:** Out of term time – Mon–Sat, 9.30–4.30pm. Sun, 10–5pm. In term: Mon–Fri, 9.30–3.30pm. Sat, 9.30–3.15pm. Sun, 1.15–2.15pm, 5–5.30pm. **Admission:** Adults £3.50, children (12–17) £2.50, children under 12 free if part of a family unit, students £2.50. Guided tours are only available through Cambridge Tourist Office Tel: 01223 457574.

ELY CATHEDRAL

The Chapter House, The College, Ely CB7 4DL
Tel: 01353 667735 Fax: 01353 665658

A wonderful example of Romanesque architecture. The Octagon and the Lady Chapel are of particular interest. There are superb medieval domestic buildings around the Cathedral. Stained glass museum, brass rubbing centre, shops and restaurants. **Location:** 15 miles N of Cambridge city centre via the A10. **Open:** Summer: 7–7pm. Winter: Mon–Sat, 7.30–6pm, Sun and week after Christmas, 7.30–5pm. Sun services: 8.15am, 10.30am and 3.45 pm. Weekday services: 7.40am, 8am & 5.30pm (Thurs only also 11.30am & 12.30pm). Admission charges apply.

ANGLESEY ABBEY AND GARDEN

Lode, Cambridge CB5 9EJ Tel: 01223 811200

Open: House: 25 March to 22 Oct: daily except Mon & Tues (but open BH Mon) 1–5pm. Garden: 5 March to 2 July, 15 Sept to 17 Oct: daily except Mon & Tues (but open BH Mon); 3 July to 17 Sept: daily 10–5.30pm. Last admission 4.30pm. Closed Good Fri.

PECKOVER HOUSE & GARDEN

North Brink, Wisbech PE13 1JR Tel: 01945 583463 Fax: 01945 583463

Open: House & garden: 1 April to 31 Oct: Sat, Sun, Wed & BH Mon 12.30 –5.30pm. Garden only: 1 April to 31 Oct: Mon, Tues & Thur 12.30–5.30pm.

WIMPOLE HALL

Arrington, Royston SG8 0BW Tel: 01223 207257 Fax: 01223 207838

Open: Hall & Garden: 18 March to 30 July, 2 Sept to 22 Oct: daily except Mon & Fri (but open Good Fri and BH Mons). Aug: daily except Mon 1–5pm (open BH Suns & Mons 11–5pm). Park: daily sunrise to sunset .

THE MANOR

Hemingford Grey, Huntingdon, Cambs PE18 9BN
Tel: 01480 463134 Fax: 01480 465026 (Mr & Mrs Peter Boston)

Built about 1130 and made famous as Green Knowe by the author Lucy Boston this house is reputedly the oldest continuously inhabited house in the country and much of the Norman house remains. It contains the Lucy Boston patchworks. The garden has topiary, one of the best collections of old roses in private hands, large herbaceous borders with many scented plants and a variety of Dykes Medal winner irises. **Open:** House: all the year by appointment. Garden: open daily all year 10–6pm (dusk in winter). **Admission:** House and Garden: Adults £4, children £1.50. Garden only: Adults £1, children 50p.

OLIVER CROMWELL'S HOUSE

29 St. Mary's Street, Ely, Cambridgeshire
Tel: 01353 662062 Fax: 01353 668518 (East Cambridgeshire District Council)

Oliver Cromwell and his family moved to Ely in 1636 and lived in the city for some ten years. Eight period rooms contain sets, exhibitions and videos about Cromwell and the Fens Drainage story. There are helmets and costumes for children to try on. Cromwell's old home is now open throughout the year and also houses the Ely Tourist Information Centre. A variety of guided tours of the city and Cromwell's House can be booked (costumed guides available). A Joint Ticket scheme in operation for the four main attractions in Ely, including Oliver Cromwell's House at a highly discounted rate. Discount vouchers to Ely shops are also given to ticket holders. Please ring for details on special events at the house and city. **Open:** Summer: 1 Apr–31 Oct, Daily, 10–5.30pm. Winter: 1 Nov–31 Mar, Mon to Sat, 10–5pm. Suns 12–4pm in winter.

UNIVERSITY BOTANIC GARDEN

Cory Lodge, Bateman Street, CB2 1JF
Tel: 01223 336265 Fax: 01223 336278 (University of Cambridge)

Forty acres of outstanding gardens with lake, glasshouses, winter garden, chronological bed and nine National Collections, including Geranium and Fritillaria. **Location:** 1 mile S of Cambridge centre. Entrance on Bateman Street. **Stations:** Cambridge Railway Station 1/4 mile. **Open:** Open all year except Christmas Day and Boxing Day 10–6pm (summer), 10–5pm (autumn & spring), 10–4pm (winter). **Admission:** Charged weekends and Bank Holidays throughout the year and weekdays Mar 1–Oct 31. All parties must be pre-booked. Pre-booked school parties and disabled people free. No reductions for parties. **Refreshments:** Tearoom in the Gilmour Building. No dogs except guide dogs. Guided tours by the Friends of the Garden available by arrangement. **E-mail:** gardens@hermes.cam.ac.uk **Internet:** http://www.plantsci.cam.ac.uk/botgdn/index.htm

PETERBOROUGH CATHEDRAL

The Chapter Office, Minster Precincts, Peterborough, Cambridgeshire PE1 1XS
Tel: 01733 343342 Fax: 01733 552465 (The Dean & Chapter)

Visit Peterborough Cathedral one of the finest Norman buildings in Europe, with a magnificent early English West Front. The 13th century painted nave ceiling is the largest in the world. Admire the exquisite fan vaulting. You may also visit the tomb of Katherine of Aragon, the first wife of Henry VIII, and see the former burial place of Mary Queen of Scots. From Sept 1999 a new shop, restaurant and visitors' centre will be open. The Tourist Information Centre is also located in the Cathedral Precincts. Open all the year, Mon–Fri 8.30–5.15pm; Sat 8.30–5.45pm; Sun 12–5.45pm. Donations are requested. Contact: Chapter Office Tel: 01733 343342.

Cheshire

Known for its cats, its cheese, its excellent roads and surprisingly varied scenery, the county of Cheshire has retained its charming rural character throughout the centuries.

The county town of Chester comes from the Latin term 'Castra Devana', meaning 'camp on the Dee'. The town lies on an elbow of the River Dee and was founded by Romans during the first century AD. The town is surrounded by

Rowton Hall

a medieval wall, packed with historic buildings, winding streets and a wealthy atmosphere.

The picturesque Cheshire Plain is the home for a multitude of pretty villages and lush countryside. Many properties such as Rowton Hall abound and here, fine views of the plains stretching across to the Welsh hills may be enjoyed.

Knutsford, with its black and white houses and winding streets, is typical of the towns clustered in the region. The whole area is a delight for the visitor.

Chester

ADLINGTON HALL

Nr Macclesfield, Cheshire SK10 4LF
Tel: 01625 820875 Fax: 01625 828756 (Mrs C Legh)

Adlington Hall is a Cheshire Manor and has been the home of the Leghs since 1315. The Great Hall was built between 1450 and 1505, the Elizabethan 'Black and White' in 1581 and the Georgian South Front in 1757. The Bernard Smith Organ was installed c1670. A 'Shell Cottage', Yew Walk, Lime Avenue, recently planted maze and rose garden. Recently restored follies include a Chinese bridge, Temple to Diana and T'ing House. Occasional organ recitals. **Location:** 5 miles N of Macclesfield on the Stockport/Macclesfield Road (A523). **Station(s)** Adlington (½m). **Open:** Throughout the year to groups by prior arrangement only. **Admission:** Hall and Gardens Adults £4, children £1.50 (over 25 people £3.50). **Refreshments:** At the Hall. Car park free.

map 8
B4

ARLEY HALL AND GARDENS

Arley, Northwich Cheshire CW9 6NA
Tel: 01565 777353 Fax: 01565 777465 (Lord & Lady Ashbrook)

Arley Hall, built about 1840, stands at the centre of an estate which has been owned by the same family for over 500 years. An important example of the early Victorian Jacobean style, it has fine plaster work and oak panelling, a magnificent library and interesting pictures, furniture and porcelain. There is a private Chapel designed by Anthony Salvin and a 15th century cruck barn. The award winning gardens overlook the park and provide great variety of style and design. Features include the double herbaceous border established in 1846, clipped Quercus Ilex and pleached lime avenues, topiary, collections of shrub roses, exotic trees, shrubs and rhododendrons. **Location:** 5 m north of Northwich; 6 m west of Knutsford; 7 m south of Warrington; 5 m off M6 at junctions 19 & 20; 5 m off M56 at junctions 9 & 10. Nearest main roads A49 and A50. **Open:** 9 Apr–1 Oct,

Gardens & Grounds: Tues–Sat & Bank Hol Mons, 11–5pm. Guided tours and parties by arrangement. Hall open one week day (please ring) and Sun 12–5pm. **Admission:** Gardens, grounds & chapel £4.40, Hall £2.50 extra. Concessions and group bookings. Also available for corporate hospitality and weddings/receptions. **Refreshments:** Restaurant and tea room. Gift shop and plant nursery. **Events/Exhibitions:** Antique fairs, Garden Festival, Craft Shows, Fireworks & Laser Concert etc., Outdoor Theatre, Christmas Events. **Conferences:** Facilities available. Corporate activities, launches, filming, weddings, themed events, countryside days etc., Private & Corporate Dinners. Shop and Plant Nursery. Woodland Walk. Facilities for disabled. Dogs allowed in gardens on leads. Picnic area. Arley Garden Festival 24–25 June 2000. Discount advance tickets available.

map 6
C1

BRAMALL HALL

Bramhall Park, Bramhall, Stockport, Cheshire, SK7 3NX
Tel: 0161 485 3708 Fax: 0161 486 6959 (Stockport Metropolitan Borough Council)

This magical Tudor manor house is set in 70 acres of parkland, with lakes, woods and gardens. The house contains 16th century wall paintings, Elizabethan fine plaster ceilings, Victorian kitchens and servant's quarters. Excellent stables, tearoom and gift shop. **Location:** 4 miles S of Stockport, off A5102. **Stations:** Cheadle Hulme. **Open:** Good Fri–30 Sept, Mon–Sat, 1–5pm. Sun & BHols, 11–5pm. 1 Oct–1 Jan, Tue–Sat, 1–4pm.

Sun & BHols, 11–4pm. Closed 25–26 Dec. 2 Jan–Easter, Sat & Sun, 12–4pm. Parties by arrangement, including out of hours bookings. **Admission:** Adults £3.50, children/OAPs £2. **Refreshments:** Stables, tearooms. **Events/Exhibitions:** Full events programme. **Conferences:** Available for corporate entertaining and civil marriages. Disabled access on ground floor, shop and tearooms.

map 8
B4

CAPESTHORNE HALL

Nr. Macclesfield, Cheshire
Tel: 01625 861 221 Fax: 01625 861 619 (Mr & Mrs W. A. Bromley-Davenport)

Capesthorne Hall has been the home of the Bromley Davenport family and their ancestors since Domesday times. The present hall dates from 1719 and contains a great variety of paintings, sculptures and furniture. The gardens, lakes and park contain many interesting features including a Georgian Chapel and an old ice house. **Location:** 3½ miles south of Alderley Edge on A34. **Open**: Hall and Gardens: April–October, Wednesday, Sunday and Bank Holidays (afternoons). **Refreshments:** Butler's Pantry plus catering by arrangement. **Admission:** Adults £6, child £2.50. Special events throughout the year. Also available for corporate hospitality, civil weddings and receptions.

map 8 B5

HOLEHIRD GARDENS

Patterdale Road (Kirkstone Pass Road), Windermere, Cumbria LA23 1NP
Tel: 01539 446008

5–acre garden of the Lakeland Horticultural Society. Open dawn to dusk throughout the year and attractive at all seasons. Wonderful views over the head of Lake Windermere to Langdale Fells beyond. Outstanding walled garden with well-stocked herbaceous borders, extensive rock gardens. Good collections of hostas, hellebores, geraniums and old roses. Specimen trees and mixed shrubberies. National Collections of astilbe, hydrangea and polystichum ferns. Maintained entirely by member volunteers. **Admission:** By donation (minimum £1 per head suggested), wardens on duty. Limited disabled access. Ample parking, coaches strictly by prior arrangement only.

CHOLMONDELEY CASTLE GARDEN

Malpas, Cheshire, SY14 8AH
Tel: 01829 720383/203 (The Marchioness of Cholmondeley)

Cholmondeley Castle is said by many to be among the most romantically beautiful gardens they have seen. Even the wild orchids, daisies and buttercups take on an aura of glamour in the beautifully landscaped setting. Visitors enter by the deer park mere - one of two strips of water which are home to many types of waterfowl and freshwater fish. The extensive pleasure gardens are dominated by the romantic Gothic Castle, built in 1801 of local sandstone. The gardens have been imaginatively laid out with fine trees and water gardens, it has been extensively replanted from the 1960's with azaleas, rhododendrons, magnolias, cornus, acer and many other acid loving plants. As well as the beautiful Temple water garden, there is a rose garden and many mixed borders. Lakeside picnic area, children's play area, rare breeds of farm animals, including llamas. Ancient private chapel in park. **Location:** Off A41 Chester/Whitchurch Road and A49 Whitchurch/Tarporley Road. **Station(s):** Crewe. **Open:** Sun 2 Apr–Thur 28 Sept 2000: Wed, Thur, Sun & Bank Hol Mons 11.30–5pm. (Closed Good Friday 21 April). **Enquiries to:** The secretary, Cholmondeley Castle (House not open to public). **Admission:** Adults £3, OAPs £2.50, children £1. Coach parties of 25 and over at reduced rates.

map 6 C/D1

DORFOLD HALL

Nantwich CW5 8LD
Tel: 01270 625245 Fax: 01270 628723 (Mr Richard Roundell)

Jacobean country house built 1616. Beautiful plaster ceilings and panelling. Interesting furniture and pictures. Attractive gardens including spectacular spring garden and summer herbaceous borders. Guided tours. **Location:** 1 mile W of Nantwich on A534 Nantwich/Wrexham Road. **Stations:** Nantwich (1½ miles). **Open:** Apr–Oct Tues and Bank Holidays Mons 2–5pm. At other times by appointment only. **Admission:** Adults £4.50, children £3.

map 6 D1

Cheshire

NT Photographic Library, Nick Meers

 ## DUNHAM MASSEY HALL

Altrincham, Cheshire
Tel: 0161 941 1025 Fax: 0161 929 7508 (The National Trust)

18th century house extensively re-worked in the early 20th century resulting in one of Britain's most sumptuous Edwardian interiors with collections of walnut furniture, paintings and magnificent Huguenot silver. One of the North West's great gardens with an Orangery, Victorian bark house and well house. The surrounding deer park was laid out in the early 18th century and contains a series of beautiful avenues and pools. **Admission:** NT members free. House and Garden: Adult £5, child £2.50, family £12.50, booked parties £4. House or garden only: Adult £3, child £1.50. Car entry: £3 per car. **Open:** House and garden open 1 Apr–1 Nov daily except house closed Thur & Fri. House open 12–5pm Apr–Sept, 4pm in Oct. Open 11am BH Mon & proceeding Sun. Garden open 11–5.30pm Apr–Sept, 4.30pm in Oct. Deer park, restaurant & shop open daily all year.

LITTLE MORETON HALL

Congleton, Cheshire CW12 4SD
Tel: 01260 272018 (The National Trust)

Begun in 1450, Little Moreton is regarded as the finest timber-framed moated manor house in England. The Chapel, Great Hall and Long Gallery, together with the Knot Garden, make Little Moreton a great day out. Location for TV films including Lady Jane and Moll Flanders. Try the local historic recipes in the restaurant and visit the shop with its extensive range of gifts. Parties welcome. Ghost Tour with supper for booked parties. Great Hall decorated for an Elizabethan Yuletide with Christmas Festivities, seasonal refreshments and shopping. Open Air theatre in July. **Admission:** Adult £4.30, child £2.10, family £10.70. **Open:** 25 Mar–5 Nov, Wed–Sun, Bank Holiday Monday 11.30–5pm. 11–26 Nov, Sat, Sun 11.30–4pm. 2–23 Dec, Sat, Sun 11.30–4pm Free entry. Tel: 01260 272018.

NESS BOTANIC GARDENS

Ness, Neston, South Wirral, Cheshire CH64 4AY
Tel: 0151 353 0123 Fax: 0151 353 1004

Pioneers in the world of plants since 1898. Beautiful Botanic Garden for all seasons with extensive displays of trees and shrubs, including Rhododendrons and Azaleas. Renowned heather, rock, terrace, water, rose and herb gardens. Visit our coffee shops which provide home-made cakes and light meals. Gift shop, plant sales area, visitor centre and picnic area. **Admission** Charge. **Location:** 6 miles from exit 4, M53, 5 miles from western end M56, off A540 Hoylake–Chester Road.

NETHER ALDERLEY MILL

Congleton Road, Nether Alderley, Macclesfield, Cheshire SK10 4TW
Tel: 01625 523012 Fax: 01625 527139 (The National Trust)

Have you visited this unique medieval flour mill? Original Elizabethan timbers support a stone flagged roof. The fully restored Victorian machinery is driven by tandem overshot wooden waterwheels and runs daily subject to availability of water. Flour grinding demonstrations on Sunday afternoons. Groups welcome (booking essential). Guided tours on request. Enjoy the sights and sounds of a working mill for a fascinating visit! **Location:** 1½ miles south of Alderley Edge on A34. **Open:** April, May and Oct: Wed, Sun and Bank Holiday Mon, 1–4.30pm. June–Sept: Tues–Sun & Bank Holiday Mon, 1–5pm.

NORTON PRIORY MUSEUM & GARDENS

Tudor Road, Manor Park, Runcorn, Cheshire WA7 1SX
Tel: 01928 569895 (The Norton Priory Museum Trust)

The beautiful 38 acre woodland gardens with an award winning walled garden are the setting for the now demolished mansion of the Brookes, built on the site of a former Augustinian priory. Excavated remains of the priory & the atmospheric 12th century undercroft can be found with displays on the medieval priory, the later houses and gardens in the museum. Contemporary sculpture is situated in the grounds. **Location:** From M56 (junction 11) turn towards Warrington and follow Norton Priory road signs. **Open:** Daily all year. Apr–Oct, Sat, Sun & Bank Hols 12–6pm; Mon to Fri 12–5pm; Nov–Mar, daily 12–4pm. Walled Garden open Mar–Oct. Closed 24/25/26 Dec, 1 Jan. Special arrangements for groups. **Admission:** Adults £3.30, concs £2, family £8.80 (2 adults & up to 3 children under 16).

LYME PARK

Disley, Stockport, SK12 2NX

Tel: 01663 762023 Infoline: 01663 766492 Fax: 01663 765035

Admission: Legh Family home for 600 years. Part of the original Elizabethan house survives with 18th and 19th century additions by Giacomo Leoni and Lewis Wyatt. Four centuries of period interiors – Mortlake tapestries, Grinling Gibbons carvings, unique collection of English clocks. Historic gardens with conservatory by Wyatt, a lake and a 'Dutch'garden. A 1,400 acre park, home to red and fallow deer. Exterior featured as Pemberley in BBC's Pride and Prejudice. **Open:** Park: April to Oct: daily 8am–8.30pm; Nov to March 8am–6pm. Garden: 24 March to 31 Oct: Fri–Tues 11–5pm, Wed & Thurs 1–5pm. House: 24 March to 31 Oct: Fri–Tues 1–5pm. BHols 11–5pm.

Admission: Park: £3.50 per car. Garden only: £2. House only: £3.50. Combined £4.50, family £12.

PEOVER HALL

Over Peover, Knutsford WA16 9HN

Tel: 01565 632358

An Elizabethan house dating from 1585. Fine carolean stables. Mainwaring chapel, 18th century landscaped park. Large garden with topiary work, also walled and herb gardens. **Open:** April to Oct: House, stables & gardens: Mons except BHols, 2–5pm. Tours of the house at 2.30pm & 3.30pm. Stables & Gardens only: Thurs 2–5pm. **Admission:** House, Stables & Gardens: Adult £3, child £2. Stables & Garden only: £2. **Location:** 4 miles south of Knutsford. Off the A50 at Whipping Stocks Inn.

RODE HALL

Church Lane, Scholar Green ST7 3QP
Tel: 01270 873237 Fax: 01270 882962
(Sir Richard Baker Wilbraham Bt)

18th century country house with Georgian stable block. Later alterations by L Wyatt and Darcy Braddell. Repton landscape and formal gardens designed by Nesfield. Fully working walled kitchen garden. Icehouse. **Location:** 5 miles south west of Congleton between A34 and A50. **Open:** Easter–end Sept, Wednesdays and Bank Holidays and by appointment. Garden only: Tuesdays and Thursdays 2–5pm. **Admission:** House, garden and kitchen garden: Adult £4, OAP £2.50. Garden and kitchen garden: Adult £2.50, OAP £1.50. (Senior citizens £2 and £1) **Refreshments:** Home-made teas.

map 8
B5

TABLEY HOUSE

Knutsford, Cheshire, WA16 0HB.
Tel: 01565 750 151 Fax: 01565 653 230
Owners: The Victoria University of Manchester

Finest Palladian mansion in the NW designed by John Carr of York for the Leicester family. The staterooms show family memorabilia, furniture by Gillow, Bullock and Chippendale and the first collection of English paintings ever made. **Location:** 2 miles W of Knutsford, entrance on A5033 (M6 Junction 19, A556). **Open:** Apr–end Oct: Thurs, Fri, Sat, Sun and Bank Hols, 2–5pm. (Last entry 4.30pm). Free car park. Main rooms and the Chapel suitable for the disabled. **Admission:** Adults £4. Child/student with card £1.50. **Refreshments:** Tearoom and shop facilities. ALL ENQUIRIES TO THE ADMINISTRATOR. **Conferences:** Small meetings, civil wedding licence.

map 6
C1

TATTON PARK

Knutsford, Cheshire WA16 6QN
Tel: 01625 534400 Fax: 01625 534403 (Cheshire County Council)

Large Regency mansion with extravagantly decorated staterooms, family rooms and servants workrooms. A superb collection of Gillow furniture, Baccarat glass and paintings by Italian and Dutch masters. Two exhibition rooms, one of which features personal memorabilia of the Egerton family. 1000 acres of deer park open to visitors with its lakes woods and open vistas, provide the setting for the magnificent mansion and help make Tatton one of England's most complete country estates. The Garden contains many unusual features and rare species of plants shrubs and trees. Considered to be one of the finest and most important gardens within the National Trust. Features include: Conservatory by Wyatt, Fernery by Paxton, Japanese, Italian and Rose gardens. The rare collection of plants including rhododendrons, tree ferns, bamboo and pines are the result of 200 years of collecting by the Egerton family. **Open: Park & Gardens:** open all year except Mondays but including Bank Holidays (Closed Christmas Day). **Farm:** Sundays only, Nov–Mar. **Mansion Old Hall:** Apr–Oct, phone for further details. Managed and Financed by Cheshire County Council.

map 6
C1

Cornwall

Cornwall is renowned for its enchanted legends and associated with names such as Merlin, King Arthur, Tristan and Isolde – the magic lives on! The fortified headland of Tintagel, the picturesque fishing villages of St Ives, Port Gaverne and Port Isaac, the torrents and rock formations of Bodmin Moor and the clenched little harbour of Boscastle – are typical of Cornwall's craggy appeal, but the full elemental power of the ocean can best be appreciated on Cornwall's twin pincers of The Lizard point and Land's End, where the splintered cliffs resound to the constant thunder of the waves.

Padstow

BOSVIGO

Bosvigo Lane, Truro, Cornwall
Tel: 01872 275774 Fax: 01872 275774 (Michael and Wendy Perry)

Unlike most Cornish Gardens, Bosvigo is a 'summer' garden. Shrubs take second place to herbaceous perennials, carefully planted to give a succession of colour from Jun through 'til Sept. The gardens comprise a series of walled or hedged 'rooms' all around the Georgian house (not open). Each room has its own colour theme. A Victorian conservatory houses a collection of semi-tender climbers and plants–a delightful place to sit and relax. This is a plantsman's garden–the harder you look, the more plants you will see. Featured in many books, magazines and on television. **Open:** Mar–end Sept, Thur–Sat, 11–6pm. **Admission:** Adults £3, children 5–15yrs £1, under 5's free. Sorry, no dogs.

map 2 C6

BURNCOOSE NURSERIES & GARDEN

Gwennap, Redruth TR16 6BJ
Tel: 01209 860316 Fax: 01209 860011 (C H Williams)

The Nurseries are set in the 30 acre woodland gardens of Burncoose. 12 acres are laid out for nursery stock production of over 3000 varieties of ornamental trees, shrubs and herbaceous plants. Specialities include camellias, azaleas, magnolias, rhododendrons and conservatory plants. The Nurseries are widely known for rarities and unusual plants. Mail order catalogue £1.50 (posted). **Location:** 2 miles southwest of Redruth on the main A393 Redruth to Falmouth road between the villages of Lanner and Ponsanooth. **Open:** Mon–Sat 9–5pm, Sun 11–5pm. Gardens and tearooms open all year (except Christmas Day). **Admission:** Nurseries free, gardens £2. **E-mail:** burncoose@eclipse.co.uk **Internet:** www.eclipse.co.uk/burncoose

map 2 C6

CAERHAYS CASTLE AND GARDENS

Gorran, St Austell PL26 6LY
Tel: 01872 501310 Fax: 01872 501870

One of the very few Nash built castles still left standing - situated within approximately 60 acres of informal woodland gardens created by J C Williams, who sponsored plant hunting expeditions to China at the turn of the century. Noted for its camellias, magnolias, rhododendrons and oaks. **English Heritage Listing:** Grade One, Outstanding. **Open:** Gardens 13th Mar–19 May 10–4pm. House 20 Mar–28 Apr, 2–4pm. Mon–Fri only. House closed on Bank Hol. Additional charity openings (Gardens only) Sun 2nd & Sun 23rd Apr, 1 May, 10–4pm. **Admission:** House £3.50, Gardens £3.50, Children £1.50, House/Gardens £6. Guided Tour by Head Gardener for groups can be arranged outside normal opening times, £4 each. **E-mail:** caerhays@eclipse.co.uk **Internet:** www.eclipse.co.uk/caerhays

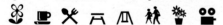

map 2 C6

LANHYDROCK HOUSE

Bodmin, Cornwall
Tel: 01208 73320 Fax: 01208 74084 (The National Trust)

Lanhydrock, one of Cornwall's grandest houses, dates back to the 17th century but much was rebuilt after a fire in 1881 destroyed all but the north wing, which includes the magnificent Long Gallery with its extraordinary plaster ceiling. A total of 49 rooms are on show today, including servants' bedrooms, kitchens, the nursery suite and the grandeur of the dining-room. Surrounding the house are formal Victorian gardens, wooded higher gardens where magnolias, rhododendrons and camellias climb the hillside. **Open:** Gardens and Park only: 1 Mar–31 Oct 2000. House: 1 Apr–31 Oct 2000 daily 11–5.30pm. Closes 5pm in October. House closed Mons (except Bank Hol Mons). **Admission:** House and gardens: Adult £6.60, child £3.30. Garden and grounds only: Adult: £3.60, child, £1.80. Family ticket (2 adults + 3 children) £16.50. Pre-arranged parties £5.50.

map 2 D5

GODOLPHIN HOUSE

Godolphin Cross, Helston, Cornwall TR13 9RE
Tel: 01736-762409 (Mrs M. Schofield)

Godolphin is of the Tudor and Stuart periods with Tudor stables. The garden retains its early raised walks. Elizabethan carp ponds are awaiting restoration. The Godolphins included Sidney, the Carolean poet and Sidney the 1st Earl, Lord High Treasurer, to Queen Anne. The 2nd Earl, Francis, owned the famous Godolphin Arabian horse, a painting of which hangs in the house. **Open:** Bank Hol Mon 2–5pm, May and Jun: Thurs 2–5pm, Jul and Sept: Tues and Thurs 2–5pm, Aug: Tues and Thurs 2–5pm, Groups of 20 and over by arrangement: Thurs 10–1pm and 2–5pm. **Admission:** Adults £3, children £1, under 5s free. Garden: Adults 50p, children free, groups of 20 or over £2.

map 2 B6

 # PENCARROW

Washaway, Bodmin PL30 3AG
Tel: 01208 841369 (The Molesworth-St Aubyn Family)

Georgian house and listed gardens, still owned and lived in by the family. A superb collection of 18th century pictures, furniture and porcelain. Mile long drive and Ancient British Encampment. Marked walks through beautiful woodland gardens, past the great granite Victorian Rockery, Italian and American gardens, Lake and Ice House. Approximately 50 acres in all. Over 700 different rhododendrons, also an internationally known specimen conifer collection. **Open:** 2 Apr–15 Oct, 1.30–5pm (1 June–10 Sept and Bank Hols 11am). **Admission:** Adults – House & Gardens £5, Gardens only £2.50. Children – House £2, Gardens: children and dogs very welcome and free. Group rate £4. NPI National Heritage Award Winner 1997 & 1998. **E-mail:** pencarrow @aol.com **Internet:** www.chycor.co.uk//pencarrow

PENDENNIS CASTLE

Falmouth, Cornwall TR11 4LP
Tel: 01326 316594 (English Heritage)

Facing the castle of St Mawes, with glorious views over the mile wide mouth of the River Fal, Pendennis Castle has stood in defence of our shores for almost 450 years. Take a guided tour through the tunnels to the Second World War Gun Battery. Explore the First World War Guardroom with its cells and see a Tudor gun deck in action complete with the sights and sounds of battle. A trip on the delightful ferry to St Mawes will make your day even more enjoyable. **Location:** On Pendennis Head 1m SE of Falmouth. **Open:** 1 Apr–31 Oct: daily, 10–6pm (5pm in October). Opens 9am July & Aug. 1 Nov–31 Mar: Wed–Sun, 10–4pm. Closed 24–26 Dec & 1 Jan. **Admission:** Adult £3.80, conc £2.90, child £1.90. (15% discount for groups of 11 or more).

map 2 C6

ST MAWES CASTLE

St Mawes, Falmouth, Cornwall TR2 3AA
Tel: 01326 270526 (English Heritage)

Designed with three huge circular bastions resembling a clover leaf, Henry VIII's picturesque fort stands in delightful sub-tropical gardens. Here you can see a remarkable collection of plants from all corners of the world. Climb to the battlements and experience the breathtaking views across the bay to Falmouth and take a trip on the ferry across the estuary to Pendennis Castle. **Location:** In St Mawes on A3078. **Open:** 1 Apr–30 Sept: daily, 10–6pm, last admission 5.30pm. 1 Oct–31 Oct: daily, 10–5pm. 1 Nov–31 Mar: Fri–Tues, 10–4pm. (Closed 24–25 Dec & 1 Jan). **Admission:** Adults £2.50, concs £1.90, child: £1.30. (15% discount for groups of 11 or more).

map 2 C6

 # ST MICHAEL'S MOUNT

Marazion, Nr Penzance, Cornwall
Tel: 01736 710507/01736 710 265 (The National Trust)

Home of Lord St Levan. Medieval and early 17th century with considerable alterations and additions in 18th and 19th century. **Location:** ½ mile from the shore at Marazion (A394), connected by causeway. 3 miles E Penzance. **Open:** 1 April–31 Oct, Mon–Fri, 10.30–5.30pm (last adm 4.45pm). **Weekends:** The castle and grounds are open most weekends during the season. These are special charity open days when National Trust members are asked to pay. Nov to end of Mar: Guided tours as tide, weather and circumstances permit. (NB: ferry boats do not operate a regular service during this period. **Admission:** Adults £4.40, children £2.20, groups £4, for 20 or more paying people.

map 2 B6

TINTAGEL CASTLE
Tintagel, Cornwall PL34 0HE
Tel: 01840 770328 (English Heritage)

A visit to Tintagel is a marvellous family experience combining legend, myth and magic. Located on Cornwall's dramatic Northern coast, this legendary castle of King Arthur is a place of mystery and romance, with breathtaking views of the Cornish coastline that inspire the imagination. Excavations prove the link between this area and the 6th century Mediterranean. **Location:** ½ mile from Tintagel Village along rough track. **Open:** Daily from 10am. Closing Apr–9 July: 6pm. 10 July–26 Aug: 7pm. 27 Aug–end Sept: 6pm. Oct: 5pm. Nov–Mar: 4pm. **Admission:** Adult £2.90, concession £2.20, child £1.50. Group discount 15% for groups of 11 or more.

TRELOWARREN HOUSE & CHAPEL
Mawgan-in-Meneage, Helston, Cornwall, TR12 6AD
Tel: 01326 221366 Fax: 01326 221834 (Sir Ferrers Vyvyan, Bt.)

Home of the Vyvyan family since 1427. Part of the house dates from early Tudor times. The Chapel, part of which is pre-Reformation and the 17th century part of the house are leased to the Trelowarren Fellowship, an ecumenical charity, for use by them as a Christian residential healing and retreat centre. (Phone for details). The Chapel and main rooms containing family portraits are open to the public at certain times. Sunday services are held in the Chapel during the holiday season. **Location:** 6 miles S of Helston, off B3293 to St. Keverne. **Open: House & Chapel:** 24 Apr–27 Sept, Wed & Bank Hol Mons, 2.15–5pm. **Admission:** Adults £1.50, children 50p (under 12 free), including entry to various exhibitions of paintings. **Events/Exhibitions:** Exhibitions of paintings. Only the ground floor is suitable for disabled.

TREVARNO ESTATE & GARDENS
Trevarno Manor, Helston, Cornwall TR13 0RU
Tel: 01326 574274 Fax: 01326 574282 (Mr M. R. Sagin & Mr N. C. Helsby)

A historic and tranquil haven protected and unspoilt for 700 years. Experience the magical atmosphere of Trevarno, an original and fascinating Cornish Estate. Beautiful Victorian and Georgian gardens, extensive collection of rare shrubs and trees, numerous garden features and follies, fascinating Gardening Museum, Handmade soap and bee-centre. Splendid Fountain Garden Conservatory tearoom. Walled gardens, woodland walks and abundant wildlife. Follow the progress of major restoration and conservation projects. **Location:** OS Ref SW6423902. Leave Helston on Penzance road, signed from B3302 junction and north of Crowntown village. **Open:** All year except Christmas Day 10.30–5pm. Groups welcome by prior arrangement. **Admission:** Gardens: Adult £3.50, OAP/disabled £3.20, children (5–14) £1.25. Museum: Donation Box.

TATE GALLERY ST IVES
Tate Gallery St Ives, Porthmeor Beach, St Ives, Cornwall TR26 1TG
Tel: 01736 796226 Fax: 01736 794480 Internet: www.tate.org.uk

Tate Gallery St Ives opened in 1993 and offers a unique introduction to modern art, where many works can be seen in the surroundings and atmosphere which inspired them. The gallery presents changing displays from the Tate Gallery Collection, focusing on the post-war modern movement St Ives is so famous for. Tate Gallery St Ives also runs the Barbara Hepworth Museum and Sculpture Garden in St Ives. **Admission:** Tate Gallery St Ives: Adults £3.90, conc £2.30. Barbara Hepworth Museum: Adults £3.50, conc £1.80. Combined: Adults £6, conc £3.30. Children under 18 free. Groups (10–30) special rates apply. **Open:** Tues–Sun 10.30–5.30pm and Mons in Jul and Aug. Bank holidays 10.30–5.30pm. Closed 24, 25, 26 December. **Refreshments:** Rooftop café, gallery shop, education services, guided tours, events and activities programme, full disabled access.

TRERICE
Nr Newquay TR8 4PG Tel: 01637 875404 Fax: 01637 879300

Open: 2 April–23 July, 10 Sept–30 Oct: daily except Tues & Sat; 24 July–9 Sept: daily. 11–5.30pm; (5pm in Oct). **Events:** send s.a.e. for programme.

ANTONY
Torpoint, Plymouth PL11 2QA Tel: 01752 812191

Open: 4 April–26 Oct: Tues, Wed, Thur & BH Mon; June, July & Aug: daily except Mon, Fri & Sat (but open BH Mon). 1.30–5.30pm; last admission 4.45. Bath Pond House can be seen by written application. Woodland Garden: open 1 March–31 October, daily 11–5.30pm.

COTEHELE
St Dominick, nr Saltash, PL12 6TA Tel: 01579 351346 Fax: 01579 351222

Open: House: 1 April–31 Oct: daily except Fri (but open Good Fri). 11–5pm (11–4.30 in Oct). Mill: 1 April–31 Oct: daily except Fri; July & Aug: daily 1.30–5.30pm. 1–6pm in July & Aug; 1.30–4.30pm in Oct. Garden: open all year, daily 11–Dusk.

Cumbria

Through the middle ages, successive kings and rulers fought over this territory. This has left the area with a multitude of Celtic monuments, Roman remains, stately homes and monastic ruins.

The Lake District dominates Cumbria, despite the attractions of other places of interest in the county. Windermere, Grasmere, Bowness, Ambleside, Kendal and Keswick are all best visited on foot. The lakes vary in character considerably, from the sombre Wastwater to the bright and breezy Windermere, the centre of most of the activities. Pastimes include hill-walking, windsurfing, rock climbing, cycling, canoeing and water-skiing.

Carlisle, set in the north of Cumbria, is a fine cathedral city which is steeped in the history of battle. The city stands imposingly as the gateway to the borders and Emporer Hadrian, Bonnie Prince Charlie and Robert the Bruce have all played a part in Carlisle's interesting past.

Loweswater

The rich land of the Eden Valley, popular with trout and salmon fishermen, complements the raw beauty of The North Pennines.

Traditional sports such as Cumberland and Westmorland wrestling and fell racing are still practised and may be seen at many of the sports shows whilst the Egremont Crab Fair hosts the annual World Gurning Championship.

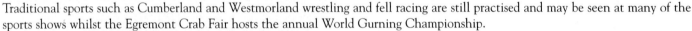

ABBOT HALL ART GALLERY

Kendal, Cumbria LA9 5AL

Tel: 01539 722464 Fax: 01539 722494 (Lake District Art Gallery & Museum Trust)

Abbot Hall is a jewel of a building in a beautiful setting on the banks of the River Kent, surrounded by a park and over looked by the ruins of Kendal Castle. This is one of Britain's finest small art galleries and a wonderful place in which to see and enjoy changing exhibitions in the elegantly proportioned rooms of a Grade I Listed Georgian building. The permanent collection at Abbot Hall alone is worth a visit. You can view 18th century paintings in their period setting, alongside furniture and objets d'art of the time. The collection of portraits of the day includes key works by George Romney, who served his apprenticeship in Kendal. The adjacent Museum of Lakeland Life is a popular family attraction with a Victorian street scene, farmhouse rooms and Arthur Ransome room. **Open:** 7 days a week 10 Feb–22 Dec 2000 10.30–5pm (reduced hours in winter).

map 11
F6

ACORN BANK GARDEN & WATERMILL

Temple Sowerby, Nr Penrith CA10 1SP

Tel: 017683 61893 Fax: 017683 61467 (The National Trust)

A walled garden renowned for its impressive herb collection of culinary and medicinal plants. There are also mixed herbaceous and rose borders and orchards containing a wide range of northern varieties of fruit tree. There are circular walks on the estate, including a circular woodland route along the Crowdundle Beck to Acorn Bank Watermill which is open to the public. Tearoom serving light refreshments, together with a shop and plant sales. **Open:** Garden Open: 1 Apr–31 Oct: daily 10–5pm, last admission 4.30. Telephone for shop/tearoom opening hours. **Admission:** Adults £2.30, children £1.20, family ticket £5.80, pre-arranged parties £1.70 per person. Car parking. **Events:** 15 Oct 2000 Apple Day.

map 11
F5

THE BEATRIX POTTER GALLERY

The Square, Hawkshead, Ambleside, Cumbria

Tel: 015394 36355 Fax: 015394 36118 (The National Trust)

An annually changing exhibition of original illustrations from Beatrix Potter's story books for children. One of many historic buildings in this picturesque village. This was once the office of the author's husband, the solicitor William Heelis and the interior remains largely unaltered since his day. **Open:** 2 Apr–31 Oct: Sun–Thur (closed Fri & Sat except Good Friday) 10.30–4.30pm. Last admission 4pm. **Admission:** By timed ticket (including NT members) Adults £3, children £1.50, family £7.50, no reduction for parties. Car & coach parking in village car park, 200m.

map 10
E6

BRANTWOOD

Coniston, Cumbria
Tel: 015394 41396 Fax: 015394 41263 (The Brantwood Trust)

Brantwood is the most beautifully situated house in the Lake District and was the home of John Ruskin from 1872 until his death in 1900. It is a constant memorial to his life and work, with continual displays of his drawings, watercolours and personal memorabilia, video programme and bookshop, glorious woodland walks, full seasonal programme of activities, events and theatre, Jumping Jenny's restaurant and tearooms, coach house craft gallery, regular sailings by Coniston Launch and Steamyacht Gondola. **Location:** 2 miles from Coniston Village, east side of Coniston Water. **Open:** Open all year–daily mid Mar–mid Nov 11–5.30pm. Winter season Wed to Sun 11–4.30pm. **Admission:** Adults £4, students £2.80, children £1. Group prices on request. **Internet:** www.brantwood.org.uk

map 10 E6

CASTLETOWN HOUSE

Rockcliffe, Carlisle, Cumbria CA6 4BN
Tel: 01228 674792 Fax: 01228 674464 (Giles Mounsey-Heysham, Esq)

Period House set in attractive gardens and grounds overlooking the River Eden. **Location:** 5 miles NW of Carlisle on Solway coast, 1 mile W of Rockcliffe village and 2 miles W of A74. Collection of Naval and Seafaring paintings. **Open:** House Only by appointment only.

map 10 E4

DALEMAIN HISTORIC HOUSE & GARDENS

Nr Penrith, Cumbria CA11 0HB
Tel: 017684 86450 Fax: 017684 86223 (Robert Hasell-McCosh)

Impressive Medieval, Tudor and Georgian house, home to the Hasell family since 1679. Fascinating interiors with fine furniture, family portraits, ceramics, dolls houses, old toys, Mrs Mouse's house and the Westmorland & Cumberland Yeomanry Museum. Delightful Gardens with many rare plants and old fashioned roses. Featured as Lowood Institution, Jane Eyre's school, in LWT's recent television production. Free parking and admission to the Licensed Restaurant and Tea Room in the Medieval Hall (log fire), the Gift Shop and the Plant Sales. Country Walk towards Dacre Church and Castle. **Open:** Sun 2 Apr–Sun 8 Oct 2000. Sun to Thur 10.30–5pm. House: 11–4pm.

map 4 E6

HOLKER HALL AND GARDENS

Cark-in-Cartmel, nr Grange-over-Sands LA11 7PL
Tel: 015395 58328 Fax: 015395 58776 (Lord and Lady Cavendish)

Holker Hall, the home of Lord and Lady Cavendish and their family, is Cumbria's premier stately home. No ropes or barriers bar your way as you look round the magnificent New Wing with its fine woodcarvings, furniture and paintings. The 25 acres of National Award winning gardens include water features, rare plants, trees and shrubs, 'World Class ... not to be missed by foreign visitors' (Good Gardens Guide). Also superb Lakeland Motor Museum, Exhibitions, 125 acre Deer Park, Adventure Playground, World's largest Slate Sundial, Picnic Area, Cafe and Gift Shop. Home of the spectacular Holker Garden Festival 2–4 June 2000. **Location:** North of Cark-in-Cartmel on B5278 from Haverthwaite; 4 miles west of Grange-over-Sands. **Stations:** Cark-in-Cartmel. **Open:** 2 Apr–31 Oct every day excluding Sat, 10–6 last admission 4.30pm. **Admission:** Various prices depending on what you want to see and do. Reduction for groups of 20 or more. **Refreshments:** Home-made cakes, sandwiches, salads in the Coach House Cafe. Free car parking.

map 10 E6

HUTTON-IN-THE-FOREST
Penrith
Tel: 017684 84449 Fax: 017684 84571 (Lord and Lady Inglewood)

The home of Lord Inglewood's family since 1605. Built around a medieval pele tower with 17th, 18th and 19th century additions. Fine English furniture, portraits, ceramics and tapestries. The lovely walled garden established in 1730 has an increasing collection of herbaceous plants, wall trained fruit trees and topiary. Also dovecote and woodland walk through magnificent specimen trees, identifiable from leaflet. **Location:** 6 miles NW of Penrith on B5305 Wigton Road (3 miles from M6 exit 41). **Stations:** Penrith. **Open:** House 12.30–4pm last entry, Thurs, Fri, Sun, and Bank Hols. 20 Apr–1 Oct. Gardens 11–5pm everyday except Sat. Groups by arrangement from Apr–Oct. **Admission:** House and Gardens: Adult £4, child £2, family £10. Gardens only: Adult £2.50, children free. **Refreshments:** Home-made light lunches & teas in Cloisters when house is open, 12–4.30pm.

map 10
E4

ISEL HALL
Cockermouth, Cumbria CA13 OQG
(The Administrator)

Pele Tower with domestic range and gardens set on north bank of River Derwent. The house is small, so groups limited to 30. **Location:** 3½ miles N.E. of Cockermouth. **Station(s):** Aspatria 9 miles; Penrith 32 miles. **Open:** Mondays, 17 April–2 October, 2–4pm. Other times by written arrangement. **Admission:** £3. No dogs. No photography inside. It is regretted there is no disabled access upstairs.

map 10
D4

LEVENS HALL
Kendal LA8 0PD
Tel: 015395 60321 Fax: 015395 60669 (C H Bagot Esq)

Elizabethan house and home of the Bagot family containing fine furniture, the earliest English patchwork (c.1708) and leather wall coverings. World famous award winning Topiary Gardens (c.1694). Collection of working model steam engines. Location for BBC TV "Wives and Daughters". **Directions:** 5 minutes drive from exit 36 of the M6. 5 miles south of Kendal on the A6. **Station:** Oxenholme. **Open:** 2 Apr–12 Oct, Sun–Thurs (including Bank Hol Mons). Garden & tearoom 10–5pm. House: noon–5pm. Last admissions 4.30pm. Closed Fri & Sat. **Admission:** House and Garden: Adults £5.30, children £2.80. Gardens only: Adults £3.90, children £2.10. **Refreshments:** Home-made light lunches and teas. We regret the house is not suitable for wheelchairs. **E-Mail:** levens.hall@farmline.com **Internet:** http://www.levenshall.co.uk

map 10
E6

MIREHOUSE
Mirehouse, Keswick CA12 4QE
Tel: 01768 772287 Fax: 01768 772287 (Mr & Mrs Spedding)

A regional winner in the 1999 NPI Heritage Awards. This house maintains its three hundred year tradition of welcome and peaceful enjoyment. Our visitors particularly appreciate the extraordinary literary and artistic connections, varied gardens and walks, natural adventure playgrounds, live classical music and the personal attention of members of the family. The Old Sawmill Tearoom is known for generous Cumbrian cooking. Catering for groups also available in the licensed Garden Hall. **Location:** A591 3½ miles N of Keswick. Good bus service. **Open:** 1 Apr–31 Oct. Gardens and tearoom: daily 10–5.30pm. Please telephone for winter opening times. House: Sun, Wed (also Fri in Aug) 2–4.30pm last entry. Also throughout the year by appointment for groups.

map 10
E5

MUNCASTER WATER MILL
Ravenglass, Cumbria CA18 1ST
Tel: 01229 717232 (Lake District Estates)

Working old Manorial Mill with 13ft overshot wheel and all milling equipment. **Location:** 1 mile north of Ravenglass on A595. **Open:** Maundy Thursday–end Oct, daily, 10–5pm. Nov–March: weekends only, 11–4pm. **Admission:** Adult £1.60, child 80p, Family £4.

RYDAL MOUNT & GARDENS
Ambleside, Cumbria LA22 9LU
Tel: 01539 433002 Fax: 01539 431738 (Rydal Mount Trustees)

The historic house of William Wordsworth from 1813 until his death in 1850, now the family home of his descendants. It contains family portraits and his personal possessions. The extensive garden, landscaped by the poet, includes terraces, rare shrubs, trees and the poet's summerhouse which overlooks beautiful Rydal Water. **Location:** 1½ miles north of Ambleside on A591 Grasmere Road. **Open:** 1 Mar–31 Oct, 9.30–5pm, 7 days a week. 1 Nov–end Feb, 10–4pm. Closed on Tuesday. **Admission:** Adult £3.75, child £1.25, OAP/Student £3.25. Groups (10+) £2.75 per person. Garden only: £1.75.

SIZERGH CASTLE & GARDEN
Kendal, Cumbria, LA8 8AE
Tel: 015395 60070 (The National Trust)

The 14th century Pele Tower rises to 60ft, containing original windows, floors and fireplaces; 16th century wings; fine panelling ceilings; French and English Furniture, china and family portraits. Extensive garden includes the largest limestone gardens owned by the Trust with Japanese maples, dwarf conifers, hardy ferns, perennials and bulbs; water garden; herbaceous borders, wild flower banks; fine autumn colour. **Location:** 3½ miles S of Kendal NW of A590/A591 Interchange. **Open:** Castle: 23 Apr–31 Oct, Sun–Thur, 1.30–5.30pm. Garden: 28 May–31 Oct, 12.30–5.30pm. **Admission:** Castle and Garden £4.60, Garden only £2.30. Family ticket £11.50. Children half price. Parties by prior arrangement. No dogs. Wheelchairs available for use in garden only.

STOTT PARK BOBBIN MILL
Low Stott Park, Ulverston, Cumbria LA12 8AX
Tel: 01539 531087 (English Heritage)

When this working mill was built in 1835 it was typical of the many mills in the Lake District which grew up to supply the spinning and weaving industry in Lancashire but have since disappeared. A remarkable opportunity to see a demonstration of the machinery and techniques of the Industrial Revolution. There is a working Static Steam Engine on Tuesday and Thursdays. **Location:** Near Newby Bridge on A590. **Open:** 1 Apr–31 Oct, daily, 10–6pm. Last tour 5pm.

www.historichouses.co.uk

49

🏛 MUNCASTER CASTLE, GARDENS & OWL CENTRE

Ravenglass, Cumbria CA18 1RQ
Tel: 01229 717 614 Fax: 01229 717 010 (Mrs P. Gordon-Duff-Pennington)

Muncaster Castle, situated on the peaceful West Coast of Cumbria has been home to the Pennington family for 800 years. Treasures include a picture painted by Gainsborough for a bet; John of Bologna's Alabaster Lady; Henry VI's drinking bowl, known as the 'Luck of Muncaster', dating from his stay at the Castle during the Wars of the Roses; and the most ornamental dinner service the Derby factory ever made. Visitors are guided around the Castle with a free audio tour, narrated by Patrick Gordon-Duff-Pennington, the present owner. The Castle stands proudly in 77 acres of splendid woodland gardens, famed for their rhododendrons and azaleas. The Georgian Terrace Walk boasts stunning views of the magnificent Lakeland fells and two recently restored Victorian summer houses. As part of a millennium programme major replanting and restoration of the gardens has taken place, ensuring colour and interest for all seasons. Around 50 species of owls are in the care of the World Owl Trust based at Muncaster. Daily at 2.30pm(March–October) a bird display and talk is given. Facilities include café, gift shops, children's play area, plant centre, church and function room, all with disabled access. The Castle is licensed for civil marriages. **Open:** Castle: Sun–Fri, 12–5pm, 19 Mar–5 Nov. Gardens & Owl Centre: Every day, all year, 10.30–6pm. **E-mail:** info@muncaster castle.co.uk **Internet:** www.muncastercastle.co.uk

map 9
D6

Derbyshire

Of all the English counties, this is probably the most traditional. Within its borders England passes from the plain country to the hill country, from the newer and softer rocks to the old and harder. As the Lake District dominates Cumbria, so the Peak District dominates Derbyshire.

Viaduct in Monsdale

The Peak District became Britain's first National Park in 1951. This vast rolling landscape stretches for an area of over five hundred square miles and is a favourite with walkers, climbers and pot-holers who congregate on the Pennine Way. The Tissington Trail is equally popular with walkers as it winds its spectacular way around this charming old village. Tissington was responsible for reviving the custom of well-dressing in the seventeenth century, as an act of thanksgiving for its deliverance from the deadly plague. Well-dressing continues to be a popular event in this area to this day.

At the Northern extremity of Derbyshire lies the former spa town of Buxton. This town is a rare gem where elegant sweeping terraces echo those found at Bath. To the southwest, the modern city of Derby is famed for its Crown Derby porcelain. Either of these towns would provide a welcome stopover point for energetic walkers to rest their weary feet.

Matlock is another fine Spa town, developed in the eighteenth century and home to some impressive buildings including the former hydrotherapy centre, perched on a hill above the town. Matlock is also an ideal base from which to venture out on the A6 as it makes its way through the stunning Derwent Gorge. Those travelling to the north of the county will be rewarded by the beauty of two great historic houses, Chatsworth and Haddon Hall.

BOLSOVER CASTLE

Bolsover, Derbyshire S44 6PR
Tel: 01246 823349 (English Heritage)

Bolsover has the air of a romantic story book castle, but is an historic house with a fascinating story to tell. Visitors can explore the enchanting 17th century mansion and 'Little Castle' with its elaborate Jacobean fireplaces, panelling and wall paintings. Discover the mock-medieval fortifications, battlements, ruined staterooms (where Charles I was entertained) and indoor riding house, one of the oldest in Europe. An inclusive audio tour brings this magical castle to life. There is a new Visitor Centre and shop and the site is now licensed to hold ceremonies. **Location:** Off M1 at junction 29, 6m from Mansfield. In Bolsover 6m E of Chesterfield on A632. **Open:** 1 Apr –30 Sept: daily, 10–6pm. 1 Oct–31 Oct: daily, 10–5pm. 1 Nov–31 Mar: Wed –Sun, 10–4pm. (Closed 24–26 Dec & 1 Jan 2001). **Admission:** Adults £4.20, concs £3.20, child £2.10. (15% discount for groups of 11 or more).

map 8
D5

CALKE ABBEY

Ticknall, Derby DE73 1LE
Tel: 01332 863822 Fax: 01332 865272

A great house with a big difference! A baroque mansion built 1701–3 for Sir John Harpur and set in a landscaped park. Little restored, Calke is preserved as a graphic illustration of the English country house in decline; contains the family's collection of natural history, a fine 18C state bed and interiors that are virtually unchanged since the 1880s. Walled garden, pleasure grounds and newly restored Orangery. Early 19C church. Historic parkland with Portland sheep and deer. **Open:** 27 Mar–1 Nov, daily except Thurs & Fri 1– 5.30pm. Last entries 5pm. House & church: 1–5.30pm. Garden: 11–5.30pm. Last entries 5pm. House, church & garden closed 12 Aug. Park: open every day, all year, vehicle charge. Shop & restaurant: as house. Christmas shop & restaurant Nov & Dec weekends 11–4pm. **Admission:** £5.10, child £2.50, family ticket £12.70, gardens only £2.40. NT members free.

map 8
C6

CHATSWORTH

Chatsworth, Bakewell, Derbyshire, DE45 1PP
Tel: 01246 582204 Fax: 01246 583536 (Chatsworth House Trust)

Chatsworth, home of the Duke and Duchess of Devonshire, is one of the great treasure houses of England. Visitors see 26 richly decorated rooms furnished with the outstanding art collection. To celebrate their 50th year at Chatsworth, the Duke and Duchess have chosen favourite treasures from their private collection to show visitors - from illuminated manuscripts to family portraits by Lucian Freud. There will also be a room devoted to Duchess Georgiana, subject of Amanda Foreman's award winning biography. 'Revelation', a new water sculpture, has recently been added to the unique assemblage of fountains, ponds and the Cascade in the 105 acre Garden. Children are thrilled by the woodland adventure playground and the farmyard, and there are award winning shops and a restaurant. The home of the Cavendish family for 450 years, and recently voted the country's favourite National Treasure, Chatsworth offers a day out that will entertain and astonish visitors of all ages. Guided tours and behind-the-scenes days are available. **Open:** 15 Mar–29 Oct 2000, 11–4.30pm. **Events:** Angling Fair 6–7 May, International Horse Trials 13–14 May, Country Fair 2–3 Sept.

map 8
C5

BLUEBELL NURSERY & WOODLAND GARDEN

Smisby, Derbyshire
Tel: 01530 413700

5 acre young Arboretum planted in the last 6 years including many specimens of rare trees and shrubs. Bring wellingtons in wet weather. **Location:** From the A511 Burton Trent to Ashby-de-la-Zouch Road, turn for Smisby by the Mother Hubbard Inn, 1 mile north-west of Ashby. Arboretum is on left after 1/2 mile Annwell Lane. Please call Tel: 01530 413700 for opening times and admission prices.

DAM FARM HOUSE

Yeldersley Lane, Ednaston, Derbyshire
Tel: 01335 360291

3 acre garden which has been extended to include a young arboretum. Beautifully situated. Contains mixed borders, scree. Unusual plants have been collected many are propagated for sale. **Location:** 5 miles south-east of Ashbourne on A52, opposite Ednaston Village turning. Gate on the right 500 yards. Please call Tel: 01335 360291 for opening times and admission prices.

EYAM HALL

Eyam, Hope Valley, Derbyshire, S32 5QW
Tel: 01433 631976 Fax: 01433 631603 (Mr R H V Wright)

This small charming manor house in the famous plague village has been the home of the Wright family since 1671 and it retains the intimate atmosphere of a much-loved private home. A Jacobean staircase, fine tapestries, family portraits and costumes are among its interior treasures. **Location:** Eyam Hall is in the centre of the village of Eyam. **Open:** Easter–Oct: Wed, Thur, Sun & BHol Mon, 11–4pm. Guided Tours. Victorian Christmas tours and Schools please phone for details. **Admission:** Adult £4, child £3, conc. £3.50, family (2+4) £12.50. Group rates with advance booking. Craft Centre Gift Shop & Buttery: in historic farmyard, with crafts people at work & local products for sale. Both open daily except Mons, all year, 10.30–5pm. **Events:** Indoor & outdoor concerts & plays -see Events Diary. **Weddings:** Eyam Hall is now licensed for civil weddings. **Internet:** www.eyamhall.co.uk

map 8
C4

HARDWICK HALL, GARDENS, PARK & MILL

The National Trust, Doe, Chesterfield, Derbyshire S44 5QJ
Tel: 01246 550430 Fax: 01246 854200 (The National Trust)

Set high on a hill in North-East Derbyshire, one of the greatest Elizabethan houses, which survives almost unchanged today. Completed 403 years ago and known to have "more glass than wall", the Hall contains one of Europe's best collections of embroideries and tapestries recorded in a 1601 inventory. A gardener's delight - the spectacular gardens, orchards and herb area are a relaxing place to spend an afternoon. The historic 300 acre parkland with woods and meadows has great walks and many attractive ponds and views. A new circular route around Miller's Pond offers mobility-impaired visitors good access. Stainsby Mill - a tranquil water powered corn mill. A mill has stood on this site since the 13th century, providing flour for the local villages and later for the Hardwick Estate. The Sixth Duke of Devonshire, owner of Hardwick, restored it in 1850. He spent the equivalent of £1,000,000 to put it into working order after years of neglect. The working mill is of advanced engineering design. **Location:** Follow brown tourist signs for Hardwick Hall from Junction 29 of the M1, 9½m southeast of Chesterfield and 7 miles northwest of Mansfield. **Open:** Hall: 1 Apr–31 Oct: Wed, Thurs, Sat, Sun & Bank Hol Mon, 12.30–5pm. Garden: 1 Apr–31 Oct: daily 12–5.30pm. Mill: 1 Apr–31 Oct: Wed, Thurs, Sat, Sun & Bank Hol Mon, 11–4.30pm (last entry 4pm). **Restaurant/Shop:** as for Hall.

map 8
D5

HARDSTOFT HERB GARDENS

Hall View Cottage, Hardstoft, Chesterfield, Derbyshire S45 8AH
Tel: 01246 854268

Consists of four display gardens with information boards and well labelled plants. **Location:** On B6039 between Holmewood & Tibshelf, 3m from J29 on M1. **Open:** Daily, 15 Mar–15 Sept, 10–5pm. Closed Tuesday (except Bank Hol). **Admission:** Adult £1, children free.

HARDWICK OLD HALL

Doe Lea, Nr Chesterfield S44 5QJ
Tel: 01246 850431 (English Heritage)

This large ruined house, finished in 1591, still displays Bess of Hardwick's innovative planning and interesting decorative plasterwork. The views from the top floor over the country park and 'New' Hall are spectacular. **Location:** 9½ miles SE of Chesterfield, off A6175, from Jct 29 / M1. **Open:** 1 Apr–31 Oct, Wed–Sun 10–6pm (5pm in October). **Admission:** Adult £2.50, concessions £1.90, child £1.30.

KEDLESTON HALL AND PARK

Kedleston Hall, Derby DE22 5JH
Tel: 01332 842191 Fax: 01332 841972 (The National Trust)

Experience the age of elegance in this neoclassical house built between 1759 and 1765 for the Curzon Family. Set in 800 acres of parkland with an 18 C pleasure ground, garden and woodland walks. Parties welcome. Introductory talks can be arranged. **Location:** 5m NW of Derby, signposted from roundabout where A38 crosses A52. **Open:** House: 1 Apr–1 Nov daily except Thurs and Fri (closed Good Fri) 12–4.30pm last admissions 4pm. Garden: same days as house 11–6pm. Park: 1 Apr–1 Nov daily 11–6pm; Nov–Dec: Sat & Sun only 12–4pm. Events: concerts and theatre. Flower Festival May Bank Hol: details from Property Manager. **Admission:** Adults £5, child £2.50, family £12.50. £1 reduction for pre-booked parties of 15+. Park & Garden only: Adults £2.20, child £1 (refundable against tickets for house); Thurs and Fri vehicle charge of £2 for park only.

map 8
C6

HADDON HALL

Bakewell, Derbyshire
Tel: 01629 812855 Fax: 01629 814379 (Haddon Hall Trust)

William the Conqueror's illegitimate son, Peverel and his descendants held Haddon for a hundred years before it passed into the hands of the Vernons. The following four centuries saw the development of the existing medieval and Tudor manor house from its Norman origins. In the late 16th century, it passed through marriage to the Manners family, later to become Dukes of Rutland, in whose possession it has remained ever since. Little has been added since the reign of Henry VIII, whose elder brother was a frequent guest and despite its time-worn steps, no other medieval house has so triumphantly withstood the passage of time. The terraced gardens, one of the chief glories of Haddon, were added during the 16th century. Now with roses, clematis and delphiniums in abundance, it is perhaps the most romantic garden in all England. A popular choice with film producers, Haddon Hall has recently appeared in: Elizabeth (1997); Jane Eyre (1996); The Prince and The Pauper (1996); Moll Flanders (1996). **Location:** On the A6, 2 miles S of Bakewell. **Open:** 1 Apr–30 Sept, everyday and Mon–Thurs in Oct. Closed Sun 16 July 2000. **Admission:** Adult £5.75, concession £4.75, child £3, family (2+3) £15. **Refreshments:** Licensed restaurant serving home-made food. **Events:** Partake Elizabethan Dancers: Sun 9 Apr, 9 July & 10 Sept. Flower Festival: 24–30 June. Craft Fair: 22–23 July and Embroiderers Guild Cushion Display: 6 May–18 June.

map 8
C5

LEA GARDENS

Lea, Matlock, Derbyshire DE4 5GH
Tel: 01629 534380 Fax: 01629 534260 (Mr & Mrs Jonathan Tye)

Visit Lea Gardens where you can see our highly acclaimed unique collection of rhododendrons, azaleas, kalmias and other plants of interest introduced from the far corners of the world. The gardens are sited on the remains of a medieval millstone quarry and cover an area of approximately four acres amidst a wooded hillside. The excellent rock gardens contain a huge variety of alpines with acers, dwarf conifers, heathers and spring bulbs. The teashop on site offers light lunches and home baking. A plant sales area reflects the contents of the garden offering up to 200 varieties of rhododendrons and azaleas. **Open:** Daily 10–7pm, 20 Mar–30 June. **Admission:** Adults £3, children 50p, season ticket £4.

MELBOURNE HALL & GARDENS

Melbourne, DE73 1EN
Tel: 01332 862502 Fax: 01332 862263

This beautiful house of history is the home of Lord and Lady Ralph Kerr. Melbourne Hall was once the home of Victorian Prime Minister William Lamb who, as 2nd Viscount Melbourne, gave his name to the famous city in Australia. One of the most famous formal gardens in Britain featuring Robert Bakewell's wrought iron 'Birdcage'. **Location:** 7 m S of Derby off the A453 in village of Melbourne. **Open:** House open every day of Aug only (except first 3 Mons) 2–5pm. Last entry 4.15pm. Garden open Apr–Sept Weds, Sats and Suns, Bank Hols Mons 2–6pm. **Refreshments:** Melbourne Hall Tearooms and Visitor centre and shops open at various times throughout the year. Car parking limited. Suitable for disabled persons. All enquiries 01332 862502.

RENISHAW HALL

Near Sheffield, Derbyshire S21 3WB
Tel: 01246 432310 (Sir Reresby Sitwell)

Home of Sir Reresby and Lady Sitwell. Seven acres of Italian style formal gardens stand in 300 acres of mature parkland, encompassing statues, shaped yew hedges, a water garden and lakes. The Sitwell museum and art gallery are located in the Georgian stables alongside craft workshops and café, furnished with contemporary art. Located 3 miles from exit 30 of the M1, equidistant from Sheffield and Chesterfield. Tours of house and gardens can be arranged. Telephone for details. **Open:** Gardens and Georgian Stables: Easter to 1 October Fridays, Saturday, Sunday and Bank Holidays 10.30–4.30pm. Free car parking.

SUDBURY HALL & MUSEUM OF CHILDHOOD

Sudbury, Ashbourne, Derbyshire
Tel: 01283 585337 Fax: 01283 585139 (The National Trust)

The ideal family day out - an intriguing house and an entertaining museum. The Hall is one of England's most individual late 17th century houses. Look at the recently opened kitchen which, last season, was used as a set for the new BBC2 drama series 'In a Land of Plenty'. The Museum contains fascinating displays about children from the 18th century onwards. Chimney climbs for adventurous youngsters plus Betty Cadbury's fine collection of toys and dolls. Parties welcome, special 'Behind the Scenes/Roof top/Conservation tours tailored to suit your requirements. Contact Property Secretary for details. **Location:** 6 m E of Uttoxeter at Jct of A50 Derby–Stoke & A515 Ashbourne. **Open:** 1 Apr–31 Oct, daily expect Mon & Tues (Open BH Mon; closed Good Fri), 1–5.30pm. **Admission:** Adult £3.70, child £1.80, family £9.20.

Devon

There is beauty in Devon, whether inland or seaward. The colour of the soil is most unusual. Nowhere else will you find earth of quite such a rich hue. Nowhere else are the hedges of the fields quite so high or quite so thick.

Devon is a land of infinite variety - in its contours as well as in its colours. Level spaces are so uncommon, cricket pitches are hard to find. It is no place for cyclists, as the hills are ominous and well spread through the whole county. To see the region properly, you should travel on foot.

The varied scenery makes Devon the perfect holiday county. The climate is almost tropical for England – the sun shines warmly, and then the rain appears! This produces lush green beauty and stunning gardens.

Romantic moorland covers vast areas of inland Devon. Dartmoor covers 365 square miles in the south. This is the land of 'The Hound of the Baskervilles'. There are many rare birds that can be seen on the moor, as well as flocks of sheep who keep the undergrowth down and small groups of wild ponies.

The coastline is truly beautiful, with long stretches of sandy beaches. There is a constant reminder of Devon's seafaring history along both coasts. Exeter, Dartmouth and Torbay all offer excellent bases for touring the south of Devon. The varied attractions and beautiful scenery allow you to relax and unwind in this slow moving county.

Barnstaple, on the north coast, is steeped in history. In the centre of the town, on the Strand is a wonderful arcade topped with a statue of Queen Anne.

Don't miss the teas!

South Pool

BICKLEIGH CASTLE

Bickleigh, Nr. Tiverton, EX16 8RP, Devon.
Tel: 01884 855363 (M.J. Boxall)

A Royalist Stronghold with 900 years of history and still lived in. The 11th century detached Chapel, Armoury Guard Room with Tudor furniture and pictures, the Great Hall, Elizabethan bedroom, 17th century farmhouse. Museum of 19th century domestic and agricultural objects and toys. Picturesque moated garden, 'spooky' tower. **Location:** 4 miles south of Tiverton, A396. **Open:** Easter Week (Easter Sun–Fri), then Wed, Sun, Bank Hol Mons to late May Bank Hol; then to early Oct daily (except Sat) 2–5pm. (Last admission 4.30pm). Parties of 20 or more by prior appointment. **Admission:** Adults £4, children (5–15) £2, family ticket £10. Very popular for wedding receptions, civil wedding licence etc. For further details please telephone the Administrator.

AVENUE COTTAGE GARDENS

Ashprington, Totnes TQ9 7UT
Tel: 01803 732769 (R.J Pitts, Esq., R.C.H. Soans, Esq.)

11 acres of garden and woodland walks. Part of 18th century landscape garden now recreated by designers/plantsmen. **Location:** 3 m SE of Totnes, 300yds beyond Ashprington Church (Sharpham Drive). **Open:** 1 Apr–30 Sept, Tues–Sat, 11–5pm. Parties by arrangement. **Refreshments:** At Durant Arms in the village. No Coaches. Limited Access for disabled persons. No wheelchairs available. Dogs on leads only.

CASTLE DROGO

Drewsteignton, Exeter, Devon, EX6 6PB
Tel: 01647 433306 Fax: 01647 433186 (The National Trust)

This granite castle, built between 1910 and 1930, is one of the most remarkable works of Lutyens. It stands at over 900 feet overlooking the wooded gorge of the river Teign with beautiful views of Dartmoor. Spectacular walks through surrounding 600 acre estate. Formal garden with roses, flowering shrubs and herbaceous borders. **Open:** 1st Apr–1st Nov daily except Fri (open good Fri). Garden, shop, tearoom open daily, 11–5pm. **Admission:** Adults £5.40. Children half price. Family ticket £13.50. Reduced rate for garden and grounds only. **Open:** Castle: 27 March to 31 Oct: daily except Fri (but open Good Fri) 11–5.30pm. Garden: all year: daily 10.30–dusk.

CADHAY
Ottery St Mary, EX11 1QT
Tel/Fax: 01404 812432 (Mr O William-Powlett)

Cadhay is approached by an avenue of lime-trees and stands in a pleasant listed garden, with herbaceous borders and excellent views over the original medieval fish ponds. Cadhay is first mentioned in the reign of Edward I. The main part of the house was built about 1550 by John Haydon who had married the de Cadhay heiress. He retained the Great Hall of an earlier house, the fine timber roof (about 1420) can be seen. An Elizabethan Long Gallery was added by John's successor in 1617, thereby forming a unique and lovely courtyard. Georgian alterations were made in the mid 18th century. **Location:** 1 mile NW of Ottery St Mary on B3176. **Open:** Late Spring & Summer Bank Hol Suns & Mons, also Tues, Weds, Thurs in July and Aug 2–6 (last adm. 5.30pm) **Admission:** Adults £4, children £2. Groups by arrangement only. **Weddings:** The house is licenced for Civil Weddings and the gardens and grounds are available for corporate entertainment.

map 3
F5

DARTMOUTH CASTLE
Dartmouth
Tel: 01803 833588

Boldly guarding the narrow entrance to the Dart Estuary this castle was among the first in England to be built for artillery. Construction began in 1481 on the site of an earlier castle which was altered and added to over the following centuries. Victorian coastal defence battery with fully equipped guns, a site exhibition and magnificent views can all be seen at the castle. **Location:** 1m (12/3 km) south east of Dartmouth. **Open:** Apr–Sept 10–6pm daily. Please phone for details for the rest of the year.

HARTLAND ABBEY & GARDENS
Nr Bideford, North Devon EX39 6DT
Tel: 01237 441264/234 Fax: 01884 861134 (Sir Hugh and Lady Stucley)

Built 1157 in beautiful valley leading to Atlantic cove. Given by Henry VIII to Keeper of his Wine Cellar whose descendants live here today. Remodelled in 18-19th C, contains spectacular architecture and murals, fascinating collections of paintings, furniture, porcelain. Documents & seals from 1160AD; Victorian & Edwardian photographs; Museum; Dairy. Paths by Gertrude Jekyll lead to Bog Garden, Victorian Fernery discovered in 1999, woodland gardens of camellias, rhododendrons etc, secret 18th C walled gardens. Walk to beach with abundant wildflowers and wildlife. Peacock, donkeys, Jacob's sheep. Cream Teas. 1998 N.P.I. National Heritage Award Winner. **Location:** Off A39, between Hartland and Quay. **Open:** May–Sept incl. Easter Sun/Mon: Weds, Thurs, Suns & BHs, plus Tues in Jul & Aug. 2–5.30pm. **Admission:** House, gardens & grounds: Adults £4.50, child £1.50. Reduction for gardens only & groups etc.

map 2
D3

FLETE
Ermington, Ivybridge, Plymouth, Devon, PL21 9NZ.
Tel: 01752 830 308 Fax: 01752 830 309
(Country Houses Association)

Built around an Elizabethan manor, with alterations in 1879 by Norman Shaw. Wonderful II drop waterfall garden, designed by Russell Page ably assisted by Laurance of Arabia in the 1920's. **Location:** 11 miles E of Plymouth, at junction of A379 and B3121. **Station(s):** Plymouth (12 miles), Totnes (14 miles). **Bus Route:** No. 93, Plymouth–Dartmouth. **Open:** May–Sept. House and Garden: Wed & Thurs, 2–5pm. (Latest admission time 4.30pm) **Admission:** Adults £3.50, children £1. Garden only: open Sat & Sun 2–5pm. **Admission:** Adults £2.50, children free. Free car park. No dogs admitted.

KILLERTON HOUSE
Broadclyst, Exeter, Devon
Tel: 01392 881345 Fax: 01392 883112

Just 6 miles from Exeter, Killerton is Devon's most popular National Trust property. Elegant 18th century house designed by John Johnson with later additions, home of the Acland family. Also on display is costume from the Killerton Dress collection in a special exhibition for 2000 'Inside Out' – a revealing exhibition on underwear. Victorian laundry. 18 acre garden landscaped by Veitch with many original plantings of specimens collected by the plant hunters William and Thomas Lobb, Ernest 'Chinese' Wilson. Killerton also has a wonderful early 19th century rustic summer house and an ice house built in 1809. Excellent facilities for the less abled. Children quiz available.

map 3
F4

POWDERHAM CASTLE

Kenton, Exeter EX6 8JQ
Tel: 01626 890243 Fax: 01626 890729 (Earl & Countess of Devon)

Powderham Castle, the historic family home of the Earl of Devon, lies in an ancient and beautiful setting beside the Exe Estuary. There are regular guided tours of the magnificent State Rooms, beautiful gardens and grounds to explore, including the Children's Secret Garden, in the old Victorian walled garden. In springtime the Woodland Garden is full of colour and later in the summer The Rose Garden provides a fragrant home to Timothy Tortoise, at 155, the World's oldest pet! Powderham's Farm Shop and Plant Centre provide an excellent regional shopping centre. Courtyard Restaurant and Gift Shop. **Open:** Every day (except Sat). Castle and grounds from 2 April–29 Oct. Guided tours every half an hour, last admission 5pm. Farm Shop at Powderham Castle – open seven days a week from March. **Admission:** Adult £5.85, Seniors £5.35, child £2.95 (5–16), family ticket £14.65 (2 Adults & 2 Children). **Location:** Signposted on A379 Exeter to Dawlish Road. Tel 01626 890243 for all information.

map 3
G5

RHS GARDEN ROSEMOOR

Great Torrington, Devon EX38 8PH
Tel: 01805 624067 Fax: 01805 624717 (Royal Horticultural Society)

Rosemoor Garden contains 40 acres of superb planting varieties in the stunning setting of the Torridge Valley. Inspirational for gardeners, or just a place of beauty and tranquillity for those who prefer to relax. Walk from the maturity of Lady Anne's old garden through the Arboretum and beside a stream in a winding rocky gorge to a magnificent lake and on to a large formal area of individual gardens, including 2000 roses of 200 different varieties. Fruit and Vegetable Garden. Exciting trails for children. <u>Location:</u> 1 mile SE of Great Torrington on the A3124. <u>Open:</u> Garden open all year 10–6pm (Oct–Mar 5pm). <u>Admission:</u> Adults £4, children under 6 yrs free, children 6–16 £1. Groups of more than 10 £3.25. One person accompanying a blind visitor or wheelchair user free. <u>Refreshments:</u> Licensed Restaurant, Picnic area, Shop and Plant Centre.

map 2 E4

TIVERTON CASTLE

Tiverton, Devon, EX16 6RP. Tel: 01884 253200/255200
Fax: 01884 253200 (Mr & Mrs A. K. Gordon)

Few buildings evoke such an immediate feeling of history as Tiverton Castle. Originally built in 1106 by Richard de Redvers, Earl of Devon, on the orders of Henry I, it was then rebuilt in stone in 1293. Now many styles of architecture down the ages, from medieval to the present day can be seen. The magnificent medieval gatehouse and tower contain Civil War armoury. Furnishings and exhibits reflect the colourful history of the Castle and with continuing restoration there is always something new and interesting to see. Old walls, new gardens. <u>Accommodation:</u> 4 superb self-catering holiday apartments. 4 keys, highly commended.

map 3 F4

TORRE ABBEY

The Kings Drive, Torquay TQ2 5JE
Tel: 01803 293593 Fax: 01803 215948 (Torbay Council)

For 800 years, Torre Abbey has been the home of Torquay's leading citizens. Founded as a monastery in 1196, the Abbey later became a country house and the Cary family's residence for nearly 300 years. As well as important monastic remains, you can see over twenty historic rooms, including the beautiful family chapel, a splendid collection of paintings and Torquay terracotta, colourful gardens and mementoes of crime writer Agatha Christie. Teas are served in the Victorian kitchen. <u>Open:</u> Daily, Easter to 1 Nov, 9.30–6pm. Last admission 5pm. <u>Internet:</u> www.torbay.gov.uk/history/torabb.htm

map 3 F5

TOTNES CASTLE

Castle Street, Totnes TQ9 5NU
Tel: 01803 864406 (English Heritage)

By the North Gate of the hill town of Totnes you will find a superb motte and bailey castle, with splendid views across the roof tops and down to the River Dart. It is a symbol of lordly feudal life and a fine example of Norman fortification. <u>Location:</u> In Totnes, on the hill overlooking the town. Access in Castle Street off west end of High Street. <u>Open:</u> 1 Apr–end Sept: daily 10–6pm. Oct: daily 10–5pm. Nov–31 Mar: Wed–Sun 10–4pm. Closed 1–2pm in winter. Closed 24–26 Dec and 1 Jan <u>Admission:</u> Adult £1.60, concession £1.20, child 80p.

map 3 F5/6

YARDE

Yarde Farm, Malborough, Kingsbridge, Devon TQ7 3BY
Tel: 01548 842367 (John and Marilyn Ayre)

Grade I listed. An outstanding example of the Devon farmstead with a Tudor Bakehouse, Elizabethan farmhouse and Queen Anne mansion under restoration. Still a family farm. <u>Location:</u> On A381 ½ mile E of Malborough. 4 miles S of Kingsbridge. <u>Open:</u> Easter–31 Sept, Sun 2–5pm. <u>Admission:</u> Adults £2, children 50p, under 5s free.

map 3 F6

UGBROOKE PARK

Chudleigh, Devon, TQ13 OAD
Tel: 01626 852179 Fax: 01626 853322 (Lord Clifford)

Beautiful scenery and quiet parkland in the heart of Devon. Original House and Church built about 1200, redesigned by Robert Adam. Home of the Cliffords of Chudleigh. Ugbrooke contains fine furniture, paintings, beautiful embroideries, porcelain, rare family military collection. Capability Brown Park with lakes, majestic trees, views to Dartmoor. Guided tours relate stories of Clifford Castles, Shakespeare's 'Black Clifford', Henry II's 'Fair Rosamund, Lady Anne Clifford who defied Cromwell, The Secret Treaty, the Cardinal's daughter, Clifford of the CABAL and tales of intrigue, espionage and bravery. <u>Location:</u> Chudleigh, Devon. <u>Open:</u> 9 July–7 Sept, Sun, Tues, Wed & Thurs. Grounds open 1–5.30pm. Guided tours of House 2pm and 3.45pm. <u>Admission:</u> Adults £4.80. Children (5–16) £2. Groups (over 20) £4.20. Private party tours/functions by arrangement.

map 3 F5

Dorset

The countryside of Dorset is bewitching. From dawn till dusk, through each season, the changing light reveals a new slant to the landscape. You could not describe the countryside as wild or grand, just charming and a little quaint, the home to beautiful thatched flint-and-chalk cottages.

Around Lyme Regis, which is at Dorset's western point, the cliffs are forbearing. The Purbeck Hills once linked the headlands of Brittany with the white cliffs of Dover.

The county town, Dorchester, is still recognized as the backdrop for Thomas Hardy's novel 'The Mayor of Casterbridge'. The high street is lined with 17th century and Georgian houses. The town has a wonderful feel to it, with many small and friendly places to eat.

North of Poole stands Wimbourne Minster, which was Thomas Hardy's home for many years. Comparisons are often drawn between Dorset and Hardy's 'Wessex' but many other authors such as Jane Austen and Sir Arthur Conan Doyle have their own connections with the area.

Cranborne, to the north of Wimbourne Minster, is a beautiful village on the edge of what used to be a royal forest and is now a stunning woodland.

The county holds a vast number of historic properties and some of the most beautiful gardens in England; they are well worth a visit.

Hardy's Cottage

ATHELHAMPTON HOUSE & GARDENS

Athelhampton, Dorchester, Dorset DT2 7LG
Tel: 01305 848363 Fax: 01305 848135 (Patrick Cooke)

Athelhampton is one of the finest 15th century manor houses and is surrounded by one of the great architectural gardens of England. The house contains many magnificently furnished rooms. The Great Hall was built in 1485 by Sir William Martyn with permission from Henry VII. The Elizabethan West Wing includes The Great Chamber, Wine Cellar, King's Room and Library. The East Wing contains The State and Yellow Bedrooms as well as The Dining Room with a fine collection of Georgian furniture. The glorious Grade I gardens, dating from 1891, are full of vistas and gain much from the fountains and River Piddle flowing through. The walled gardens include the world famous topiary pyramids and two garden pavilions designed by Francis Inigo Thomas. Fine collections of tulips, magnolias, roses, clematis and lilies can be seen in season. A 15th century Dovecote and a 19th century Toll House are also situated in the grounds. Visited often by Thomas Hardy, Athelhampton is at the heart of Dorset's heritage. Recently used as a location for the BBC Antiques Roadshow. **Location:** Off the A35 at Northbrook Junction, 5 miles East of Dorchester. Ordnance Survey Grid Reference SY770942. **Open:** Mar–Oct daily (except Sat) 10.30–5pm. Nov–Feb, Sun 10.30–5pm. Restaurant serving lunches, cream teas and refreshments. Carvery on Sun. Gift shop and free car park. **Admission:** House & Gardens: Adult £5.40, OAPs £4.95, children £1.50, family £12. Pre-booked Group Rate (min 12) £3.95. Garden Only: Adults/OAPs £3.80. **Weddings:** Also available for Wedding Receptions and Private Functions. **Internet:** www.athelhampton.co.uk

map 3
T4

CHIFFCHAFFS

Chaffeymoor, Bourton, Gillingham, SP8 5BY, Dorset.
Tel: 01747 840841(Mr & Mrs K. R. Potts)

The garden surrounds a typical 400 year old stone Dorset cottage, with a very wide range of bulbs, alpines, herbaceous trees and shrubs, many of them unusual. It is planted for long periods of interest and divided into small individual gardens with many surprise views. In addition, a woodland garden with azaleas, camellias, rhododendrons, bog primulas and daffodils, unusual trees and shrubs. The bluebells are particularly beautiful in the spring. **Location:** 3 miles E of Wincanton, just off A303. **Open:** 30 Mar–30 Oct. Every Wed, Thurs, Bank Hol Weekends and Suns: 5 Mar, 2, 16, 23 & 30 Apr, 7, 21 & 28 May, 4 & 18 June, 2 July, 6 & 27 Aug, 3 Sept and 1 Oct; 2–5.30pm. Also by appointment. Groups welcome. **Admission:** £2. **Refreshments:** By arrangement.

map 3
J3

CHRISTCHURCH PRIORY

Quay Road, Christchurch, Dorset BH23 1BU
Tel: 01202 485804 Fax: 01202 488645

A medieval monastic church begun in 1094. Famous for the "Miraculous Beam", Norman nave, turret, monks' quire, Jesse reredos, Lady Chapel, chantries, 15th century bell tower and St Michael's Loft, a former school, now a museum. Guided tours can be arranged. **Admission:** Donations invited of £1 per adult and 20p per student. Charge to ascend tower: adult 50p, child/student 30p; same for museum. **Open:** Every day except 25 Dec subject to church services: weekdays 9.30–5pm, Sun 2.15–5pm. Church Services: Sun: 8am Holy Communion, 9.45am Sung Eucharist, 11.15am Choral Matins & sermon, 6.30pm Choral Evensong & sermon. Weekdays: 7.30am morning prayer, 8am Holy Communion. Thurs 11 Holy Communion, 5.30 daily, evening prayer. **E-mail:** hugh.m.williams @ukgateway.net **Internet:** www.resort–guide.co.uk/christchurch–priory

map 3
K4

COMPTON ACRES GARDENS

Canford Cliffs Road, Poole, Dorset
Tel: 01202 700778 Fax: 01202 707537 (Mr L. Green)

Compton Acres is set in a delightful area of Canford Cliffs in Poole, overlooking Poole Harbour and the Purbeck Hills beyond. Covering nearly ten acres, the nine gardens include an Italian Garden, an authentic Japanese Garden, a Rock and Water Garden and a Woodland Walk. The Tea Rooms and Terrace Brasserie serve a variety of food throughout the day, with our gift shop, ice cream parlour and well stocked Garden Centre. Compton Acres is one of the south's top attractions. **Location:** Off the B3065 onto Canford Cliffs Road. **Open:** 1 Mar–end Oct. **Admission:** Adult £4.95, senior citizen £3.95, child £2.95. Group rates 20+, adult £4.45, senior citizen £3.45, child £2.45. **E-mail:** sales@comptonacres.co.uk **Internet:** www.comptonacres.co.uk

map 3
K5

CRANBORNE MANOR GARDEN

Cranborne, Wimborne, Dorset BH21 5PP
Tel: 01725 517248, Fax: 01725 517862
(The Viscount and Viscountess Cranborne)

Walled gardens, yew hedges and lawns; wild garden with spring bulbs, herb garden, Jacobean mount garden, flowering cherries and collection of old-fashioned and specie roses. Beautiful and historic garden laid out in the 17th century by John Tradescant and much embellished in the 20th century. **Location:** 18 miles N of Bournemouth B3078; 16 miles S of Salisbury A354, B3081. **Open:** Garden Centre open Mon–Sat 9–5pm, Sun 10–5pm. Something for every gardener, but specialising in old-fashioned and specie roses, herbs, ornamental pots and garden furniture. Garden only Mar–Sept, Wed 9–5pm. South Court occasionally closed. Free car park. **Internet:** www.cranborne.co.uk **E-mail:** gardencentre@cranborne.co.uk

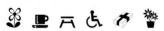

map 3
K5

HORN PARK GARDENS

Horn Park, Beaminster, Dorset
Tel: 01308 862 212 (Mr & Mrs John Kirkpatrick)

Large and beautiful garden. House built 1910 by a pupil of Lutyens – unique position, magnificent view to sea. Plantsman's garden, unusual trees, shrubs and plants in rock, water gardens terraces and herbaceous borders. Woodland Garden, Bluebell Woods, Wild flower meadow with over 160 species including orchids. Plants for sale. In RHS "Twelve Beautiful Gardens" calendar for 1998. Wedding receptions. **Location:** 1.5 miles N of Beaminster on A3066. **Station(s):** Crewkerne. **Open:** 1 Apr–31 Oct. Every Sun–Thur incl., 2–6pm & Bank Hol Mons. **Admission:** Adults £3. (Under 16 and wheelchair users free). Groups welcome any day or time, by prior arrangement, with teas if booked. Dogs on leads.

map 3
H4

DEANS COURT GARDEN

Deans Court, Wimborne, BH21 1EE, Dorset.
Wimborne Tourist Info: 01202 886116 (Sir Michael & Lady Hanham)

13 peaceful acres a few minutes walk south of the Minster. Free parking, specimen trees, lawns, borders, herb garden and kitchen garden with long serpentine wall. Chemical–free produce usually for sale also interesting herbaceous plants. Rose garden opening on 17th June. Wholefood teas in garden or in Housekeeper's room (down steps). **Location:** OS Ref. SZ 010 997. **Open:** Easter Sun 23 Apr 2–6pm; Easter Mon 24 Apr 10–6pm; Sun 30 Apr 2–6pm; Mon 1 May 10–6pm; Sun 28 May 2–6pm; Mon 29 May, 17–18 June, Sun 23 July 10–6pm. Organic Gardening Weekend: 5–6 Aug, Sun 27 Aug & Sun 17 Sept 2–6pm. Mon 28 Aug 10–6pm. **Admission:** Adults £2; children (5–15) 50p; OAPs £1.50. Groups by arrangement. **House:** Open by prior written appointment but not on days when garden is open. Prices on request.

map 3
K4

FORDE ABBEY AND GARDENS
Forde Abbey, Chard, Somerset TA20 4LU
Tel: 01460 221290, Fax: 01460 220296 (Mr M Roper)

Dating back to 1146 Forde Abbey is the finest example of a Cistercian monastery still standing today. It was transformed into a family home by Sir Edmund Prideaux in 1650 and has remained as such ever since. The house contains a magnificent set of 17th century tapestries taken from the Raphael cartoons drawn for the Sistine Chapel in Rome. There are also many wonderfully intricate Cromwellian plaster ceilings throughout the house. The Abbey is surrounded by 30 acres of award winning gardens with many unusual plants and shrubs. In the spring the garden is awash with spring bulbs, and throughout the season there is always something of interest including azaleas, magnolias, herbaceous borders, rock garden, bog garden and fully functioning kitchen garden. **Location:** 1 mile E of Chard Junction, 4 miles SE of Chard signposted off A30. **Open:** Gardens open daily throughout the year 10–4.30pm (last admission). House open 1–4.30pm Tuesday, Wednesday, Thursday, Sunday & Bank Holiday afternoons 1 April–31 Oct. **Admission:** House and gardens: Please telephone for details. **Refreshments:** Undercroft open for light lunches and teas 11–4.30 daily 1 April–end Oct.

map 3
H4

 KINGSTON LACY HOUSE, PARK & GARDEN
Wimborne, Dorset BH21 4EA
Tel: 01202 883402 Fax: 01202 882402 (The National Trust)

Beautiful 17th century house containing an outstanding collection of paintings, including works by Van Dyck, Titian and Brueghel. Fascinating interiors including the fabulous gilded leather Spanish Room. Exhibition of Egyptian artefacts from 3000BC. 250 acres of wooded parkland with splendid Red Devon cattle. Woodland walks. NT shop and restaurant. Dogs welcome in park and woods only. On B3082, Blandford Wimborne road. 1.5 miles from Wimborne. **Open:** House: 1 Apr–29 Oct 2000, daily except Thur & Fri, 12–5.30pm (last admission 4.30) Garden and Park: 1 Apr–29 Oct 2000, daily 11–6pm. For further information on events and winter openings please contact Kingston Lacy House, Wimborne, Dorset BH21 4EA. Tel No: 01202 883402. For an Events leaflet, please send s.a.e. to Kingston Lacy House.

map 3
K4

KINGSTON MAURWARD GARDENS
Dorchester, Dorset DT2 8PY
Tel: 01305 215003 Fax: 01305 215001

Kingston Maurward Gardens are set deep in Hardy's Dorset and are listed on the English Heritage Register of Gardens. The 35 acres of classical 18th century parkland and lawns sweep majestically down to the lake from the Georgian house. The Edwardian Gardens include a croquet lawn, rose garden, herbaceous borders and large displays of tender perennials including national collections of Penstemons and Salvias. Stone terraces, balustrading and yew hedges have been used to create many intimate gardens and carefully planned vistas. The walled demonstration garden is planted with a superb collection of hedges and plants suitable for growing in Dorset. Lakeside nature and tree trails, Animal Park, guided tours and lectures, conference centre, restaurant, visitor centre and plant sales. **Open:** 14 Mar–31 Oct, seven days a week from 10–5.30pm.

 map 3
J5

MAPPERTON
Mapperton, Beaminster, Dorset DT8 3NR
Tel: 01308 862645 Fax: 01308 863348 (Earl & Countess of Sandwich)

Terraced valley gardens surround charming Tudor/Jacobean manor house, stable blocks, dovecote and All Saints' Church. Pevsner's Dorset guide says, "There can hardly be anywhere a more enchanting manorial group than Mapperton". Above, the Orangery and Italianate formal garden with fountain court and topiary. Below, a 17th century summer house and fishponds. Lower garden with specimen shrubs and trees. Magnificent walks and views. Shop with plants, pots and gift items. Featured in Country Life, Country Living, Daily Telegraph and used as film location. **Location:** 1 m off B3163, 2 m off B3066. **Station:** Crewkerne. **Open:** Mar–Oct daily 2–6pm. **Admission:** Adults £3.50, under 18s £1.50, under 5s free. House open to group tours by appointment, adults £3.50. **E-mail:** mapperton@dial.pipex.com **Internet:** www.mapperton.com

MILTON ABBEY CHURCH
Milton Abbas, Nr. Blandford, Dorset, DT11 0BP
Tel: 01258 880489 (Organising Secretary)

A Church has stood here for over 1000 years. The present Abbey dates from the 14/15th century. The 18th century Gothic style house was built to compliment the Abbey & ancient Abbots Hall. Exterior by Sir William Chambers, interior in classic style by James Wyatt. Idyllic tranquil setting in the heart of Dorset, 1/2 mile from 200 year old 'new' village of Milton Abbas with its identical cottages. The Abbey is situated in grounds of Milton Abbey School and owned by diocese of Salisbury. **Location:** 3¹/2 from A354 (Puddletown to Blandford road). **Open:** Abbey Church throughout the year. House and grounds: Easter, mid July–end of August, 10–6pm. **Admission:** Adults £1.75, Children free. when house and grounds are open. At other times donations are invited.

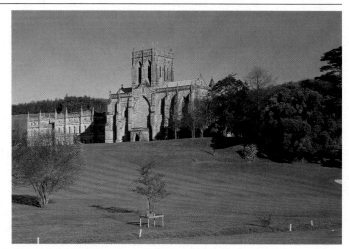

MINTERNE GARDENS
Minterne Magna, Nr Dorchester, Dorset, DT2 7AU
Tel: 01300 341 370 (The Lord Digby)

If you want a formal immaculate garden, do not come to Minterne, but if you want to wander peacefully through 20 wild woodland acres, where magnolias, rhododendrons, eucryphias, hydrangeas, water plants & water lilies, provide a new vista at each turn, and where ducks enhance the small lakes and cascades, then you will be welcome at Minterne, the home of the Churchill & Digby families for 350 years. **Location:** On A352 Dorchester/Sherborne Rd 2 miles N of Cerne Abbas. **Open:** Daily, 28 March–10 November 10–7pm. **Admission:** Adults £3 (Acc. children free).

THE OLD RECTORY
Litton Cheney, Dorset
Tel: 01308 482 383 (Mr & Mrs Hugh Lindsay)

Greatly varied garden with small walled garden, partly paved with a prolific quince tree. A steep path leads to 4 acres of beautiful natural woodland on steep slope with springs, streams and ponds, primulas, native plants, wild flower lawn. (Stout shoes recommended). **Location:** 1 mile S of A35. 10 miles from Dorchester. 6 miles from Bridport. **Open:** For NGS. Also open with Little Cheney Gardens. Private visits also welcome by appointment, Apr–June. **Admission:** Charges apply. Please phone for details. Limited parking for infirm and elderly, otherwise park in village and follow signs. Plants available for sale.

THE PRIEST'S HOUSE MUSEUM & GARDEN
23–27 High Street, Wimborne, Dorset BH21 1HR
Tel: 01202 882533

Award winning museum housed in a historic town house. A series of period rooms takes the visitor back through the centuries. With hands-on activities in the Archaeology and Childhood Galleries and special exhibitions and events through the year, there is plenty to do. New for 2000 the East Dorset Villages Gallery. Our award-winning garden is a tranquil retreat and the Tea Room offers home made cakes (June to September). **Open:** 1 Apr–31 Oct: Mon–Sat, 10.30–5pm. Sundays: June to Sept and Bank Hols. **Admission:** Adult £2.20, senior citizens, students £1.75 and children £1, family ticket £5.50.

PURSE CAUNDLE MANOR
Purse Caundle, Nr. Sherborne, Dorset, DT9 5DY
Tel: 01963 250400 (Michael de Pelet Esq)

Interesting 15th/16th century Manor House. Lived in as a family home. Great Hall with minstrel gallery; Winter Parlour; Solar with oriel; bedchambers; garden. **Location:** 4 miles E of Sherborne; ¼ mile S of A30. **Open:** Thursdays by appointment only. May–Sept. Coaches welcomed by appointment. **Admission:** £2.50. Children free. Free car park. **Refreshments:** Home-made cream teas by prior arrangement at £2 each for coach parties.

LULWORTH CASTLE

The Lulworth Estate, East Lulworth, Wareham, Dorset BH20 5QS
Tel: 01929 400352 Fax: 01929 400563 (Mr & Mrs Weld)

A 17th century hunting lodge restored by English Heritage after the fire of 1929. Features include a gallery devoted to the Weld family, owners of the Castle and Estate since 1641. The kitchen and wine cellar have been furnished and the history of the building is brought to life through a video presentation. The Chapel of St Mary in the Castle grounds is reputed to be one of the finest pieces of architecture in Dorset. It is the first free standing Roman Catholic Church to be built in England since the Reformation and contains an exhibition of 18th & 19th century vestments, church and recusant silver. A short walk from the Castle & Chapel is the Children's Summer Farm, Play Area & Woodland Walk. The Stables have been converted to house the licensed Café serving morning coffee, light lunches and traditional cream teas. The Courtyard Shop offers a wide range of unusual gift

items. Coach & car parking is free as is access to the Shop & Café. There is a series of special events throughout the year and facilities are available for corporate hospitality, conferences, wedding receptions and private parties. **Open:** Summer 10–6pm, Winter 10–4pm. Last admission 90 minutes before closing in Summer. Open Sun–Fri, All year. Closed 24 & 25 December. **Admission:** (From 1 Apr) Adult £4.50, concessions £3.50, children (5–16 yrs) £3, family £12 (children under 5 free). Groups (10–200): Adult £4.05, concessions £3.15, children (5–16 yrs) £2.70. **Events:** 23 Apr: Easter Bunny Hunt. 13–14 May: Country Gardening & Food Fair. 25 June: Classic Car Event. 29–30 July: Lulworth Horse Trials & Country Fair. 22–24 Sept: International Floral Design Show & Competition.

PARNHAM HOUSE & GARDEN

Parnham, Beaminster, Dorset

Tel: 01308 862 204 Fax: 01308 863 444 (Owner: John & Jennie Makepeace Contact: The House Manager Cdr Bruce Hunter–Inglis)

Parnham is a jewel of a Dorset manor dating from 1540 and embellished and enlarged by Nash in 1810. It is a working and friendly house, imaginatively restored and lived in by John and Jennie Makepeace. Built of golden hamstone in a river valley of wooded parkland, this noble house is surrounded by 14 acres of landscaped gardens; grand terraces, balustrading and courtyards with twin gazebos overlook fifty topiaried yews, bisected by water rills, to a small lake with many grand old trees. To the north there are herbaceous borders and everywhere distinctive and unusual plant combinations reflect the personal style of Jennie Makepeace, who has restored and replanted much of the garden in recent years. Inside, the rooms relate to the growth of the house over the centuries; their many fine features - stained glass, panelling and beautiful ceilings - provide the perfect setting for the superb Makepeace furniture shown in them. The Workshop is an essential part of a visit and provides an opportunity to see unique pieces in the making. In 1954, Parnham's remaining estates were sold and by 1976 the house faced an uncertain future. The internationally recognised furniture-designer and seminal force in the newly-emerging crafts movement in Britain, John Makepeace, bought the house and moved his workshops here. Parnham was given a new and exciting future and has become unique as a Mecca for modern design where superlative craftsmanship flourishes. Furniture made at Parnham is collected worldwide by private clients, corporations and museums. **Location:** Parnham is on the A3066, 5 miles N of Bridport, ½ m S of Beaminster. **Station:** Crewkerne 6 m; Dorchester 20 m. **Open:** 2 Apr–31 Oct: Suns, Tues, Weds, Thurs & BHols, 10–5pm. **Admission:** Adults £5.50, children (5–15) £2.50, Under 5's free. Groups: with guided tour: £5.50 less £1 per head for groups over 20 in number.

map 3 H4

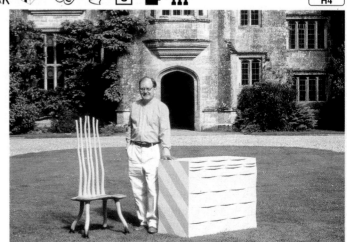

ST CATHERINE'S CHAPEL

Abbotsbury, Dorset
Tel: 01179 750700 (English Heritage)

A small stone chapel, set on a hilltop, with an unusual roof and small turret used as a lighthouse. **Location:** ½ mile S of Abbotsbury by pedestrian track to the hilltop. **Open:** Any reasonable times. For further information on admission please contact the S.W. regional office.

SHERBORNE OLD CASTLE

Castleton, Sherborne DT9 3SA
Tel: 01935 812730 (English Heritage)

The ruins of this 12th century castle are a testament to the 16 days it took Cromwell to capture it during the Civil War, after which it was abandoned. A gatehouse, some graceful arcading and decorative windows survive. **Location:** ½m E of Sherborne off B3145. ½m N of the 1594 castle. **Open:** 1 Apr–30 Sept, 10–6pm. 1–31 Oct, 10–5pm. 1 Nov–31 Mar, 10–4pm (but closed Mondays and Tuesdays). **Admission:** Adult £1.60, concessions £1.20, children (under 5's free) 80p.

SHERBORNE CASTLE

Sherborne DT9 3PY
Tel: 01935 813182 Fax: 01935 816727 (Sherborne Castle Estates)

Built by Sir Walter Raleigh in 1594, the Castle contains a fine collection of pictures, porcelain and furniture. Set in glorious lake lands and gardens it has been the home of the Digby family since 1617. **Location:** 5 miles east of Yeovil off A30 to south, Station Sherborne. **Open:** 1 Apr–31 Oct 2000. Grounds, tearoom and shop: every day except Weds from 12.30pm with last admission at 5pm. Castle: Tues, Thurs, Sat & Suns plus Bank Hol Mons from 12.30pm with last admission at 4.30pm. Throughout the season we will be pleased to make arrangements for party bookings (15+) during normal opening hours and other days if possible. Tel: 01935 813182 or write to: Castle and Events Manager, Sherbourne Castle Estate Office, Cheap Street, Sherbourne, Dorset DT9 3PY **E-mail:** graham_rogers@talk21.com

SANDFORD ORCAS MANOR HOUSE

The Manor House, Sandford Orcas, Sherborne, Dorset DT9 4SB.
Tel: 01963 220206 (Sir Mervyn Medlycott, Bt.)

Tudor Manor House in remarkable original state of preservation, with gatehouse, spiral staircases and Tudor and Jacobean panelling. Fine collection of 14th–17th century stained glass, Queen Anne and Chippendale furniture, Elizabethan and Georgian needlework and 17th century Dutch paintings. Terraced gardens, with fine mature trees, topiary and herb garden. **Location:** 2 miles N or Sherborne, entrance next to church. **Open:** Easter Mon 10–6pm then May–Sept: Suns 2–6pm & Mons 10–6pm. **Admission:** £2.50, children £1. Pre-booked parties (of 10 or more) at reduced rates on other days if preferred.

WOLFETON HOUSE

Dorchester, Dorset DT2 9QN
Tel: 01305 263 500 Fax: 01305 265090 (Capt. NTLL Thimbleby)

A fine medieval and Elizabethan Manor House lying in the water-meadows near the confluence of the Rivers Cerne and Frome. It was much embellished around 1580 and has splendid plaster ceilings, fireplaces and panelling of that date. See the Great Hall, stairs and chamber; parlour, dining room, chapel and cyder house. The medieval gatehouse has two unmatched and older towers. There are many fine works of art. **Location:** 1.5 miles from Dorchester on Yeovil road (A37); indicated by Historic House signs. **Station(s):** Dorchester South and West, 1.75 miles. **Open:** 15 July–15 Sept. Mon & Thurs. Groups at any time by appointment throughout the year. **Admission:** Charges not available at time of going to press. **Refreshments:** Ploughman's lunches, teas, evening meals for groups by arrangement. Cyder for sale. Available for weddings, parties etc.

CLOUDS HILL

Wareham, Dorset BH20 7NQ Tel: 01929 405616

Open: 2 April to 29 Oct: daily except Mon, Tues & Sat (but open BH Mons) 12–5pm or dusk if earlier; no electric light. Groups wishing to visit at other times must tel. in advance. **Admission:** £2.30. No reduction for groups or children. Unsuitable for coaches or trailer caravans. No WC

HARDY'S COTTAGE

Higher Bockhampton, nr Dorchester DT2 8QJ Tel: 01305 262366

Open: 2 April to 31 Oct: daily except Fri & Sat (but open Good Fri) 11–5pm (or dusk if earlier). Cottage is 10min walk through woods from car park. **Admission:** £2.60. No reduction for children or parties. School parties and coaches by arrangement only. No WC. Hardy's works on sale.

CORFE CASTLE

Corfe Castle, Wareham BH20 5EZ Tel/fax: 01929 481294

Open: Daily, (closed 25, 26 Dec and for 2 days at end Jan). 5–25 March: daily 10–4.30pm; 26 March to 29 Oct: 10–5.30pm; 30 Oct to 3 March 2001: 11–3.30pm. **Admission:** £4, children £2; family tickets £10 (2 adults & 3 children)/£6 (1 adult & 3 children). Groups £3.50, children £1.80. Car & coach-parking available at Castle View off A351; also at Norden park & ride and West St (not NT).

MAX GATE

Alington Avenue, Dorchester, Dorset Tel: 01305 262538 Fax: 01305 250978

Open: 2 April to 27 Sept: Mon, Wed & Sun 2–5pm. Note: Only dining and drawing room open. Private visits, tours and seminars by schools, colleges and literary societies by appointment with the tenants, Mr & Mrs Andrew Leah. **Admission:** £2.10, child £1.10. No reduction for groups. No WC

County Durham

A county of moors and rivers, County Durham is renowned for its fascinating heritage and magnificent scenery. One of the most famous of its vistas can be seen in the city of Durham itself, where the mighty towers of the cathedral stand silhouetted over the River Wear. Durham Cathedral has huge dimensions with 900 year old columns, piers and ribbed vaults.

The city was built in its entirety in

Low Force Waterfall

the year 995 on 'Dunholm' or Island Hill, a rocky peninsula quite unique to Durham. To this day, the ancient centre of Durham is reached by a series of bridges that connect the older buildings with the modern town that has developed over the centuries.

Moving westwards from this historic city, the beautiful moorland scenery features a series of stunning Pennine valleys and spectacular waterfalls.

AUCKLAND CASTLE

Bishop Auckland, Co Durham, DL14 7NR
Tel: 01388 601627

Principal country residence of the Bishops of Durham since Norman times and now the official residence of the present day Bishops. State Rooms, Chapel and Exhibition area available to visitors. Also access to the adjacent Bishop's park and 18th century Deerhouse. **Open:** 1 May–16 July: Friday and Sunday 2–5pm. 17 July–31 Aug: every day except Saturday 2–5pm. September: Friday and Sunday 2–5pm. Also the same hours on Bank Holiday Mondays. **Admission:** Adults £3, children over 12 and over 60's £2, children under 12 free. Excellent venues for concerts, exhibitions, conferences and meetings. **E-mail:** auckland.castle@zetnet.co.uk **Internet:** www.auckland–castle.co.uk

DURHAM CASTLE

Durham, DH1 3RW
Tel: 01913 743 800 Fax: 01913 747 470 (The University of Durham)

Durham Castle, the former home of the Prince Bishop of Durham, was founded in the 1070s. Since 1832 it has been the foundation College of the University of Durham. With the Cathedral it is a World Heritage Site. Important features include the Norman Chapel (1072), the Great Hall (1284), the Norman Doorway (1540s). With its 14th century style Keep it is a fine example of a Motte and Bailey Castle. In vacations the Castle is a conference and holiday centre and prestige venue for banquets etc. **Location:** In the centre of the city (adjoining Cathedral). **Station(s):** Durham (½ mile) **Open:** Guided tours only Apr–June daily 2–4pm. July–Sept daily 10–12 noon and 2–4pm. Oct–Mar Mon, Wed, Sat, Sun 2–4pm. **Admission:** charges apply.

RABY CASTLE

Staindrop, Darlington, Co. Durham, DL2 3AY
Tel: 01833 660 202 Fax: 01833 660169 (The Lord Barnard, T.D.).

Celebrating nearly 1000 years of history, Raby is without doubt one of the most impressive castles in all of England. Legend has it was founded by King Canute in early 11th century, being built by the powerful Nevills during the 14th century and remaining in the ownership of the present Lord Barnard's family since 1626. Housing a fabulous Art collection, and sumptuous interior, it is situated amidst a 200 acre Deer Park in the foothills of the dramatic North Pennines. Beautiful walled gardens frame picturesque views of the Castle and the valley beyond, with the 18th century stable block containing a stunning collection of horse drawn coaches. A new Adventure Playground, complete with aerial runway located near to the Castle's celebrated Tea Rooms and Gift Shop means that Raby has

something for everyone to enjoy. **Location:** 1 mile N of Staindrop village, on the Barnard Castle-Bishop Auckland Road (A688). **Station(s):** Bishop Auckland & Darlington. **Open:** Easter and Bank Holiday Weekends Sat–Wed, 1–5pm. May and Sept: Wed and Sun only, 1–5pm. July–August: Daily except Sats, 1–5pm. Private groups by arrangement, Mon–Fri, Easter–Sept: Park and Gardens 11–5.30pm. **Admission: Castle, Park & Gardens:** Adults £5, children (5–15) £2, OAP/NUS £4, Family (2 adults & 3 children) £12. **Park & Gardens:** Adults £3, other £2. Park and Gardens Season Ticket: Adult £12, other £10. Groups (20+) welcome by arrangement. **Refreshments:** Tea at the Stables. Picnic area. **E-mail:** admin @rabycastle.com **Internet:** www.rabycastle.com

Essex

Dotted between nature's mosaic, the inland towns of Essex, such as Coggeshall, Dedham and Ingatstone, wait patiently for visitors. Like old gentlemen bursting with incredible stories of battle, war and witchcraft to tell, they sit silently, anxious to be asked.

The towns on the coast have well defined characters of their own. The quayside of Maldon, locally known as the Hythe, is an ideal place to view the Thames sailing barges. Travel to Burnham-On-Crouch, which is the sailing home of Essex.

The last week in August is Burnham Sailing Week, when the whole place heaves with sailors and nautical groupies. With its flat landscape, Essex is a pleasurable place to explore on foot or bike. Visitors are able to truly appreciate its gentle patchwork countryside and experience its wider, soft-hued horizon.

Dedham

AUDLEY END HOUSE

Saffron Waldon, Essex CB11 4JF
Tel: 01799 522842 (English Heritage)

"Too large for a King but might do for a Lord Treasurer", was how King James I described Audley End, built by his own Lord Treasurer Thomas Howard first Earl of Suffolk. Come and see its wonderful palatial interiors and famous picture collection. Stroll in 'Capability' Brown's fine landscaped parkland with its enchanting follies and colourful Parterre Garden. Also visit the newly opened kitchen garden. **Location:** 1m W of Saffron Walden on B1383 (M1 exits 8, 9 Northbound only & 10) **Open:** Park & Garden: 1 Apr–30 Sept: Wed–Sun & B Hols, 11–6pm. House: 1 Apr–30 Sept: Wed–Sun & B Hols, 1–6pm. Last adm. 5pm. Park & House: 1–31 Oct: Wed–Sun, 10–3pm. Site closes at 4.30pm. **Admission:** House & Grounds: Adult £6.50, concs £4.90, child £3.30, family £16.30. Grounds only: Adult £4.50, concs £3.40, child £2.30, family £11.30.

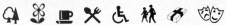
map 5 F2

THE GARDENS OF EASTON LODGE

Warwick House, Easton Lodge, Great Dunmow, Essex CM6 2BB
Tel: 01371 876979 Fax: 01371 876979 (Brian & Diana Creasey)

Beautiful gardens set in 23 acres. Visit the Italian gardens, designed by Harold Peto in 1902 for 'Daisy' Countess of Warwick (Edward VII's close friend), abandoned in 1950: restoration commenced 1993. Other features include - Peto Pavilion, herringbone and cobbled courtyard with fountain; Glade (formerly Japanese Garden); ruined Shelley Pavilion and tree house; Millennium Yew and Box sundial. World War 2 airfield. In the dovecote, study the history of the house, garden and owners over 400 years. Visitors comments (1999): "Magical", "Fascinating", "Riveting and so Romantic", "Superb", "Brilliant", "It's a dream we hope to often return to", "Merveilleux jardin pour rever".

map 5 G3

RHS GARDEN HYDE HALL

Rettendon, Chelmsford, Essex CM3 8ET
Tel: 01245 400256 (Royal Horticultural Society)

A charming hilltop garden which extends to over 24 acres. Highlights include the spring bulbs, the modern all and intermediate bearded irises in late May and the rope walk of climbing roses and large beds ablaze with floribunda and hybrid tea roses in midsummer. There is also a small plant centre and delightful hot and cold meals are available in the Essex thatched barn when the garden is open. **Open:** 24 March–31 Oct. 24 March–August: 11–6pm & Sept–Oct: 11–5pm. **Admission:** Adults £3, children (6–16yrs) 70p. RHS Members free and one guest.

map 5 G3

HYLANDS HOUSE, PARK & GARDENS

Hylands Park, Writtle, Chelmsford, Essex. CM2 8WF
Tel: 01245 606812

This beautiful villa, with its neoclassical exterior is surrounded by over 500 acres of parkland, including formal gardens. The house reopened at Easter 1999 after a period of restoration work. The Library, Drawing Room and Salon have been restored to their appearance in the early Victorian period. The entrance hall was the subject of work in 1995 to restore it to its Georgian origins. It is possible to view the unrestored Banqueting room on the ground floor. There is an exhibition detailing the restoration work and the history of the house. **Location:** SW of Chelmsford. Signposted on the A1016. **Open:** Sun, Mon & Bank Hols, 11–6pm. **Admission:** Adults £3, children under 12 yrs free, conc £2. **Refreshments:** Tearoom open Sundays throughout the year. Hylands Park & Gardens are open daily 8–5pm throughout the year.

C map 5 G3

HEDINGHAM CASTLE

Castle Hedingham, Nr. Halstead, Essex CO9 3DJ
Tel: 01787 460261 Fax: 01787 461473 (The Hon. Thomas Lindsay)

One of the finest and best preserved Norman keeps in England, it was built in 1140 by Aubrey de Vere. The keep walls are 12ft thick at the base, and is approached by a beautiful Tudor bridge which spans the dry moat surrounding the inner bailey. This was built in 1496 to replace the drawbridge, by the 13th Earl of Oxford, one of Henry VII's chief commanders at the battle of Bosworth. Visited by King Henry VII, King Henry VIII and Queen Elizabeth I and besieged by King John. Home of the de Veres, Earls of Oxford for 550 years, and still owned by their descendent, The Honourable Thomas Lindsay. The Banqueting Hall, reached from the first floor by a beautiful spiral staircase, 13ft wide in circumference and constructed round a central column, has a splendid Minstrels' Gallery and timbered ceiling supported by a magnificent central arch, 28ft wide, the

finest Norman arch in England. Beautifully kept grounds with peaceful lakeside and woodland walks. Large picnic area. Light refreshments served inside the keep. Hog Roast on Bank Holiday weekends. **Location:** 40km (24 miles) SE of Cambridge, approached along the A1017 and B1058. Within easy reach of A12, M11 and M25. (60 miles from London). **Open:** Week before Easter to the end of Oct, Daily 10–5pm. Open all year round for private parties. **Admission:** Adults £3.50, children £2.50 (5–15), family £10.50 (2 adults & 5 children). Except for special events, please telephone for prices. **Events:** Grounds open to the public in Feb/March to view the snowdrops (please telephone to confirm opening times). Admission price includes entrance to the keep and a free glass of mulled wine! Various events planned throughout the year such as, Jousting Tournaments, Medieval Displays, with music and dance, including Falconry and historical drama.

map 5
G2

 # INGATESTONE HALL

Hall Lane, Ingatestone, Essex CM4 9NR
Tel: 01277 353010, Fax: 01245 248979 (Lord Petre)

Tudor mansion in 11 acres of grounds, built by Sir William Petre, Secretary of State to four monarchs. The house continues to be the home of his descendants and contains furniture, pictures and memorabilia accumulated over the centuries. The house retains its original form and appearance including two priests' hiding places. **Location:** From London end of Ingatestone High Street, take Station Lane. House is half a mile beyond the level crossing. **Open:** Easter–end Sept. Sat, Sun and Bank Holidays. 1–6pm Plus (school hols only) Wed, Thurs and Fri 1–6pm. **Admission:** Adults £3.50 OAPs/students £3, children 5–16 £2 (under 5s free) parties 20 or more 50p per head reduction. **Refreshments:** Tearoom. Car park adjacent to gates. 200m walk to house. Gift shop. No dogs (except guide dogs). The upper floor and some rooms downstairs are inaccessible to wheelchairs.

map 5 G3

LAYER MARNEY TOWER

Nr Colchester, Essex CO5 9US
Tel & Fax: 01206 330 784 (Mr Nicholas Charrington)

Lord Marney's 1520 masterpiece is the tallest Tudor gate house in the country. Visitors may climb the tower for excellent views of the Essex countryside. Explore the formal gardens and visit the Long Gallery, Corsellis Room and church. The Medieval Barn has rare breed farm animals and the deer are on the farm walk. Guided tours are available by arrangement (minimum cost of 25 people). The Long Gallery and Corsellis Rooms may be hired for corporate days, weddings, receptions, banquets or concerts. **Location:** 6 miles S of Colchester, signpost off the B1022 Colchester–Maldon Road. **Open:** 2 Apr–1 Oct 2000: everyday except Saturday 12pm–5pm. Bank Holiday Sundays and Mondays 11–6pm. Groups anytime by arrangement. **Admission:** Adults £3.50, children £2, family ticket £10. **Refreshments:** Stable tearoom.

map 5 H3

THE SIR ALFRED MUNNINGS ART MUSEUM

Castle House, Dedham, Essex CO7 6AZ
Tel: 01206 322127 Fax: 01206 322127 (Castle House Trust)

Castle House and its collection is a fitting memorial to Sir Alfred Munnings who lived at Castle House from 1919 until his death. Castle House, a mixture of Tudor and Georgian periods, has been restored, with Munnings' original furniture, and stands in spacious well-maintained gardens. A collection representative of Munnings' life span of work. Each season there is a special exhibition. **Location:** ¾ mile from Dedham Village. **Station(s):** Colchester, Manningtree, Ipswich. **Open:** Extended Season: Easter Sunday –first Sunday in October, Wed, Sun & Bank Hol Mons. Also Thurs and Sats in Aug, 2–5pm. **Admission:** Adult £3, conc £2, child 50p. Private parties by arrangement. Free car park.

map 5 H2

SHALOM HALL

Layer Breton, Nr Colchester, Essex
Tel: 01206 330338 Fax: 0207 831 9607 (Lady Phoebe Hillingdon)

19th century house containing a collection of 17th and 18th century French furniture, porcelain and portraits by famous English artists including Thomas Gainsborough, Sir Joshua Reynolds etc. **Location:** 7 miles southwest of Colchester, 2 miles from A12. **Open:** August Mon–Fri 10–1pm, 2.30–5.30pm. **Admission:** Free.

map 5 H3

VALENCE HOUSE MUSEUM & ART GALLERY

Becontree Avenue, Dagenham, Essex
Tel: 020 8227 5293 Fax: 020 8227 5293 (Barking & Dagenham Council)

The only remaining manor house in Dagenham, partially surrounded by a moat. Dates from 15th century. There is an attractive herb garden to the west of the house. **Location:** On the south side of Becontree Avenue, ½ mile west of A1112 at Becontree Heath. **Open:** Tues–Fri, 9.30–1pm & 2–4.30pm. Sats 10–4pm. **Admission:** Free.

map 5 F4

Gloucestershire

The picturesque honey coloured cottages of the Cotswolds are quite charming. It is easy to see why Gloucestershire attracts thousands of visitors every year, with its quaint blend of meandering lanes and fine churches.

Many Cotswold villages were established as early as the twelfth century, with money from the medieval wool trade. The landscape is breathtaking, with cottages built of mellow stone nestling in the rolling hills.

The cities of Gloucester and Cheltenham are well worth exploring. Situated on the River Severn, Gloucester is dominated by its imposing Norman Cathedral, the scene of the coronation of Henry III and famous for its wonderful early fan vaulting.

Bibury

Cheltenham is a city of elegance which becomes the centre of the horse racing world during Gold Cup week. In the 18th century, the high society flocked to the spa town to "take the waters". There are many fine examples of Regency-style architecture in and around the town.

To the south-east is the charming town of Cirencester, known as the capital of the Cotswolds.

The Forest of Dean, one of England's last remaining ancient woodlands, lies between the River Wye and the River Severn. For those interested in contemporary art, the Forest of Dean Sculpture Trail is a pleasant way in which to explore the surrounding woodland whilst admiring a number of creative artworks.

BARNSLEY HOUSE GARDEN

Barnsley House, Nr. Cirencester, Glos GL7 5EE
Tel: 01285 740561 Fax: 01285 740628
(Charles & Denzil Verey)

Old garden re-planned since 1960 by Rosemary Verey inside 1770 wall. 4½ acres. **Special features:** Spring bulbs & blossom, laburnum walk (in flower late May–early June), mixed borders, autumn colour and berries, knot garden, decorative potager. Tuscan Temple & Gothick Summerhouse (both 1770's). House 1697 – not open. Plants, garden furniture & antiques for sale. **Location:** 4 miles northeast of Cirencester, on B4425. **Open:** 1 Feb–16 Dec, Mon, Wed, Thur & Sat 10am–5.30pm (Tues & Fri, shop only). **Admission:** Garden £3.75, OAPs & Students £3, Season Ticket £10. Children under 16 free. Guided tour by appointment extra.

map 4
B3

BATSFORD ARBORETUM

Batsford Park, Moreton-in-Marsh, Gloucestershire.
Tel: 01386 701441 Fax: 01608 650290 (The Batsford Foundation)

The arboretum set in 55 acres of Cotswold countryside contains over 1500 trees with species from all over the world. The change in mood throughout the year never fails to seduce and excite the visitor with its tranquil beauty and Japanese influence. Spring carpets the ground with snowdrops. Narcissi and daffodils whilst the cherries and magnolias put on their finest display. In summer explore the bamboo groves, fine bronze statues and waterside planting. Experience the Autumn explosion when all the trees put on their finale display. **Location:** Off A44 Moreton-in-Marsh, Eversham Road. **Open:** Daily Mar–Nov. **Admission:** Adult £3.50, seniors £3, child free. Also: Cotswold Falconry Centre – Garden Centre – Tearooms. **Internet:** www.batsford –arboretum.co.u.k.

map 4
B2

CHAVENAGE

Tetbury, Gloucestershire GL8 8XP
Tel: 01666 502329 Fax: 01453 836778 (David Lowsley-Williams, Esq.)

Elizabethan House (1576) set in the tranquil Cotswold countryside with Cromwellian associations. 16th and 17th century furniture and tapestries. Personally conducted tours, by the owner or his family. **Location:** 2 miles N of Tetbury, signposted off A46 (Bath–Stroud) or B4014. **Open:** Thurs, Sun and Bank Hols, 2–5pm. May – end Sept plus Easter Sun and Mon. **Admission:** Adults £4, children half-price. Parties by appointment as shown or other dates and times to suit. **Refreshments:** Catering for parties by arrangement. **Conferences:** Wedding receptions, dinners, corporate hospitality, also available for film and photographic location.

map 4
A3

CHEDWORTH ROMAN VILLA

Yanworth, Cheltenham
Tel: 01242 890256 Fax: 01242 840544 (The National Trust)

Chedworth Roman Villa is one of the finest Roman-period sites in Britain. Nestling in a wooded combe in the Cotswolds, it contains the ruins of a large, opulent country house of the 4th century. There are some very special features surviving–fine mosaics, a water shrine with running spring, two bath-houses, several hypocaust systems (Roman central heating) and many artefacts in the site museum. There is a ten minute video introduction to the site and a new audio tour which guides the visitor around the villa. There are various events and open days during the year and archaeological work continues. Visit Chedworth for a flavour of life in 4th century Britain. **Open:** Mar–Apr, Weds–Sun 11–4pm, BHols & Event Days 10–5pm. May–Sept, Tues–Sun 10–5pm. Oct–19 Nov, Weds–Sun 11–4pm. **Admission:** Adult £3.40, child £1.70, family £8.50. **Location:** 20 mins from Cirencester.

map 4
B3

BERKELEY CASTLE

Gloucestershire, GL13 9BQ
Tel: 01453 810332 (Mr R J G Berkeley)

England's most Historic Home and Oldest Inhabited Castle. Completed in 1153 by Lord Maurice Berkeley at the command of Henry II and for nearly 850 years the home of the Berkeley family. 24 generations have gradually transformed a savage Norman fortress into a truly stately home. The castle is a home and not a museum. Enjoy the castle at leisure or join one of the regular one-hour guided tours covering the dungeon, the cell where Edward II was murdered, the medieval kitchens, the magnificent Great Hall and the State Apartments with their fine collections of pictures by primarily English and Dutch masters, tapestries, furniture of an interesting diversity, silver and porcelain. Splendid Elizabethan Terraced Gardens and sweeping lawns surround the castle, Tropical Butterfly House with hundreds of exotic butterflies in free flight – an oasis of colour and tranquillity. Facilities include free coach and parks, picnic lawn and two gift shops. Tearooms for refreshments, light lunches and afternoon teas. **Location:** Midway between Bristol and Gloucester, just off A38, M5 junctions 13 or 14. **Open:** April & May: Tues–Sun 2–5pm; June & Sept: Tues–Sat 11–5pm, Sun 2–5pm; July & Aug: Mon–Sat 11–5pm, Sun 2–5pm; Oct: Sun only 2–5pm; Bank Holiday Mondays 11–5pm. **Admission:** Castle & Gardens: Adult £5.40, child £2.90, senior citizen £4.40. Pre-booked parties 25 or more: Adult £4.90, child £2.60, senior citizen £4.10, family ticket £14.50 (2 adults & 2 children). Gardens only: Adult £2, child £1. Butterfly Farm: Adult £2, child/OAP £1, family ticket £4.50 (2 adults & 2 children), school groups 80p.

map 3
J1

FRAMPTON COURT

Frampton-on-Severn, Gloucester GL2 7EU
Tel: 01452 740267 Messages/Fax: 01452 740698 (Mrs H. Clifford)

Listed Grade I, by Vanburgh. 1732. Stately family home of the Cliffords who have lived at Frampton since granted land by William the Conquerer, 1066. Fine collection of the original period furniture, tapestries, needlework and porcelain. Panelled throughout. Fine views over well kept parkland to extensive lake. A famous Gothic orangery, now self-catering holiday lets, stands in the garden reflected in a long Dutch ornamental canal similar to Westbury. Special bed and breakfast by appointment £45. Tel: Before 10.30am, between 1–2pm and after 7pm. The original well known floral water colours by the gifted 19th century great Aunts hang in the house. These inspired the book "The Frampton Flora". **Open:** All year by appointment £4.50. Tel: 01452 740267. Near jct. 13 of M5 motorway. Signposted.

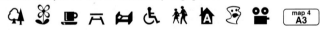

map 4
A3

HARDWICKE COURT

Nr Gloucester, Glos
Tel: 01452 720212 (C G M Lloyd-Baker)

Late Georgian house designed by Robert Smirke, built in 1816–1817. Entrance Hall, Drawing Room, Library and Dining Room open. **Location:** 5 miles S of Gloucester on A38 (between M5 access 12 S only and 13). **Open:** Easter Mon-end Sept, Mon only 2–4pm other times by prior written agreement. **Admission:** £2, parking for cars only. Not suitable for disabled.

map 4
A3

HODGES BARN GARDENS

Shipton Moyne, Tetbury, Gloucestershire GL8 8PR
Tel: 01666 880202 Fax: 01666 880373 (Mrs Amanda Hornby)

Hodges Barn is a 15th century Cotswold stone dovecote converted into a charming family home surrounded by "one of the finest private gardens in England". Spring bulbs, magnolias and flowering trees are followed by a superb collection of old fashioned and climbing roses and many mixed shrub and herbaceous beds. **Open:** 1 Apr–19 Aug: Mon, Tues, Fri 2–5pm. **Admission:** Adults £3, children free. Dogs on leads.

HORTON COURT

Horton, Nr Chipping Sodbury B17 6QR
Tel: 01985 843600 (The National Trust)

A Cotswold manor house with 12th century Norman hall and early Renaissance features. Of particular interest is the late perpendicular ambulatory, detached from the house. Norman hall and ambulatory only shown. **Location:** 3 miles north-east of Chipping Sodbury. ¾miles north of Horton, 1 mile west of A46. **Open:** 3 Apr–30 Oct, Wed & Sat, 2–6pm or dusk if earlier. **Admission:** Charges apply, children half price.

Gloucestershire

KIFTSGATE COURT GARDENS

Chipping Campden, Gloucestershire GL55 6LW
Tel: 01386 438777 Fax: 01386 438777 (Mr & Mrs J G. Chambers)

Garden set on the edge of the Cotswold escarpment with fine views. Many unusual shrubs and plants including tree peonies, abutilous, specie and old fashioned roses. New water garden in the old tennis court. **Location:** 3 miles NE of Chipping Campden. **Open:** Apr–May & Aug–Sept; Wed, Thurs and Sun, 2–6pm. June–July; Wed, Thurs, Sat and Sun, 12noon–6pm. Bank Hols Mon 2–6pm. **Admission:** Adults £4, children £1. **Refreshments:** Home-made teas throughout the season and light lunch in June and July. Coach by appointment only. Unusual plants for sale on open days.

map 4 B2

MISARDEN PARK GARDENS

Miserden, Stroud, Gloucestershire
Tel: 01285 821303, Fax: 01285 821530 (Major M T N H Wills)

Spring flowers, shrubs, fine topiary (some designed by Sir Edwin Lutyens) and herbaceous borders within a walled garden, roses and specimen trees. 17th century manor house (not open), stunning position overlooking Golden Valley. New summerhouse and rill. **Location:** Miserden 7 miles from Gloucester, Cheltenham, Stroud & Cirencester; 3 miles off A417 (signed). **Open:** Every Tues, Wed & Thurs from 1 Apr–30 Sept, 10–5pm. Nurseries adjacent to garden open daily except Mons. **Admission:** Adults £3, (guided tour extra), children (accompanied) free. Reductions for parties (of 20 or more) by appointment.

map 4 A3

OWLPEN MANOR

Owlpen, Nr Uley, Gloucestershire, GL11 5BZ
Tel: 01453 860261 Fax: 01453 860819 (Mr & Mrs C N Mander)

Romantic Tudor manor house (1450–1616), home of the Mander family. Magnificent Great Hall, Jacobean solar wing, unique painted textiles in a room haunted by Queen Margaret of Anjou (in 1471), and family and Cotswold Arts and Crafts collections. The formal terraced garden (1723) has fine yew topiary, parterres and mill pond walk. Medieval outbuildings include the Cyder House Restaurant (open daily), the Grist Mill and Court House (now holiday cottages) and a richly-detailed Victorian church. The house lies at the bottom of a picturesque wooded valley under the edge of the Cotswolds, with miles of walks. **House open:** 2–5pm, April 1–October 15, every day except Mondays (but open on Bank Holiday Mondays). *"Owlpen in Gloucestershire - ah what a dream is there!"* – Vita Sackville-West. **Internet:** http://www.owlpen.com/ **E-mail:** sales@owlpen.com

map 4 A3

PAINSWICK ROCOCO GARDENS

The Stables, Painswick House, Painswick, Gloucestershire GL6 6TH
Tel & Fax: 01452 813204 (Painswick Rococo Garden Trust)

Painswick Rococo Garden is a unique survivor from a brief period of 18th century garden design. It is set in a hidden Cotswold valley near the picturesque, historic wool town of Painswick. The garden boasts charming contemporary buildings, a large kitchen garden, herbaceous borders, woodland walks and wonderful views of the surrounding countryside. One of its most noted features is the magnificent carpet of snowdrops during late winter, early spring. Newly planted maze. **Open:** Gardens from 12 Jan–30 Nov, Wed–Sun, plus Bank Hol Mons 11–5pm; daily from May to Sept. **Admission:** Adult £3.30, senior £3, child £1.75. The Coach House contains the restaurant/tearooms and gift shop is open Wednesday to Sunday. Ample car parking. The garden is a registered charity. **E-mail:** painsgard@aol.com **Internet:** www.beta.co.uk/painswick

map 4 A3

RODMARTON MANOR

Cirencester, Gloucestershire GL7 6PF
Tel: 01285 841253 Fax 01285 841298 (Mr & Mrs Simon Biddulph)

The house is a unique example of the Cotswold Arts and Crafts and was built and furnished with local materials entirely by hand. The garden is a series of outdoor rooms. There are hedges, topiary, a troughery, a rockery, lawns, magnificent herbaceous borders and kitchen garden all in a romantic setting. **Location:** Off A433 6m west of Cirencester. **Open:** House and Garden open Wed, Sat and Bank Hol Mons 10 May–30 Aug 2–5pm. Groups please book. Guided tours of house can be booked for groups of 20 or more people at other times. Groups of 20 or more are welcome to visit the garden by appointment at other times. Guided tours of garden can also be booked. **Admission:** House and Garden £6 (children under 14 £3). Minimum group charge for house £120. Garden only £2.50 (accompanied children under 14 free).

map 4 A3

MILL DENE GARDEN

Old Mill Dene, Blockley, Moreton-in-Marxh GL56 9HU
Tel: 01386 700457 Fax: 01386 700526 (Mr & Mrs B S Dare)

In a naturally beautiful situation this 2½ acre Cotswold water-mill garden has been designed and planted by the owner. Steep lawned terraces rise from the mill-pool, stream and grotto; wander through a rose-walk to the cricket lawn, then to the potager at the top. All the garden has glimpses of the church as a back-drop and views over the Cotswold Hills. Plenty of seats encourage contemplation of tranquil water and vistas. **Location:** From A44 Bourton on the Hill, take turn to Blockley. 1⅛ miles down hill, turn left behind 30mph sign labelled cul-de-sac. Please telephone for opening details and admission charges.

ST MARY'S CHURCH

Kempley
Tel: 01179 750 700

A delightful Norman church with superb wall paintings from the 12–14th centuries which were only discovered beneath white wash in 1871. **Location:** On minor road. 1½ miles south–east of Much Marcle A449. **Open:** 1 Apr–30 Sept, open daily 10–6pm. 1 Oct–31 Mar, open daily 10–4pm. Closed 24–26 December and 1 January. **Admission:** Free.

STANWAY HOUSE

Cheltenham, Gloucestershire GL54 5PQ
Tel: 01386 584469 (Lord Neidpath)

The jewel of Cotswold Manor houses is very much a home rather than a museum and the centre of a working landed estate, which has changed hands once in 1275 years. The mellow Jacobean architecture, the typical squire's family portraits, the exquisite Gatehouse, the old Brewery, medieval Tithe Barn, the extensive gardens, arboretum pleasure grounds and formal landscape contribute to the timeless charm of what Arthur Negus considered one of the most beautiful and romantic houses in England. **Location:** 1 mile off B4632 Chelteham/Broadway road; on B4077 Toddington/Stow-on-the-Wold road: M5 junction 9. **Open & Admission:** Please phone for details of opening times and admission charges. **Refreshments:** Teas in Old Bakehouse in the village (01386 584204).

SEZINCOTE

Moreton-in-Marsh, Gloucestershire GL56 9AW
(Mr & Mrs D Peake)

Oriental water garden by Repton and Daniell with trees of unusual size. House in Indian style, inspiration of Royal Pavilion, Brighton. **Location:** 1 mile W of Moreton-in-Marsh on A44 to Evesham; turn left by lodge before Bourton-on-the-Hill. **Station(s):** Moreton-in-Marsh **Open:** Garden Thurs, Fri & Bank Hol Mons 2–6pm (or dusk if earlier) throughout the year, except Dec. House May, June, July and Sept, Thurs and Fri 2.30–6pm parties by appointment. Open in aid of National Gardens Scheme Sun July 9th 2–6pm. **Admission:** House and garden £5; garden only £3.50, children £1, under 5s free. **Refreshments:** Hotels and restaurants in Moreton-in-Marsh. No dogs except guide dogs for the blind.

SUDELEY CASTLE

Winchcombe, Cheltenham, Gloucestershire GL54 5JD
Tel: 01242 602 308 (Lord & Lady Ashcombe)

Sudeley Castle is one of England's great historic houses with royal connections stretching back 1000 years. For more information, opening times, prices and beautiful colour photography please turn to pages 76 & 77.

WHITTINGTON COURT

Whittington, Nr Cheltenham, Gloucestershire GL54 4HF
Tel: 01242 820556 (Mrs J L Stringer)

Small Elizabethan stone-built manor house with family possessions. **Location:** 4 miles E of Cheltenham on A40. **Open:** Sat 22 Apr–Sun 7 May and Sat 12 Aug–Bank Hol Mon 28 Aug inclusive. **Admission:** Adults £3, OAPs £2.50, children £1. Open to parties by arrangement.

DYRHAM PARK

nr Chippenham SN14 8ER
Tel: Property Office 0117 937 2501; Warden's Office 01225 891364

Open: 1 April to 29 Oct: daily except Wed & Thur, 12–5.30pm. Garden as house: 11–5.30pm or dusk if earlier. Park: daily (closed 25 Dec) 12–5.30pm or dusk if earlier (opens 11 when garden open). Note: Property closed 7–9 July.

HIDCOTE MANOR GARDEN

Hidcote Bartrim, nr Chipping Campden GL55 6LR
Tel: 01386 438333, Restaurant 01386 438703 Fax: 01386 438817

Open: 1 April to end of May, Aug to 5 Nov: daily except Tues & Fri; June & July: daily except Fri. April to end Sept 11–7pm, Oct 11–6pm; last admission 1hr before closing or dusk if earlier. Event: send s.a.e. for details. **Admission:** £5.60; family £14. Coach and groups by appointment only (tel. 01386 438333); no group reduction. No picnicking and no games in garden. Free car park 100m.

SNOWSHILL MANOR

Snowshill, nr Broadway WR12 7JU Tel: 01386 852410

Open: 1 April to 29 Oct: daily except Mons & Tues 12–5pm; last admission 45 min before clossing. Note: Entry to house is by timed ticket. Grounds: as house 11–5pm. Tel. for details of special interest days. **Admission:** £6; family £15. Grounds, restaurant & shop only £3. Coach and school groups by written appointment only. Photography only by written arrangement with Curator.

WESTBURY COURT GARDEN

Westbury-on-Severn, Gloucestershire Tel: 01452 760461

Open: 1 April to 29 Oct: daily except Mon & Tues (but open BH Mons) 11–6pm. Other months by appointment. Events: send s.a.e. for details. **Admission:** £2.80. Free car park. Groups of 15+ by written appointment; no group reduction.

SUDELEY CASTLE

Winchcombe, Cheltenham, Gloucestershire GL54 5JD
Tel: 01242 602 308 (Lord & Lady Ashcombe)

Sudeley Castle, surrounded by ten beautiful gardens, winner of the HHA/Christies Garden of the Year Award, is the romantic home of Lord and Lady Ashcombe and the Dent-Brocklehurst family. Henry VIII, Anne Boleyn, Lady Jane Grey and Elizabeth I stayed here. Charles I sought refuge here and Prince Rupert of the Rhine made it his headquarters during the Civil War. Former home of Queen Katherine Parr, her tomb can be seen in the Castle Church. The Castle houses an impressive collection of pictures and furniture and includes works by Van Dyck, Turner and Sir Joshua Reynolds. **Open:** 4 Mar–29 Oct: Gardens, Exhibition Centre, Plant Centre and Shop: 10.30–5.30pm. Castle Apartments and Church: 1 Apr–29 Oct 11–5pm and Restaurant: 10.30–5pm. Group and private tours out of season by arrangement. **Admission:** Castle and gardens: Adults £6.20, concessions £5.20, children (5–15yrs) £3.20. Group rates (min 20): Adults £5.20, concessions £4.20, children (5–15yrs) £3.20. Gardens and Exhibition Only: Adults £4.70, concessions £3.70, children (5–15yrs) £2.50. Family ticket (2 adults and 2 children) £17. Guided Tours and Garden Tours available (pre-booking required). **Events:** Call for full programme. **Accommodation:** Complex of 14 holiday cottages within walking distance of the castle.

map 4
B2

Hampshire

Curled in the semi circle formed by the Western Downs, the Hampshire Downs and the South Downs and sheltered from the Channel winds by the pearl and emerald hills of the Isle of Wight, the county of Hampshire basks in as mellow a climate as any part of the British Isles. The unassuming county town of Winchester was the one time capital of England and is home to a beautiful cathedral and many points of historic interest.

Hampshire's new forest, 145 square miles of heath and woodland, is the largest area of unenclosed land in Southern Britain. William the Conqueror's 'new' forest, despite its name, is one of the few primeval oak woods in England. The New Forest was a popular hunting ground for Norman kings and is the home of the Rufus Stone, where William II was shot dead. Numerous shaggy New Forest ponies and over 1,500 fallow deer may be seen rambling through the woodlands.

Chawton Church

AVINGTON PARK

Winchester, Hampshire SO21 1DB
Tel: 01962 779260 Fax: 01962 779864 (Mrs C P S Bullen)

Avington Park is a Palladian mansion, where both Charles II and George IV stayed at various times. It was enlarged in 1670 with the addition of two wings and a classical portico surmounted by three statues. The State Rooms on view include the magnificent silk and gilded Ballroom, hand painted Drawing Room, Library and Hall. In a delightful parkland and lakeside setting, it adjoins an exquisite Georgian church, which may be visited. **Open:** May to September 2.30–5pm, Sundays and Bank Holiday Monday. Last tour 5pm. **Admission:** Adults £3.50, children £1.50. Coaches welcome by appointment all year. **E-mail:** sarah@avingtonpark.co.uk **Internet:** www.avingtonpark.co.uk

JANE AUSTEN'S HOUSE

Chawton, Alton GU34 1SD
Tel/Fax: 01420 83262 (Jane Austin Memorial Fund)

17th century house where Jane Austen wrote or revised her six great novels. The house contains many items associated with her and her family, documents and letters, first editions of the novels, pictures, portraits and furniture. Pleasant garden, suitable for picnics, bakehouse with brick oven and wash tub, houses Jane's donkey carriage. **Location:** Just S of A31, 1 mile SW of Alton, signposted Chawton. **Open:** 1 Mar–1 Jan daily. Jan & Feb, Sat & Sun 11–4.30pm. Closed Christmas Day and Boxing Day. **Admission:** Adult £3, child (8–18) 50p, concessions £2.50.

BREAMORE HOUSE

Nr. Fordingbridge, Hampshire SP6 2DF
Tel: 01725 512468 (Sir Edward Hulse)

Elizabethan Manor House (1583) with fine collections of paintings, tapestries, furniture. Countryside Museum takes the visitor back to when a village was self-sufficient. Exhibition of Rural Arts and Agricultural machinery. **Location:** 3 miles N of Fordingbridge off the main Bournemouth Road (A338) 8 miles S of Salisbury. **Open:** 2 Apr–30 Sept 2000. House 2–5.30pm Countryside Museum 1–5.30pm. Other times by appointment. **Admission:** Combined ticket adults £5, children £3.50, reduced rate for parties and OAPs. **Refreshments:** Home-made snacks and teas available from midday.

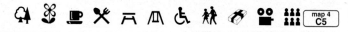

EXBURY GARDENS

Nr Southampton SO45 1AZ, Tel: 01703 891203
Fax: 01703 243380 (E.L. de Rothschild, Esq.)

Described as 'Heaven with the gates open', this 200 acres garden, created by Lionel de Rothschild, contains magnificent displays of rhododendrons, azaleas and other woodland shrubs. Free 'Trail Guides' in Spring, Summer and Autumn to encourage the visitor to see newly planted areas, making this a beautiful day out any time. **Location:** Exbury village, south drive from Jct.2 M27 west of Southampton. Turn W off A326 at Didben Purlieu towards Beaulieu. **Open:** Daily, 27 Feb–31 Oct, 10–5.30pm (dusk if earlier). Free entry to Gift shop and Plant Centre. Please phone for admission charges.

FAMILY TREES

Sandy Lane, Shedfield, Hampshire, SO32 2HQ
Tel: 01329 834 812
(Philip House)

Wide variety of fruit for the connoisseur. Trained tree specialists; standards, espaliers, cordons etc. Other trees, old-fashioned and climbing roses, and evergreens. Free catalogue from Family Trees (as above). **Location:** See map in free catalogue. **Station(s):** Botley (2.5 miles). **Open:** Mid Oct–end Apr, Wed & Sat, 9.30am–12.30. **Admission:** No charge. No minimum order. Courier dispatch for next day delivery.

BROADLANDS
Romsey, Hampshire SO51 9ZD
Tel: 01794 505010

One of the finest examples of mid–Georgian architecture in England, Broadlands stands serenely in Capability Brown parkland on the banks of the River Test. Country residence of the famous Victorian Prime Minister, Lord Palmerston, and later home of Queen Victoria's great grandson, Earl Mountbatten of Burma. Visitors may view the House with its countless mementoes of the Mountbatten and Palmerston eras and its fine collection of art, furniture, porcelain and sculpture. History is brought vividly to life by means of the Mountbatten Exhibition and the audiovisual presentation. **Open:** Daily 12 June–1 Sept, 12–5.30pm (last adm. 4pm). **Admission:** Adult £5.50, senior citizen £4.70, student £4.70, disabled £4.70, child 12–16 £3.85 & children under 12 free. For group rate please call the number detailed above. **E-mail:** admin@broadlands.net **Internet:** www.broadlands.net

map 4 C6

GILBERT WHITE'S HOUSE & THE OATES MUSEUM
'The Wakes', Selborne, Nr. Alton, Hampshire, GU34 3JH
Tel: 01420 511275

Charming 18th century house and glorious garden, home of famous naturalist Rev. Gilbert White. Furnished rooms and original manuscript. Also fascinating museum on Capt. Lawrence Oates, hero of Scott's ill-fated Antarctic Expedition. Tea Parlour. Excellent shop. Plant sales. **Open:** 11–5 daily. 1 Jan–24 Dec. Groups welcome all year and summer evenings. **Admission:** Adults £4, OAPs £3.50, children £1, group rates also. **Events:** Unusual Plants Fair 17 & 18 June 2000. Picnic to 'Jazz in June' 17 June 2000. Mulled Wine & Christmas Shopping Day 26 November 2000.

map 4 D5

HIGHCLERE CASTLE
Newbury RG20 9RN
Tel: 01635 253210

Designed by Charles Barry in the 1830s at the same time as he was building the Houses of Parliament. This soaring pinnacled mansion provided a perfect setting for the 3rd Earl of Carnarvon, one of the great hosts of Queen Victoria's reign. Old master paintings mix with portraits by Van Dyck and 18th century painters. The 5th Earl of Carnarvon, discovered the Tomb of Tutankhamun with Howard Carter.
FURTHER INFORMATION, OPENING TIMES AND DATES WITH PHOTOGRAPHY CAN BE SEEN UNDER THE COUNTY OF BERKSHIRE.

HALL FARM HOUSE
Bentworth, Alton, Hampshire GU34 5JU
Tel: 01420 564010 (A.C & M.C Brooking)

map 4 D5

THE SIR HAROLD HILLIER GARDENS & ARBORETUM
Jermyns Lane Ampfield, Nr Romsey, Hampshire
Tel: 01794 368787 Fax: 01794 368027

Set in the rolling Hampshire countryside between Winchester and the market town of Romsey, The Sir Harold Hillier Gardens & Arboretum comprises the greatest collection of wild and cultivated woody plants in the world. Established in 1953, by the late Sir Harold Hillier, the 180 acre Hampshire County Council managed public garden features 11 National Plant Collections, Champion Trees and the largest Winter Garden in Europe. A garden for all seasons. **Location:** 3 miles NE of Romsey on A3090. **Open:** All year except Christmas Bank Hol. Apr–Oct: weekdays 10.30–6pm; weekends & Bank Hols: 9.30–6pm. Nov–Mar 10.30–dusk. **Admission:** Adults: Apr–Oct £4.25, Nov–Mar £3.25. Senior Citizens: Apr–Oct £3.75, Nov–Mar £2.75. Child (5–16): £1. Under 5's Free. Group rates available. Free car parking. Regret no dogs. **Internet:** www.hillier.hants.gov.uk

map 4 C6

BEAULIEU

Beaulieu, Brockenhurst, Hampshire SO42 7ZN
Tel: 01590 612345 Fax: 01590 612624 Internet: www.beaulieu.co.uk

Beaulieu is set in the heart of the New Forest and is a place that gives enormous pleasure to people with an interest in seeing history of all kinds. Overlooking the Beaulieu River, Palace House has been Lord Montagu's ancestral home since 1538. The House was once the Great Gatehouse of Beaulieu Abbey and its monastic origins are reflected in such features as the fan vaulted ceilings. The House also contains many of the Montagu family treasures, portraits and personal photographs. Beaulieu Abbey was founded in 1204 and although most of the buildings have been destroyed, much of beauty and interest remains. The Domus, which houses an exhibition of monastic life, is home to embroidered wall hangings designed and created by Belinda, Lady Montagu, depicting the story of the Abbey since its foundation. Beaulieu is also home of the world famous National Motor Museum which traces the story of motoring from 1894 to the present day. 250 vehicles are on display including legendary World Record breakers such as Bluebird and Golden Arrow plus Veteran, Vintage and Classic cars and motorcycles. When visiting Beaulieu arrangements can be made to view the Estate's own vineyards. Visits, which can be arranged between Apr–Oct, must be pre–booked at least one week in advance with the Beaulieu Estate office. Beaulieu also offers a comprehensive range of facilities for conferences and corporate hospitality functions. In addition, Beaulieu has a 4x4 track and facilities which are suitable for team building activities, company days out, exhibitions, outdoor events and product lauches. **Open:** Daily 10–5pm except May–Sept 10–6pm. Closed Christmas Day. **Location:** By car take M27 to junction 2 then follow the Brown Tourist Signs. **Admission:** Please phone for details on 01590 612345.

map 4
C6

Hampshire

HOUGHTON LODGE GARDENS

Stockbridge, Hampshire SO20 6LQ
Tel: 01264 810177 (Capt & Mrs M W Busk)

Landscaped pleasure grounds and fine trees surround unique 18th C 'Cottage Ornée' beside the River Test with lovely views over the tranquil and unspoilt valley. Featured in BBC TV's "David Copperfield". Chalkcob walls shelter the 1 acre kitchen garden with ancient espaliered fruit trees, glasshouses and newly established herb garden. THE HYDROPONICUM SHOWS HOW TO GARDEN EASILY AT HOME WITHOUT SOIL OR PESTICIDES. **Location:** 1½ miles south of A30 at Stockbridge on minor road to Houghton village. **Station(s):** Winchester, Andover. **Open:** Mar–Sept, Sat, Sun & Bank Holidays 10–5pm, Mon, Tues, Thurs and Fri 2–5pm or by appointment. House by appointment. **Admission:** £5 (Children free). Special group discounts. Visitor centre with hydroponics shop serves free refreshments. **E-mail:** T.Grimshaw@aol.com **Website:** www.hydroponicum.co.uk

map 4 C5

LANGLEY BOXWOOD NURSERY

Rake, Nr Liss, Hampshire GU33 7JL
Tel: 01730 894467 Fax: 01730 894703 (Elizabeth Braimbridge)

This small nursery, in a beautiful setting, specialises in box-growing, offering a chance to see together a unique range of old and new varieties, hedging, topiary, specimens and rarities. Some taxus also. **National Collection – Buxus.** Descriptive list available (4 x 1st class stamps). **Location:** Off B2070 (old A3) 3 miles south of Liphook. Ring for directions. **Open:** Mon–Fri 9–4.30pm, Sat – enquire by telephone first. **E-mail:** langbox@msn.com **Internet:** www.boxwood.co.uk

map 4 D6

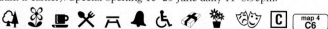

MOTTISFONT ABBEY

Mottisfont, Nr Romsey, Hants, SO51 OLP
Tel: 01794 340757 Fax: 01794 341492 (The National Trust)

The abbey and garden form the central point of an 809 hectare estate which includes most of the village of Mottisfont, farmland and woods. It is possible to walk along a tributary of the River Test which flows through the garden, forming a superb and tranquil setting for a 12th century Augustinian priory, which, after the Dissolution, became a house. It contains the spring or 'font' from which the place-name is derived. The magnificent trees, walled garden and the national collection of old-fashioned roses combine to provide interest throughout the seasons. The abbey contains a drawing room decorated by Rex Whistler and the cellarium of the old priory. In 1996 the Trust acquired Derek Hill's 20th-century picture collection. **Open:** 18 Mar–1 Nov: Sat–Wed, 12–6pm (or dusk if earlier). Special opening 10–25 June daily 11–8.30pm.

C map 4 C6

SOMERLEY

Ringwood, Hampshire BH24 3PL
Tel: 01425 480819 Fax: 01425 478613

Sitting on the edge of the New Forest in the heart of Hampshire, Somerley, home of the Sixth Earl and Countess of Normanton is situated in 7,000 acres of stunning countryside. Although never open to the public, Somerley is available for corporate events and its location along with its seclusion and privacy, provide the perfect environment for conferences and meetings, product launches, lunches and dinners, activity and team building days (the estate boasts a hugely challenging off road driving course) and film and photographic work.

Somerley only ever hosts one event at a time so exclusivity in an outstanding setting is always guaranteed. From groups as small as 8 to perhaps a large dinner for 120, the style of attention and personal service go hand in hand with the splendour of the house and estate itself. Housing a magnificent art and porcelain collection, Somerley, albeit impressively splendid, still retains the warmth and character of a family home. **E-mail:** info@somerley.com **Internet:** www.somerley.com

C map 4 D7

82 www.historichouses.co.uk

STRATFIELD SAYE HOUSE

Stratfield Saye, Nr Reading, Hampshire RG27 OAS
Tel: 01256 882882 (The Duke of Wellington)

Home of the Dukes of Wellington since 1817. The house and exhibition pay tribute to Arthur Wellesley, the first and Great Duke – soldier and statesman. **House:** Contains a unique collection of paintings, furniture and personal effects of the Great Duke. **Wellington Exhibition:** Depicts the life and times of the Great Duke and features his magnificent funeral carriage. **Grounds:** Include gardens and the grave of Copenhagen, the Duke's favourite charger which carried him throughout the Battle of Waterloo. **Location:** 1 mile W of A33 between Basingstoke & Reading (turn off at Wellington Arms Hotel); signposted. **Open:** June, July & Aug, daily except Mon & Tues. Grounds & Exhibition: 11.30–5pm. House 12–3pm. Last admission 3pm. Groups: by arrangement, June, July & Aug: Mon & Tues. Sept: Mon–Fri. **Admission:** Adult £5.50, child £2.50, OAP £5.

ST AGATHA'S CHURCH

Market Way, Portsmouth, Hants
Tel & Fax: 01329 230330

A grand Italianate basilica of 1894, built for the famous Anglo Catholic priest, Fr R Dolling. Interior enriched with marble, alabaster, polished granite, carved stone and coloured glass. The apse displays a magnificent sgraffito mural c.1901, by Heywood Sumner, described by the late Sir Nikolaus Pevsner as "one of Portsmouth's few major works of art". Fine furnishings, many rescued from redundant churches. Guides available. **Location:** By Cascades Shopping Centre. On route for Historic Ships. **Open:** Sat, Sun, Wed Jun–Sept 10–3pm. Sat, Sun Oct–May 10–2pm. Traditional High Mass every Sunday, 11am (B.C.P. & English Missal). Other times by arrangement. **Admission:** Free. Nave available for hire subject to availability.

WINCHESTER CATHEDRAL

Winchester SO23 9LS
Tel: 01962 853137 Fax: 01962 841519

The cathedral was founded in 1079 on a site where Christian worship had already been offered for over 400 years. Among its treasures are the 12th century illuminated Winchester Bible, the font, medieval wall paintings and six chantry chapels. **Location:** Winchester city centre. **Open:** 8.30–6.30pm. East end closes 5pm. Access may be restricted during services. **Admission:** Donations recommended. Adults £2.50, OAPs/Students £2, children 50p. Group tours – additional 50p, should be booked through the education centre. (Tel: 01962 866854 or 01962 853137).

UPPARK

South Harting, Petersfield, Hampshire GU31 5QR
Tel: 01730 825415 Fax: 01730 825873 (The National Trust)

An extensive award-winning, exhibition shows the exciting work which restored this beautiful house and its treasures following the disastrous 1989 fire. The elegant, fully restored mid-18th century interior houses the rescued Grand Tour paintings, fine ceramics, textiles, furniture and famous dolls' house. Nostalgic servants rooms as they were in 1874 when H G Wells' mother was housekeeper. The restored garden, high on the South Downs with magnificent views, is in the Picturesque style - primarily foliage, with flowering shrubs, under-planted bulbs, perennials, herbaceous plants. **Location:** 5 miles SE of Petersfield (B2146). **Open:** 2 Apr–31 Oct; daily except Fri & Sat. Exhibition, Shop, Restaurant & Grounds 11.30–5.30pm. House: 1–5pm (4pm Oct). **Admission:** Adults £5.50; family ticket £13.75. Groups must book.

THE VYNE

Vyne Road, Sherborne St John, Basingstoke, Hampshire RG24 9HL
Tel: 01256 881337 Fax: 01256 881720 (The National Trust)

Built in the early 16th century in beautiful diaper brickwork by William Sandys, Lord Chamberlain to Henry VIII. Passed to the Chute family in the mid-17th century resulting in extensive alterations. Tudor chapel contains extremely fine renaissance glass and majolica floor tiles. A wealth of tudor panelling and collections of furniture, ceramics and textiles. Herbaceous borders, lawns sloping down to lake and surrounded by parkland. Woodland walks. Refreshments. **Open:** Tues–Thur, Sat & Sun (also Good Fri & Bank Hol Mons). Grounds: Weekends in Feb–Mar, 11–4pm. 1 Apr–29 Oct, 11–6pm. House: 1 Apr–29 Oct, 1–5pm. Last admission ½hr before closing. **Admission:** House & Grounds £5. Grounds only £3. **E-mail:** svygen@smtp.ntrust.org.uk

Hereford & Worcester

Ross-on-Wye

Right against the Welsh border lies the old county of Herefordshire. The River Wye winds its way across this rugged land of pastoral landscapes, offering excellent salmon fishing. Situated along its meandering route is the city of Hereford with its beautiful Norman cathedral that towers above the River Wye. The spectacular Black Mountains lie to the South West along the Welsh borders, where trickling streams run through fertile valleys.

Worcester is famous for its fine timber buildings and its porcelain, particularly in Friar Street and New Street which houses the best examples of such architecture. Greyfriars and the Commandery are particularly worthy of a mention. Like Hereford, Worcester is dominated by a beautiful cathedral with an especially fine crypt. This wondrous place is also renowned for hosting a wide variety of musical events.

AVONCROFT MUSEUM OF HISTORIC BUILDINGS

Stoke Heath, Bromsgrove, Worcestershire B60 4JR
Tel: 01527 831363/831886 Fax: 01527 876934 (Council of Management)

25 buildings of historic, architectural and social value authentically restored and re-erected on 15-acre rural site. Covering 7 centuries, it ranges from the magnificently carved timber roof of the Priory of Worcester Cathedral, now gracing a fine new Guesten Hall, to a 1946 Pre-Fab, authentically furnished. English life over the centuries is illustrated – early agriculture by a range of timber-framed buildings, including a working windmill; the local 19th century industries of nail and chain-making; and many aspects of domestic social life. We also house the National Telephone Kiosk Collection. **Location:** At Stoke heath 2 miles south of Bromsgrove. **Open:** March–Nov from 10.30am. Some days closed. **Admission:** Adult £4.60, senior citizen £3.70, child £2.30. Group Rates: Adult £3.70, senior citizen £3.10, child £1.75. Under fives are free.

BURTON COURT

Eardisland, Nr Leominster, Herefordshire HR6 9DN
Tel: 01544 388231 (Lt. Cmdr. & Mrs. R. M. Simpson)

A typical squire's house, built around the surprising survival of a 14th century hall. The East Front re-designed by Sir Clough Williams-Ellis in 1912. Some European and Oriental costume, natural history specimens and models including a children's working model fairground and model railway. Pick your soft fruit in season. **Location:** 5 miles W of Leominster signposted on A44. **Open:** Spring Bank Holiday to end September, Wed, Thur, Sat, Sun, Bank Holiday Mon 2.30–6pm. **Admission:** Adults £2.50, children £2. **Refreshments:** Teas by arrangement. **Conferences:** Subject to availability.

EASTNOR CASTLE
Eastnor, Ledbury, Herefordshire HR8 1RL
Tel: 01531 633160 Fax: 01531 631776 (Mr J. Hervey–Bathurst)

Home of the Hervey-Bathurst family, this magnificent Georgian Castle was built by their ancestors in 1812. Eastnor is dramatically situated in a 5000 acre sporting estate in The Malvern Hills. The lavish Italianate and Gothic interiors have recently been restored to critical acclaim. Unique collection of medieval armour, tapestries, furniture and pictures by Van Dyck, Kneller, Romney & Watts. Castellated terraces descend to a beautiful lake and the castle is surrounded by a famous arboretum containing many rare mature trees and 300 acre Deer Park which is used successfully for large outdoor events and concerts.

Location: 5 miles from junction 2 of M50. 2 miles east of Ledbury on A438 Tewkesbury Road. **Open:** 23 Apr–8 Oct on Sun and Bank Holiday Mon plus every day in Jul and Aug, except Sat. **Admission:** Castle and Grounds: Adults: £4.75, children £2.50. Reduced rates for groups, families and grounds only. Eastnor Castle is also available for exclusive corporate and private entertainment, activity and teambuilding days, product launches, private parties and dinners, wedding ceremonies, receptions and luxury accommodation for small groups.

map 7
G1

THE COMMANDERY
Sidbury, Worcester
Tel: 01905 361821 Fax: 01905 361822 (Worcester City Council)

The first view of the Commandery is deceptive for behind the small timber-framed entrance is a stunning complex of buildings dating from the medieval to Georgian periods. Originally founded in 1085 as a monastic hospital the Commandery later became the family home of the Wylde's whose Stuart lifestyle is reflected in period room settings. In 1651 the Commandery assumed national importance when it housed the Royalist headquarters at the battle of Worcester. This role is reflected in our award winning civil war museum, returning visitors to the days of Cavaliers and Roundheads. The Commandery plays host to a varied events programme with living history, lectures, family days and theatre. New from May 2000 - a special exhibition for the Millennium.

HARTLEBURY CASTLE

Nr Kidderminster, Worcester, Hereford & Worcester DT11 7XX
Tel: 01299 250410 (State Rooms Secretary) 01299 250416 (Museum)

Home of the Bishops of Worcester for over 1,000 years. Fortified in 13th century, rebuilt after sacking in Civil War and gothicised in 18th century. State Rooms include medieval Great Hall, Hurd Library and Saloon. Fine plaster work and collection of episcopal portraits. Also County Museum in North Wing. **Location:** In village of Hartlebury, 5 mile south of Kidderminster, 10 miles N of Worcester off A449. **Station:** Kidderminster 4 miles. **Open:** County Museum: Mar–Nov, Mon–Thurs 10–5pm, Fri & Sun 2–5pm. Closed Good Friday. State rooms: Open Tuesday, Wednesday and Thursday please contact the museum for details. **Admission:** County Museum: Adults £2.20, concessions £1.10, family tickets £6.

HELLENS

Much Marcle, Ledbury, Herefordshire HR8 2LY
Tel: 01531 660 668 (The Pennington Mellor Munthe Charity Trust)

Built first as a monastery and then as a stone fortress in 1292 by Mortimer, Earl of March, with Tudor, Jacobean and Stuart additions, this manorial house has been lived in ever since by descendants of the original builder. Visited by the Black Prince, Bloody Mary and the family ghost (a priest murdered during the Civil War). Interesting family paintings relics and heirlooms from the Civil War and possessions of the Audleys, Walwyns and Whartons as well as Anne Boleyn. Also beautiful 17th century woodwork carved by the 'King's Carpenter' John Abel. All these historical stories incorporated into guided tours, revealing the loves and lives of those who lived and died here. Goods and chattels virtually unchanged and certainly not modernised. **Open:** Good Friday–2 Oct, Wed, Sat, Sun and Bank Hol Mons. Guided tours only on the hour 2–5pm (last tour 4pm). Other times by appointment with the custodian. **Admission:** Adults £3.50, children £1.50 (must be accompanied by an adult).

HARVINGTON HALL

Harvington, Kidderminster, Worcestershire DY10 4LR
Tel: 01562 777846 (the Roman Catholic Archdiocese of Birmingham)

Moated medieval and Elizabethan manor house containing secret hiding places and rare wall paintings. Georgian Chapel in garden with 18th century altar, rails and organ. **Location:** 3 miles SE of Kidderminster, ½ mile from the junction of A448 and A450 at Mustow Green. **Station(s):** Nearest Kidderminster. **Open:** Mar and Oct, Sat & Sun, Apr to Sept, Wed–Sun. Bank Holiday Mondays. The Hall is available every day for pre-booked schools or groups and for meetings, conferences or wedding breakfasts. **Admission:** Adults £3.80, OAPs £2.50, children £2.50, family ticket £10.50, garden only £1. Free car parking. **Events:** Outdoor play – July. Craft Fair – Mar and Nov. Pilgrimage – early Sept. Wassail – December. Other events and reconstructions to be arranged. Occasionally the Hall may be closed for a private function, up to date information available by phone.

map 4 A1

HERGEST CROFT GARDENS

Kington, Herefordshire HR5 3EG
Tel: 01544 230160 Fax: 01544 230160 (W.L. Banks, Esq.)

Spring bulbs to autumn colour, a garden for all seasons. Old-fashioned kitchen garden; spring and summer borders, roses. Over 59 champion trees and shrubs in one of the finest collections in the British Isles. National Collections of birches, maples and zelkovas. Rhododendrons up to 30ft. **Location:** On outskirts W of Kington off Rhayader Road (A44) (signposted to Hergest at W end of bypass). **Station(s):** Leominster–14 miles. **Open:** 1 Apr–31 Oct 1.30–6pm. **Admission:** Adult £3.50, children under 16 free. Groups of 20+ by appointment anytime £3. Guided tours available (pre-booked). Season tickets £12, access Apr–Mar. **Refreshments:** Home-made light lunches (pre-booked for groups) and teas. **Events:** Mon 1 May Flower Fair: plant stalls, special events. (£5 admission). Gift shop: Attractive gifts. Plant sales: Rare, unusual trees and shrubs. **Internet:** www.hergest.co.uk

map 7 G2

HOPTON COURT

Hopton Court, Cleobury Mortimer, Kidderminister, DY14 OEF
Tel: 01299 270734 Fax: 01299 271132 (C. R. D Woodward)

Substantial changes were made to the house and grounds from 1798 to 1803. The works were supervised by John Nash and Humphrey Repton. Around 1820, a conservatory (graded II* in 1995) of cast-iron and glass was built. To the northeast of the house lies the stable block incorporating the Coach House. Both the Conservatory and the Coach House were renovated in 1997. Three rooms in the house and the Conservatory are licensed for civil ceremonies. The Conservatory is open four days a year without appointment, at other times by prior appointment. **Admission:** £3.50. The Coach House is available for receptions.

map 4 A4

HOW CAPLE COURT GARDEN

How Caple, HR1 4SX, Hereford & Worcester.
Tel: 01989 740 612 Fax: 01989 740 611 (Mr & Mrs Roger Lee)

Discover 11.5 acres of delightful Edwardian gardens set high above the River Wye. The planting is formal and woodland with a unique atmosphere of peace and tranquillity. The nursery has a wide variety of rose shrubs and herbaceous plants. The stable shop offers a selection of dried and silk flowers and How Caple preserves and pickles. **Location:** B4224, Ross-on-Wye (4.5 miles), Hereford (9 miles). **Open:** March–Oct, 9–5pm. Closed Nov–end Feb. **Admission:** Adults £2.50, children £1.25. Parties welcome by appointment. Dogs on leads welcome. **Refreshments:** Teashop open daily offering home made cakes.

map 7 G1

KENTCHURCH COURT

Nr. Pontrilas, Hereford, Herefordshire, HR2 0DB
Tel: 01981 240 228 (Mr & Mrs John Lucas-Scudamore)

Fortified border manor house altered by Nash. Part of the original 14th century house still survives. Pictures and Grinling Gibbons carving. Owen Glendower's tower. Game shooting and shooting parties. Also wine appreciation weekends. **Location:** Off B4347, 3 miles SE of Pontrilas. Monmouth (12 miles). Hereford (14 miles). Abergavenny (14 miles). On left bank of River Monnow. **Open:** May–Sept. All visitors by appointment only. **Admission:** Adults £4, children £4. **Refreshments:** At Kentchurch Court by appointment. **Accommodation:** By appointment.

map 7 G2

LANGSTONE COURT

Llangarron, Ross on Wye, Herefordshire
Tel: 01989 770254 (R M C Jones Esq.)

Mostly late 17th century house with older parts. Interesting staircases, panelling and ceilings. **Location:** Ross on Wye 5 miles, Llangarron 1 miles. **Open:** Wednesdays & Thursdays 11–3pm between May 20–August 31, spring and summer bank holidays. **Admission:** Free.

map 7 H1

LITTLE MALVERN COURT

Nr Malvern, Hereford & Worcester, WR14 4JN
Tel: 01684 892988 Fax: 01684 893057 (Mrs Berington)

14th century Prior's Hall once attached to 12th century Benedictine Priory, with Victorian addition by Hansom. Family and European paintings and furniture. Collection of 18th and 19th century needlework. Home of the Berington family by descent since the Dissolution. 10 acres of former monastic grounds. Magnificent views, lake, garden rooms, terrace. Wide variety of spring bulbs, old fashioned roses, shrubs and trees. **Location:** 3 m S of Great Malvern on Upton-on-Severn Road (A4104). **Open:** 19 April–20 July, Wed and Thurs 2.15–5pm, parties by prior arrangement. Guided tours – last admission 4.30pm. **Admission:** Adults: house and garden £4.50; house or garden only £3.50. Children: house and garden £2; house or garden only £1. **Refreshments:** Home-made teas only available for parties by arrangement. Partially suitable for wheelchairs in garden.

map 4
A2

MAWLEY HALL

Cleobury Mortimer, Nr. Kidderminster, Worcestershire, DY14 8PN

18th century house attributed to Francis Smith. Fine plasterwork and panelling. **Location:** 1 mile S of Cleobury Mortimer (A4117). 7 miles W of Bewdley. **Open:** 10 Apr–13 July, Mon & Thur, 2.30–5pm. Visitors are requested to give advanced notice to Mrs R Sharp, Bennet House, 54 St. James' Street, London SW1A 1JT. Tel: 0171 495 6702 **Admission:** £3.

map 4
A1

 # SPETCHLEY PARK GARDEN

Spetchley Park, Worcester, Hereford & Worcester WR5 1RS
Tel: 01905 345224 (Spetchley Gardens Charitable Trust)

This lovely 30 acre garden is a plantsman's delight, with a large collection of trees, shrubs and plants, many of which are rare or unusual. There is colour and interest throughout the months that the garden is open to visitors. The park contains red and fallow deer. This is truly a garden for seasons. April and May produce a wonderful display of daffodils and other bulbs, and are also the months of flowering trees and shrubs, many rare or unusual. The large collection of roses come into their own in June and July, whilst July, August and September reveal the great herbaceous borders in all their glory. Late September sees the start of the Autumn tints. **Location:** 3 miles E of Worcester on Stratford-upon-Avon Road (A422). **Open:** Gardens: 1 Apr–30 Sept. Tues–Fri 11–5pm, Suns 2–5pm. Bank Hols 11–5pm. Closed all Sats & all other Mons. **Admission:** Adults £3.20, children £1.60, concessions for pre-booked parties. **Refreshments:** Tea in the garden. Regret no dogs. House not open.

map 4
A2

 # MOCCAS COURT

Moccas, Herefordshire, HR2 9LH
Tel: 01981 500 381 (Trustees of Baunton Trust)

Built by Anthony Keck in 1775 overlooking the River Wye, decoration including the round room and oval stair by Robert Adam. Scene of famous 17th century romance and destination of epic night ride from London. Set in 'Capability' Brown parkland with an attractive walk to The Scar Rapids. **Location:** 10 miles E of Hay on Wye. 13 miles W of Hereford on the River Wye. 1 mile off B4352. **Station(s):** Hereford. **Open:** House & Gardens: Apr–Sept, Thurs, 2–6pm. **Admission:** £2.00. **Refreshments:** Food and drink available at the Red Lion Hotel, Bredwardine, by pre-booking only. **Accommodation:** Available at the Red Lion Hotel, Bredwardine. Disabled access in the garden only.

map 7
G2

WORCESTER CATHEDRAL

College Green, Worcester, Worcestershire, WR1 2LA
Tel: 01905 28854 Fax: 01905 611139 (Dean & Chapter)

Beside the River Severn, facing the Malvern Hills. Built between 1084 and 1375. Norman Crypt and Chapter House. Early English Quire, Perpendicular Tower. Monastic buildings include the Refectory (now College Hall and open on request during August), Cloisters, remains of Guesten Hall and Dormitories. Tombs of King John and Prince Arthur. Elgar memorial window. Misericords. **Location:** Centre of Worcester. Main roads Oxford and Stratford to Wales. 3 miles M5, Junction 7. **Station(s):** Foregate Street (easier). Shrub Hill (taxi). **Open:** Every day, 7.30–6pm. Choral Evensong daily (except Thurs and school hols). **Admission:** FREE. Suggested donation £2. **Guided tours:** Visits Officer 01905 28854. **E-mail:** worcestercathedral@compuserve.com

map 4
A2

Hertfordshire

A land of woods, streams and cornfields – a gracious countryside, undulating, varied, typically English, strangely remote and rich in historic monuments – Hertfordshire is a county which retains its ancient character in the midst of rapid development.

With the development of high speed trains, Hertfordshire has become a favourite area for commuters. Part of the county lies inside of the M25, down to Borehamwood, whilst the rest stretches up north into the open countryside.

St Albans today is a thriving market town, steeped in beauty and historic memories. It has seen more than its fair share of history through the years. St Albans was fought over twice during the War of the Roses and the area in front of the abbey's gate was a medieval meeting place and focus of rioting during the Peasant's Revolt of 1381. The cathedral, one of the longest in Britain, is an excellent example of medieval architecture. The town has an air of affluence best appreciated on foot.

Capel Manor

Nearby, there are many vestiges of the country's heritage and architecture. Hatfield House is surrounded by beautiful parkland and is a fine example of a Jacobean house. The new towns of Welwyn Garden City and Hemel Hempstead are located close by and form a stark contrast to the many historical areas in this region.

ASHRIDGE

Berkhamsted, Hertfordshire HP4 1NS
Tel: 01442 843491, Fax: 01442 841209
(Governors of Ashridge)

150 acres of both parkland and intimate smaller gardens. The landscape influenced by Humphry Repton. Mature trees combined with unique features e.g. Beech Houses with windows and doors in a Pink and Grey Garden, Grotto – Ferns planted between Herts Pudding Stone. **Location:** 3½ miles N of Berkhamsted (A4251), 1 miles S of Little Gaddesden. **Station(s):** Berkhamsted. **Open:** Gardens open Easter, Apr–Sept Sat & Sun & B/Holidays 2–6pm. **Admission:** Gardens: Adults £2 Children/OAP £1. **Conferences:** For information please contact Carol Johnston, Conference Manager (01442 841027).

`map 4 E3`

CATHEDRAL AND ABBEY CHURCH OF SAINT ALBAN

St Albans, Hertfordshire AL1 1BY.
Tel: 01727 860780 Fax: 01727 850944 (Dean and Cathedral Council of St Albans)

Standing in the centre of the historic city of St Albans, the Cathedral is the imposing and beautiful abbey church of a Benedictine monastery founded by King Offa in 793 on the site of execution of St Alban, first British martyr (died c.250). The present church was built in 1077 using Roman brick from nearby Verulamium. Became the parish church of St Albans in 1539 and a cathedral in 1877. **Admission:** Free. Spectacular multi-image audiovisual show (£1.50 adults/£1 children). Shop and Refectory Restaurant. Guided Tours available. All enquiries 01727 860780. **E-mail:** cathedra@alban.u-net.com. **Internet:** www.stalbans cathedral.org.uk

`map 4 E3`

CROMER WINDMILL

Ardeley, Stevenage, Hertfordshire SG2 7QA
Tel: 01279 843301 (Hertfordshire Building Preservation Trust)

Hertfordshire's last surviving Post Mill now fully restored, with grants from English Heritage and Heritage Lottery Fund. Short video for visitors showing method of working. ½ hour video available on loan, with brochure giving history of Mill. Disabled access, adequate parking, no lavatories, literature and tea towels on sale. **Open:** Sundays, Bank Holidays, 2 and 4 Saturday 2.30–5pm mid May–mid Sept. Special parties by arrangement. Cristina Harrison 01279 843301. **Admission:** Adults £1.50, children 25p. **Location:** OSS TL304287. On the B1037 between Stevenage and Cottered.

`map 5 F3`

GORHAMBURY

St Albans, Hertfordshire AL3 6AH
Tel: 01727 854051 Fax: 01727 843675 (The Earl of Verulam)

Mansion built 1777–84 in classical style by Sir Robert Taylor, 16th century enamelled glass and historic portraits. **Location:** 2 miles W of St Albans, entrance off A4147 at Roman Theatre. **Station(s):** St Albans **Open:** May–Sept, Thurs 2–5. Last tour of house 4.15pm. Gardens open with the house. **Admission:** House and Gardens Adults £6, children £3, OAPs £4. Guided tours only. Parties by prior arrangement, Thurs £5, other days £6.

`map 4 E3`

HATFIELD HOUSE, PARK & GARDENS

Hatfield, Hertfordshire AL9 5NQ
Tel: 01707 262823, Fax: 01707 275719 (Contact – The Curator)

Hatfield House was built by Robert Cecil, 1st Earl of Salisbury and Chief Minister to King James I, in 1611. This celebrated Jacobean house, which stands in its own Great Park, has been in the Cecil family ever since and is the home of the Marquess of Salisbury. The State Rooms are rich in world-famous paintings, exquisite furniture, fine tapestries and historic armour. Superb examples of Jacobean craftsmanship can be found throughout the house. Within the delightful gardens stand the surviving wing of the Royal Palace of Hatfield (1497), were Elizabeth I spent much of her childhood. Today, the Marchioness of Salisbury continues to recreate and maintain the beautiful gardens in a style that reflects their Jacobean history. **Location:** 21 miles N of London - A1(M) Junction 4, 2m. Signed off A414 & A1000. Opposite Hatfield railway station (Kings Cross 25mins). **Open:** 25 March–24 September (closed Good Friday, but open BH Mondays). House: Tue–Thur: guided tours only, 12–4pm. Sat & Sun: no guided tours, 1–4.30pm. Bank Hols: no guided tours, 11–4.30pm. Park: Daily, except Fri, 10.30–8pm. Fri: 11–6pm. West Gardens: Tue–Sun: 11–6pm. East Gardens: Fri(Connoisseurs' Day): 11–6pm. Shop: Tue–Sat: 11–5.30pm. Sun: 1–5.30pm. Restaurant: Tue–Sun 10.30–5.30pm. **Admission:** (except at major events) House, Park & West Gardens (not Fri): Adult £6.20, child £3.10, booked party (20+) £5.20. Park only (not Fri): Adult £1.80, child 90p. Connoisseurs' Day (Fri): Park & Gardens (East & West): £5.20. House Tour, Park & Gardens: booked parties only (20+) £9.20. **Major Events:** Living Crafts: 4–7 May. Festival of Gardening: 24–25 June, Art in Clay, 4–6 Aug, Country Homes & Gardens Show, 8–10 Sept.

KNEBWORTH HOUSE

Knebworth, Hertfordshire
Tel: 01438 812661 (The Lord Cobbold)

Home of the Lytton family since 1490 and still a lived-in family house. Transformed in early Victorian times by Edward Bulwer–Lytton, the author, poet, dramatist and statesman, into the unique High Gothic fantasy house of today, complete with turrets, griffins and gargoyles. Home of Constance Lytton, the Suffragette, and Robert Lytton, the Viceroy of India who proclaimed Queen Victoria Empress of India at the Great Delhi Durbar of 1877. Visited by Queen Elizabeth I, Charles Dickens and Sir Winston Churchill. The interior contains many different styles, including the Jacobean Banqueting Hall, the Regency elegance of Mrs Bulwer–Lytton's bedroom, the Victorian State Drawing Room and the Edwardian designs of Sir Edwin Lutyens in the Entrance Hall, Dining Parlour and Library. 25 acres of beautiful gardens, simplified by Lutyens, including pollarded lime avenues, formal rose garden, maze and Gertrude Jekyll herb garden. 250 acres of gracious parkland, with herds of red and sika deer, includes extensive children's adventure playground and miniature railway. Special events staged throughout the summer. World famous for its huge open-air rock concerts, and used as a film location for Batman, the Shooting Party, Wilde, Jane Eyre and the Canterville Ghost, amongst others. **Location:** Direct access off A1(M) junction 7 (Stevenage South A602). 28 miles N of London. 12 miles N of M25 junction 23. **Open:** Daily: 15 Apr–1 May, 27 May–4 June & 8 July–3 Sept. Weekends & Bank Hols: 6–21 May. Weekends only: 10 June–2 July & 9 Sept–1 Oct inclusive. **Times:** Park, Gardens & Playground 11–5.30pm. House & Raj Exhibition 12–5pm. (last admission 4.30pm). **E-mail:** info@knebworthhouse.com **Internet:** www.knebworthhouse.com

THE GARDENS OF THE ROSE

Chiswell Green, St Albans, Herts AL2 3NR
Tel: 01727 850461, Fax: 01727 850360 (The Royal National Rose Society)

The Royal National Rose Society's Gardens provide a wonderful display of one of the best and most important collections of roses in the world. There are some 30,000 roses in 1800 different varieties. The Society has introduced many companion plants which harmonise with the roses including over 100 varieties of clematis. The garden, named for the Society's Patron HM The Queen Mother, contains a fascinating collection of old garden roses. Various cultivation trials show just how easy roses are to grow and new roses can be viewed in the International Trial Ground. **Open:** 27 May–24 Sept, Mon–Sats 9–5pm. Sun & Bank Hols. 10–6pm. **E-mail:** mail@rnrs.org.uk **Internet:** roses.co.uk

BENINGTON LORDSHIP

Benington
Tel: 01438 869668 Fax: 01438 869622 (Mr & Mrs C.H.A Bott)

Hilldrop garden on castle ruins overlooking lakes. Amazing April display of Scillas, scented rose garden, hidden rock/water garden, spectacular borders, ornamental kitchen garden, nursery. **Location:** 5m E of Stevenage, in Benington Village. **Open:** Please phone to confirm times, dates and prices.

OLD GORHAMBURY HOUSE

St Albans, Hertfordshire
Tel: 01604 730320 (English Heritage)

The remains of this Elizabethan mansion, particularly the porch of the Great Hall, illustrate the impact of the Renaissance on English architecture. **Location:** ¼ mile west of Gorhambury House and accessible only through private drive from A4147 at St Albans (2 miles). **Open:** May–Sept, Thursday only, 2–5pm. At any other times by appointment only. **Admission:** Free.

SCOTT'S GROTTO

Scott's Road, Ware, Herts SG12 9SQ
Tel: 01920 464131, 01992 584322 (East Hertfordshire District Council)

Grotto, summerhouse and garden built 1760–73 by Quaker poet John Scott. Described by English Heritage as 'one of the finest grottos in England.' Now extensively restored by The Ware Society. **Location:** Scott's Road, Ware (off A119 Hertford Road). **Station:** Ware/Liverpool Street line. **Open:** Every Sat beginning of Apr–Sept and Easter, Spring and Summer Bank Hol Mons 2–4.30pm. **Admission:** Free but donation of £1 requested. Please park in Amwell End car park by level crossing (300 yards away) and walk up Scott's Road. Advisable to wear flat shoes and bring a torch. Parties by prior arrangement.

SHAW'S CORNER

Ayot St Lawrence, Nr Welwyn, Herts AL6 9BX
Tel: 01438 820307 (The National Trust)

The home of George Bernard Shaw from 1906 until his death in 1950. The rooms remain much as he left them, with many literary and personal effects evoking the individuality and genius of this great dramatist. The garden has richly planted borders and views over the Hertfordshire countryside. **Open:** 1 Apr–29 Oct: daily except Mon & Tues (but closed Good Fri and open Bank Hol Mon) 1–5pm. **Admission:** £3.50, family ticket £8.75. **Location:** At SW end of village, 2 miles NE of Wheathampstead: approx. 2 miles from B653. **E-mail:** www.tscgen@smtp.ntrust.org.uk

ST. PAULS WALDEN BURY

Hitchin, Herts. SG4 8BP
Tel: 01438 871218/871229. Fax: As telephone. (Bowes Lyon)

Formal landscape garden, laid out around 1730, covering about 40 acres. Listed Grade I. Avenues and rides span woodland gardens leading to temples, statues, lake and ponds. There are also more recent flower gardens, best from Apr–Jul. This is the childhood home of Queen Elizabeth, the Queen Mother. **Open:** Suns, 18 Apr, 16 May, 13 Jun 2–7pm. Adults £2.50, children 50p. Home-made teas. Lakeside Concert Jul to be announced. Also by appointment, £5 entry. Proceeds go to charity. **E-mail:** Boweslyon@aol.com

Isle of Wight

Nunwell House

The Isle of Wight is an extremely popular destination. Its magnificent landscape is complemented by some unique scenery, such as the stunning Needles. The old capital of Carisbrooke is home to the 11th century Norman castle where Charles I was imprisoned in 1647. Visitors will be fascinated by the history and splendour of Osborne House, designed by Prince Albert.

The Isle of Wight's popular resorts are Sandown, Shanklin and Newport, renowned for their golden beaches. The quaint village of Godshill is often frequented by day-trippers as it offers pleasant tearooms, a model village and other attractions. The island is a famous base for sailing, the big highlight of the sailing calendar being Cowes Week.

CARISBROOKE CASTLE

Newport, Isle of Wight PO30 1XY
Tel: 01983 522107 (English Heritage)

Royal fortress and prison to King Charles I, Carisbrooke is set dramatically on a sweeping ridge at the very heart of the Isle of Wight. One of the most popular attractions are the famous Carisbrooke donkeys. See them tread the huge wheel in the medieval well house, much as donkeys would have done in the 18th century, and meet them in the Donkey Centre. Discover the popular interactive exhibitions and museum, which trace the history of the castle. The island's World War I Memorial chapel offers a moment of contemplation before admiring the breathtaking views from the castle walls. **Location:** 1¼ m SW of Newport. **Open:** 1 Apr–30 Sept: daily, 10–6pm, 1 Oct–31 Oct: daily, 10–5pm, 1 Nov–31 Mar: 10–4pm. (Closed 24–25 Dec and 1 Jan) **Admission:** Adults £4.50, concs. £3.40, child £2.30, family £11.30 (15% discount for groups of 11 or more).

 `map 4 C7`

DEACONS NURSERY (H.H)

Moor View, Godshill, PO38 3HW, Isle of Wight
Tel: 01983 840 750 Fax: 01983 523 575 (G. D. Deacon & B. H. Deacon)

Specialist national fruit tree growers. Trees and bushes sent anywhere so send NOW for a FREE catalogue. Over 300 varieties of apples on various types of root stocks from M27 (4ft), M26 (8ft) to M25 (18ft). Plus Pears, Peaches, Nectarines, Plums, Gages, Cherries, Soft Fruits and an unusual selection of Family Trees. Celebrate the year 2000 with Deacons specially developed millennium apple tree on M26 at £15.95 delivered (will grow to 8ft). Many special offers. Catalogue always available (stamp appreciated). Many varieties of grapes; dessert and wine, plus Hybrid Hops and nuts of all types. **Location:** The picturesque village of Godshill. Deacons Nursery is in Moor View off School Crescent (behind the only school). **Open:** Winter – Mon–Fri, 8–4pm & Sat, 8–1pm. Summer – Mon–Fri, 8–5pm.

 `map 4 C7`

NUNWELL HOUSE & GARDENS

Coach Lane, Brading, Isle of Wight
Tel: 01983 407240 (Col. & Mrs J A Aylmer)

Nunwell House has been a family home for 5 centuries and reflects much island and architectural history. Finely furnished with Jacobean and Georgian wings. Lovely setting with Channel views and 5 acres of tranquil gardens. Special family military collections. **Location:** 1 mile from Brading turning off A3055 signed; 3 mile S of Ryde. **Station:** Brading. **Open:** 28/29 May then 3 July–6 Sept, Mon, Tues & Weds 1–5pm with House tours at 1.30, 2.30 and 3.30pm. **Admission:** £4 (includes guide book) – reductions for senior citizens, children and parties. Gardens only £2.50. **Refreshments:** Picnic areas: large parties may book catering in advance. Parties welcome out of season if booked. Large car park. Regret no dogs.

   `map 4 C7`

OSBORNE HOUSE

East Cowes, Isle of Wight PO32 6JY
Tel: 01983 200022 (English Heritage)

Visit the magnificent Osborne House, the beloved seaside retreat of Queen Victoria, and gain insight into the private family life of Britain's longest reigning monarch. The Royal Apartments have been preserved almost unaltered since Victoria died here in 1901. The Swiss Cottage, a chalet built in the grounds for the children, gives a fascinating insight into the children's lives and there is an authentic Victorian carriage to take visitors between house and cottage. **Location:** 1m SE of East Cowes. **Open:** 1 Apr–30 Sept: House daily, 10–5pm. Grounds daily, 10–6pm. 1 Oct–31 Oct: House & Grounds daily, 10–5pm. Telephone for details of our winter guided tours, pre-booking essential. **Admission:** House & Grounds: Adults £6.90, concs £5.20, child £3.50, family £17.30. Grounds only: Adults £3.50, concs £2.60, child £1.80. (15% discount for groups of 11 or more).

Kent

The fruitful fields of the lowlands and the inspiring contours of the downland ridges present a typical picture of England, as the idealist would have it. The county boasts fine countryside, picturesque villages, an elegant spa town, the white cliffs and a county town which is one of the most venerable in England.

Canterbury, on the River Stour, is the centre of the Anglican church and seat of the Archbishop of Canterbury. The cathedral houses a magnificent collection of twelfth and thirteenth century stained glass and the tomb of the Black Prince.

Kent's seaside towns of Whitstable, Margate and Broadstairs are an odd combination of the nostalgic and frivolous. Viking Bay is just one of several sandy coves that dent Thanet's eastern shore. Between Broadstairs and Margate you'll find Stone, Joss, Kingsgate and Botany Bay, with Louisa Bay to the south – all quiet gems.

Matfield Village Green

BELMONT

Belmont Park, Throwley, Faversham, Kent ME13 0HH
Tel: 01795 890202 (Harris (Belmont) Charity)

Charming late 18th century mansion by Samuel Wyatt set in fine parkland. Seat of the Harris family since 1801 when it was acquired by General George Harris, the victor of Seringapatam. The delightfully furnished house contains interesting mementoes of the family's connections with India and colonies, plus the fifth Lord Harris's fine clock collection. There is a walled garden and a pinetum containing some fine specimens of trees and a small grotto. In the spring the rhododendrons and azaleas give a blaze of colour and these are followed by the hydrangeas. There is also a charming pets' cemetery. Tearoom and gifts. **Location:** 4½ miles south-southwest of Faversham, off A251 (signed from Badlesmere). **Open:** 23 Apr–30 Sept 2000, Sat, Sun & Bank Hols from 2–5pm. (Last admission 4.30pm). Groups on Tue & Thur by appointment. **Admission:** House & garden: Adult £5.25, OAP £4.75, child (2–16 yrs) £2.50. Garden: Adult £2.75, OAP £2.75, child £1. Cream tea £2.95.

map 5 H5

DODDINGTON PLACE GARDENS

Sittingbourne, Kent ME9 0BB
Tel/Fax: 01795 886101 (Mr and Mrs Richard Oldfield)

10 acres of landscaped gardens in an area of outstanding natural beauty. Woodland garden (spectacular in May/June), an Edwardian rock garden, formal terraces with mixed borders, impressive clipped yew hedges, a new folly, fine trees and lawns. **Location:** 4 miles from A2 and A20. 5 miles from Faversham. 6 miles from Sittingbourne, 9 miles from Canterbury. **Station(s):** Sittingbourne, Faversham. **Open:** May–Aug: Suns 2–6pm Weds and Bank Hol Mons 11–6pm. Groups also on other days by prior arrangement. **Admission:** Adults £3, children 50p, group rate £2.50 coaches by prior arrangement. Restaurant serving morning coffee, lunches, afternoon teas. Gift shop and restaurant open to non garden visitors.

map 5 H5

GAD'S HILL PLACE

Rochester, Kent ME3 7PA
Tel: 01474 822366 (Gad's Hill School Ltd)

Grade 1 listed building, built in 1780. Home of Charles Dickens from 1857 to 1870. **Location:** On A226; 3 miles from Rochester, 4 miles from Gravesend. **Station:** Higham (1½ m) **Open:** 1st Sun in month Apr–Oct and Bank Hol Sun (incl. Easter) 2–5pm. During Rochester Dickens Festivals (June and Dec) 11–4.30pm. At other times by arrangement. Parties welcome. Rooms, including newly restored conservatory, can be hired for weddings/parties (wedding licence). Free coach/car parking. **Admission:** £2.50, child £1.50 parties by arrangement. Proceeds to restoration fund. **Refreshments:** Sundays, cream teas; Dickens Weekends, Dickensian refreshments; other catering by arrangement.

map 5 G4

COBHAM HALL

Cobham, Nr Gravesend, Kent DA12 3BL
Tel: 01474 823371 Fax: 01474 822995/824171

'One of the largest, finest and most important houses in Kent', Cobham Hall is an outstandingly beautiful, red brick mansion in Elizabethan, Jacobean, Carolean and 18th century styles, set in 150 acres of parkland. It yields much of interest to the student of art, architecture and history. The Elizabethan wings were begun in 1584 whilst the central section contains the Gilt Hall, wonderfully decorated by John Webb, Inigo Jones' most celebrated pupil, 1654. Further rooms were decorated by James Wyatt in the 18th century. Cobham Hall, now a girls' school, has been visited by several of the English monarchs from Elizabeth I to Edward VIII, later Duke of Windsor. Charles Dickens used to walk through the grounds from his house in Higham to the Leather Bottle pub in Cobham Village. In 1883, the Hon Ivo Bligh, later the 8th Earl of Darnley, led the victorious English cricket team against Australia bringing home the 'Ashes' to Cobham. Gardens: Landscaped for the 4th Earl by Humphry Repton, the gardens are gradually being restored by the Cobham Hall Heritage Trust. The gardens are particularly delighful in Spring, when they are resplendent with daffodils and a myriad of rare bulbs. **Location:** By A2/M2, between Gravesend & Rochester, 8 miles from Jct 2 on the M25. **Open** 29 Mar; 2, 5, 9, 12, 16, 19, 21, 22 & 23 Apr; 12, 16, 19, 23, 26 & 30 July; 2, 6, 9, 12, 13, 16, 20, 23, 27, 28, 30 Aug; 21 & 22 Oct. All tours guided. Please call to check dates & times. **Admission:** £3.50/£2.50. **Events/Exhibitions:** 2 Apr & 16 July: National Garden Scheme Days. 21–24 Apr & 21–22 Oct Medway Craft Show. Many through year, please phone for details. **Excellent venue for conferences.** **E-mail:** smithk@cobhamhall.com

DOVER CASTLE

Dover, Kent CT16 1HU
Tel: 01304 211067 (English Heritage)

The special highlight of a visit to Dover Castle is the recently opened network of secret wartime underground tunnels which functioned as the nerve centre for the evacuation of Dunkirk. There is even a hospital where visitors can experience the sights, sounds and smells of life underground. However, there's as much to see above ground as there is below. Visitors will unlock over 2,000 years of history when they explore Henry II's Keep and new reconstruction of the Tudor Court preparing for the arrival of Henry VIII in 1539. Also explore the Royal Regiment Museum, Saxon Church and Roman lighthouse. **Location:** On East side of Dover. **Open:** 1 Apr–30 Sept: daily 10–6pm. 1 Oct–31 Oct: daily, 10–5pm, 1 Nov–31 Mar: 10–4pm. (closed 24–25 Dec & 1 Jan) **Admission:** Adult £6.90, concs £5.20, child £3.50, family £17.30 (15% discount for groups of 11 or more).

DOWN HOUSE: HOME OF CHARLES DARWIN

Downe, Kent BR6 7JT
Tel: 01689 859119 (English Heritage)

Explore the home of the 19th century's most influential scientist, Charles Darwin. It was in his study that he wrote the scientific works that first scandalised and then revolutionised the Victorian World in 1859; *On the Origin of Species by means of Natural Selection*. Today his study remains full of the notebooks and journals from his voyage of discovery, that took him most famously to the Galapagos Islands. **Location:** In Luxted Road, Downe off A21 near Biggin Hill. **Open:** 1 Nov–31 Mar: Wed–Sun, 10–4pm. 1 Apr–30 Sept: Wed–Sun, 10–6pm. 1–31 Oct: Wed–Sun, 10–5pm. Open B Hols. Closed 24–28 Dec, 1 Jan–7 Feb 2001. **Admission:** Adults £5.50, concs £4.10, child £2.80 (15% discount for groups of 11 or more). Groups over 11 pre-book please call 01689 859119. All visitors must pre-book at least one day in advance on: 0870 6030145 from 12 July–17 Sept.

FINCHCOCKS

Goudhurst, Kent TN17 1HH
Tel: 01580 211702, Fax: 01580 211007 (Mr & Mrs Richard Burnett)

Georgian manor in beautiful garden, housing a magnificent collection of ninety historical keyboard instruments. Many of these are fully restored and played whenever the house is open in entertaining musical tours. Pictures, prints and exhibition 'The Lost Pleasure Gardens'. **Location:** Off A262 1½ west of Goudhurst, 10 miles from Tunbridge Wells. **Open:** Easter–end of Sept, Suns and BH Mons and Wed and Thurs in Aug: 2–6pm. **Admission:** Adult £6.50, children £4, family ticket £14. **Garden only:** £2. Free parking. **Refreshments:** Teas. **Reserved Visits:** Groups and individuals most days April–October. **Events:** Finchcocks Festival: weekends in September. Craft & Garden Fairs: end of May–October. **Civil Marriages and Receptions:** Available for functions.

GOODNESTONE PARK GARDENS

Goodnestone Park, Canterbury, Kent CT3 1PL
Tel & Fax: 01304 840107

The home of Lord and Lady FitzWalter, Goodnestone Park Gardens covers approximately fourteen acres. The formal area around the house with fine old specimen trees, leads into a small arboretum with an avenue of limes. This adjoins a mature woodland area, with a 1920's rockery and pond. Finally, the walled garden; with some of the walls dating back to the 17th century. This area has been redesigned and planted during the last 30 years, with changes and new plantings continuing all the time. Jane Austen was a frequent visitor, her brother marrying a daughter of the house. **Open:** 27 Mar–27 Oct: weekdays 11–5pm, Sun 12–6pm. Closed Tues & Sat. **Admission:** Adults £3, child (under 12) 30p, OAP's £2.50, Family Ticket (2 Adults & 2 children under 12) £4.50. Disabled in wheelchair £1. Season ticket £12.50. Parties of 20+: (unguided) £2.50, (guided) £3.50.

GREAT COMP GARDEN

Comp Lane, St. Mary's Platt, Borough Green, Sevenoaks, Kent TN15 8QS
Tel: 01732 886 154/882 669 (Great Comp Charitable Trust)

Skilfully designed 7 acre garden of exceptional beauty, surrounding a fine early 17th century manor house. Sweeping lawns, romantic ruins and tranquil woodland walks guide the visitor through areas of different character. The extensive collection of trees, shrubs and perennials offer inspiration and pleasure and include many which are rarely seen. The Italian Garden, completed in 1994 offers shelter to the more tender species of plants including Salvias, Bottlebrushes and Cordelines and is at its most colourful during the summer months. The nursery offers a wide and unusual range of plants, most of which can be seen growing in the garden. **Open:** Apr–Oct, daily, 11–6pm. **Admission:** Charges apply.

GROOMBRIDGE PLACE

Groombridge Place, Groombridge, Nr. Royal Tunbridge Wells, Kent TN3 9QG
Tel: 01892 863999 Fax: 01892 863996 (Blenheim Asset Management Ltd)

Winner of South East England Tourist Board Visitor Attraction of the Year 1997. Surrounded by acres of breathtaking parkland, Groombridge Place has an intriguing history stretching back to medieval times. Flanked by a medieval moat, with a classical 17th century manor as its backdrop, the beautiful formal gardens boast a rich variety of "rooms", together with extensive herbaceous borders. High above the walled gardens and estate vineyard, hidden from view, lies The Enchanted Forest, where magic and fantasy await discovery. Here are secret mysterious gardens to challenge and delight your imagination and reward your mind's ingenuity. **Location:** On B2110, (off A264), 4 miles south west of Tunbridge Wells, 9 miles east of East Grinstead. **Open:** April–October 2000 Daily 9–6pm. **Admission:** Adults £7.50, children/senior citizens £6.50. **Special Events:** London to Brighton Classic Car Run: Sun 4 June. Take to the skies Hot Air Balloons & Kites: Sun 18 June. Wings, Wheels & Steam 2000: Sun 6 Aug. King Henry V & His Archers: Sun 3 Sept. Millennium Kent Hot Air Balloon Classic: Sun 10 Sept. **Internet:** www.groombridgeplace.com

mmap 5
F5

HEVER CASTLE AND GARDENS

Nr Edenbridge, Kent TN8 7NG
Tel: 01732 865224 Fax: 01732 866796 (Hever Castle Ltd)

Hever Castle is a romantic 13th century moated castle, once the childhood home of Anne Boleyn. In 1903, William Waldorf Astor bought the castle and created beautiful gardens. He filled the castle with wonderful furniture, paintings and tapestries which visitors can enjoy today. The spectacular award-winning gardens include topiary, Italian and Tudor gardens, a 110 metre herbaceous border and a lake. A yew maze (open May–Oct) and a unique water maze (open April–Oct) are also in the gardens. The Miniature Model Houses Exhibition must also be seen. **Location:** Hever Castle is 30 miles from London, 3 miles SE of Edenbridge. Exit M25 junctions 5 or 6. Stations: Edenbridge Town 3 miles (taxis available), Hever 1 mile (no taxis). **Open:** Daily 1 Mar–30 Nov. Gardens open 11am. Castle opens 12 noon. Last admission 5pm. Final exit 6pm. Mar & Nov 11–4pm. **Admission:** Castle and garden ticket, Gardens only ticket and family ticket. Group discounts also available (minimum 15). Pre-booked guided tours of the castle available for groups. **Refreshments:** Two licensed self-service restaurants serving hot and cold food throughout the day. Picnics welcome. **Events:** Special events includes May Day Music and Dance: 29–30 April & 1 May, Merrie England Weekend: 27–29 May and Patchwork & Quilting Exhibition: 8–10 Sept. **Conferences:** Exclusive luxury conference facilities available in the Tudor Village. **E-mail:** mail@hevercastle.co.uk **Internet:** www.hever castle.co.uk

map 5
F5

HALL PLACE

Bourne Road, Bexley, DA5 1PQ, Kent
Tel: 01322 526 574 Fax: 01322 522 921
(Bexley Council)

Historic house built in 1540, with additions c.1650. Museum and other exhibitions. Outstanding rose, rock and herb gardens and floral bedding displays. Conservatories, parkland and topiary. **Location:** Near the junction of A2 and A223. **Station(s):** Bexley (half a mile). **Open:** House: Mon–Sat, 10–5pm (4.15pm in winter). British Summer Time only – Suns, 2–6pm. Park & Grounds: Daily during the daylight during the year. **Admission:** Free. **Refreshments:** At café & restaurant.

map 5 F4

IGHTHAM MOTE

Ivy Hatch, Sevenoaks, Kent TN15 ONT
Tel: 01732 810378 Fax: 01732 811029

Ightham Mote, a moated medieval manor house, originates from the 14th century. Grade I Listed building and a Scheduled Monument constructed largely from oak timbers and local ragstone. Bequeathed to the National Trust in 1985 by an American businessman, Charles Henry Robinson, and the focus of the largest conservation project ever undertaken by the Trust on a house of this age and fragility. Visitors are able to visit ' Conservation in Action' Exhibition in the Visitor Reception building. Free Introductory Talks and Garden Tours are often available. Estate walks. Booked special guided tours for groups of 15 or more on open weekday mornings only. **Open:** 2 Apr–30 Oct, daily except Tues & Sat, 11–5.30pm (last entry 4.30pm) incl. Sun & BHols. **Admission:** House & Gardens: Adult £5, child £2.50, family ticket £12.50. **Refreshments:** Tea Pavilion & Shop.

map 5 G5

KNOLE

Sevenoaks, Kent
Tel: 01732 462100 Fax: 01732 465528 (The National Trust)

Tour 13 magnificent state rooms in one of the great treasure houses of England - a 'calendar' house dating from the 15th century with 365 rooms, 52 staircases and 7 courtyards. Find the treasures of kings and queens; exquisite silver furniture, fragile tapestries, rare carpets and other unique furniture including the first 'Knole' settee, state beds and even an early royal loo! Enjoy the extensive deer park throughout the year by courtesy of Lord Sackville. **Location:** located off M25 at south end of Sevenoaks, Kent. **Open:** 1 Apr–29 Oct: Wed–Sat, 12–4pm (last entry 3.30pm). Sun & BH Mon & Fri, 11–5pm (last entry 4pm). **Admission:** Adult £5, child £2.50, family £12.50, group £4.25. Car park £2.50 - members free.

map 5 F5

LADHAM HOUSE

Ladham Road, Goudhurst, Kent
Tel: 01580 211203 Fax: 01580 212596
(Mr and Mrs Alastair Jessel)

Privately owned family house set in 10 acres of rolling lawns, fine specimen trees, rhododendrons, azaleas, camellias, shrubs and magnolias. Arboretum and newly cleared woodland walk; spectacular twin mixed borders. Fountain garden and bog garden. Fine views. Restored old rock garden with waterfall. **Location:** 10 miles east of Tunbridge Wells, 1 mile east of Goudhurst off A262 Goudhurst–Ashford road, signposted from B2079 Marden–Horsmonden road. **Open:** For NGS Sun 30 Apr, 21 May 1–5.30pm and 6 July 6–9pm. At all other times by appt. Coach parties welcomed. Superb marquee site for weddings and private parties. **Admission:** Adults £3 incl. glass of wine, children under 12 50p. Free parking. **Refreshments:** Available on NGS open days and at other times by arrangement.

map 5 G5

LEEDS CASTLE AND GARDENS

Maidstone, Kent ME17 1PL.
Tel: 01622 765400 Fax: 01622 735616 (Leeds Castle Foundation)

Standing majestically on two islands in the middle of a natural lake, Leeds Castle is one of England's oldest and most romantic stately homes. Known as "the loveliest Castle in the world", Leeds was home to six of the medieval Queens of England, and most famous of monarchs, King Henry VIII. It now contains a magnificent collection of furnishings, tapestries and paintings. Leeds Castle is surrounded by 500 acres of rolling parkland and superb gardens which include a Wood Garden with meandering streams and the Culpeper Garden – many people's idea of the perfect English country garden. Opened in May 1999, the terraced, Mediterranean-style Lady Baillie Garden has

intimate suntraps and stunning views over the Great Water. Other attractions at the Castle include a unique Dog Collar Museum, a maze and secret underground grotto, greenhouses, a vineyard and an exotic bird aviary housing more than 100 species of rare and endangered birds. **Events:** An extensive programme of events include Open Air Concerts on 24 June and 1 July, the Festival of English Food & Wine on 13–14 May and the Balloon & Vintage Car Weekend on 9–10 Sept. **Location:** 4 miles east of Maidstone, M20/A20 Junction 8. **Open:** All year (except 24 June, 1 July and 25 Dec 2000). **Admission:** Please phone 01622 765400 for details. **Internet:** www.leeds–castle.co.uk

GREAT MAYTHAM HALL

Rolvenden, Cranbrook, Kent, TN17 4NE.
Tel: 01580 241 346 Fax: 01580 241 038
(Country Houses Association)

Built in 1910 by Sir Edwin Lutyens. **Location:** Half a mile S of Rolvenden Village, on road to Rolvenden Layne. **Station(s):** Headcorn (10 miles), Staplehurst (10 miles). **Open:** May–Sept, Wed & Thurs, 2–5pm. (Last entry 4.30pm). **Admission:** Adults £3.50, children £1.75. Free car park. No dogs admitted. Groups by arrangement. Up to 20 £3.50pp, over 20 £4pp, including tea & biscuits.

LULLINGSTONE CASTLE

Eynsford, Kent DA14 0JA
Tel: 01322 862114 (Guy Hart Dyke, Esq) Fax: 01322 862115

Family portraits, armour, Henry VII gatehouse, church, herb garden. **Location:** In the Darenth valley via Eynsford on A225. **Station:** Eynsford (½ m) **Open:** Castle and grounds May–Aug: Sat, Sun & Bank Hols (2–6pm). Booked parties over 25 persons by arrangement. Telephone for enquiries or bookings. **Admission:** Adults £4, children £1.50, OAPs £3, family £10. Free car parking.

map 5 F4

OWL HOUSE GARDENS

Lamberhurst, Kent TN3 8LY
Tel: 01892 890230 Fax: 01892 891290 (Maureen, Marchioness of Dufferin & Ava)

The Owl House Gardens were created by Maureen Marchioness of Dufferin and Ava over a period of forty five years. The 16th century timber framed wool smugglers cottage was surrounded by a cabbage patch and ploughed fields when the property was purchased in 1952. It now comprises sixteen acres of romantic gardens. In Spring the expansive lawns are filled with daffodils and the trees with apple and cherry blossom, and the woodland gardens a carpet of bluebells and primroses. The water gardens have recently been restored and improved and in May are encircled by Rhododendrons, Azaleas and Camellias. The walled gardens have been replanted to include a herbaceous border to give more colour in the summer along with many roses. After Lady Dufferins death at the age of 91 in 1998 her family have continued to evolve these unique Gardens. They are now available for weddings and also private and corporate entertainment. The new tea rooms provide light lunches and teas. **Location:** 8 miles SE of Tunbridge Wells; 1 mile from Lamberhurst off A21. **Station(s):** Tunbridge Wells or Wadhurst. **Open:** Daily except Christmas Day and New Years Day. **Admission:** Adult £4, children £1. Coach parties welcome by appointment. Dogs welcome on leads. Tea rooms closed Tuesdays & Thursdays from 1 Oct–1 March. Gardens may close some Saturdays during Mar–Sept. If you intend to visit on Saturdays during the period please ring to check if Gardens are open. Picnic area, gifts & souvenirs, plant sales, wheelchair access and free parking.

map 5 G5

MOUNT EPHRAIM GARDENS

Hernhill, Nr Faversham, Kent
Tel: 01227 751496 Fax: 01227 750940 (Mr & Mrs E S Dawes & Mrs M N Dawes)

8 acres of superb gardens set in the heart of family run orchards. The gardens offer an attractive balance of formal and informal with a herbaceous border, a topiary, a Japanese style rock garden, a water garden, rose terraces and a lake. Vineyard and orchard trails to follow. **Location:** 1 mile off M2, A2 or A299. **Open:** Easter–Sept. Mon, Wed, Thurs, Sat & Sun, 11–6pm. Bank Holidays 11–6pm. Groups at all times by arrangement. House open by appointment for groups of approximately 20–25.

THE NEW COLLEGE OF COBHAM

Cobham, Nr Gravesend, Kent DA12 3BX
Tel: 01474 812503 (The New College of Cobham Trust)

Almshouses based on medieval chantry built 1362, part rebuilt 1598. Originally endowed by Sir John de Cobham and descendants. **Location:** 4 miles W of Rochester; 4 miles SE of Gravesend; 1½ miles from junction Shorne-Cobham (A2). In Cobham rear of Church of Mary Magdelene. **Station(s):** Sole St (1 mile). **Open:** Apr–Sept, daily 10–7pm. Oct–Mar, daily 10–4pm. **Refreshments:** Afternoon teas by prior arrangement. Guided tours and historical talk by prior arrangement.

map 5 G4

PENSHURST PLACE AND GARDENS

Penshurst, Nr Tonbridge, Kent TN11 8DG
Tel: 01892 870307 Fax: 01892 870866 (Viscount & Viscountess De L'Isle)

The Ancestral home of the Sidney Family since 1552, with a history going back six and a half centuries, Penshurst Place has been described as "the grandest and most perfectly preserved example of a fortified manor house in all England". See the awe-inspiring medieval Barons Hall with its 60ft high chestnut beamed roof, where Kings, Queens, noblemen, poets and great soldiers have all dined. The Staterooms contain fine collections of tapestries, furniture, portraits, porcelain and armour from the 15th, 16th, 17th and 18th centuries. They chart the history of the family whose forebears include the Elizabethan poet, courtier and soldier, Sir Philip Sidney. On his death in 1586 he was accorded the honour of a state funeral at St Pauls Cathedral, the first commoner to receive such a tribute and not to be repeated until the death of Nelson and later, Sir Winston Churchill. The Gardens, first laid out in the 16th century have remarkably remained virtually unaltered during 400 years. A network of trimmed yew hedges and flower terraces make up the 10 acre patchwork of individual garden rooms designed to give colour all year round. Other features include a toy museum, adventure playground, shop, plant centre, restaurant, 200 acre park with lakes and a nature trail. Penshurst Place offers an exquisite arena for corporate and private entertainment amidst beautiful Kent countryside. **Open:** Weekends from 4 Mar. Daily: 1 Apr–31 Oct. Grounds: 10.30–6pm. House: 12–5pm. Shop & Plant Centre: 10.30–6pm. **Admission:** House & Gardens: Adults £6, OAPs £5.50, child (5–16) £4, family ticket £16. Adult party (20+) £5.30. Gardens only: Adults £4.50, OAPs £4, child (5–16) £3.50, family ticket £13. Garden season ticket £22. House Tours: Adults £6, child £3.20. Garden Tours: Adults £6.50, child £4. House & Garden Tours: Adults £7. **E-mail:** enquiries@ penshurstplace.com **Internet:** www.penshurstplace.com

map 5
F5

PATTYNDENNE MANOR

Goudhurst, Kent TN17 2QU
Tel: 01580 211361 (Mr & Mrs D C Spearing)

One of the great timber houses of England, built of oak trees before Columbus discovered America. Special architectural features include banqueting hall, dragon beams, upturned oak trees, enormous fireplaces, 13c prison, pleasant gardens. Connected with Henry VIII. Lived in as a family house, furnished, lecture tour by owner. Ghosts (occasionally). **Location:** 1 miles S of Goudhurst on W side of B2079. **Open:** Open to groups by prior appointment (Groups 20–55 people). Connoisseur's tour also possible. **Admission:** £4.50 **Refreshments:** Light refreshments available.

RIVERHILL HOUSE GARDENS

Riverhill, Sevenoaks, Kent TN15 ORR
Tel 01732 458802/452557 Fax: 01732 458802 (The Rogers Family)

A lived in family home. Panelled rooms, portraits and interesting memorabilia. Historic hillside garden with sheltered terraces. Rhododendrons, azaleas and bluebells in natural woodland. Rare trees. **Location:** Close to Knole. 2 miles S of Sevenoaks on A225. **Station:** Sevenoaks. **Open:** April, May & June only. Gardens: Every Wed, Sun and all Bank Hol weekends during above period. 12–6pm. The house is also open but only to pre-booked groups of adults, 20 upwards, any day during above period. **Admission:** Gardens: Adults £2.50, child 50p. House & Garden: £3.50. **Refreshments:** Home-made teas on open days, Ploughmans lunches, teas etc by arrangement for party bookings any day in April, May or June. No dogs. Unsuitable for disabled. Specialising year round in country house luncheon and dinner parties for from 12–24 visitors.

map 5
F5

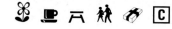SCOTNEY CASTLE GARDEN

Lamberhurst, Tunbridge Wells, Kent TN3 8JN
Tel: 01892 891081 Fax: 01892 890110 (The National Trust)

One of England's most romantic gardens designed in the picturesque style, surrounding the ruins of a 14th century moated castle. Rhododendrons, azaleas, roses, water-lilies and wisteria flower in profusion. Also renowned for its autumn colour. The surrounding estate, open all year, has many country walks. **Location:** located off A21 south of Lamberhurst village. **Open:** 4–26 Mar: weekends only 12–4pm. 1 Apr–29 Oct (Old Castle May–mid Sept): Wed–Fri, 11–6pm. Sat–Sun, 2–6pm. BH Sun & Mon, 12–6pm (closed Good Fri). Last admission 1hr before close. **Admission:** Adult £4.20, child £2.10, family £10.50. Pre-booked groups £3.60.

map 5
G5

 SMALLHYTHE PLACE

Smallhythe, Tenterden, Kent TN30 7NG
Tel/Fax: 01580 762334 (National Trust)

Home of Shakespearean actress Dame Ellen Terry, containing personal and theatrical memories. Also garden and barn theatre. **Location:** OS Ref. TQ893 300. 2 miles south of Tenterden on east side of Rye road B2082. **Open:** 1 Apr–31 Oct 2000, 1.30–6pm. **Admission:** Adult £3.10, child £1.55, family £7.55.

map 5
H6

THE THEATRE ROYAL

102 High Street, Chatham, Kent ME4 4BY
Tel: 01634 831028 (Chatham Theatre Royal Trust Ltd)

The Theatre Royal, built in 1899 to accommodate 3000 people, is Kent's finest surviving Victorian Theatre. No expense was spared in its construction or furnishing and it played host to many top stars of their day. In 1955 the curtain finally fell and the building converted to shops and warehousing. Threatened with demolition in the early 1990s the near derelict building was listed and purchased by a charitable trust who are working to reopen it as a first class venue. This gives the public an ideal opportunity to see restoration work in progress. The theatre is open for guided tours most weekdays and groups are welcome any day or time by appointment. Admission is by donation.

map 5
G4

TONBRIDGE CASTLE

Tonbridge, Kent TN9 1BG
Tel: 01732 770929 Fax: 01732 770449 (Tonbridge & Malling Borough Council)

A fine example of the layout of a Norman Motte and Bailey Castle set in landscaped gardens overlooking the River Medway. The site is clearly interpreted. Tours are available from the Tourist Information Centre. **Location:** In town centre off High Street. **Station(s):** Tonbridge (Main line Charing Cross). **Open:** Apr–Sept Mon–Sat 9–5pm, Sun and BH 10.30–5pm; Oct–Mar, Mon–Fri 9–5pm, Sat 9–4pm, Sun 10.30–4pm. Last tours 1 hr before closing time. Self guided headset tours available from the Tourist Information Centre £1.50 per head with comp. guide book. Gatehouse closed until September 2000. **Refreshments:** Nearby. **Accommodation:** Nearby.

map 5
G5

SQUERRYES COURT

Manor House & Gardens, Westerham, Kent TN16 1SJ
Tel: 01959 562345/563118 Fax: 01959 565949 (Mr J St. A Warde)

Squerryes Court is a beautiful, privately owned Manor House built in 1681 in a parkland setting. The house was acquired by the Warde family in 1731 and is lived in by the same family today. The Old Master paintings, furniture, porcelain and tapestries were collected by the Wardes in the 18th century. The lovely gardens, landscaped in the 18th century, are interesting throughout the year with a lake, spring bulbs, borders, recently restored formal garden, topiary and 18th century dovecote. **Location:** Western outskirts of Westerham signposted from A25. Junctions 5 & 6 M25 10 mins. **Station(s):** Oxted or Sevenoaks. **Open:** 1 Apr–30 Sept. Wed, Sat, Sun & BH Mon. Garden: 12–5.30pm.

House 1.30–5.30pm (last entry 5pm). **Admission:** House and Grounds: Adults £4.20, OAPs £3.80, children (under 14) £2.50. Garden only: Adults £2.50, OAPs £2.20, children (under 14) £1.50. Parties over 20 (any day) by arrangement House and Grounds £3.60. Garden only £2.20. Guided (small extra charge). Pre-booked lunches/teas. Restaurant licence. **Refreshments:** Home-made teas served in Old Library from 2–5pm on open days. **Conferences:** House and Grounds are available for private hire all year e.g. marquee wedding receptions, corporate conferences, luncheons, dinners, promotions, launches, clay pigeon shoots. Dogs on leads in grounds only. Free parking at house.

map 5
F5

⊞ WALMER CASTLE & GARDENS

Kingsdown Road, Walmer, Deal, Kent CT14 7LJ
Tel: 01304 364288 (English Heritage)

Walmer Castle was originally built by Henry VIII to defend the south coast but has since been transformed into an elegant stately home. As the residence of the Lords Warden of the Cinque Ports, Walmer was used by the Duke of Wellington (don't miss the Duke's famous 'Wellington boots') and is still used today by HM the Queen Mother. Many of her rooms are open to view. Recently opened are the Queen Mother's Gardens that commemorate her 95th birthday. The gardens are stunning in summer and the herbaceous borders are exceptional. **Location:** On coast S of Walmer on A258. **Open:** 1 Apr–30 Sept: daily, 10–6pm. 1 Oct–31 Oct: daily, 10–5pm. 1 Nov–31 Mar: Wed–Sun 10–4pm. Closed Jan and Feb and when Lord Warden is in residence. **Admission:** Adults £4.50, concs £3.40, child: £2.30. (15% discount for groups of 11 or more).

PORT LYMPNE WILD ANIMAL PARK, MANSION & GARDENS

Lympne, Hythe CT21 4PD
Tel: 01303 264647 Fax: 01303 264944 (John Aspinall, Esq)

Location: 3 m W of Hythe; 6 m W of Folkestone; 7 m SE of Ashford exit 11 off M20.

YALDING ORGANIC GARDENS

Benover Road, Yalding, Near Maidstone, Kent ME18 6EX
Tel: 01622 814650

These beautiful, much acclaimed gardens, take you on a fascinating tour through garden history. You start in medieval times and journey to the present day through fourteen individual gardens. Beautifully laid out and interpreted, the gardens encourage reflection on mankind's experience of gardening over the centuries. Guided tours may be taken or you can wander at your leisure. Gift shop, plant sales and organic cafe. The gardens are run by HDRA, Europe's largest organic organisation which promotes organic gardening. **Open:** May–Sept: Wed–Sun, 10–5pm. Weekends only in April and October. Also open at Easter and all Bank Holiday Mondays. **Admission:** Adults £3, accompanied children (under 16) Free. Discounts for groups.

❧ CHARTWELL

Westerham TN16 1PS Tel: Information 01732 866368

The family home of Sir Winston Churchill from 1924 to the end of his life. **Open:** House, garden & studio: 1 April to 29 Oct: daily 11–5 (except Mon & Tues, but open BH Mon); last admission 4.30. July & Aug only Tues–Sun 11–5pm. **Admission:** Adults £5.50, child £2.75. Family ticket £13.75.

❧ EMMETTS GARDEN

Ide Hill, Sevenoaks TN14 6AY Tel: 01732 750367 Enquiries 01732 868381

An informal, hillside garden boasts the highest tree top in Kent. **Open:** 1 April to 31 May: Wed–Sun, plus BH Mon & Good Fri 11–5.30. Last admission 4.30. Events: for details of concerts and other events tel. 01892 891001. **Admission:** Adult £3.20, child £1.50. Family £8.

❧ QUEBEC HOUSE

Westerham TN16 1TD Tel: (Regional Office) 01892 890651

General Wolfe spent his early years in this gabled red brick 17th century house. **Open:** 2 April to 31 Oct: Tues & Sun only 2–6. Parties by arrangement; please write to tenant. **Admission:** Adult £2.50, child £1.25. Family ticket £6.25. Groups £2.10.

❧ SISSINGHURST CASTLE GARDEN

Sissinghurst, nr Cranbrook TN17 2AB

Tel: 01580 715330 Infoline: 01580 712850

Open: April to 15 Oct: Tues to Fri 1–6.30; Sat, Sun & Good Fri 10–5.30. Closed Mon, incl. BH. Ticket office & exhibition open at 12 on Tues–Fri. (The garden is less crowded in April, Sept & Oct, also Wed to Fri after 4pm).

❧ SMALLHYTHE PLACE

Smallhythe, Tenterden TN30 7NG Tel: 01580 762334

This early 16th century half-timbered house was home to Shakespearean actress Ellen Terry from 1899–1928. **Open:** 1 April to 31 Oct: daily except Thur & Fri (but open Good Fri) 1.30–6pm, or dusk if earlier. (The Barn Theatre may be closed some days at short notice). **Admission:** Adult £3.10, child £1.55. Family ticket £7.55.

❧ STONEACRE

Otham, Maidstone ME15 8RS Tel: 01622 862871

A half-timbered mainly late 15th century yeoman's house, with great hall and crownpost & newly restored cottage style garden. **Open:** 1 April to 28 Oct: Wed & Sat 2–6. Last admission 5pm. **Admission:** Adult £2.50, child £1.25. Groups £2.10. Family ticket £6.25.

Lancashire

Ribble Valley

Lancashire is well endowed with beauty, charm and even grandeur – and much maligned by its image of dreary industrial mines, mills, ugly towns and smoke blackened countryside. There is farming land with great expanses of cornfields, meadows, pleasant vales and bare moorlands, whilst in the north it shares some of the finest mountain and lake scenery in Britain. Inland, the Forest of Bowland and the Ribble Valley both offer fantastic views.

Southport, a beautiful seaside resort, is famous for its annual international flower show. It is a lively and cosmopolitan town.

The historic county town of Lancaster is tiny when compared to Liverpool and Manchester, but it boasts a long history. The Romans named it after their camp over the River Lune.

Today, its university and cultural life still thrive and the Norman castle, Georgian streets, Lune Aqueduct and a smattering of museums will fascinate the traveller.

BROWSHOLME HALL

Nr Clitheroe, Lancashire BB7 3DE
Tel: 01254 826719 Fax: 01254 826739 (Robert Redmayne Parker)

Built in 1507 and set in a landscaped park, the Ancestral home of the Parker family, with an Elizabethan façade and Regency West Wing recast by Sir Jeffrey Wyatville. Portraits (incl. Devis & Romney), a major collection of furniture, arms, stained glass and other strange antiquities from stone age axes to fragment of a zepellin. **Location:** 5 miles NW of Clitheroe: off B6243; Bashall Eaves–Whitewell signposted. **Open:** 2–4pm Spring Bank Hol Sun and Bank Hol Mon, 1–15 July (except Mondays) and 15 Aug–Aug Bank Hol Mon (except Mondays). **Admission:** Adults £3.50, children £1. Booked parties particularly welcome by appointment. **Internet:** www.browsholme.co.uk

map 11
F7

BLACKBURN CATHEDRAL

Blackburn BB7 3DG
Tel:01254 51491 Fax: 01254 667309

Blackburn Cathedral is set on a historic Saxon site in the town centre. Built as the Parish Church in 1826, subsequent extensions give a uniqueness to both interior and exterior. Features including the lantern tower, central altar with corona above, fine Walker organ, stained glass from medieval period onwards. Recent restoration work gives a new magnificence. **Location:** 9 miles E of M6 / Jct 31, via A59 and A677, city centre. **Open:** Mon–Fri 9–5.30pm. Sat 9.30–4pm. Sun 8–5pm. **Admission:** Donations.

GAWTHORPE HALL

Padiham, Nr Burnley, Lancashire BB12 8UA
Tel: 01282 771004 Fax: 01282 770178 (The National Trust)

An Elizabethan gem in the heart of industrial Lancashire. The Rachel Kay-Shuttleworth textile collections exhibited. Portrait collection loaned by National Portrait Gallery. Events and exhibitions during high season. **Open:** Hall 1 Apr–31 Oct: daily except Mon and Fri, open Good Fri & BH Mon. 1–5pm. Last admission 4.30pm. Garden: all year, daily 10–6pm. Tearoom open as Hall 12.30–5pm. **Admission:** Hall: adults £3, children £1.30, family ticket £8, concessions £1.50 (charges maybe subject to change). Garden: free. Parties by prior arrangement. Free parking 150m. Hall not suitable for baby-packs or pushchairs. **Location:** ¼ mile out of Padiham on A671 to Burnley. Bus services from Burnley (Barracks & Manchester Road Tel: 01282 423125.) Railway station 2m (Rose Grove). Managed by Lancashire County Council. Free to NT members.

map 8
B3

HOGHTON TOWER

Nr Preston PR5 OSH
Tel: 01254 852986 Fax: 01254 852109

Hoghton Tower is the home of the 14th Baronet Sir Bernard de Hoghton. It is one of the most dramatic looking houses in Lancashire. There have been 3 houses on the present site stretching back to 1100 AD whilst the estates have remained in unbroken succession since the Norman conquest. The grounds are sited on the hill commanding extensive views of the sea, the Lakes and north Wales. There are also some walled gardens. Location: M6 Jct 28, 10 mins. 6 miles SE of Preston, E of A675. **Open:** All Bank Hols & July, Aug & Sept, Mon–Thur, 11–4pm & Sun, 1–5pm. **Admission:** Charges apply.

LEIGHTON HALL

Carnforth LA5 9ST
Tel: 01524 734474 Fax: 01524 720357

The Hall's neo–Gothic façade was superimposed on an 18th century house, which in turn, had been built on the ruins of the original medieval house. Leighton Hall is situated in a bowl of parkland, with a panoramic view of the Lakeland fells rising behind it. Connoisseurs of furniture will enjoy the 18th century pieces by Gillow of Lancaster. The main garden has a continuous herbaceous border and rose covered walls. **Location:** 3 miles N of Carnforth. 1½ mile W of A6. **Open:** May–September, Tue–Fri & Sun 2–5pm and BH Mons. Groups 25+ may be pre–booked at any time. **Admission:** Charges apply.

ROSSENDALE MUSEUM

Whitaker Park, Rawtenstall, Rossendale, Lancashire BB4 6RE
Tel: 01706 217777 Fax: 01706 250037 (Rossendale Borough Council)

Former 19th century mill owner's house set in Whitaker Park. Displays include fine and decorative art, natural history, costume and local history. Disabled access to ground floor. Audio guide. **Location:** Off A681, ¼ mile from Rawtenstall centre. **Open:** Mon–Fri: 1–5pm; Sat 10–5pm (Apr–Oct), 10–4pm (Nov–Mar); Sun 12–5pm (Apr–Oct), 12–4pm (Nov–Mar); Bank Hols 1–5pm. Closed Christmas Day, Boxing Day and New Year's Day. **Admission:** Free.

RUFFORD OLD HALL

Rufford, Nr Ormskirk, L40 1SG
Tel: 01704 821254 Fax: 01704 821254 (The National Trust)

Come and enjoy the former ancestral home of the Lords of the Manor of Rufford, one of Lancashire's finest 16th century buildings. There's a glorious garden, kitchen restaurant and shop and within the House, a wide variety of tapestries, arms, armour and paintings. The Great Hall has an intricately carved movable wooden screen and dramatic hammerbeam roof. **Location:** 7 miles N of Ormskirk, in the village of Rufford on E side of A59. **Open:** 1 Apr–1 Nov, Sat–Wed 1–5pm. Also open Thurs 1 Jun, and all Thurs in Aug. Garden: same days 12–5.30pm. **Admission:** House and garden £3.80, children £1.90, family ticket £9.50. Garden only: £2. Gift shop, wheelchair, food, picnic site.

TOWNHEAD HOUSE

Slaidburn, Clitheroe, Lancashire
Tel: 01772 421566

Notice is hereby given that part of Townhead House (unfurnished) a Grade II* Listed Building at Slaidburn, near Clitheroe will be open to the Public for viewing on: 21–24 Apr, 28 Apr–1 May, 26–29 May, 30 June–3 July, 28–31 July, 25–28 Aug, 22–24 Sept 2000. On each occasion the House will be open between the hours of 2–5pm. A £1 charge will be made for entry. For further information, apply to: John Forrester, Chartered Surveyor and Land Agent, First Floor, 19/21 Chapel Brow, Leyland, Preston PR5 2NH Tel: 01772 421566

STONYHURST COLLEGE

Stonyhurst, Clitheroe. Lancashire BB7 9PZ
Tel: 01254 826345 Fax: 01254 826732

The original house (situated close to the picturesque village of Hurst Green in the beautiful Ribble Valley) dates from the late 16th century. Set in extensive grounds which include ornamental gardens. The College is a co-educational Catholic boarding & day school, founded by the Society of Jesus in 1593. **Location:** Just off the B6243 (Longridge–Clitheroe) on the outskirts of Hurst Green. 10 miles from junction 31 on M6. **Station(s):** Preston. **Open:** House weekly 17 July–28 Aug, daily except Fri (incl. Aug Bank Hol Mon) 1–5pm. Grounds and Gardens weekly 1 July–28 Aug, daily except Fri (incl. Aug BHol Mon) 1–5pm. **Admission:** House and Grounds £4.50, child (4–14) £3.50 (under 4 free), senior citizens £3.50. Grounds only £1. **Refreshments:** Refreshments/Gift shop: Limited facilities for disabled. Coach parties & evening groups by prior arrangement. No dogs permitted.

TOWNELEY HALL ART GALLERY & MUSEUMS

Burnley, Lancashire, BB11 3RQ
Tel: 01282 424213 Fax: 01282 436138 (Burnley Borough Council)

The former home of the Towneley family, dating from the 14th century, has been an Art Gallery and Museum since 1903. Collections include oak furniture, 18th and 19th century paintings and decorative arts. Loan exhibitions. There is a Natural History Centre with aquarium and nature trails in the grounds. A separate museum of Local Crafts and Industries is housed in the former brew-house. **Location:** ½ mile SE of Burnley on the Burnley/Todmorden Road (A671). Station(s): Burnley Central (1½ miles). **Open:** All the year Mon–Fri 10–5pm, Sun 12–5pm, closed Sat throughout year and Christmas–New Year. Guided tours available Tuesday, Wednesday and Thursday at 3pm (small charge). There maybe some restrictions due to redevelopment work late 1999 and 2000. **Admission:** Free. **Refreshments:** At cafe on grounds.

TURTON TOWER

Chapeltown Road, Turton, Bolton, Lancashire, BL7 0HG
Tel: 01204 852 203 Fax: 01204 853 759
(Lancashire County Museum Service)

A Lancashire country house dating from medieval times incorporating reconstructed period rooms and a substantial collection of English and Continental domestic wood furniture complemented by an exhibition gallery, tearoom, gift shop, outdoor theatre and other events. Demonstration workshops. Organised guided tours and school tours available. Woodland gardens. **Open:** May–Sept: Sat/Sun 1–5pm, Mon–Thur 10–12pm, 1–5pm. Oct–Mar: Sat–Wed 1–4pm, Apr: Sat–Wed 2–5pm. Nov and Feb: Sun 1–4pm.

Leicestershire

Within its borders, the Midland plain falters and dies and the level stretches of East Anglia merge into gentle, undulating countryside. This is the charm of Leicestershire – simplicity of landscape, a green and pleasant land with few industrial blots to mar its peaceful expanse.

Of the many picturesque and interesting corners of Leicestershire, two are frequently overlooked. The first is linked with a date almost as well known as 1066. In 1485, Richard III was defeated and slain by Henry of Richmond at Bosworth Field. The actual site of the battle is not the little town of Market Bosworth – but between Shenton and Sutton Cheney.

The other is Charnwood Forest. Compared with the mountains of Cumbria, these hills are insignificant, but the eyes delight at the scraggy rocks jutting out abruptly through the fern clad miniature mountains. Picturesque

Town Hall Square, Leicestershire

villages nestle into the countryside, such as Woodhouse Eaves, Newtown Linford and Swithland, with its world famous quarry of blue slate.

Leicester, one of England's cleanest cities, is home to great antiquity. The Old Town Hall is one of Britain's oldest buildings. Here, under the magnificent oak beamed roof, Shakespeare recited his verses to Queen Elizabeth. Traditionally the home of King Lear, with the old Roman walls still standing, the city during Saxon times was the seat of East Mercian Bishops and during the reign of the House of Lancaster, possessed a royal castle. But of Leicester's greatest pride, only the outer walls remain of the abbey where Wolsey came to lay his bones.

If you like to walk, the wolds around Melton Mowbray offer wonderful opportunities. Melton Mowbray is a very pretty market town, offering many interesting little shops and cosy places to eat.

BELVOIR CASTLE

Nr Grantham, Lincolnshire NG32 1PD
Tel: 01476 870262 (Duke of Rutland)

Seat of the Dukes of Rutland since Henry VIII's time and rebuilt by Wyatt in 1816. A castle in the grand style, commanding magnificent views over the Vale of Belvoir. The name dates back to the famous Norman Castle that stood on this site. Many notable art treasures, and interesting military relics. The Statue gardens contain many beautiful 17th century sculptures. Flowers in bloom throughout most of the season. Medieval Jousting Tournaments and other weekend events. Conference and filming facilities. Banquets, school visits, private parties. **Location:** 7 m WSW of Grantham, between A607 (to Melton Mowbray) and A52 (to Nottingham). **Open:** 1 Apr–31 Oct, Tues, Wed, Thurs, Sat, Sun and Bank Holidays 11–5pm. Other times for groups by appointment. **Admission:** Adults £5.25, children £3, seniors £4. Parties 20+: Adults £4, Seniors £3.50, Family Ticket £14.50. School parties £2.50. Privilege Card holders – party rate. Ticket office and catering facilities in the Castle close approximately 30 mins before the Castle. Guide books are on sale at the ticket office or inside the Castle, or by post £3.50 include. post and packing. We regret that dogs are not permitted (except guide dogs). Leaflet sent free on application.

map 8
E6

KAYES GARDEN NURSERY

1700 Melton Road, Rearsby, Leicester, Leicestershire LE7 4YR
Tel: 01664 424578 (Mrs Hazel Kaye)

Set in the lovely rural Wreake Valley, this all-year garden houses an extensive collection of interesting and unusual hardy plants. A long pergola leads the visitor into the garden and forms a backdrop to the double herbaceous borders. Mixed beds beyond are filled with a wide range of herbaceous plants, shrubs and shrub roses in subtle colour coordinated groups. A stream dissects the garden and ends in a large wild life pond alive with a myriad of dragonflies. Aromatic herbs surround a much favoured seat which looks out across one of the garden ponds towards flower beds shaded by old fruit trees, where hellebores, ferns and many other shade loving plants abound. **Open:** Mar–Oct incl. Tues–Sat 10–5pm Sun 10am–noon. Nov–Feb incl. Fri & Sat 10–4.30. Closed Dec 25–Jan 31 incl. **Admission:** Entrance to garden £2. Coach parties welcome by appointment.

map 8 D6

 # THE MANOR HOUSE

Manor Road, Donington-Le-Heath, Coalville, Leicestershire LE67 2FW
Tel: 01530 831259 (Leicestershire Museums, Arts and Records Service)

A fine Medieval Manor House dating back to about 1280. The house has fascinating grounds surrounding the house including period herb gardens and a miniature maze. The adjoining Barn Tea Room serves tempting home-made delights and light lunches. A programme of special events and exhibitions for all ages runs throughout the season. Admission to the Manor House is free. There is plenty of free parking. Disabled access is on the ground floor of the Manor House, the gardens and Barn Tea Room. **Open:** Wed before the Easter Bank Holiday, then daily until 30 Sept inclusive, 11–5pm. Oct–Mar, 11–3pm.

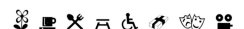

LYDDINGTON BEDE HOUSE

Blue Coat Lane, Lyddington, Uppingham LE15 9LZ
Tel:01572 822438 (English Heritage)

Set among golden–stone cottages, the Bede House was originally a medieval palace of the Bishop of Lincoln. It was later converted into an alms house. **Location:** In Lyddington, 6 miles N of Corby, 1 mile E of A6003. **Open:** Please phone for opening times and admission charges.

 # STANFORD HALL

Lutterworth, Leicestershire, LE17 6DH
Tel: 01788 860250, Fax: 01788 860870 (The Lady Braye)

William and Mary house, fine pictures (including the Stuart Collection), furniture and family costumes. Replica 1898 flying machine, motorcycle museum, rose garden, nature trail. Craft centre (most Sundays). **Location:** M1 exit 18, M1 exit 19 (from/to North only); M6 exit at A14/M1(N) junction. **Open:** Easter–end Sept, Sats, Suns, Bank Hol Mons and Tues following 2.30–5.30pm (last admission 5pm). On Bank Hols and event days open 12 noon (house 2.30pm). **Admission:** House and grounds: Adult £4, child £2. Grounds only: Adult £2.30, child £1. Prices subject to increase on some event days. Parties (min 20): Adult £3.70, child £1.80. Museum: Adult £1, child 35p. **Refreshments:** Home-made teas. Light lunches most Sundays. Suppers, teas, lunches for pre-booked parties any day during season.

map 4 C1

WARTNABY GARDENS

Melton Mowbray, Leicestershire LE14 3HY
Tel: 01664 822296 Fax: 01664 822900 (Lord & Lady King)

This garden has delightful little gardens within it, including a white garden, a sunken garden and a purple border of shrubs and roses, and there are good herbaceous borders, climbers and old-fashioned roses. A large pond has an adjacent bog garden with primulas, ferns, astilbes and several varieties of willow. There is an arboretum with a good collection of trees and shrub roses, and alongside the drive is a beech hedge in a Grecian pattern. Greenhouses, a fruit and vegetable garden with rose arches and cordon fruit. **Location:** OS Ref. SK709 228, 4 miles northwest of Melton Mowbray. From A606 turn west in Ab Kettleby for Wartnaby. **Open:** June, Sundays 11–4pm. Parties by appointment, weekdays (except Wednesdays). Open days: Sun 30 April & Sun 25 June, 11–4pm. Plant sales: 25 June only. **Admission:** Adult £2.50, children free.

Lincolnshire

In this county the fens and the great stretches of southern waterways come into their own, revealing a land where field upon field extends over unending acres of plain, to a distant skyline tinged to deepest red by the setting sun. The Spalding Fens, where the endless acres of red, white, blue and variegated yellow tulips wave majestically under the

The view from Bluestone Heath Road

power of stiff breezes and the mixed holdings of daffodils, narcissi and hyacinths have an intoxicating effect, mingle like an eastern carpet at your feet.

The windmills of England are fast disappearing but many are still to be found in the Lincolnshire fens. A visit to the old town of Boston, with its magnificent parish church and a well rounded climb to the top of the 272 foot high lantern tower, reveals the splendour of the fens and the array of ancient windmills dotting a landscape which is forever divided into long straight fields of varying colours.

During the middle ages profits from the wool industry

enabled the development of towns such as Lincoln, the county town, which still houses many fine, historic buildings. Lincoln sits on a cliff above the River Witham. The whole city seems to rise out of the flat fens, with the towers of Lincoln Cathedral being visible for many miles around. The Romans first settled here in AD48 and the historic flavour of the city still remains.

There are many pretty towns in Lincolnshire: Grantham is the site of a wonderful medieval church and an alternative shrine is to the place where Margaret Thatcher was born! Stamford, in the very southern point, is a beautiful little town, with spires, antique shops, splendid churches and a quarry of little lanes and cobbled alleys.

Lincolnshire is also home to a large coastline. It shares The Wash with Norfolk and houses the popular seaside resort of Skegness, which attracts many holiday-makers in the height of the season.

AUBOURN HALL

Aubourn, Nr. Lincoln, Lincolnshire, LN5 9DZ
Tel: 01522 788 270

Late 16th century house attributed to J. Smythson (Jnr). Important carved staircase and panelled rooms. Lovely garden with deep borders, roses, pond and lawns. **Open:** For charity July–Aug, Wed, 2–5pm. **Admission:** £3, OAPs £2.50. Disabled access to gardens only.

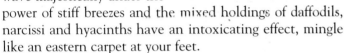

map 9 E5

AYSCOUGHFEE HALL MUSEUM & GARDENS

Churchgate, Spalding, Lincolnshire.
Tel: 01775 725468 Fax: 01775 762715

Ayscoughfee Hall is a late-Medieval wool merchants house set in five acres of walled gardens. The Hall is on the east bank of the River Welland five minutes walk from Spalding town centre. The fully Registered 'Museum of South Holland Life' is housed within the Hall and has galleries on local villages, the history of Spalding, agriculture and horticulture. The Museum also includes a gallery dedicated to Matthew Flinders, the District's most famous son, and many specimens from the important Ashley Maples bird collection are on display. **Open:** Garden cafe open seasonally, Mar–Sept. Museum open: Mon–Sat 10–5pm. Sun & BHols 11–5pm. Exhibitions of local artist's work in the Geest Gallery, change monthly. The Spalding Tourist Information Centre is also housed within Ayscoughfee Hall. Hall closed winter weekends (Nov–Feb).

map 9 6F

BURGHLEY HOUSE

Stamford
Tel: 01780 752451 Fax: 01780 480125 (Burghley House Trustees)

The finest example of later Elizabethan architecture in England, built (1565–1587) by William Cecil, the most able and trusted adviser to Queen Elizabeth I. Eighteen magnificent staterooms are open to visitors. Those painted by Antonio Verrio in the late 17th century form one of the greatest decorated suites in England. Burghley is a sumptuous Treasure House and contains one of the finest private collections of 17th century Italian paintings in the world. **Location:** 1 m SE of Stamford, clearly signposted from the A1 and all approaches. Station(s): Stamford (1 mile) Peterborough (10 miles). **Open:** 1 Apr–3 Oct daily, 11–4.30pm except 4 Sept and during horse trials. **Admission:** Charges apply.

Lincolnshire

DODDINGTON HALL
Doddington, Lincoln LN6 4RU
Tel: 01522 694308 (A Jarvis)

Doddington Hall is a superb Elizabethan Mansion surrounded by walled gardens and courtyards and entered through a Tudor Gate House. It stands today as it was built, and its fascinating contents reflect 400 years of unbroken family occupation with fine china, textiles, furniture and family portraits. The gardens contain magnificent box-edged parterres, sumptuous borders and a wonderful succession of spring flowering bulbs that give colour in all seasons. **Open:** Gardens only: Sundays 2–6pm 20 Feb–30 Apr. House and Gardens: Weds, Suns and Bank Hol Mons 2–6pm May–Sept. Parties and school parties at other times by appointment. **Admission:** Adults: house and gardens £4.30, gardens only £2.15. Children: house and gardens £2.15, gardens only £1.10, family ticket £11.75.

map 8 E5

ELSHAM HALL COUNTRY AND WILDLIFE PARK AND ELSHAM HALL BARN THEATRE
Brigg, North Lincolnshire DN20 OQZ
Tel: 01652 688698 Fax: 01652 688240 (Park Manager: Robert Elwes)

Beautiful lakes and gardens; miniature zoo; giant carp; falconry centre; wild butterfly walkway; adventure playground; mini–beast talks, garden and working craft centre: Granary tearooms and restaurant; animal farm, museum and art gallery; caravan site; ten National Awards. Also excellent new theatre with indoor winter and new outdoor summer programme with various festivals. **Location:** Near Brigg M180 Jct 5, near Humberside Airport. **Station(s):** Barnetby. **Open:** Times and prices on application. Contact Manager. **Refreshments:** Granary Tearooms, ice cream shop, restaurant, banqueting. **Conferences:** Conference facility. Licensed for civil weddings, medieval banquets and corporate entertainments/paintballing.

map 8 E3

LINCOLN CASTLE
Castle Hill, Tel: 01522 511068
(Recreational Services Dept., Lincolnshire County Council)

Built by William the Conqueror in 1608, the Castle with its towers, walls and gatehouses, dominates the bail, alongside Lincoln's great Cathedral. The 1215 Magna Carta, sealed by King John at Runnymeade, is set in an informative exhibition. The administration of law and order is well established here with a history stretching back over 900 years. Visitors may attend Crown Court sittings on most weekdays. Encompassed within the walls is a unique Victorian prison chapel where incarceration can be 'experienced'. Events throughout the year. **Location:** Opposite west front of Lincoln Cathedral in the centre of Historic Lincoln. **Open:** Winter: Mon–Sat 9.30–last admission 3.30pm. British Summer Time: as winter but last admission 4.30pm. Closed Christmas Day, Boxing Day and New Year's Day. **Admission:** Adults £2.50, children 16 & under £1, family ticket £6.50.

MARSTON HALL
Grantham
Tel: 01400 250225 (The Rev Henry Thorold, FSA) or 01400 250167 (Mrs Ballaam)

Tudor manor house with Georgian interiors, held by Thorold family since 14th century. Interesting pictures and furniture. Romantic garden with long walks and avenues, high hedges enclosing herbaceous borders and vegetables. Gothick gazebo and ancient trees. **Open:** Suns, 13 & 20 June, 25 July 1999, 2–6pm and by appointment. **Admission:** House & garden £2.50. **Refreshments:** Home-made cream teas. In aid of local causes. **Location:** 6 miles NW of Grantham.

map 8 E6

NORMANBY HALL
Normanby, Scunthorpe, North Lincolnshire DN15 9HU
Tel: 01724 720588 Fax: 01724 721248 (North Lincolnshire Council)

The restored working Victorian Walled Garden is growing produce for the 'big house', as it would have been done 100 years ago. Set in 300 acres of park, visitors can also see the Regency Mansion, designed by Sir Robert Smirke, which the Garden was built to serve. The rooms of the Hall are displayed in styles depicting the Regency, Victorian and Edwardian eras. Costume from the Museum Service's collections is also exhibited. **Location:** OS Ref. SE886 166. 4 miles North of Scunthorpe off B1430. Tours by arrangement. **Open:** Hall & Farming Museum: 27 Mar–1 Oct, daily, 1–5pm. Park: All year, daily, 9am–dusk. Walled Garden: All year, daily, 11–5pm (4pm winter). **Admission:** Summer Season: Adults £2.90, concs £1.90, family ticket (2 adults, 3 children) £8, half price for North Lincolnshire residents. Winter Season: £2.20 per car.

map 8 3E

BELTON HOUSE
Grantham NG32 2LS
Tel: 01476 566116 Fax: 01476 579071

Admission: £5.30 adults, £2.60 child, £13.20 family, groups £4.30. **Open:** 1 April to 31 Oct: daily except Mon & Tues (but closed Good Fri and open BH Mon) House: 1–5.30pm; Garden & park (incl. adventure playground): 11–5.30pm (last admission 5pm). Park only: all year on foot only from Lion Lodge gates. Note: No access from this entrance to house, garden or adventure playground. Park may occasionally be closed for special events. Bellmount Woods: daily, access from a separate car park. **Events:** send a s.a.e. for details. **Restaurant** Licensed restaurant as house 12–5pm. Open for functions and booked groups throughout year; write (with s.a.e.) for details.

TATTERSHALL CASTLE
Tattershall, Lincoln LN4 4LR
Tel: 01526 342543

Admission: £3 adults, £1.50 child, £7.50 family, but accompanied children free in July & Aug. Groups £2.60. Coach groups must book. **Open:** House: 15 April to 2 July & 15 July to 31 Oct: daily except Thur & Fri; 6 Nov to 19 Dec: Sat & Sun. 3 April to 31 Oct: 10.30–5.30pm; 4 Nov to 17 Dec: 12–4pm. Closed 3–14 July. Ground floor of castle may occasionally be closed for functions or events, tel. to check. **Events:** send s.a.e. for details. **Restaurant**. Picnicking welcome in grounds.

GUNBY HALL
Gunby, Spilsby PE23 5SS
Tel: 01526 342543
Open: 5 April to Sept: Wed 2–6pm.

London

Regents Park and Lake

L ondon is beautiful even when the sky is grey. St Paul's, rising above the drabness of Victorian warehouses and offices, adorns a city where Wren churches tucked away in odd corners and the halls of city companies are exquisite gems of craftsmanship.

Johnson declared that someone who is tired of London must be tired of life. The social and cultural heart of the city has long been the bustling West End, where the contagious lively ambience lasts long into the night in the street cafés and restaurants.

It is also possible to snatch a moment's reflection in one of London's great parks such as Hyde Park, Regents Park or Richmond Park. It is sometimes easy to forget that these verdant glades are just a stone's throw from the bustle of a capital city.

Today more than ever, London whets the appetite for living.

APSLEY HOUSE, THE WELLINGTON MUSEUM

Hyde Park Corner, London, W1V 9FA
Tel: 0171 499 5676 Fax: 0171 493 6576

Apsley House was designed by Robert Adam 1771–78 for Baron Apsley. Known as 'No. 1 London' because of its position just past the toll-gate into the Capital from the West, it was bought by the Duke of Wellington in 1817. The Duke enlarged the house, notably adding on the spectacular 90' long Waterloo Gallery. The lavish gilt and silk interiors, now restored to their former glory, house his magnificent collection: paintings (many from the Spanish Royal Collection and including works by Velazquez, Goya, Rubens, Brueghel, Lawrence, Wilkie, Dutch and Flemish masters), porcelain, silver, sculpture, furniture, medals and memorabilia. **Open:** Tue–Sun 11–5pm. **Admission:** Adults £4.50, concessions £3, both including soundguide, pre-booked groups £2.50/head, children under 18 free.

map 5
J6

BANQUETING HOUSE

Whitehall Palace, London
Tel: 020 7930 4179

From the days of Henry VIII until its destruction by fire in 1698, the Palace of Whitehall was the Sovereign's main London residence. The only part to survive that fire was the Banqueting House. It is also the only building in Whitehall that is open to the public and it offers an oasis of peace and tranquillity amidst the bustle of Westminster. The Banqueting House was built in 1622 from a design by Inigo Jones, the leading architect of the time. The beautiful vaults beneath are known as the Undercroft–a favourite haunt of James I. When Charles I came to the throne, he further enhanced the building's interior by commissioning the Flemish painter, Rubens, to paint the ceiling. In 1635 Ruben's nine canvasses, including two measuring 28x20 feet and two measuring 40x10 feet, were finally put in place. These exquisite paintings are still intact and provide a spectacular sight for today's visitors. Just as the Banqueting House featured in Charles I's early career as King, so it was to feature at the end of his reign. On 30 January 1649 on a high platform outside the north end of the building, Charles I was beheaded, the only British Monarch ever to suffer such a fate. **Location:** London underground–Westminster (District/Circle line) Embankment (District/Circle, Northern & Bakerloo lines), Charing Cross (Northern, Bakerloo & Jubilee lines). BR–Charing Cross. **Open:** Mon–Sat 10–5pm. Closed Suns, 24–26 Dec, 1 Jan, Good Friday & other public holidays & at short notice for Government Functions. **Admission:** Adults £3.60, senior citizens/students £2.80, child under 16 yrs £2.30, under 5s free. From 1 April: Adults £3.80, senior citizens/students £3, children £2.30. **Website:** www.hrp.org.uk

map 5
J6

The Royal Collection © 1999, H. M. Queen Elizabeth II

BUCKINGHAM PALACE

London, SW1A 1AA
Tel: The Visitor Office 020 7839 1377 Fax: 020 7930 9625

Buckingham Palace, Windsor Castle and the Palace of Holyroodhouse are the Official residences of the Sovereign and are used by The Queen as both home and office. The Queen's personal standard flies when Her Majesty is in residence. Furnished with works of art from the Royal Collection, these buildings are used extensively by The Queen for State ceremonies and official entertaining. They are opened to the public as much as these commitments allow. **THE STATE ROOMS:** Are opened daily from 6 Aug–1 Oct 9.30–4.30pm. Tickets can be obtained during Aug–Sept from the Ticket Office in Green Park but are subject to availability. <u>Admission:</u> Adult £10.50, children (under 17) £5, senior citizens (over 60) £8. To pre book your tickets telephone the Visitor Office 0171 839 1377. All tickets booked in advance are

£10.50 and are subject to a small transaction fee. Disabled visitors are very welcome and should telephone in advance for information on access. **THE QUEEN'S GALLERY:** The Queen's Gallery is closed for refurbishment and will reopen in 2002, the Golden Jubilee year. **THE ROYAL MEWS:** Is one of the finest working stables in existence. It offers a unique opportunity for visitors to see a working department of the Royal Household. The Monarch's magnificent Carriages and Coaches including the Gold State Coach are housed here, together with their horses and State liveries. <u>Open:</u> All year Mon, Tues, Wed, Thurs 12–4pm. Last admission 3.30pm. Extra days and hours are added in the summer months.

The Gold State Coach
The Royal Collection © 1999, H. M. Queen Elizabeth II

The Throne Room
The Royal Collection © 1999, H. M. Queen Elizabeth II/Derry Moore

map 5
J6

The White Drawing Room   The Royal Collection © 1999, H. M. Queen Elizabeth II/Derry Moore

The Grand Staircase   The Royal Collection © 1999, H. M. Queen Elizabeth II/Derry Moore

BOSTON MANOR HOUSE

Boston Manor Road, Brentford, Middlesex, TW8 9JX
Tel: 020 8560 5441 Fax: 020 8583 4595 (Hounslow Cultural and Community Services)

Boston Manor House is set in Boston Manor Park, which borders the Grand Union Canal. It is a fine Jacobean Manor built in 1623, extended in 1670 when the Clitherow family bought the house. It was their family home until 1924. Boston Manor is renowned for its fine English Renaissance plaster ceilings in the State Rooms on the first floor. The Drawing Room has a magnificent ceiling divided into panels representing the senses, the elements, peace, plenty, war and peace and faith, hope and charity. These rooms are furnished with items on loan from Gunnersbury Park Museum. The ground floor rooms date from the early 19th century and house part of the local collection of paintings. The ground floor dining room and library are available for letting for private functions, small wedding receptions and seminars. When not in use they may be viewed by visitors. **Station(s):** Underground Boston Manor, Piccadilly Line 200 yards north of House. **Open:** Sat, Sun, Bank Hol Mons and from the first Sat in April to the last Sun in October, 2.30–5pm. Children must be accompanied by an adult. **Admission:** Free. Parking in Boston Manor Road.

map 4
E4

BURGH HOUSE

New End Square, Hampstead, London, NW3 1LT
Tel: 0171 431 0144 Fax: 0171 435 8817 (London Borough of Camden)

A Grade I listed building erected in 1703, in the heart of old Hampstead. Home to many notable professional people before the war. Re-opened in 1979, it houses the Hampstead Museum, an Art Gallery with regularly changing exhibitions and a panelled Music Room popular for weddings, (the house is licensed), wedding receptions, seminars and conferences. Also used for recitals, talks, local society meetings, book fairs and other events. Licensed basement Buttery and award-winning Gertrude Jekyll -inspired terrace garden. Buttery reservations on 0171 431 2516. **Station(s):** Hampstead or Hampstead Heath. **Buses:** 24, 46, 168, 210, 268, C11. **Open:** Wed–Sun 12–5pm. Saturdays by appointment only. Bank Hols 2–5pm. Buttery: 11–5.30pm. Closed Christmas/New Year, Good Friday & Easter Mon. **Admission:** Free to House/Museum. **Refreshments:** The Buttery.

map 5
F4

CARLYLE'S HOUSE

24 Cheyne Row, Chelsea, London SW3 5HL
Tel: 020 7352 7087 (The National Trust)

Part of a terrace in a quiet backwater of Chelsea, this Queen Anne house was the home of writer and historian Thomas Carlyle from 1834 until his death. The house, which contains the original furniture and many books, portraits and relics of his day, was visited by many illustrious Victorians, including Chopin, Dickens, Tennyson and George Eliot. The restored Victorian walled garden also reflects the Carlyle's life here. **Open:** 1 Apr–31 Oct: Wed to Sun (but open Bank Hol Mon) 11–5pm. Last admission 4.30pm. Closed Good Fri. Price: £3.50; child £1.75.

map 5
J7

COLLEGE OF ARMS

Queen Victoria Street, London, EC4V 4BT
Tel: 0171 248 2762 Fax: 248 6448(College of Arms)

Mansion built in 1670s to house English Officers of Arms and panelled Earl Marshal's Court. Official repository of Armorial Bearings and Pedigrees of English, Welsh, Northern Ireland and Commonwealth families, with records covering 500 years. **Location:** S of St. Paul's Cathedral **Station(s):** Blackfriars or St Pauls. **Open:** Earl Marshal's Court: All year (except public holidays and State and special occasions), Mon–Fri, 10–4pm. Record Room: Open for tours (groups of up to 20) by special arrangement in advance with Officer in Waiting. (Fee by negotiation). **Admission:** Free. Officer in Waiting available to take enquiries concerning grants of Arms and genealogy.

map 5
J6

CHELSEA PHYSIC GARDEN

66 Royal Hospital Road, London, SW3 4HS
Tel: 020 7352 5646 (The Chelsea Physic Garden Company)

The second oldest botanic garden in the country, founded in 1673 including notable collection of medicinal plants, comprises 4 acres densely packed with c. 6,500 plants, many rare and unusual. **Location:** Swan Walk, off Royal Hospital Road, Chelsea; near junction of Royal Hospital Road and Chelsea Embankment. **Station(s):** Sloane Square – underground. **Open:** Apr–end Oct, Suns, 2–6pm, Wed 12–5pm. Also 12–5pm in Chelsea Flower Show Week and Chelsea Festival Week. Open at other times for subscribing friends and groups by appointment. **Admission:** Adults £4, children/students/unemployed £2. Garden accessible for disabled and wheelchairs via 66 Royal Hospital Road. Parking in street on Sun and on other days across Albert Bridge in Battersea Park. **Refreshments:** Home-made teas. No dogs (except guide dogs). **Internet:** www.cpgarden.demon.co.uk

 map 5 J7

 # CHISWICK HOUSE

Burlington Lane, Chiswick, London, W4
Tel: 020 8995 0508 (English Heritage)

Lord Burlington's internationally celebrated villa never fails to inspire a sense of awe in all who visit. An exhibition on the ground floor reveals why this villa and its gardens are so important to the history of British architecture and an audio-tour will escort you through the fine interiors, including the lavish Blue Velvet Room. The Italianate grounds are equally impressive and have, at every turn, something to surprise and delight – including statues, temples, obelisks and urns. **Location:** Burlington Lane, W4. **Open:** 1 Nov–31 Mar: Wed–Sun, 10–4pm. 1 Apr–30 Sept: daily 10–6pm. 1–31 Oct: daily, 10–5pm. 1 Nov–31 Mar: Wed–Sun, 10–4pm. Closed 24–26 Dec & 1–18 Jan. **Admission:** Adults £3.30, concs £2.50, child £1.70 (15% discount for groups of 11 or more).

 map 5 H7

THE DE MORGAN FOUNDATION

Old Battersea House, 30 Vicarage Crescent, Battersea, SW11 3LD
Tel/Fax: 0171 371 8385

A substantial part of The De Morgan Foundation collection of ceramics by William De Morgan and Pre Raphaelite paintings and drawings by Evelyn De Morgan (née Pickering), her uncle Roddam Spencer Stanhope, J. M. Strudwick and Cadogan Cowper are displayed on the ground floor of Old Battersea House – a Wren-style building which is privately occupied. **Location:** Battersea, London SW11. **Open:** Admission by appointment only, usually Wednesday mornings. All visits are guided. **Admission:** £2.50 (optional catalogue £1.50). Parties – max. 30 (split into two groups of 15). Apply to The De Morgan Foundation, 56 Bradbourne Street, London, SW6 3TE.

 map 5 J7

 # FENTON HOUSE

Windmill Hill, Hampstead, London NW3 6RT.
Tel: 020 7435 3471 (The National Trust)

A late 17th century house with an outstanding collection of porcelain and early keyboard instruments, most of which are in working order. The delightful walled garden includes fine displays of roses, an orchard and vegetable garden. **Open:** 1 Apr–31 Oct: Sat, Sun & Bank Hol Mon 11–5pm; Wed, Thurs & Fri 2–5pm; last admission 30 minutes before closing. **Admission:** £4.20; family ticket £10.50. **Location:** Visitor's entrance on W side of Hampstead Grove. **E-mail:** tfehse@smtp.ntrust.org.uk

 map 4 E4

GEFFRYE MUSEUM

Kingsland Road, London E2 8EA
Tel: 020 7739 9893 Fax: 020 7729 5647

The Geffrye Museum presents the changing style of English middle class living rooms from 1600 to the present day through a series of period room settings. The displays lead the visitor on a walk through time, from the 17th century with oak furniture and panelling, past the refined elegance of the Georgian rooms and the ornate style of the Victorian parlour, to 20th century art deco and modern style. The museum is set in elegant 18th century almshouses surrounded by attractive gardens including an award winning walled herb garden and a series of period garden rooms. **Open:** Tues–Sat, 10–5pm. Suns & BHol Mons 12pm–5pm. **Admission:** Free. **Exhibitions/Events:** Temporary exhibitions & special activities for all ages throughout the year. **Facilities:** Restaurant, shop & reference library.

 map 5 K6

ELTHAM PALACE
Eltham, London SE9 5QE
Tel: 020 8294 2548 (English Heritage)

A master piece of *Moderne* design, Eltham Palace dramatically shows the glamour and allure of 1930's style. Bathe in the light flooding from a spectacular glazed dome in the Entrance Hall, as it highlights the beautiful blackbean veneer and figurative marquetry. Step into Virginia's magnificent gold-leaf and onyx bathroom, and wander throughout the house discovering the 'ocean liner' style veneered interior with custom designed furniture. A Chinese sliding screen is all that separated the chic '30s Art Deco from the Medieval Great Hall. **Open:** 1 Nov–31 Mar: Wed–Fri & Sun, 10–4pm. 1 April–30 Sept: Wed–Fri & Sun, 10–6pm. 1–31 Oct: Wed–Fri & Sun, 10–5pm. Open BH Mons throughout the year. Closed 24–26 Dec & 1 Jan 2001. **Admission:** House & Garden: Adult £5.90, concession £4.40, child £3. Gardens only: Adult £3.50, concession £2.60, child £1.80.

map 5
F4

GREENWICH – OBSERVATORY

National Maritime Museum, Romney Road, Greenwich, SE10 9NF
Tel: 020 8312 6565 (24hr infomation line) Fax: 020 8312 6632

The Millennium starts here on the Greenwich Meridian. See the Astronomer Royal's apartments. Charming Wren building. Watch the time ball fall at 1 o'clock. Harrison's amazing clocks. The nearby National Maritime Museum's modern new extension opened Easter 1999 with features on exploration, Nelson, trade and empire, passenger liners and the global garden. **Location:** Off A2. River boats from central London. **Station(s):** Maze Hill (BR) Cutty Sark (DLR) **Open:** Daily (except 24–26 Dec) 10–5pm. **Admission:** Observatory: Adult £6, student/OAP £4.80, child free. National Maritime Museum: Adult £7.50, student/OAP £6, child free. **Internet:** www.nmm.ac.uk

map 5
J6

HOGARTH'S HOUSE
Hogarth Lane, Great West Road, Chiswick, London, W4 2QN
Tel: 020 8994 6757 Fax: 020 8583 4595 (Hogarth House Foundation)

50 yards from Hogarth Roundabout stands Hogarth's House, 1749–1764 the country home of artist, William Hogarth. Known as 'his little country box by the Thames'. Here he escaped the noise and dirt of London, in summer for the peace and quiet of the countryside. In 1764 he was buried in St Nicholas Churchyard, Chiswick where David Garrick, the actor, inscribed a tomb with verses. His wife, her cousin and Hogarth's sister lived on in the house. The house became derelict by 1891. In 1904 Hogarth's House opened as a museum commemorating his life and work including his most famous engravings. In 1997, the Tercentenary of his birth, money was raised together with a lottery grant from the National Heritage Memorial Fund which enabled the house to be restored and a small extension built for special exhibitions. **Location:** West of Hogarth Roundabout, A4, Great West Road. **Station(s):** BR Chiswick (from Waterloo) – ½ mile. Turnham Green Underground, District Line – 1 mile. **Open:** Tue–Fri: 1–5pm. (Nov–Mar, 1–4pm). Sat & Sun: 1–6pm. (Nov–Mar, 1–5pm). Closed Mondays (excluding Bank Hols), Good Friday and all of January. **Admission:** Free. Parties by arrangement. Parking as for Chiswick House Grounds – signed, named spaces in Axis Business Centre behind house.

map 5
H7

HAMPTON COURT PALACE

East Molesey, Surrey KT8 9AU
Tel: 020 8781 9500

With its 500 years of royal history Hampton Court Palace has been home to some of Britain's most famous kings and queens and also the setting for many great historical events. When viewed from the west, Hampton Court is still the red brick Tudor palace of Henry VIII, yet from the east it represents the stately Baroque façade designed by Sir Christopher Wren for William III. The sumptuous interiors reflect the different tastes of its royal residents and are furnished with great works of art, many still in the positions for which they were originally intended. Discover the delights that this marvellous palace has to offer – the recently restored Privy Garden, the 16th century Tudor kitchens and the Mantegna's, a series of nine paintings that represent some of the most important Italian Renaissance works of art in the world. Costumed guides give lively and informative tours of the stunning interiors of the King's Apartments, giving a unique insight into the daily lives of the kings and their courtiers. **Location:** Take Exit 12 & A308 from M25 or Exit 10 onto the A307. **Station:** Hampton Court 32 minutes from London Waterloo via Clapham Junction. **Open:** Mid Mar–Mid Oct, Tue–Sun 9.30–6pm, Mon 10.15–6pm. Mid Oct–Mid Mar, Tue–Sun 9.30–4.30pm, Mon 10.15–4.30pm. Closed 24–26 Dec inclusive. **Admission:** Adults £10.50, senior citizens/students: £8, child under 16yrs £7, child under 5yrs free, family ticket (up to 2 adults & 3 children): £31.40. **Events/Exhibitions:** Special events for everyone throughout the year, including storytelling, family trails, special tours and hands-on demonstrations. Take a tour by Lantern light in the Autumn and celebrate Christmas Tudor style with entertainment, dancing and a feast fit for Henry VIII. **Internet:** www.hrp.org.uk

map 4
E4

KENSINGTON PALACE STATE APARTMENTS

Kensington, London
Tel: 020 7937 9561

Situated in the peaceful surroundings of Kensington Gardens, Kensington Palace State Apartments are open to the public. The history of the Palace dates back to 1689 when the newly crowned William III and Mary II commissioned Sir Christopher Wren to convert the then Nottingham House into a Royal Palace. The palace was again altered when George I had the artist William Kent paint the magnificent trompe l'oeil ceilings and staircases which can still be enjoyed at this most intimate of Royal Palaces. Other highlights include the Cupola room where Queen Victoria was baptised and the recently restored King's Gallery. The State Apartments are home to 'Dressing for Royalty' – a stunning presentation of Royal Court and Ceremonial Dress dating from the 18th century, which allows visitors to experience the excitement of preparing for Court – from invitation to presentation. There is also a dazzling selection of 16 dresses owned and worn by HM Queen Elizabeth II. **Location:** On the edge of Hyde Park, just off Kensington High Street. **Open:** Summer; 10–last entry 5pm. Open every day. Winter; 10–last entry 4pm. **Admission:** Adults £8.50, concessions £6.70, child £6.10, family £26.10. **Refreshments:** Available all day in the Orangery. **Events/Exhibitions:** From 1 Oct–31 Mar 2000, a special exhibition 'Diana, Princess of Wales – A Collection of her Dresses', featuring 14 exquisite dresses designed by leading couturiers, which capture her extraordinary style. Highlights include the black dress worn by the Princess when she danced with John Travolta. Price increase by £1 during this period. **Internet:** www.hrp.org.uk

map 5
J6

KEATS HOUSE

Keats Grove, Hampstead, London, NW3 2RR
Tel: 0171 435 2062 Fax: 0171 431 9293 (Corporation of London)

Keats House was built in 1815–1816. The poet John Keats lived here from 1818–1820 and wrote many of his best known poems, including 'Ode to a Nightingale', during this time. The house has letters, books and personal items belonging to the poet and his fiancée Fanny Browne. **Open:** Please telephone for current opening hours. Keats House will be closed for essential repairs from 13 December 1999–23 April 2000. **Location:** S end of Hampstead Heath, near South End Green. **Station(s):** BR – Hampstead Heath. Underground – Belsize Park/Hampstead. Bus: 24, 46, C11, C12, (alight South End Green), 268 (alight Downshire Hill). **Admission:** On application.

map 5 F4

KEW GARDENS, ROYAL BOTANIC GARDENS

Kew, Richmond, Surrey, TW9 3AB
Tel: 0181 940 1171 Fax: 0181 332 5197 (Royal Botanic Gardens)

At any time of the year, Kew's 300 acres offer many special attractions: bluebells in the spring; colourful displays in the summer; beautiful autumnal tints. With some of the largest glasshouses in the world displaying thousands of exotic plants, there is always something to enjoy. The Palm House simulates the multi-layered nature of a tropical rainforest with a canopy of palms and climbers. **Station(s):** Kew Gardens District Line, Kew Bridge British Rail. **Open:** Kew: Daily (except Christmas Day & New Years Day) 9.30am. Tel: 0181 940 1171. Wakehurst Place: Daily (except Christmas Day & New Years Day), 10.00am. Tel: 01444 894066. Closing times for both properties vary according to season; ring for details. **Admission:** Charges apply.

KENWOOD HOUSE

Hampstead, London NW3 7JR
Tel: 020 8348 1286 (English Heritage)

Discover a true hidden gem amongst the multitude of attractions in London and visit Kenwood, a neoclassical house containing one of the finest private collections of paintings ever given to the nation. With important works by many world-famous artists, including Rembrandt, Vermeer, Turner, Reynolds and Gainsborough, a visit to Kenwood is a must for art lovers. In the 1760s the house was re-modelled by Robert Adam and the breathtaking library is one of his finest achievements. Outside, the sloping lawns and ornamental lake form a spectacular backdrop for our programme of hugely popular lakeside concerts with their dramatic firework finales. **Location:** Hampstead Lane NW3. **Open:** 1 Nov–31 Mar: daily, 10–4pm. 1 Apr–30 Sept: daily, 10–6pm. 1 Oct–31 Oct: daily, 10–5pm. 1 Nov–31 Mar: daily, 10–4pm. Open until 8pm on Sun in Aug. Closed 24–25 Dec & 1 Jan. **Admission:** Free.

 map 5 J4

LEIGHTON HOUSE MUSEUM & ART GALLERY

12 Holland Park Road, London, W14 8LZ
Tel: 0171 602 3316 Fax: 0171 371 2467

Leighton House was the first of the magnificent Studio Houses to have been built in the Holland Park area and today is open to the public as a museum of High Victorian Art. The home of the great classical painter and President of the Royal Academy, Frederic Lord Leighton, was designed by George Aitchison. The Arab Hall, is the centrepiece of Leighton House with dazzling gilt mosaics and authentic Isnik tiles. Temporary exhibitions are held throughout the year. **Nearest Underground:** High Street Kensington. **Buses:** 9, 9a, 10, 27, 28, 49. **Open:** All year, daily except Tues, 11–5.30pm. Open spring & summer BHols. **Admission:** Free. Donations welcome. The house may be booked for concerts, lectures, receptions and private functions.

 map 5 J6

LINLEY SAMBOURNE HOUSE

18 Stafford Terrace, London, W8 7BH
Tel: 0171 937 0663 (Ans Machine) Fax: 0171 371 2467 (The Royal Borough of Kensington & Chelsea)

The home of Linley Sambourne (1844–1910), chief political cartoonist at 'Punch' Magazine. A unique survival of a late Victorian town house. The original decoration and furnishings have been preserved together with many of Sambourne's own cartoons and photographs, as well as works by other artists of the period. **Location:** 18 Stafford Terrace. **Station(s):** London Underground – Kensington High St. **Buses:** 9, 10, 27, 28, 49, 52, 70. **Open:** 1 Mar–31 Oct. Wed, 10–4pm (Last entry 3.30pm). Sun, House viewed by guided tours only at 2.15pm, 3.15pm & 4.15pm (Tours last approx 45 mins). Pre-booking not essential. Numbers limited to 12. Groups of 12 or more at other times by prior arrangement. **Admission:** Adults £3.50, children (under 16) £2, concessions £2.50, family ticket £10.

 map 5 J7

MARBLE HILL HOUSE

Richmond Road, Twickenham, London TW1 2NL
Tel: 020 8892 5115 (English Heritage)

Explore this magnificent Palladian Thames-side villa with its 66 acres of parkland. Admire the Great Room with its lavishly gilded decoration and architectural paintings by Pannini. See the important collection of early Georgian paintings and furniture and the Lazenby Bequest Chinoiserie display. The inclusive audio tour, exhibition and film will reveal the history of this beautiful house and its residents. Marble Hill House was originally built for the Countess of Suffolk, mistress to King George II. Today it offers a wonderful riverside backdrop for a programme of spectacular open-air concerts. **Location:** Richmond Road, Twickenham. **Open:** 1 Nov–31 Mar: Wed–Sun, 10–4pm. 1 Apr–30 Sept: daily, 10–6pm. 1–31 Oct, daily, 10–5pm. Closed 24–26 Dec & 1–18 Jan. **Admission:** Adult £3.30, concs £2.50, child £1.70. (15% discount for groups of 11).

 map 4 E4

MUSEUM OF GARDEN HISTORY

Lambeth Palace Road, London SE1 7LB
Tel: 020 7401 8865 Fax: 020 7401 8869 (The Tradescant Trust)

Fascinating permanent exhibition of the history of gardens, collection of ancient tools and re-created 17th century garden displaying flowers and shrubs of the period – seeds of which may be purchased in the Shop. Plus knowledgeable staff, gift shop, café and tombs of the Tradescants and Captain Bligh of the Bounty. Lectures, courses, concerts and art exhibitions held regularly throughout the year. **Location:** Lambeth Palace Road. **Station(s):** Waterloo or Victoria, then 507 Red Arrow bus, alight Lambeth Palace. **Open:** Mon–Fri, 10.30–5pm. Sun 10.30–5pm. Closed Sat. Closed 2nd Sun in Dec to 1st Sun in Mar. **Admission:** Free. Donations appreciated. **Refreshments:** Tea, coffee, light lunches. Parties catered for but prior booking essential. Literature sent on request with SAE. **Internet:** www.museumgardenhistory.org

map 5
J7

PITSHANGER MANOR & GALLERY

Mattock Lane, Ealing, London W5 5EQ
Tel: 0181 567 1227 Fax: 0181 567 0595

Pitshanger Manor and Gallery is set in the beautiful surroundings of Walpole Park, Ealing in West London. The Manor's most illustrious owner was the architect Sir John Soane (1753–1837), 'Architect and Surveyor' to the Bank of England. He rebuilt most of the house to create a Regency villa using highly individual ideas in design and decoration. The house is continually being restored and refurbished to its early 19th century style. A Victorian wing houses a large collection of Martinware pottery. Pitshanger Manor and Gallery is open to the public as a historic house and cultural centre. Adjacent to the manor is a newly refurbished contemporary art gallery, programming a wide range of changing exhibitions. Please phone for current exhibition programme. **Open:** Tues–Sat 10–5pm. Closed Sun and Mon. Also closed Christmas, Easter and New Year. **Admission:** FREE Parties by arrangement.

map 5
H6

MUSEUM OF FULHAM PALACE

Bishops Avenue, Fulham, London SW6 6EA
Tel: 0171 736 3233 (Museum & Tours) 0181 748 3020 x4930 (Functions)
(L.B. of Hammersmith & Fulham & Fulham Palace Trust)

A Tudor courtyard, a herb garden and a history going back 5000 years. You can find all these at Fulham Palace, once the home of the Bishop of London. The building is a charming mixture of periods (Tudor with Georgian additions and Victorian chapel). Three rooms available for functions. The museum in part of the Palace tells the story of this ancient site; the displays include paintings, archaeology, garden history and a fascinating scale model of the building. The gardens, famous in the 17th century under Bishop Compton who introduced plants from Virginia, now contain over 40 specimen trees and a knot garden of herbs. **Open:** Gardens open daylight hours. Museum open Mar–Oct: Wed–Sun 2–5pm; Nov–Feb: Thurs–Sun 1–4pm.

OSTERLEY PARK

Jersey Road, Isleworth, Middlesex, London TW7 4RB
Tel: 020 8568 7714 (The National Trust)
Recorded Visitor Information 01494 755566

Although originally a Tudor house, Osterley was transformed into what we see today by Robert Adam in 1761. The spectacular interiors contain one of Britain's most complete examples of his work and include exceptional plasterwork, carpets and furniture. The house also has an interesting kitchen. The house is set in extensive park and farmlands. **Open:** House: 1 Apr–29 Oct; Wed to Sun 1–4.30pm but open Bank Hol Mon. Closed Good Fri. Last admission 4.30. Park and Pleasure grounds open all year 9–7.30pm or sunset if earlier. **Admission:** £4.20; family ticket £10.50. Tearoom and shop available. **E-mail:** www.tosgen@smtp.ntrust.org.uk

map 4
E4

ROYAL SOCIETY OF ARTS

8 John Adam Street, London WC2N 6EZ
Tel: 020 7930 5115 Fax: 020 7321 0271

The house of the Royal Society of Arts was designed especially for the society by Robert Adam in the early 1770's. One of the few remaining buildings from the original Adelphi development its Georgian façade conceals many unexpected delights of both traditional and contemporary architecture. Designed as one of London's earliest debating chambers, the Great Room is one of the most spectacular theatres in the city. The Benjamin Franklin Room is spacious and elegant, featuring an antique chandelier and two Adam fireplaces. The Vaults were originally designed as river front warehouses. Now fully restored they offer a striking contrast to the splendour of the rooms above. All rooms maybe hired for meetings, receptions and weddings.

map 5
J6

THE MUSEUM OF THE ORDER OF ST. JOHN AT ST. JOHN'S GATE

St. John's Lane, Clerkenwell, London, EC1M 4DA
Tel: 020 7253 6644 Fax: 020 7336 0587

Take a tour round the Priory of the Knights Hospitallers with its Tudor Gate house, 16C Church and Norman Crypt. Warrior monks set out from here to fight for the faith and tend the sick in hospitals on the great medieval pilgrim routes. Illuminated manuscripts, silver, canon and armour are among the Order's treasures on display in the Museum. In more recent time, the St. John Ambulance first aid movement was founded here and spread to over 45 countries around the globe. A new interactive gallery tells its story. **Station:** 5 mins walk from Farringdon Underground. **Open:** Museum: Mon–Fri, 10–5pm. Sat, 10–4pm. Tours of the buildings: 11am & 2.30pm, Tue Fri & Sat. **Admission:** Free to Museum, donations of £4 (£3 OAP) requested for tours. Charity Reg No: 1077265. **Website:** www.sja.org.uk

map 5
J6

SIR JOHN SOANE'S MUSEUM

13 Lincoln's Inn Fields, London WC2A 3BP
Tel: 0171 430 0175 Fax: 0171 831 3957
(Trustees of Sir John Soane's Museum)

Built by the leading architect Sir John Soane, RA, in 1812–1813, as his private residence. Contains his collection of antiquities and works of art. **Stations(s):** London Underground – Holborn. **Open:** Tues–Sat, 10–5pm. Lecture tours, Sat 2.30pm, Max. 22 people. Tickets £3, on a first come, first served basis from 2pm, no groups. Groups welcome at other times by prior arrangement (Tel: 0171 405 2107). Late evening opening on first Tues of each month, 6–9pm. Also library and architectural drawings collection by appointment. Closed Bank Hols. **Admission:** Free but donations welcome. **Events/Exhibitions:** Changing exhibitions of drawings in the 'Soane Gallery'. **Internet:** www.soane.org

map 5
J6

TOWER OF LONDON

Tower Hill, London
Tel: 0171 709 0765

Begun by William the Conqueror in 1078 to help secure London, the chief city of his new realm, the Tower of London has served as a royal residence, fortress, mint, armoury and more infamously a prison and place of execution. Since the seventeenth century, the Crown Jewels have been on public display at various locations in the Tower; today visitors can see them in all their glory in the magnificent new Jewel House. **Location:** Underground to Tower Hill or buses 15, 25, 42, 78, 100, D1. Included on all major sightseeing tours. **Open:** 9–5pm, Mar– Sept. 9–4pm, Oct–Feb. The Tower opens at 10 am on Sundays throughout the year. **Admission:** Charges apply. Groups: Call 0181 781 9540 for special features and rates. Further information: Call 0171 709 0765.

SOMERSET HOUSE WITH THE COURTAULD GALLERY & THE GILBERT COLLECTION

Strand, London WC2R 0RN
Courtauld Gallery Tel: 020 7848 2526 Gilbert Collection Tel: 020 7240 4080 Somerset House Tel: 020 7845 4600

Somerset House, Sir William Chambers' masterpiece, is open to the public for the first time. Situated between Covent Garden and the South Bank, it will take its place as one of Europe's great centres for art and culture, where visitors can also enjoy long-hidden classical interiors and architectural vistas. A new museum for the Gilbert Collection joins the Courtauld Gallery on the site. The Courtyard is now a venue for performing arts and events. Opens May 2000. **The Gilbert Collection** is London's newest museum of the decorative arts. Given to the nation by Sir Arthur Gilbert, the magnificent collections of European silver, gold snuffboxes and Italian mosaics are pre-eminent in the world. Opens May 2000. **The Courtauld Gallery**, part of the Courtauld Institute of Art, has one of the most important collections

of Impressionist paintings in the world. It re-opened in 1998 restored to its full splendour, with more of the Renaissance to 20th century collections on display. Now Open. **Location:** Entrances Strand or Victoria Embankment. **Open:** Somerset House daily except 25 Dec. Courtauld and Gilbert: Mon–Sat except bank holiday Mons 10–6pm, Sun and bank holiday Mons 12–6pm, closed 1 Jan and 24–26 Dec. **Admission:** Somerset House free except special exhibitions and events; Courtauld or Gilbert: Adult £4 each (£7 joint ticket), OAP £3 each (£5 joint ticket), pre-booked groups £3 each (£6 joint ticket), disabled and helper £2 each person (£4 each person joint ticket). Under 18 and UK full-time students free. Mon 10–2pm everyone free.

map 5
J6

SPENCER HOUSE

27 St James's Place, London, SW1A 1NR
Tel: 020 7514 1964 Fax: 020 7409 2952

Spencer House, built 1756–1766, for the first Earl Spencer, an ancestor of Diana, Princess of Wales (1961–97) is London's finest surviving 18th century private palace. The construction of the House involved some of the greatest artists and craftsmen of the day, including the Palladian architect John Vardy and James 'Athenian' Stuart. The House has now regained the full splendour of its 18th century appearance after a ten year programme of restoration undertaken by RIT Capital Partners plc, under the Chairmanship of Lord Rothschild. Spencer House is now partly used as offices and as a place where entertainments can be held in the historic setting of the state rooms, where the remarkable restoration is complemented by a magnificent collection of paintings and furniture. The House is open to the public on Sun and is available for private and corporate entertaining during the rest of the week. **Station(s):** Green Park. **Open:** Every Sun, except during Jan & Aug, 10.30am–5.30pm. Tours last approx. 1 hour (Last tour 4.45pm). Tickets available at door from 10.30 on day. Enquiry Line: 020 7499 8620. **Admission:** Adults £6, concessions £5 (students/Friends of the Royal Academy, Tate and V&A, all with cards/children 10–16; under 10 not admitted). **Internet:** www.spencerhouse.co.uk

map 5
J6

STRAWBERRY HILL HOUSE
Waldegrave Road, Strawberry Hill, Twickenham, Middlesex.
Tel: 020 8240 4114 Fax: 020 8255 6174 (St. Mary's College):

Horace Walpole converted a modest house into a fantasy villa. It is widely regarded as the first substantial building of the Gothic Revival, and as such internationally known and admired. A century later Lady Waldegrave added a magnificent wing to Walpole's original structure. Guided tours take approximately 75 minutes and it is worth coming to see this unique house. These magnificent rooms can also be hired for corporate events, wedding receptions and conferences both day and residential. **Open:** Advance group bookings by appointment only are taken throughout the year and the House is open to the general public on Suns from Easter to Mid October, between 2pm and 3.30pm. This information was correct at the time of going to print, please phone 0181 240 4224 for up to the minute information. **Admission:** The ticket price is £4.75 concessions for OAP's, a maximum of 20 people per tour, the house is not suitable for disabled or children under 14 years of age. For information regarding advance group bookings or functions, please call the conference office on 0181 240 4114/0181 240 4311 or 0181 240 4044.

map 4
E4

SYON PARK

Syon House & Gardens, Syon Park, Brentford, Middlesex TW8 8JF
Tel: 0181 560 0883 Fax: 0181 568 0936

Sir John Betjeman described Syon House as "The Grand Architectural Walk". Syon House is the London home of the Duke of Northumberland, whose family have lived here since the late 16th century. The present house is Tudor in origin, having been built by Lord Protector Somerset on the site of a medieval Abbey. It was in the Long Gallery that Lady Jane Grey was offered the Crown and at Syon where some of Charles 1st's children were imprisoned during the Civil War. The first Duke of Northumberland commissioned Robert Adam in 1761 to remodel the interior into the magnificent suite of State rooms on view today. The magnificent 200 acres of parkland beside the Thames, was landscaped by Capability Brown. Within it there are 30 acres of gardens which incorporate 'The Great Conservatory', (shown above) designed by Charles Fowler in the 1820s, the Rose Garden and over 200 species of rare trees. Syon House and the Great Conservatory can be hired for civil wedding ceremonies, receptions and corporate/private functions. All wedding receptions are held in the Great Conservatory but marquees can be erected for larger corporate/private functions for example, balls or fashion shows, for up to 1000 guests. Please call the Estate Office on the above number for more details. **Open:** House 11–5pm, Wed, Thurs, Suns and Bank Hols, 15 Mar–29 Oct. Gardens open daily 10–5.30pm or dusk except 25–26 Dec. Party rates, guide service if required.

map 4
E4

SOUTHSIDE HOUSE
3 Woodhayes Road, Wimbledon, SW19 4RJ
Tel: 0181 946 7643 (The Pennington Mellor Munthe Charity Trust)

Built by Robert Pennington in 1665 after the death of his first born in the Plague. The family befriended or were related to many distinguished names through the centuries; amongst others Ann Boleyn's descendants, Nelson and the Hamiltons, the infamous "Hell-fire Duke of Wharton" and Natalie, the widowed Queen of Serbia. Family portraits and possessions of theirs are on show. Bedroom prepared for Prince of Wales in 1750 and gifts to John Pennington–family 'Scarlet Pimpernel'. In 1907 the heiress, Hilda Pennington Mellor married Axel Munthe the Swedish doctor and philanthropist. After the Second World War Hilda and her sons Viking and Malcolm restored the house. Haunted by his vision of a bombed out Europe, Malcolm who had lived extraordinary adventures during the war, determined to make a cultural ark of the family inheritance, and with minimal resources but fine aesthetical sense made good the war damage. Guided tours give reality and excitement to the old family histories. **Location:** On S. Side of Wimbledon Common (B281) Opposite Crooked Billet Inn. **Open:** 2 Jan–24 Jun, Wed, Sat, Sun & Bank Holiday Mons. Guided tours on the hour 2–5pm (last tour 5pm). Also open for private parties by arrangement with the Administrator from 1 Dec–24 Jun. **Admissions:** Adults £5, (child accompanied by adult £2).

map 5 F4

THE WALLACE COLLECTION
Hertford House, Manchester Square, London
Tel: 020 7563 9500 Fax: 0171 224 2155

The Wallace Collection is a national museum, displaying superb works of art against the opulent backdrop of a late eighteenth century town house. In the richly decorated rooms are fine Old Masters, one of the greatest collections of French 18th century pictures, porcelain and furniture in the world and a remarkable armoury. In June 2000 the museum is celebrating its centenary with the opening of four new galleries, educational facilities and a Sculpture Garden Restaurant, to offer visitors greater access to and enjoyment of the outstanding Collection. **Location:** Manchester Square (behind Selfridges). **Station:** Bond Street. **Open:** Mon–Fri, 10–5pm. Sun, 2–5pm. Free lectures on the collection, daily. Galleries accessible to wheelchair users, who are advised to phone before visits (ext.23). Wheelchairs available on request. **Admission:** Free (donations). **Internet:** www.wallace–collection.com

map 5 J6

THE TRAVELLERS CLUB
106 Pall Mall, London, SW1Y 5EP
Tel: 020 7930 8688 Fax: 020 7930 2019

The Club House was designed by 34 yr. old Charles Barry. His design broke architectural precedent, the Pall Mall façade being derived from the Palazzo Pandolfino in Florence, causing considerable comment in its day. Barry went on to design the Houses of Parliament. **Location:** 106 Pall Mall. **Station(s):** London Underground: Piccadilly Circus, Charing Cross. **Open:** By prior appointment only, Mon–Fri, 10–12noon. Closed Bank Hols, August and Christmas. **Admission:** Adults £8 by prior appointment. **Refreshments:** Included.

map 5 J6

2 WILLOW ROAD
2 Willow Road, Hampstead, London NW3 1TH
Tel: 020 7435 6166 (The National Trust)

The former home of Erno Goldfinger, designed and built by him in 1939. One of Britain's most important examples of modernist architecture, the house is filled with furniture also designed by Goldfinger. The interesting art collection includes work by Henry Moore and Max Ernst. **Open:** 30 Mar–28 Oct: Thurs, Fri & Sat 12–5pm. Last admission 4pm. Guided tours every 45 minutes from 12.15 until 4pm. **Admission:** £4.20. No parking at house. Limited on-street parking. **E-mail:** twlgen@smtp.ntrust.org.uk

map 4 E4

Greater Manchester

Halli'th'Wood

Manchester houses a buzzing cultural scene with museums such as Salford Museum and Art Gallery, the Manchester Museum and the Jewish Museum all offering a fascinating insight into the heritage and tradition of this area.

Classical concerts, ballet, theatre, ethnic festivals and clubs famous for test cricketers and other sportsmen are all part of its legend. The rivalry between Manchester City Football Club and the internationally renowned Manchester United has continued throughout the centuries.

At the start of this new millennium, historic edifices are being spruced up, architects are transforming the old mills, new buildings are springing up and the canals have been cleared and are attracting the colourful barges and small boats again.

In 1830, the railway to Liverpool was opened and carried the first passenger trains in the world. Years later, the Victorian Gothic architecture still dominates the city.

At night, Manchester is particularly convivial with Canal Street offering a plethora of friendly pubs in which to sample a beverage. It has become an increasingly popular destination for weekend breaks as it is home to a number of vibrant nightclubs such as Cream and the Paradise Factory which attract youth from across the continents ready to dance the night away to the European beats.

For those who do not frequent museums, pubs and nightclubs, Manchester's array of shops and boutiques are certain to add appeal. The Old Trafford Centre is a huge mall with a range of shops to please all ages and with the infamous prison Strangeways nearby, Manchester is not a place to shoplift!

Salford Museum & Art Gallery

HEATON HALL

Heaton Park, Prestwich, Manchester, Lancashire, M25 2SW
Tel: 0161 773 1231/234 1456 Fax: 0161 236 7369
(Manchester City Art Galleries)

Set in 650 acres of rolling parkland, Heaton Hall is a magnificent Grade I listed building described as 'the finest house of its period in Lancashire and one of the finest in the country'. Designed by James Wyatt in 1772, the building's beautifully restored 18th century interiors are furnished with fine paintings and furniture of the period. A superb collection of Wyatt furniture from Heveningham Hall in Suffolk is also a highlight. The unique circular Pompeiian Room, elegant Music Room and annual art exhibition are also not to be missed. **Open:** Easter–Oct. **Admission:** free. Please call for details.

map 8 B4

MANCHESTER CATHEDRAL

Manchester M3 1SX
Tel: 0161 833 2220 Fax:0161 839 6226

In addition to regular worship and daily offices, there are frequent professional concerts, day schools, organ recitals, guided tours and brass-rubbing. The Cathedral contains a wealth of beautiful carvings and has the widest medieval nave in Britain. **Location:** Manchester city centre. **Open:** Daily. **Admission:** Donations.

SMITHILLS HALL

Off Smithills Dean Road, Bolton, BL1 7ND
Tel: 01204 841265 (Bolton Museum, Art Gallery & Aquarium)

14th century manor house. Highlights include the Great Hall with its open timber roof, and Tudor linenfold panelling in the withdrawing room. **Open:** Apr–Sept, Tues–Sat 11–5pm, Sun 2–5pm. Closed: Mondays except Bank Holidays. Oct–March, closed to the general public. Open to pre-booked party tours. **Admission:** Adults £2, concs £1, groups £1.50.

HALL I'TH' WOOD

GREEN WAY, OFF CROMPTON WAY, BOLTON BL1 8UA TEL: 01204 301159
Late Medieval Merchants House which became the home of Samuel Crompton in 1779 where he invented the Spinning Mule. **Open:** Apr–Sept, Tues–Sat 11–5pm, Sun 2–5pm. Closed: Mondays except Bank Holidays. Oct–March, closed to the general public. Open to pre-booked party tours. **Admission:** Adults £2, concs £1, groups £1.50.

Norfolk

Norfolk is one of England's most peaceful counties. This flat county boasts some of the most glorious coastline which has a unique network of inland waterways, tranquil heaths, woodland and hedgerows.

Norfolk remains unspoilt by man or time. This reflects in the county town, Norwich, which to this day is one of the best preserved towns in England. In the 9th century, Norwich was fortified by the Saxons and the medieval street plan remains.

The Norfolk Broads National Park attracts birdwatchers and boaters from around the country. The Broads to the east, best seen on a boat, contain many slow moving shallow rivers which meander through the countryside, until they join the coast around the popular holiday resort of Great Yarmouth.

Kings Lynn

FAIRHAVEN WOODLAND & WATER GARDEN

South Walsham, Nr Norwich, Norfolk NR13 6EA
Tel & Fax: 01603 270449 (G.E. Debbage)

Delightful natural garden with private inner Broad. 950 year old oak tree. Spring/early Summer - shrubs, spring bulbs, skunk cabbage, primroses, wood anemones and bluebells. Largest collection of naturalised Candelabra Primulas in Britain. Azaleas and Rhododendrons. 92 species of woodland, garden and water birds. Summer - Hydrangeas, shrubs, foxgloves, wildflowers, butterflies, dragonflies. Autumn - Rich shades of russet, red and gold. Winter walks - Bright frosty mornings, colourful berries, reflections in the Broad. **Location:** 9 miles NE of Norwich on the B1140. **Open:** Daily 10–9pm, Wed & Thurs May to end of August. Boat trips Easter–end Oct. **Refreshments:** Tea room, gift shop, plant sales & children's nature trail. **Admission:** Adults £3, Senior Citizens./Conc. £2.70, children £1. Under 5s free. Wildlife Sanctuary £1. Season Tickets: Family £25, Single £10.

HOUGHTON HALL

Kings Lynn
Tel: 01485 528569 (The Marquess of Cholmondeley)

The Home of the Marquess of Cholmondeley, Houghton Hall was built in the 18th century for Sir Robert Walpole by Colen Campbell and Thomas Ripley, with interior decoration by William Kent and is regarded as one of the finest examples of Palladian architecture in England. Houghton was later inherited by the 1st Marquess of Cholmondeley through his grandmother, Sir Robert's daughter. Situated in beautiful parkland, the house contains magnificent furniture, pictures and china. Pleasure grounds. A private collection of 20,000 model soldiers and militaria. Newly restored walled garden. **Location:** 13 miles E of King's Lynn; 10 miles W of Fakenham off A148. **Open:** Thurs, Sun and Bank Hol. Mon from 23 April–24 September. Park and grounds, soldier museum, walled garden, tearoom and shop: 1–5.30pm. House: 2–5.30pm. Last admission 5pm. **Admission:** Adult £6, child £3. Excluding House Adult £3.50, child £2.

HOLKHAM HALL

Wells-next-the-Sea, Norfolk NR23 1AB
Tel: 01328 710227, Fax: 01328 711707 (The Earl of Leicester)

One of Britain's most majestic stately homes, situated in a 3,000 acre deer park, on the beautiful north Norfolk coast. This celebrated Palladian style mansion, based on designs by William Kent, was built between 1734 and 1764 by Thomas Coke, 1st Earl of Leicester. The magnificent alabaster entrance hall rises the full height of the building and in the richly and splendidly decorated Staterooms are Greek and Roman statues, brought back by the 1st Earl from his Grand Tour of Europe, fine furniture by William Kent and paintings by Rubens, Van Dyck, Claude, Poussin and Gainsborough. In addition to the Hall there is a Bygones Museum in the original stable block, History of Farming Exhibition in the porters' lodge and Holkham Nursery Gardens in the 18th century walled kitchen garden. **Location:** 2 miles W of Wells-next-the-Sea. S off the A149. **Open:** Suns–Thurs (incl.) 28 May–28 Sept 1–5pm. Plus Easter, May, Spring & Summer Bank Hols. Sun & Mon 11.30–5pm. (last admission 4.45pm). **Admission:** Hall: Adults £4, children £2. Bygones: Adults £4, children £2. Combined ticket: Adults £6, children £3. Reduction on parties of 20 or more. Private tours of the Hall by arrangement. **Refreshments**: Restaurant. Gift shop and pottery.

map 9
H6

EUSTON HALL

(Nr.Thetford), Suffolk
Tel: 01842 766366 (The Duke and Duchess of Grafton)

Euston Hall – Home of the Duke and Duchess of Grafton. The 18th century country house contains a famous collection of paintings including works by Stubbs, Van Dyck, Lely and Kneller. The pleasure grounds were laid out by John Evelyn and William Kent, lakes by Capability Brown. 17th century parish church in Wren style. Watermill, craft shop, picnic area. **Location:** A1088; 3 miles S Thetford. **Open:** June 1–Sept 28 Thurs only 2.30–5pm, also Sun June 25 and Sept 3, 2.30–5pm. **Admission:** Adults £3, children 50p, OAPs £2.50. Parties of 12 or more £2.50 per head. **Refreshments:** Teas in Old Kitchen.

map 5
H1

HOVETON HALL GARDENS

Hoveton Hall, Norwich, Norfolk.
Tel: 01603 782798 Fax. 01603 784564

Hoveton Hall Gardens – 15 acres of rhododendron and azalea filled woodland, laced with streams leading to a lake. Daffodils galore in Spring. Formal walled herbaceous and vegetable gardens. Morning coffee, light lunches and delicious home-made teas. **Open:** Easter Sun to mid Sept, Wed, Fri, Sun and Bank Hol Mons 11–5.30pm. Coaches welcome by appointment.

map 9
J6

SANDRINGHAM HOUSE, MUSEUM & GROUNDS

Estate Office, Sandringham, Norfolk PE35 6EN
Tel: 01553 772675 (Her Majesty The Queen)

Sandringham is the charming country retreat of Her Majesty The Queen hidden in the heart of sixty acres of beautiful wooded grounds. All the main ground floor rooms used by The Royal Family, full of their treasured ornaments, portraits and furniture, are open to the public. More Royal possessions dating back more than a century are displayed in the Museum housed in the old stable and coach houses. Glades, dells, lakes and lawns are surrounded by magnificent trees and bordered by colourful shrubs and flowers. **Location:** 8 m NE of King's Lynn (off A148). **Open:** House: from 1 April–20 July 1999 daily 11–4.45pm (Grounds and Museum 24 July), reopens 5 August–3 October, daily 10.30 (Museum 11am) to 5pm. Grounds and Museums open weekends in October. **Admission:** Charges apply.

map 9
G6

MANNINGTON HALL

Saxthorpe, Norfolk
Tel: 01263 584175, Fax: 01263 761214 (Lord and Lady Walpole)

15th century moated house and Saxon church ruins set in attractive gardens. Outstanding rose gardens. Extensive walks and trails around the estate. **Location:** 2 miles N of Saxthorpe, near B1149; 18 miles NW of Norwich; 9 miles from coast. **Open:** Walks daily all year; Garden May–Sept Sun 12–5pm. Also June–Aug Wed, Thurs and Fri 11–5. **Admission:** Adults £3, children (accompanied children under 16) free OAPs/students £2.50. House open by prior appointment only. **Refreshments:** Coffee, salad lunches and home-made teas.

map 9
J6

WOLTERTON PARK

Erpingham, Norfolk
Tel: 01263 584175, Fax: 01263 761214 (Lord and Lady Walpole)

Extensive historic park with lake and 18th century Mansion house. **Location:** Near Erpingham, signposted from A140 Norwich to Cromer Road. **Station(s):** Gunton. **Open:** Park open all year, daily 9–5pm or dusk if earlier. 2000 Hall: Fridays from April 28, 2–5pm (last entry 4pm). For Sundays and events see local press. **Admission:** Park £2 per car. Hall: £5. **Refreshments:** Pub at drive gate. **Events/Exhibitions:** Yes. **Accommodation:** Limited. **Conferences:** Yes.

map 9
J6

❧ BLICKLING HALL, GARDEN & PARK

Blickling, Norwich NR11 6NF Tel: 01263 738030 Fax: 01263 731660

Open: House: 8 April to 29 Oct: daily except Mon & Tues (but open BH Mons) 1–4.30pm. Garden: 8 April to 29 Oct as house. Aug Tues–Sun; 2 Nov to 17 Dec: Thur–Sun 11–4pm. Park and woods: daily dawn to dusk. **Events:** tel. or send s.a.e. for details. **Admission:** £6.50. Groups £5.20. Groups must book with s.a.e. to Property Manager. Garden only: £3.70. Free access to South Front, shop, restaurant and plant centre. Coarse fishing in lake; permits from Warden, tel. 01263 734181.

❧ FELBRIGG HALL, GARDEN & PARK

Felbrigg, Roughton, Norwich NR11 8PR Tel: 01263 837444

Open: House: 1 April to 31 Oct: daily except Thur & Fri 1–5pm; BH

Mons & BH Suns 11–5pm. Garden: as house 11–5.30pm. Woodland, lakeside walks and parkland: daily (closed Christmas Day) dawn to dusk. **Events:** send s.a.e. for details or contact Events Box Office (tel. 01263 838297). **Admission:** House & garden: Adult £5.70, child £2.80, family £14.20. Groups (except Sun) £4.70; book with s.a.e. to Property Manager. Garden only £2.20. **Restaurant.**

❧ OXBURGH HALL, GARDEN & ESTATE

Oxborough, King's Lynn PE33 9PS Tel: 01366 328258 Fax: 01366 328066

Open: House: 1 April to 31 Oct: daily except Thur & Fri 1–5pm; BH Mon 11–5pm. Garden: 4–26 March: Sat & Sun; 1 April to 31 July, 1 Sept to 29 Oct: daily except Thur & Fri; Aug daily. 6 to 21 April to 31 Oct 11–5.30pm. **Events:** send s.a.e. for full details. **Admission:** House, garden & estate: £5.30, booked groups £4.20; book with s.a.e. to Administrator. Garden & estate only: £2.60.

Northamptonshire

Northamptonshire is a gently undulating county where church spires and grand estates nestle amongst rolling hills rising to a lofty height of seven hundred feet above sea level in places. Its beautiful landscape comprises waterways, ancient woodlands and rivers. Visitors can enjoy a hearty pub lunch after a morning of guided walks or cycling through the meandering valleys.

Oundle

The impressive town of Northampton is the setting for Holy Sepulchre, one of only four surviving round Norman churches in England. A fine display of works of art by Henry Moore and Graham Sutherland may be seen at St Matthew's church in Kingsley.

Cottesbrooke Hall

As you walk around, it is easy to appreciate the spacious, ordered layout of this town, created after Northampton was destroyed by a huge fire in the seventeenth century.

Travelling further east, St James' Church in Thrapston is often frequented by historians as the family coat of arms of Sir John Washington, relative of the first American president, is depicted.

Those wishing to explore the county's national treasures must visit the many historic properties in the area. Althorp, the home of the Spencer family, Holdenby House with its magnificent gardens and Rockingham Castle, built by William the Conqueror are all fine examples of Northamptonshire's rich heritage.

BOUGHTON HOUSE

Boughton House, Kettering, Northamptonshire.
Tel: 01536 515731 Fax: 01536 417255 E-mail: llt@boughtonhouse.org.uk (Duke of Buccleuch)

Northamptonshire home of the Duke of Buccleuch and his Montagu ancestors since 1528. A 500 year old Tudor Monastic building, gradually enlarged until French style addition of 1695 led the sobriquet "The English Versailles". Outstanding collection of fine arts from the world renowned Buccleuch Collection including 16th century carpets, 17th, 18th century French and English furniture, tapestries, porcelain and painted ceilings and notable works of art including works by El Greco, Murillo, Caracci and over 40 Van Dyck paintings. There is an incomparable Armoury and Ceremonial Coach. Extensive parkland with historic avenues of trees, woodlands, lakes and riverside walks. There is a Plant Centre in attractive old walled garden and tearooms in the attractively refurbished Stable Block adjacent to the House, which together with the Adventure

Woodland Play area and Gift Shop are open weekends and daily throughout August. **Internet:** Award winning site gives full information, a 'virtual' tour of House and details of our group visits and educational facilities (Heritage Education Trust, Sandford Award Winner 1988, 1993 and 1998) www.boughtonhouse.org.uk. **Open: House and Park:** Daily (including Fri) 1 Aug–1 Sept. Park from 1pm, House 2pm, last entry 4.30pm. Staterooms strictly by pre-booked appointment, telephone 01536 515731 for details. **Park:** Daily (except Fri) 1 May–1 Sept, 1–5pm Plant Centre, Adventure Play area, tearoom open daily in Aug and weekends during park opening. Educational groups throughout the year, by prior appointment. **Admission:** House and Park: Adults £6, OAP/child £5. Park only: Adults £1.50, OAP/child £1. Wheelchair visitors free.

map 4
D1

 COTTESBROOKE HALL AND GARDENS

Nr Northampton, Northants NN6 8PF
Tel: 01604 505808 Fax: 01604 505619 (Captain & Mrs John Macdonald-Buchanan)

Architecturally magnificent Queen Anne house commenced in 1702. Renowned picture collection, particularly of sporting and equestrian subjects. Fine English and Continental furniture and porcelain. Main vista aligned on celebrated 7th century Saxon church at Brixworth. House reputed to be the pattern for Jane Austen's 'Mansfield Park'. Celebrated gardens of great variety including herbaceous borders, water and wild gardens, fine old cedars and specimen trees. The magnolia, cherry and acer collections are notable, as also are the several fine vistas across the park. **Location:** 10 miles N of Northampton (A14–A1/M1 Link Road), near Creaton on A5199, near Brixworth on A508. **Open:** Easter to end Sept. **House and Gardens:** Thurs and Bank Hol Mon afternoons, in addition first Sun of each month May–Sept 2–5.30pm. Last admission 5pm. **Gardens Only:** Tues, Wed and Fri afternoons 2–5.30pm. Last admission 5pm. **Admission: House and Gardens:** Adults £4. **Gardens Only:** £2.50; children half price. **Refreshments:** Tearoom open 2.30–5pm. Gardens, but not house, suitable for disabled. Car park. Plants for sale. No dogs. **PRIVATE BOOKINGS:** Available for group visits to the house and gardens, or gardens only, on any other day during the season, except weekends, by prior appointment. **Lunches/refreshments** Available for groups by prior arrangement. Please telephone for information. **Functions and Banquets:** Evening and lunchtime functions, details upon request.

map 4
D1

ALTHORP

The history of Althorp is the history of a family. The Spencers have lived and died here for nearly five centuries and twenty generations.

Since the death of Diana, Princess of Wales, Althorp has become known across the world, but before that tragic event, connoisseurs had heard of this most classic of English stately homes on account of the magnificence of its contents and the beauty of its setting.

Next to the mansion at Althorp lies the honey-coloured stable block, a truly breathtaking building which at one time accommodated up to 100 horses and 40 grooms. The stables are now the setting for the Exhibition celebrating the life of Diana, Princess of Wales and honouring her memory after her death. The freshness and modernity of the facilities are a unique tribute to a woman who captivated the world in her all-too-brief existence.

All visitors are invited to view the House, Exhibition and Grounds as well as the Island in the Round Oval where Diana, Princess of Wales is laid to rest.

Althorp is clearly signed from junction 16 of the M1. The Park is located 5 miles west of Northampton off the A428.

Open daily, 1st July to 30th August 2000, 9am to 5pm. Last admission at 4pm.
At the time of booking visitors will be asked to state a preference for a morning or an afternoon visit.
Advance booking is strongly recommended.

Admission

	Pre-booked	Paying at the Gate *(subject to availability)*
Adults	£10.00	£11.00
Senior Citizens	£7.50	£8.50
Children (5–17)	£5.00	£5.00
Children under 5 free		

All the profits from visitor activity at Althorp are donated to the **Diana, Princess of Wales Memorial Fund,** subject to a minimum annual donation of £50,000.

Group visits by arrangement only.

Please contact our dedicated booking line (24 hour service)

Tel: +44 (0)870 167 9000

Althorp, Northampton NN7 4HQ Tel: +44 (0)1604 770107 Fax: +44 (0)1604 770042

www.althorp.com

CASTLE ASHBY

Northampton NN7 1LQ
Tel: 01604 696696 Fax: 01604 696516

The lands at Castle Ashby were given to the Compton family in 1512 by Henry VIII. In 1574 Queen Elizabeth 1 gave William, Lord Compton, permission to demolish the derelict 13th century castle and build the present House on this site. The original plan of the House was in the shape of an 'E' in honour of Queen Elizabeth and in 1625 the courtyard was enclosed by a screen designed by Inigo Jones. Castle Ashby is still the home of the Compton family, the 7th Marquess of Northampton being the 27th generation. The Castle and the Compton family have a fascinating history; related by marriage to most of the aristocratic families in this country. These liaisons are still remembered in the names given to each of the bedrooms. Castle Ashby stands at the heart of a 10,000 acre working estate, surrounded by 200 acres of beautiful parkland. It is not open to the public and is the only Stately Home truely available on an exclusive basis with 26 exquisite ensuite bedrooms. Despite its seclusion and tranquillity, Ashby is capable of hosting the most sophisticated event, whilst clients are cared for by experienced professionals. Our aim is to provide discreet service with a touch of informality to allow guests to experience the enjoyment of using the house as if it were their own. Located 55 miles from London the Capability Brown landscape contains many superb walks and lakes for fishing. Horse-riding, clay shooting and carriage driving are also accessible. The vast gardens incorporate a Triumphal Arch, Orangery, Italian Gardens and Camellia Houses.

map 4
D2

CANONS ASHBY HOUSE

Canons Ashby, Daventry NN11 3SD
Tel: 01327 860044

Open: House: 11 Apr–1 Nov: Sat–Wed incl. Bank Holiday Mons (closed Good Fri) 1–5.30pm or dusk if earlier. Last admission 5pm. Park, gardens & church: same days as house 12–5.30pm, access through garden. **Events:** details from Property Manager (s.a.e. please). **Admission:** £3.60, children £1.80, family ticket £8.90. Discount for parties; contact Property Manager. Donation box for church. Parking 200m; coaches and parties should pre-book in writing with the Property Manager.

COTON MANOR GARDEN

Nr Guilsborough, Northamptonshire NN6 8RQ
Tel: 01604 740219 Fax: 01604 740838 (Mr & Mrs Ian Pasley-Tyler)

Traditional old English garden set in unspoilt countryside, with yew and holly hedges, extensive herbaceous borders, rose garden, water garden, herb garden, woodland garden, famous bluebell wood (early May) and recently established wild flower meadow. **Location:** 10 miles N of Northampton and 11 miles SE of Rugby. Follow tourist signs on A428 and A5199 (formerly A50). **Station(s):** Northampton, Long Buckby. **Open:** 1 Apr–30 Sept daily Wed–Sun and Bank Hol Mons 12–5.30pm. **Admission:** Adults £3.50, senior citizens £3, children £2. **Refreshments:** Restaurant serving home-made lunches and teas. **Events/Exhibitions:** Unusual plants propagated from the garden for sale during season.

`map 4 D1`

HADDONSTONE SHOW GARDEN

The Forge House, Church Lane, East Haddon, Northampton, NN6 8DB
Tel: 01604 770711 Fax: 01604 770027 (Haddonstone Limited)

See Haddonstone's classic garden ornaments in the beautiful setting of the walled manor gardens – including urns, troughs, fountains, statuary, bird baths, sundials, obelisks, columns and balustrading. Featured on BBC Gardeners' World, the garden is on different levels with shrub roses, ground cover plants, conifers, clematis and climbers. In 1998 the new Jubilee Garden opened, complete with temple, pavilion and Gothic Grotto. **Location:** 7 miles NW of Northampton off A428. **Open:** Mon–Fri 9–5.30pm closed weekends, Bank Hols and Christmas period. **Admission:** Free. Groups must apply in writing for permission to visit.

`map 4 D1`

KELMARSH HALL

Kelmarsh, Northampton, Northants NN6 9LU
Tel & Fax: 01604 686543 (Kelmarsh Hall Estate Preservation Trust)

1732 Palladian house by Gibbs. Chinese Room with wallpaper from 1740s. Entrance lodges by Wyatt. Interesting gardens with lake and woodland walks. Herd of British White Cattle. **Location:** 12 miles N of Northampton; 5 miles S of Market Harborough on A508/A14 (J2). **Open:** Suns and Bank Hols between 12 April and 31 August 2.30-5pm. **Admission:** Adults £3.50, OAPs £3, children/garden only £2. Group bookings by arrangement. **Refreshments:** Home-made teas. Private functions, wedding receptions.

`map 4 D1`

HOLDENBY HOUSE GARDENS & FALCONRY CENTRE

Holdenby, Northampton, Northants NN6 8DJ
Tel: 01604 770074 Fax: 01604 770962 (Mr & Mrs James Lowther. Administrator: Sarah Maughan)

Just across the fields from Althorp lies Holdenby, a house whose royal connections go back over 400 years. Built by Sir Christopher Hatton to entertain Elizabeth I, this once largest house in England became the palace of James I and the prison of his son Charles I. Today the house is a family home and a splendid backdrop to a beautiful garden and Falconry Centre. Wander through Rosemary Verey's Elizabethan Garden and Rupert Golby's Fragrant Walk. Evoke the feeling of the 17th century by visiting the 17th century Farmstead. Then sit back to watch our magnificent birds of prey soar over this pastoral scene of so much history. Shop, Teas, Childrens Attractions. **Location:** 7 miles NW of Northampton, off A428 & A5199. M1 exit 15a or 18. **Station:** Northampton. **Open:** April–end Sept. Gardens and Falconry: Sundays 1–5pm. Bank Holiday Suns and Mons 1–6pm. Daily (except Saturday) in July and August, 1–5pm. House open: 24 Apr, 29 May, 28 Aug, 1–6pm or by appointment. **Admission:** Gardens & Falconry Centre: Adults £3, Child £1.75, OAP £2.50. Bank Holiday Events: Adults £4, Child £2, OAP £3.50. Bank Holiday Events with House Open: Adults £5, child £3, OAP £4.50. Private Tours - ring for prices. **Events:** Victorian: Easter, Falconry and Plant Fair: May, Medieval: August. Please ring for details.

`map 4 D1`

LAMPORT HALL & GARDENS

Lamport, Northamptonshire, NN6 9HD
Tel: 01604 686 272 Fax: 01604 686 224 (Lamport Hall Preservation Trust Ltd)

Built for the Isham family. The South West front is a rare example of John Webb, pupil of Inigo Jones and was built in 1655 with wings added in 1732 and 1740. The fine rooms include the High Room of 1655 with magnificent plasterwork, the 18th century Library with books from the 16th century, the early 19th century Cabinet Room containing rare Venetian cabinets, the exquisitely panelled Oak Room and the Victorian Dining Room where refreshments are served. The Hall contains a wealth of outstanding books, paintings, furniture and china. Set in spacious wooded parkland with tranquil gardens, including a remarkable rock garden where the 10th Baronet introduced the first garden gnomes to England and an Italian garden and box bower. **Location:** 8 miles north of Northampton on A508. **Open:** Easter–1 Oct, Sun & Bank Hol Mons, 2.15–5.15pm. 21–22 Oct, 2.15–5.15pm. Last tour/admission 4.00pm. Aug, Mon–Sat for one tour only at 3.30pm. **Group Visits:** Welcome at anytime by prior arrangement. **Admission:** Adults £4, senior citizens £3.50, children £2. **Refreshments:** Home-made teas. **Events:** Please telephone for a free brochure. **Conferences:** Available for conferences/corporate hospitality.

map 4 D1

THE PREBENDAL MANOR HOUSE

Nassington, Nr. Peterborough, Northamptonshire, PE8 0QG
Tel: 01780 782 575 (Mrs J. Baile)

Grade 1 listed and dating from the early 13th century the Prebendal Manor is the oldest house in Northamptonshire, steeped in history and still retaining many architectural features. Unique to the region are the 14th century re-created medieval gardens which include a rose arbour, herber, flowery mead, and medieval fish ponds. Also included are the 15th century dovecote and tithe barn museum. Home-made teas. Lunches to order. **Location:** 6 miles N of Oundle, 7 miles S of Stamford, 8 miles W of Peterborough. **Open & Admission:** Please telephone for details of opening times and admission charges.

SULGRAVE MANOR

Manor Road, Sulgrave, Banbury, Oxon OX17 2SD
Tel: 01295 760205 (Sulgrage Manor Board)

The home of George Washington's Ancestors. A delightful 16th Century Manor House presenting a typical walthy man's home and gardens in Elizabethan times. "A perfect illustration of how a house should be shown to the public" – Nigel Nicholson, Great Houses of Britain. **Location:** Sulgrave Village is off Banbury/Northampton Road (B4525); 5 m from Banbury junction of M40, 12 m from Northampton junction of M1; 7 m NE of Banbury. **Open:** Weekdays open every day except Weds. 1 Apr–31 Oct 2–5.30pm. Bank Hols and the month of August: 10.30–1pm and 2–5.30pm. 27–31 Dec: 10.30–1pm and 2–4.30pm. Please note: Last admissions are one hour before closing times. Closed: Christmas Day, Boxing Day and the whole of January. **Admission:** Charges apply.

SOUTHWICK HALL

(Christopher Capron)
Southwick, Peterborough, Northants PE8 5BL
Tel: 01832 274064 (W.J. Richardson)Manager

A family home since 1300, retaining medieval building dating from 1300, with Tudor rebuilding and 18th century additions. Exhibitions: Victorian and Edwardian life; collections of agricultural and carpentry tools, named bricks and local archeological finds and fossils. **Location:** 3 miles N of Oundle; 4 miles E of Bulwick. **Open:** Bank Holidays (Sunday & Monday) Apr 23–24 & 30, May 1 & 28–29, Aug 27–28 and Weds May–Aug, 2–5pm. Parties at other times (Easter–Aug) by arrangement with the Manager. **Admission:** Adults £3.50, OAPs £3, children £2 (all inclusive). **Refreshments:** Teas available.

map 8 E7

Northumberland

Northumberland is steeped in the past; with its boundaries on two sides – the River Tweed and the Cheviot Hills separating it from Scotland – it was the scene of many fierce battles as armies came along the original route of today's A1.

Parts of Hadrian's Wall, built by the Roman emperor of that name, still straddle the wild, undulating moorland. Romans would have difficulty in recognising some of the terrain today, modern man having planted large pine forests and built an artificial lake.

Northumberland has glorious scenery – The National Park is famous for its unspoilt rugged beauty and its stark, dramatic coastline is spectacular. Viking invasions drove the monks from Holy Island (Lindisfarne). The Farne Islands are now a nature reserve for seals and seabirds. Villages with fascinating names cluster round ancient crosses, runic inscriptions still visible; water mills and old smithies are reminders of past trades.

Lindisfarne Castle

BAMBURGH CASTLE

Bamburgh ME69 7DF
Tel: 01669 620314

Bamburgh Castle is the home of Lady Armstrong and her family. The earliest reference to Bamburgh shows the craggy citadel to have been a royal centre by AD 547. The public rooms contain many exhibits, including the collections of armoury on loan from HM Tower of London. Porcelain, china , jade, furniture from many periods, oils, water – colours and a host of interesting items are all contained within one of the most important buildings of Britain's national heritage. **Location:** 42m N of Newcastle–upon–Tyne. 6m E of Belford by B1342 from A1 at Belford. **Open:** April–October daily 11–5pm. Last entry 4.30pm. **Admission:** Adult £4, child £1.50, OAP £3. Groups: Adult £3, child £1, OAPs £2. Groups up to 16 – min. payment £30.

CHIPCHASE CASTLE & GARDENS

Wark on Tyne, Hexham, Northumberland
Tel: 01434 230203, Fax: 01434 230740 (Mrs P J Torday)

An imposing 17th and 18th century Castle with 14th century Pele Tower set in formal and informal gardens. A chapel stands in the park. One walled garden is now a nursery specialising in unusual perennials. **Location:** 2 miles S of Wark on the Barrasford Road **Open:** Castle: 1-28 June, daily 2-5pm. Tours by arrangement at other times. Gardens and Nursery: Easter-31 July, Thurs to Sun and Bank Hols 10-5. **Admission:** Castle £3, gardens £1.50, nursery free.

BELSAY HALL, CASTLE & GARDENS

Belsay, Northumberland NE20 0DX
Tel: 01661 881636 (English Heritage)

Explore a ruined castle, manor house and neoclassical hall all set amidst 30 acres of magnificent landscaped grounds – a great and varied day out for all who visit. The beautiful honey-coloured stone from which the Belsay Hall is built came from its own quarries which have since become the unusual setting for one of the series of spectacular gardens, deservedly listed Grade I in the Register of Gardens. Enjoy the mix of formal and informal; rhododendrons, magnolias, ornate terraces and even a winter garden are among Belsay's special features. **Location:** In Belsay, 14m NW of Newcastle on A696. **Open:** 1 Apr–30 Sept: daily, 10am-6pm. 1 Oct–31 Oct: daily, 10–5pm. 1 Nov–31 Mar: daily 10–4pm. (Closed 24–26 Dec). Open 1 Jan 2000. **Admission:** Adults £3.90, concs £2.90, child £2 (15% discount for groups of 11 or more).

SEATON DELAVAL HALL

Seaton Sluice, Whitley Bay, Northumberland NE26 4QR
Tel: 0191 237 0786/1493 (The Lord Hastings)

The home of Lord and Lady Hastings near Seaton Sluice is the last and most sensational mansion designed by Sir John Vanbrugh, builder of Blenheim Palace and Castle Howard. It was erected between 1718 and 1728 and comprises a high turreted block flanked by arcaded wings which form a vast forecourt. The centre block was gutted by fire in 1822 but was partially restored in 1862 and again in 1959–62 and 1999. The east wing contains immense stables. The coach house and ice house are nearby. Behind the house lie beautiful varied gardens with a spectacular parterre and a unique Norman Church. **Open:** May–August Bank Holidays, June–30 Sept Wednesday and Sunday. **Admission:** Adult £3, concessions £2.50, children £1. **Refreshments:** Tearoom. Free car park.

WARKWORTH CASTLE

Warkworth, Morpeth, Northumberland NE66 0UJ
Tel: 01665 711423 (English Heritage)

The great towering keep of this 15th century castle, once the home of the mighty Percy family, dominates the town and River Coquet. **Location:** 7 miles south of Alnwick on A1068. **Open:** 1 Apr–30 Sept, 10–6pm. 1–31 Oct, 10–5pm. 1 Nov–31 Mar, 10–4pm. Closed Christmas eve, Christmas day, Boxing day and New Years day. **Admission:** Adult £2.40, concessions £1.80, children £1.20. 15% discount on groups of 11 or more.

CHILLINGHAM CASTLE & GARDENS

Chillingham, Northumberland NE66 5NJ
Tel: 01668 215359 Fax: 01668 215463 (Sir Humprey Wakefield Bt)

This medieval family fortress remains home since the 1200's to the same family including the Earls Grey and Tankerville. Complete with alarming dungeon and even a torture chamber, the castle displays many remarkable restoration techniques alongside antique furnishings, paintings, tapestries, arms and armour. Wrapped in the nation's history it occupied a strategic position as fortress during Northumberland's bloody border feuds, often besieged and at many times enjoying the patronage of royal visitors. The Italian ornamental garden, landscaped avenues and gate lodges were created by Sir Jeffrey Wyatville, fresh from his triumphs at Windsor Castle. The castle grounds command breathtaking views of the surrounding countryside. As you walk to the lake you will see, according to the season, drifts of snowdrops, daffodils or bluebells and an astonishing display of rhododendrons. **Location:** 12 miles N of Alnwick, signposted from A1 and A697. **Open:** Good Fri–Easter Mon & 1 May–30 Sept, 12–5pm. Open 7 days a week July & Aug. Closed Tue–May, Jun–Sept. All year for groups by arrangement. **Admission:** Adults £4.50, OAPs £4. Children free when accompanied. Parties (10 +) £3.80. Coaches welcome. **Refreshments:** Tearoom within the castle. Restaurant facilities available to groups by prior arrangement. **Events/Exhibitions:** Musical and theatrical events regularly planned. **Accommodation:** Private family suites of rooms available within the castle. Coaching rooms available for let in original stable buildings. **Conferences:** Facilities within castle for presentations. Access for disabled may be difficult due to number of stairs.

map 11
G2

ALNWICK CASTLE

Alnwick, Northumberland NE66 1NQ

Tel: 01665 510777 24 hour Information Line: 01665 511100 Fax: 01665 510876 (His Grace the Duke of Northumberland)

Set in stunning landscape, designed by Capability Brown, Alnwick Castle is the home of the Duke of Northumberland. Owned by his family since 1309. This beautiful and awe-inspiring Castle was a major defence against invading Scottish armies in the middle ages. Visitors arriving through the massive and imposing Medieval Barbican are then treated to views of one of the finest Castles in England. Beautifully kept grounds are the wonderful setting for the Keep, which was restored by the first Duke in the 18th century to create a Fortress on the outside and a luxurious stately home on the inside. The grounds also contain the Museum of Northumberland Fusiliers, telling the story from 1674 to the present day. The Postern Tower displays one of the finest archeological collections in private hands and the Constable's Tower an exhibition on the Percy Tenantry Volunteers, who were formed in response to the threat from Napoleon's France. Furnishings and decoration were of the highest quality with paintings by Canaletto, Van Dyck and Titian hanging on the walls. **Guest Hall:** Alnwick Castle Guest Hall is one of the chief buildings of Anthony Salvin's 19th century restoration. Built as a magnificent coach house, it has throughout its history served as a venue for entertainment. This splendid Guest Hall is available for Conferences, Corporate Entertaining, Wedding Receptions, Concerts, Dinner Dances and Theatre Productions. Please note that the Guest Hall is not open to Castle visitors. <u>Location:</u> 35 miles from Newcastle on the A1. Accessible by public transport. <u>Open:</u> Daily 11–5pm (last admission 4.15pm). 15 Apr–27 Oct. <u>Education:</u> Programmes of activities for schools and colleges. <u>Parking:</u> Free <u>Events:</u> include the Unique Northumberland Millennium Festival 24–25 June. <u>E-mail:</u> enquiries@alnwickcastle.com

map 11
H2

Nottinghamshire

The river Trent and its tributaries are the determining factors to the scenery of Nottinghamshire. The county is shaped like an elongated oval, through the eastern half of which the broad sleepy Trent flows without haste in a placid pastoral landscape – a county fertile in crops and fields of thousands of head of cattle.

Nottinghamshire is perhaps most famous for the traditions surrounding Robin Hood and Sherwood forest. Indeed the entire county was once swathed in this dense forest which is now confined to an area of some twenty miles. The tree alleged to have been frequented by Robin Hood and his merry men, still stands (albeit on crutches!) in Sherwood Forest Country Park. This part of the forest has survived almost untouched for centuries and it is easy to conjurer up images of this thirteenth century rogue astride his trustworthy stead.

To the South of Sherwood Forest lies the city of Nottingham, which once commanded a ford over the river. Famous for centuries for its lace and textiles, Nottingham today is a lively and thriving city where life congregates at Market Square or at the annual Goose Fair held each October. Nottingham also has one of the most successful of the new universities established after World War II.

Nottingham

CARLTON HALL

Carlton-on-Trent, Nottinghamshire NG23 6LP
Tel: 01636 821421 Fax: 01636 821554

Mid 18th century house by Joseph Pocklington of Newark. Stables attributed to Carr of York. Family home occupied by the same family since 1832. Magnificent drawing room. **Location:** 7 miles north of Newark off A1. Opposite the church. **Open:** By appointment only. **Admission:** Hall and Garden: £3.50. Minimum charge for a group £35.

  `map 8 D6`

NEWARK TOWN HALL

Market Place, Newark, Nottinghamshire
Tel: 01636 680 333 Fax: 01636 640 967 (Newark Town Council)

One of the finest Georgian Town Halls in the country, the building has recently been refurbished in sympathy with 'John Carr's original concept. On display is the Town's collection of Civic Plate, silver dating generally from the 17th and 18th century, including the 'Newark Monteith' and the Newark 'Siege Pieces'. Other items of interest are some early historical records and various paintings including a collection by the artist Joseph Paul. **Location:** Market Place, Newark. Located on A1 and A46. **Station(s):** Newark Castle. Northgate (½ mile). **Open:** All year, Mon–Fri, 10–12noon & 2–4pm. Open at other times for groups by appointment. Closed: Sat, Sun, Bank Hol Mons & Tue following and Christmas week.

NORWOOD PARK

Norwood Park, Southwell, Nottinghamshire NG25 OPF
Tel: 01636 815649 Fax: 01636 815702 (Sir John and Lady Starkey)

Delightful Georgian country house and stables, set in a medieval deer Park with ancient oaks, fishponds and eyecatcher Temple overlooking apple orchards and the cricket ground, Norwood Park is the ideal venue for events of all kinds. The charming reception rooms of the house are perfect for weddings, meetings and dinners, while the Stables Gallery complex is a unique and spacious setting for events such as dances and conferences. The grounds are varied and ideal for filming, shows and activity days. The USA designed golf course and practice area is a recent bonus to the facilities offered at Norwood Park. **Contact:** Sarah Dodd - Events Manager. **E-mail:** Starkey@farmline. com **Internet:** members.farmline.com/norwood_park/

PAPPLEWICK HALL

Nr. Nottingham, NG15 8FE, Nottinghamshire
Tel: 0115 963 3491 Fax: 0115 964 2767 (Dr R. Godwin-Austen)

Fine Adam house built 1784 with lovely plasterwork ceilings. Park and woodland garden, particularly known for its rhododendrons. **Location:** 6 miles N of Nottingham, off A69. 2 miles from Junction 27, M1. **Open:** 1st, 3rd & 5th Weds in the month. **Refreshments:** By arrangement. **Events/Exhibitions:** 3rd Sat in June – annual fête and maypole dancing. **Conferences:** Up to 30 people. **Admission:** £5.

Oxfordshire

Oxfordshire will appeal to the lover of noble architecture. The churches stand out as the most consistently handsome of any county of England. The manor houses which represent every period of architecture, cry out to be discovered. And then there is Oxford – the city of dreaming spires which still maintain a medieval character.

Oxford's architectural beauty is best appreciated on foot. Some of the finest examples of college architecture are to be found around Radcliffe Square and the Bodelian Library, crowned by its famous domed Baroque rotunda.

Oxford's college buildings are quite unique, and many of them have retained their original features over several centuries. The city is a wonderful place in which to spend a few relaxing hours. Once you have taken your fill of wondrous architecture, why not take a riverside walk, or, if the sun shines, go punting on the river.

Around Oxford, the Vale of the White Horse, White Horse Hill and Uffington are all worth visiting. Standing in the heart of the Vale, the village of Uffington provides a good vantage point, overlooking this great prehistoric horse.

Oxford Botanic Garden

 ## ARDINGTON HOUSE

Ardington House, Wantage, Oxfordshire
Tel: 01235 821566 Fax: 01235 821151 (The Baring Family)

Home of the Baring family. Early 18th century beautifully symmetrical house with exceptionally fine brickwork. The entrance is dominated by the Imperial Staircase – two flights of stairs coming back into one. These are very rare and the Ardington Staircase is a magnificent example. The Hall and Dining Room have original panelling. Cornices and woodwork in the Hall are beautiful and the Dining Room has a plaster work ceiling. Attractive garden, river and stable yard. Weddings, dinner parties. FOR FURTHER INFORMATION, OPENING TIMES AND PHOTOGRAPHY, PLEASE TURN TO PAGE 148.

map 4 C4

 ## BROUGHTON CASTLE

Banbury, Oxfordshire OX15 5EB
Tel & Fax: 01295 276070 (the Lord Saye and Sele)

The home of the family of Lord and Lady Saye & Sele for 600 years. Surrounded by a moat, it was built in 1300 and greatly enlarged in 1550. It contains fine panelling and fireplaces, splendid plaster ceilings and good period furniture. Civil War Parliamentarian connections. Beautiful walled gardens, with old roses, shrubs and herbaceous borders. **Location:** 2 miles W of Banbury on the B4035 Shipston-on-Stour Road. **Open:** Weds and Suns 21 May–13 Sept. Also Thurs in July and August. Bank Hol Suns and Bank Hol Mons (including Easter) 2–5pm. Groups welcome on any day and at any time during the year, by appointment. Telephone/Fax 01295 276070 or 01869 337126. **Admission:** Adult £4, senior citizens £3.50, students £3.50, children £2. Groups reduced rates. Tearoom and shop. **E-mail:** admin@ broughtoncastle.demon.co.uk **Internet:** www.broughtoncastle.demon.co.uk

map 4 C2

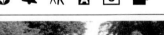 ## BUSCOT PARK

Faringdon, Oxfordshire SN7 8BU
Tel: 01367 240786 Fax: 01367 241794 (Lord Faringdon)

The late 18th century neoclassical house contains the Faringdon Collection of paintings and furniture. The park features a water garden, designed in the early 20th century by Harold Peto. **Open:** House & grounds: 3 Apr–29 Sept, Wed–Fri 2–6pm (incl. Good Fri and also open Easter Sat & Sun). Also open every 2nd & 4th Sat and immediately following Sun in each month 2–6pm. Last admission to house 5.30pm. Grounds only: 1 Apr–end Sept: open as house but also Mon (but not Bank Hol. Mon) & Tue 2–6pm. **Admission:** House & grounds £4.40. Grounds only £3.30. Children half price. Parties must book in writing or by fax. Unsuitable for wheelchair users due to gradients, gravel paths and steps to house. Tearoom open same days as house 2.30–5.30pm. No dogs allowed. **Location:** Between Lechlade and Faringdon, on A417. **E-mail:** estbuscot@aol.com **Internet:** www.faringdon–coll.com

map 4 B4

ARDINGTON HOUSE

Ardington House, Wantage, Oxfordshire
Tel: 01235 821566 Fax: 01235 821151 (The Baring Family)

Home of the Baring family. Early 18th century beautifully symmetrical house with exceptionally fine brickwork. The entrance is dominated by the Imperial Staircase – two flights of stairs coming back into one. These are very rare and the Ardington Staircase is a magnificent example. The Hall and Dining Room have original panelling. Cornices and woodwork in the Hall are beautiful and the Dining Room has a plaster work ceiling. Attractive garden, river and stable yard. Weddings, dinner parties and small conferences. **Open:** 1–5 May, 8–12 May, 1–4 August, 7–11 August and 14–17 August. Also Bank Holiday Mondays 2.30–4.30pm.

map 4
C4

BLENHEIM PALACE

Woodstock, OX20 1PX

Tel: 01993 811325 (24hrs info) Fax: 01993 813527 (His Grace the Duke of Marlborough)

Blenheim Palace, home of the 11th Duke of Marlborough and birthplace of Sir Winston Churchill, was built for John Churchill, 1st Duke of Marlborough in recognition of his great victory over the French at the Battle of Blenheim, 1704. FOR FURTHER INFORMATION, OPENING TIMES AND PHOTOGRAPHY, PLEASE TURN TO PAGE 150 & 151.

DITCHLEY PARK

Enstone, Chipping Norton, Oxfordshire OX7 4ER

Tel: 01608 677346, Fax: 01608 677399 (Ditchley Foundation)

Third in size and date of the great 18th century houses of Oxfordshire, Ditchley is famous for its splendid interior decorations (William Kent and Henry Flitcroft). For three and a half centuries the home of the Lee family and their descendants – Ditchley was frequently visited at weekends by Sir Winston Churchill during World War II. It has now been restored, furnished and equipped as a conference centre devoted to the study of issues of concern to the people on both sides of the Atlantic. **Location:** 1½ miles W of A44 at Kiddington; 2 miles from Charlbury (B4437). **Station(s):** Charlbury (2 miles) **Open:** Group visits by prior arrangement with the Bursar, Mon to Thurs afternoons only. Closed July-mid Sept. **Admission:** Entry fee £5 per person, minimum charge £40. **Internet:** www.ditchley.org

map 4 C3

FAWLEY COURT

Henley-on-Thames, Oxon RG9 3AE

Tel: 01491 574917 Fax: 01491 411587 (Congregation of Marian Fathers)

Designed by Sir Christopher Wren, built in 1684 for Col W Freeman, decorated by Grinling Gibbons and by James Wyatt. The Museum consists of a library, various documents of the Polish kings, a very well preserved collection of historical sabres and many memorable military objects of the Polish army. Paintings, early books, numismatic collections, arms and armour. **Location:** 1 mile north of Henley-on-Thames east to A4155 to Marlow. **Open:** Mar–Oct Wed, Thurs & Sun, 2–5pm. Other dates by arrangement. Closed Easter and Whitsuntide weeks and Nov–Feb. **Admission:** House, museum and grounds: Adults £4, OAPs £3, child £1.50, groups (min 12) £3.

map 4 D4

KELMSCOTT MANOR

Kelmscott, Nr. Lechlade, Oxfordshire, GL7 3HJ.

Tel: 01367 252 486 Fax: 01367 253 754 (Society of Antiquaries)

Kelmscott Manor was the country home of William Morris – poet, craftsman and socialist – from 1871 until his death in 1896. It is the most evocative of all his houses and continues to delight with the charm of its architecture, the fascination of its contents and the charm of its garden, which has recently undergone extensive restoration and now contains many fine examples of plants and flowers which would have been an inspiration to Morris. **Location:** 2 miles SE of Lechlade, on the Lechlade/Faringdon Road. **Open:** Apr–Sept, Wed 11am–1pm, 2–5pm. The 3rd Sat in Apr, May, June and Sept, 2–5pm. The 1st and 3rd Sat in July & Aug, 2–5pm. Thurs & Fri – private group visits. **Admission:** Adults £6, Children £3, Students £3. **Events/Exhibitions:** Centenary exhibition "William Morris at Kelmscott". Gift shop and bookshop.

map 4 B3

 KINGSTON BAGPUIZE HOUSE

Nr Abingdon, Oxfordshire OX13 5AX

Tel: 01865 820259 Fax: 01865 821659 (Mr and Mrs Francis Grant)

Beautiful 1660's manor house remodelled in early 1700's in red brick with stone facings. Cantilevered staircase and finely proportioned panelled rooms. Set in mature parkland, the gardens contain a notable collection of plants including rare trees, shrubs, perennials and bulbs. Available for functions. **Location:** In Kingston Bagpuize village, S of A420/A415 intersection. Abingdon 5 miles, Oxford 9 miles. **Station(s):** Oxford or Didcot. **Open:** Mar 12, 26; Apr 8, 9, 22, 23, 24, 29, 30; May 1, 13, 14, 27, 28, 29; Jun 10, 11, 25; Jul 8, 9, 22, 23; Aug 9, 12, 13, 26, 27, 28; Sept 6, 9, 10, 23, 24; Oct 8, 22. 2–5.30pm (tours of house 2.30pm to 4.45pm). Garden: Last entry 5pm. **Admission:** House & Garden: Adult £3.50, OAP £3, child £2.50. Garden only £1.50 (under 5s not admitted to house but free to garden). Groups welcome by appointment. Wheelchairs garden only. No dogs. **Refreshments:** Home-made teas.

map 4 C3

NUFFIELD PLACE

Huntercombe, Henley-on-Thames, Oxon RG9 5RY

Tel: 01491 641224(Nuffield College/Friends of Nuffield Place)

Home from 1933–63 of William Morris, Lord Nuffield, car manufacturer and philanthropist. A rare survival of a complete upper-middle class home of the 1930's, retaining majority of furniture and contents acquired on taking up residence. Fine quality rugs, clocks, tapestries and custom-made furniture. Four acre gardens, laid out around 1914 when house was built, contain mature trees, yew hedges, rose pergola, rockery and pond. **Location:** Approximately 7 miles Henley-on-Thames just off A4130 to Oxford. Coach service X39 Oxford/ Henley. **Open:** May–Sept every 2nd and 4th Sun 2–5pm. **Admission:** Adults £3, concession £2, children 50p. Garden only £1. Parties by arrangement. **Refreshments:** Home-made teas. Ground floor and gardens suitable for disabled. No disabled lavatory.

map 4 D4

BLENHEIM PALACE

Woodstock, OX20 1PX
Tel: 01993 811325 (24hrs information) Fax: 01993 813527 (His Grace the Duke of Marlborough)

Blenheim Palace, home of the 11th Duke of Marlborough and birthplace of Sir Winston Churchill, was built for John Churchill, 1st Duke of Marlborough in recognition of his great victory over the French at the Battle of Blenheim, 1704. The Palace, designed by Sir John Vanbrugh, is set in 2,100 acres of parkland landscaped by "Capability" Brown and is one of the finest examples of English Baroque. The collection comprises tapestries, paintings, sculpture and fine furniture set in magnificent gilded staterooms. The Gardens are renowned for their beauty and include the formal Water Terraces, Italian Garden, Rose Garden and Arboretum. In the Pleasure Gardens are the Butterfly House, adventure play area, cafeteria and a shop, as well as the Marlborough Maze, the world's largest symbolic hedge maze. An inclusive ticket covers the Palace Tour, park, gardens, train, nature trail and car parking. Close to Oxford and next to the historic town of Woodstock, the Palace is easily accessible by car, train and coach. In 2000, events include Craft Fairs at the May Day and August Bank Holiday weekends, Firework Concerts, and the Blenheim International Horse Trials (7–10 Sept). **Open:** 13 March–31 Oct 10–5.30pm (last admission 4.45pm) Licensed Restaurant and self-service Cafeterias. **Conferences:** The Orangery and Spencer Churchill Rooms offer luxurious conferences and corporate hospitality facilities overlooking the Italian Garden, throughout the year. **Education:** A Sandford Award holder since 1982. **Admission:** Please phone for details. **Internet:** www.blenheimpalace.com **E-mail:** administration@blenheim palace.com

map 4
C3

The South Front from the Cricket Pavilion

The Marlborough Maze

MAPLEDURHAM HOUSE & WATERMILL

Nr. Reading, Oxfordshire, RG4 7TR Tel: 01189 723 350
Fax: 01189 724 016 (The Mapledurham Trust)

Late 16th century Elizabethan home of the Blount family. Original plaster ceiling, great oak staircase, fine collection of paintings and private chapel in Strawberry Hill Gothick added in 1797. The 15th century Watermill is fully restored and producing flour and bran which are sold in the gift shop. **Location:** 4 miles NW of Reading on North bank of River Thames. Signposted from A4074. **Open:** Easter–end Sept. Midweek parties by arrangement. **Admission:** Please phone for details. **Refreshments:** Tearooms serving cream teas. **Events/ Exhibitions:** By arrangement. **Conferences:** By arrangement. **Accommodation:** 11 self-catering holiday cottages. Wedding receptions by arrangement. Car parking and picnic area. **E-mail:** mtrust@aol.com or maple@mapledurham.co.uk **Internet:** www.mapledurham.co.uk

UNIVERSITY OF OXFORD BOTANIC GARDEN

Rose Lane, Oxford, Oxfordshire
01865 276920 Fax: 01865 276920 (University of Oxford)

The University of Oxford Botanic Garden is the oldest botanic garden in Britain. For more than 375 years this Walled Garden, built before the English Civil War, has stood on the bank of the River Cherwell in the centre of Oxford. It has evolved from a seventeenth century collection of medical herbs to the most compact yet diverse collection of plants in the world. In addition to the botanical family beds and the National Collection of Euphorbias, there is a range of glasshouses including a Tropical Lily House, Palm House and Arid House. Outside the original Walled Garden there are herbaceous borders, a newly restored bog garden and a rock garden. **Open:** Open all year (except Good Fri and Christmas Day). Apr–Sept 9–5pm. Oct–Mar 9–4.30pm. Last admission 4.15pm. **Admission:** £2: Apr–Aug. **E-mail:** postmaster@botanic–garden.ox.ac.uk

ROUSHAM HOUSE

Rousham, Steeple Aston, Oxfordshire OX6 3QX
Tel: 01869 347110 or 0860 360407 (C Cottrell-Dormer Esq.)

Rousham House was built by Sir Robert Dormer in 1635 and the shooting holes were put in the doors while it was a Royalist garrison in the Civil War. Sir Robert's successors were Masters of Ceremonies at Court during eight reigns and employed Court artists and architects to embellish Rousham. The house stands above the River Cherwell one mile from Hopcrofts Holt, near the road from Chipping Norton to Bicester. It contains 150 portraits and other pictures and much fine contemporary furniture. Rooms were decorated by William Kent (1738) and Roberts of Oxford (1765). The garden is Kent's only surviving landscape design with classic buildings, cascades, statues and vistas in thirty acres of hanging woods above the Cherwell. Wonderful herbaceous borders, pigeon house and small parterre. Fine herd of rare Long-Horn cattle in the park. Wear sensible shoes and bring a picnic and Rousham is yours for the day. **Location:** 12 miles N of Oxford; E of A4260; S of B4030. **Station:** Heyford (1 mile). **Open:** Apr–Sept inclusive Wed, Sun & Bank Hols 2–4.30pm. Gardens only every day all year 10–4.30pm. No children under 15. No dogs. Groups by arrangement on other days. **Admission:** House: Adults £3. Garden £3.

STONOR PARK
Nr Henley-on-Thames, Oxfordshire RG9 6HF
Tel: 01491 638587, Fax: 01491 638587 (Lord and Lady Camoys)

Home of Lord and Lady Camoys and the Stonor family for over 800 year with it's own medieval Chapel where mass is still celebrated today. Sanctuary for St. Edmund Campion in 1581. A family home containing fine family portraits; rare items of furniture, paintings, drawings, tapestries and bronzes from Britain, Europe and America. Beautiful hillside gardens. **Location:** On B480 5 miles north of Henley-on-Thames. **Open:** 2 Apr–24 Sept: Suns & Bank Hol Mons 2–5.30pm. July–August: Weds & Sats 27 May & 26 Aug, 2–5.30pm. Groups welcome by arrangement. **Admission:** House & Gardens: Adults £4.50, child under 14 free. Adult Groups (minimum 12) £4. Private groups (minimum 20) £5. Gardens only: £2.50. **Refreshments:** Tearoom. Group lunches and suppers by arrangement.

map 4
D4

WALLINGFORD CASTLE GARDENS
Castle Street, Wallingford, Oxfordshire
Tel: 01491 835 373 Fax: 01491 826 550 (Wallingford Town Council)

These gardens are situated on part of the site of Wallingford Castle, which was built by William the Conqueror and demolished by Oliver Cromwell in 1652. The remains of St. Nicholas Priory are a feature of the Gardens, which is a haven of beauty and tranquillity and has a well-established wildlife area. **Location:** Bear Lane, Castle Street,

Wallingford, Oxfordshire. **Open:** Apr–Oct, 10–6pm. Nov–Mar, 10–3pm. **Admission:** Free. **Events/Exhibitions:** Band concerts some Sundays in summer. Telephone for details. 'Britain in Bloom' winner 1993, 1996, 1997 and 1998. Car parking in the town. **Tourist Information Office:** 01491 826 972.

map 4
C4

ASHDOWN HOUSE
Lambourn, Newbury RG16 7RE Tel: 01488 72584

Open: Hall, stairway, roof and grounds only: April–end Oct: Wed & Sat. Guided tours only; at 2.15pm, 3.15pm & 4.15pm from front door. Woodland: all year: daily except Fri, dawn to dusk. **Admission:** £2.10. Woodland free. No reduction for groups, which must book in writing. Car park 250m. No WC. **E-mail:** tadgen@smtp.ntrust.org.uk

GREYS COURT
Rotherfield Greys, Henley-on-Thames RG9 4PG
Tel: 01491 628529 or (Infoline)01494 755564

Open: House (part of ground floor only): 1 April–end Sept: Wed, Thur & Fri (closed Good Fri) 2–6pm. Garden: 1 April–end Sept: Tue–Sat & BH Mons (closed Good Fri) 2–6pm. **Admission:** £4.60. child £2.30; family £11.50. Garden only £3.20; family £8. Parking 220m. No reduction for coach groups, which must book in advance. **Events:** for details send s.a.e. to The Box Office, PO Box 180, High Wycombe, Bucks HP14 4XT. **E-mail:** tgrgen@smtp.ntrust.org.uk

CHASTLETON HOUSE
Chastleton, Moreton-in-Marsh GL56 0SU
Tel: 01608 674355 or 01494 755572 (Bookings)

Open: 1 April–28 Oct: daily except Sun, Mon & Tues 1–5pm. Last admission 1hr before closing. Note: Admission for all visitors (incl. NT members) by timed ticket, which must be booked in advance; write to the ticket office (do not include payment) or tel. 01494 755572, Mon to Fri 1.30–4.30pm from 1 Feb 2000. **Admission:** Adult £5.10, child £2.55, family £12.75. Groups (min 11, max. 25) by written arrangement only. No access for coaches. Car park on hill 270m from house; return walk includes a short but steep hill. **E-mail:** tchgen@smtp .ntrust.org.uk

GREAT COXWELL BARN
Great Coxwell, Faringdon, Oxfordshire Tel: 01793 762209

Open: Daily at reasonable hours. **Admission:** 50p. No WC. **E-mail:** tbcjaw@smtp.ntrust.org.uk

WATERPERRY GARDENS

Nr Wheatley, Oxfordshire OX33 1JZ
Tel: 01844 339226/254 Fax:01844 339883

The peaceful gardens at Waterperry feature a magnificent herbaceous border, shrub and heather borders, alpine and rock gardens, a formal garden and a new rose garden. Together with stately trees, a river to walk by and a quiet Saxon Church to visit – all set in 83 acres of unspoilt Oxfordshire. The long established herbaceous and alpine nurseries provide year round interest. For the experienced gardener, the novice, or those who have no garden of their own, here is a chance to share, enjoy and admire the order and beauty of careful cultivation. Garden Shop and Plant Centre with exceptionally wide range of plants, shrubs etc produced in the nurseries for sale. Main agents for Haddonstone, Pots and Pithoi and Whichford Pottery. The Pear Tree Teashop provides a delicious selection of freshly prepared food made on the premises. Serving hot and cold light lunches, morning coffee, cream teas etc. Wine licence. The Art in Action Gallery exhibits and sells quality ceramics, wood, glass, paintings, jewellery, textiles, etchings and engravings. **Location:** 9 miles from Oxford, 50 miles from London (M40 Junction 8), 42 miles from Birmingham (M40 Junction 8a). Well signposted locally with Tourist Board symbol. **Station(s):** Oxford & Thame Parkway. **Open:** Gardens & Shop: Apr–Oct 9–5.30pm, Nov–Mar 9–5pm. Pear Tree Teashop: Apr–Oct 10–5pm, Nov–Mar 10–4pm. Art in Action Gallery: Apr–Oct 9–5pm, Nov–Mar 9–4.30pm. **Open Daily** except Christmas and New Year Holidays. Open only to Art in Action visitors (enquiries 0171 381 3192) 20–23 July. The Pear Tree Teashop will close from 19 July–24 July incl. **Admission:** Apr–Oct Adults £3.40, senior citizens £2.90, parties (20+) £2.90. Nov–Mar £1.60 all categories. Coaches by appointment only.

map 4
D3

Shropshire

This county is a hidden treasure, a real gem for visitors although it remains off the main tourist routes. The hills and mountains to the west separate Shropshire and Wales. The north of the county is home to seven beautiful lakes, which are wonderful for walking and home to a large number of birds.

Shrewsbury sits in a large loop of the River Severn. This made an excellent defence system during the frontier battles between England and Wales. Within the town is a wealth of medieval buildings and monuments. There are many timber framed buildings, narrow streets and a charming old market square.

Ludlow retains a huge amount of geological interest, with several fossils having been found around there, that are now on display in the museum. Many pretty shops and half-timbered Tudor buildings are located in the town.

Above: Old Market Hall, Shrewsbury

BOSCOBEL HOUSE & THE ROYAL OAK

Shifnal, Shropshire ST19 9AR
Tel: 01902 850244 (English Heritage)

Discover the fascinating history of the fully restored and refurbished lodge and famous 'Royal Oak' tree where the future King Charles II hid from Cromwell's troops in 1651. The panelled rooms, secret hiding places and pretty gardens lend a truly romantic character. A fascinating guided tour and an award winning exhibition also cover the later additions to the site – a Victorian farmhouse, dairy, smithy and farmyard complete with resident ducks and geese. **Location:** On classified road between A41 and A5, 8m NW of Wolverhampton. **Open:** 1 Apr–30 Nov 2000. Closed from the end of November 2000 until April 2001. **Admission:** Adults £4.30, concs £3.20, child £2.20. (15% discount for groups of 11 or more).

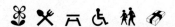

map 8
B7

BURFORD HOUSE GARDENS

Tenbury Wells, Worcestershire, WR15, 8HQ
Tel: 01584 810 777 Fax: 01584 810 673 (C. Chesshire)

The sweeping lawns and plantsman's paradise of Burford House Gardens are set in the picturesque valleys of the River Teme and Ledwyche Brook. The late Georgian bridge over the Ledwyche has been restored, leading to a new wildflower garden down to the heavenly spot where the two rivers meet. The grass garden has been redesigned, a bamboo collection planted and the National Collection of Clematis of over 200 varieties continues to grow. Also on site is **Treasures of Tenbury Garden Centre/Nursery** growing over 300 varieties of clematis and many of the unusual plants that can be seen in the gardens; specialising in quality plants for sale, pots, tools and friendly practical advice; **Burford House Gallery:** contemporary and one botanical art show annually; **Gift Shop:** decorative and functional gifts, books and cards; **Mulu** exotic plants; **Jungle Giants** bamboos. **Refreshments: Burford Buttery**, serving a wide selection of home-made cakes, pastries, hot and cold meals, teas and coffees. Seating 120 inside (including Buttery Marquee), 40 outside. Evening Bistro, Thurs–Sat. **Location:** Tenbury Wells, Worcestershire, WR15 8HQ (off A456, 1 mile west of Tenbury Wells, 8 miles from Ludlow). **Car Parking:** Free parking for 120 cars, 10 coaches. **Open:** All year daily 10–6pm (last entry into gardens 5pm); evenings by arrangement. **Admission:** Adults £3.50, children £1.00; groups of 10+ £3. **E-mail:** treasures@burford.co.uk

map 7
F1

HAWKSTONE HISTORIC PARK & FOLLIES

Weston-under-Redcastle, Nr Shrewsbury, Shropshire, SY4 5UY
Tel: 01939 200 611 Fax: 01939 200 311 (Hawkstone Park Leisure Ltd.)

Few places in the world can claim to be truly unique. However, Hawkstone Park with its well hidden pathways, concealed grotto, secret tunnels and magical collection of follies earns that right. A giant theatre in landscape - it was originally one of the most visited landscapes in Britain and is the only Grade I landscape in Shropshire. Work to restore the Park to its former glory began in April 1991 after a 100 year closure. Visitors are once more privileged to enter the Hawkstone Labyrinth. Folly buildings, it has been said 'indulge a natural urge to express eccentricity with the resources of wealth and imagination". It is a description which sits perfectly on the shoulders of the hills of Hawkstone. Sir Roland Hill started it all in the 18th century with his son Richard "The Great Hill", not only taking over but also increasing the tempo and arranged for some 15 miles of paths and some of the best collections of follies in the world to be constructed in the grounds of their ancestral home. At the turn of the 19th century the Hills could no longer accommodate the growing number of

sightseers to the Hall. As a result an inn, now the Hawkstone Park Hotel, was opened and guided tours were organised. Hawkstone, according to one top writer, became "the inspiration for Longleat, Wombourne and other stately homes which attract visitors". Little has changed since then. The Park is full of attractions, surprises and features. You can, for example, tread the timeless stone steps, see the dramatic cliffs and rocks, towers, monuments, tunnels, passageways, precipice rocks, paths, rustic sofas and romantic secret valleys. Even the Duke of Wellington was a regular visitor. It takes about 3 hours to complete the whole tour of the Park. <u>Location:</u> 12 miles N of Shrewsbury, off A49. <u>Open:</u> 1 Apr–2 July: Wed–Sun & Bank Hols incl. 3 July–3 Sept: Mon–Sun incl. 4 Sept–29 Oct: Wed–Sun incl. <u>Admission:</u> Adults £5, child £3, senior citizen £4. Family £14. Small additional charges apply on Bank Holidays and special events. Special reduced rates for groups. Gift shop, tearoom and hotel & golf course adjacent. Please wear sensible shoes. Guided tours by arrangement.

map 6
D1

DAVENPORT HOUSE

Worfield, Nr Bridgnorth, Shropshire
Tel: 01746 716221 Fax: 01746 716021 (Roger Murphy)

A grade 1 listed country manor house of 1726 by the architect Francis Smith of Warwick, built out of Henry Davenport's profits from the India trade. The House sits within an extensive estate setting, typical of Shropshire, one of England's loveliest counties. A popular regional venue for civil marriage ceremonies and wedding receptions, noted for a combination of high quality cuisine and a friendly, relaxed management style, Davenport House is also a frequent venue for corporate events of all kinds and group social entertainment. The house opens as a restaurant for parties of two upwards on Wednesday evenings, by advance booking only.

HODNET HALL GARDENS

Hodnet, Market Drayton, Shropshire TF9 3NN
Tel: 01630 685202 Fax: 01630 685853 (Mr & Mrs A.E.H. Heber-Percy)

60+ acres of landscaped gardens, renowned to be amongst the finest in the country. Woodland walks amidst forest trees, shrubs and flowers alongside a daisy chain of ornamental pools. Light lunch or afternoon tea in the 17th century tearooms, adjacent to which is a gift shop. The walled Kitchen Garden grows a wide range of flowers and produce which are available for sale during the appropriate season. Disabled visitors are especially welcome. Guided tours and evening parties by appointment. **Location:** A53 (Shrewsbury–Market Drayton): A442 (Telford–Whitchurch): M6 exits 12 & 15: M54 exit 3. **Open:** 1 April–30 Sept. Tues–Sun & Bank Holiday Mons 12–5pm. **Admission:** Adult £3.25, OAPs £2.75, child £1.20. Special rates for parties (prebook please).

IRONBRIDGE GORGE MUSEUMS

Ironbridge, Telford, Shropshire TF8 7AW
Tel: 01952 433522 or 432166 (w/ends) Fax: 01952 432204 (Independent Museum Trust)

Scene of pioneering events which led to the Industrial Revolution. The Ironbridge Gorge is home to 9 unique museums set in 6 square miles of stunning scenery. These include Jackfield Tile Museum, Coalport China Museum and a recreated Victorian Town where you can chat to the locals as they go about their daily business. You'll need 2 days here. **Location:** OS Ref. SJ666 037. Telford, Shropshire via M6/M54. **Open:** All Year: daily from 10am (closed 24/25 Dec & 1 Jan) Please telephone for winter details before visit. **Admission:** Passport tickets which allows admission to all museums; Adult £9.50, child/student £5.50, 60+ £8.50, family £29. Prices valid until Easter 2000. Group discounts also available. Freephone: 0800 590258 for a free colour guide. **Internet:** www.ironbridge.org.uk

ROWLEY'S HOUSE MUSEUM

Barker Street, Shrewsbury, Shropshire
Tel: 01743 361196 Fax: 01743 358411 (Shrewsbury and Atcham Borough Council)

Major regional museum displaying varied collections in timber-framed 16th century warehouse and adjoining 17th century brick mansion. Archaeology, including Roman Wroxeter; geology; costume; natural and local history; temporary exhibitions including contemporary arts and crafts. **Open:** Tue–Sat 10–5pm; Summer Suns and Bank Hol Mons 10–4pm. Closed Christmas/New Year period.

SHIPTON HALL

Much Wenlock, Shropshire, TF13 6JZ.
Tel: 01746 785 225 Fax: 01746 785 125 (J. N. R. N. Bishop)

Delightful Elizabethan stone manor house c.1587 with Georgian additions. Interesting Rococo and Gothic plaster work by T. F. Pritchard. Stone walled garden, medieval dovecote and parish church dating from late Saxon period. Family home. **Location:** In Shipton, 6 miles SW of Much Wenlock near junction B4378 & B4368. **Station(s):** Craven Arms (10 miles), Telford (14 miles), Ludlow (14 miles). **Open:** Easter–end Sept, Thurs. Not Sun, except Bank Hol Suns & Mons (except Christmas & New Year) 2.30–5.30pm. Also by appointment throughout the year for parties of 20+. **Admission:** House & Garden: Adults £3, children £1.50, parties of 20+ less 10%. **Refreshments:** Teas/buffets by prior arrangement.

OLD COLEHURST MANOR

Colehurst, Market Drayton, Shropshire TF9 2JB
Tel: 01630 638833 Fax: 01630 638647 (Bjorn Teksnes Lord of the Manor)

Undoubtedly one of the best period houses you will ever have the pleasure of visiting. The reasons... Perhaps because we are a living home where visitors are welcomed as guests. There is no staid formality here. The rooms seen are all used by the family and their pets. Even the animals themselves greet you and often accompany the tour. The beautiful timber frame house, lovingly restored by the present Lord of the Manor and his lady has a warmth and a tactile quality, which we encourage by having no roped off areas or 'private' signs. During your personal tour you will see priest holes and beautiful period furniture blending with our family belongings. Tales will be told of the history, restoration and the spirits of the house. For those who enjoy gardens, Bjorn's rose, clematis, herb and knot gardens are a delight, and not to forget one of the finest exotic plant collectors in Shropshire. Our dining room and old library make an atmospheric setting for one of Maria, Lady of the Manor's teas or light lunches, all home baked in our 17th century kitchens, and not forgetting our speciality dishes from the past and the unique 17th century experience. **Location:** Follow brown signs on A41–A53 and A529. Stations: Stoke–on–Trent 12 miles, Shrewsbury 17 miles, Air: Manchester airport, 1½ hours. Jacobean weekends, civil weddings, wedding receptions and conference facilities. Great Hall capacity 75, Dining Room capacity 20. **Open:** 1 Apr–30 Sept: Weds, Thurs & Sun 12–5pm, last tour 4pm. 1 Oct–31 Mar by appt only. **Admission:** Adult £4, child £2.75, Family Ticket £11.50. Group min 20 max 50: Adult £3.50. No photography in house. Restaurant by appt only. Guided tours obligatory. Limited parking for cars. **E-mail:** old–coldhurst–manor@talk21.com **Internet:** www.colehurst.co.uk

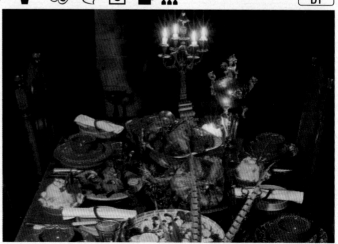

SHREWSBURY CASTLE & SHROPSHIRE REGIMENTAL MUSEUM

Castle Street, Shrewsbury, Shropshire
Tel: 01743 358516 Fax:01743 358411

Norman castle with substantial alterations by Thomas Telford in the eighteenth century. The Great Hall now houses the collections of the Shropshire Regimental Museums plus graphic displays on the history of the castle. **Open:** Museum, Tue–Sat & summer Suns, 10–4.30pm. Please phone for details of opening times Dec–Feb. Free admission to the grounds Mon–Sat (and summer Suns).

map 6
1E

WESTON PARK

Weston-U-Lizard, Nr Shifnal, Shropshire
Tel: 01952 850207 Fax: 01952 850430 (Weston Park Foundation)

Nestled in 1,000 acres of "Capability" Brown Parkland and formal gardens this superb Stately Home, built in 1671 and designed by Lady Wilbraham, contains a magnificent collection of treasures, including work by Van Dyck, Lely and Gainsborough. The house has 28 historic bedrooms, available on an exclusive basis for conferences and private parties. An extensive event programme available during the summer, including a balloon festival, outdoor symphony firework concert and a game and country sports fair. The Parkland includes a deer park, woodland adventure playground, pets corner and miniature railway. The Old Stables, now renovated into a tearoom and licensed bar, serves lunch and afternoon tea. **Location:** Situated on A5, 8 miles M6 Junction 12 and 3 miles M54 Junction 3. **Open & Admission:** For opening details and charges please telephone 01952 850207.

STOKESAY CASTLE

Craven Arms, Shropshire SY7 9AH
Tel: 01588 672544 (English Heritage)

A visit to Stokesay guarantees a day out to remember. Take a trip back in time with our free audio tour or relax in the charming 'cottage' style garden framed by the tranquil Welsh borders scenery. Historically, the castle represents the country's finest example of a fortified manor house built in a style that owes more to fashion than to fortification. The solid walls and crenellated battlements form part of an ostentatious building programme begun by the wool merchant, Lawrence of Ludlow in 1281. The majority of features familiar to the original owner can still be seen including the Great Hall that once echoed to the sounds of feasts and banquets. **Location:** 7m NW of Ludlow off A49. **Open:** 1 April–30 Sept: daily, 10–6pm. 1 Oct–31 Oct: daily, 10–5pm. 1 Nov–31 Mar: Wed–Sun, 10–4pm. Closed 1–2pm in winter. (Closed 24–26 Dec & 1 Jan 2001). **Admission:** Adults £3.50, concs £2.60, child £1.80. (15% discount for groups of 11 or more).

map 7
F2

WALCOT HALL

Lydbury North, Nr. Bishops Castle, SY7 8AZ, Shropshire.
Tel: 0171 581 2782 Fax 0171 589 0195 (C. R. W. Parish)

Built by Sir William Chambers for Lord Clive of India, Walcot Hall possesses a free-standing Ballroom; stable yard with twin clock towers; extensive walled garden and wonderful arboretum noted for its rhododendrons, azaleas, specimen trees and spectacular setting. **Location:** 3 miles E of Bishops Castle, on B4385, half a mile outside Lydbury North. **Station:** Craven Arms. **Open:** Arboretum open 12–4.30pm, Fri, Sat and Sun, Apr 1–Oct 31. House by appointment except National Garden scheme open day 28–29 May 2000, 2–6pm. **Admission:** Adults £3, children (under 15) free. Collect tickets from Powis Arms, beside main gate. **Accommodation:** All year holiday flats. Estate suitable for film and photographic locations, Marriage Licence, Ballroom available for receptions, conferences, concerts and parties.

map 7
F2

ATTINGHAM PARK

Shrewsbury SY4 4TP Tel: 01743 708123 Fax: 01743 708150

Open: House: 24 March to 31 Oct: daily except Wed & Thur 1.30–5pm; (BH Mon 11–5pm). Deer park & grounds: Daily (closed 25 Dec). March to end Oct: daily 8–9pm. **Events:** Send s.a.e. for programme. **Admission:** House & park: £4; family ticket £10. Booked groups £4.20. Park & grounds only: £2. **Restaurant.**

BENTHALL HALL

Broseley TF12 5RX Tel: 01952 882159

Open: 2 April to 27 Sept: Wed, Sun & BH Mon 1.30–5.30pm. House and/or garden for groups by prior arrangement. **Events:** church services most Suns 3.15pm; visitors welcome. **Admission:** £3, children £1.

Garden only £2. Booked groups £2.50 (min 22 people/£55). Parking 150m. Coaches by appointment. **Restaurant.**

DUDMASTON

Quatt, nr Bridgnorth WV15 6QN Tel: 01746 780866 Fax: 01746 780744

Open: 28 March to 29 Sept: Tues, Wed & Sun plus BH Mons 2–5.30pm. Garden: as house and Mons 12–6pm. Booked groups Thur. **Events:** send s.a.e. for details. **Admission:** House & garden £3.75, children £2.25; family ticket £9. Booked Groups £2.90. Garden only £2.75. Parking 100m. **Restaurant.**

MORVILLE HALL

Bridgnorth WV16 5NB Tel: 01743 708100

Open: By written appointment only.

Somerset

Glastonbury Tor

There is more scenic variety in Somerset than in any other part of the West Country – impressive moorland, verdant hills, romantic coastal reaches, combes, woodlands and flats. Two towns in Somerset – Taunton and Wells – dominate the county. Both are set in a time lock which tourists and developers thankfully fail to crack.

The nearby Mendip Hills are characterised by chasms and caverns while the neighbouring Quantock Hills with their clear streams and grazing deer are the heartlands of Somerset. This is a region of verdant glens, thatched pubs and village greens.

The mood changes dramatically at Exmoor, a protected wilderness which extends as far as the coast, where the cliffs and sea create a perfect setting. Bath was transformed by the Romans. It was the first spa town in the 18th century. Today it remains ever popular.

BARFORD PARK

Enmore TA5 1AG
Tel: 01278 671269

Set in a large garden and looking out across a ha-ha to a park dotted with fine trees, it presents a scene of peaceful domesticity, a miniature country seat on a scale appropriate today. The well-proportioned rooms, with contemporary furniture, are all in daily family use. The walled flower garden is in full view from the house, and the woodland and water gardens and archery glade with their handsome trees form a perfect setting for the stone and red-brick Queen Anne building. **Location:** 5m W of Bridgwater. **Open:** May–Sept by appointment. **Admission:** Charges not available at the time of going to press. **Refreshments:** Teas and buffet luncheons for groups, by appointment.

map 3
G3

JOHN BARSTAPLE ALMSHOUSE

Old Market St, Bristol, BS2 OEU
Tel: 01179 265 777 (Bristol Municipal Charities)

Victorian almshouse with garden courtyard. Location: Half a mile from Bristol city centre, on A4. **Station(s):** Bristol Temple Meads. **Open:** Garden & Exterior buildings only (now extensively renovated): Weekdays all year, 10am–1pm. By appointment only telephone 0117 9265777. **Admission:** Free. The almshouses are occupied mainly by elderly residents and their rights for privacy should be respected.

map 3
H2

THE BISHOP'S PALACE

Wells, Somerset, BA5 2PD
Tel: 01749 678 691 (The Church Commissioners)

The fortified and moated medieval palace unites the early 13th century first floor hall (known as The Henderson Rooms), the late 13th century Chapel and the now ruined Great Hall, also the 15th century wing which is today the private residence of the Bishop of Bath and Wells. The extensive grounds, where rise the springs that give Wells its name, are a beautiful setting for borders of herbaceous plants, roses, shrubs, mature trees and the Jubilee Arboretum. The Moat is home to a collection of waterfowl and swans. **Location:** City of Wells: enter from the Market Place through the Bishop's Eye or from the Cathedral Cloisters, over the Drawbridge. **Station(s):** Bath and Bristol. **Open:**

The Henderson Rooms, Bishop's Chapel and Grounds: 1 Apr–31 Oct, Tues, Wed, Thurs, Fri 10.30–6pm and Sun 2–6pm and most days in Aug, 10.30–6pm. As this is a private house, the Trustees reserve the right to alter these times on rare occasions. **Admission:** As advertised – Guided and educational tours by arrangement with the Manager. **Refreshments:** A restaurant service is available in the Undercroft using fresh produce from the Palace gardens, unless prior bookings are made. **Events/Exhibitions:** Wedding receptions a speciality. Open air theatre. **Conferences:** Conferences, training courses and seminars by arrangement with the manager.

map 3
H3

COMBE SYDENHAM COUNTRY PARK

Monksilver, Taunton, Somerset, TA4 4JG
Tel: 01984 656 284 Fax: 01984 656 273

Built in 1580 on the site of the monastic settlement, home of Elizabeth Sydenham, wife of Sir Francis Drake. Beautifully restored Courtroom and Cornmill. Elizabethan-style gardens. Deer park. Play area, Woodland walks with the 'Alice' Trail and the 'Ancient' Trail of Trees. Fish farm. Picnic area. **Open:** Country Park Walks, play area & woods: 1 Apr–30 Sept everyday. Guided tour of West wing of House, Gardens and Cornmill 23 Apr–30 Sept, Mon, Weds, Thurs at 1.30pm. Booklets for Self guided 'Alice' Trail and the 'Ancient' Trail of Trees available for sale 1–1.30pm on tour days. Group bookings available (min 20). **Admission:** Country Park £3 per vehicle. Guided tour, adults £5, children £2.

map 3 G3

CROWE HALL

Widcombe Hill, Bath, Somerset, BA2 6AR
Tel: 01225 310322 (John Barratt)

Elegant George V classical Bath villa, retaining grandiose mid-Victorian portico and great hall. Fine 18th century and Regency furniture: interesting old paintings and china. 10 acres of romantic gardens cascading down hillside. Terraces, Victorian grotto, ancient trees. **Location:** Approx. ¼ mile on right up Widcombe Hill, 1 mile from Guildhall. **Open: Garden:** 19 March, 16 April, 7 & 21 May, 11 June, 16 July and groups by appointment. **House:** By appointment only, £2. **Admission:** House or Garden only £2; House and Garden £4. **Refreshments:** Teas on opening days and by appointment. Dogs welcome.

map 3 V16

DODINGTON HALL

Nr. Nether Stowey, Bridgwater, Somerset
Tel: 01278 741 400
(Lady Gass, Occupier: P.Quinn)

Small Tudor manor house on the lower slopes of the Quantock Hills. Great hall with oak roof. Carved stone fireplace. Semi-formal garden with roses and shrubs. **Location:** ½ mile from A39, 11 miles from Bridgwater. 7 miles from Williton. **Open:** Sat 20 May–Mon 29 May inclusive, 2–5pm. **Admission:** Donations for charity. Parking for 15 cars. Regret unsuitable for disabled.

map 3 G3

EAST LAMBROOK MANOR GARDEN

South Petherton, Somerset Tel: 01460 240 328
Fax: 01460 242 344 (Mr & Mrs Robert Williams)

This Grade I listed garden is one of the best loved in Britain. It was the home of the late Margery Fish. It is also the subject of many books, articles and television and radio programmes. The 17th century malthouse has been developed to provide modern facilities for visitors retaining its unique character. During the summer months, as well as cream teas there are also exhibitions by well known local artists. The garden contains the National Collection of Geraniums. **Location:** Off A303. 2 miles N of South Petherton. **Open:** All year round, Mon–Sat, 10–5pm. **Admission:** Adults £2.50, students/children 50p, OAPs £2. **E-mail:** elambrook@aol.com **Internet:** www.margeryfish.com

map 3 H4

FAIRFIELD

Stogursey, Bridgwater, Somerset
Tel: 01278 732251 Fax: 01278 732277 (Lady Gass)

Elizabethan House of medieval origin, undergoing extensive repairs. Woodland garden. Location: 11 miles W of Bridgwater, 8 miles E of Williton. From A39 Bridgwater/Minehead turn N; house 1 mile W of Stogursey. **Open:** House open in summer (when repairs allow) for groups by appointment only. Garden open for NGS and other charities on dates advertised in spring. **Admission:** Donations for charity. Disabled access. No dogs, except guide dogs. Parking for 30 cars. Unsuitable for coaches.

map 3 G3

GAULDEN MANOR

Tolland, Lydeard St Lawrence, Nr Taunton, Somerset TA4 3PN
Tel: 01984 667213 (James Le Gendre Starkie)

Small historic red sandstone Manor House of great charm. A real home lived in and shown by the owners. Past seat of the Turberville family immortalised by Thomas Hardy. Great Hall has magnificent plaster ceiling and oak screen to room known as the chapel. Fine antique furniture and many hand embroideries worked by the wife of owner. Interesting grounds include rose gardens, bog garden with primulas and moisture loving plants, butterfly and herb garden. Visitors return year after year to enjoy this oasis of peace and quiet set amid superb countryside. **Location:** 9 miles NW of Taunton signposted from A358 and B3224. **Open:** Garden: June 8–Aug 28 on Thurs, Sun & Bank Hols, 2–5pm. House & Garden: July 2–Aug 28 on Thurs, Sun & Bank Hols, 2–5pm. Parties on other days by prior arrangement. **Admission:** Adults: house and garden £4.20. Garden only £3, children £1.

map 3 G3

GLASTONBURY ABBEY

Abbey Gatehouse, Magdalene Street, Glastonbury, Somerset
Tel: 01458 832267 Fax: 01458 832267 (Glastonbury Abbey Estate)

Traditionally the oldest Christian sanctuary in Britain and legendary burial place of King Arthur. Magnificent Abbey ruins set in 36 acres of glorious Somerset parkland. Visit our Award winning museum to see model of pre-reformation abbey and the Othery Cope. From April to October meet Brother Cleeve (actor) who will tell you how the monks used to live and feed. **Open:** Daily 9.30–6pm or dusk if earlier (except Christmas Day). June, July and Aug: open 9am. Dec, Jan and Feb: open 10am. Car and coach park adjoins our entrance. **Admission:** Adults £3, child (5–15yrs inc) £1. **E-mail:** glastonbury.abbey@dial.pipex.com **Internet:** www.glastonburyabbey.com

map 3 H3

GLENCOT HOUSE

Glencot Lane, Wookey Hole, Nr Wells, Somerset BA5 1BH
Tel: 01749 677160 Fax: 01749 670210 (Mrs M J Attia)

Idyllically situated in 18 acres of gardens and parkland with river frontage this elegantly furnished hotel offers high class accommodation, good food and friendly service. Over the past 15 years the gardens have been restored. There is a secret garden, rose walk, cascade and several other water features. **Open:** Wednesdays, 1 Apr–30 Sept, 11–5pm. **Refreshments:** light meals and refreshments available. **Location:** From Wells follow the signs to Wookey Hole drive through the village past the caves around the corner, take the first turning on the left along Titlands Lane, proceed for ½ a mile and you will find the entrance to Glencot Gardens through a white gate on the left. **E-mail:** glencot@ukonline.co.uk **Internet:** www.web.ukonline.co.uk/glencot

map 3 H3

HESTERCOMBE GARDENS

Hestercombe, Cheddon Fitzpaine, Taunton, Somerset TA2 8LG
Tel: 01823 413923 Fax: 01823 413747

Over three centuries of garden history are encompassed in Hestercombe's fifty acres of formal gardens and parkland near Cheddon Fitzpaine, Taunton. The unique Edwardian gardens, designed by Sir Edwin Lutyens and planted by Gertrude Jekyll, were completed in 1906. With terraces, pools and an orangery, they are the supreme example of their famous partnership. These gardens are now reunited with Hestercombe's secret Landscape Garden, which opened in the Spring of 1997 for the first time in 125 years. Created by Coplestone Warre Bampfyide in 1750s, these Georgian pleasure grounds comprise forty acres of lakes, temples and delightful woodland walks. **Location:** 4m NE of Taunton off A361. **Open:** Daily 10–last admission 5pm. **Admission:** Adults £3.60, children (5–15) £1. Groups and coaches by prior arrangement only.

map 3 G3

MAUNSEL HOUSE

North Newton, Nr Bridgwater, Somerset TA7 O8U
Tel: 01278 661076

This imposing 13th century manor house was partly built before the Norman Conquest, but latterly around a Great Hall erected in 1420. Geoffrey Chaucer wrote part of The Canterbury Tales whilst staying at the house. Maunsel House is the ancestral seat of the Slade family and is now the home of the 7th baronet, Sir Benjamin Slade. Wedding receptions, private and garden parties, conferences, functions, filming, fashion shows, archery, clay pigeon shooting, equestrian events. **Location:** OS Ref: ST302 303, Bridgwater 4m, Bristol 20 miles, Taunton 7 m, M5/J24, turn left North Petherton 2½ m SE of A38 at North Petherton. Gardens only 1 Apr–1 Oct (to include Easter). £2 (Honesty Box) Suns 2–5.30pm. **Open:** Coach and group parties welcomed by appointment. **Admission:** For further info tel: 0171 352 1132 (office hrs). **Internet:** www.sirbenslade.co.uk

map 3 G3

HATCH COURT

Hatch Beauchamp, Taunton, Somerset, TA3 6AA
Tel: 01823 480 120 Fax: 01823 480 058 (Dr & Mrs Robin Odgers)

A most attractive and unusual Grade I listed Bath stone Palladian mansion, surrounded by extensive gardens, beautiful parkland with a herd of fallow deer and stunning views over the Somerset countryside. A much loved and lived-in family home, shown by present members of the family (youngest aged 10), containing fine furniture, paintings and a unique semicircular china room and a small private military museum. **Location:** 6 miles SE Taunton, off A358. **Open & Admission:** Please phone for details, opening times and admission charges. **Refreshments:** Full catering available. **Conferences:** Functions, promotions, etc. Full facilities and experienced staff. Entire gardens – wheelchair accessible.

MILTON LODGE GARDENS

Old Bristol Road, Wells, Somerset
Tel: 01749 672168 (Mr D C Tudway Quilter)

Grade II listed terraced garden dating from 1906, with outstanding views of Wells Cathedral and Vale of Avalon. Mixed borders, roses, fine trees. Separate 8 acre early XIX century arboretum. **Location:** ½m N of Wells. From A39 Bristol-Wells turn N up Old Bristol Road; free car park first gate on left. **Open:** Garden and arboretum only Easter–end Oct daily (except Sat) 2–5pm. Parties and coaches by prior arrangement. **Admission:** Adults £2.50, children (under 14) free. Open on certain Suns in aid of National Gardens Scheme. **Refreshments:** Teas available Suns and Bank Hols Apr-Sept. No dogs.

map 3 H3

MUSEUM OF COSTUME & ASSEMBLY ROOMS

Bennett Street, Bath, Somerset
Tel: 01225 477789 Fax: 01225 477743 (National Trust)

The Assembly Rooms in Bath are open to the public daily when not in use for functions (admission free) and everyday in August. They are also popular for dinners, dances, concerts and conferences. The magnificent interior consists of a splendid Ball Room, Tea Room and Card Room, connected by two fine octagonal rooms. They are managed by Bath and North East Somerset Council, which runs a full conference service. The building houses one of the finest collections of fashionable dress in the country, the Museum of Costume (admission charge). Its extensive displays cover the history of fashion from the late 16th century to the present day, interpreted by hand-held audio guides at no extra charge. The shop sells noted publications and gifts. **Open:** All year, 10–5pm. Closed 25/26 Dec. Last admission ½ hr before closing. **Internet:** www.museumofcostume.co.uk

NUMBER 1, ROYAL CRESCENT

Bath, Avon.
Tel: 01225 428 126 Fax: 01225 481 850 (Bath Preservation Trust)

Number 1 was the first house built in the Royal Crescent in 1767 and is a fine example of John Wood the Younger's Palladian architecture. Visitors can see a grand town house of the late 18th century with authentic furniture, paintings and carpets. There is a study, dining room, lady's bedroom, drawing room, kitchen and museum shop. **Location:** Bath, upper town, close to the Assembly Rooms. **Open:** Mid Feb–end Oct, Tues–Sun, 10.30–5pm. Nov, Tue–Sun, 10.30–4pm. Last admission 30 mins before closing. Private tours out of hours if required by arrangement with the Administrator. Open Bank Hols and Bath Festival Mon. Closed Good Fri. **Admission:** Adults £4, children/students/OAPs £3, all groups £2.50, family ticket £10. **Internet:** www.bath–preservation–trust.org.uk

 map 4 A4

KENTSFORD HOUSE

Washford, Watchet, Somerset.
(Wyndham Estate)

House open only by written appointment with Mr R. Dibble. **Open:** Gardens Tues and Bank Hols. 14 Mar–29 Aug. **Admission:** Entry to the house £2. Gardens free.

 map 3 G3

ORCHARD WYNDHAM

Williton, Taunton, Somerset TA4 4HH
Tel: 01984 632309 Fax: 01984 633526 (Wyndham Est Office)

English Manor House. Family home for 700 years encapsulating continuous building and alteration from 14th to 20th centuries. **Location:** 1 mile from A39 at Williton. **Open:** House and gardens Thurs, Fri and Bank Hol Mon in August 2000 2–5pm. Guided tours only, last tour 4pm. Limited showing space within the house: to avoid disappointment please advance book places on tour by telephone or fax. House unsuitable for wheelchairs. Narrow road suitable for light vehicles only. **Admission:** Adults £4. Children under 12 £1.

 map 3 G3

BARRINGTON COURT

Barrington, nr Ilminster TA19 0NQ Tel: 01460 241938

Open: March and Oct: Sat & Sun 11–4.30pm; 21 April to 31 Sept: daily except Fri 11–5.30pm. Coach groups by appointment only. For further information, please tel. 0891 33525.

CLEVEDON COURT

Tickenham Road, Clevedon, North Somerset BS21 6QU Tel: 01275 872257

Open: 2 April to 28 Sept: Wed, Thur, Sun & BH Mons 2–5pm. **Admission:** Adults £4, concessions £2. **Restaurant**.

COLERIDGE COTTAGE

35 Lime Street, Nether Stowey, Bridgwater TA5 1NQ Tel: 01278 732662

Open: 2 April to 31 Oct: daily except Mon, Fri & Sat 2–5pm. In winter by written application to the Custodian. **Admission:** Adults £2.60, concessions £1.

DUNSTER CASTLE

Dunster, nr Minehead TA24 6SL Tel: 01643 821314

Open: Castle: 11 April to 27 Sept: daily except Thur & Fri. March to Sept 11–5pm; Oct 11–4pm. Garden and park: daily (closed 25 Dec). Jan to March, Oct to Dec 11–4pm; April to Sept 10–5pm. **Restaurant.**

LYTES CARY MANOR

Nr Charlton Mackrell, Somerton TA11 7HU Tel: Regional Office 01985 843600

Open: 1 April to 30 Oct: Mon, Wed & Sat 2–6 or dusk if earlier.

MONTACUTE HOUSE

Montacute TA15 6XP Tel: 01935 823289

Open: House: 1 April to 31 Oct: daily except Tues 12–5.30pm. Garden & park: 1 April to 30 Oct: daily except Tues; 1 Nov to March 2001: daily except Mon & Tues. March to Oct 11–5.30pm; Nov to March 11.30–4pm. **Events:** for details of all events tel: 01985 843601. **Restaurant.**

Staffordshire

If there is a Cinderella of the shires with beauty undiscovered, it is Staffordshire. Large numbers of people still cherish an utterly wrong impression of the county because of its famous "potteries" and industrial towns. It contains some of Britain's fairest treasures.

The Dove flows beside a string of market towns and hamlets; gems of lovely unspoiled England. Picturesque Ellastone, which lies below the lofty limestone ridge of the Weaver Hills was George Eliot's scene for 'Adam Bede' – high above is the quaint Wooton with its great park.

The capital of North Staffordshire is the town of Stoke-on-Trent, immortalised in the work of Arnold Bennett. Some of the finest porcelain in the world originates from this area and there are plenty of museums devoted to the development of this craft. For those interested in more energetic pastimes, the theme park at Alton Towers lies just fifteen miles to the east.

Lichfield, the birthplace of Dr. Samuel Johnson, is famous for its distinctive, three-spired cathedral, built in the thirteenth century and housing some magnificent Belgian stained glass.

ANCIENT HIGH HOUSE

Greengate Street, Stafford, Staffordshire, ST16 2JA
Tel: 01785 619619 Fax: 01785 619136 (Stafford Borough Council)

The Ancient High House is the largest timber-framed town house in England. It was built in 1595 by the Dorrington family. Its most famous visitor was King Charles 1, who stayed here in 1642. Now a registered museum, the fascinating history of the house is described in a series of displays. The top floor contains the Museum of the Staffordshire Yeomanry. Stafford's Tourist Information Centre is on the ground floor. An attractive gift shop is on the first floor, adjacent to the temporary exhibition area. **Location:** Town centre. **Admission:** Phone for prices. **E-mail:** TIC@staffordbc.gov.uk **Internet:** www.staffordbc.gov.uk

map 8 B6

BARLASTON HALL

Barlaston, Staffs ST12 9AT
Tel: 01782 372749 Fax: 01782 372391 (Mr and Mrs James Hall)

Barlaston Hall is a mid-eighteenth century palladian villa, attributed to the architect Sir Robert Taylor, extensively restored during the 1990s with the support of English Heritage. The four public rooms, open to visitors, contain some fine examples of eighteenth century plaster work. **Open:** By appointment to groups of 10–30. **Admission:** £3.50 per head including refreshments. If you wish to visit the hall, please write or fax giving details of your group including numbers, range or possible dates and a telephone contact. Recorded message with other opening times on above number.

map 8 B6

DUNWOOD HALL

Longsdon, Nr Leek, Staffordshire ST9 9AR
Tel: 01538 385071

Dunwood Hall is a private lived-in country house on the Staffordshire, Cheshire, Derbyshire borders near the Peak District. It is a listed building, recorded in Pevsner and is an unspoiled example of the Victorian neo-Gothic period, both inside and out. Built 1871 by the Pugin-influenced architect Robert Scrivener. Outstanding is the high–galleried hall with original Minton-tiled floor. The unique stone architecture, period décor, secluded gardens and the steepled stable–block (listed), all make a venue with authentic Victorian ambience. Interested Societies or groups are welcome for private visits. Dunwood Hall is in Longsdon, 3 miles West of Leek on the A53 to Stoke-On-Trent. **Open:** All year by arrangement. **Accommodation:** B & B available. **Admission:** £3–£5 (garden/house/guided tours) Home–made Refreshments.

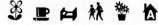

map 8 B5

CHILLINGTON HALL

Nr Wolverhampton, Staffordshire WV8 1RE
Tel: 01902 850236 (Mr & Mrs John Giffard)

Georgian house. Part 1724 (Francis Smith); part 1785 (Sir John Soane). Fine saloon. The lake in the park was created by 'Capability' Brown. The bridges by Brown and Paine and the Grecian and Roman Temples, together with the eye-catching Sham House, as well as many fine trees add great interest to the four mile walk around the lake. Dogs welcome in grounds if kept on lead. **Location:** 4 miles SW of A5 at Gailey; 2 miles Brewood. Best approach is from A449 (Jct 12, M6 Jct 2, M54) through Coven (no entry at Codsall Wood). **Open:** June–31 Aug Thurs (also Suns in Aug) 2–5pm open Easter Sun & Suns preceding May and late Spring Bank Holidays 2–5pm. Parties of at least 15 other days by arrangement. **Admission:** Adults £3, (grounds only £1.50) children half-price.

map 8 B7

THE DOROTHY CLIVE GARDEN

Willoughbridge, Market Drayton, Shropshire, TF9 4EU
Tel: 01630 647237 Fax: 01630 647902 (Willoughbridge Garden Trust)

The garden is known for its woodland plantings, established in a disused gravel quarry. A spectacular waterfall cascades between mature rhododendrons, azaleas and choice woodland plants. A south facing hillside garden provides views of surrounding countryside. A scree garden, water features and colourful summer borders are among the many delights. **Location:** A51, midway between Nantwich and Stone, 2 miles south of Woore. **Open:** Garden only: 1 Apr–31 Oct, daily 10–5.30pm. **Admission:** Adults £3, senior citizens £2.50, children up to 11 yrs free, 11–16 yrs £1. Free car park. **Refreshments:** Tearoom open daily. Beverages, home baking and light snacks.

FORD GREEN HALL

Ford Green Road, Smallthorne, Stoke-on-Trent, Staffordshire.
Tel: 01782 233 195 Fax: 01782 233 194
(Stoke-on-Trent City Council)

A timber-framed farmhouse built for the Ford family in 1624, with eighteenth century brick additions. The house is furnished according to inventories of the 17th and 18th century to give a flavour of the domestic life of the Ford family. **Location:** Smallthorne on B5051 Burslem-Endon Road. **Station(s):** Nearest Stoke-on-Trent. **Open:** Sunday–Thursday 1–5pm. Closed 25 Dec–1 Jan. **Admission:** Adult £1.50, concessions £1.00. Group/Coach parties by appointment. **Refreshments:** Small tearoom garden. **Events/Exhibitions:** Wide variety of events held throughout the year. Small parties by prior arrangement. **Internet:** www.stoke.gov.uk/fordgreenhall (Events listing available)

SANDON HALL

Sandon, Stafford, Staffordshire
Tel/Fax: 01889 508004 (The Earl of Harrowby)

Situated in the heart of Staffordshire and surrounded by 400 acres of parkland, this elegant neo-Jacobean house is a superb venue for a wide range of functions and for visits. Sandon Hall, ancestral home of the Earl of Harrowby, is steeped in history and contains many letters, clothes and furnishings of national importance which can be viewed in the museum. The 50 acre garden is landscaped and is especially beautiful in May/June, while the rolling parkland, laid out in the mid-18th century, is a visual delight throughout the seasons. **Location:** 5 miles NE of Stafford on A51, 10 mins from Jct 14, M6. **Open:** Throughout the year in booked groups only. **Admission:** Guided Tour £4 (concessions £3.50). Gardens £1.50 (concessions £1). **Refreshments:** Tea and cakes or Ploughman's Lunch – advance booking essential.

IZAAK WALTON'S COTTAGE

Worston Lane, Shallowford, Nr. Great Bridgeford,
Stafford, Staffordshire, ST15 0PA
Tel: 01785 760 278 (Stafford Borough Council)

Izaak Walton's Cottage was bequeathed to Stafford by this famous author of the 'Compleat Angler'. It is a delightful timber-framed, thatched cottage and registered museum. It has a series of angling displays showing how the equipment for this sport developed over the years. The events programme takes place each summer, both in the cottage and within its' beautiful garden. It has facilities for disabled visitors, although gravel paths can make access difficult. There are refreshment facilities. **Open:** Apr – Oct.

STAFFORD CASTLE & VISITOR CENTRE

Newport Road, Stafford, Staffordshire, ST16 1DJ
Tel: 01785 257 698 (Stafford Borough Council)

Stafford Castle is the impressive site of a Norman motte and bailey fortress. A later stone castle was destroyed during the Civil War, after being defended by Lady Isabel Stafford. It was partly rebuilt in the early 19th century and although now a ruin, is an important example of Gothic Revival architecture. A series of trail boards tell the story of the site. The Visitor Centre displays artefacts from a series of archaeological excavations. An audiovisual presentation narrated by Robert Hardy sets the scene. A collection of chain mail and other objects are fun to try on. A herb garden and attractive gift shop complete this interesting corner of Staffordshire. Picnic area, disabled access and guided tours available.

THE SHUGBOROUGH ESTATE

Milford, Nr. Stafford, ST17 0XB, Staffordshire.
Tel: 01889 881 388 Fax: 01889 881323 (Staffordshire County Council)

Shugborough is the magnificent 900 acre ancestral home of the 5th Earl of Lichfield, known world-wide as Patrick Lichfield the leading photographer. The 18th century mansion house contains a fine collection of ceramics, silver, paintings and French furniture. Part of the house is still lived in by the Earl. Visitors can enjoy the 18 acre Grade 1 Historic garden with its Edwardian Rose Garden and terraces. A unique collection of neo-classical monuments by James Stuart can be found in the parkland. Other attractions include the County Museum, housed in the original servants' quarters. The working laundry, kitchens and brewhouse have all been lovingly restored and are staffed by costumed guides. Shugborough Park Farm is a Georgian working farm which features an agricultural museum, restored working corn mill and a rare breeds centre. In the kitchen visitors can see bread baked in brick ovens and cheese and butter being made in the dairy. A lively collection of themed tours are in operation for the coach market and an award-winning educational programme for schools. From April to December an exciting events programme is in operation. Shugborough is an ideal venue for weddings, meetings, conferences, corporate activity days and product launches. **Location:** 6 miles E of Stafford on A513. 10 mins from M6, Jct 13. **Station:** Stafford. **Open:** 25 Mar–1 Oct (daily except Mons but open BH Mons) 11–5pm. Oct Suns only. All year to booked parties. **Admission:** Adults £4, concs £3, Voyager ticket (all 3 sites) Adults £8, concs £6, family £18. Site entry £2 per vehicle. **Conferences:** Facilities available. Please contact Mrs Anne Wood. **E-mail:** shugborough. promotions@staffordshire.gov.uk **Internet:** www.staffordshire.gov.uk

map 8
B6

TAMWORTH CASTLE

The Holloway, Tamworth, Staffordshire B79 7LR
Tel: 01827 709626 Fax: 01827 709630 (Tamworth Borough Council)

Dramatic Norman castle with 15 rooms open to the public, set in attractive town centre park noted for its floral terraces. Includes Great Hall, Dungeon and Haunted Bedroom featuring *Living Images*. "The Tamworth Story" – interactive exhibition telling the town's history from Roman times to the present day. **Location:** Town centre, in Castle Pleasure Grounds; 15 miles NE of Birmingham. **Station:** Tamworth. **Open:** Mon–Sat 10–5.30pm and Sun 2–5.30pm (last admission 4.30pm). Please check opening times after 1 November. **Admission:** Adults £4.20, concessions £2.10 and family ticket £11.60. **Events:** Approx 20 special events are held annually. Many are on Bank Holidays. **Internet:** www. tamworthcastle.co.uk

map 8
C7

WHITMORE HALL

Whitmore, Nr Newcastle-under-Lyme, Staffordshire ST5 5HW.
Tel: 01782 680478 Fax: 01782 680906 (Guy Cavenagh-Mainwaring Esq)

Whitmore Hall is a Grade 1 listed building, designated as a house of outstanding architectural and historical interest, and is a fine example of a small Carolinian Manor House, although parts of the Hall date back to a much earlier period. It has been the owner's family home for over 950 years and has continuous family portraits dating back to 1624. A special feature of Whitmore is the extremely rare example of a late Elizabethan stable block. The exterior grounds include a beautiful home park with a lime avenue leading to the house. **Location:** 4 miles from Newcastle-under-Lyme, on A53 to Market Drayton. **Open:** 1 May–31 August, Tues, Wed and Bank Hols, 2–5.30pm. **Admission:** Adult £3, child 50p.

map 8
A6

Suffolk

Suffolk

Those who delight in wide open spaces, blowing winds and delicate, shifting colour will find their paradise in Suffolk. There is a lyrical, quirky quality to the names of streets, villages and towns in Suffolk. The charmed villages and seaside towns of Orford, Somerleyton, Walberswick, Southwold and Aldeburgh remain resolutely unspoilt and almost Dickensian in appearance despite their seasonal popularity. Aldeburgh wakes up for three weeks in June to play host to East Anglia's most compelling cultural gathering, the Aldeburgh Festival, and then promptly falls back to sleep again.

The county has suffered changing fortunes, but a testament to former immense wealth can be seen in the huge churches, which dwarf all that now surrounds them. The town of Dunwich used to have thirteen of these mini-cathedrals, but due to fierce erosion they, along with the entire town and its once great port, have been lost.......to the sea!

Snape Maltings

THE ANCIENT HOUSE

Clare, Suffolk CO10 8NY
Tel: The Landmark Trust: 01628 825920
(Leased to the Landmark Trust by Clare Parish Council)

A 14th century house extended in the 15th and 17th centuries, decorated with high relief pargeting. Half of the building is managed by the Landmark Trust, which lets buildings for self-catering holidays. **Open:** By appointment only, and for Clare Arts Festival, w/c 17th June 2000. Tel: 01628 825920 for details. The other half is run as a Museum. **Open:** Contact Clare Museum Tel: 01787 277662 for details. **Accommodation:** Available for up to two people for self-catering holidays. Telephone: 01628 825925 for Bookings. Full details of the Ancient House and 167 other historic buildings are featured in the Landmark Handbook (price £9.50, refundable against a booking) from the Landmark Trust, Shottesbrooke, Maidenhead, Berkshire SL6 3SW. **Internet:** www.landmarktrust.co.uk

map 8 B6

HAUGHLEY PARK

Nr Stowmarket, Suffolk IP14 3JY
Tel: 01359 240701 (Mr & Mrs R J Williams)

Imposing red-brick Jacobean manor house of 1620, set in gardens, park and woodland. Unaltered three storey east front with five gables topped with crow steps and finials. North end rebuilt in Georgian style, 1820. Six acres of well-tended gardens including walled kitchen garden. Nearby 17th century brick and timber barn restored as meeting rooms. Three woodland walks (1.5 to 2.5 miles) through old broadleaf and pine woodland with bluebells, lily of the valley, rhododendron, azaleas and camellias. **Location:** 4 miles W of Stowmarket signed off A14 (Haughley Park, not Haughley). **Open:** Gardens: May–Sept, Tues and Sundays 30 Apr and May 2–5.30pm. House: by appointment (01359 240701) May–Sept, Tues 2–5.30pm. **Admission:** Adults £2, children £1.

map 5 H1

CHRISTCHURCH MANSION

Christchurch Park, Ipswich, Suffolk
Tel: 01473 433544 Fax: 01473 433564 (Ipswich Borough Council)

A fine tudor house set in beautiful parkland. Period rooms furnished in styles from 16th to 19th centuries. Outstanding collections of china, clocks and furniture. Paintings by Gainsborough, Constable and other Suffolk artists. Attached, the Wolsey Art Gallery shows a lively temporary exhibition programme. **Location:** Christchurch Park, near centre of Ipswich. **Station(s):** Ipswich (1.25 miles). **Open:** Tues–Sat, 10–5pm (dusk in winter). Sun 2.30–4.30pm (dusk in winter). Also open Bank Hol Mons. Closed 24–26 Dec, 1 Jan & Good Fri. **Admission:** Free.

map 5 H2

HENGRAVE HALL CENTRE

Hengrave Hall, Bury St Edmunds, Suffolk
Tel: 01284 701561 Fax: 01284 702950 (Religious of the Assumption)

Hengrave Hall is a Tudor mansion of stone and brick built between 1525 and 1538. Former home to the Kytson and Gage families, it was visited by Elizabeth I on her Suffolk Progress. Set in 45 acres of cultivated grounds, the Hall is now run as a Conference and Retreat Centre by the Hengrave Community of Reconciliation. The ancient church with Saxon tower adjoins the Hall and continues to be used for daily prayer. **Location:** 3.5 miles NW of Bury St Edmunds on the A1101. Enquire: The Warden for: tours (by appointment); conference facilities (day/ residential); retreats, programme of events; schools' programme. **E-mail:** co-ordinator@hengravehallcentre.org.uk **Internet:** www.hengravehallcentre.org.uk

map 5 G1

HELMINGHAM HALL GARDENS

The Estate Office, Helmingham Hall, Stowmarket, Suffolk IP14 6EF
Tel: 01473 890363 Fax: 01473 890776

Completed in 1510, the Hall has been the home of the Tollemache family continuously to the present day. There are two superb gardens that extend to several acres set in 400 acres of ancient parkland containing herds of Red and Fallow deer and Highland cattle. The main garden is surrounded by its own Saxon moat and 1740 wall, with wide herbaceous borders and planted tunnels intersecting an immaculate kitchen garden; the second is a very special rose garden enclosed within high yew hedges with a herb and knot garden containing plants grown in England before 1750. Listed Grade I by English Heritage. **Open:** 30 Apr–10 Sept 2000, Sun only 2–6pm. Also by appointment only for groups, Wed 2–5pm. **Admission:** Adults £3.75, children £2, groups 30+ £3.25 (£3.75 on Wed). Please call 01473 890363 to make an appointment.

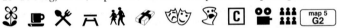

map 5
H2

IPSWICH MUSEUM

Ipswich, Suffolk, IP1 3QH.
Tel: 01473 433550 (Ipswich Borough Council)

Geology and natural history of Suffolk; Mankind galleries covering Africa, Asia, America and the Pacific. 'Romans in Suffolk' and 'Anglo-Saxons in Ipswich' exhibitions. **Location:** High Street in Ipswich town centre. **Station(s):** Ipswich. **Open:** Tues–Sat, 10–5pm. Closed Dec 24, 25 & 26, Jan 1 & Good Friday. Closed Bank Holidays. Temporary exhibition programme. **Admission:** Free.

map 5
H2

KENTWELL HALL

Long Melford, Suffolk, CO10 9BA,
Tel:01787 310207. Fax: 01787 379318 (Mrs Phillips)

A mellow redbrick moated Tudor Mansion. Exterior little changed from when it was built. Interior shows changes of successive family occupiers. Fine service buildings; Moat House with dairy, bakehouse and brewhouse. Moated Walled Garden with potager and herb garden. Lived in family home. Famous for RECREATIONS OF DOMESTIC TUDOR LIFE on selected weekends throughout season. Also Rare Breeds Farm. **Open:** Gardens & Farm only: 5–26 Mar. House, Gardens & Farm: 2–20 Apr, Suns only 7 May–11 June. Daily 12 July–8 Sept. Suns only 10 Sept–29 Oct & daily 22–27 Oct, usually 12–5pm. Re-Creations: Great Annual Re-Creations, 18 June–9 July (Sats & Suns only, plus Fri 7 July) plus Mini Re-Creations: 8–9 Apr, 21 Apr–1 May, 27–29 May, 5–6 Aug, 25–28 Aug, 23–24 Sept & 14–15 Oct. Telephone for opening times.

map 5
G2

OTLEY HALL

Otley, Nr Ipswich, Suffolk IP6 9PA
Tel: 01473 890264 Fax: 01473 890803 (Mr Nicholas & Mrs Ann Hagger)

A stunning medieval moated hall, grade 1 listed and a family home. Rich in history and architectural detail: ornately carved beams, superb linenfold panelling and 16 C wall paintings. Home of the Gosnold family for some 300 years from 1401. Bartholomew Gosnold voyaged to the New World in 1602 and named Cape Cod and Martha's Vineyard. He returned in 1606/7 to found the Jamestown colony, the first English-speaking settlement in the US, 13 years before the *Mayflower* landed. He is also linked to Shakespeare. The house is set in 10 acres of gardens. They include parts of a design by Francis Inigo Thomas (1866–1950): an H-canal, nutteries, croquet lawn, rose garden and moat walk. There are also historically accurate medieval/Tudor recreations designed by Sylvia Landsberg, author of *The Medieval Garden*, including a knot garden that symbolises the Universe, 25 beds representing 25 civilisations. Care has been taken to encourage growth of wild flowers and hedges, and preserve the habitats of native wildlife. There are newly constructed woodland walks with over 60 varieties of holly; collections of hostas, grasses and asters; and some surprises. **Open:** Bank Hol Suns and Mons, 12.30–6pm; Gardens only Mons from 10 Apr–25 Sept, 2–5pm. **Admission:** Adult £4.50, child £2.50. Garden Days: Adult £2.80, OAP £2.60, child £1. Coach parties welcome by appointment for private guided tours. Also available for Wedding Receptions, Conferences and Seminars, Corporate Entertainment, Concerts and Theatrical Productions.

map 5
H2

SOMERLEYTON HALL & GARDENS

Somerleyton, Lowestoft, Suffolk NR32 5QQ
Tel: 01502 730224 Fax: 01502 732143 (The Rt. Hon. Lord Somerleyton GCVO)

Home of Lord and Lady Somerleyton, Somerleyton Hall is a splendid early Victorian mansion built in Anglo-Italian style with lavish architectural features, magnificent carved stonework and fine state rooms. Paintings by Landseer, Wright of Derby and Stanfield, wood carvings by Willcox of Warwick and Grinling Gibbons. The justly renowned 12 acre gardens feature an 1846 yew hedge maze, glasshouses by Paxton, fine statuary, pergola, walled garden, Vulliamy tower clock, magnificent specimen trees and beautiful borders. Also Loggia Tea Rooms. **Location:** 5 miles NW Lowestoft B1074. **Open:** Easter Sunday–end Sept, Thursdays, Sundays and Bank Holidays plus Tuesdays and Wednesdays during July and August. Gardens 12.30–5.30pm, Hall 1–5pm. Coach parties welcome, private tours and functions by arrangement. **Internet:** www.somerleyton.co.uk

 map 9 K7

SHRUBLAND PARK GARDENS

Shrubland Park, Coddenham, Ipswich, Suffolk
Tel: 01473 830221 Fax: 01473 832202 (Lord De Saumarez)

The extensive formal garden of Shrubland Park is one of the finest examples of an Italianate garden in England. Much use is made of evergreens clipped into architectural shapes to complement the hard landscaping of the masonry. Pines, cedars, holly and holm oak soften this formal structure and add to the Italian flavour. Sir Charles Barry exploited the chalk escarpment overlooking the Gipping Valley to create one of his famous achievements, the magnificent 'Grand Descent' which links the Hall to the lower gardens through a series of terraces. **Location:** 6 miles north of Ipswich to the east of A14/A140 Beacon Hill junction. **Open:** Suns 2–5pm from 9 Apr–24 Sept 2000 inclusive, plus Bank Hol Mons. **Admission:** Adults £2.50, children and seniors £1.50. Guided tours by arrangement. Toilet facilities but no refreshments. Limited suitability for wheelchairs.

 map 5 H2

EUSTON HALL

(Nr. Thetford), Suffolk
Tel: 01842 766366 (The Duke and Duchess of Grafton)

Euston Hall – Home of the Duke and Duchess of Grafton. The 18th century country house contains a famous collection of paintings including works by Stubbs, Van Dyck, Lely and Kneller. The pleasure grounds were laid out by John Evelyn and William Kent, lakes by Capability Brown. 17th century parish church in Wren style. Watermill, craft shop, picnic area. **Location:** A1088; 3 miles S Thetford. **Open:** June 1–Sept 28 Thurs only 2.30–5pm, also Sun June 25 and Sept 3, 2.30–5pm. **Admission:** Adults £3, children 50p, OAPs £2.50. Parties of 12 or more £2.50 per head. **Refreshments:** Teas in Old Kitchen.

map 5 H1

WINGFIELD OLD COLLEGE & GARDENS

Wingfield, Nr Stradbroke, Suffolk IP21 5RA
Tel: 01379 384888 Fax: 01379 388082 (Mr & Mrs Ian Chance)

This delightful medieval house with walled gardens offers a unique Arts and Heritage experience. Spectacular medieval Great Hall. Exhibitions of contemporary art in the new College Yard galleries plus permanent collections of textiles, ceramics and garden sculpture. Some of history's colourful characters associated with the Old College are the Black Prince, William de la Pole and Mary Tudor. Summer 2000 - 17th century walled garden restoration project. **Location:** Signposted off B1118 (Off the A140 Ipswich/Norwich trunk road) and the B1116 (Harleston–Fressingfield). **Open:** Easter Sat–end Sept Sats, Suns, Bank Hol Mons 2–6pm. **Admission:** Adults £3.80, seniors £3, children/students £1.50, family ticket £9. **Refreshments:** Cream teas and homemade cakes.

 map 5 H1

WYKEN HALL

Stanton, Bury St.Edmunds, Suffolk IP31 2DW
Tel: 01359 250287 Fax: 01359 252256

The garden, vineyard, country store and vineyard restaurant at Wyken are at the heart of an old Suffolk manor that dates back to Domesday. The garden, set among old flint walls and fine trees, embraces herb and knot gardens, an old-fashioned rose garden, maze, nuttery and gazebo set in a wild garden with spring bulbs. The Leaping Hare Vineyard Restaurant in the 400 year old barn serves Wyken's award-winning wines and is the 1998 Good Food Guide's 'Vineyard Restaurant of the Year'. The Country Store offers an unique collection of textiles, pottery and baskets from the Suffolk Craft Society. A walk through ancient woodland leads to the vineyard. **Open:** Weds–Sun 10–6pm and for dinner Fri–Sat. Garden closed on Saturdays.

 map 5 H1

ICKWORTH HOUSE, PARK & GARDEN

Ickworth, The Rotunda, Horringer, Bury St Edmunds IP29 5QE
Tel: Property Office 01284 735270

Open: 18 March to 29 Oct: daily except Mon & Thur (but open BH Mons) 1–5pm. Garden: 18 March to 29 Oct: daily; 1 Nov to end March 2001: daily except Sat & Sun 10–5pm; 1 Nov to end March 2001: 10–4pm. Park: daily 7–7pm.

LAVENHAM: THE GUILDHALL OF CORPUS CHRISTI

Market Place, Lavenham, Sudbury CO10 9QZ Tel: 01787 247646

Open: March to Nov: daily (closed Good Fri) 11–4pm. The building, or parts of it, may be closed ocassionally for community use.

MELFORD HALL

Long Melford, Sudbury CO10 9AH Tel: 01787 880286

Open: April & Oct: Sat, Sun & Bank Hol Mons; May to end Sept; daily except Mon & Tues (but open BH Mons) 2–5.30pm.

THEATRE ROYAL

Westgate Street, Bury St Edmunds, Suffolk IP33 1QR Tel: 01284 755127
Fax: 01284 706035

Open: Daily, except Sun & BHols 10.30–3.30pm. No access when theatrical activity in progress. Check in advance that theatre is open, tel. 01284 769505.

Surrey

A county of sandy heaths and spacious commons, Surrey commands wide views of the chequered Weald where oak and elm thrive.

Leafy lanes, steep and twisted, are an attractive feature of Surrey towns. The town planners seem to have determinedly built roads around both natural resources and old buildings, giving each town an intricate cobweb of infrastructure and genuine charm.

Surrey's verdant beauty was appreciated amongst some of the most prestigious literary figures of the past. Jane Austen, Sheridan, Keats and EM Forster gained inspiration from this county. Explore the cobbled charm of Surrey's Georgian capital, Guildford, or the tiny streets of hidden villages and you will feel equally as inspired.

River Wey, Guildford

CLANDON PARK

West Clandon, Guildford, Surrey, GU4 7RQ
Tel: 01483 222482 Fax: 01483 223176 (The National Trust)

An outstanding Palladian country house of dramatic contrasts; from the magnificent neoclassical marble hall to the Maori Meeting House in the garden; the opulent saloon to the old kitchen, complete with old range, below stairs. All this adds up to a fascinating insight into the different lifestyles of the ruling and serving classes in the 18th century. The house is rightly acclaimed for housing the famous Gubbay Collection of porcelain, furniture and needlework, as well as Onslow family pictures and furniture, the Mortlake tapestries and the Ivo Forde collection of Meissen Italian comedy figures. The garden has a grotto and parterre and there is a gift shop and licensed restaurant. **Location:** At West Clandon on the A247, 3 miles E of Guildford. B Rail Clandon 1 mile. **Open:** 2 Apr–31 Oct, Tue, Wed, Thur, Sun plus Bank Hols & Easter 11.30–4.30pm.

CLAREMONT

Claremont Drive, Esher, Surrey, KT10 9LY
Tel: 01372 467 841 Fax: 01372 471 109
(The Claremont Fan Court Foundation Limited)

Excellent example of Palladian style. Built in 1772 by 'Capability' Brown for Clive of India. Henry Holland and John Soane were responsible for the interior decoration. It is now an independent co-educational school. **Location:** ½ mile SW of Esher on A307, Esher-Cobham Road. **Open:** Feb–Nov, first complete weekend (Sat–Sun) in each month (except first Sat in July), 2–5pm. Last tour 4.30 pm. **Admission:** Adults £3, children/OAPs £2. Reduced rates for parties. Guided tours and souvenirs. **E-mail:** mansion@claremont–school.co.uk **Internet:** www.claremont–school.co.uk

CROYDON PALACE

Old Palace School, Old Palace Road, Croydon, Surrey, CR0 1AX
Tel: 020 8688 2027 / 020 8680 0467 Fax: 020 8680 5877
(The Whitgift Foundation)

Seat of the Archbishops of Canterbury since 871 AD. 15th century Banqueting Hall and Guardroom. Tudor Chapel. Norman Undercroft. **Location:** In Croydon Old Town, adjacent to the Parish Church. **Station(s):** East Croydon or West Croydon. **Open:** Conducted Tours only. Doors open 1.45pm. Tours at 2.15pm. 10–15 Apr & 29 May–3 June & 10–15 July & 17–22 July. **Admission:** Adults £4.00, children/OAPs £3, family £10. Includes tea served in the Undercroft. Parties catered for by prior arrangement (Tel: 020 8680 0467). Souvenir shop. Unsuitable for wheelchairs. **E-mail:** awb@soton.ac.uk

FARNHAM CASTLE

Farnham, Surrey GU7 0AG
Tel: 01252 721194 Fax: 01252 711283 (Church Commissioners)

Bishop's Palace built in Norman times by Henry of Blois, with Tudor and Jacobean additions. Formerly the seat of the Bishops of Winchester. Fine Great Hall re-modelled at the Restoration. Features include the Renaissance brickwork of Wayneflete's tower and the 17th century chapel. **Location:** ½ miles N of Town Centre on A287. **Station(s):** Farnham. **Open:** All year round, Weds 2–4pm; parties at other times by arrangement. All visitors given guided tours. Centrally heated in winter. **Admission:** Adults £1.50, OAPs/children/students 80p, reductions for parties. **Conferences:** Please contact Conference Organiser. Centrally heated in winter. Not readily accessible by wheelchair.

GODDARDS

Abinger Common, Dorking, Surrey, RH5 6TH
Tel: The Landmark Trust: 01628 825920
(Leased to the Landmark Trust by the Lutyens Trust)

Built by Sir Edwin Lutyens in 1898–1900. Garden by Gertrude Jekyll. Managed and maintained by the Landmark Trust, which lets buildings for self-catering holidays. **Open:** By appointment only. Must be booked in advance, including parking, which is very limited. Visits booked for Wed afternoons from the Wed after Easter until last Wed of Oct between 2–6pm. **Admission:** Tickets £3, obtainable from Mrs Baker on 01306 730871, Mon–Fri, 9–6pm. Visitors will have access to part of the house and garden only. **Accommodation:** Available for up to 12 people. Tel: 01628 825925 for bookings. Full details of Goddards and 168 other historic buildings are featured in The Landmark Handbook (price £9.50 refundable against a booking) from The Landmark Trust, Shottesbrooke, Maidenhead, Berkshire, SL6 3SW. **Internet:** www.landmarktrust.co.uk

map 4
E5

GREAT FOSTERS

Stroude Road, Egham, Surrey
Tel: 01784 433822 Fax: 01784 472455

Probably built as a Royal Hunting lodge in Windsor Forest, very much a stately home since the 16th century, today Great Fosters is a prestigious hotel. It is evident in the mullioned windows, tall chimneys and brick finials, while the Saxon moat – crossed by a Japanese bridge – surrounds three sides of the formal gardens complete with topiary, statuary and a charming rose garden. Within are fine oak beams and panelling, Jacobean chimney pieces, superb tapestries and a rare oakwell staircase leading to the Tower. Some guest bedrooms are particularly magnificent – one Italian styled with gilt furnishings and damask walls, others with moulded ceilings, beautiful antiques and Persian rugs. Close to M25, Heathrow and M3. London 40 minutes by rail. **E-mail:** GreatFosters@compuserve.com **Internet:** www.great–fosters.co.uk

map 4
E4

GUILDFORD HOUSE GALLERY

155 High Street, Guildford, Surrey, GU1 3AJ
Tel: 01483 444740, Fax: 01483 444742 (Guildford Borough Council)

A beautifully restored 17th century town house with a number of original features including a finely carved staircase, panelled rooms and decorative plaster ceilings. A varied temporary exhibition programme including paintings, photography and craft work. Exhibition and events leaflet available. Lecture and workshop programme. Details on application. **Location:** Central Guildford on High Street. Public car parks nearby off pedestrianised High Street. **Open:** Tues–Sat 10–4.45pm **Admission:** Free. **Refreshments:** Old kitchen tearoom. **Gallery Shop:** with attractive selection of cards, craftwork and other publications. **E-mail:** guildfordhouse@remote.guildford.gov.uk **Internet:** guildford borough.co.uk/pages/leisure/culture/housgall/housegt.htm.

map 4
E5

HAMPTON COURT PALACE

East Molesey, KT8 9AY
Tel: 0181 781 9500

The Splendour of Cardinal Wolsey's house, begun in 1514, surpasses that of many a Royal Palace, so it was not surprising that Henry VIII obtained it prior to Wolsey's fall from power. Henry VIII enlarged it; Charles I lived in it as a prisoner; Charles I repaired it; William III and Mary I rebuilt it to a design by Sir Christopher Wren and Queen Victoria opened it to the public. PLEASE LOOK UNDER LONDON SECTION FOR FULL INFORMATION DETAILS AND PHOTOGRAPHY.

HAM HOUSE

Ham Street, Richmond, Surrey TW10 7RS
Tel: 020 8940 1950 Fax: 020 8332 6903 (The National Trust)

Set in beautiful gardens by the Thames, Ham House is one of the finest 17th century houses in Europe, with exquisite furniture, textiles and paintings. **Location:** South bank of River Thames. West of A307 at Petersham. **Station(s):** BR/London Underground – Richmond (2m by road). BR - Kingston (2m by road). **Buses:** 65, 371 (both passing Richmond & Kingston stns.). **Open:** 1 Apr–29 Oct: daily except Thurs & Fri 1–5pm. Last admission ½ hr before closing. Garden: all year daily except Thurs & Fri 10.30–6pm or dusk if earlier. Closed 25–26 Dec & 1 Jan. **Admission:** Adults £5, Child £2, Family £12.50. Pre-booked parties on application. **Refreshments:** Orangery Restaurant – self-service (Tel: 020 8940 0735). Open Sat–Wed, 11am–5.30pm. Disabled visitors may park near entrance. Disabled toilet.

map 12
U22

HATCHLANDS PARK

East Clandon, Guildford, Surrey GU4 7RT
Tel: 01483 222482 Fax: 01483 223176

Built in 1758 for Admiral Boscawen and set in a beautiful Repton park offering a variety of park and woodland walks, Hatchlands contains splendid interiors by Robert Adam, his first commission in a country house in England. It houses the Cobbe Collection, the world's largest group of early keyboard instruments associated with famous composers, e.g. Purcell, JC Bach, Chopin, Mahler, Elgar and Marie Antoinette. Small garden by Gertrude Jekyll, gift shop, licensed restaurant. Audio Guide. Lunchtime recitals most Wednesdays. **Location:** 5 miles E of Guildford, on A246 Guildford–Leatherhead Road. **Open:** 2 Apr–31 Oct, walks daily 11–6pm. House: Tues, Wed, Thurs, Sun plus BH Mons and all Fris in Aug 2–5.30pm. **Events:** Second weekend in July 2000 Hatchlands Hat Trick Open Air Concerts Tel: 01372 451596.

map 4
E5

LOSELEY PARK

Guildford, Surrey, GU3 1HS
Tel: 01483 304 440 Fax: 01483 302 036 (Mr & Mrs Michael More-Molyneux)

Loseley House was built in 1562 by Sir William More, a direct ancestor of the present owner. It is a fine example of Elizabethan architecture, dignified and beautiful, set amid magnificent parkland. Inside are many fine works of art, including panelling from Henry VIII's Nonsuch Palace, paintings and tapestries. The glorious 2.5 acre Walled Garden features an award-winning Rose Garden (with over 1,000 bushes, mainly old-fashioned varieties), a Herb Garden (divided into sections for culinary, medicinal, dyeing, cosmetic and ornamental purposes), a Flower Garden, a Vegetable Garden, a Fountain Garden and also Moat Walk. The Garden has been carefully planted to create interest and colour throughout the year. **Location:** 2 miles south of Guildford. (Take B3000 off A3 through Compton). 2 miles north of Godalming (off B3100). OS Ref. SU975 471. **Station(s):** Farncombe 1.5 miles. Guildford 2 miles. **Admission: House & Gardens:** Adult £5, child £3, concession £4. **Gardens only:** Adult £2.50, child £1.50, concession £2. Group rates available. **Open: Garden, Shop & Tea Room:** 1 May–30 Sept, Wed–Sat & Bank Hol, 11–5pm. Plus Sun in June, July & Aug. **House:** 29 May–31 Aug, Wed–Sun & Bank Hol, 2–5pm (last tour 4pm). **Refreshments:** Courtyard Tea Room serves light lunches and teas. **Corporate:** The Tithe Barn is available for conferences, company days, private parties and wedding receptions. The House and Tithe Barn are licensed for Civil wedding ceremonies. Chapel. New for 2000: House & Garden: open on Sun in June, July & August. Lakeside walks & picnic area.

map 4
E5

PAINSHILL LANDSCAPE GARDEN

Portsmouth Road, Cobham, Surrey KT11 1JE
Tel: 01932 868113 Fax: 01932 868001 (Painshill Park Trust)

One of Europe's finest eighteenth century landscape gardens. Designed to surprise and mystify, leaving visitors spellbound at every turn. Walk around the 14 acre Serpentine lake. A Gothic temple, Chinese bridge, crystal grotto, Turkish tent, replanted shrubberies all disappear and reappear as the walk proceeds. **Location:** W of Cobham of A245; 200 metres E of A307 roundabout. Visitor entrance: Between Streets, Cobham. **Open:** April–Oct daily except Mon (open Bank Hols). 10.30–6.00pm (last entry 4.30pm). Nov–Mar daily except Mon & Fri, Christmas Day & Boxing Day. 11–4pm dusk if earlier. (Last entry 3pm) **Admission:** Adults £3.80, concessions £3.30, children 5–16 £1.50. School groups must arrange with Education Department 01932 866743, prices vary. Adult groups of 10+ £3 (**must pre-book phone 01932 868113**). No dogs please.

RHS GARDEN WISLEY

Wisley, Woking, Surrey GU23 6QB
Tel: 01483 224234 (Royal Horticultural Society)

A world famous garden which extends to 240 acres and provides a unique chance to glean new ideas and inspiration. The Alpine Meadow, carpeted with wild daffodils in spring, Battleston Hill, brilliant with rhododendrons in early summer, the heathers and autumnal tints together with the glasshouses, trials and model gardens are all features for which the garden is renowned. But what makes Wisley unique is that it is not just beautiful to look at. As the showpiece of the Royal Horticultural Society, the Garden is a source of not only practical advice but also over 9,000 plants available in the Plant Centre. **Location:** Wisley is just off M25 Jct 10, on the A3. **Open:** Every day of the year (except Christmas Day) though please note, Sundays are for Members only. **Further Information phone 01483 224234. E-mail:** joannec@rhs.org.uk

TITSEY PLACE AND GARDENS

Titsey Hill, Oxted, Surrey RH8 OSD
Tel: 01273 407056 (The Trustees of the Titsey Foundation)

Historic Mansion House. Situated outside Limpsfield, Surrey. Extensive formal and informal gardens containing Victorian Walled Garden, lakes, fountains and rose gardens. Outstanding features of this House include important paintings and object d'art. Home of the Gresham and Leveson Gower Family since the 16th century. **Location:** A25 Oxted to Westerham, at main traffic lights in Limpsfield turn left and then at the bottom of Limpsfield High Street on sharp bend, turn left in to Bluehouse Lane and then first right in to Water Lane. Under motorway and turn right in to Titsey Park. **Open:** Between 15 May–30 Sept on Weds and Suns. 1–5pm and Summer Bank Hols. Also Easter Mon (garden only). Guided tours of the House at 2pm, 3pm and 4pm. Private parties by prior arrangement. **Admission:** House and garden £4.50, garden only £2. Contact: Kate Moisson. Limited access to house, infinite capacity in garden.

Sussex

Of all the counties Sussex is the easiest to visualise. Sussex lies in four parallel strips – the northern boundary being forest, the next strip the clay Weald, then the smooth green line of the downs and lastly, the coastline of chalk-cliff and low plain – each sublime in its own way.

East Sussex is dramatically beautiful. Inland, the rolling Downs provide a chalky background to the mysterious figure of the Long Man of Wilmington whilst on the coast lies Brighton, an intensely lively place which is often described as "London By The Sea".

West Sussex plays host to the historic town of Chichester where four atmospheric bustling streets meet at a central 16th century market cross. Chichester's cathedral is also worth a visit and its majestic spire dominates the surrounding countryside.

Lewes

ANNE OF CLEVES HOUSE

52 Southover High Street, Lewes, Sussex BN7 1JA
Tel: 01273 474 610 Fax: 01273 486 990 (Sussex Past)

This beautiful 16th century timber-framed Wealden hall-house contains wide-ranging collections of Sussex interest. Furnished rooms give an impression of life in the 17th and 18th centuries. Exhibits include artefacts from nearby Lewes Priory, Sussex pottery, Wealden ironwork and kitchen equipment. **Station(s):** Lewes (10 mins walk). **Bus route:** Adjacent. Bus station 15 mins walk away. **Open:** 4 Jan–20 Feb: Tues, Thurs & Sat 10–5pm. 21 Feb–5 Nov: Sat, 10–5pm; Sun 12–5pm. 6 Nov–31 Dec (ex 24–27): Tues–Sat, 10–5pm; Sun 12–5pm. **Admission:** Adults £2.50, children £1.10, OAP/Student £2.30, family (2+2) £6.70; combined ticket with Lewes Castle available. 50% discount to EH members. No dogs. **E-mail:** castle@sussexpast.co.uk

BENTLEY HOUSE & GARDENS

Halland, Nr. Lewes, East Sussex, BN8 5AF
Tel: 01825 840573 (East Sussex County Council) Fax: 01825 841322

Bentley House dates back to early 18th century times and was built on land granted to James Gage by the Archbishop of Canterbury, with the permission of Henry VIII. The family of Lord Gage was linked with Bentley from that time until 1904. The estate was purchased by Gerald Askew in 1937 and during the 1960s he and his wife, Mary, added two double height Palladian rooms to the original farmhouse. The architect who advised them was Raymond Erith, who had worked on 10 Downing Street. The drawing room contains mid 18th century Chinese wallpaper and gilt furniture. The Bird Room contains a collection of wildfowl paintings by Philip Rickman. The gardens at Bentley have been created as a series of 'rooms' divided by Yew hedges, specialising in many old-fashioned roses including the Bourbons, the Gallicas and the Damask. Nearby 6 stone sphinxes stand along a broad grass

walk where daffodils bloom in spring. **Location:** 7 miles northeast of Lewes, signposted on A22, A26 & B2192. **Open:** 20 Mar–31 Oct, daily 10.30–4.30pm (last admissions). House opens 12noon daily 1 Apr–31 Oct. **Admission:** 2000 prices: Adults £4.80, senior/student £3.80, child (4–15) £3, family (2A+4C) £14.50, 10% discount for groups 11+. Special rates for disabled (wheelchairs available). Admission price allows entry to House, Gardens, Grounds, Wildfowl Reserve, Motor Museum, History of Bentley Exhibition, Woodland Walk, Children's Adventure Play Area. Picnic area, Gift shop complimented by resident crafts people, Education Centre with audio visual. **Refreshments:** Licensed tearooms. **Conferences:** Civil wedding ceremonies. Ample free parking. Dogs allowed in this area only. **E-mail:** barrysutherland@pavilion.co.uk **Internet:** www.bentley.org.uk

ARUNDEL CASTLE

Arundel, West Sussex, BN18 9AB.
Tel: 01903 883136 Fax: 01903 884581 (Arundel Castle Trustees Ltd)

A Castle has overlooked the picturesque South Downs town of Arundel and River Arun for almost 1000 years. The Castle is set in spacious and beautiful landscaped grounds and features a fully restored Victorian kitchen garden. The original Castle suffered some destruction by Cromwell's troops during the Civil War. With restoration and later additions, the Arundel Castle of today is quite magnificent and houses a very fine collection of furniture dating from the 16th century, tapestries, clocks and paintings by Canaletto, Gainsborough, Van Dyck and many other masters. There is such a wealth of treasures to see – the Library with its spectacular carved and vaulted ceiling, the Bedrooms including the suite refurbished for Queen Victoria and Prince Albert with its sumptuous gilt state bed, the Dining Room, the Picture Gallery and much, much more. **Open:** From 2 April until the last Friday in October, 12–5pm, the last admission on any day is at 4pm. The Castle is closed on Good Friday and Saturdays. Delicious home-made lunches and afternoon teas are served daily in the restaurant. Pre-booked parties are welcome and menus are available on request. Gifts and mementoes, chosen especially by the Countess of Arundel, can be purchased in the shop which is open at the same time as the Castle. For further information please contact: The Comptroller, Arundel Castle, West Sussex BN18 9AB. Tel: 01903 883136/882173. Fax: 01903 884581.

map 4 E6

ARCHITECTURAL PLANTS CHICHESTER

Lidsey Road Nursery, Woodgate, Chichester, West Sussex PO20 6SU
Tel: 01243 545008 Fax: 01243 545009 (Christine Shaw)

Architectural Plants has been trading for some 10 years now. The Chichester Branch was set up in 1997 to cope with the increasing demand for exotic and unusual hardy plants and also to extend propagation and the growing on of larger numbers of our home grown, broad-leaved, garden sized trees. The Nursery also specialises in Seaside Plants - tough and exotic specimens that will thrive in these difficult conditions and survive salt-laden winds and fierce winter gales. **Open:** The Chichester Nursery is open Monday to Friday from 9am to 5pm, Closed Saturday, open Sunday from 10am to 4pm.

map 4 E5/6

CHICHESTER CATHEDRAL

West Street, Chichester, West Sussex, PO19 1PX
Tel: 01243 782595 Fax: 01243 536190 (The Dean and Chapter of Chichester)

In the heart of the city, this fine Cathedral has been a centre of Christian worship and community life for 900 years and is the site of the Shrine of St Richard of Chichester. Its treasures range from Romanesque stone carvings to 20th century works of art by Sutherland, Feibusch, Procktor, Chagall, Skelton, Piper, Ursula Benker-Schirmer and Philip Jackson. Treasury. **Location:** Centre of city, British Rail, A27, A286. **Open:** Summer 7.30–7pm; Winter 7.30–5pm. Choral Evensong daily (except Wed) during term time. **Admission:** Free; suggested donations adults £2, children 50p. **Conferences:** Medieval Vicars' Hall (for 100 people max). Loop system during Cathedral services; touch and hearing centre and braille guide for the blind. Guide dogs only. Parking in city car and coach parks. Contact: Mrs Jenny Thom.

map 4 D6

1066 BATTLE OF HASTINGS ABBEY & BATTLEFIELD

Battle, East Sussex TN33 0AD
Tel: 01424 773792 (English Heritage)

Battle Abbey stands at one of the turning points in history, 1066 and the Battle of Hastings. A free interactive audio tour will lead you around the battlefield itself and you can even stand on the exact spot where King Harold fell. As the sounds of the battle ring in your ears, you can retrace the lines of conflict and discover where the English army watched the advancing enemy. Explore the impressive abbey ruins then walk the abbey walls to the Great Gatehouse and climb the spiral staircase to the exhibition about abbey life in the Middle Ages. **Location:** At south end of Battle High Street. Battle is reached by road by turning off A21 onto the A2100. **Open:** 1 Apr–30 Sept: daily, 10–6pm, 1 Oct–31 Oct: daily, 10–5pm, 1 Nov–31 Mar: 10–4pm. (Closed 24–5 Dec and 1 Jan) **Admission:** Adults £4, concs £3, child £2, family £10 (15% discount for groups of 11 or more).

map 5 G6

BORDE HILL GARDEN

Balcombe Road, Haywards Heath, West Sussex RH16 1XP
Tel: 01444 450326 Fax: 01444 440427

Visitor Attraction of the Year 1999 SEETB. A garden of contrast that captures the imagination and delights the senses. This truly global garden, established in the early 1900s set in 200 acres of spectacular parkland, contains a phenomenal range of rare trees, shrubs and perennials. The sub-tropical Round Dell and the Italian Garden lead to the Garden of Allah and on to the romantic English Rose Garden. A Heritage Lottery Grant has enabled a "renaissance", with extensive replanting, the creation of a wildlife pond and a new Mediterranean garden, restoration of Victorian greenhouses and pathways for disabled access. Blooms Plant Centre & Tea Room. Jeremy's Restaurant. **Open:** Daily All year incl Christmas Day 10–6pm. **Admission:** Adults £4.50, child £1.75, groups 20+ £4, family ticket £11, guided tours available. **Internet:** www.bordehill.co.uk

map 5 F6

FISHBOURNE ROMAN PALACE

Salthill Road, Fishbourne, Chichester, Sussex PO19 3QR
Tel: 01243 785 859 Fax: 01243 539 266 (Sussex Past)

First occupied as a military base in AD43, Fishbourne's sumptuous palace was built around AD75. Remains include 20 spectacular mosaics and its story is told in the museum and by an audiovisual programme. The Roman garden has been replanted to its original plan and now features a Roman gardening museum. There is also an Education Centre and shop. **Station(s):** Fishbourne (5 mins walk). **Bus route:** 5 mins walk away. **Open:** 3 Jan–6 Feb & 16–31 Dec: Sat & Sun 10–4pm. 7 Feb–15 Dec: daily 10–5pm (Mar–Jul & Sept–Oct) 10–6pm (Aug) 10–4pm (Feb, Nov–Dec). **Admission:** Adults £4.40, children (5–15) £2.30. Students/OAP £3.70, disabled £3.50, family (2+2) £11.50. 50% discount to EH members. **Refreshments:** Cafeteria. Picnic area. Suitable for disabled. Parking and toilets. No dogs. **E-mail:** adminfish@sussexpast.co.uk

map 4 D6

CHARLESTON

Firle, Nr Lewes, East Sussex
Tel: 01323 811265 (Visitor Information) Fax: 01323 811628

Charleston was the home of Vanessa Bell, the sister of Virginia Woolf, and Duncan Grant from 1916 until Grant's death in 1978. The house became a 'Bloomsbury' outpost, full of intellectuals, artists and writers; walls, furniture and ceramics were decorated by the artists with their own designs, strongly influenced by post impressionism and interior decoration styles in France and Italy. The walled garden displays a vivid collection of contrasting plants and flowers **Location:** Signposted off the A27, 6 miles E of Lewes, between the villages of Firle and Selmeston. **Open:** 1 Apr–29 Oct, Weds to Sun & Bank Holiday Mons 2–5pm. Jul & Aug Wed–Sat 11.30–5pm, Sun & Bank Holiday Mons 2–5pm. Guided tours Weds–Sats; unguided Suns & Bank Holiday Mons. Connoisseur Fridays; in-depth tour of the house including Vanessa Bell's studio and the kitchen, not July and Aug. **Admission:** House/Garden: Adult £5.50, children £4, Connoisseur Fridays £6.50, Concessions £4 Wed & Thurs only. Organised groups should telephone 01323 811626 for rates and information. **Refreshments:** Tea and cakes available Wed to Sun. **Events/Exhibitions:** The Charleston Festival 25–29 May. Literature, art and theatre. The Charleston Gallery; explores Charleston's history and influence on contemporary art. The shop is Craft's Council selected; applied art and books. No disabled access beyond ground floor. Disabled toilet. No dogs. No film, video or photography in the house.

map 5
F6

GOODWOOD HOUSE

Goodwood, Chichester, West Sussex PO18 0PX
Tel: 01243 755048 Fax: 01243 755005 (The Duke of Richmond)

Richly refurbished country home of the Lennox sisters featured in the acclaimed BBC real life drama series 'Aristocrats'. The unparalleled collection includes commissioned works by Canaletto and Stubbs, French furniture, and the unique Sèvres Bird Services. **Location:** 3½ miles NE of Chichester. **Open:** Suns and Mons from 2 Apr–25 Sept, and on Sun–Thurs 6–31 Aug. 1–5pm. Closed on Special Event Days in Apr, May, 18–19, 25–26 June, 1–3 Aug and 17 Sept. **Please check Recorded Information:** 01243 755040). Groups welcome on Open Days. All groups must book. Guided tours for groups on Mon mornings by arrangement and on Connoisseurs' Days. **Admission:** Adult £6, child (12–18) £3. Groups (20–200) Guided £8, Open Days £5. **Refreshments** and teas. Free coach/car park.

map 4
D6

DENMANS GARDEN

Denmans Lane, Fontwell, Nr Arundel, West Sussex BN18 0SU
Tel: 01243 542808, Fax: 01243 544064 (Mr John Brookes)

Unique 20th century garden artistically planted with emphasis on colour, shape and texture. Individual plantings within the garden are allowed to self-seed and ramble, often in gravel. A remarkable and unique collection of plants - glass areas for tender species. **Location:** Between Arundel and Chichester, turn off A27 into Denmans Lane (W of Fontwell racecourse). **Station(s):** Barnham (2 miles). **Open:** Daily from 1 March–31 October including all Bank Hols 9–5pm. Coaches by appointment. **Admission:** Adults £2.80, children £1.50, senior citizens £2.50. Groups of 15 or more £2.20 (1999 prices). **Refreshments:** Restaurant open 11–5pm. Plant centre. No dogs. National Gardens Scheme.

map 4
E6

MARLIPINS MUSEUM

High Street, Shoreham-by-Sea, Sussex BN43 5DA
Tel: 01273 462994

Shoreham's local and especially its maritime history are explored at Marlipins, itself an important historic Norman building believed to have once been used as a Customs House. It has a beautiful chequer-work facade of Caen Stone and inside, much of the original timberwork of the building is open to view. The maritime gallery contains many superb nautical models and fine paintings, while the rest of the museum houses exhibits dating back to Man's earliest occupation of the area. The development of Shoreham's airport and life in the town during the war years feature prominently in the displays. **Open:** 1 May–30 Sept: Tues–Sat, 10.30–4.30pm. Sun 2.30–4.30pm. **Admission:** Adults £1.50, children 75p, senior citizen/student £1.00.

map 4
E6

FIRLE PLACE

Nr Lewes, East Sussex BN8 6LP
Tel (Recorded Information): 01273 858335 Fax: 01273 858188 (Viscount Gage)

House: Firle Place is the home of the Gage family, and has been for over 500 years. It is set at the foot of the South Downs within its own parkland. This unique House contains a magnificent collection of Old Master Paintings, Fine English and European furniture and an impressive collection of Serves porcelain mainly collected by the 3rd Earl Cowper from Panshanger. **Restaurant - 01273 858307:** Enjoy the licensed restaurant and tea terrace with views over the gardens for luncheon and cream teas. **Events and other Enquiries - 01273 858567.** The Tudor Great Hall lends itself to Private dinners with drinks in the Billiard room or on the Terrace which can incorporate a private tour of the house. The paddock area is ideal for erecting a marquee and the Park can be used for larger events using the House as a backdrop. **Location:** 5 miles SE of Lewes on A27 Brighton/Eastbourne. **Station:** Lewes. **Open:** 23, 24, 30 April & 1 May then 17 May–28 Sept: Wed, Thurs, Sun & Bank Hol Mons, 2–4.30pm. Groups must pre-book. Private tours by arrangement. **Admission:** Adult £4, child £2, disabled £2. Connoisseur's Day first Wed June–Sept, £4.85. Car park adjacent to house. Restaurant. Shop. Wheelchair access to ground floor. **E-mail:** gage@firleplace.co.uk

map 5
F6

GLYNDE PLACE

Glynde, Lewes, East Sussex, BN8 6SX
Tel: 01273 858 224 Fax: 01273 858 224 (Viscount & Viscountess Hampden)

Set below the ancient hill fort of Mount Caburn, Glynde Place is a magnificent example of Elizabethan architecture and is the manor house of an estate which has been in the same family since the 12th century. Built in 1569 of Sussex flint and Caen stone round a courtyard, the house commands exceptionally fine views of the South Downs. Amongst the collections of 17th and 18th century portraits of the Trevor family, a collection of Italian old masters brought back by Thomas Brand on his Grand Tour and a room dedicated to Sir Henry Brand, Speaker of the House of Commons 1872–1884. The house is still the family home of the Brands and can be enjoyed as such. **Location:** In Glynde village, 4 miles SE of Lewes, on A27. **Station(s):** Within easy walking distance of Glynde station, with hourly services to Lewes, Brighton and Eastbourne.

Open: Gardens only: Easter Day & Easter Mon and Sun in April. **House and gardens:** May, Sun and Bank Hols only; Jun-Sept, Wed, Sun & Aug Bank Hol only. July & Aug also Thurs. Guided tours for parties (25 or more) can be booked on a regular open day (£2.50 per person) or on a non-open day (£5 per person). Contact Lord Hampden on 01273 858 224. House open 2pm. Last admission 4.45pm. **Admission:** Adults £4, children £2. Free parking. **Refreshments:** Sussex cream teas in Georgian Stable block. Parties to book in advance as above. Exhibition of watercolours and prints by local artists and shop. **Exhibitions:** 'Harbert Morley and the Great Rebellion 1638–1660', the story of the part played by the owner of Glynde Place during the Civil War. **Weddings:** Glynde Place can be hired for a civil wedding.

map 5
F6

 # GREAT DIXTER HOUSE AND GARDENS

Northiam, Nr Rye, East Sussex TN31 6PH.
Tel: 01797 252 878 Fax. 01797 252 879 (Mr Christopher Lloyd)

Great Dixter, birthplace and home of gardening writer Christopher Lloyd, was built in 1460 and boasts one of the largest surviving timber–framed halls in the country. Lutyens was employed to restore both the house and gardens in 1910. The gardens are now the hallmark of Christopher Lloyd with an exciting combination of meadows, ponds, topiary and the famous Long Border and Exotic Garden. **Location:** signposted off the A28 in Northiam. **Open:** 1 Apr–29 Oct; Tues–Sun 2–5pm; open Bank Hol. Mon. **Admission:** House & Gardens: Adult £6, child £1.50. Gardens only: Adult £4.50, child £1. **Refreshments & facilities:** Pre–packed refreshments, partial disabled access, free parking, plant nursery. All enquiries to Elaine Francis, Business Manager. **E-mail:** greatdixter@compuserve.com

map 5
G6

LEWES CASTLE

Barbican House, 169 High Street, Lewes, Sussex, BN7 1YE
Tel: 01273 486 290 Fax: 01273 486 990 (Sussex Past)

Lewes' imposing Norman castle provides an invigorating climb rewarded by magnificent views. Adjacent Barbican House Museum follows the progress of Sussex people from their earliest beginnings. The Lewes Living History Model is a superb scale model of Victorian Lewes and an audio-visual presentation. There is also an Education Centre and shop. **Station(s):** Lewes (7 mins walk). **Bus route:** Adjacent. Bus station 10 mins walk away. **Open:** Daily (except Christmas & Boxing Day), 10–5.30pm. (Sun & Bank Hols 11–5.30pm). **Admission:** Adults £3.70, child (5–15) £1.90, OAP/student £3.20, family (2+2) £10.50. 50% discount to EH members. Joint ticket with 'Anne of Cleves House': Adult £5, children £2.60. 50% discount to EH members. Audio tours 50p + deposit. No dogs. **E-mail:** castle@sussexpast.co.uk

map 5
F6

HIGH BEECHES GARDENS

Handcross, West Sussex RH17 6HQ
Tel: 01444 400589 (High Beeches Gardens Conservation Trust. Reg. non profit making Charity No. 299134)

Help us to preserve these twenty acres of enchanting landscaped woodland and water gardens, with Magnolias, Rhododendrons and Azaleas, in Spring. In Autumn, one of the most brilliant gardens for leaf colour. Gentians and Primulas are naturalised. Many rare plants. Tree trail. Four acres of natural wildflower meadows recommended by Christopher Lloyd. This long established landscape garden, in the 'natural' style, has been declared Grade II* and outstanding by English Heritage, as one of the best preserved, and best maintained, examples of landscape design dating from the early 20th century. Originally planted by a member of the well known Loder family, and developed on an enchanting site in the Sussex Wealden Ghyls, among mature oak trees and natural streams, this was an essentially private and secret place, known only to the priveleged few. Since 1966 the gardens have been cared for by the Boscawen/Bray family, and they have successfully preserved their magically peaceful and remote atmosphere. The Boscawens are talented amateur botanists, and much travelled, and they have greatly enriched the already important plant collections, while preserving the essential character of the gardens. They will personally guide groups booked in advance. **Location:** 1 mile east of A23 at Handcross, on B2110. **Open:** Gardens only: 1–5pm, 24 Mar–30 June & 1 Sept–31 Oct. Daily except Weds. Mon and Tues only in July & August. **Admission:** Adults £4. Accompanied children free. **Refreshments:** Hot and cold drinks, ice cream and biscuits in Gate Lodge. Sadly, gardens not suitable for wheelchairs. Regret no dogs. **Events:** Please enquire for Event Days, plant sales, and group bookings.

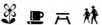

map 5
F6

MERRIMENTS GARDENS

Hawkhurst Road, Hurst Green, East Sussex TN19 7RA
Tel: 01580 860666 Fax: 01580 860324 (Weeks Family with Mark Buchele)

"Gardened naturally, free from the restrictions of institute, experimenting continuously and always permitting nature to have its say." Set in 4 acres of gently sloping Wealden farmland, a naturalistic garden which never fails to delight. Deep curved borders richly planted and colour themed. An abundance of rare plants will startle the visitor with sheer originally. **Admission:** £2.50 **Open:** 2 April–end October. Daily 10–5pm. **E-mail:** info@merriments.co.uk **Website:** www.merriments.co.uk

map 5
G6

MICHELHAM PRIORY

Upper Dicker, Hailsham, Sussex, BN27 3QS
Tel: 01323 844 224 Fax: 01323 844 030 (Sussex Past)

Enclosed by a medieval moat, the remains of this beautiful Augustinian Priory are incorporated into a splendid Tudor mansion featuring a fascinating array of exhibits. Superb gardens are enhanced by a 14th century gatehouse, water mill, physic herb and cloister gardens, smithy, rope museum and dramatic Elizabethan Great Barn. **Location:** O.S. map ref: OS 198 TQ 558093. **Station(s):** Polegate (3 miles). Berwick (2 miles). **Buses:** Bus route (1.5 miles). **Open:** Wed–Sun. 15 Mar–29 Oct. Mar & Oct, 10.30–4pm. Apr–July & Sept, 10.30–5pm. Daily in Aug, 10.30–5.30pm. **Admission:** Adults £4.40, children £2.30, OAP £3.80, family (2+2)£11.40. (50% discount to English Heritage members). **Refreshments:** Tearoom/restaurant. Picnic area. Museum, education centre and shop. Dogs are admitted in car park. **E-mail:** adminmich@sussexpast.co.uk

map 5
F6

LEONARDSLEE GARDENS

Lower Beeding, Nr Horsham RH13 6PP
Tel: 01403 891212 Fax: 01403 891305 (Mr Robin Loder)

Leonardslee Gardens, created and maintained by the Loder family since 1889, are set in a peaceful 240-acre valley. There are delightful walks around seven beautiful lakes, giving rise to glorious views and reflections. Camellias, magnolias and the early rhododendrons provide colour in April, while in May it becomes a veritable paradise, with banks of sumptuous rhododendrons and azaleas overhanging the paths which are fringed with bluebells. Also in May, the Rock Garden becomes a Kaleidoscope of colour with Japanese evergreen azaleas and ancient dwarf conifers. Superb flowering trees and interesting wildflowers enhance the tranquillity of summer and the mellow seasonal tints of autumn complete the season. The fascinating Bonsai collection shows this oriental living art-form to perfection. Many visitors are surprised to see the wallabies, which have been used as environmentally–friendly mowing machines for over 100 years! Axis Fallow and Sika Deer roam in the parks and wildfowl are seen on the lakes. The Loder family collection of Victorian Motor Cars (1895–1900) has some fine examples–all in running order–from the dawn of motoring! There is a licensed restaurant and a café for refreshments, as well as a gift shop and a wide selection of plants for sale. **Open:** Daily 1 Apr–31 Oct, 9.30–6pm. **Admission:** May (weekends & bank hols) £6, May (weekdays) £5, all other times £4. Children (age 5–15) £2.50.

map 4
E6

PARHAM HOUSE & GARDENS

Parham Park, near Pulborough, West Sussex. Tel: 01903 742021
Info Line: 01903 744888 Fax: 01903 746557(Parham Park Ltd)

A much-loved family home open from April–October on Wednesdays, Thursdays, Sundays and Bank Holiday Mondays (with private guided visits on Tuesday or Friday afternoons, and Wednesday or Thursday mornings.) Our Big Kitchen opens from 12 noon for light lunches and delicious cream teas. Complementing the panelled rooms containing beautiful furniture, paintings and needlework are fresh flower arrangements. Spend a peaceful afternoon strolling through our award-winning gardens, with walled garden containing greenhouse, orchard, potager and herbiary, try your hand at the brick and turf maze! **Events:** Annual Garden Weekend: 15/16 July; Open Air Theatre: Romeo & Juliet: 5–8 July, also Sheridan's "The Rivals": 12 Aug. **E-mail:** parham@dial.pipex.com **Internet:** www.parhaminsussex.co.uk

map 4 E6

PASHLEY MANOR GARDENS

Pashley Manor, Ticehurst, Nr Wadhurst, E. Sussex TN5 7HE
Tel: 01580 200888 Fax: 01580 200102 (Mr and Mrs J. Sellick)

Pashley Manor is a Grade I Tudor and Georgian house with magnificent gardens offering a sumptuous blend of romantic landscaping, imaginative plantings and fine old trees, fountains, springs and large ponds. This is a quintessentially English Garden of a very individual character with exceptional views to the surrounding valleyed fields. Many eras of English history are reflected here, typifying the tradition of the English Country House and its garden. Home-made lunches/teas. Wine licence. **Admission:** £5, Concessions/Groups £4.50. **Open:** Tues, Wed, Thurs, Sat & Bank Hol Mons. 8 Apr–30 Sept 2000. **Location:** On B2099 between A21 and Ticehurst village. **Events:** Tulip Festival: 27 Apr–1 May. Summer Flower Festival: 15–18 June. Plant Fairs: 21 May & 13 Aug. Sculpture Week: 13–19 May.

map 5 G6

PALLANT HOUSE GALLERY

9, North Pallant, Chichester, West Sussex, PO19 1TJ
Tel: 01243 774557 Fax: 01243 536038

Meticulously restored Queen Anne town house with eight rooms decorated and furnished in styles from early Georgian to late Victorian. Also Georgian style gardens and important displays of Bow Porcelain (1747–1775) and Modern British Art (1920–1980). **Location:** Chichester City centre. **Open:** All year Tues–Sat 10–5pm, also open Sun & Bank Hols: 12.30–5pm. **Admission:** Adults £4, over 60s £3, students/ UB40 £2.50. **Refreshments:** Victorian Kitchen Café. **Events/Exhibitions:** Major exhibitions held throughout the year, please call for details. **E-mail:** pallant@pallant.co.uk

map 4 D6

PRESTON MANOR

Preston Drove, Brighton BN1 6SD
Tel: 01273 292770 Fax: 01273 292771 (Brighton & Hove Council)

Experience the charms of this delightful Manor House which powerfully evokes the atmosphere of an Edwardian gentry home both 'Upstairs' and 'Downstairs'. There are more than twenty rooms to explore over four floors, from the superbly renovated servants' quarters and butler's pantry in the basement to the day nursery and attic bedrooms on the top floor. Situated adjacent to Preston Park, the Manor also comprises picturesque walled gardens and a pets' cemetery. **Location:** 2 miles north of Brighton on the A23 London Road. **Open:** Daily Tues–Sat 10–5pm, Sun 2–5pm, Mon 1–5pm (Bank Holidays 10–5pm). Closed 25 & 26 Dec and Good Friday. **Admission:** Adults £3.10, children £1.95, conc. £2.60. Please call for details of family and group tickets. (Prices valid until 31.3.2000)

map 5 F6

THE PRIEST HOUSE

North Lane, West Hoathly, Sussex RH19 4PP
Tel: 01342 810479

The Priest House nestles in the picturesque village of West Hoathly, on the edge of Ashdown Forest. Originally a 15th century timber-framed farmhouse with central open hall, it was modernised in Elizabethan times with stone chimneys and a ceiling in the hall. Later additions created a substantial yeoman's dwelling. Standing in the beautiful surroundings of a traditional cottage garden, the house has a dramatic roof of Horsham stone. Its furnished rooms, including a kitchen, contain a fascinating array of 17th and 18th century domestic furniture, needlework and household items. In the formal herb garden, there are over 150 herbs used in medicine and folklore. **Open:** 1 March–31 Oct, Mon–Sat, 11–5.30pm, Sun 2–5.30pm. **Admission:** Adults £2.50, children £1.20, OAP/student £2.30.

map 5 F5

WILMINGTON PRIORY

Wilmington, Nr Eastbourne, East Sussex BN26 5SW
Tel: The Landmark Trust: 01628 825920
(Leased to the Landmark Trust by Sussex Archaelogical Society)

Founded by the Benedictines in the 11th century, the surviving, much altered buildings date largely from the 14th century. Managed and maintained by the Landmark Trust, which lets buildings for self-catering holidays. **Open:** The grounds, ruins, porch and crypt on 30 days between April and October. The whole property including interiors on 8 of these days. Telephone: 01628 825920 for details. **Accommodation:** Available for up to six people for self-catering holidays. Tel: 01628 825925 for Bookings. Full details of Wilmington Priory and 167 other historic buildings are featured in The Landmark Handbook (price £9.50 refundable against a booking) from The Landmark Trust, Shottesbrooke, Maidenhead, Berkshire, SL6 3SW. **Internet:** www.landmarktrust.co.uk

 map 4 E5

THE ROYAL PAVILION

Brighton, East Sussex BN1 1EE
01273 290900, Fax: 01273 292871 (Brighton & Hove Council)

The Royal Pavilion, the famous seaside palace of King George IV, is one of the most exotically beautiful buildings in the British Isles. Originally a simple farmhouse, in 1787 architect Henry Holland created a neoclassical villa on the site. From 1815–1822, the Pavilion was transformed by John Nash into its current distinctive Indian style complete with Chinese-inspired interiors. Magnificent decorations and fantastic furnishings have been re-created in an extensive restoration programme. From the opulence of the main State Rooms to the charm of the first floor bedroom suites, the Royal Pavilion is filled with astonishing colours and superb craftsmanship. Witness the magnificence of the Music Room with its domed ceiling of gilded shell shapes, and the dramatic Banqueting Room lit by a huge crystal chandelier held by a silvered dragon. The Banqueting Room ceiling will be unveiled in its full Regency glory in January 2000 when scaffolding comes down after a year of restoration. Visitors will also have the opportunity to discover more about life behind the scenes at the Palace during the last 200 years with a new interactive multimedia visitor interpretation programme. The Royal Pavilion is an ideal location for filming and photography, from fashion shoots to corporate videos. Rooms are also available for hire for corporate and private functions and civil wedding ceremonies. **Location:** In centre of Brighton (Old Steine). **Station(s):** Brighton (1/2 mile). **Open:** Daily (except 25 & 26 Dec) June–Sept 10–6pm, Oct–May 10–5pm. **Admission:** Adults £4.50, children £2.75 students/OAPs £3.25. Please call for details of family and group tickets. (Prices valid until 31.3.2000). **Refreshments:** Regency teas and light lunches in Queen Adelaide tearooms with balcony providing sweeping views over the Regency gardens. **Events/Exhibitions:** A popular winter programme of events.

map 5
F6

SAINT HILL MANOR

Saint Hill Road, East Grinstead, West Sussex RH19 4JY
Tel: 01342 326711 (contact Liz Nyegaard)

Fine Sussex sandstone house built in 1792 and situated near the breathtaking Ashdown Forest. Saint Hill Manor's final owner, acclaimed author and humanitarian, L. Ron Hubbard, lived here for many years with his family. Under his direction extensive renovations were carried out uncovering exquisite period features hidden for over a century. Fine wood panelling, marble fireplaces, Georgian windows and plasterwork ceilings have been expertly restored to their original beauty. Outstanding features of this lovely house include a complete library of Mr. Hubbard's work, the elegant Winter Garden and the delightful Monkey Room, housing John Spencer Churchill's 100ft mural depicting many famous characters as monkeys, including his uncle Sir Winston Churchill. 59 acres of landscaped gardens, lake and woodlands. **Location:** Off A22, N of East Grinstead, down Imberhorne Lane. Straight into Saint Hill Road, 300 yds on right. Stations: East Grinstead. Owner: Church of Scientology. **Open:** All year. Daily, 2–5pm. Tours on the hour or by appointment. Group parties welcome. Parking for coaches and cars. **Admission:** Free. **Events/Exhibitions:** Choir evening, Saturday 8th April. Outdoor production of Sheridan's "The Rivals", Sunday afternoon, 25th June. Telephone for details. Summer concerts on the terrace, musical evenings throughout the year. Business conference and wedding reception facilities available in Saint Hill Manor. Also Saint Hill Castle seats up to 600 theatre style and 300 for dinner. Also available as a film location.

map 5
F5

SHEFFIELD PARK GARDEN

Sheffield Park, East Sussex TN22 3QX
Tel: 01825 790231 Fax: 01825 791264

A magnificent 120 acre landscaped garden, laid out in the 18th century and extended with the advice of the famous landscape designers 'Capability' Brown and Humphrey Repton. There are four lakes linked by cascades and waterfalls and the garden is renowned for stunning displays of daffodils, bluebells, rhododendrons and azaleas in Spring, and in Autumn the garden is transformed by a blaze of colour. The North American trees and shrubs produce a display of gold, orange and crimson reflected in the lakes. The garden was further developed early this century by its owner, Arthur G. Soames, who planted on an ambitious scale much of what the visitor sees today including rare and exotic trees and shrubs. **Open:** Jan–Feb: Sat & Sun 10.30–4pm. March–end of Oct: Daily 10.30–6pm (except Mons, but open BH Mons). Nov–Dec: Daily 10.30–4pm (except Mon).

map 5 F6

THE WEALD & DOWNLAND OPEN AIR MUSEUM

Singleton, Nr Chichester, West Sussex
Tel: 01243 811348

Over 40 historic buildings in one beautiful Downland park vividly demonstrate the homes and workplaces of the past. Buildings, furnished interiors and complete work environments bring the past to life. Bayleaf medieval farmstead is complete with furnishings, animals, fields and gardens, the Victorian school is intact and the working 17th century watermill produces flour daily. Constantly evolving this museum is the only one to be Designated as outstanding in West Sussex. Summer open-air theatre and evening arts programme. **Location:** 6 miles N of Chichester on A286 just S of Singleton. **Open:** 1 Mar–31 Oct daily 10.30–6pm, 1 Nov–28 Feb, Wed, Sat and Sun only 10.30–4pm, 26 Dec–1 Jan daily 10.30–4pm. **Admission:** Charged. Parties by arrangement (group rates available). **Refreshments:** Light refreshments. **Internet:** www.wealddown.co.uk

map 4 D6

WEST DEAN GARDENS

The Edward James Foundation, Estate Office, West Dean, Chichester, West Sussex PO18 0QZ
Tel: 01243 818210 Fax: 01243 811342

Extensive downland garden with 300ft pergola, herbaceous borders and bedding displays. Victorian Walled Kitchen Garden with unusual vegetables, herbs, cut flowers, fruit collection and 16 original glasshouses and frames. These include vineries, fig and peach houses and an outstanding collection of chilli peppers together with extensive floral display houses. Park Walk (2¼ miles) through landscaped parkland and the 45 acre St Roche's Arboretum. Visitor Centre (free entry) houses quality licensed restaurant, garden shop and plant sales. Group bookings/guided tours can be arranged by appointment.

Location: 6 miles north of Chichester on A286. **Open:** Daily Mar–Oct inclusive. 11–5pm: March, April and October. 10.30–5pm: May–Sept. Last admission 4.30pm. **Admission:** Adults £4, over 60's £3.50, children £2, pre-booked parties 20+ £3.50 each. **Refreshments:** Restaurant. **Events:** Garden Event: 24–25 June. Chilli Fiesta: 12–13 Aug. Totally Tomato Show: 9–10 Sept. Apple Day: 15 October. Coach/car parking. No dogs. **E-mail:** westdean@pavilion.co.uk **Website:** http//www.westdean.org.uk/

map 4 D6

Warwickshire

Of mountains, valleys and other natural beauties, Warwickshire has few. However, from a historical aspect, Warwickshire is the most fortunate of counties. The names of Warwickshire towns read like chapters in a history book: Stratford Upon Avon, Warwick, Kenilworth, Rugby and Coventry.

The town of Warwick retains some superb examples of medieval architecture, despite being partly destroyed by a huge fire in the late seventeenth century. Some of the finest buildings are to be found around the High Street and in Northgate Street.

The springs of Royal Leamington Spa, to the East of Warwick, were frequented by royalty when Queen Victoria visited the fashionable town in 1838. Nearby Kenilworth Castle

Kenilworth Castle

was constructed during Norman times and vastly altered by Elizabeth I's favourite, the Earl of Leicester. It then became renowned as a place of fine music and pageantry.

But it is for its association with William Shakespeare that Warwickshire is invariably best known. The town of Stratford-Upon-Avon stands central to "Shakespeare Country", with its many examples of Shakespearean heritage.

BADDESLEY CLINTON HALL

Rising Lane, Baddesley Clinton Village, Knowle, Solihull, West Midlands
Tel: 01564 783294 Fax: 01564 782706 (The National Trust)

A romantic and atmospheric moated manor house dating from the 15th century and little changed since 1634. The interiors reflect the house's heyday in the Elizabethan era, when it was a haven for persecuted Catholics – there are no fewer than 3 priest-holes. There is a delightful garden, ponds, lake walk and nature trail. **Open:** House: 1 Mar–29 Oct, daily except Mon & Tues (open Good Fri and BH. Mon). Mar, Apr & Oct 1.30–5pm, May–end Sept 1.30–5.30pm. Grounds: 13 Feb–17 Dec daily except Mon & Tues (open Good Fri and BH. Mon). 13–27 Feb 12–4.30pm; Mar, Apr & Oct 12–5pm; May–end Sept 12–5.30pm and Nov–17 Dec 12–4.30pm. Shop and Licensed Restaurant. Party lunches & dinners arranged. Picnic tables near entrance. Coaches welcome.

map 4 B1

HONINGTON HALL

Shipston-on-Stour, Warwickshire CV36 5AA
Tel: 01608 661434, Fax: 01608 663717 (Benjamin Wiggin Esq)

This fine Caroline manor house was built in the early 1680s for the Parker family. It was modified in the mid 18th century with the introduction within of exceptional and lavish plasterwork and the insertion of an octagonal saloon. It is set in 15 acres of grounds. **Location:** 10 miles S of Stratford-on-Avon; ½ mile E of A3400. **Open:** June, July, Aug, Weds & Bank Hol Mons 2.30–5pm. Parties at other times by appointment. **Admission:** Adults £3, children £1.50.

ARBURY HALL

Nuneaton, Warwickshire, CV10 7PT
Tel: 02476 382804, Fax: 02476 641147 (The Rt. Hon. The Viscount Daventry)

Arbury Hall has been the seat of the Newdegate family for over 400 years and is the ancestral home of Viscount and Viscountess Daventry. This Tudor/Elizabethan House was Gothicised by Sir Roger Newdigate in the 18th century and is regarded as the 'Gothic Gem' of the Midlands. The Hall contains a fine collection of both Oriental and Chelsea porcelain, portraits by Lely, Reynolds, Devis and Romney and furniture by Chippendale and Hepplewhite. FOR FURTHER DETAILS, OPENING TIMES AND PHOTOGRAPHY, PLEASE TURN TO PAGE 190.

map 4 B2

ARBURY HALL

Nuneaton, Warwickshire, CV10 7PT
Tel: 02476 382804, Fax: 02476 641147 (The Rt. Hon. The Viscount Daventry)

Arbury Hall has been the seat of the Newdegate family for over 400 years and is the ancestral home of Viscount and Viscountess Daventry. This Tudor/Elizabethan House was Gothicised by Sir Roger Newdigate in the 18th century and is regarded as the 'Gothic Gem' of the Midlands. The Hall contains a fine collection of both Oriental and Chelsea porcelain, portraits by Lely, Reynolds, Devis and Romney and furniture by Chippendale and Hepplewhite. The principal rooms, with their soaring fan vaulted ceilings and plunging pendants and filigree tracery, stand as a most breathtaking and complete example of early Gothic Revival architecture and provide a most unique and fascinating venue for Corporate entertaining, Product Launches, Receptions, Fashion Shoots and Activity days. Exclusive use of this historic Hall, it's Gardens and Parkland is offered to clients. The Hall stands in the middle of beautiful Parkland with landscaped gardens of rolling lawns, lakes and winding wooded walks. **Location:** 2 miles SW of Nuneaton off B4102. **Station(s):** Nuneaton. **Open:** All the year round on Tuesdays, Wednesdays and Thursdays only for Corporate Functions and Events. Pre–booked parties for 25 and over on Tuesdays, Wednesdays and Thursdays only from Easter–end Sept and the Hall and Gardens open on Bank Holiday Weekends only (Sun & Mon) from Easter–Sept. Hall: 2–5.30pm. Gardens: 2–6pm. **Admission:** Adults £4.50, children £2.50, Family ticket £10. **Events:** Special Party Rates and Corporate Events by arrangement with the Administrator; Tel: 02476 382804 Fax: 02476 641147. Wheelchair access ground floor only. Gravel paths. Free car park.

map 8
C7

 CHARLECOTE PARK

Warwick CV35 9ER
Tel: 01789 470 277, Fax: 01789 470 544

Home of the Lucy family since 1247. Present house built in 1550's. Queen Elizabeth I visited. Victorian interiors; objects from Fonthill Abbey. Park landscaped by Capability Brown. Jacob sheep. Red and fallow deer, reputedly poached by Shakespeare. **Open:** 21 Apr–5 Nov, Fri–Tues, 11–6pm. House open 12–5pm. Shop and restaurant 11–5.30pm. **Admission:** Adult £5.40, child (5–16) £2.70. Family ticket £13.50. Special group rate £4.40 (weekdays only for parties 15+). Evening guided tours for pre-booked parties £6.50 (including NT members; minimum charge £115 for party). Wheelchair facilities: All ground floor rooms accessible including Orangery and shop. Parking. Lavatories. **Refreshments:** Morning coffee, lunches, afternoon teas in restaurant (licensed). Picnic in deer park only. Changing and feeding room. No dogs allowed.

map 4 B2

THE HILLER GARDEN

Dunnington Heath Farm, Nr. Alcester, Warwickshire B49 5PD
Tel: 01789 490991 Fax: 01789 490439 (A. H. Hiller & Son Ltd)

Among gravelled walks, large beds display an extensive range of unusual herbaceous perennials providing colour and interest throughout the year in this two acre garden near Ragley Hall. The Rose Gardens, at the peak of their beauty from the end of June, hold a collection of some 200 old-fashioned, species, modern shrub, rugosa and English roses in settings appropriate to their characters. There is a well-stocked plant sales area, a garden gift shop, farm shop and licensed tearooms. **Location:** 2 miles south of Ragley Hall on B4088 (formerly A435/A441 junction). **Open:** Daily (except Christmas and New Year), 10–5pm. **Admission:** Free. **Refreshments:** Morning coffee, light lunches, afternoon teas in the Garden Tea Rooms (licensed).

map 4 B2

 COUGHTON COURT HOUSE & GARDENS

Alcester, Warwickshire B49 5JA
Tel: 01789 400 777 Fax: 01789 765 544 Tel: 01789 762435(Visitor Information)

Coughton Court has been the home of the Throckmorton family since the 15th century. The house contains one of the best collections of portraits and memorabilia of one family from Tudor times to the present day. There are two churches in the grounds to visit and magnificent 1½ acre flower garden together with a lake and riverside walks, an orchard and bog garden. Gunpowder Plot Exhibition. **Location:** 2 miles north of Alcester, on A435. **Open:** Mid Mar–End Oct. Please contact Visitor Information Line for 2000 opening times & admission prices.

map 4 B2

KENILWORTH CASTLE

Kenilworth, Warks CV8 1NE
Tel 01926 852078 (English Heritage)

Explore England's finest and most extensive castle ruins. Wander through rooms used to lavishly entertain Queen Elizabeth I. Learn of the building's links with Henry V, who retired here return from his victorious expedition to Agincourt. Today you can view the marvellous Norman keep and John of Gaunt's Great Hall, once rivalling London's Westminster Hall in palatial grandeur. An audio tour, and interactive model of the Castle, provide a fascinating insight into the development of the Castle through the centuries. **Location:** Off A46. Follow A452 to Kenilworth town centre. **Open:** 1 Apr–30 Sept: daily, 10–6pm, 1 Oct–31 Oct: daily, 10–5pm, 1 Nov–31 Mar: daily, 10–4pm (closed 24/26 Dec 2000 & 1 Jan 2001). **Admission:** Adults £3.60, concs £2.70, child £1.80. (15% discount for groups of 11 or more). **Refreshments:** Tea room: open Apr–Oct daily.

map 4 B1

LORD LEYCESTER HOSPITAL

High Street, Warwick, Warwickshire, CV34 4BH
Tel: 01926 491 422 Fax: 01926 491 422 (The Governors of Lord Leycester Hospital)

In 1571, Robert Dudley, Earl of Leycester, founded his hospital for twelve old soldiers in the buildings of the Guilds, which had been dispersed in 1546. The buildings have been restored to their original condition: the Great Hall of King James, the Guildhall (museum), the Chaplain's Hall (Queen's Own Hussars Regimental Museum), the Brethren's Kitchen and the Chapel of St James. A new Knot Garden has been created to celebrate the Millennium. The recently restored historic Master's Garden is now open to the public (April–30 Sept £1 donation please). The Hospital, with its medieval galleried courtyard, featured in the TV serials 'Pride and Prejudice', 'Tom Jones', 'Moll Flanders' and 'Dangerfield'. **Location:** West Gate of Warwick (A429). **Station(s):** Warwick (¾m). **Open:** All year, Tues–Sun, 10–5pm (Summer) and 10–4pm (Winter). Open BH Mons, closed Good Fri and Christmas Day. **Admission:** Adult £2.95, children (under 14) £1.75, OAP/Student £2.25. Free car park.

map 4 B1

STONELEIGH ABBEY

Estate Office, Kenilworth, Warwickshire CV8 2LF
Tel: 01926 858585 Fax: 01926 850724 (Stoneleigh Abbey Ltd)

Re-opening in 2000, after two years renovation work, Stoneleigh Abbey is one of the finest country house estates in the Midlands. Visitors will experience a wealth of architectural styles spanning more than 600 years: the magnificent state rooms and chapel of the 18th century Baroque West Wing designed by Francis Smith of Warwick; the medieval Gatehouse, one of very few complete monastic gatehouses left; the Gothic Revival style Regency Stables; 690 acres of grounds and parkland with the River Avon flowing through, displaying the design influences of Humphry Repton and other major landscape designers. Other attractions include a visitor centre and a riverside conservatory serving light refreshments. A series of special events will be staged throughout the season.

map 4 B1

RAGLEY HALL
Alcester, Warwickshire B49 5NJ
Tel: 01789 762090 Fax: 01789 764791 (Marquess of Hertford)

Ragley Hall, a byword for splendour and elegance and the Warwickshire home of The Marquess and Marchioness of Hertford and their family is one of the great English houses displaying unmissable beauty at every turn. The grandeur of its facades are only surpassed by the breathtaking beauty of its Great Hall and rooms. The Hall was designed by Robert Hooke in 1680 and is one of the earliest and loveliest of England's great Palladian Houses. It contains some of the finest Baroque plasterwork by James Gibb, and Graham Rust's stunning mural 'The Temptation'. On show are some of the finest antique porcelain and furniture. Ragley is a working estate with more than 6000 acres of land. The House is situated in 27 acres of gardens which were designed by Capability Brown and include the beautiful Rose Garden. Near to the Hall are working stables housing a carriage collection dating back to 1760 and a display of harnesses and assorted historical equestrian equipment. There is a lake and picnic area, and for the children an Adventure Wood, Woodland Walk, 3D Maze and for the younger children an additional playground. **Location:** 8 miles South of Stratford-upon-Avon. <u>Open:</u> 13 Apr–1 Oct. House: Thurs, Fri, Sun 12.30–5pm (last entry 4.30pm). Sat 11–3.30pm (last entry 3pm). Bank Holiday Mons 11–5pm (last entry 4.30pm). The Park and Gardens open Thurs–Sun 10–6pm (last entry 4.45pm) and everyday between 23 July–1 Sept. **Admission:** Adults £5, senior citizens and Orange Badge Holders £4.50, children £3.50, this includes entry into the House. Season Tickets also available.

map 4
B2

Mary Arden's House

THE SHAKESPEARE HOUSES IN AND AROUND STRATFORD-UPON-AVON

The Shakespeare Centre, Henley Street, Stratford-upon-Avon, Warks CV37 6QW.
Tel: 01789 204016 Fax: 01789 296083

Five beautifully preserved Tudor houses, all associated with William Shakespeare and his family. In Town: **Shakespeare's Birthplace**, Henley Street. Half-timbered house where William Shakespeare was born in 1564. Visitor's centre showing highly acclaimed exhibition **William Shakespeare, His Life and Background**. **Nash's House and New Place**, Chapel Street. Nash's House was the home of Shakespeare's grand-daughter, Elizabeth Hall and contains exceptional furnishings. Upstairs there are displays about the history of Stratford. Also site and gardens of **New Place** (including Elizabethan style Knott Garden and Shakespeare's Great Garden), where Shakespeare lived in retirement. Discover why the house was demolished and see the foundations and grounds of his final Stratford home. **Hall's Croft**, Old Town. Impressive 16th century house and garden, with Jacobean additions. Owned by Dr John Hall who married Shakespeare's eldest daughter, Susanna. Includes exhibitions about medicine in Shakespeare's time and beautiful walled garden with mulberry tree and herb garden. Out of Town: **Anne Hathaway's Cottage**, Shottery. Picturesque thatched farmhouse cottage which belonged to the family of Shakespeare's wife. Contains the famous Hathaway bed and the other original furniture. Outside lies a beautiful English cottage garden, orchard and the Shakespeare Tree Garden. **Mary Arden's House** and **Shakespeare's Countryside Museum**, Wilmcote. This striking farmhouse was Shakespeare's mother's family home and offers a fascinating insight into rural farm life in the Tudor period. See also, falconry displays, working blacksmith, prize-winning livestock and Glebe Farm's kitchen of 1900. **Open:** Daily all year round except 23–26 Dec. Inclusive tickets available to three in-town, or all five houses. The Shakespeare Birthplace Trust is a Registered Charity, No. 209302.

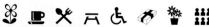

map 4
B2

Shakespeare's Birthplace

Anne Hathaway's Cottage

WARWICK CASTLE

Warwick, Warwickshire, CV34 4QU
Tel: 01926 406600 Internet: www.warwick–castle.co.uk

Never in a thousand years will you believe what's happened over the last ten centuries. From the days of William the Conqueror to the reign of Queen Victoria, Warwick Castle has provided a backdrop for a world of treason, treachery and murder. With a thousand years waiting to unfold before your eyes, come and discover the secret life of England for yourself. In our Kingmaker attraction, join a mediaeval household and see a 15th century army prepare for the Earl of Warwick's final battle. Or enter the Ghost Tower, where it is said that the unquiet spirit of Sir Fulke Greville roams. A ghostly reminder of his brutal murder at the hands of a once loyal manservant. Descend the narrow steps into the dungeon and discover the cruel secrets of the torture chamber. Step forward in time and marvel at the grandeur of the State Rooms, including the Great Hall which houses some of history's most stunning artefacts. Move a few hundred years on to witness the perfect manners and hidden indiscretions of Daisy, Countess of Warwick and friends at the Royal Weekend Party 1898. Then stroll around 60 acres of grounds, beautifully landscaped by Capability Brown. Warwick Castle has seen it all. Now it's your turn.

map 4
B1

West Midlands

The West Midlands are famously known as having been at the heart of The Industrial Revolution in the nineteenth century. The city of Birmingham was the base for a wide range of manufacturing trades and oversaw the vast growth in factories and associated housing for its workers.

Meriden

Today, Birmingham has established itself as a city of culture, with a thriving arts scene: The City of Birmingham Symphony Orchestra has a worldwide reputation for excellence and in recent times, The Royal Sadler's Wells have relocated their Ballet Company to Birmingham, in order to benefit from their excellent facilities. For lovers of Pre-Raphaelite art, the City Museum and Art Gallery offers the perfect opportunity to indulge in the works of, among others, Ford Maddox Brown and Sir Edward Burne-Jones.

On the outskirts of the city, the National Exhibition Centre is the venue for many of today's popular events. Indeed, in the last year it has hosted a wide variety of shows ranging from fashion exhibitions to car conventions. It is also a renowned music venue: various popular and classical artists have performed concerts at the Centre.

Britain's first completely modern cathedral, at Coventry, arose out of the ruins of the bombed city centre after the Second World War. Sir Basil Spence's fine building is adorned with superb sculptures by Jacob Epstein and Graham Sutherland.

ASTON HALL

Trinity Road, Aston, Birmingham, West Midlands, B6 6JD
Tel: 0121 327 0062 (Birmingham Museums & Arts)

A magnificent Jacobean mansion built by Sir Thomas Holte between 1618–1635, Aston Hall has period interiors from the 17th, 18th and 19th centuries, containing fine furniture, paintings, textiles and metalwork. Decorative highlights include the ceiling and frieze of the Great Dining Room, and the carved oak Great Stairs. On the staircase balustrade, sharp-eyed visitors will spot the traces of Roundhead cannon shot, fired during the Civil War siege. **Open:** Apr–Oct, daily, 2–5pm. **Guided Tours:** By appointment only. **Admission:** Free. Please quote Ref no. HHCG00.

map 8
B7

BIRMINGHAM BOTANICAL GARDENS & GLASSHOUSES

Westbourne Road, Edgbaston, Birmingham, West Midlands B15 3TR
Tel: 0121 454 1860 Fax: 0121 454 7835 E-Mail: admin@bham-bot-gdns.demon.co.uk

The Gardens are a 15 acre 'Oasis of Delight' with the finest collection of plants in the Midlands. The Tropical House, full of rainforest vegetation, includes many economic plants. Palms, tree ferns and orchids are displayed in the Palm House. The Orangery features citrus fruits and conservatory plants while the Cactus House conveys a desert scene. There is colourful bedding on the Terrace plus Rhododendron, Rose, Rock, Herb and Cottage Gardens, Trials Ground, Historic Gardens and the National Bonsai Collection. Children's Playgrounds and Aviaries. Gallery. The 'Shop at the Gardens' has a wide range of gifts, souvenirs and plants. Refreshments in the Pavilion. Bands play summer Sunday afternoons. Open daily.

map 4
B1

BLAKESLEY HALL

Blakesley Road, Yardley, Birmingham, West Midlands, B25 8RN.
Tel: 0121 783 2193 (Birmingham Museums & Arts)

Blakesley Hall closes on 31 October. Throughout the year 2000, Blakesley Hall will undertake a major redevelopment, to improve the facilities and services to the public. The museum will be open again in April 2001. For more information please contact the Community Museums Department, Birmingham Museum & Art Gallery, Chamberlain Square, Birmingham B3 3DH. Tel: 0121 303 4698

map 8
B7

CASTLE BROMWICH HALL GARDENS

Chester Road, Castle Bromwich, Birmingham, West Midlands
Tel/Fax: 0121 749 4100

The gardens are a cultural gem and a unique example of early 18th century garden design, restored to their original splendour. Succeeding generations developed and enhanced the gardens, including 'An Elegant Kitchen and Fruit Garden', with many interesting historical vegetables; a 'Ladies Border' with plants of the period; a 'Wilderness' of mature trees underplanted with interesting specimen plants to provide a woodland atmosphere, plus a 'Holly Maze' of 19th century design. Major restoration of the original Green House and Summer House, at either end of the long Holly Walk, together with the classic surrounding walls, enhance the beauty of the gardens. Guided tours. **Open:** pm, Easter–end Sept. Closed Mon & Fri. Internet: www.cbhgt.swinternet.co.uk

map 8
C7

COVENTRY CATHEDRAL

Coventry
Tel: 01203 227597

The remains of the blackened medieval Cathedral, bombed in 1940, stand beside the new Cathedral designed by Basil Spence, consecrated in 1962. Modern works of art include a huge tapestry by Graham Sutherland, a stained glass window by John Piper and a bronze sculpture by Epstein. **Location:** Coventry city centre. **Admission:** Donations for the Cathedral. **Open:** 9–5pm daily. Please phone for Sunday opening times.

SOHO HOUSE

Soho Avenue, Handsworth, Birmingham B18 5LB, West Midlands. Tel: 0121 554 9122 (Birmingham Museums & Arts)

The former home of industrial pioneer Matthew Boulton, who lived at Soho House from 1766 to 1809. It was also the meeting place of some of the most important scientists, engineers and thinkers of the time, The Lunar Society. Possibly the first centrally heated house in England since Roman times, Soho House has been carefully restored to its 18th century glory and contains some of Boulton's own furniture. **Open:** All year. **Times:** Tue–Sat, 10–5pm. Sun, 12 noon–5pm. Closed Mon except Bank Holidays. **Admission:** Adults £2.50, concessions £2, family ticket £6.50. 10% discount for groups of 10 or more. Please quote Ref no. HHCG00.

map 8
B7

HAGLEY HALL

Hagley, Worcestershire DY9 9LG
Tel: 01562 882408 Fax: 01562 882632 (The Viscount Cobham)

The last of the great Palladian Houses, designed by Sanderson Miller and completed in 1760. The house contains the finest example of Rococo plasterwork by Francesco Vassali and a unique collection of 18th century furniture and family portraits including works by Van Dyck, Reynolds and Lely. **Location:** Just off A456 Birmingham to Kidderminster, 12 m from Birmingham within easy reach M5 (exit 3 or 4), M6 or M42. **Station(s):** Hagley (1 m) (not Suns); Stourbridge Junction (2 m). **Open:** Mon 3 Jan–Thurs 27 Jan inclusive; Sun 30 Jan–Sun 27 Feb (excluding all Sats); Fri 21–Thurs 27 Apr inclusive; Sun 28 May–Wed 31 May inclusive; Sun 27–Wed 30 Aug inclusive. **Admission:** Charges apply. **Refreshments:** Tea available in the house. **Conferences:** Specialists in corporate entertaining and conferences throughout the year.

map 4
A1

WIGHTWICK MANOR

Wightwick Bank, Wolverhampton WV6 8EE

Tel: 01902 761108 Fax: 01902 764663

Open: House: 1 March to 31 Dec and March 2000: Thur & Sat (but open BHols for ground floor only) 2.30–5.30pm. Note: Viewing is by timed ticket, issued at front door from 2pm, and by guided tour only. Many of the contents are fragile and some rooms cannot always be shown, so tours vary. Garden: Wed & Thur 11–6pm; Sat, BH Sun & BHols Mon 1–6pm. Other days by appointment. Events: send s.a.e. for details. **Admission:** £5.40; students £2.70. No reduction for groups. Garden only: £2.40. Parking: only room for one coach in lay-by outside main gate; car park (120m) at bottom of Wightwick Bank (please do not park in Elmsdale opposite the property). **Restaurant:** Tea-room, Wed & Thur 11–5pm, Sat & BHols 1–5pm.

Wiltshire

Wiltshire covers a vast and varied area. It remains largely unknown as a county and few visitors are intimate with its great bare sweeps of downland and the smooth lines of the uplands, where bygone tribes first trod the straight tracks and left their camps, dykes and burial mounds. Its gentle and limpid streams flow through the little hamlets and the scores of picturesque villages. In 1220, Salisbury was founded. This tranquil city is the home to Salisbury Cathedral; a wonderful example of Gothic architecture which has the tallest spire in England. This majestic building dwarfs the charming streets that are strewn haphazardly at its foot and overlooks one of this country's most beautiful closes.

Castle Combe

CHARLTON PARK HOUSE

Malmesbury, Wiltshire SN16 9DG
(The Earl of Suffolk and Berkshire)

Jacobean/Georgian mansion, built for the Earls of Suffolk, 1607, altered by Matthew Brettingham the Younger, c.1770. **Location:** 1¹/2 miles NE Malmesbury. Entry only by signed entrance on A429, Malmesbury/Cirencester road. No access from Charlton village. **Open:** 1 May–30 Sept: Mon 2–4pm. Viewing of Great Hall. Staircase and saloon. **Admission:** Adults £1, children/OAP 50p. Car parking limited. Unsuitable for wheelchairs. No dogs. No picnicking.

map 3 K1

THE PETO GARDEN AT IFORD MANOR

Bradford-on-Avon, Wiltshire, BA15 2BA
Tel: 01225 863 146 Fax: 01225 862 364 (Mrs Cartwright-Hignett)

This Grade 1 Italian-style award winning garden was the home of Harold A Peto, the well known Edwardian architect and landscape gardener. Situated beside the River Frome, this unique and romantic hillside garden is characterised by steps, terraces, sculpture and magnificent rural views. **Location:** 7 miles S of Bath via A36. **Open:** Easter Sun–Mon, Apr & Oct, Sun only. May–Sept, Sat–Sun & Tue–Thur & Bank Hol Mon, 2–5pm. **Admission:** Adults £3, children (10+) and OAPs £2.50. Children under 10 not admitted at weekends. **Refreshments:** Saturdays and Sundays, May–Aug only, 2–5pm.

 map 3 J2

HAMPTWORTH LODGE

Landford, Nr Salisbury, Wiltshire SP5 2EA
Tel: 01794 390215 (Mr N Anderson)

Rebuilt Jacobean Manor, with period furniture, including clocks. **Location:** 10 miles SE of Salisbury on the C44 road linking Downton on A338, Salisbury-Bournemouth to Landford on A36, Salisbury-Southampton. **Open:** House and garden daily, except Sundays. Monday March 30 to Thursday April 30 1998 (inclusive). Conducted parties only 2.30 and 3.45. Coaches by appointment only Apr 1–Sept 30. By appointment all year, 18 hole golf course 01794 390155. **Admission:** £3.50, under 11s free. No special arrangement for parties, but about 15 is the maximum. **Refreshments:** Downtown, Salisbury; nil in house. Car parking; disabled ground floor only.

 map 4 B6

HEALE GARDEN & PLANT CENTRE

Middle Woodford, Salisbury SP4 6NT
Tel: 01722 782504 (Mr & Mrs Guy Rasch)

1st Winner of Christie's/HHA Garden of the Year award. Early Carolean manor house where King Charles II hid during his escape. The garden provides a wonderfully varied collection of plants, shrub, musk and other roses, growing in the formal setting of clipped hedges and mellow stonework, at their best in June and July. Particularly lovely in Spring and Autumn is the water garden, planted with magnificent Magnolia and Acers, surrounding an authentic Japanese Tea House and Nikko Bridge which create an exciting focus in this part of the garden. Stunning winter aconites and snowdrops. **Location:** 4 m N of Salisbury on the Woodford Valley road between A345 and A360. Midway between Salisbury, Wilton and Stonehenge. **Open:** Garden, Plant Centre and shop open throughout the year, 10–5pm. **Admission:** Adults £3, accompanied children under 14 free.

 map 4 B5

BOWOOD HOUSE AND GARDENS

The Estate Office, Bowood, Calne, Wiltshire SN11 0LZ
Tel: 01249 812102 Fax: 01249 821757

Bowood House is the magnificent family home of the Marquis and Marchioness of Lansdowne and was designed by Robert Adam in the 18th century. On display in the exhibion rooms upstairs is a remarkable collection of family heirlooms built up over 250 years. Part of the house was demolished in 1955, leaving a perfectly proportioned Georgian home, much of which is open to visitors. Robert Adam's magnificent Diocletian wing contains a splendid library, the laboratory where Joseph Priestley discovered oxygen gas in 1774, the orangery, now a picture gallery, the Chapel and a sculpture gallery. Among the family treasures shown in the numerous exhibition rooms are Georgian costumes, including Lord Byron's Albanian dress; Victoriana; Indiana and superb collections of watercolours, miniatures and jewellery. The House is set in one of the most beautiful parks in England. Over 2,000 acres of gardens and grounds were landscaped by 'Capability' Brown between 1762 and 1768, and are embellished with a Doric temple, a cascade, a pinetum and an arboretum. The Rhododendron Gardens are open for six weeks during the flowering season, from late April to early June. All the walks have seats. For children, Bowood offers a truly outstanding Adventure Playground, complete with life–size pirate ship, giant slides, chutes and high level rope walks. **Admission:** Adults £5.70, senior citizens £4.70, children £3.50. Party rates: Adults £4.80, senior citizens £4.10, children £3. <u>**Open:**</u> daily from 1 April–29 October. Rhododendron Walks: Adults/OAPs £3, children free; cost per person £2 if combined with a visit to the House and Gardens on the same day. <u>**Internet:**</u> www.bowood-estate.co.uk

map 3
K2

CORSHAM COURT

Corsham, Wiltshire SN13 0BZ
Tel/Fax: 01249 701610 (J Methuen-Campbell Esq)

Since 1745 Corsham Court has been the home of the Methuen family, based on an Elizabethan house dating from 1582. It was bought by Paul Methuen to house a collection of 16th and 17th century Italian and Flemish master paintings and statuary. In the middle of the 19th century, the house was enlarged to receive a second collection purchased in Florence, principally of fashionable old masters and stone-inlaid furniture. The surviving collection includes works by Van Dyck and Lippi, which hang alongside family portraits by Reynolds. The Picture Gallery was designed as a triple cube and boasts a rare ornate ceiling attributed to Lancelot 'Capability' Brown. The Georgian State Rooms were furnished by Thomas Chippendale and others during late 19th century. The Gardens have magnificent views, particularly East, providing a tranquil aspect over the Park. The grounds comprise sweeping lawns and formal areas with a rose garden, lily pond and herbaceous borders. There are beautiful specimen trees including the Great Plane, cedars, beeches and oaks dating back to the original 18th century plantings by 'Capability' Brown and Repton. **Location:** Signposted 4 miles west of Chippenham from the A4 Bath Road. **Open:** Throughout the year to groups of 15 or more persons by appointment. Otherwise, open 20 Mar–30 Sept daily except Mondays (but including Bank Hols) from 11–5.30pm. 1 Oct–19 Mar open weekends from 2–4.30pm. Closed December. Last entry 30 minutes before close. **Admission:** Adults £4.50, OAP's £3.50, child £1.00, group rates £3.50. **Refreshments:** Available at Johnsons Bakery nearby. **Internet:** www.touristnetuk.com

map 3
J2

LONGLEAT

Warminster, Wiltshire, BA12 7NW
Tel: 01985 844400 Fax: 01985 844885 (The Marquess of Bath)

Nestling within magnificent 'Capability' Brown landscaped grounds in the heart of Wiltshire, Longleat House is widely regarded as one of the finest examples of high Elizabethan architecture in Britain and one of the most beautiful stately homes open to the public. This magnificent Elizabethan property, built by Sir John Thynne and substantially completed by 1580, has been the home of the same family ever since. The House contains many treasures including paintings by Tintoretto and Wootton, exquisite Flemish tapestries, fine French furniture, as well as elaborate ceilings by John Dibblee Crace incorporating paintings from the 'School of Titian'. The Murals in the family apartments in the West Wing were painted by Alexander Thynn, the present Marquess, and are fascinating and remarkable additions to the collections. Apart from the ancestral home, Longleat is also renowned for its Safari Park, the first of its kind outside Africa. Here, visitors have the rare opportunity to see hundreds of animals in a natural woodland and parkland setting. Amongst the most magnificent sights are the famous pride of lions, a white tiger, giraffe, wolves, elephants and zebras. Also roaming free around the park are Longleat's monkeys, rhinos and camels. New animals are constantly being introduced or born so each visit always brings new surprises. Other attractions that shouldn't be missed include the 'World's Longest Hedge Maze', the children's Adventure Castle, Longleat Railway, the Safari Boats (to view sea lions and hippos) and the Needlecraft Centre. In fact there's so much to see and do for all the family, we recommend a second visit! **Open:** The House is open 1 Apr–31 Dec (excl. Christmas Day) with pre-booked groups only from Jan–Mar. The Safari Park and all other attractions are open from 1 Apr–29 Oct. Please telephone or contact our website for opening times & further information. **Internet:** www.longleat.co.uk

map 3
J3

LUCKINGTON COURT

Luckington, Chippenham, Wiltshire SN14 6PQ
Tel: 01666 840205 (The Hon Mrs Trevor Horn)

Mainly Queen Anne with magnificent group of ancient buildings. Beautiful mainly formal garden with fine collection of ornamental trees and shrubs. Home of the Bennet family in the BBC TV adaptation 'Pride and Prejudice'. **Location:** 6 miles W of Malmesbury on B4040 Bristol Road. **Open:** All through the year Weds 2–5pm, garden only. Open Sunday 30 Apr 2000, 2.30–5pm. Collection box for National Gardens' Scheme. Inside view by appointment 3 weeks in advance. **Admission:** Outside gardens only £1, house £2. **Refreshments:** Teas in garden or house (in aid of Luckington Parish Church) on Sun 2 May only.

map 3
J2

AVEBURY MANOR AND GARDEN

Nr Marlborough SN8 1RF Tel: 01672 539250

Open: House: 2 Apr–31 Oct: Tues, Wed, Sun & BH Mons 2–5.30pm; last admission 5pm or dusk if earlier. Garden: 2 Apr–31 Oct: daily except Mon & Thur (but open BH Mons) 11–5.30pm.

GREAT CHALFIELD MANOR

Nr Melksham SN12 8NJ Tel: 01225 782239

Open: 4 April to 29 Oct: Tues–Thur by guided tours only at 12.15pm, 2.15pm, 3.45pm & 4.30pm.

LACOCK ABBEY

Lacock, Nr Chippenham SN15 2LG Tel: Abbey 01249 730227

Open: Museum, cloisters & grounds: 26 Feb–29 Oct: daily (closed Good Fri) 11–5.30pm. Abbey: April–29 Oct: daily, except Tues, 1–5.30pm. Museum open some winter weekends. Tel. for details.

SALISBURY CATHEDRAL

The Close, Salisbury SP1 2EJ
Tel: 01722 555120 Fax: 01722 555116

Salisbury Cathedral is probably the finest medieval building in Britain, with the highest spire, the best preserved Magna Carta, the unique 13th century frieze of bible stories in the Chapter House and Europe's oldest working clock. Boy and girl choristers sing daily services, continuing a tradition of music that goes back over 750 years. Volunteer guides conduct tours of the Cathedral most days, special tours for pre-booked parties include the roof old tower, workshops, stained glass windows and vestments. **Location:** In The Close, just south of the city centre. **Open:** 7am every day of the year. Closing time: Jan–May & Sept–Dec: 6.15pm. June, July & Aug: 8.15pm. Every Sun: 6.15pm. **E-mail:** visitors@salcath.co.uk **Website:** www.salisbury cathedral.org.uk

map 3
K3

Photography, Steve Day

WILTON HOUSE

The Estate Office, Wilton, Salisbury, Wiltshire SP2 0BJ
Tel: 01722 746720 Fax: 01722 744447 (The Earl of Pembroke)

Wilton House stands on the site of the 9th century nunnery founded by King Alfred. This in turn was replaced by a 12th century Benedictine abbey which, including its surrounding lands, was surrendered during the Dissolution of the monasteries. Now home to the 17th Earl of Pembroke, Wilton House provides a fascinating insight on British history. Marvel at Inigo Jones' magnificent state rooms and admire the world famous art collection. Perhaps the most striking room in the house is the Double Cube, sixty feet long by thirty feet wide and thirty feet high. This room, among others, has offered film-makers the perfect setting for many major movies amongst which are, *The Madness* of *King George, Sense and Sensibility* and *Mrs Brown*. Created within the atmospheric setting of the old indoor riding school, the Visitor Centre provides the starting point for your tour of Wilton House. The modern interpretative displays, including the Tudor kitchen, Victorian laundry and award-winning introductory film bring history to life. Enjoy 'the Wareham Bears' - 200 miniature costumed teddy bears. Relax in 21 acres of landscaped parkland, water and rose gardens beside the River Nadder and Palladian Bridge. **Open:** Daily from 10 Apr–29 Oct 2000. 10.30–5.30pm (last admission 4.30pm). **E-mail:** tourism@wiltonhouse. com **Internet:** www.wiltonhouse.com

map 4
B5

STOURHEAD

Stourton, Warminster, BA12 6QD, Wiltshire.
Tel: 01747 841 152 Fax: 01747 841 152 (The National Trust)

Stourhead combines Britain's foremost landscape garden with a fine Palladian mansion. Stourhead Garden is one of the most famous examples of the early 18th century English landscape movement. Planned in the belief that it was "Tiresome for the foot to travel, to where the eye had already been", the garden continually surprises the visitor with fresh glimpses of its enchanting lakes and temples. The House was designed in 1721 for Henry Hoare by Colen Campbell. Its contents include a collection of furniture designed by the younger Chippendale and many fine works of art. Interesting features of the estate include two Iron Age hill forts and King Alfred's Tower, a 160 ft high red brick folly. This tower offers magnificent views across the three counties of Wiltshire, Somerset and Dorset. **Location:** Stourton, off B3092, 3 miles NW of A303 (Mere). 2hrs from London, 1.5 hrs from Exeter. **Open:** Garden: All Year Daily, 9–7pm (or dusk if earlier), except 20–23 July (Fête Champêtre), when gardens close at 5pm (last admission 4pm). House: 1 Apr–29 Oct, Sat–Wed, 12–5.30pm or dusk if earlier (last admission 5pm). King Alfred's Tower: 1 Apr–29 Oct: Tues–Fri 2–5.30pm. Sat, Sun, Good Friday & Bank Holiday Mon 11.30–5.30pm (or dusk if earlier). Plant Centre: Open Apr–Sept, 12–6pm. 01747 840 894. **Admission:** Garden or House: Adult £4.60, children £2.60, group (15 or more) £4.10, family £10. (2 adults & up to 3 children). Combined Garden and House: Adult £8, children £3.80, group £7.70, family £20. Large coach and car park. Guided Tours: Pre-booked garden tours are available on request throughout the year. King Alfred's Tower: Adult £1.50, child 70p. **Events:** Held throughout the year. Please phone for leaflet.

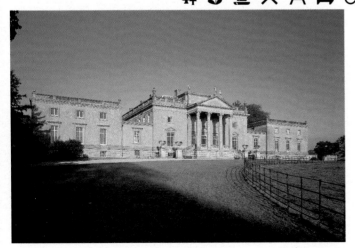

Yorkshire

Yorkshire nowadays is sub-divided into various administrative areas. Pleasure-seekers can happily forget this contemporary arrangement. North Yorkshire hosts two national parks, an excellent spa town in Harrogate, Knaresborough – the oldest town mentioned in the Doomsday book and enchanting small cities such as Ripon.

Between the Lake District and the North York Moors lie the Yorkshire Dales with their farming landscape.

Mount Grace Priory, English Heritage

The capital of the whole region – York – has retained so much of its medieval structure that walking into its centre is like entering a museum. Home to England's largest medieval church, the wonderfully gothic York Minster houses the largest collection of medieval stained glass in Britain and embodies history, with its 18 medieval churches, 2 mile long medieval city walls, elegant Jacobean and Georgian architecture and fine museums.

ASKE HALL

Aske, Richmond, North Yorkshire DL10 5HJ
Tel: 01748 850391 Fax: 01748 823252 (The Marquess of Zetland)

The Hall – a Georgian gem – nestles in Capability Brown parkland with lake, follies, meadows, woods and a new terraced garden, the visionary creation of Lady Zetland described as the most ambitious gardening scheme of the day! It has been the family seat of the Dundas family for over 200 years and boasts an impressive collection of 18th century furniture, paintings and porcelain. **Location:** 2 m from A1 on the Richmond/Gilling West Road (B6274) **Stations:** Darlington 13 m away. **Admission:** £6 – for groups of 15+ by appointment only. "A Taste of Gentility", a tour followed by Yorkshire afternoon tea in the Regency dining room on Weds in July & Aug £15pp. Booking essential Tel: 01748 850391 for further details. **Events/Exhibitions:** Telephone for programme. **Conferences:** Suitable for up to a capacity of 100.

map 11
H5

THE BAR CONVENT

17 Blossom Street, York YO24 1AQ
Tel: 01904 643238 Fax: 01904 631792

The Bar Convent is an elegant Georgian building (1787) located on the corner of Blossom St and Nunnery Lane. It houses a beautiful neo-classical chapel (1769); both were designed by Thomas Atkinson. The Bar Convent Museum outlines the early history of Christianity in the North of England and also tells the story of Mary Ward, the foundress of the Institute of the Blessed Virgin Mary (IBVM). There are guided museum tours on Mon-Fri at 10.30am and 2.30pm. There is a cafe which serves coffee, tea and wine as well as hot meals (9.30–4.00pm Mon–Sat). There is a small souvenir and gift shop. Conference and residential facilities are available to groups; please contact the Business manager on 01904 643238.

map 8
D2

BOLTON ABBEY

Skipton, North Yorkshire, BD23 6EX. Tel: 01756 710 227
Fax 01756 710 535 (Trustees of the Chatsworth Settlement)

The Yorkshire Estate of the Duke and Duchess of Devonshire. The Augustine Bolton Priory was founded in 1154 and is now partly parish church. Other historic buildings include the 13th century Barden Tower – formerly owned by the Cliffords of Skipton. The Estate offers spectacular walks in some of the most beautiful countryside in England – along the riverside, on the heather moors and Nature Trails in Strid Wood (S.S.S.I.) renowned for its bird life and rare plants. **Location:** On B6160, N from the roundabout junction with the A59 Skipton-Harrogate Road, 23 miles from Leeds. **Station(s):** Skipton & Ilkley. **Open:** All year. **Admission:** Charges apply. Motorised chairs available. **Refreshments:** Restaurant and 2 tearooms. **Accommodation:** Farmhouse B&B, self-catering cottage, hotel.

BROCKFIELD HALL

Warthill, York, North Yorkshire YO19 5XJ
Tel: 01904 489298 (Lord and Lady Martin Fitzalan Howard)

A fine late Georgian house designed by Peter Atkinson, whose father had been assistant to John Carr of York, for Benjamin Agar Esq. Begun in 1804, its outstanding feature is an oval entrance hall with a fine cantilevered stone staircase curving past an impressive Venetian window. It is the happy family home of Lord and Lady Martin Fitzalan Howard. He is the brother of the 17th Duke of Norfolk and son of the late Baroness Beaumont of Carlton Towers, Selby. There are some interesting portraits of her old Roman catholic family, the Stapletons, and some good furniture. **Location:** 5 miles east of York, off A166 or A64 **Open:** August 1–31st 2000, 1pm–4pm except Mondays, other times by appointment. **Admission:** Adults £3.50, children £1.

map 11
J7

BOLTON CASTLE

Leyburn, North Yorkshire, DL8 4ET
Tel: 01969 623 981 Fax: 01969 623 332
(Hon. Mr & Mrs Harry Orde-Powlett)

Completed in 1399, Bolton Castle celebrated its 600th anniversary last year. Originally the stronghold of the Scrope family, the castle has a wealth of history. Mary, Queen of Scots was imprisoned here for 6 months shortly after her arrival in England. Medieval garden and vineyard also open to the public. Also tearoom and gift shop. **Location:** Just off A684, 6 miles W of Leyburn. **Open:** Daily throughout year 10–5pm or dusk if earlier. **Admission:** Guided tour by arrangement for groups of 15+. Adults £4, OAP/children £3, family ticket £10 (2 adults & 2 children). **Refreshments:** Tearoom – meals available, picnic area. Wedding licence. **E-mail:** harry@boltoncastle.co.uk **Internet:** www .boltoncastle.co.uk

map 8 B1

BRAMHAM PARK

Wetherby, West Yorkshire, LS23 6ND
Tel: 01937 844265/846005 Fax: 01937 845923/846006 (G. F. Lane Fox)

The Queen Anne house is 5 miles south of Wetherby on the A1, 10 miles from Leeds and 15 miles from York. The grand design of the gardens (66 acres) and pleasure grounds (100 acres) are the only example of a formal, early 18th century landscape in the British Isles. Unexpected views and grand vistas, framed by monumental hedges and trees, delight the visitor, while temples, ornamental ponds and cascades focus the attention. The profusion of spring and summer wild flowers give a constant variety of colour and include many rare species.

Location: 5 miles south of Wetherby, on A1. **Open:** Every day from 2 Feb–30 Sept, 10.30–5.30pm (closed for Bramham Horse Trials 5–11 June). Gardens: open every day. House: open by appointment only for parties 6+. **Admission:** Adult £2.95, senior citizen/children under 16 £1.95. Under 5's free. For further information contact: The Estate Office, Bramham Park, Wetherby, West Yorkshire LS23 6ND Tel: 01937 844 265. **Refreshments:** Picnics in grounds permitted. Packed lunches available (must be pre-booked).

map 11 H7

BRODSWORTH HALL

Brodsworth, Nr. Doncaster, South Yorkshire DN5 7XY
Tel: 01302 722598 Fax: 01302 337165 (English Heritage)

Brodsworth Hall is an outstanding example of a Victorian country house. Within its grand Italianate exterior, visitors can glimpse a vanished way of life viewing over 30 rooms ranging from the sumptuous family reception to the plain but functional servants' wing. A pervasive sense of faded grandeur and of time past adds an element of enchantment to the Hall. The restored Victorian gardens form the ideal setting. **Location:** 5 m NW of Doncaster, A635 from Junction 37, A1(M). **Open:** 1 Apr–5 Nov, Tues–Sun & Bank Hols, 1–6pm. Last admission 5pm. Gardens, tearoom & shop from noon. Pre-booked guided tours from 10am. 6 Nov–26 Mar 2000 Winter weekends only, garden, shop & tearoom 11–4pm. **Admission:** Hall & Gardens: Adults £5, concs £3.80, child £2.50. Gardens: Adults £2.60, concs £2, child £1.30. Gardens (Winter): Adults £1.60, concs £1.20, child 80p.

map 8 B3

BURTON AGNES HALL

Burton Agnes, Diffield, East Yorks YO25 0ND
Tel: 01262 490 324 Fax: 01262 490 513 (Burton Agnes Hall Preservation Trust Ltd).

The Hall is a magnificent example of late Elizabethan architecture - still lived in by descendants of the family who built it in 1598. There are wonderful carvings, lovely furniture and a fine collection of modern French and English paintings of the Impressionist Schools. The walled garden contains a potager, maze, herbaceous borders, campanula collection, jungle garden and giant games set in coloured gardens. Also woodland gardens and walk, children's corner, Norman manor house, donkey wheel and gift shop. **Location:** 6 miles SW of Bridlington on Driffield/Bridlington Rd (A166). **Open:** Apr 1–Oct 31 daily 11–5pm. **Admission:** Adults £4.50, OAPs £4, children £2.25. **Gardens only:** Adults £2.25, OAPs £2, children £1. **Refreshments:** Licensed cafeteria. Teas, light lunches & refreshments.

CASTLE HOWARD

Nr York, North Yorkshire YO60 7DA
Tel: 01653 648444 Fax: 01653 648501 (The Hon. Simon Howard)

Magnificent palace designed by Vanbrugh in 1699. One of Britain's most spectacular stately homes. Impressive Great Hall and beautiful rooms are filled with fine furniture, paintings and objets d'art. Extensive grounds with lakes and colourful woodland. Rose garden, plant centre, adventure playground. **Location:** 15 m NE of York; 3 m off A64; 6 m W of Malton; 22 m from Scarborough. **Open:** Daily 17 Mar–5 Nov. Grounds from 10am, house from 11am. Last admission 4.30pm. **Admission:** Adult £7.50, child £4.50, OAP £6.75. Groups (min. 12 people): Adult £6.50, child £4, OAP £6. Grounds only: Adult £4.50, child £2.50 **Refreshments:** Licensed cafeteria in House, Lakeside Café. Café and shops facilities in Stable Courtyard. **E-mail:** mec@castlehoward.co.uk **Internet:** www.castlehoward.co.uk

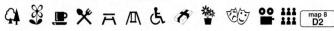

CONSTABLE BURTON HALL

Constable Burton, Leyburn, North Yorkshire DL8 5LJ
Tel: 01677 450428 Fax: 01677 450622 (Mr Charles Wyvill)

Situated 3 miles east of Leyburn on the A684 and 6 miles west of the A1. A large romantic garden surrounded by 18th century parkland with a superb John Carr house (not open). Fine trees, woodland walks, garden trails and nature trails, rockery with an interesting collection of alpines and extensive shrubs and roses. Set in beautiful countryside at the entrance to Wensleydale. **Open:** Gardens Mar 25–Oct 17 daily 9–6pm. **Admission:** Please phone for details. Group tours of the house and gardens available by Phil Robinson, The Dales Plantsman. Tel: 01677 460225. **Events:** Special Event - Tulip Festival 30 Apr–1 May.

DUNCOMBE PARK

Helmsley, Ryedale, York, North Yorks YO62 5EB
Tel: 01439 770213 Fax: 01439 771114

Visit Lord and Lady Feversham's restored family home in the North York Moors National Park. Built on a virgin plateau in 1713 overlooking both Norman Castle and river Valley it is surrounded by 35 acres of 'spectacularly beautiful' 18th century landscaped gardens and 400 acres of rolling, Arcadian parkland with National Nature Reserve and veteran trees. **Location:** Just off Helmsley Market Place, along A170 (Scarborough–Thirsk road). **Open:** 2 Apr–29 Oct, Apr/Oct: Sun–Thurs, May–Sept: Sun–Fri. House & Garden: 10.30–6pm. Tearoom, shop and walks 10.30–5.30pm. **Admission:** House & Garden: adult £6, conc. £5, child (10–16) £3, family (2+2) £13.50, groups £4.50. Gardens and parkland: adult £4, child £2. Parkland: adult £2, child £1. Season ticket (2+2) £35. Duncombe Park is available for weddings and corporate entertainment.

FAIRFAX HOUSE

Castlegate, York, YO1 9RN, North Yorkshire
Tel: 01904 655 543 Fax: 01904 652 262 (York Civic Trust)

An 18th century house designed by John Carr of York, and described as a class architectural masterpiece of its age. Certainly one of the finest town houses in England and saved from near collapse by the York Civic Trust who restored it to its former glory during 1982/84. In addition to the superbly decorated plaster work, wood and wrought iron, the house is now home for an outstanding collection of 18th century furniture and clocks, formed by the late Noel Terry. Described by Christie's as one of the finest private collections of this century, it enhances and complements the house and helps to create a very special 'lived in' feeling. Their regular set-piece exhibitions bring the House to life in a very tangible way. Special displays for the coming year. **Location:** Centre of York, follow signs for Castle Area and Jorvik Centre. **Station(s):** York (10 mins walk). **Open:** 26 Feb–6 Jan, Mon–Thurs &

Sat, 11am–5pm, Sun 1.30–5pm. Last admission 4.30pm. Fri, guided tours only 11am and 2pm. Special evening tours, connoisseur visits and private dinners welcomed by arrangement with the Director. **Admission:** Adults £4, children £1.50, OAPs/students £3.50. Adult parties (pre-booked 15+) £3, children £1.25. **Events/Exhibitions:** Eat, Drink and Be Merry, The British at Table 1600–2000: 26 Feb–4 June 2000. The Keeping of Christmas: 2 Dec–6 Jan 2001. **Conferences:** By arrangement with the Director. Public car park within 50 yards. Suitable for disabled persons only with assistance (by telephoning beforehand, staff can be available to help). A small gift shop offers selected antiques, publications and gifts. Opening times are the same as the house.

map 8
D2

HAREWOOD HOUSE

The Harewood Estate, Leeds, West Yorkshire, LS17 9LQ
Tel: 0113 218 1010 Fax: 0113 218 1002 (Earl & Countess of Harewood)

Award-winning Harewood! Renowned for its stunning architecture; exquisite interiors; outstanding collections; beautiful gardens and 'Capability' Brown landscape; popular lakeside Bird Garden and wide variety of special events throughout the season. **Location:** A61, between Leeds and Harrogate. **Open:** 1 Apr–29 Oct, daily. Grounds & Bird Garden: 10am. House: 11am, last admissions 4pm. **Admission:** Adult £7.25, OAP £6.50, Children £5, Family £25. **Events/Exhibitions:** New for 2000 - a major Chippendale exhibition featuring exquisite samples of his work, including the newly restored 'Chippendale State Bed - unseen for 150 years! Outdoor events range from concerts to car rallies, and inside the House, by appointment, are 'behind the scenes' and specialist guided tours. Telephone for details. **E-mail:** business@harewood.org **Internet:** www.harewood.org

HOVINGHAM HALL

Hovingham, York, North Yorkshire YO62 4LU
Tel: 01653 628206 Fax: 01653 628668 (Sir Marcus Worsley)

Palladian House built c.1760 by Thomas Worsley to his own design. Unique entry by huge riding school. Visitors see family portraits and rooms in everyday use; also the extensive garden with magnificent yew hedges and dove-cot and the private cricket ground, said to be the oldest in England. **Location:** 20 miles N of York on Malton/Helmsley Road (B1257). **Open:** Open for parties of 15 or more *by written appointment* only Apr–end Sept 1999. Tues, Wed and Thurs 11–7pm. **Admission:** £4, children £2. **Refreshments:** At the Hall by arrangement. Meals at the Worsley Arms Hotel, Hovingham. **E-mail:** office@hovingham.co.uk

HARLOW CARR BOTANICAL GARDENS

Crag Lane, Harrogate, North Yorkshire HG3 1QB
Tel: 01423 565418 Fax: 01423 530663 (Northern Horticultural Society)

Sixty-eight acre headquarters of the Northern Horticultural Society. Vegetable, fruit and flower trials. Rock, foliage, scented, winter and heather gardens. Alpines, herbaceous beds, display houses, fern house, streamside, woodland and arboretum. National collections, Museum of Gardening, Model Village, library, childrens' play area. Fully licensed restaurant, plant and gift centre. Picnic area. Courses, exhibitions, displays, walks and talks held on a regular basis throughout the year. Ample free coach parking, shelters, seating and hard surface pathways. Driver facilities vouchers. **Location:** 1½ miles W of town centre on B6162 Otley road. **Open:** Daily from 9.30am. Last admission dusk. **Admission:** Adults £4, OAPs and groups of 20+ £3. Children free. **Internet:** www.harlowcarr.fsnet.co.uk

THE SUE RYDER HOME, HICKLETON HALL

Hickleton, Doncaster DN5 7BB
Tel: 01709 892070

The Home cares for 20 elderly residents and 33 disabled patients (from 40 years and above). This fine Georgian Mansion built in the 1740's, to a design by James Paine, is set in 12 acres of formal garden. The present garden design is by Inigo Thomas c 1866–1950 and laid out in the early 1900's. **Location:** 6 miles west of Doncaster on the A635 Doncaster/Barnsley Road. **Open:** Individuals wishing to visit Hickleton Hall and Gardens may do so, Mon–Fri 2–4pm with prior arrangement. **Refreshments:** Hotels and restaurants in Doncaster.

KNARESBOROUGH CASTLE & MUSEUM

Knaresborough, North Yorkshire
Tel: 01423 556130 Fax: 01423 556130 (Duchy of Lancaster)

Ruins of 14th century castle standing high above the town. Local history museum housed in Tudor Courthouse. Gallery devoted to the Civil War. **Location:** 5 miles east of Harrogate off A59. **Open:** Good Friday–1 Oct: Daily 10.30–5pm. **Admission:** Adults £2, child £1.25, concessions £1.50. Family £5.50. Groups (10+) £1.50. **E-mail:** lg31@harrogate.gov.uk

LEDSTON HALL

Hall Lane, Ledston, Castleford, WF10 2BB, West Yorkshire
Tel: 01423 523 423 Fax: 01423 521 373 (G. H. H. Wheler)

17th century mansion with some earlier work. **Location:** 2 miles N of Castleford, off A656. **Station(s):** Castleford (2 ¾ miles). **Open:** Exterior only: May–Aug, Mon–Fri, 9–4pm. Other days by appointment. **Refreshments:** Chequers Inn, Ledsham (1 mile).

NEWBURGH PRIORY

Coxwold, York, North Yorkshire, YO6 4AS
Tel: 01347 868 435 (Sir George Wombwell, Bt.)

One of the North's most interesting historic houses. Originally built in 1145 with alterations in 1568 and 1720–1760, the Priory has been the home of one family and its descendants since 1538. The house contains the tomb of Oliver Cromwell (his third daughter, Mary, was married to Viscount Fauconberg, the owner from 1647–1700). In the grounds there is a really beautiful water garden full of rare alpines, other plants and rhododendrons. **Location:** 5 miles from Easingwold, off A19, 9 miles from Thirsk. **Open: House & Grounds:** 2 Apr–28 June, Sun & Wed & Bank Hol Mons Easter. House open 2.30–4.45pm. Grounds open 2–6pm. Open at other times for parties of 25+ by appointment with the Administrator. **Admission:** House & Grounds: Adults £4, children £1. Grounds only: Adults £2, children free. **Refreshments:** Afternoon tea is served in the original Old Priory Kitchens.

NORTON CONYERS

Ripon, North Yorkshire, HG4 5EQ
Tel: 01765 640333 Fax: 01765 692772 (Sir James and Lady Graham)

Visited by Charlotte Brontë, Norton Conyers is an original of 'Thornfield Hall' in 'Jane Eyre' and a family legend was an inspiration for the mad Mrs Rochester. Another visitor was James II when Duke of York, in 1679. The room and the bed he and his wife traditionally used are still to be seen. 376 years of occupation by the Grahams (they bought it in 1624) have given the house a noticeably friendly atmosphere. Family portraits, furniture, ceramics and costumes. The paintings in the Great Hall include a celebrated John Ferneley, 'The Quorn Hunt', painted in 1822. The 18th century walled garden, with Orangery and herbaceous borders, includes a plant sales area, specialising in unusual hardy plants. Pick your own fruit in season; please check beforehand. **Location:** Near Wath, 4 miles N of Ripon, 3 miles from A1. **Open:** House and garden: all Suns and Bank Hol Mons 23 Apr–3 Sept. Daily 3–8 July. The house is open 2–5pm, the garden 11.30–5pm. **Admission:** Adults £3, children (10–16) and OAPs £2.50. Prices for parties on application. Garden is free (donations welcome); a charge is, however, made at charity openings. **Refreshments:** Teas are available at garden charity openings. Dogs (except guide dogs) in grounds and garden only and must be on a lead. Photography by owners' written permission only. No high-heeled shoes in house, please. Wheelchair access ground floor only.

Yorkshire

NEWBY HALL & GARDENS
Ripon, North Yorkshire, HG4 5AE
Tel: 01423 322 583 Fax: 01423 324 452 (R. E. J. Compton)

The family home of Mr and Mrs Robin Compton is one of Yorkshire's renowned Adam houses. It is set amidst 25 acres of award-winning gardens full of rare and beautiful plants. Famous double herbaceous borders with formal compartmented gardens, including a species rose garden, water and rock garden, the Autumn Garden and the tranquillity of Sylvia's Garden – truly a 'Garden for all Seasons'. **Location:** 4 miles SE of Ripon on Boroughbridge Road (B6265). 3 miles W of A1. Harrogate (14 miles). York (20 miles). Leeds (35 miles). Skipton (32 miles). **Station(s):** Harrogate or York. **Open:** House & Garden: 1 Apr–30 Sept, Tues–Sun and Bank Hol Mons. **Admission:** Charges apply.

NORMANBY HALL
Normanby, Scunthorpe, North Lincolnshire DN15 9HU
Tel: 01724 720588 Fax: 01724 721248 (North Lincolnshire Council)

The restored working Victorian Walled Garden is growing produce for the 'big house', as it would have been done 100 years ago. Set in 300 acres of park, visitors can also see the Regency Mansion, designed by Sir Robert Smirke, which the Garden was built to serve. The rooms of the Hall are displayed in styles depicting the Regency, Victorian and Edwardian eras. Costume from the Museum Service's collections is also exhibited. FURTHER INFORMATION, OPENING TIMES AND DATES WITH PHOTOGRAPHY CAN BE SEEN ON PAGE 114.

NUNNINGTON HALL
Nunnington, York, North Yorkshire YO62 5UY
Tel: 01439 748283 Fax: 01439 748284

Sheltered in a lovely walled garden on a quiet riverbank is this delightful 17th century manor house. It is easy to see why it has remained a much lovely family home for over 400 years. A magnificent oak panelled hall leads to cosy family living rooms, the nursery and maid's room. Explore the attics and discover the amazing Carlisle Collection of miniature rooms each exquisitely furnished to one eighth life size. **Open:** 1 Apr–29 Oct. April, May, Sept & Oct: daily except Mon and Tues 1.30–5pm. (4.30pm Apr & Oct). June–Aug: daily except Mon 1.30–5pm. Open Good Fri and Bank Hol Mons. **Admission:** Adult £4, child £2, family £10 (2 adults and up to 3 children). Garden: Adult £1.50, children free. Group: £3 per person (minimum 15 paying). **Tearooms:** Seating 72, plus 60 in the Tea Garden. Not licensed. Open 12.30–5pm.

map 8 D1

PLUMPTON ROCKS
Plumpton, Knaresborough, North Yorkshire HG5 8NA
Tel: 01423 863950 (Edward de Plumpton Hunter)

Owned by the Plumpton Family for over 750 years. This Grade 2* listed garden extends to over 30 acres and includes an idyllic lake, dramatic Millstone Grit rock formations, romantic woodland walks winding through bluebells and rhododendrons. Declared by English Heritage to be of outstanding interest. Painted by Turner, Girtin and Hodges. Used in numerous television productions including Emmerdale Farm, Heartbeat and the Muppet Show. Described by Queen Mary as 'Heaven on Earth'. **Location:** Situated midway between Harrogate and Wetherby on the A661 one mile south east of that road's junction with the Harrogate Southern Bypass A658. **Open:** March–Oct: Sat, Sun and Bank Holidays 11–6pm. **Admission:** Adults £1.50, children and senior citizens £1.

map 8 C2

RIEVAULX ABBEY
Helmsley, North Yorkshire YO6 5LB
Tel: 01439 798228 (English Heritage)

Visit the spectacular remains of the first Cistercian monastery in Northern England and experience the unrivalled peace and serenity of its setting in the beautiful wooded valley of the River Rye. Imaginations will be fired as you listen to our audio tour while exploring the extensive remains; the soaring graceful arches silhouetted against the sky will take the breath away. Also, new interactive exhibition. **Location:** In Rievaulx, 2¼ m W of Helmsley on minor road off B1257. **Open:** 1 Apr–30 Sept: daily, 10–6pm. Open 9.30–7pm, July–Aug. 1 Oct–31 Oct: daily, 10–5pm, 1 Nov–31 Mar: daily, 10–4pm. Closed 24–26 Dec. **Admission:** Adults £3.40, concs £2.60, child £1.70. (15% discount for groups of 11 or more).

 map 8 D1

RIEVAULX TERRACE & TEMPLE
Rievaulx, Helmsley, York, YO6 5LJ
Tel: 01439 748283 Fax: 01439 748284

A ½ mile long grass covered terrace and adjoining woodlands with vistas over Rievaulx Abbey (English Heritage) and Rye Valley to Ryedale and the Hambleton Hills. There are two mid-18th century temples: the Ionic Temples has elaborate ceiling paintings and fine 18th century furniture. **Note:** No access to Rievaulx Abbey from Terrace. No access to property Nov–end of March. **Open:** 1 Apr–29 Oct. Apr & Oct: daily 10.30–4pm. June, July, Aug & Sept: daily 10.30–5pm. Open Good Fri and Bank Hol Mons. **Admission:** Adult £3, child £1.50, family £7.50 (2 adults and upto 3 children). Groups: £2 per person (minimum of 15 paying). **Refreshments:** Ice cream only. Teas at Nunnington Hall 7m (see entry for Nunnington).

map 8 D1

RIPLEY CASTLE
Ripley Castle Estate, Harrogate, North Yorkshire.
Tel: 01423 770152 Fax: 01423 771745 (Sir Thomas and Lady Ingilby)

Ripley Castle has been home to the Ingilby family for twenty-six generations and Sir Thomas and Lady Ingilby together with their five children continue the tradition. The guided tours are amusing and informative, following the lives and loves of one family for over 670 years. The historic Gatehouse, 550 years old in 2000 still bears bullet marks from Cromwell's Army after the Battle of Marston Moor. The Old Tower houses splendid armour, books, panelling and a Priest's Hiding Hole. FOR FURTHER DETAILS, OPENING TIMES AND PHOTOGRAPHY, PLEASE TURN TO PAGE 214 & 215.

SHANDY HALL

Coxwold, York, North Yorkshire, YO61 4AD
Tel: 01347 868 465 (The Laurence Sterne Trust)

Here in 1760–1767 the witty and eccentric parson Laurence Sterne wrote 'Tristram Shandy' and 'A Sentimental Journey'. Shandy Hall was built as a timber-framed open-hall in the mid-15th century and added to by Sterne in the 18th century. Not a museum but a lived-in house where you are sure of a personal welcome. Surrounded by a walled garden full of old-fashioned roses and cottage-garden plants. Also one acre of wild garden in an old quarry. **Location:** 20 miles north of York. **Open:** June–Sept. Wed 2–4.30pm. Sun 2.30–4.30pm. Other times by appointment. Gardens open every day 1 May–30 Sept, except Sat, 11–4.30pm. **Admission:** Adults £3.50. Garden only £2.50. children half price. **Refreshments:** In village. **Exhibitions:** June–Sept, paintings and pots, by local artists. Unusual plants for sale.

map 8 D1

SHIBDEN HALL

Lister's Road, Halifax, HX3 6XG, West Yorkshire
Tel: 01422 352 246 Fax: 01422 348 440(Calderdale M.B.C. Leisure Services)

Allow yourself to drift into 600 years of history ... a world without electricity ... where craftsmen worked in wood and iron ... a house where you sense the family has just gone out ... allowing you to enjoy a sense of the past at Shibden Hall, Halifax's Historic Home. Set in 90 acres of park, Shibden Hall provides a whole day of entertainment. **Location:** 2 km outside Halifax, on A58 Leeds Road. **Buses:** 548/549 Brighouse, 508 Leeds, 681/682 Bradford. **Open:** Mar–Nov, Mon–Sat, 10–5pm. Sun, 12–5pm. Last admission 4.30pm. Contact for winter opening hours. **Admission:** (From April 1999) Adults £2, children £1, OAPs £1, family ticket £5. Group rate for pre-booked party. **Refreshments:** Tearoom. Shop, amusements, toilets, car park, disabled access.

map 8 B3

SKIPTON CASTLE

Skipton, North Yorkshire BD23 1AQ
Tel: 01756 792442 Fax 01756 796100

For over 900 years Skipton Castle has survived wars and seiges. Once home of the famous Clifford Lords, it is one of the best preserved and most complete medieval castles in England. Fully roofed, it is a fascinating and delightful place to explore - from the atmospheric Dungeon to the great Watch Tower, from the beautiful conduit court to the ancient Chapel. **Location:** Centre of Skipton. **Open:** Daily, 10am (Sun 12noon). Last admission at 6pm (Oct–Feb, 4pm). Closed Christmas Day. **Admission:** Adults £4.20, children (5–17) £2.10, children (under 5) free, OAPs and students £3.60. Family ticket: 2 adults & up to 3 children £11.50. Free tour sheets available in 8 languages. Guides are provided for pre-booked parties at no extra charge. Large car & coach park off nearby High Street. **Internet:** www.skiptoncastle.co.uk

map 8 B2

LOTHERTON HALL

Aberford, Yorkshire, LS25 3EB
Tel: 0113 281 3259 Fax: 0113 281 2100 (Leeds City Council)

Modest late Victorian and Edwardian country house of great charm and character, formerly the home of the Gascoigne family. Fine collections of furniture, silver, pottery and porcelain, paintings, sculpture and costume, including many family heirlooms. Famous period gardens with a deer park and bird garden. **Location:** 1mile E of A1 at Aberford, on the Towton Road (B1217). **Open:** 1 Apr–31 Oct, Tues–Sat 10–5pm, Sun 1–5pm. 1 Nov–31 Mar, Tues–Sat 10–4pm, Sun 12–4pm Closed Jan & Feb, closed Mons. **Admission:** Please contact for details of admission prices. **Refreshments:** Cafe in stable block.

SION HILL HALL

Kirby Wiske, Nr Thirsk, North Yorkshire YO7 4EU
Tel: 01845 587206 Fax: 01845 587486 (H.W. Mawer Trust)

The Hall was designed in 1912 by the renowned York Architect Walter H Brierley, "the Lutyens of the North". With its fine lines, unique character and superb layout, the Hall was designated by the Royal Institute of British Architects as being of "outstanding Architectural Merit". Sion Hill contains the H W Mawer collection of fine furniture, porcelain, paintings and clocks in superb room settings. **Location:** Signed off A167; 6 miles S of Northallerton: 4 miles W of Thirsk, 6 miles E of A1 via A61. **Open:** Good Fri–end Sept, Wed–Sun incl. & Bank Holiday Mons. 1–5pm, last entry 4pm. **Admission:** Adult £4, Conc. £3.50, children under 12 free if accompanied by adult. Seperate Attractions: Falconry Centre: Tel: 01845 587522, Tearoom: Tel: 01845 587071 & Antiques Centre: Tel: 01845 587071. All open daily 1 Mar–31 Oct, 10.30–5.30pm.

map 8 C1

RIPLEY CASTLE

Ripley Castle Estate, Harrogate, North Yorkshire.
Tel: 01423 770152   Fax: 01423 771745 (Sir Thomas and Lady Ingilby)

Ripley Castle has been home to the Ingilby family for twenty-six generations and Sir Thomas and Lady Ingilby together with their five children continue the tradition. The guided tours are amusing and informative, following the lives and loves of one family for over 670 years. The historic Gatehouse, 550 years old in 2000 still bears bullet marks from Cromwell's Army after the Battle of Marston Moor. The Old Tower houses splendid armour, books, panelling and a Priest's Hiding Hole. The Knight's Chamber is a remarkable Tudor room that was completed in 1555 and the original oak ceiling and wall panelling create a wonderful atmosphere of antiquity. In the Georgian wing you can appreciate the fine paintings, china, furnishings and chandeliers collected by the family over the Centuries. The extensive Victorian Walled Gardens have been transformed and are a colourful delight through every Season. In the Kitchen Gardens you can see an extensive selection of rare vegetables from the Henry Doubleday Research Association. The restored Victorian Hot Houses are home to a tropical plant collection with cacti, ferns and exotic fruits. In the Spring you can enjoy 15,000 flowering bulbs which create a blaze of colour and the National Hyacinth Collection whose scent is breathtaking. The Castle and Gardens lie at the heart of the Ripley Estate with an extensive deer park and panoramic lakes. **Open:** 10.30–4pm (Last Tour 3pm). June, July & Aug: open daily. Sept–May: Tues, Thurs, Sat & Sun. Gardens open daily 10–5pm. Groups welcome all year round by prior arrangement. **Admission:** Adults £5, senior citizens £4, children (up to 16yrs) £2.50.

map 8
C2

SEWERBY HALL & GARDENS

Church Lane, Sewerby, Bridlington, YO15 1EA
Tel: Estate Office:01262 673 769 Hall: 01262 677 874
(East Riding of Yorkshire Council)

Sewerby Hall and Gardens, set in 50 acres of parkland overlooking Bridlington Bay, dates back to 1715. The Georgian House, with its 19th century Orangery, is now the Museum of East Yorkshire and contains history/archaeology displays, art galleries and an Amy Johnson Room with a collection of her trophies and mementos. The grounds include the magnificent walled Old English and Rose gardens and host many events all year round. Activities for all the family include a children's zoo and play areas, golf, putting, bowls, plus woodland and clifftop walks. **Location:** Bridlington, 2m NE. **Station:** Bridlington (2.5 miles). **Open:** Hall: 2 Apr–31 Oct, 10–6pm daily. Off peak 6 Mar–30 Mar and 1 Nov–19 Dec 1999, Sat–Tues. Gardens and zoo open throughout the year. **Refreshments:** Traditional tearooms.

SHEFFIELD BOTANICAL GARDENS

Clarkhouse Road, Sheffield, S10 2LN. Contact: Sheffield City Council, Meersbrook Park. Tel: 0114 250 0500 Fax: 0114 255 2375

Designed in 1833 by Robert Marnock, the original curator, the Gardens (listed Grade II by English Heritage) are a fine example of the Victorian 'Gardenseque' style. Particularly impressive is the straight promenade up to the 'Paxton Pavilions', an important example of early metal and glass curvilinear structure. Occupying 7.6 hectares in the south-west of the city, the Gardens contain around 5,000 species of plants, including the national collections of Weigela and Diervilla. In addition to the Pavilions, the Gardens contain the highest concentration of listed structures in Sheffield. **Open:** Daily, except Christmas, Boxing & New Year's Days. **Admission:** Free. **Refreshments:** For pre-arranged guided tours. **Events/Exhibitions:** Frequently, held by the Friends of the Botanic Gardens and specialist horticultural societies. **Conferences:** Facilities for 80 people.

SUTTON PARK

Sutton–on–the–Forest, York YO61 1DP
Tel: 01347 810249/811239 Fax: 01347 811251 (Sir Reginald & Lady Sheffield)

The prettiest house & gardens in Yorkshire. Sutton Park is a charming example of early Georgian architecture with a warm lived-in feeling. Plasterwork by Cortese, fine paintings, lovely 18th century furniture, important collection of porcelain. Award–winning GARDENS. Herbaceous and rose borders full of interesting plants. Georgian Ice House, and Nature Trail. **Open:** House: Every Sun & Weds 2 Apr–27 Sept. Also Good Fri–Easter Mon 21–24 Apr & all BH Mons 1.30–5pm. Coach Parties to book please. Private parties by appt. Gardens: Daily 2 Apr–end Sept 11–5pm. **Admission:** House & Garden: Adults £4.50, OAP's/Students £4, child £2.50. Garden only: Adults £2, OAP's £1.50, child 50p. Private parties £5pp. Tearooms open House open days 12–5pm. Disabled access grounds only. **E-mail:** suttonpark@fsbdial.co.uk **Internet:** www.statelyhome.co.uk

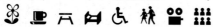

THORP PERROW ARBORETUM

Bedale, North Yorkshire, DL8 2PR
Tel: 01677 425 323 Fax: 01677 425 323 (Sir John Ropner, Bt.)

Thorp Perrow, the country home of Sir John and Lady Ropner, contains the finest arboretum in the north of England. A collection of over 1,000 varieties of trees and shrubs including some of the largest and rarest in the country. It is also the home of three National Collections – ash, lime and walnut – and is becoming a popular attraction for all the family. The arboretum comprises 85 acres of landscaped grounds with a lake, grassy glades, tree trails and woodland walks. Thousands of daffodils carpet the ground in spring, while the summer is noted for bold drifts of wild flowers and the autumn brings glorious and vibrant colour. Nature trail. Children's trail. Tearoom and information centre. Childrens play area. Plant centre. Electric wheelchair available. The impressive Georgian mansion at Thorp

Perrow makes an ideal venue for private or corporate hospitality. Whether it be for conferences, seminars, product launches, cocktail parties, or just a private weekend, there are rooms to suit every occasion. For activity days or product launches, the magnificent parkland setting with its two ornamental lakes lends itself to a host of outdoor pursuits that can be arranged upon request. **Location:** Well–Ripon Road, S of Bedale. O.S. map ref: SE258851. 4 miles from Leeming Bar on A1. **Open:** All year, dawn-dusk. Guided tours available. Tel: 01677 425 323. **Admission:** Please contact the Arboretum Office for admission prices. Free car and coach park. **Refreshments:** Tearoom. Picnic area. Dogs permitted on a lead. **E-mail:** ropner.thorp@btinternet.com

SCARBOROUGH CASTLE

Castle Road, Scarborough YO11 1HY
Tel: 01723 372451 (English Heritage)

Spectacular coastal views from the walls of this enormous 12th century castle. The buttressed castle walls stretch out along the cliff edge and the remains of the great rectangular stone keep, still stand to over three storeys high. There is also the site of a 4th century Roman signal station. The castle was frequently attacked, but despite being blasted by cannons of the Civil War and bombarded from the sea during World War 1, it is still a spectacular place to visit. **Location:** Castle road, east of town centre. **Open:** Please phone for opening times and admission charges.

TEMPLE NEWSAM HOUSE

Leeds, West Yorkshire, LS15 0AE
Tel: 0113 264 7321 Fax: 0113 260 2285 (Leeds City Council)

The magnificent Tudor-Jacobean house was the birthplace of Lord Darnley, husband of Mary, Queen of Scots and later became the home of the Ingram family, Viscounts Irwin. There are over 30 historic interiors (many newly restored), including a spectacular Picture Gallery, with superlative paintings, furniture (including the Chippendale Society collection), silver and ceramics. The thousand acre Capability Brown park (free) contains a home farm with rare breeds of animals, sensational displays of rhododendrons and azaleas (May & June), national collections of delphiniums and phlox (July & Aug), chrysanthemums (Sept) and roses (all summer). Guided tours available. Gift shop. There is limited disabled access. **Open:** Please contact for details of 1998 opening times and admission charges.

WILBERFORCE HOUSE

25 High Street, Kingston-upon-Hull, East Yorkshire, HU1 1EP
Tel: 01482 613 902 Fax: 01482 613 710 (Kingston-upon-Hull City Council)
Internet: www.hulcc.gov.uk/museums/index.htm

Hull's oldest and most famous museum is a brick-built 17th century merchant's house in the centre of the old town. The birthplace of William Wilberforce (1759–1833), known worldwide for his fight to abolish slavery. The main displays within the museum tell the horrific story of slavery and Wilberforce's fight to abolish it. Wilberforce House is much more than just a reminder of slavery. The building contains survivals of every stage in its history: the oak-panelled 17th century rooms on the first floor; the 18th century staircase with elaborate rococo plasterwork ceilings and the Victorian parlour. The famous collection of Hull silver is displayed in the adjoining Georgian house. **Location:** In the centre of Hull's Old Town. **Open:** All year. Mon–Sat, 10–5pm. Sun, 1.30–4.30pm. **Admission:** Free.

map 9 F3

TREASURER'S HOUSE

Chapter House Street, York YO1 2JD Tel: 01904 624247

Open: 1 April to 31 Oct: daily except Fri 10.30–5pm. Last admission 4.30pm. **Events:** contact Property Manager for details of function hire and full calendar of special events. Licensed for civil weddings. **Admission:** Adults £3.50, concessions £1.75. Family ticket £8.50.

EAST RIDDLESHAM HALL

Bradford Road, Keighley BD20 5EL Tel: 01535 607075

Open: 1 April to 5 Nov: daily except Mons, Thurs & Fri 12–5pm. Sat 1–5pm.

BENINGBROUGH HALL & GARDENS

Shipton-by-Beningbrough, York YO6 1DD Tel: 01904 470666

Open: 1 April to 29 Oct: Sat to Wed, Good Fri & Fri in July and Aug. House: 12–5pm. Last admission 4.30pm. Grounds: 12–5.30pm. Last admission 5pm. Licensed for wedding ceremonies and receptions; please contact Assistant Property Manager for details. **Admission:** Adults £5, concessions £2.50. Family ticket £12.50. Garden only: Adults £3.50, concessions £1.70.

NOSTELL PRIORY

Doncaster Road, Nostell, nr Wakefield WF4 1QE
Tel: 01924 863892 Fax: 01924 865282

Closed for Year 2000.

FOUNTAINS ABBEY
& STUDLEY ROYAL WATER GARDEN

Fountains, Ripon HG4 3DY Estate Office tel: 01765 608888

Open: Abbey & water garden: open all year daily except Fri in Nov, Dec, Jan and 24/25 Dec. April to Sept: 10–7pm (closes at 4pm on 9/10 July & 7 Aug); Oct to March 2001: 10–5pm (dusk if earlier). Closed 1 Jan 2001. Last admission 1hr before closing. Deer park: open all year daily during daylight hours. Floodlighting: Abbey is floodlit on Fri & Sat evenings until 10pm, 27 Aug to 16 Oct. Fountains Hall & St Mary's Church: restoration in progress, apply to Estate Office for opening times. Charge may be reduced on and around event days (9/10 July) due to restricted access to parts of estate. Events: extensive programme of concerts, plays, walks & talks available all year, incl. Shakespeare theatre; Music by Moonlight; outdoor promenade entertainment. Details from Box Office (tel. 01765 609999). All outside events wheelchair-accessible.

ORMESBY HALL

Ormesby, Middlesbrough TS7 9AS Tel: 01642 324188 Fax: 01642 300937

Open: 2 April to 29 Oct: daily except Mon, Fri & Sat (but open Good Fri, & BH Mons) 2–5pm. Events: Telephone or send sae for full programme. Hall licensed for wedding ceremonies. **Admission:** Adults £3.50, concessions £1.70. Family ticket £8.50.

GREAT
Houses
&
Gardens
OF YORKSHIRE

Explore Yorkshire's Heritage

The Great Houses & Gardens of Yorkshire are a group of over 30 fine houses and gardens, situated throughout the Yorkshire region and open to visitors.

Discover the wonderfully rich and varied heritage of this rewarding area. Grand stately homes, elegant country houses and fascinating museums all of which lie waiting to be explored with their unrivalled collections of art and furniture. Many of their treasures were gathered during the Grand Tour of Europe, a cultural mecca and part of every nobleman's education during the eighteenth and nineteenth centuries. These enchanting objects are still a source of wonder for the modern day visitor and will continue to delight for generations to come.

The architectural splendour of these great houses is complemented further by the beauty of Yorkshire's famous gardens and landscapes. Those seeking peace and tranquillity will surely find it here.

This is a selection of the Great Houses and Gardens of Yorkshire that are featured in this guide

1. Brodsworth Hall & Gardens (EH)
2. Ormesby Hall (NT)
3. Temple Newsam House
4. Lotherton Hall
5. Oakwell Hall Country Park
5. Red House Museum
6. Kirkstall Abbey
7. East Riddlesden Hall (NT)
8. Harewood House
9. Harlow Carr Botanical Gardens
10. Ripley Castle
11. Fountains Abbey & Studley Royal (NT)
12. Middleham Castle (EH)
13. Bolton Castle
14. Constable Burton Gardens
15. Richmond Castle (EH)
16. Mount Grace Priory (EH)
17. Whitby Abbey (EH)
18. Scarborough Castle (EH)

19. Pickering Castle (EH)
20. Nunnington Hall (NT)
21. Duncombe Park
21. Helmsley Castle (EH)
21. Helmsley Walled Garden
22. Rievaulx Abbey (EH)
22. Rievaulx Terrace & Temples (NT)
23. Byland Abbey (EH)
24. Skipton Castle
25. Sledmere House
26. Sewerby Hall & Gardens
27. Beningbrough Hall & Gardens (NT)
28. Treasurer's House (NT)
28. Clifford's Tower (EH)
29. Wilberforce House
30. Castle Howard
31. Newby Hall & Gardens
32. Shibden Hall
33. Burton Agnes Hall & Gardens

Wales

The North West landscape has a dramatic quality reflected in its history. In prehistoric times, Anglesey was a stronghold of the religious elite known as the Druids. Roman and Norman invasions concentrated on the coast, leaving the mountains to the Welsh. These wild areas are the centre of the Welsh language and culture.

The dominant feature of North Wales is Snowdon, the highest mountains in Wales. Snowdonia National Park extends dramatically from the Snowdonia massif south beyond Dolgellau, with thickly wooded valleys, mountain lakes, moors and estuaries. To the east are the softer Clywdian Hills and unspoilt coastlines can be enjoyed on Anglesey and the beautiful Llyn Peninsula, where the Welsh language is still spoken.

Above: Marloes. Right: Harlech Castle. Bottom: Nant Gwynant

South and mid Wales are less homogenous regions than North Wales. Most of the population live in the southeast corner. To the west is Pembrokeshire, the loveliest stretch of Welsh coastline. To the north the industrial valleys give way to the wide hills of the Brecon Beacons and the rural heartlands of Central Wales.

Magnificent coastal scenery marks the Pembrokeshire Coast National Park and cliff backed Gower Peninsula, while Cardigan Bay and Carmarten Bay offer quieter beaches. Walkers can enjoy grassy uplands in the Brecon Beacons and gentler country in the leafy Wye Valley. Urban life is concentrated in the southeast of Wales, where old mining towns line the valley north of Cardiff, the capital.

ABERGLASNEY GARDENS
Llangathen SA32 8QH
Tel & Fax: 01558 668998 (Aberglasney Restoration Trust)

Aberglasney is a 'garden lost in time'. Spectacularly set in the beautiful Towy Valley of Carmarthenshire, the gardens have been an inspiration for poetry since 1477. Celebrated by John Dyer in his poem 'The Country Walk', this garden is a unique survival in Britain. Featured in a BBC TV series and the subject of a book published by Weidenfeld and Nicolson, the gardens have first class horticultural and aesthetic qualities and a mysterious history. Set within eight acres are six different garden spaces, including three walled gardens, at its centre is the unique Elizabethan and Jacobean 'cloister' garden, from the parapet walk above there are views of an ornamental pool, walled gardens and ancient gatehouse. Rare specimen trees planted in the early 19th century still survive, although the greatest arboreal creation is the magnificent yew tunnel. Its hauntingly beautiful and unspoiled pastoral landscape makes it one of the most fascinating gardens in the UK. The gardens are between Llandeilo and Carmarthen at the village of Llangathen. **Open:** Daily Apr–Oct 2000. **E-mail:** marketing@aberglasney.org.uk

map 7
H4

BLAENAVON IRONWORK
North Street, Blaenavon
Enquiries Tel: 01495 792615
(Cadw: Welsh Historic Monuments)

This site is not only one of Europe's best-preserved 18th century ironworks, but a milestone in the history of the Industrial Revolution. Built in the 1780's, the ironworks were at the cutting edge of new technology. Visitors can still trace the entire process of production, which involved the harnessing of steam power to blow the blast furnaces, and the movement by water balance tower. The human side is represented at Stack Square, a community of small terrace dwellings built for pioneer ironworkers.

map 3
G1

CAERLEON ROMAN BATHS & AMPHITHEATRE
High Street, Caerleon NP6 1AE
Enquiries Tel: 01633 422518
(Cadw: Welsh Historic Monuments)

Caerleon is Britain's most fascinating and revealing Roman site. It was founded in AD75 as one of only three bases in Britain for the Roman's legionary troops. These elite soldiers enjoyed the conveniences of an entire township, complete with amphitheatre and bath house. The excavated remains of their barrack blocks – the only examples currently visible in Europe – stand in green fields near the fortress baths, a giant leisure complex equivalent to today's sports and leisure centre. The well-preserved amphitheatre, with seating for 6,000 was the setting for bloody combat involving wild beasts and gladiators.

map 7
J2

CAERPHILLY CASTLE
Caerphilly, Mid Glamorgan, CF83 1JD
Enquiries Tel: 01222 883143
(Cadw: Welsh Historic Monuments)

The largest castle in Wales, with extensive water defences and a famous leaning tower, was built by the De Clare family to defend their territory against the armies of Llewelyn, the last Welsh Prince of Wales. The effectiveness of the finished work is proved by the fact that throughout its long and colourful history, the castle has never been taken by attackers. Due to conservation work in 1776, a large amount of the castle remains undamaged, giving visitors a fascinating insight into medieval life. During the summer reconstructions of warfare, including working replica siege engines, provide an exhilarating and entertaining day out for all the family.

map 7
J3

CAREW CASTLE & TIDAL MILL
Carew, Nr. Tenby, Pembrokeshire, Wales
Tel/Fax: 01646 651 782
(Pembrokeshire Coast National Park)

A magnificent Norman castle and later an Elizabethan residence. Royal links with Henry Tudor, setting for Great Tournament of 1507. The Mill is the only restored tidal mill in Wales. Automatic talking points explaining milling process. Special exhibition 'The Story of Milling'. **Location:** 4 miles E of Pembroke. **Station(s):** Pembroke. **Open:** Easter-end Oct, daily. **Admission:** Please phone for details. **E-mail:** tracy@carew–pcnp.freeserve.co.uk **Internet:** http://www.pembrokeshirecoast.org

map 7
H6

Carreg Cennen Castle

Trapp, Dyfed, SA19 6TS
Enquiries Tel: 01558 822291
(Cadw: Welsh Historic Monuments)

Spectacularly situated on a remote crag 300 feet above the River Cennen, this castle has for centuries been sought out by visitors who enjoy mystery and the dramatically picturesque. The site's origins are lost in ancient obscurity, but in the cave under the castle, which can be explored with torches, prehistoric human remains have been discovered. Other finds at the castle include Roman coins and it is believed that the existing castle is built on top of an Iron Age hill fort. The stone fortress we see today was started by a Norman knight, on top of a Welsh castle constructed by The Lord Rhys, the most famous Prince of South Wales.

map 7 H4

Usk Castle

Usk, Monmouthshire
Tel: 01291 672563 (J.H.L. Humphreys)

Romantic, ruined norman castle overlooking the picturesque town of Usk. Inner and outer baileys, towers and earthwork defences. Surrounded by enchanting gardens (open under NGS and Usk Gardens open days) incorporating the Castle House, the former medieval gatehouse, as lived in by the current owner. **Location:** OS Ref SO 376 011, off Monmouth Road in Usk, opposite Fire Station. **Open:** Castle ruins: daily 11–5pm. Group bookings by appointment only. Gardens & Castle House: open to small groups by prior appointment. **Admission:** Castle ruins: Adults £2, children free. House & Garden: Adults £5, children £2.

map 7 H2

Castell Coch

Tongwynlais, Nr Cardiff, South Glamorgan, CF4 7JS
Enquiries Tel: 01222 810101
(Cadw: Welsh Historic Monuments)

One of the most distinctive and memorable castles in Wales, this spectacular building peeks out from the treetops of a cliff towering over the Taff valley near Cardiff. The original medieval castle was rebuilt by the third Lord Bute, who spared no expense on its reconstruction and decoration. From the exterior's re-creation of a medieval fortress complete with conical-roofed towers, the amazed visitor enters the breathtaking apartments of Lord and Lady Bute. Although the castle was intended only for occasional use as a country retreat, the interior is richly and exquisitely carved and painted with scenes from fables and fantasies, all of which are immaculately preserved.

map 7 J3

Chepstow Castle

Chepstow, Gwent NP6 5EZ
Enquiries Tel: 01291 624065
(Cadw: Welsh Historic Monuments)

It comes as quite a surprise to find a great castle in the pretty border town of Chepstow. But on a cliff overlooking the river Wye stands the earliest datable stone fortification in Britain; the great stone keep built by William the Conqueror's most trusted general. Since guarding the border was always an important task, Chepstow castle was developed and enlarged over the centuries in a series of modernisations and gives visitors the opportunity to trace centuries of history in its imposing stones. It was in use up to the Civil War and afterwards was used to keep Henry Marten under house arrest for signing the death warrant of Charles I.

map 7 J4

Chirk Castle

Chirk, Wrexham, Wales
Tel: 01691 777701 Fax: 01691 774706 (The National Trust)

Chirk Castle is a magnificent marcher fortress close to the Welsh border, which has been lived in continuously since it was built in 1295. A dramatic dungeon was hollowed out of the rock and circular towers provide defensive viewpoints over the surrounding countryside. Chirk has elegant state rooms containing Adam style furniture, tapestries and portraits as well as excellent examples of Pugin's work. The castle gardens were voted National Trust Garden of the Year in 1999, a fragrant stroll amongst the roses, yews, flowering trees and shrubs will allow the visitor to appreciate the fine views over the surrounding countryside.

map 6 D2

Cilgerran Castle

Cilgerran, Dyfed SA13 2SF
Enquiries Tel: 01239 615007 (Cadw: Welsh Historic Monuments)

Sitting on a high, rocky crag above the meeting-point of two rivers, Cilgerran Castle has the perfect defensive position and is so spectacular that it became a popular subject for romantic artists such as Turner. The earliest castle on this site was built by a Norman lord who married Princess Nest, a famous Welsh beauty. When raiders came to assassinate her husband in his bed, Nest helped him to escape, although she and her children were kidnapped. The castle has had a long and chequered history, passing from English to Welsh hands and back again many times during the long wars for the conquest of Wales. The Castle we see today was the work of the English Marshal family, who extended and strengthened the fortress over a period of two hundred years.

map 7 G5

Cresselly

Kilgetty, Pembrokeshire, Wales SA68 0SP
Fax: 01646 687045 (HDR Harrison-Allen Esq.)

Home of the Allen family for 250 years. The house dates to 1770 with matching wings from 1869 and contains good plasterwork and fittings of both periods. The Allens are of particular interest for their close association to the Wedgwood family. **Location:** In the Pembrokeshire National Park, off the A4075. OS Ref SN0 606. **Open:** 28 days between May and September. Please write or fax 01646 687045 for details. **Admission:** Adults £3.50. No children under 12. Wedding receptions and functions in house or marquee for 20 to 300 persons. Dinners, private or corporate events in historic dining room. Guided tours only. Ample parking for cars (coaches by arrangement only). No dogs. Bed and breakfast and dinner by arrangement. Two double en suite with four-poster bed, single, twin and children by arrangement.

map 7 H6

Dinefwr Park

Llandeilo, Carmarthenshire
Tel: 01558 823902 Fax: 01558 822036 (The National Trust)

An eighteenth century landscape park and ancient deer park surrounding Newton House originally built in 1660 but now with a Victorian Gothic facade. An exhibition explains the importance of Dinefwr in the history of Wales. The Fountain Garden is currently under restoration. There are fine views over the Towy Valley, with an ice house and boardwalk which is suitable for families and wheelchair users. The historically famous Dinefwr White Park cattle can be seen in the deer park. There is also access to the old Dinefwr Castle, owned by the Wildlife Trust West Wales. Guided tours of Newton House/Deer Park by arrangement - small charge applicable. **Admission:** House & Park: Adult £3, child £1.50, family £7.50, Group £2.60. Park only: Adult £2, child £1, family £5. National Trust members free.

map 7 H4

KIDWELLY CASTLE

Kidwelly, Dyfed SA17 5BQ
Enquiries Tel: 01554 890104
(Cadw: Welsh Historic Monuments)

Perched high above the river Gwendraeth, looking out towards Laugharne across the Taf estuary, Kidwelly's early Norman earth and timber castle could be reached by boat, making it difficult to besiege. However, The Lord Rhys, Prince of South Wales, captured and burned the castle, which did not return to Norman hands until 1244 when the construction of a stone fortress was started. Over the following centuries, the castle and its walled town passed into different hands and was added to and modernised by the Dukes of Lancaster and then by the most powerful man in early Tudor Wales, Sir Rhys ap Thomas.

map 7
H5

LAMPHEY BISHOP'S PALACE

Lamphey, Nr Pembroke SA71 5NT
Enquiries Tel: 01646 672224
(Cadw: Welsh Historic Monuments)

The medieval bishops of St David's built themselves a magnificent retreat away from the worries of Church and State. Here, amongst fish ponds, fruit orchards, vegetable gardens and sweeping parklands, they could enjoy the life of country gentlemen. The palace was improved over two centuries, though it is mainly the work of Henry De Gower, bishop of St Davids from 1328 to 1347, who built the splendid Great Hall. Later additions include a Tudor chapel with a fine, five-light east window.

map 7
H6

LAUGHARNE CASTLE

Laugharne, Dyfed
Enquiries Tel: 01994 427906 (Cadw: Welsh Historic Monuments)

Looking out over the estuary that Dylan Thomas was to make famous for its beauty, is Laugharne's "castle, brown as owls". Like its neighbours at Kidwelly and Llansteffan, Laugharne is built on the site of an early Norman earth and timber fort, and was rebuilt in stone during the Middle Ages by the local Lord, Guy de Brian. As the castle passed down through succeeding generations of the family, it was added to and strengthened. By the reign of Elizabeth I, the castle had fallen into disrepair, and it was modernised in the Tudor style by Sir John Perrot, who was tried for treason. In this century, the castle was rented out to author Richard Hughes who wrote his novel "In Hazard" in the castle's gazebo, where Dylan Thomas later wrote "Portrait of the Artist as a Young Dog."

map 7
H5

LLANVIHANGEL COURT

Nr Abergavenny, Monmouthshire, NP7 8DH
Tel: 01873 890 217 (Mrs Julia Johnson)

A Grade 1 listed Tudor Manor of 15th century origins. Beautiful early 17th century plaster ceilings and panelling and magnificent yew staircase, leading to a bedroom where Charles I is reputed to have stayed during the Civil War. Remodelled during the 1650s by John Arnold. The main entrance overlooks 17th century terraces and steps. Unusual stables from the same period with turned wood pillars. **Location:** 4 miles north of Abergavenny on A465. **Open:** 8 Aug–1 Sept inclusive, or by appointment. **Admission:** Adults £4, children (5–15) and OAPs £2.50.

map 7
H2

THE NATIONAL BOTANIC GARDEN OF WALES

Middleton Hall, Llanarthne, Carmarthenshire, Wales SA32 8HG
Tel: 01558 668768 Fax: 01558 668933

The National Botanic Garden of Wales is the first national botanic garden to be created in the United Kingdom for more than two hundred years. Set in the eighteenth century parkland of the former Middleton Hall, on the edge of the Towy Valley, the Garden of Wales commands spectacular views over the surrounding Carmarthenshire countryside. This is an area rich in history and culture, famed for its gentle beauty. The Garden's creation is dedicated to horticulture, science, education and leisure driven by the vision of a twenty first century centre of international botanical significance. The centrepiece is the Great Glasshouse, designed by Norman Foster and Partners, which houses plants from the mediterranean ecosystems of the world within a landscape which uses innovative design to incorporate cliff faces and water walls. The Great Glasshouse is surrounded by a necklace of lakes, a 220 metre long herbaceous Broadwalk with a rill and fountains, ancient woodland walks, a Water Discovery Centre, Lifelong Learning Centre and Middleton Square with its revolving theatre, café, restaurant and shop. Visitors will be able to view the creation of the Double Walled Garden and areas of habitat dedicated to the woods and moorlands of the world. **Internet:** www.gardenof wales.org.uk

map 7
H5

OXWICH CASTLE

Oxwich, Nr Swansea, West Glamorgan
Enquiries Tel: 01792 390359 (Cadw: Welsh Historic Monuments)

On a headland overlooking Oxwich Bay in the beautiful Gower peninsula, stands Oxwich Castle. A Tudor mansion, rather than a medieval fortress, its impressive gatehouse emblazoned with the Mansel family's coat of arms was added more as a show of pride than for military purposes. Like many successful gentlemen, Sir Rice Mansel remodelled his ancestral home in the modern Tudor style, with his son continuing the building programme by adding a stupendous multi-storey wing during Queen Elizabeth's reign. During conservation work on the castle, a magnificent gold and jewelled brooch was discovered, which may once have been part of King Edward II's lost royal treasure. How it came to be at Oxwich remains an intriguing mystery.

    map 7 J4

RAGLAN CASTLE

Raglan, Gwent, NP5 2BT
Enquiries Tel: 01291 690228
(Cadw: Welsh Historic Monuments)

A monument to medieval family pride, this imposing fortress-palace was built by the Herbert family. The water-moated Great Yellow Tower was built by Sir William, "The Blue Knight of Gwent", a veteran of Agincourt. His son, William Herbert continued the construction of the majority of the existing castle, using profits he made by importing French wine. William was one of the leading Yorkist supporters in the Wars of the Roses and was so well trusted by King Edward IV that he was given custody of young Henry Tudor, later King Henry VII, who was brought up at Raglan. William's loyalty as the King's right-hand man in Wales brought a string of titles and estates, but Raglan remained the family's stronghold.

    map 7 H2

PENHOW CASTLE

Nr Newport, South Wales NP6 3AD
Tel: 01633 400800 Fax: 01633 400990 (Stephen Weeks)

Wales' Oldest Lived-in Castle holds 8 awards for its careful restoration and interpretation. First home in Britain of the Seymour family, this enchanting Knight's border fortress now presents a glimpse into eight centuries of changing Castle life. Visitors cross the drawbridge to explore restored period rooms from battlements to kitchens, guided by acclaimed Walkman audio tours included free (also French & German). **Location:** A48 midway b/w Chepstow and Newport; M4 Jct 24. **Open:** Good Fri-end Sept, Wed–Sun incl. & Bank Hols, 10–5.15pm (last admission). Aug–open daily. Winter, Wed only 10–4pm and selected Sun pm's 1–4pm. Open all year for groups, Evening Candlelit Tours and school visits. Special Christmas Tours 15 Nov–5 Jan. **Admission:** Adult £3.60, child (5-16) £2.30, family (2+2) £9.50. Group discount 10% for 20+. **E-mail:** castles@compuserve.com

 map 7 J2

PENYCLAWDD COURT

Llanfihangel Crucorney, Abergavenny, Monmouthshire, NP7 7LB
Tel: 01873 890719 Fax: 01873 890848 (Mrs Julia Evans)

This Grade I listed Medieval Manor House dates from 1400 with an imposing Jacobean extension. The authentic restoration of the property has won a number of prestigious awards. The gardens, while compact, contain some fascinating features; herb and knot gardens and a recently planted maze of unique design. Abutting the gardens is a Norman Motte and Bailey, a scheduled Ancient Monument, dating from about 1070. **Location:** Approximately 4 miles north of Abergavenny, ¼ mile west of A465. **Open:** Thur, Fri, Sat, Sun and Bank Holidays from 1pm, last entry 4pm. **Admission:** Adults £3, concessions £2. Accommodation available. Researched Tudor Feasts (20 people). Groups and school parties by arrangement. Schools programmes based upon National Curriculum Tudor/Stuart period. No dogs at any time.

   map 7 H2

 PICTON CASTLE & WOODLAND GARDENS

Haverfordwest, Pembrokeshire, Wales, SA62 4AS
Tel/Fax: 01437 751 326 (Picton Castle Trust)

Built in the 13th century, home of the Philipps family, the Castle retains it external appearance but was remodelled inside, above the undercroft in the 1750's and extended around 1800. The woodland and walled gardens cover 40 acres and are part of The Royal Horticultural Society access scheme for beautiful gardens. Events include art exhibitions and spring and autumn plant sales. **Location:** OS Ref. SN011 135. 4 m E of Haverfordwest just off A40. **Open: Castle:** April–Sept. Closed Mon & Sat except Bank Hol, open all other afternoons for guided tours. **Garden & Gallery:** April–Oct. Tues–Sun inclusive. 10.30–5pm. **Admission: Castle, Garden & Gallery:** Adults £4, OAPs £3.50, children £1. **Garden & Gallery:** Adults £2.75, OAPs £2.50, children £1. Reduced prices for groups of 20 or more by prior appointment.

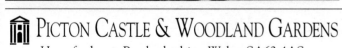 map 7 H6

ST DAVIDS BISHOP'S PALACE

St Davids SA62 6PE
Enquiries Tel: 01437 720517
(Cadw: Welsh Historic Monuments)

Even in ruin, this imposing palace, standing next to St Davids Cathedral, still conveys the affluence and power of the medieval church. Largely the work of Bishop De Gower, no expense was spared in creating a grand residence fit for a major figure of both Church and State. De Gower's palace boasted two sets of state rooms ranged around a courtyard, one for his own use, the other for ceremonious entertainment. The palace is richly embellished with lavish stone carvings. Particularly fine are its arcaded parapets, decorated with chequered stonework.

map 7 G7

ST. DAVIDS CATHEDRAL

The Deanery, The Close, St. Davids, Pembrokeshire, Wales
Tel: 01437 720 199 Fax: 01437 721 885 (The Dean and Chapter)

This cathedral, begun in 1181, is at least the fourth church to have been built on a site reputed to be that on which St. David himself founded a monastic settlement in the 6th century. The outstanding features of the building are the magnificent ceilings – oak in the Nave, painted in the Choir and Presbytery – and the sloping floor. The stalls of the Chapter of the cathedral contain medieval misericords and the Chapter is unique in having the reigning Sovereign as a member. The cathedral has been an important place of pilgrimage for nearly fourteen centuries. In 1124, Pope Calixtus II declared that two pilgrimages to St. Davids were equal to one to Rome and that three were equal to one to Jerusalem itself.

 map 7 G7

STRATA FLORIDA ABBEY

Ystrad Meurig, Pontrhydfendigaid SY25 6BT
Enquiries Tel: 01974 831261
(Cadw: Welsh Historic Monuments)

None of the Cistercians' Welsh abbeys preserves that original spirit of remoteness more strongly than Strata Florida. There is much to captivate the visitor at this evocative, historically important site. The abbey, founded in the 12th century, grew to become a powerhouse of Welsh culture, patronised by princes and poets. Although in ruin, Strata Florida displays much evidence of its former status, including a wonderful carved doorway and beautiful medieval tiles.

map 7 F4

TINTERN ABBEY

Tintern NP6 6SE
Enquiries Tel: 01291 689251
(Cadw: Welsh Historic Monuments)

Founded by Cistercian monks in 1131 and largely rebuilt by Roger Bigod, Lord of nearby Chepstow Castle in the 13th century, Tintern Abbey encompasses grand design and architectural detail of great finesse. The shell stands open almost to its full height, an outstanding example of the elaborate 'decorated' style of Gothic architecture. Visitors are captivated by the vast windows, with their delicate tracery and the wealth of detail on the walls, doorways and soaring archways. Tintern has inspired artists and poets like JMW Turner and William Wordsworth.

map 7 H1

TRETOWER COURT AND CASTLE

Crickhowell, Powys NP8 2RF
Enquiries Tel: 01874 730279 (Cadw: Welsh Historic Monuments)

In the quiet foothills of the Black Mountains stands a unique example of a family's building through the centuries. Alongside the castle which had protected them for 300 years, the Vaughan family built a manor house which was later extended and enlarged into a medieval mansion with elaborately timbered roofs and a galleried courtyard. During the Wars of the Roses, the house was fortified to enable the family to live there in safety. They continued to do so until the seventeenth century, when the great poet Henry Vaughan drew inspiration from his wonderfully well-preserved family home and its beautiful surroundings. Now visitors can also enjoy the re-created medieval garden that was featured in the television programme "Geoff Hamilton's Paradise Gardens."

 map 7 H2

WEOBLEY CASTLE

Llanrhidian, Nr Swansea, West Glamorgan SA3 1HB
Enquiries Tel: 01792 390012
(Cadw: Welsh Historic Monuments)

This fortified manor house perches above the wild northern coast of the beautiful Gower peninsula, looking over the marshes towards the Loughor estuary. It dates from the medieval thirteenth and fourteenth centuries, a rare survivor from those wild and often troubled times. Weobley was designed to be a comfortable home for the knightly de la Bere family, but its defensive tower and turrets provided a safe shelter in times of trouble. In Tudor times, Sir Rhys ap Thomas, the most powerful man in Wales added the two-storey porch block, providing a more stately entrance to the hall and private apartments.

map 7 J5

USK CASTLE

Usk, Monmouthshire
Tel: 01291 672563 (J.H.L. Humphreys)

Romantic, ruined norman castle overlooking the picturesque town of Usk. Inner and outer baileys, towers and earthwork defences. Surrounded by enchanting gardens (open under NGS and Usk Gardens open days) incorporating the Castle House, the former medieval gatehouse, as lived in by the current owner. **Location:** OS Ref SO 376 011, off Monmouth Road in Usk, opposite Fire Station. **Open:** Castle ruins: daily 11–5pm. Group bookings by appointment only. Gardens & Castle House: open to small groups by prior appointment. **Admission:** Castle ruins: Adults £2, children free. House & Garden: Adults £5, children £2.

 map 7 H2

WHITE CASTLE

Llantilio Crossenny, Gwent NP7 8UD
Enquiries Tel: 01600 780380
(Cadw: Welsh Historic Monuments)

One of a trio of castles built by the Normans to protect the route into Wales from Hereford, White Castle is the classic medieval castle. Standing on a low hill, its six towers and curtain wall are surrounded by a water-filled moat with drawbridge. It was built to house a garrison which, along with troops from Grosmont and Skenfrith castles, was responsible for the defence of the border against the rebellious Welsh. During Llewelyn the Last's attacks into the established Marcher lands of South Wales, the Three Castles were repaired and readied for war, but never saw action. After Henry Bolingbroke became King Henry IV, the castles, which were part of his Duchy of Lancaster, became the property of the Crown.

map 7 H2

TREDEGAR HOUSE & PARK
Newport, South Wales NP10 8YW
Tel: 01633 815880 Fax: 01633 815895 (Newport County Borough Council)

Set in 90 acres of award winning gardens and parkland, Tredegar House is one of the architectural wonders of Wales. For more than five hundred years it was the ancestral home of the Morgans, later Lords Tredegar. The medieval stone house, of which one wing survives, was rebuilt in brick by William Morgan between 1664 and 1672. Tredegar with its lavish interiors would be a symbol of the Morgan family wealth for the next 250 years, during which time they were a dominant influence on the political, social and economic life of the counties of Brecon, Glamorgan and Monmouth. The lavish lifestyle of the family in the 1930s and 40s saw the House sold together with its contents and the surrounding estate in 1951. For the twenty-three years it would be home to a girls' boarding school, until it was purchased in 1974 by Newport Borough Council, who embarked on an ambitious programme of restoration. Visitors to Tredegar can now discover what life was like for the Morgans 'above' stairs and their army of servants 'below' stairs in more than thirty restored rooms. **Location:** SW of Newport, signposted from M4, junction 28, A48. **Open:** From Good Friday–end Sept, Wed–Sun. Daily during Aug and weekends in Oct. Also/open for special Halloween tours and leading up to Christmas. **Admission:** Adult £3.95, concession £3, child £2, family (2 adults & 3 children) £10.50. Party Rates: adult £3.50, concessions £2.50 (pre-booked only). Special Victorian tours for school parties. **Refreshments:** Available in the Brewhouse Tearoom.

BEAUMARIS CASTLE

Beaumaris, Anglesey, Gwynedd, LL58 8AP
Enquiries Tel: 01248 810361
(Cadw: Welsh Historic Monuments)

This lovely castle overlooks the Menai Straits between Anglesey and the North Wales mainland, guarding an important medieval trade route. It was built by Edward I to complete his chain of coastal fortresses and served as Anglesey's garrison, protecting the island and its precious grain stores against invaders. The castle was ingeniously designed to use the straits' tides to both fill the defensive moat and to enable large ships to sail right up to the castle gate at high tide. The castle's picturesque setting and unusual design have drawn visitors for centuries, including Princess Victoria, later to be Queen, who visited for a Royal Eisteddfod in 1832.

map 6
C4

BODNANT GARDEN

Tal Y Cafn, Nr Colwyn Bay, Conwy LL28 5RE
Tel: 01492 650460 Fax: 01492 650448 (The National Trust)

Eighty acres of magnificent garden in the beautiful Conwy Valley comprising formal lawns and borders, Italianate terraces and The Dell which contains the Wild Garden and Pinetum. Daffodils and spring bulbs in March and April; Rhododendrons, camellias and magnolias in April and May with the famous original Laburnum Arch and azaleas flowering mid May–mid June. The summer months give a colourful show of herbaceous borders, roses, hydrangeas, water lilies and climbers, which is followed by the superb autumn colours in October. **Open:** 18 Mar–31 Oct, daily 10–5pm (last adm. 4.30pm). **Admission:** Adult £5, child £2.50. **Refreshments:** Morning coffee, light lunches and afternoon teas available from the Pavilion. Ample car and coach parking facilities. **Internet:** www.oxalis.co.uk/bodnant.htm

map 6
C4

BODELWYDDAN CASTLE

Bodelwyddan, Denbighshire, Wales LL18 5YA
Tel: 01745 584060 Fax: 01745 584563 (Bodelwyddan Castle Trust)

Set against the beauty of the Clwydian hills this magnificently refurbished victorian country house is the welsh home of the National Portrait Gallery. Opulent surroundings feature furniture from the Victoria & Albert Museum and sculpture from the Royal Academy. Children of all ages will enjoy the amusements, puzzles and inventions displayed in the hands on victorian games gallery. Throughout the year the house features a varied programme of exhibitions. Outside guests can explore the woodland trail, stroll in the gardens or simply enjoy the breathtaking views. **Open:** All year except Fri during the season and Mon & Fri at other times, Bodelwyddan Castle is the venue for a memorable day out. **Admission:** Adult £4.50, conc £3.50, child under 16 £2.50, Family £12 (2 adults & 2 children). Grounds only: Adult £2, child 50p.

map 6
C3

BODRHYDDAN

Rhuddlan, Denbighshire
Tel: 01745 590414 Fax: 01745 590155 (Lord Langford)

The home of Lord Langford and his family. Bodrhyddan is basically a 17th century house with 19th century additions by the famous architect William Eden Nesfield, although traces of an earlier building exist. The house has been in the hands of the same family since it was built over 500 years ago. There are notable pieces or armour, pictures, period furniture, a 3000 year old mummy, a formal parterre, a woodland garden and attractive picnic areas. Teas are available. Bodrhyddan is a Grade I listing making it one of few in Wales to remain in private hands. **Location:** OS Ref. SJ045 788. On the A5151 midway between Dyserth and Rhuddlan, 4 miles SE of Rhyl. **Open:** Jun–Sept inclusive, Tue & Thur, 2–5.30pm. **Admission:** Adult £4, child £2. Coach parties and receptions by special arrangement. Partially suitable for disabled. Tearoom. Guided tours only. Ample parking.

map 6
C2

CAERNARFON CASTLE

Caernarfon, Gwynedd, LL55 2AY
Enquiries Tel: 01286 677617
(Cadw: Welsh Historic Monuments)

This most impressive of Edward I's Welsh defences was built near the Roman fort of Segontium, mentioned in the ancient tales of the Mabinogion. Its unique polygonal towers with decorative coloured stone bands echo the walls of the great city of Constantinople and marked the castle as a special place. Indeed, it was intended to be the official residence of the King's chief representative in the Principality and is inextricably linked with the Princes of Wales since it is the birthplace of Edward's heir, Edward Caernarfon, first English Prince of Wales. The twentieth century has seen it rise again to prominence as the site of the Investiture of both this century's Princes of Wales.

map 6
C5

CONWY CASTLE

Conwy, Gwynedd, LL32 8AY
Enquiries Tel: 01492 592358
(Cadw: Welsh Historic Monuments)

This finest and most complete example of a fortified town and castle was constructed after the second Welsh war of independence by Edward I, whose apartments are in the castle's Inner Ward. Edward believed in building walled towns alongside his castles to create small pockets of English dominance in Wales. The town not only housed the community needed to supply the castle, but increased local prosperity and acted as the focal point of local government. Conwy is a classic example of this philosophy, cleverly designed to have 21 "circuit-breaker" towers along the town walls which enabled defenders to isolate an attacking force and ward them off effectively.

map 6
C4

CRICCIETH CASTLE

Criccieth, Gwynedd LL52 0DP
Enquiries Tel: 01766 522227
(Cadw: Welsh Historic Monuments)

Set high on a rocky headland overlooking Cardigan Bay, this is the most striking of the castles built by the native Welsh Princes. Llewelyn the Great built the first castle here, during his long campaign against the English annexation of Wales. When his grandson, Llewelyn the Last continued the struggle, he extended and strengthened Criccieth's defences. Over a century later, during the revolt of Owain Glyndwr, the rebel army was besieged in the castle, but were able to hold out due to the castle's position overlooking the sea, since provisions could be brought in by boat.

map 6
D5

CYMER ABBEY

Dolgellau, Gwynedd LL40 2HE
Enquiries Tel: 01341 422854
(Cadw: Welsh Historic Monuments)

The serene ruins stand in a lovely setting beside the River Mawddach. Even by the austere standards of the Cistercians, life must have been hard at Cymer – the abbey suffered badly during the troubled 13th century, the wars between England and Wales probably accounting for the failure to complete the original plan of the church. Cymer rewards visitors with a telling insight into the way of life of this enterprising order of monks. Particularly impressive are its great windows, arches and an unusual tower.

map 6
E4

DOLBADARN CASTLE

Llanberis, Gwynedd
Enquiries Tel: 01222 500200
(Cadw: Welsh Historic Monuments)

This Welsh fortress is so picturesque that artists have come from far and wide to try and capture its lonely majesty. The castle was built by Llewelyn the Great to guard the Llanberis Pass that leads into the heart of Snowdonia, the traditional Welsh stronghold. A mighty round keep with a cunning spiral staircase which reverses direction halfway, to confuse invaders; it stands between two lakes, with the mountains of Snowdonia at its back. Yet the haunting beauty of the castle is only one of the reasons for a visit. For it was here that Llewelyn the Last imprisoned his brother Owain Goch for 22 years as a punishment for attempting to overthrow him.

DENBIGH CASTLE

Denbigh, Clwyd
Enquiries Tel: 01745 813385
(Cadw: Welsh Historic Monuments)

Encircling a rocky outcrop overlooking the Vale of Clwyd, Denbigh Castle is built on the site of a traditional Welsh court. At the end of Llewelyn the Last's wars of Welsh independence against Edward I, the English king gave Denbigh to his campaign commander, Henry de Lacy. Together they planned a castle and walled town similar to Edward's own fortresses along the north Welsh coast. Sadly, Henry never finished building the finely decorated gatehouse, the castle's final crowning glory, due to the death of his son in the castle well. In later years, as Denbigh passed into the hands of several powerful owners, the castle saw many famous visitors, including King Charles I.

map 7
J3

DOLWYDDELAN CASTLE

Dolwyddelan, Gwynedd
Enquiries Tel: 01690 750366
(Cadw: Welsh Historic Monuments)

Tradition claims Dolwyddelan as the birthplace of Llewelyn ap Iorwerth, Llewelyn the Great; the Prince who united Wales. However, the stone keep that now stands was probably re-built by Llewelyn to guard the road into the heart of the stronghold of Snowdonia and Gwynedd through the strategically important Lledyr Valley. The castle would also have watched over Llewelyn's precious cattle pastures, since this was a time of war when cattle were essential battle supplies that were easily moved to support hungry armies. When Edward 1st took the castle during the Welsh wars for independence under Llewelyn the Last, he outfitted the garrison in white snow camouflage and made some additions to the existing structure.

map 6
D4

ERDDIG HALL, GARDEN & COUNTRY PARK

Erddig, Nr Wrexham LL13 0YT
Tel: 01978 355314 Fax: 01978 313333 (Owner)

One of the most fascinating houses in Britain, not least because of the unusually close relationship between the family and their servants. The range of outbuildings includes: joiner's shop, smithy, sawmill, stables, bakehouse, laundry and kitchen, while the stunning state rooms display 18th and 19th century furniture and furnishings. The large walled garden has been restored to its 18th century formal design with Victorian parterre and yew walk. **Open:** 25 Mar–1 Nov daily, except Thurs & Fri but open Good Fri. Garden: 11–6pm. House: 12–5pm. July & Aug Garden: 10–6pm. 7 Oct–1 Nov Garden: 11–5pm. House: 12–4pm. Last admission to House an hour before closing. **Admission:** All inclusive ticket: Adult £6, child £3, family £15. Belowstairs (incl. outbuildings & garden) ticket: Adult £4, child £2, family £10. **E-mail:** erddig@ntrust.org.uk

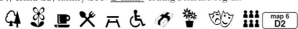

map 6
D2

GWYDIR CASTLE

Gwydir Castle, Llanrwst, Gwynedd.
Tel: 01492 641687 Fax: 01492 641687 (Mr and Mrs Welford)

Gwydir Castle is situated in the beautiful Conwy Valley and is set within a Grade 1 listed, 10 acre garden. Built by the illustrious Wynn family c.1500, Gwydir is a fine example of a Tudor courtyard house, incorporating re-used medieval material from the dissolved Abbey of Maenan. Further additions date from c.1600 and c.1826. The important 1640's panelled Dining Room has now been reinstated, following its repatriation from the New York Metropolitan Museum. **Location:** ½ mile W Of Llanrwst on A5106. **Open:** 1 Mar–31 Oct, daily 10–5pm. Occasional weddings on Saturdays. Limited opening at other times. **Admission:** Adults £3, children £1.50. Guided tours & refreshments by arrangement. Group discount 10%.

map 6 C4

HARLECH CASTLE

Harlech, Gwynedd LL46 2YH
Enquiries Tel: 01766 780552
(Cadw: Welsh Historic Monuments)

Famed in song and story, Harlech is enshrined in the history of Wales. This is the "castle of lost causes" where a handful of defenders could hold off an army; a fortress which has been the last refuge for defiant, valiant men and women who have refused to compromise their principles. Built by Edward I, it had a clever channel connecting it to the sea, with a water gate and protected walkway to the castle allowing supplies to be brought in by boat. The castle was besieged in the 15th century when it was the headquarters and court of rebel leader, Owain Glyndwr; and again during the Wars of the Roses when it was the last Lancastrian stronghold in Wales to fall to the Yorkists.

map 6 D4

PENNARTH FAWR
MEDIEVAL HALL-HOUSE

Chwilog, Pwllheli, Gwynedd.
Enquiries Tel: 01222 500200
(Cadw: Welsh Historic Monuments)

Near Criccieth stands this fascinating example of the home of a medieval gentleman. From outside, the modest building gives few clues to the glorious interior which was lovingly restored earlier this century. Incredibly, this house remained in a single family for over 400 years after it was built in the mid-fourteenth century by a local Welsh gentleman. One member of the family, Hugh Gwyn, was High Sheriff of Caernarvonshire at the end of Queen Elizabeth I's reign, and it was he who modernised the house by adding the large fireplace in the east wall which bears his coat of arms.

PLAS BRONDANW GARDENS

Llanfrothen, Nr. Penrhyndeudraeth, Gwynedd, Wales.
Tel: 01766 771 136 (The Second Portmeirion Foundation)

Created by Sir Clough Williams-Ellis, architect of Portmeirion, below his ancestral home. Italian inspired gardens with spectacular mountain views, topiary and folly tower. **Location:** 2 miles north of Penrhyndeudraeth. ¼ mile off the A4085 on Croesor Road. **Open:** All year, daily, 9–5pm. **Admission:** Adults £1.50, children 25p.

map 6 D4

PLAS MAWR, CONWY

Conwy, Gwynedd LL32 8DE
Tel: 01492 580167 (Cadw: Welsh Historic Monuments)

Within the town of Conwy, best-known for its great medieval fortifications of castle and walls, hides a perfect Elizabethan jewel. Plas Mawr is the best-preserved Elizabethan town house in Britain, famous for the quality and quantity of its plasterwork decoration. Plas Mawr is a fascinating and unique place which gives visitors a chance to peek into the lives of the Tudor gentry and their servants. This was the fast moving time, when the creation of increased wealth among merchants and the gentry meant that private homes such as Plas Mawr could be decorated and furnished lavishly. Cadw gives visitors the opportunity to enjoy all of this through an audio tour which also explains the amazing process of restoration the house has been through.

map 6 C4

PORTMEIRION VILLAGE & GARDENS

Portmeirion, Gwynedd, Wales LL48 6ET
Tel: 01766 770000 Fax: 01766 771331

Sir Clough Williams-Ellis aimed to show at Porteirion that one could "…*develop even a very beautiful place without defiling it.*" Located on the shores of Cardigan Bay in North Wales, Portmeirion has seven shops inlcuding one selling Portmeirion Pottery seconds, plus restuarants, gardens and miles of beaches. Surrounding the village are the Gwyllt woodland and gardens containing rare Himalayan flowering treees. All the houses in the village are let as part of the Portmeirion Hotel. **Open:** The village is open every day all year round. **Location:** It is located off the A487 at Minffordd between Penrhyndeudraeth and Porthmadog. **Admission:** Adults £4.50, children £2.25, senior citizens £3.30. **E-mail:** info@portmeirion–village.com **Internet:** www.portmeirion.com

map 6 D4

RHUDDLAN CASTLE
Rhuddlan, Clwyd
Tel: 01745 590777
(Cadw: Welsh Historic Monuments)

One of the first castles built by Edward I in his programme to fortify the North Wales coast, a man-made channel three miles long linked Rhuddlan to the sea, giving supply ships access to the castle. This was reputed to be Queen Eleanor's favourite castle and indeed, it seems that she and King Edward spent a large amount of time here. It was in Rhuddlan that Edward made a treaty with the Welsh Lords and persuaded them to accept his baby son, recently born in Caernarfon Castle, as the Prince of Wales by promising them that their new Lord would be born in Wales, with an unblemished character and unable to speak a word of English.

map 6
C3

RUG CHAPEL & LLANGAR CHURCH
C/o Coronation Cottage, Rug, Corwen LL21 9BT
Enquiries Tel: 01490 412025
(Cadw: Welsh Historic Monuments)

Rug is a rare example of a little altered 17th century private chapel. Carved angels appear as part of an elaborate roof, decorated from end to end. The skills of local artists and wood carvers can even be seen in the bench ends, which are decorated with fantastic carvings. Nearby Llangar Church is even older. The small, idyllically located medieval building retains many ancient features, including extensive 15th century wall paintings, a 17th century figure of death, old beams, box pews, pulpit and minstrels gallery.

map 6
D3

VALLE CRUCIS ABBEY
Llangollen
Enquiries Tel: 01978 860326
(Cadw: Welsh Historic Monuments)

The Cistercian abbey founded in the 13th century, lies in green fields beneath Llangollen's deep sided mountains. Many original features remain including the glorious west front complete with richly carved doorway and a beautiful rose window. Other well preserved features include the east end of the abbey (which still overlooks the monks' original fishpond) and lovely chapter house with its striking rib-vaulted roof. Valle Crucis, the "Abbey of the Cross", is named after Eliseg's Pillar, a nearby 9th century Christian memorial cross.

map 6
D2

CHIRK CASTLE
Chirk, Wrexham LL14 5AF Tel: 01691 777701 Fax: 01691 774706

Open: 29 March to 29 Oct: daily except Mon & Tues (but open BH Mon) 12–5pm; 2 Oct to 29 Oct: 11–5pm. Garden: Mar–Sept: 11–6pm; last admission 4.30pm. **Events:** send s.a.e for details of programme, which includes open–air plays, family fun days and snowdrop walks.which includes open–air plays, family fun days and snowdrop walks. **Admission:** Adult £5, concessions £2.50. Family £12.50.

COLBY WOODLAND GARDENS
Stepaside, Narberth, Pembrokeshire Tel: 01834 811885

Open: 1 April to 4 Nov: daily 10–5pm. **Admission:** Adults £2.80, concessions £1.40. Family ticket £7.

PENRHYN CASTLE
Bangor LL57 4HN Tel: 01248 353084 Infoline: 01248 371337

Open: 22 March to 5 Nov: daily except Tues. March to June, Sept to Oct 12–5pm, July & Aug 11–5pm (last audio tour 4pm). Grounds and stable block exhibitions: March to June, Sept to Oct 11–5.30pm, July & Aug 10–5.30pm; last admission to house & grounds 4.30pm. **Events:** send s.a.e. for details or tel. Infoline. **Admission:** Adult £5, concessions £2.50. Family ticket £12.50.

PLAS NEWYDD
Llanfairpwll, Anglesey LL61 6DQ Tel: 01248 714795

Open: House: 1 April to 1 Nov: daily except Thur & Fri 12–5pm. Garden: as house 11–5.30pm. Rhododendron Garden 27 March to early June only; woodland walk and marine walk open all year. **Events:** send s.a.e for full details of varied programme. **Admission:** Adult £4.50, concessions £2.25. Family ticket £11. Groups £3.70.

POWIS CASTLE & GARDEN
Welshpool SY21 8RF Tel: 01938 554338 Fax/Infoline: 01938 554336

Open: Castle & Museum: 27 March to 30 June, 1 Sept to 31 Oct: daily except Mon & Tues; July & Aug: daily except Mon (but open all BH Mons). Castle & Museum: 1–5pm. Garden: as castle & museum, 11–6pm. Last admission to castle, garden & museum each 30mins before closing. **Events:** varied programme, tel. for details. **Admission:** Adult £7.50, concessions £3.75. Family ticket £18.75. Groups £6.50. Garden only: Adult £5, child £2.50. Family ticket £12.50. Groups £4. No group rates on Suns or BH Mons.

TUDOR MERCHANTS HOUSE
Quay Mill, Tenby SA70 7BX Tel: 01834 842279

Open: 1 April to 30 Sept: daily except Weds 10–5pm. Suns 1–5pm.

The National Trust for Scotland

Please note that opening times are subject to change. For current details please telephone 0131 226 5922

ALLOA TOWER, Alloa, Clackmannanshire. Open: Good Fri–Easter Mon and 1 May–30 Sep, daily 1.30–5.30.

ANGUS FOLK MUSEUM, Kirkwynd, Glamis, Forfar, Angus DD8 1RT. Open: Good Fri–Easter Mon and 1 May–30 Sep, daily 11–5.

ARDUAINE GARDEN, Arduaine, By Oban, Argyll PA34 4XQ. Open: all year, daily 9.30–sunset.

BACHELORS' CLUB, Sandgate Street, Tarbolton KA5 5RB. Open: Good Fri–30 Sep, daily 11.30–5; weekends in Oct, 11.30–5

BANNOCKBURN, Glasgow Road, Stirling FK7 0LJ. Open: site, all year, daily. Heritage Centre and shop, 1–31 Mar and 1 Nov–23 Dec, daily 11–3; 1 Apr–31 Oct, daily 10–5.30.

BARRIE'S BIRTHPLACE, 9 Brechin Road, Kirriemuir, Angus DD8 4BX. Open: Good Fri–Easter Mon and 1 May–30 Sep, Mon–Sat 11–5.30 Sun 1.30–5.30.

BARRY MILL, Barry, Carnoustie, Angus DD7 7RJ. Open: Good Fri–Easter Mon and 1 May–30 Sep, daily 11–5.

BRANKLYN GARDEN, 116 Dundee Road, Perth PH2 7BB. Open: 1 Mar–31 Oct, daily 9.30–sunset.

BRODICK CASTLE AND GOATFELL, Isle of Arran, KA27 8HY. Open: castle, 1 Apr (or Good Fri if earlier)–31 Oct, daily 11.30–5.

BRODIE CASTLE, Brodie, Forres IV36 0TE. Open: castle, 1 Apr (or Good Fri if earlier)–30 Sep, Mon–Sat 11–5.30, Sun 1.30–5.30.

BROUGHTON HOUSE AND GARDEN, 12 High Street, Kirkcudbright DG6 4JX. Open: 1 Apr (or Good Fri if earlier)–31 Oct, daily 1–5.30.

CARLYLE'S BIRTHPLACE, The Arched House, Ecclefechan, Lockerbie DG11 3DG. Open: 1 May–30 Sep, Fri–Mon 1.30–5.30.

CASTLE FRASER, Sauchen, Inverurie AB51 7LD. Open: castle, Good Fri–Easter Mon, 1 May–30 Jun and 1–30 Sep, daily 1.30–5.30; 1 Jul–31 Aug, daily 11–5.30; weekends in Oct, 1.30–5.30 (last admission 4.45).

CRATHES CASTLE AND GARDEN, Banchory AB31 3QJ. Open: castle, Visitor Centre, shop and licensed restaurant, 1 Apr (or Good Fri if earlier)–31 Oct, daily 11–5.30 (last admission–castle 4.45).

CULLODEN, NTS Visitor Centre, Culloden Moor, Inverness IV1 2ED.

Open: site, all year, daily. Visitor Centre, 1 Feb–31 Mar and 1 Nov–30 Dec (except 25/26 Dec), daily 10–4; 1 Apr–31 Oct, daily 9–6.

CULROSS, Fife, off A985, 12M West of Forth Road Bridge. Open: Palace, 1 Apr (or Good Fri if earlier)–30 Sep, daily 11–5 (last admission 4). Town House and Study, same dates, 1.30–5 and weekends in Oct, 11–5.

CULZEAN CASTLE AND COUNTRY PARK, Maybole KA19 8LE. Open: castle, Visitor Centre, licensed restaurant and shops, 1 Apr (or Good Fri if earlier)–31 Oct, daily 10.30–5.30 (last admission 5)

DRUM CASTLE, Drumoak, By Banchory AB31 3EY. Open : Good Fri–Easter Mon and 1 May–30 Sep, daily 1.30–5.30; weekends in Oct, 1.30–5.30 (last admission 4.45). Garden, same dates, daily 10–6. Grounds, all year, daily 9.30–sunset.

FALKLAND PALACE, GARDEN AND TOWN HALL, Falkland, Cupar, Fife KY15 7BU. Open: palace and garden, 1 Apr (or Good Fri if earlier)–31 Oct, Mon–Sat 11–5.30, Sun 1.30–5.30 (last admission–palace 4.30,–garden 5).

FYVIE CASTLE, Fyvie, Turriff AB53 8JS. Open: castle, 1 Apr (or Good Fri if earlier)–30 Jun and 1–30 Sep, daily 1.30–5.30; 1 Jul–31 Aug daily 11–5.30; weekends in Oct, 1.30–5.30 .

THE GEORGIAN HOUSE, 7 Charlotte Square, Edinburgh EH2 4DR. Open: 1 Apr (or Good Fri if earlier)–31 Oct, Mon–Sat 10–5, Sun 2–5

GLADSTONE'S LAND, 477B Lawnmarket, Edinburgh EH1 2NT. Open: 1 Apr (or Good Fri if earlier)–31 Oct, Mon–Sat 10–5, Sun 2–5

GLENCOE, NTS Visitor Centre, Glencoe, Ballachulish PA39 4HX. Open: site, all year, daily. Visitor Centre and snack-bar, 1 Apr (or Good Fri if earlier) to 18 May and 1 Sep–31 Oct, daily 10–5; 19 May–31 Aug, daily 9.30–5.30 .

GLENFINNAN MONUMENT, NTS Information Centre, Glenfinnan PH37 4LT. Open: site, all year, daily. Visitor Centre and snack-bar, 1 Apr (or Good Fri if earlier)–18 May and 1 Sep–31 Oct, daily 10–1 and 2–5; 19 May–31 Aug, daily 9.30–6 (snack-bar 10–6).

GREENBANK GARDEN, Flenders Road, Clarkston, Glasgow G76 8RB. Open: all year, daily 9.30–sunset, except 25/26 Dec and 1/2 Jan. Shop and tearoom, 1 Apr (or Good Fri if earlier)–31 Oct, daily 11–5; 1 Nov–31 Mar, Sat/Sun 2–4. House open 1 Apr–31 Oct, Suns only 2–4 and during special events (subject–functions in progress). No dogs in garden, please.

HADDO HOUSE, Ellon, Aberdeenshire AB41 0ER. Open: house, Good Fri–Easter Mon and 1 May–30 Sep, daily 1.30–5.30; weekends in Oct, 1.30–5.30 (last admission 4.45); shop and Stables.

THE HILL HOUSE, Upper Colquhoun Street, Helensburgh G84 9AJ. Open 1 Apr (or Good Fri if earlier)–31 Oct, daily 1.30–5.30 (last admission 5); tearoom, 1.30–4.30.

HILL OF TARVIT MANSIONHOUSE, Cupar, Fife KY15 5PB. Open: house, Good Fri–Easter Mon and 1 May–30 Sep, daily 1.30–5.30; weekends in Oct, 1.30–5.30 (last admission 4.45). Garden and grounds, all year, daily 9.30–sunset.

HOUSE OF THE BINNS, Linlithgow, West Lothian EH49 7NA. Open: house, 1 May–30 Sep, daily except Fri, 1.30–5.30 (last admission 5). Parkland, 1 Apr–31 Oct, daily 9.30–7; 1 Nov–31 Mar, daily 9.30–4.

HOUSE OF DUN, Montrose, Angus DD10 9LQ. Open: house and shop, Good Fri–Easter Mon and 1 May–30 Sep, daily 1.30–5.30; weekends in Oct, 1.30–5.30 (last admission 5).

HUGH MILLER'S COTTAGE, Cromarty, IV11 8XA. Open: 1 May–30 Sep, Mon–Sat 10–1 and 2–5.30, Sun 2–5.30.

INVEREWE GARDEN, Poolewe IV22 2LQ. Open: garden, 15 March–31 Oct, daily 9.30am–9pm; 1 Nov–14 Mar, daily 9.30–5. Visitor Centre and shop, 15 Mar–31 Oct, daily 9.30–5.30. Licensed restaurant, same dates, daily 10–5. Guided garden walks, 15 Mar–30 Sep, Mon–Fri at 1.30. No dogs in garden please. No shaded car parking.

KELLIE CASTLE AND GARDEN, Pittenweem, Fife KKY10 2RF. Open castle, Good Fri–Easter Mon and 1 May–30 Sep, daily 1.30–5.30; weekends in Oct, 1.30–5.30 (last admission 4.45). Garden and grounds, all year, daily 9.30–sunset. .

KILLIECRANKIE, NTS Visitor Centre, Killiecrankie, Pitlochry PH16 5LG. Open: site, all year, daily. Visitor Centre, shop and snack-bar, 1 Apr (or Good Fri if earlier)–31 Oct, daily 10–5.30.

LEITH HALL AND GARDEN, Huntly AB54 4NQ. Open: house and tearoom, Good Fri–Easter Mon and 1 May–30 Sep, daily 1.30–5.30; weekends in Oct, 1.30–5.30 (last admission 4.45). Garden and grounds all year, daily 9.30–sunset.

PITMEDDEN GARDEN, Ellon AB41 0PD. Open: garden, Visitor Centre, museum, tearoom, grounds and other facilities, 1 May–30 Sep, daily 10–5.30 (last admission 5).

PRESTON MILL AND PHANTASSIE DOOCOT, East Linton, East Lothian, EH40 3DS. Open: Good Fri–Easter Mon, 1 May–30 Sep, Mon–Sat 11–1 and 2–5, Sun 1.30–5; weekends in Oct, 1.30–4.

PRIORWOOD GARDEN AND DRIED FLOWER SHOP, Melrose TD6 9PX. Open: 1 Apr (or Good Fri if earlier)–30 Sep, Mon–Sat 10–5.30, Sun 1.30–5.30; 1 Oct–24 Dec, Mon–Sat 10–4, Sun 1.30–4.

ROBERT SMAIL'S PRINTING WORKS, 7/9 High Street, Innerleithen EH44 6HA. Open: Good Fri–Easter Mon and 1 May–30 Sep, Mon–Sat 10–1 and 2–5, Sun 2–5; weekends in Oct, Sat 10–1 and 2–5, Sun 2–5 (last admission 45 mins before closing, morning and afternoon).

SOUTER JOHNNIE'S COTTAGE, Main Road, Kirkoswald KA19 8HY. Open: Good Fri–30 Sept, daily 11.30–5; weekends in Oct, 11.30–5 (last admission 4.30).

THE TENEMENT HOUSE, 145 Buccleuch Street, Glasgow G3 6QN. Open 1 Mar–31 Oct, daily 2–5 (last admission 4.30) Very restricted parking.

THREAVE GARDEN AND ESTATE, Castle Douglas DG7 1RX. Open: estate and garden, all year, daily 9.30–sunset. Walled garden and glasshouses, all year, daily 9.30–5.

TORRIDON, N of A896, 9M SW of Kinlochewe. Open: Countryside Centre, 1 May–30 Sep, Mon–Sat 10–5, Sun 2–5. Estate, Deer Park and Deer Museum (unstaffed), all year, daily.

WEAVER'S COTTAGE, The Cross, Kilbarchan PA10 2JG. Open: Good Fri–30 Sep, daily 1.30–5.30; weekends in Oct, 1.30–5.30

Scotland

Southeast of the Highland boundary fault line lies a part of Scotland very different in character from its northern neighbour. If the Highlands embody the romance of Scotland, the Lowlands are the powerhouse. Lowlanders have always prospered in agriculture and more recently, in industry and commerce.

The Lowlands are traditionally all the land south of the fault line stretching northeast from Loch Lomond to Stonehaven. Confusingly, they include plenty of wild upland country. The region illustrates best the diversity of Scotland's magnificent scenery. The wooded valleys and winding rivers of the border give way to the stern moorland hills of the

Above: River Tweed. Below: Forth Bridge. Bottom: Isle of Skye

Cheviots and Lammermuirs.

Lively little fishing villages cling to the rocky east coast, while the Clyde coast and its islands are dotted with cheerful holiday towns. Inland lie the Trossachs: these romantic mountains surrounding Loch Lomond are a magnet for walkers and well within reach of Glasgow.

Scotland is renowned for its rich and diverse selection of the arts. The National Museum of Scotland displays both international collections of human and cultural history, archaeology, geology and the decorative arts whilst in the Western Isles of Scotland lies An Lanntair, an arts centre devoted to local artists and musicians.

 # ABBOTSFORD

Melrose, Borders, Scotland, TD6 9BQ.
Tel: 01896 752 043 Fax: 01896 752 916

The house of Sir Walter Scott, containing many historical relics collected by him. **Location:** 3 miles W of Melrose; S of A72; 5 miles E of Selkirk. **Station(s):** No railway. **Open:** Third Monday in March–31 Oct: Mon–Sat, 10–5pm. Jun–Sept: Sun, 10–5pm. Mar–May & Oct: Sun, 2–5pm. **Admission:** Adults £3.80, children £1.40. Coach Party: Adults £2.80, children £1.40. **Refreshments:** Tea shop. Gift shop. Cars with wheelchairs or disabled enter by private entrance.

 # AYTON CASTLE

Eyemouth, Berwickshire, Scotland, , TD14 5RD.
Tel: 018907 81212 Fax: 018907 81550
(Ayton Castle Maintenance Fund)

A Victorian castle built in red sandstone in 1846, which has been fully restored and is now lived in by the family owners. **Open:** 10 May–13 Sept: Sun, 2–5pm. At other times by appointment. **Admission:** £3, Children (under 15) free. **Events/Exhibitions:** Occasionally.

 # BLAIRQUHAN CASTLE & GARDENS

Straiton, Maybole, KA19 7LZ, Ayrshire, Scotland
Tel: 016557 70239 Fax: 016557 70278 (James Hunter Blair)

Magnificent Regency Castle approached by a 3 mile long private drive beside the River Girvan. Walled gardens and pinetum. Picture gallery. Shop. Tree Trail. **Location:** 14 miles S of Ayr, off A77. Entrance Lodge is on B7045, 1/2 mile S of Kirkmichael. **Open:** 15 July–13 Aug, daily except Mons, 1.30–4.15pm. **Admission:** Adults £5, children £3, OAPs £4. Parties by arrangement any time of the year. **Refreshments:** Tearoom. Car parking. Wheelchair access – around gardens and principal floors of the Castle. **Internet:** www.blairquhan.co.uk **E-mail:** enquiries@blairquhan.co.uk

CALLENDAR HOUSE

Callendar Park, Falkirk, Scotland, FK1 1YR
Tel: 01324 503 770 (Falkirk Council)

Imposing mansion within attractive parkland with a 900 year history. Facilities include a working kitchen of 1825 where costumed interpreters carry out daily chores, including cooking based on 1820's recipes. **Exhibition area:** 'Story of Callendar House', plus two temporary galleries, with regularly changing exhibitions. Permanent Exhibition 'William Forbes Falkirk' with working 1820's general store, clockmaker and printer. There is also a history research centre, gift shop and the Georgian tea shop at the Stables. **Location:** E of Falkirk town centre, on A803 Callendar Road. **Open:** Jan–Dec: Mon–Sat, 10–5pm. Apr–Sept: Sun, 2–5pm. Open all public hols. **Admission:** Adults £2.50, children £1, OAPs £1. Last admission 4pm.

 # BOWHILL

Selkirk, Borders TD7 5ET
Tel: 01750 22204 Fax: 01750 22204 (Buccleuch Heritage Trust)

Scottish Borders home of the Scotts of Buccleuch. Paintings by Guardi, Canaletto, Claude, Gainsborough, Reynolds and Raeburn. Superb furniture, porcelain. Monmouth, Sir Walter Scott, Queen Victoria relics. Victorian kitchen. Audiovisual. Theatre. Adventure Woodland. Nature trails. **Location:** 3 miles west of Selkirk on A708. Edinburgh, Carlisle & Newcastle approx 1.5 hrs by road. **Open:** House: 1–31 Jul, daily 1–4.30pm. Open by appointment at additional times for educational groups. Country park: 22 Apr–28 Aug daily except Fri, 12–5pm. Open on Fri in July with House. Last entry 45 mins before closing. (Heritage Education Trust, Sandford Award Winner 1993, 1998.) **Admission:** House & Country Park: Adults £4.50, children £2, OAP & groups £4. Wheelchair users & children under 5 free. Country Park £2. **Refreshments:** Gift shop, tearoom.

CRAIGDARROCH HOUSE

Moniaive, DG3 4JB Dumfries & Galloway, Scotland
Tel: 01848 200 202 (J. H. A Sykes)

William Adam house built for Annie Laurie. **Location:** 2 miles W of Moniaive, on B729. **Open:** All July, 2–4pm. **Admission:** £2. Please note: no public conveniences.

map 10
C3

GOSFORD HOUSE

Longniddry, EH32 OPY, East Lothian, Scotland Tel: 01875 870 201
Fax: 01875 870 620 (The Wemyss & March Estates Management Co. Ltd)

Robert Adam designed the Central block and Wings, which were later demolished. Two Wings rebuilt in 1890 by William Young. The 1800 roof was part burnt (military occupation) in 1940, but was restored in 1987. North Wing now roofless. South Wing is family home and contains famous Marble Hall (Staffordshire Alabaster). Parts of South Wing are open. Fine collection of paintings and works of art. Surrounding gardens redeveloping. Extensive policies, artificial ponds; geese and other wildfowl breeding. **Location:** On A198 between Aberlady and Longniddry. NW of Haddington. **Station(s):** Longniddry (2.5 miles). **Open:** June-July, Wed, Sat–Sun, 2–5pm. **Admission:** Adults £2.50, children 75p. **Refreshments:** Hotels in Aberlady.

DALMENY HOUSE

South Queensferry, Edinburgh, Scotland, EH30 9TQ.
Tel: 0131 331 1888 Fax: 0131 331 1788 (Earl of Rosebery)

Home of the Earls of Rosebery, set in beautiful parkland on the Firth of Forth. Scotland's first gothic revival house. Rothschild Collection of 18th century French furniture and decorative art. Portraits by Reynolds, Gainsborough, Raeburn and Lawrence. Goya tapestries. Napoleonic Collection. **Location:** 7 miles N of Edinburgh, signposted off A90. **Buses:** St. Andrew Square Bus Station to Chapel Gate (1 mile from house). **Open to public:** July & August, Sun, Mon & Tues 2–5.30pm. Special parties at other times by arrangement. **Admission:** Adults £4, children (10–16) £2, children under 10–free, OAPs £3.50, students £3, groups (min. 20) £3. Corporate events welcome throughout the year including product launches, dinners, outdoor activities. **Internet:** www.edinburgh.org

map 13
G5

FLOORS CASTLE

Kelso, TD5 7SF, Scotland
Tel: 01573 223 333 Fax: 01573 226 056 (Duke of Roxburghe)

Scotland's largest inhabited castle, built in 1721 by William Adam and remodelled by Playfair. Outstanding collection of French furniture, stunning tapestries and works of art. Beautiful Chinese and European porcelain and a unique Victorian collection of birds. **Location:** N of Kelso. **Station(s):** Berwick-upon-Tweed. **Open:** 21 April–29 October daily. 10am–4.30pm. **Admission:** Please contact for admission prices. Party rates on request. **Refreshments:** Restaurant and coffee shop.

Events/ Exhibitions: Family Fun Day with massed pipe bands on 27 Aug. **Accommodation:** At nearby Roxburghe Hotel & Golf Course. **Conferences:** Millennium Parterre open for Easter 2000. Facilities available including dinners, receptions, product launches and outdoor events. Free parking, walled garden, woodland & river walks and garden centre.

map 13
J6

The Royal Collection © 1999, H. M. Queen Elizabeth II/John Freeman

THE PALACE OF HOLYROODHOUSE

Edinburgh EH8 8DX, Scotland
Tel: 0131 556 7371 Information Line (24 hours): 0131 556 1096 Fax: 0131 557 5256

The Palace of Holyroodhouse, Buckingham Palace and Windsor Castle and are the Official residences of the Sovereign and are used by The Queen as both home and office. The Queen's personal standard flies when Her Majesty is in residence. Furnished with works of art from the Royal Collection, these buildings are used extensively by The Queen for State ceremonies, and official entertaining. They are opened to the public as much as these commitments allow. At the End of the Royal Mile stands the Palace of Holyroodhouse. Set against the spectacular backdrop of Arthur's Seat, Holyroodhouse has evolved from a medieval fortress into a baroque residence. The Royal Apartments, an extensive suite of rooms, epitomise the elegance and grandeur of this ancient and noble house, and contrast with the historic tower apartments of Mary, Queen of Scots' which are steeped in intrigue and sorrow. These intimate rooms where she lived on her return from France in 1561, witnessed the murder of David Rizzio, her favourite secretary, by her jealous husband, Lord Darnley and his accomplices. **Open:** Every day, except Good Friday, Christmas Day, Boxing Day and during Royal Visits. 9.30–5.15pm Apr–Oct, 9.30–3.45pm Nov–Mar. **Admission:** Adults £6, senior citizens (over 60) £4.50 and children (under 17) £3. Family ticket (2 adults and 2 under 17) £13.50.

The Royal Dining Room
The Royal Collection © 1999, H. M. Queen Elizabeth II/Antonia Reeves

Mary, Queen of Scots'
The Royal Collection © 1999, H. M. Queen Elizabeth II

map 13
G5

www.historichouses.co.uk

The Palace of Holyroodhouse   The Royal Collection © 1999, H. M. Queen Elizabeth II/John Freeman

Mary, Queen of Scots' Bedchamber   The Royal Collection © 1999, H. M. Queen Elizabeth II/Antonia Reeves

HOPETOUN HOUSE

South Queensferry, West Lothian, Scotland, EH30, 9SL
Tel: 0131 331 2451 Fax: 0131 319 1885 (Hopetoun House Preservation Trust)

Hopetoun House is a unique gem of Europe's architectural heritage and undoubtedly 'Scotland's Finest Stately Home'. Situated on the shores of the Firth of Forth, it is one of the most splendid examples of the work of Scottish architects Sir William Bruce and William Adam. The Bruce House has fine carving, wainscoting and ceiling painting, while in contrast the Adam interior, with opulent gilding and classical motifs reflect the aristocratic grandeur of the early 18th century. The House is set in 100 acres of rolling parkland including woodland walks, the Red Deer Park, the Spring Garden with a profusion of wild flowers, and numerous picturesque picnic spots. Panoramic views can be seen from the rooftop platform. **Location:** 2 miles from Forth Road Bridge. 10 miles from Edinburgh. **Open:** Daily 31 Mar–1 Oct 10–5.30pm. Last admission 4.30pm. Winter by appointment only for groups of 15+. **Admission:** Adults £5.30, children (5–16yrs) £2.70, OAP/students £4.70, groups £4.50, family £15. Under 5s free. **Refreshments:** Delicious meals and snacks served in the recently converted Stables Restaurant.

map 13
G5

Drumlanrig Castle, Gardens & Country Park

Nr Thornhill, Dumfries & Galloway, Scotland DG3 4AQ
Tel: 01848 330248 Fax: 01848 331682 (His Grace The Duke of Buccleuch & Queensberry K.T.)

Exquisite pink sandstone castle built by William Douglas, 1st Duke of Queensberry. 1679–91. Renowned art collection, including work by Holbein, Leonardo and Rembrandt. Versailles furniture, relics of Bonnie Prince Charlie. Douglas family historical exhibition. Working forge. Extensive gardens and woodlands superbly landscaped. Craft centre. Cycle museum. **Open:** Castle: Easter Saturday–13 Aug inclusive & 26–31 August 7 days, weekdays 11–4pm, Sun 12–4pm. 1–30 Sept by appointment. Country Park: Easter Saturday–30 Sept inclusive, 7 days, 11–5pm. For further details telephone: 01848 330248. Countryside Service: 01848 331555. **Admission:** Adults: Castle and country park £6, country park £3. Child: Castle and country park £2. Senior citizens: Castle and country park £4, country park £3. Family (2 adults, 4 children) £14. Pre-booked parties (minimum 20) Normal time £4, outwith normal time £8. Wheelchairs free. **E-mail:** bre@ drumlanrigcastle.org.uk

map 13
F7

LAURISTON CASTLE

Edinburgh, Lothian, Scotland
Tel: 0131 336 1921

A 1590s Scottish tower house with substantial additions from 1824 by the architect William Burn, the castle stands in 30 acres of parkland and tranquil gardens which enjoy a spectacular view across the Firth of Forth. The remarkably complete Edwardian interior was designed by the castle's last owner, William Robert Reid, who was the proprietor of the important Edinburgh cabinet making business, Morison & Company. Reid was both a connoisseur and a collector. Between 1903, when he purchased Lauriston and his death in 1919, he filled the castle with superb collections of eighteenth century Italian furniture (principally from Naples and Sicily), Derbyshire Blue John, Sheffield Plate, Caucasion carpets and rugs, clocks, porcelain, Mezzotint prints, tapestries, textiles and items of decorative art. There are also many items of fine furniture made by Morison & Co during the 1890s. The Castle is preserved exactly as left in 1926 at the death of Reid's widow, Margaret Johnston Reid, who gave it in Trust to the Nation. To enter Lauriston is to step across a threshold in time into the home of a wealthy and cultured family in the years before the Great War. **Located:** Cramond Road South, Davidson's Mains some three miles from the centre of Edinburgh. **Open:** April–October daily, except Friday, 11–1pm, 2–5pm, November–March, Saturday and Sunday only 2–4pm. Visit is by guided tour only. Tours take about 50 minutes. Last admission 40 minutes before each closing time. **Cost:** Admission charge (concessions available). Tel: 0131 336 2060. Free admission to grounds and car parking.

map 13
G5

MANDERSTON

Duns, TD11 3PP, Berwickshire, Scotland.
Tel: 01361 883 450 Fax: 01361 882 010 (Lord & Lady Palmer)

Manderston, the home of Lord and Lady Palmer is an Edwardian mansion set in 56 acres of formal gardens (Scottish Borders).The only silver staircase in the world, insights into life at the turn of the century both 'upstairs' and 'downstairs'. Formal and woodland gardens, stables, Racing Room, Biscuit Tin Museum, Marble Dairy, lakeside walks. Tearoom serving cream teas on open days and gift shop. **Location:** 12 miles W of Berwick-upon-Tweed. **Open:** 11 May–28 Sept: Thurs & Sun, 2–5pm. Also Mons 29 May & 28 Aug 2–5pm. Group visits any time of year by appointment. **Admission:** Please phone 01361 883450 for details. **Refreshments:** Tearoom serving cream teas on open days. **Conferences:** Available as a corporate and location venue. **E-mail:** palmer@ manderston.demon.co.uk **Internet:** http://www.manderston.demon.co.uk

map 13 J5/6

LENNOXLOVE HOUSE

Haddington, East Lothian, Scotland, EH41 4NZ
Tel: 01620 823 720 Fax: 01620 825 112 (Duke of Hamilton)

Lennoxlove House, home of the Duke of Hamilton, dates from the 14th century and is set in 600 acres of woodland about 20 minutes drive from Edinburgh. The original Tower with its splendid Great Hall was known as Lethington Tower, but later renamed Lennoxlove after Frances Stewart, Duchess of Lennox, a favourite of Charles II. The house is home to the Hamilton Palace collection of furniture, paintings and porcelain as well as historic mementoes of Mary, Queen of Scots, including her silver casket, sapphire ring and a death mask. **Open: House & Grounds:** Easter Weekend-end Oct. Guided tours – Wed, (Most Saturdays – please check), Sun, 2–4.30pm. Private groups by arrangement. **Refreshments:** Garden Cafe serves morning coffee, lunch and afternoon tea. **E-mail:** lennoxlove@compuserve.com

MAYBOLE CASTLE

High Street, Maybole, Ayrshire KA19 7BX
Tel: 01655 883765 (The Trustees of The Seventh Marquess of Ailsa)

Historic 16th century town house of the Kennedy family. **Location:** High Street, Maybole on A77. **Open:** May–Sept. Sun, 3–4pm. At other times by appointment. **Admission:** Adult £2, concs. £1.

map 10 B2

NEWLISTON

Kirkliston, West Lothian, Scotland EH29 9EB
Tel: 0131 333 3231 Fax: 0131 335 3596 (Mrs Caroline Maclachlan)

Late Robert Adam house. Costumes on display. 18th century designed landscape, rhododendrons, azaleas and water features. On Sundays tea is in the Edinburgh Cookery School in the William Adam Coach House. Also on Sundays there is a ride-on steam model railway from 2–5pm. An inventory of Chattels not on public display can be inspected and such chattels can be viewed by request when the house is open to the public. **Location:** 8 miles west of Edinburgh, 3 miles south of the Forth Road Bridge, off the B800. **Open:** 3 May–4 June: Wed–Sun, 2–6pm. Also by appointment. **Admission:** Adults £1.50, child/OAP 50p, students £1.

map 13 G5

RAMMERSCALES

Lockerbie, Dumfriesshire, Scotland, DG11 1LD
Tel: 01387 811 988 Fax: 01387 810 940
(M. A. Bell Macdonald)

Georgian manor house dated 1760 set on high ground with fine views over Annandale. Pleasant policies and a typical walled garden of the period. There are Jacobite relics and links with Flora Macdonald retained in the family. There is also a collection of works by modern artists. **Location:** 5 miles W of Lockerbie (M6/A74). 2.5 miles S of Lochmaben on B7020. **Open:** Last week of July–first 3 weeks of August (except Sats) 2–5pm. **Admission:** £5.

map 10 D3

MELLERSTAIN HOUSE

Gordon, Berwickshire, Borders, Scotland, TD3 6LG
Tel: 01573 410 225 Fax: 01573 410636 (The Mellerstain Trust)

Scotland's famous Adam mansion. Beautifully decorated and furnished interiors. Terraced gardens and lake. Gift shop. **Location:** 9 miles NE of Melrose. 7 miles NW of Kelso. 37 miles SE of Edinburgh. **Open:** 21 April–30 Sept, daily except Sats. 12.30–5pm. (Last admission 4.30pm). Groups at other times by appointment. **Admission:** Adults £4.50, seniors £3.50, child £2.00. Groups (20+) £3.50 prior booking required. Apply Administrator. Free parking. **Refreshments:** Tearooms. **Events/Exhibitions:** 4 June: Vintage Car Rally. Permanent exhibition of Antique Dolls and Toys. Wheelchair access to principal rooms. **E-mail:** mellerstain.house@virgin.net **Internet:** http://muses.calligrafix.co.uk/mellerstain

map 13 J6

PAXTON HOUSE & COUNTRY PARK

Paxton, Nr Berwick upon Tweed, Scottish Borders TD15 1SZ
Tel: 01289 386291 Fax: 01289 386660 (The Paxton Trust)

Award-winning 18th century Palladian Country House built in 1758 to the design of John and James Adam for a Prussian Princess. The largest Picture Gallery in a Scottish Country House, an outstation for the National Galleries of Scotland plus the greatest collection of Chippendale Furniture in Scotland. 80 acres of woodland, parkland, gardens and riverside walks include picnic areas, adventure playground, croquet, children's 'nature detective trails', highland cattle, shetland ponies and an observation hide from which you can watch the red squirrels. **Location:** Just 4 miles from the A1 Berwick upon Tweed bypass. **Open:** Daily 1 Apr–31 Oct, House 11.15–5pm, last tour 4.15pm. Shops, Tearoom and Exhibitions, 10–5pm, Grounds 10–Sunset. **Admission:** Adults £5, children £2.50. **E-mail:** info@paxtonhouse.com **Internet:** www.paxtonhouse.com

map 13 K6

ROSSLYN CHAPEL

Rosslyn Chapel Trust, Roslin, Midlothian EH25 9PU
Tel: 0131 440 2159 Fax: 0131 440 1979 (The Earl of Rosslyn)

This most remarkable of churches was founded in 1446 by William St Clair, Prince of Orkney. Set in the woods of Roslin Glen and overlooking the River Esk, the Chapel is renowned for its richly carved interior and world famous apprentice pillar. Visitors to the chapel can enjoy a walk in some of Scotland's most romantic scenery. As Sir Walter Scott wrote: 'A morning of leisure can scarcely be anywhere more delightfully spent than in the woods of Rosslyn'. The chapel is available for weddings throughout the year. **Location:** OS Ref. NT275 630. 6m S of Edinburgh off A701. Follow B7006. **Open:** All year: Mon–Sat 10–5pm. Sun 12–4.45pm.

ROYAL BOTANIC GARDEN

20a Inverleith Row, Edinburgh EH3 5LR
Tel: 0131 552 7171 Fax: 0131 552 0382

Scotland's premier garden. Discover the wonders of the plant kingdom in over 70 acres of beautifully landscaped grounds including the world famous Rock Garden, the Pringle Chinese Collection and the amazing Glasshouse Experience featuring Britain's tallest palmhouse. **Location:** Off A902, 1 mile north of the city centre. **Open:** Daily. January & November: 9.30–4pm. February & October: 9.30–5pm. March & September: 9.30–6pm. April–August: 9.30–7pm. **Admission:** Free, donations welcome.

SORN CASTLE

Sorn, Mauchline, Ayrshire.
Tel: Cluttons 01505 612 124 (R. G. McIntyre's Trust)

Dating from 14th century, the Castle stands on a cliff on the River Ayr. The 18th and 19th century additions are of the same pink sandstone quarried from the river banks. The woodlands and grounds were laid out in the 18th century with fine hardwood trees, rhododendrons and azaleas. The Castle is essentially a family home with fine examples of Scottish paintings and artefacts. **Location:** 4 miles E of Mauchline, on B743. **Open:** Castle: Sat 15 July–12 Aug, 2–4pm or by appointment. Grounds: 1 Apr–30 Oct. **Admission:** Adults £3.50.

map 12 E6

THE TOWER OF HALLBAR

Braidwood Road, Braidwood, Lanarkshire, Scotland
Tel: 020 7930 8030 Fax: 020 7930 2295 (The Vivat Trust)

A sixteenth-century defensive tower and Bothy built in response to the 1535 Act of Parliament, advising landlords to construct a tower, 30 foot square to protect themselves from the lawlessness of the Border reivers. Converted into self-catering holiday accommodation and decorated in keeping with its history, by The Vivat Trust, Hallbar sleeps up to seven people, including facilities for a disabled person and their carer. **Location:** 45 minutes outside Glasgow, on B7056 in Braidwood. **Open:** Every Saturday afternoon 2–3pm year round, by appointment, and for four Open Days a year. **Admission:** Free.

map 13 F6

YESTER HOUSE

Gifford, East Lothian EH41 4JH
Tel: 01620 810241 Fax: 01620 810650 (Francis Menotti)

Splendid neoclassical House designed by James Smith, set on the edge of the Lammermuir Hills. For centuries the seat of the Marquesses of Tweedale. Fine 18th century interiors by William and Robert Adam, including the Great Saloon which is a perfect example of their style. Formal gardens were laid out in the 17th century and provide a beautiful natural setting to this day. The House has been extensively restored and sumptuously furnished by the current owner. **Open:** House and Chapel: 30 & 31 Oct, 2–5pm. **Admission:** House & Garden: Adults £4, children £1.50, OAPs £2.50. Garden only £1. Chapel only £1.

map 13 H5

TRAQUAIR HOUSE

Innerleithen, Peeblesshire, Scotland EH44 6PW
Tel: 01896 830 323 Fax: 01896 830 639 (Mrs F. Maxwell Stuart)

Traquair is Scotland's oldest inhabited and most romantic house, spanning over 1000 years of Scottish history. Once a pleasure ground for Scottish kings in times of peace, then a refuge for Catholic priests in times of terror, the Stuarts of Traquair supported Mary, Queen of Scots and the Jacobite cause without counting the cost. Imprisoned, tried and isolated for their beliefs, their home, untouched by time, reflects the tranquillity of their family life. In one of the 'modern' wings (completed in 1680) visitors can also see an 18th century working brewery, which was resurrected by the 20th Laird and now produces the world renowned Traquair House Ale. In the grounds there is also a brewery museum with shop, maze, craft workshops, 1745 Cottage Restaurant and extensive woodland walks. **Open:** 22 April–31 Oct, daily. 12.30–5.30pm. Jun–Aug, 10.30–5.30pm. **E-mail:** enquiries@ traquair.co.uk **Website:** www.traquair.co.uk

map 13
H6

THIRLESTANE CASTLE

Lauder, Berwickshire, Scottish Borders TD2 6RU
Tel: 01578 722 430 Fax: 01578 722 761 (Thirlestane Castle Trust)

One of the seven 'Great Houses of Scotland', Thirlestane was the seat of the Earls and Duke of Lauderdale. It has unsurpassed 17th century ceilings, a restored picture collection, Maitland family treasures, historic toys and a country life exhibition. Woodland picnic tables, tearoom and gift shop. **Location:** Off A68 at Lauder, 28 miles south of Edinburgh. **Open:** 21 Apr–31 Oct Daily except Sat 11–5pm. Last admission 4.15pm each open day. **Admission:** Adults £5. Family (parents and own school age children) £12. Grounds only £1.50. Party discounts available, also booked tours at other times by arrangement. Free parking. Visit us on the World Wide Web at www.great–houses– scotland.co.uk **E-mail:** thirlestane@great–houses–scotland.co.uk

map 13
H6

WINTON HOUSE

Pencaitland, Tranent, East Lothian, Scotland EH34 5AT
Tel: 01620 824986 Fax: 01620 823961 (The Winton Trust)

A masterpiece of the Scottish Renaissance with famous stone twisted chimneys and magnificent plaster ceilings. A family home, still after 500 years with many treasures inside, including paintings by some of Scotland's most notable artists, fine furniture and a family exhibition of costumes and photographs. Specimen trees, terraced gardens and café. **Location:** OS Ref NT439695. 14 miles SE of Edinburgh off the A1 at Tranent. Lodge gates S of New Winton (B6355). **Open:** Second and third weekends in April, May and Sept; 12noon–5pm other times by prior arrangement. **Admission:** Adult £4.50, child £2, conc £3.80. Groups should pre book (10+). **Email:** email@wintonhouse.co.uk

map 13
H5

BALCARRES

Colinsburgh, Fife, Scotland
Tel: 01333 340 206 (Balcarres Trust)

16th century house with 19th century additions by Burn and Bryce. Woodland and terraced garden. **Location:** ½ mile N of Colinsburgh. **Open:** Woodlands and Lower Garden: 7–23 Feb & 28 Mar–17 June, daily except Suns. West Garden: 5–17 Jun, daily except Suns. 2–5pm. House not open except by written appointment and 17 Apr–2 May **Admission:** Gardens only – Adults £2.50, children £1.50. House – £4.50. Car park. Suitable for disabled persons, no wheelchairs provided.

map 13
H4

BOLFRACKS GARDEN

Aberfeldy, Perthshire PH15 2EX
Tel: 01887 820207 (M. J. D. Hutchison)

The Garden, approximately four acres, overlooks the upper Tay Valley with splendid views over the river to the hills beyond. A walled garden of an acre contains a wide variety of flowering trees, shrubs and perennials including a good collection of old fashioned rambler and shrub roses. A less formal garden with a burn and lots of peat wall arrangements contains very many ericaceous plants including rhododendrons particularly dwarf, heaths, dwarf conifers. Primulas, moeonopisis, celmisias and gentians all do well. Masses of bulbs in spring and good autumn colour. **Open:** Apr–Oct, 10–6pm. **Admission** £2.50.

map 13
F3

BLAIR CASTLE

Blair Atholl, Pitlochry, Perthshire, Scotland PH18 5TI
Tel: 01796 481 207 Fax: 01796 481 487

Scotland's most visited historic house is home of the Atholl Highlanders, Britain's only private army. The Castle boasts 30 fascinating rooms containing a unique collection of beautiful furniture, fine paintings, arms and armour, china, costumes, lace and other treasures. Explore extensive grounds with walks, nature trails, deer park and enjoy the rare wildlife that exists in its natural habitat. 18th century walled garden restoration project. **Location:** 8 miles NW of Pitlochry, off A9. **Station:** Blair Atholl (half a mile). **Open:** Castle & Grounds: 1 Apr–26 Oct, daily 10–6pm. Last admission 5pm. **Admission:** Castle: Adults £6, children £4, Senior Citizens £5. Grounds £2, children £1. Family tickets. Reduced rates and guided tours for parties by prior arrangements.

map 13
F2

BRAEMAR CASTLE

Braemar, Grampian, AB35 5XR, Scotland.
Tel/Fax:013397 41219 (Braemer Castle)

Built in 1628 by the Earl of Mar. Attacked and burned by the celebrated Black Colonel (John Farquharson of Inverey) in 1689. Repaired by the government and garrisoned with English troops after the rising of 1745. Later transformed by the Farquharsons of Invercauld, who had purchased it in 1732, into a fully furnished private residence of unusual charm. L-plan castle of fairy tale proportions, with round central tower and spiral staircase. Barrel-vaulted ceilings, massive iron 'Yett' and underground pit (prison). Remarkable star-shaped defensive curtain wall. Much valuable furniture, paintings and items of Scottish historical interest. **Location:** Half a mile NE of Braemar on A93. **Open:** Easter-late Oct, daily (except Fri), 10–6pm. **Admission:** Charges apply. **E-mail:** invercauld@aol.com

CASTLE MENZIES

Weem, Aberfeldy, PH15 2JD, Perthshire, Scotland.
Tel: 01887 820 982 (Menzies Charitable Trust)

Magnificent example of a 16th century 'Z' plan fortified house, seat of Chiefs of Clan Menzies for over 400 years and now nearing completion of its restoration from an empty ruin. It was involved in the turbulent history of the Central Highlands. 'Bonnie Prince Charlie' was given hospitality here on his way north to Culloden in 1746. Visitors can explore the whole of the 16th century building, together with part of the 19th century addition. Small clan museum and gift shop. **Location:** 1.5 miles from Aberfeldy, on B846. **Open:** 1 Apr–14 Oct 2000, Mon-Sat, 10.30–5pm. Sun, 2–5pm. Last admission 4.30pm. **Admission:** Adult £3, OAPs £2.50, children £1.50 (reduction for groups). **Refreshments:** Tearoom.

map 13
F3

DRUMMOND CASTLE GARDENS

Muthill Crieff, Tayside, Scotland, PH5 2AA
Tel: 01764 681 257/433 Fax: 01764 681 550

The gardens of Drummond Castle, first laid out in the early 17th century by John Drummond, 2nd Earl of Perth, are said to be among the finest formal gardens in Europe. A spectacular view can be obtained from the upper terrace, overlooking a magnificent example of an early Victorian parterre in the form of a St. Andrew's Cross. The gardens you see today were renewed by Phyllis Astor in the early 1950's, preserving features such as the ancient yew hedges and the copper beech trees planted by Queen Victoria to commemorate her visit in 1842. The multi-faceted sundial by John Mylne, Master Mason to Charles I, has been the centrepiece since 1630. The gardens recently featured in United Artists 'Rob Roy'. **Location:** Entrance 2 miles S of Crieff, on A822 Muthill Road. **Open:** May–Oct & Easter Weekend, daily, 2–6pm. (Last admission 5pm). **Admission:** Adults £3, children £1.50, OAPs £2. **E-mail:** thegardens@drummondcastle.sol.co.uk

map 13 F4

GLAMIS CASTLE

Glamis, Angus, Scotland DD8 1RJ
Tel: 01307 840 393 Fax: 01307 840 733

Glamis Castle is the family home of the Earls of Strathmore and Kinghorne and has been a royal residence since 1372. It is the childhood home of Her Majesty Queen Elizabeth The Queen Mother, the birthplace of Her Royal Highness The Princess Margaret and the legendary setting of Shakespeare's play 'Macbeth'. The Castle, a five-storey 'L' shaped tower block, was originally a royal hunting lodge. It was remodelled in the 17th century and is built of pink sandstone. It contains the Great Hall, with its magnificent plasterwork ceiling dated 1621, a beautiful family Chapel constructed inside the Castle in 1688 and the Royal Apartments which have been used by Her Majesty Queen Elizabeth The Queen Mother. Glamis provides a majestic setting for corporate hospitality. **Location:** Glamis, 6 miles West of Forfar, A94. **Open:** 2 Apr–12 Nov, daily 10.30–5.30pm (July & Aug from 10am). Last admission 4.45pm. Nov 10.30–4pm. **Admission:** Adults £6, children (5–16) £3, OAPs £4.50, family £16.50. Grounds only: Adults £3, children/OAP £1.50. Party rates (min 20), adult £5, OAP £4, child £2.50. **Facilities:** Licensed self-service restaurant, seating for 96. Picnic area, four shops, magnificent grounds, garden, nature trail and Pinetum. Ample parking. **E-mail:** glamis@great-houses–scotland.co.uk

map 13 H3

BRANKLYN GARDEN

Dundee Road, Perth PH2 7BB
Tel: 01738 625535 (The National Trust for Scotland)

Small but magnificent garden with an impressive collection of rare and unusual plants. Among the most breathtaking is the Himalayan blue poppy, *Meconopsis x sheldonii*. There is a rock garden with purple maple and the rare golden *Cedrus*. Seasonal highlights in May and June are the alpines and rhododendrons and in autumn the fiery red *Acer palmatum*. **Location:** On A85 at 116 Dundee Road, Perth. **Open:** Daily, 9.30–Sunset. 1 Mar–31 Oct. **Admission:** Charges apply.

MEGGINCH CASTLE GARDENS

Megginch Castle, Errol, Perthshire PH2 7SW
Tel: 01821 642222 Fax: 01821 642708 (Lady Strange & Capt Drummond of Megginch)

Gardens of 15th century Castle, 1000 year old yews, walled kitchen garden and 'Astrological Garden'. 19th century parterre, flower borders, rose garden, lilacs, daffodils, rhododendrons and topiary. **Location:** 8 miles east of Perth on A90. **Open:** Apr–Oct on Weds, Aug every day 2–5pm. **Admission:** Adult £2.50, child £1.

map 13
G3

STOBHALL

Guildtown, Perthshire, Scotland, (Earl of Perth)
Tel: 01738 451111

Gardens and policies. Chapel with 17th century painted ceiling. **Location:** 8 miles N of Perth on A93. **Open:** Mid May–mid June, 1–5pm. **Admission:** Adults £2, children £1.

map 13
G3

WHITHORN PRIORY

Whithorn
Tel:01988 500508 (Historic Scotland)

Part of the 'Whithorn Cradle of Christianity' attraction. The site of the first Christian church in Scotland. Founded as 'Canadian Casa' by Sir Ninian in the early 5th century it later became the cathedral church of Galloway. In the museum is a fine collection of early Christian stones including the Monreith Cross. Visitor Centre and archaeological dig. **Location:** At Whithorn on the A746. **Open:** Please phone for details, 01988 500700. **Admission:** Joint ticket by Whithorn Trust gives entry to the Priory, Priory museum and archaeological dig.

SCONE PALACE

Scone, Perth, PH2 6BD, Perthshire.
Tel: 01738 552300 (The Earl of Mansfield) Fax: 01738 552588

Situated 2 miles outside Perth, Scone was the ancient crowning place of the Kings of Scotland and the home of the Stone of Destiny. The present Palace was remodelled in the early nineteenth century, using the structure of the 1580 Palace and remains the home of the Earl and Countess of Mansfield. The State Rooms house unique collections of ivories, paintings, clocks, furniture, porcelain and Vernis Martin. The grounds contain magnificent collections of shrubs, the Murray Star Tartan Maze and woodland walks through the famed pinetum; many species were first introduced by David Douglas (of Douglas Fir fame).

The magnificence of the Palace and its contents are complemented by an attractive gift shop, restaurants and adventure playground. Scone is ideal for any family visit and can also provide a exciting venue for corporate and incentive hospitality, both in the Palace or outside in the grounds or Parklands running down to the River Tay. **Open:** 7 Apr–23 Oct, 9.30–5.15pm (last admission 4.45pm). **Admission:** Adults £5.60, children £3.30, OAP/students £4.80, family £17. Groups (20+): Adults £5.10, children £2.80, OAP/students £4.40. **E-mail:** sconepalace@cqm.co.uk **Internet:** www.scone–palace.co.uk

map 13
G3

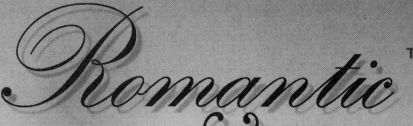

Romantic & HISTORIC

DUNVEGAN CASTLE

WELCOME TO THE ISLE OF SKYE

THE HOME OF THE CHIEFS OF MACLEOD FOR NEARLY 800 YEARS

*Any visit to this enchanted Isle must be deemed incomplete
without savouring the wealth of history offered by Dunvegan Castle.*

LICENSED RESTAURANT	CLAN EXHIBITION
TWO CRAFT AND SOUVENIR SHOPS	ITEMS BELONGING TO BONNIE PRINCE CHARLIE
CASTLE WATER GARDENS	LOCH BOAT TRIPS
AUDIO-VISUAL THEATRE	FAMOUS SEAL COLONY
PEDIGREE HIGHLAND CATTLE FOLD	ST KILDA CONNECTION WOOLLEN SHOP
MACLEOD OF DUNVEGAN QUALITY CLOTHES AND KILT SHOP	

OPENING TIMES

Mid March - End October
Castle, Gardens, Craft Shop & Restaurant, Monday - Sunday 10.00am - 5.30pm (last entry into Castle - 5.00pm)
Winter opening: November - Mid March
Castle and Gardens, Monday - Sunday 11.00am - 4.00pm (last entry into Castle at 3.30pm)
Telephone: 01470 521206 Website: http://www.dunvegancastle.com

ARMADALE CASTLE GARDENS & MUSEUM OF THE ISLES

Armadale Castle, Sleat, Isle of Skye, Highland Region IV45 8RS
Tel: 01471 844305 Fax: 01471 844275 (Clan Donald Lands Trust)

The Clan Donald Lands Trust are the custodians of the beautiful 20,000 acre Armadale Estate on the South peninsular of Skye opposite Knoydart and half an hour by car ferry from Mallaig. The 48 acre gardens, surrounded by sea on three sides, are set around the sculptured ruins of Armadale Castle. They are remarkable, due to the warm generally frost-free climate of the West Highlands, with the Gulf Stream allowing these sheltered gardens to flourish with exotic trees, shrubs and flowers. Enjoy a complete experience to Armadale by visiting the Museum of the Isles within the grounds. Our Head Gardener would be delighted to guide small groups on request. **Internet:** www.cland.demon.co.uk

map 14 **B6**

CAWDOR CASTLE

Nairn, Scotland, IV12 5RD (The Dowager Countess Cawdor)
Tel: 01667 404615 Fax: 01667 404674

The most romantic castle in the Highlands. The 14th century keep, fortified in the 15th century and impressive additions, mainly 17th century, form a massive fortress. Gardens, nature trails and splendid grounds. Shakespearean memories of Macbeth. **Location:** S of Nairn on B9090 between Inverness and Nairn. **Station(s):** Nairn (5m) and Inverness (14m). **Open:** 1 May–8 Oct, daily, 10–5.30pm. Last admission 5pm. **Admission:** Adults £5.60, children (5–15) £3, OAPs & disabled £4.60. Groups: Adult (20+) £5.10, children (5–15, 20+) £2.50, family (2 adults & up to 5 children) £16.50. Blind people free. Gardens, grounds & nature trails only: £2.90. **Refreshments:** Licensed restaurant, snack bar. Gift shop, bookshop and wool shop. Picnic area, 9-hole golf course and nature trails. No dogs allowed in Castle or Grounds. **E-mail:** cawdor.castle@btinternet.com

map 15 **F5**

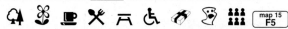

CULLODEN HOUSE HOTEL

Inverness, Inverness-shire, Scotland IV2 7BZ
Tel: 01463 790461 Fax: 01463 792181 (Major R H Gillis/Patricia Davies)

As capital of the Highlands, Inverness increasingly provided metropolitan sophistications and diversions as the town attracted wealthy families from all over the Highlands to settle. The finest of the country houses in the neighbourhood of Inverness still survives, Culloden House, an exquisite Georgian mansion set in open parkland. It was originally a Jacobean castle, where in 1746 Bonnie Prince Charlie requisitioned the building for his headquarters just prior to the tragic battle, the battle which is forever etched into the history books of England and Scotland. The imposing Palladian mansion is set in 40 acres of parkland and gardens on the edge of Inverness, the capital of the Highlands, perfectly positioned for your headquarters of conquest and discovery. The Garden Pavilion, with easy access to the main house, offers seclusion and privacy in four gracious luxury suites, and is an appropriate setting for functions. There are an abundance of visitor attractions within easy reach of the hotel. Arranged championship golf, on-site tennis, croquet, fishing, clay and pheasant shooting, mountain climbing, skiing in season, horse-riding and pony trekking. **Accommodation:** Twenty eight charming bedrooms each uniquely decorated in understated comfort - your private domain with room service just a call away. **E-mail:** info@cullodenhouse.co.uk **Internet:** www.cullodenhouse.co.uk

map 15 **F5**

DUNROBIN CASTLE

Golspie, Sutherland KW10 6SF Scotland
Tel: 01408 633177 Fax: 01408 634081 (The Sutherland Trust)

Dunrobin Castle is the most northerly of Scotland's Great Castles and seat of the Earls of Sutherland (Earldom created c.1235). The keep dates from c.1300 and there are additions from the 17–19th centuries, the biggest being in 1845 when the castle was remodelled by Sir Charles Barry, who had just completed the Houses of Parliament. A serious fire in 1915 caused a lot of damage and gave Sir Robert Lorimer a chance to re-design and re-decorate all the major rooms. The Castle is filled with fine furniture, superb paintings, fine china and family memorabilia. The rooms and corridors are decorated with flowers from the garden which is overlooked by most of them. The Dining room contains the outstanding family silver. The whole building has a friendly, 'lived in' atmosphere. The beautiful gardens were laid out by Barry at the same time as he re-modelled the castle and are of French formal design. In recent years, they have been improved and restored and are one of the few remaining formal gardens in Scotland. The castle and gardens are set next to the sea and there are lovely walks along the beach and the surrounding woodlands. The garden contains an eccentric museum, unlike anything else in the UK. This must be seen, even by those who disapprove of the activities it displays! Regular falconry displays also in the garden. **Location:** OS Ref: NC850 010.50m N of Inverness on A9. 1m NE of Golspie. **Open:** 1 Apr–31 May & 1–15 Oct: Mon–Sat 10.30–4.30pm. Sun 12–4.30pm. Last entry 4pm. 1 Jun–30 Sept; Mon–Sat 10.30–5.30pm. Sun, 12–5.30pm. Last entry 5pm. **Admission:** Adult £5.50, child £4, OAP £4. Groups–Adult £5, child £4, OAP £4. Family (2 adults and 2 children) £16. Open all year round for pre-booked groups. **Refreshments:** Tearooms seating 90. **Events:** 20 Aug Vintage Car Rally. A variety of evening and lunchtime functions can be arranged on request. All functions are accompanied by good quality local music.

map 13
F3

CRAIGSTON CASTLE

Turriff AB5 7PX, Aberdeenshire
Tel: 01888 551228 (William Pratesi Urquhart of Craigston)

Built between 1604–1607 by John Urquhart, Craigston Castle is still owned and lived in, by the Urquhart family. Few changes have been made to the castle's exterior of which the main feature is the sculptured balcony, unique in Scottish architecture. The interior decoration dates mainly from the 19th century but features unique carved wooden panels from the 17th century. The drawing room contains mirrors from the Palace of Versailles. Open by appointment for parties: contact Mrs Morrison on 01888 551640. **Open:** Sat 18 June–Sun 3 July 2000 (excl Mon–Tues) and Sat 27 Aug–Sun 11 Sept (excl Mon–Tues). **Admission:** Adults £3.50, OAPs £2.50, children £1.

map 15 J5

DELGATIE CASTLE

Delgatie, Turriff, Aberdeenshire, Scotland
Tel: 01888 563479 Fax: 01888 563479 (Delgatie Castle Trust)

Delgatie Castle dating from approx. 1030 has been lovingly restored over the last 50 years by the late Capt. and Mrs Hay of Delgatie and is not a museum, but a well loved home. Paintings, armoury and Victorian clothes are on display. It is reputed to have the widest turnpike stair of 97 steps and the original painted ceilings dating 1592/1597 are considered some of the finest in Scotland. Mary Queen of Scots stayed here after the Battle of Corrichie in 1562. The Castle is the official Clan Hay Centre. Pretty tearoom in the old Castle kitchen offers the best in homebaking and meals. **Open:** Daily from the 2 Apr–25 Oct, 10–5pm. **Admission:** Adults £2.50, OAP and children £1.50. Open all year for prebooked tours.

map 15 J5

THE DOUNE OF ROTHIEMURCHUS

Rothiemurchus Estate, By Aviemore, Inverness-shire PH22 1QH.
Tel: 01479 812345 Fax: 01479 811778 (J.P. Grant of Rothiemurchus)

The family home of The Grants of Rothiemurchus was nearly lost as a ruin and has been under an ambitious repair programme since 1975. This exciting project may be visited on selected Mondays throughout the year. Book with the Information Desk for a longer 2 hour "Highland Lady" tour which explores the haunts of Elizabeth Grant of Rothiemurchus, born 1797, author of "Memoirs of a Highland Lady" who vividly described the Doune and its surroundings from the memories of her childhood. **Location:** 2 m S of Aviemore on E bank of Spey river. **Open:** Grounds: May-Aug, Mon 10–12.30pm and 2–4.30pm. Also first Monday of the month in winter. **Admission:** Charges apply. **E-mail:** rothie@enterprise.net **Internet:** www.aviemore.co.uk/rothiemurchus.htm

DOCHFOUR GARDENS

Dochfour, Inverness IV3 8GY
Tel: 01463 861218 Fax: 01463 861366 (Dochfour Estate)

Victorian garden near Inverness, with grassed terraces and panoramic views over Loch Dochfour. Magnificent specimen trees, naturalised daffodils, rhododendrons and azaleas, water garden, extensive yew hedges, walled kitchen garden. 6 miles SW of Inverness on A82 to Fort William. **Open:** Mon–Fri Apr–Sept 10–5pm Garden Walk. **Admission:** Charges apply. Parking free. HOUSE NOT OPEN. Coaches by prior arrangement only.

DUFF HOUSE COUNTRY HOUSE GALLERY

Banff, Banffshire, Scotland, AB45 3SX.
Tel: 01261 818 181 Fax: 01261 818 900

Duff House is one of the most imposing and palatial country houses in Scotland, with a classical façade and a grand staircase leading to the main entrance. It remained in the hands of the Duffs, Dukes of Fife, until 1906 when the family presented the house and park to Banff and Macduff, consigning its contents to the saleroom. Set in acres of parkland, by the banks of River Deveron, Duff House is one of the glories of the North East. **Location:** Banff. 47 miles NE of Aberdeen on A947. **Open:** 1 Apr–31 Oct, daily, 11–5pm. 1 Nov–31 Mar, Thur–Sun, 11–4pm. **Admission:** Charges apply.

DUNROBIN CASTLE

Golspie, Sutherland KW10 6SF Scotland
Tel: 01408 633177 Fax: 01408 634081 (The Sutherland Trust)

Dunrobin Castle is the most northerly of Scotland's Great Castles and seat of the Earls of Sutherland (Earldom created c.1235). The keep dates from c.1300 and there are additions from the 17–19th centuries, the biggest being in 1845 when the castle was remodelled by Sir Charles Barry, who had just completed the Houses of Parliament. A serious fire in 1915 caused a lot of damage and gave Sir Robert Lorimer a chance to re-design and re-decorate all the major rooms. FOR FURTHER DETAILS, OPENING TIMES AND PHOTOGRAPHY, PLEASE TURN TO PAGE 248 & 249.

DUNVEGAN CASTLE

Dunvegan, Isle of Skye Scotland, IV55 8WF
Tel: 01470 521206 Fax: 01470 521205

Any visit to this enchanted Isle must be deemed incomplete without savouring the wealth of history offered by Dunvegan Castle, the home of the Chiefs of Macleod for nearly 800 years. Dunvegan Castle is a Fortress stronghold in an idyllic lochside setting with dramatic scenery where seals play and eagles soar. Other attractions include gardens, craft shops, boat trips, restaurant, loch cruises and pedigree highland cattle. **Location:** Dunvegan Village (1 mile), 23 miles W of Portree on the Isle of Skye. **Open:** Mon 23 Mar–Sat 31 Oct Mon–Sun 10–5.30pm. Last admission 5pm. **Admission:** Castle & Gardens Adults £5, children £2.50, parties/OAPs/students £4.50. Gardens only Adults £3.50, children £2. FOR FURTHER INFORMATION PLEASE SEE ADVERT ON PAGE 246.

FASQUE

Fettercairn, Laurencekirk, AB30 1DN, Kincardineshire,
Tel: 01561 340 202/ 340 569 Fax: 01561 340 569(Charles Gladstone)

Fasque is a spectacular example of a Victorian 'Upstairs-Downstairs' stately home. Bought by Sir John Gladstone in 1829, it was home to William Gladstone, four times Prime Minister, for much of his life. In front of the house red deer roam in the park and behind the hills dramatically towards the Highlands. Inside, very little has changed since Sir John's days. Fasque is not a museum, but rather an unspoilt old family home. Visit the kitchen, laundry, bakery, knives hall and buttery. You'll find a wealth of domestic articles from a bygone age. Climb the famous double cantilever staircase and wander through the magnificent drawing room, library and bedrooms. Explore a Victorian gamekeeper's hut, complete with man trap, or discover our exhibition of William Gladstone memorabilia. Groups and Coach Parties welcome.

map 13 J2

INVERARAY CASTLE

Cherry Park, Inveraray, Argyll, Scotland, PA32 8XE
Tel: 01499 302 203 Fax: 01499 302 421
(Home of the Duke and Duchess of Argyll)

Since the early 15th century Inveraray Castle has been the Headquarters of the Clan Campbell. The present Castle was built in the third quarter of the 18th century by Roger Morris and Robert Mylne. The Great Hall and Armoury, the State Rooms, tapestries, pictures and the 18th century furniture and Old Kitchen are shown. Those interested in Campbell Genealogy and History will find a visit to The Campbell Room especially enjoyable. <u>Location:</u> ¼ mile NE of Inveraray by Loch Fyne. 61 miles NW of Glasgow. <u>Open:</u> 1 Apr–8 Oct.

map 12 D4

MOUNT STUART HOUSE & GARDENS

Mount Stuart, Isle of Bute, Scotland, PA20 9LR
Tel: 01700 503877 Fax: 01700 505313 Internet: www.mountstuart.com

Award winning Mount Stuart, one of Britain's most spectacular High Victorian Gothic houses, is the magnificent architectural fantasy of the 3rd Marquess of Bute (1847–1900) and the Scottish architect Robert Rowand Anderson. The scale and ambition of Mount Stuart is equalled only by Bute's collaboration with William Burges to restore Cardiff Castle and Castell Coch. The profusion of astrological designs, stained glass and marble is breathtaking, and all combine to envelop the visitor in the mystique and history of the house. Fabulous interiors and architectural detail. Set in 300 acres of stunning woodlands, mature Victorian pinetum, arboretum and exotic gardens. Facilities include shop, tearoom, adventure play and picnic areas, audio-visual, assisted wheelchair access, guided tours of house and gardens. Mount Stuart is easily accessible and can be reached by frequent ferry service from Wemyss Bay, Renfrewshire or Colintraive in Argyll. Regular bus service from Rothesay to Mount Stuart. <u>Open:</u> May–Sept, daily except Tue & Thurs. Gardens: 10–5pm, House: 11–4.30pm (Last tour 3.30pm). <u>Admission:</u> Adults: £6, child: £2.50, family: £15. Season: £15. Senior citizen/student/group rates given.

map 12 D6

Ireland

Top: Glin Castle. Left: Mount Usher. Below: Powerscourt

Ireland is fast becoming one of most popular places to visit. For such a tiny island it has a vast history steeped in romanticism, valour, poverty, poetry and music.

From the stark craggy cliffs on the west coast of Galway to the calm running waters of the River Liffey in Dublin, Ireland offers contrasting territory that is both breathtaking and serene. Looking out on the barren lands of Connemara is to view a land still untouched by the modern world.

Music is an integral part of Irish life and can be heard on the streets drifting from the bars – another integral part of Irish life! The joviality and talk in the pubs is mingled with the live music that is played by the locals. It would also serve music lovers who visit Ireland to attend where possible a 'Fleadh' (pronounced 'Fla') which is a festival of music offering the opportunity to find great 'craic' (fun!)

The weather can be contrary but this is a secondary concern when you discover all that Ireland has to offer.

ARDGILLAN VICTORIAN GARDEN

Balbriggan, Co Dublin, Ireland
Tel: 00 353 1 849 2212 Fax: 00 353 1 849 2786

The park consists of 82ha of rolling pasture land, mixed woodland and gardens. The Walled Garden of 1ha is unique in being sub-divided by two free standing walls, one of which has the unusual feature of a series of 20 alcoves for the growing of tender fruits. Each section has a specific theme including a Herb garden, Vegetable Potager, an Irish cottage garden and fruit garden. There is a magnificent Victorian conservatory overlooking the Rose Garden with its wide selection of old and new varieties. **Location:** 30km north of Dublin city. **Open:** All year 10–5pm. Guided tour each Thursday at 3pm during June, July and August. **Admission:** Guided Tours £3.

ANTRIM CASTLE GARDENS

Randalstown Road, Antrim (Antrim Borough Council)
Tel: 01849 428000 Fax: 01849 460 360

Antrim Castle Gardens boasts ownership of one of the earliest examples of an Anglo-Dutch water garden within the British Isles. It contains exceptional examples of ornamental canals, an ancient motte and a parterre garden. The parterre garden has preserved the timeless atmosphere of the 17th century formal garden. It has been planted with fine examples of 17th century plants which were originally used for culinary and medicinal purposes. An interpretative display in the foyer of Clotworthy Arts Centre outlines the process of the gardens' restoration. **Open:** Mon–Fri, 9.30am–9.30pm, Sat 10am–5pm. Jul–Aug, Sun 2–5pm. Admission: Free access to gardens. Guided tours available for groups; rates available on request.

ARDGILLAN CASTLE

Balbriggan, Co Dublin, Ireland
Tel: 00 353 1 849 2212 Fax: 00 353 1 849 2786 (Fingal County Council)

Location: 30km north of Dublin off the N1. **Open:** All year. July & August: daily. 1 Apr–end May & Sept: Tues–Sun & Public Holidays, 11–6pm. 1 Oct–31 Mar: Tues–Sun & Public Holidays, 11–4.30pm. Closed 23 Dec–1 Jan. **Admission:** Castle by guided tour only: Adult £3, concessions £2. Family £6.50. Groups (10+) £2.

BANTRY HOUSE

Bantry, Co. Cork, Ireland
Tel: 00 353 2 750 047 Fax: 00 353 2 750 795 (Egerton Shelswell-White)

Partly Georgian mansion standing at edge of Bantry Bay, with beautiful views. Seat of family of White, formerly Earls of Bantry. Unique collection of tapestries, furniture, etc. Terraces and statuary in the Italian style in the grounds. Restoration work in progress. **Location:** In outskirts of Bantry (1/2 mile). 56 miles SW of Cork. **Open:** Daily, 9–6pm, 1 March–31 Oct. **Admission:** **House & Grounds:** Adults £6, children (up to 14) accompanied by parents free, OAPs £4.50, students

£4. **Grounds only:** £2. **Groups (20+) House & Grounds:** £4. **Refreshments:** Tearoom, Bed & Breakfast and dinner. **Events/Exhibitions:** 1796 Bantry French Armada (permanent exhibition). West Cork Chamber Music Festival 26 June for ten days. **Accommodation:** B&B and dinner. Nine rooms en suite. **Conferences:** Facilities available. Shop.

BIRR CASTLE DEMESNE & IRELAND'S HISTORIC SCIENCE CENTRE

Birr, Co Offaly, Ireland
Tel: 00 353 509 20336 Fax: 00 353 509 21583

Ireland's Historic Science Centre includes demesne, telescope and galleries of discovery. **Admission:** Adult IR£5 or Euros5.70, child IR£2.50 or Euros3.20, senior citizen IR£3.50 or Euros4.45, student IR£3.50 or Euros4.45, Family (2 adults & 2 children) IR£12 or Euros15.20. Guided tours (must be pre-booked) IR£25 or 32. Groups (20+): Adult IR£4 or Euros5, child IR£2.20 or Euros2.80, senior citizen IR£3 or Euros3.80, student IR£2.50 or Euros3.20. **Open:** 9.30–6pm or dusk if earlier. **E-mail:** info@birrcastle.com **Internet:** www.birrcastle.com

map 16
C4

BOTANIC GARDENS

Stranmillis Road, Belfast, Antrim, Northern Ireland
Tel/Fax: 028 90 324902 (Belfast City Council)

The Botanic Gardens are situated in the south of the city adjacent to Queens University. Established in 1828 the gardens house an exquisite Palm House, the earliest example of a curvilinear glass house. The unique Tropical Ravine houses many rare and exotic plants. The magnificent herbaceous borders are reported to be one of the longest examples in Ireland, perfectly situated alongside the famous rose garden which has a wide collection of interesting varieties. **Open:** The gardens open at 8am, closing at sunset. **Admission:** is FREE. Guided Tours are available for a small charge. For information contact 028 90 324902.

map 16
D3

CASTLE COOLE

Enniskillen, Co. Fermanagh, Northern Ireland
Tel: 02866 322690 Fax: 02866 325665

Castle Coole is credited with being the finest neo-classical house in Ireland. Its interior was created by some of the leading craftsmen of the 18th century. Marble chimneys by Westmacott, plasterwork by Rose and scagliola columns by Bartoli. Magnificent state rooms, include the State Bedroom prepared for a visit by George IV. Visitors can also enjoy walks through The Grand Yard, Servants Quarters and view the original Belmore Coach. Gift shop and tearoom available. **Open:** Easter (Good Fri–Easter Tues) Apr, May & Sept: Sat, Sun, Bank Hols 1–6pm; Groups mid-week by appointment. Jun–Aug: daily 1–6pm (except Thurs). Last tour 5.15pm. **Admission:** Car Park: Free. House tours: Adult £3, child £1.50, family £8, adult party £2.50, child party £1.25. **Events:** Coole Fest 2000: Festival of Music, Arts & Heritage 1–4 June. **E-mail:** ucasco@smtp.ntrust.org.uk **Website:** www.nationaltrust.org.uk

map 16
3C

DUBLIN WRITERS MUSEUM

18 Parnell Square, Dublin 1, Ireland
Tel: 00 353 1 872 2077 Fax: 00 353 1 872 2231

The Dublin Writers Museum is located in a splendidly restored 18th century house. It uniquely represents that great body of Irish writers – in prose, poetry and drama – which has contributed so much to the world of literature over the years. **Location:** Dublin city centre – 5 mins. walk from O'Connell St. **Open:** All year except 24/25/26 Dec. Mon–Sat 10–5pm. Sun & Public Hols 11–5pm. Late opening Jun–Aug, Mon–Fri 10–6pm. **Admission:** Adults £3.10, children £1.45, concessions £2.60, family £8.50. Group rates (20+): Adults £2.60, children £1.20, concessions £2.20.

map 16
D4

GLIN CASTLE

Glin, Co Limerick, Ireland
Tel: 00 353 68 34173 Fax: 00 353 68 34364 (Bob Duff)

Experience life as it is lived in an historic Irish castle, home of the Knight of Glin. The 29th Knight of Glin and Madam FitzGerald welcome you to their home. Glin Castle stands proudly in the middle of its 500 acre wooded demesne on the banks of the river Shannon. The toy-fortress like quality is echoed by its three sets of battlemented Gothic folly lodges, one of which is a tea and craft shop. The present Glin Castle which succeeds the medieval ruin in the village of Glin was built in the late 18th century with entertaining in mind. The entrance hall with a screen of Corinthian pillars has a superb neo-classical plaster ceiling and the enfilade of reception rooms are filled with a unique collection of Irish 18th century mahogany furniture. Family portraits and Irish pictures line the walls, and the library bookcase has a secret door leading to the hall and the very rare flying staircase. Formal pleasure grounds surround the castle and magnolia campbell and sophora tetraptera as well as camellias and drifts of daffodils make a splendid spring garden, while other magnificent trees and shrubs come into their own in the summer. Visitors are welcomed for dinner, overnight stays and breakfast. Tours of the castle and garden together with luncheon or dinner can be arranged for groups, but reservation in advance is essential. The castle and gardens are open to the public during May and June from 10–12noon and from 2–4pm. For those who want total privacy, occasional lets of the castle, fully-staffed can also be arranged. **E-mail:** knight@iol.ie

map 16
B5

FERNHILL GARDEN

Sandyford, Co. Dublin, Ireland
Tel: 00 353 12 956 000 (Mrs Sally Walker)

A garden for all seasons, 200 years old in Robinsonion style with over 4,000 species and varieties of trees, shrubs and plants. Dogs not allowed. **Location:** Sandyford, Co. Dublin. **Open:** Mar–Oct, Tue–Sat, 11am–5pm. Sun 2–6pm. **Admission:** Adults £3, Children £1, OAPs £2.

HAMWOOD

Hamwood, Dunboyne, Co Meath
Tel: (01) 8255210 (Major C.R.F. Hamilton)

Situated 3km from Dunboyne on Maynooth Road (beside Ballymacoll Stud). **Open:** House: 1 Mar–31 Aug 2–6pm. Gardens: Open 3rd Sun of each month Mar–Sept 2–6pm. Groups by arrangements. Hamwood is an 18th century house built in the Palladian style in 1779 by Charles Hamilton, wine importer and later Land Agent for the Duke of Leinster. The house was built at a cost of £2,500 with all the timber used in the construction coming from Memel in Russia and was one of the first in Ireland to be roofed with dry slating. The house contains a fine collection of 18th century furniture, mirrors and pictures of historical interest. Hamwood was also the home of Eva and Letitia Hamilton, artists of the 1920–1960 period and now the home of their nephew. The garden is one of the least known in Meath but is among the most fascinating.

THE JAMES JOYCE MUSEUM

The Joyce Tower, Sandycove, Co. Dublin, Ireland
Tel: 00 353 1 280 9265 Fax: 00 353 1 280 9265

The Joyce Tower is one of a series of Martello Towers built to withstand an invasion by Napoleon. James Joyce's brief stay here inspired the opening of his great masterpiece, Ulysses, whose first chapter is set in this very tower. The gun platform and living room are much as he described them in his book. It now houses the James Joyce Museum, a modern exhibition devoted to the life and works of the famous writer. **Location:** Sandycove Point on sea front, 1 mile from Dun Laoghaire. **Station(s):** DART to Sandycove. **Buses:** 8 (to Sandycove). **Open:** Apr–Oct, Mon–Sat, 10–1pm & 2–5pm. Suns and public hols, 2–6pm. **Admission:** Adults £2.70, children £1.40, concessions £2.20, family £7.95. Groups prices (20+): Adults £2.20, children £1.10, concessions £1.90, by prior arrangement.

map 16
D4

KING HOUSE

Boyle, Co Roscommon, Ireland
Tel: 079 63242 Fax: 079 63243 (Roscommon County Council)

This beautifully restored 18th century mansion is architecturally unique as it is the only fully vaulted domestic house in Britain or Ireland. Now open to the public, it allows visitors to discover the world of Gaelic kings, landlords, craftsmen and soldiers. Explore the past of King House, its inhabitants and the region in this fully interactive historical tour which is spread throughout this once home of the Earls of Kingston. **Open:** April–Mid October daily, late October weekends 10am to last admission at 5pm (house closes at 6pm).

map 16
C3

JAPANESE GARDENS & ST FIACHRA'S GARDEN

Tully, Co. Kildare, Ireland
Tel: 00 353 45 521617 Fax: 00 353 45 522964 (Irish National Stud)

(Both gardens are situated in the grounds of The Irish National Stud Farm). The Japanese Gardens were designed between 1906-1910, they symbolise the 'Life of Man' from the Cradle to the Grave. Now almost 100 years later, The Irish National Stud have created an Irish garden to celebrate the Millennium - St Fiachra's Garden. This garden seeks to capture the power of the Irish landscape in its rawest state, that of rock & water. **Location:** 1 mile outside Kildare town. 30 miles from Dublin off the M/N7. Easy access by rail and bus. **Open:** 12 Feb–12 Nov (Thereafter by booking only). **Admission:** which incl. all 3 attractions: Adults £6, students/OAPs £4.50, children (under 12) £3, family (2 adults & 4 children under 12) £14. **Refreshments:** Yum Yum's Restaurant & Craft shop. Recently restored coach & car park.

map 16
D4

KYLEMORE ABBEY & GARDENS

Connemara, Co Galway, Ireland
Tel: 00 353 95 41146 Fax: 00 353 95 41145

Set in the heart of the Connemara mountains is the renowned KYLEMORE ABBEY ESTATE. Its fame to date is derived from its status as a premier tourist attraction, international girls' boarding school, magnificent Gothic church, tranquil surrounds, superb restaurant and one of the finest craft shops in Ireland. The six acre Victorian Walled Garden opened to the public in Spring 1999, while under restoration. FOR FURTHER DETAILS, OPENING TIMES AND PHOTOGRAPHY, PLEASE TURN TO PAGE 225.

LISMORE CASTLE GARDENS

Lismore, Co. Waterford, Ireland
Tel: 00 353 58 54424 Fax: 00 353 58 54896 (Lismore Estates)

Lismore Castle has been the Irish home of the Dukes of Devonshire since 1753 and at one time belonged to Sir Walter Raleigh. The gardens are set in seven acres within the 17th century outer defensive walls and have spectacular views of the castle. There is also a fine collection of specimen magnolias, camellias, rhododendrons and a remarkable yew walk where Edmund Spenser is said to have written the "Faerie Queen". Throughout the open season there is always plenty to see in this fascinating and beautiful garden. **Location:** Lismore, 45 miles W of Waterford. 35 miles NE of Cork (1 hour). **Open:** 22 Apr–15 Oct. **Admission:** Adults £3, children (under 16) £1.50. Reduced rates for groups of 20+: Adults £2.50, children £1.30.

map 16
C6

KYLEMORE ABBEY & GARDENS

Connemara, Co Galway, Ireland
Tel: 00 353 95 41146 Fax: 00 353 95 41145

Set in the heart of the Connemara mountains is the renowned KYLEMORE ABBEY ESTATE. Its fame to date is derived from its status as a premier tourist attraction, international girls' boarding school, magnificent Gothic church, tranquil surrounds, superb restaurant and one of the finest craft shops in Ireland. The six acre Victorian Walled Garden opened to the public in Spring 1999, while under restoration. This garden was the most impressive in Ireland. The walls stretch for over half a mile to enclose: the kitchen garden, the flower garden, gardener's cottage, bothy and the impressive glass (hot) house complex. All of these features and more are being restored in phases over the next few years. The Benedictine Nuns at Kylemore continue to work tirelessly at restoring the estate and opening it to the education and enjoyment of all who visit, carrying on the unique Benedictine tradition, spanning over 1,500 years of warmth and hospitality. A VISIT TO THE WEST OF IRELAND IS NOT COMPLETE WITHOUT VISITING KYLEMORE ABBEY AND GARDEN. **Open:** Abbey, Grounds & Gothic Church: All year (Closed Good Friday and Christmas Week). Shop and Restaurant: Mar–Nov (Closed Good Friday). Garden: Easter–Oct. **E-mail:** enquiries@kylemoreabbey.ie **Internet:** www.kylemoreabbey. com

map 16
B4

MALAHIDE CASTLE

Malahide, Co Dublin
Tel: 00 353 1 846 2184 Fax: 00 353 1 846 2537

Malahide Castle, set on 250 acres of parkland in the pretty seaside town of Malahide, was both a fortress and a private home for nearly 800 years and is an interesting mix of architectural styles. The Talbot family lived here from 1185 to 1973, when the last Lord Talbot died. The house is furnished with beautiful period furniture together with an extensive collection of Irish portrait paintings, mainly from the National Gallery. **Open:** Apr–Oct: Mon–Sat 10–5pm, Sun & Public Hols 11–6pm. Nov–Mar: Mon–Fri 10–5pm, Sat, Sun & Public Hols 2–5pm. Closed for tours daily 12.45–2pm. **Admission:** Adults £3.15, children £1.75, concs £2.65, family £8.75. Group (20+): Adults £2.65, children £1.55, concs £2.20.

map 16 D4

MOUNT USHER

Ashford, Co Wicklow
Tel: 00 353 404 40205/40116 Fax: 00 353 404 40205 (Mrs Madelaine Jay)

Laid out along the banks of the river Vartry, Mount Usher represents the Robinsonian style, i.e. informality and natural design. Trees and shrubs introduced from many parts of the world are planted in harmony with woodland and shade loving plants. The river, with its weirs and waterfalls, is enhanced by attractive suspension bridges from which spectacular views may be enjoyed. The Gardens cover 20 acres and comprise of over 5000 different species of plants, most serving as host to a variety of birds and other wildlife. To the professional gardener, the lover of nature or the casual tourist, a visit to Mount Usher is sure to be a memorable one. **Location:** Ashford, on the main Dublin to Rosslare Road N11, 50km from Dublin. 115km from Rosslare. **Open:** Mid Mar–end Oct. **Admission:** Adults £3.50, OAP, students, child £2.50 (Special group rates for 20+).

map 16 D5

MUCKROSS HOUSE, GARDENS & TRADITIONAL FARMS
INCORPORATING MUCROS CRAFTS CENTRE

National Park, Killarney, Kerry
Tel: 00 353 64 31440 Fax: 00 353 64 33926 (Trustees of Muckross House)

Muckross House is a magnificent Victorian mansion, situated on the shores of Muckross Lake and set amidst the splendid and spectacular landscape of Killarney National Park. The exquisitely furnished rooms portray the lifestyles of the gentry, including Queen Victoria's boudoir and bedroom as it was when she visited in 1861. The Gardens of Muckross are famed for their beauty worldwide. Muckross Traditional Farms is an exciting outdoor representation of the lifestyles and farming traditions of a rural community of the 1930s. Three separate working farms, complete with animals, poultry and traditional farm machinery will help you relive the past when all work was carried out using traditional methods. Muckross Vintage Coach, visitors to the Farms can enjoy a Free trip around the site on a beautiful Vintage Coach. Visit the magnificent newly opened 'Mucros Crafts Centre', with full Restaurant and Craft Shop. **Location:** 3.5m from Killarney, on the Kenmare road. **Open:** Daily, all year. 9–5.30pm, 9–7pm Jul/Aug (Farms Mar–Oct) **Admission:** Adult Ir£4, students Ir£1.60. Group rate for 20+ Ir£3. Family Ir£10. Ditto for Muckross Traditional Farms. Substantial savings on joint tickets. Gardens free. **Website:** www.muckross–house.ie

map 16 B6

NEWBRIDGE HOUSE

Donabate, Co. Dublin, Ireland
Tel: 00 353 1 8436534 Fax: 00 353 1 8462537

This delightful 18th century mansion is set on 350 acres of parkland, 12 miles north of the city centre and boasts one of the finest Georgian interiors in Ireland. The house appears more or less as it did 150 years ago. It was built in 1737, to a design by Richard Castle, for the Archbishop of Dublin and contains elaborate stucco plasterwork by Robert West. The grounds contain a 29 acre traditional farm complete with farmyard animals, a delight to any young visitor and perfect for school tours and large groups. **Open:** Apr–Sept: Tues–Sat 10–5pm, Sun & Public Hols 2–6pm, closed Mons. Oct–Mar: Sat, Sun, Public Hols 2–5pm. Closed for tours daily 1–2pm. Coffee shop remains open **Admission:** Adult £3, children £1.65, concs £2.60, family £8.25. Group (20+): Adult £2.60, children £1.40, concs £2.20.

map 16 D4

NEWMAN HOUSE

85–86 St Stephen's Green, Dublin 2
Tel: 00 353 706 7422 Fax: 00 353 706 7211 (University College Dublin)

Numbers 85 and 86 St Stephen's Green are two of the finest Georgian houses in the city of Dublin. Each house contains a series of spectacular 18th century stucco interiors. By good fortune these remarkable buildings were united in common ownership in the 19th century when they were acquired by the Catholic University of Ireland, the precursor of modern University College Dublin. The building was named in honour of John Henry Newman, the University's first rector. The great English poet Gerard Manley Hopkins spent the last years of his life at Newman House and James Joyce was a student here from 1899–1902. Recently restored to its former grandeur, Newman House offers the visitor a unique combination of visual splendour and evocative literary associations. **Open:** June, July &Aug only, Tues–Fri 12–5pm, Sat 2–5pm, Sun 11–2pm. The rest of the year tours by appointment only.

map 16 D4

POWERSCOURT GARDENS & WATERFALL

Enniskerry, Co. Wicklow, Ireland
Tel: 00 353 204 6000 Fax: 00 353 286 3561

Just 12 miles south of Dublin, in the foothills of the Wicklow Mountains, lies Powerscourt Estate. Its 20 hectares of gardens are famous the world over. It is a sublime blend of formal gardens, sweeping terraces, statuary and ornamental lakes, together with secret hollows, rambling walks, walled gardens and over 200 variations of trees and shrubs. The shell of the 18th century house gutted by fire in 1974 has an innovative new use: incorporating a terrace restaurant overlooking the spectacular gardens, speciality shops and an exhibition on the Estate and Gardens. Powerscourt Waterfall (5km from Gardens) is Ireland's highest. **E-mail:** gardens@powerscourt.ie **Internet:** www.powerscourt.ie

map 16 D4

SEAFORDE GARDENS

Seaforde, Downpatrick, Co. Down, BT30 8PG, Northern Ireland
Tel: (028) 4481 1225 Fax: (028) 4481 1370 (Patrick Forde)

Over 600 trees and shrubs, container grown. Many camellias and rhododendrons. National collection of Eucryphius. Tropical butterfly house with hundreds of free flying butterflies. The 18th century walled gardens and pleasure grounds contain a vast collection of trees and shrubs. Many very rare. Huge rhododendrons. The Hornbeam maze is the oldest in Ireland. **Location:** On A24, Ballynahinch–Newcastle road. **Open:** Easter–end Sept, Mon–Sat 10–5pm. Sun 1–6pm.

map 16 E3

STROKESTOWN PARK HOUSE & GARDENS

Strokestown, Co Roscommon, Ireland
Tel: 00 353 78 33013 Fax: 00 353 78 33712 **E-mail:** info@strokestownpark.ie

Strokestown Park was the home of the Pakenham Mahon family from the 1660's to 1979. The house retains most its original furnishings and is viewed by guided tour. The Famine Museum uses original documents and letters relating to the time of the Famine on the Strokestown Park Estate to explain the history of The Great Irish Famine and to draw parallels with the occurrence of famine in the Developing World today. The 4½ acre walled pleasure garden has been faithfully restored to its original splendour. Home of the longest herbaceous border in Ireland & UK. **Open:** House, gardens & Famine Museum 1 Apr–31 Oct, every day, 11–5.30pm (flexible for groups). **Admission:** Charges apply. Reduced rates for families, senior citizens, unemployed and groups. Parking. Wheelchair access to museum and garden.

map 16 C4

TALBOT BOTANIC GARDEN

Malahide Castle Demesne, Malahide, Co Dublin, Ireland
Tel: 00 353 1 872 7777 Fax: 00 353 1 872 7530

Botanical Garden located within Malahide Demesne, containing over 4,000 species of non ericaceous plants with a comprehensive collection of Southern Hemisphere plants, many rare and unusual. The gardens were largely created by Lord Milo Talbot from 1948 to 1973 and cover an area of 9ha including the Walled Garden of 1.6ha. It includes many tender shrub borders, alpine yard, pond and 7 glasshouses including a most elegant Victorian Conservatory. The collection continues to expand with the addition of new species and varieties. **Location:** 16km north of Dublin city. **Open:** 1 May–30 Sept: Daily 2–5pm. Guided tour Wed at 2pm. Groups by appointment. **Admission:** Adults £2.

map 16 4D

SHANNON HERITAGE 'A COMMON CELTIC PAST'

Central Reservations Bunratty Castle & Folk Park, Bunratty, Co. Clare, Ireland
Tel: 00 353 61 360 788   Fax: 00 353 61 361 020

'A Common Celtic Past' is a concept which links each of the products in the Shannon Heritage portfolio together in a time line. The story which is thereby created brings the visitor into the magic and mystery of the Prehistoric, Celtic, Viking, Anglo Norman, Anglo and native Irish societies starting 5000 years ago and continuing to the present day. Please call 00 353 61 360 788 for further details.

TULLYNALLY CASTLE & GARDENS

Castlepollard, Co. Westmeath, Ireland.
Tel: 00 353 44 61159/61289 Fax: 00 353 44 61856
(Thomas & Valerie Pakenham)

Home of the Pakenhams (later Earls of Longford) since the 17th century. The original house is now incorporated in a huge rambling gothic revival castle. 30 acres of romantic woodland and walled gardens are also open to the public. **Location:** 1.5 miles outside Castlepollard on Granard Road. **Station(s):** Mullingar. **House open:** 15 June–30 July, 2–6pm. Pre-booked groups admitted at other times. **Gardens:** May–August, 2–6pm. **Admission:** House & Gardens: Adults £4.50, children £2.50, groups £4. Gardens only: Adults £3, children £1. **Refreshments:** Tearoom open May–August daily 2–6pm. **E-mail:** tpakenham@tinet.ie

map 16 C4

Channel Islands

With a wealth of wonderful scenery, magnificent coastlines, historic buildings, natural and man-made attractions plus mouthwatering local produce, the Channel Islands provide a memorable destination that is distinctly different.

Guernsey held a particularly enchanting ceremony at the end of last year. The Millennium Eve Carnival began with a true Guernsey 'budloe' style boat burning in St Peter Port Harbour, then a torchlit procession and a magical parade of light and music through the streets of St Peter Port. There was also an Octopussy Big Top, situated on North Beach, with an early evening cabaret, live bands, DJs, sideshows and various artists. At Beau Sejour on the 1st July 2000, a Gala Concert will be held. This will be a fantastic musical event featuring the Guernsey Symphony Orchestra, the Guernsey Choral Society, the Guernsey Sinfonia Chorus and the Guernsey Youth Choir. The groups will all join together for a performance of Beethoven's Symphony No. 9.

The island of Jersey will also hold various musical events between the 6th and 9th of April when the Jazz Festival takes

Above: St. Aubins Harbour, Jersey

place. The Jersey International Food Festival, held between 13th and 21st May 2000, gives visitors the chance to taste the finest local produce and experience the skills of top Jersey Chefs. The Battle of Flowers parade is held on 10th August 2000 and features floats covered in flowers, musicians, dancers and carnival queens.

A fine destination for all the family, the island offers a plethora of fun activities and attractions such as Jersey Zoo. Last year, the zoo celebrated its 40th anniversary as it was founded in 1959 by the celebrated author and naturalist, Gerald Durrell. With over one hundred species including Andean bears, ring-tailed coatis and short-clawed otters, visitors are both treated to an exciting experience and reminded of the diversity of the animal kingdom.

Above: A view of the Bay in Jersey

SAUSMAREZ MANOR - HISTORIC HOUSE, SCULPTURE PARK & SUBTROPICAL GARDEN

St Martin, Guernsey, Channel Islands GY4 6SG
Tel: 01481 235571 Fax: 01481 235572 (Peter de Sausmarez)

Regarded as the finest example of Queen Anne Colonial Architecture in Europe and the first example of American cultural influence in Britain. Built at the bequest of Sir Edmund Andros 1st Governor of New York, 1714 (also Governor of North Carolina, Massachusetts, Virginia, New Jersey and New England etc). Still the seat of the Seigneurs de Sausmarez since C1220. One of only 21 houses in Britain recommended by the Courvoisier Book of the Best in the world and in the top 20 houses as judged by the AA and NPI in '95. Also in the grounds are a lush subtropical woodland garden, a 9 hole par 3 pitch and putt course, petland and the 3rd largest dedicated Dolls House collection in Britain. Regularly used for celebrations, receptions and special horticultural, architectural and artistic visits and conventions.

The remarkable Sculpture Park and Path is set in the Formal Gardens and in and around the small lakes and the subtropical woodland amongst the bamboo groves, Tree Ferns, Lilies, Hibiscus, Magnolias, 320 Camellias, Rhododendrons, Fuchsias, Giant Echiums, Cyclamen and Banana Trees. The Sculpture Park is regarded by the 70 or so exhibitors as the most beautiful setting they have seen, where the 180 pieces in a constantly changing permanent exhibition sit so happily. The work that is bought is sent all over the world and are constantly having to be replaced. The Sculptors are members of the Royal Society of British Sculptors and the Society of Portrait Sculptors augmented by French, German, Italian, Irish and Channel Island artists. **Internet:** www.guernsey.org/sausmarez

map 3 H6

Belgium

If you happen to doze off and miss your stop as the Eurostar gently rolls along to Paris, then you could wake up in the neighbouring land of Belgium. Whilst France may be renowned for its many vintages of wine, here the preferred beverage is of a more golden hue and is produced in the many breweries across the country. North of Brussels, Antwerp was nominated as the Cultural Capital of Europe in 1993. It may be more renowned for its artistic associations, however, the city is home to a number of beers, such as the local tipple, De Koninck. Made from malt, without the addition of maize or other brewing sugars, the beer is widely-consumed as an everyday drink. A strong, dark beer is produced 30 kilometres away in the village of Meer. Poorter is a top-fermenting beer, bottled to look like Flemish gin (genever) and dedicated to the community of Hoogstraten.

The Westmalle Abbey is situated in the village of Malle and the monastery is a self-contained community dating from

around 1900. Real Trappist beers such as the dubbel are produced here. With its dark malt and sugary characteristics, it is chestnut in colour with exotic hints of banana and passion fruit.

The perfect place to sample one of these brews is by one of the terraces in Brussels' convivial 'Grand-Place'. Set in the capital city, the market place is one of the most enchanting town squares in Europe and has attracted the admiration of writers such as Victor Hugo and Charles Baudelaire. With its impressive Town Hall and attractive set of Guild Houses, this is an ideal place to relax with a hot 'gaufre' (waffle) and admire the fine architecture.

Belgium

CASTLES OF AIGREMONT & WARFUSEE

Aigremont – Les Awirs, 4400 Flemalle, Belgium   **Warfusee** – 4470 St Georges s/Meuse, Belgium
Tel: 00 32 (0)4 336 1687 Fax: 00 32 (0)4 337 0801 (Mme Renard-Ortmans)

Château D'Aigremont: Aigremont lies on the river Meuse and was built in 1715 by a wealthy canon. The house features classic architecture of the Mosane region and terraced gardens. The interior is beautifully decorated with remarkable examples of eighteenth century panelling and a collection of paintings and trompe l'oeil . There is also a collection of furniture, tapestries, paintings, painted ivory miniatures and small wooden objects from Spa. Meals and teas held within the rooms of the house (Groups only by pre-booking). **Location:** On Liege-Namur motorway (E42), exit 4, towards Flemalle, drive 2km and take signposted route to the right. **Open:** 1 April to 31 October, Sundays 10–12noon, and 2–6pm. 1st July to 31st August: every day except Monday. OPEN THROUGHOUT THE YEAR TO GROUPS BY PRIOR ARRANGEMENT.

Château De Warfusee: A major part of Wallonie's heritage. One of the most beautiful buildings in the Mosane region, built in 1754 by the architect Jean Gilles Jacob. Former residence of the prince-bishop Charles Nicolas d'Oultremont, the rooms at Warfusee remain decorated as they were at the time. Magnificent rooms decorated with tapestries. Also features a collection of furniture, paintings, porcelain, silverware, bookshelves and family treasures. The house is still occupied by the same family to this day. A superb park surrounds the house. After your visit, it is possible to have lunch in the rooms at Aigremont house. **Location:** Between Liege and Huy, on the E42 motorway. **Open:** Throughout the year by prior arrangement only for groups (min 25 people). Guided tours. Closed on Sundays.

map 261
1

CHATEAU-FORT (CASTLE OF BOUILLON)

Bte Postale 13, B6830 Bouillon, Belgium
Tel: 00 32 61 466 257 Fax: 00 32 61 468 285

The most interesting feudal castle in Belgium, this fortress probably goes back to 8C, but the first records date from 988. Its existence was made immortal by heroic Godfrey of Bouillon, leader of the First Crusade in 1096 and proclaimed King of Jerusalem. **Open:** Jan, Feb, Dec weekdays 1–5pm, weekends 10–5pm. Mar, Oct, Nov, 10–5pm. Apr–Jun, Sep, 10–6pm. Jul & Aug 9.30–7pm on Mon and Thurs. 9.30–10pm the other days. During the Christmas holidays and Spring holiday, 10–5pm weather permitting. Closed 25 Dec and 1 Jan. Possibility to combine with the museums and the archeoscope. **Admission:** Adult BF150, child BF80. Seniorcard BF140 . Studentcard BF120. Groups (20 pers.): Adult BF130, child (6–12yrs) BF70, student (13–18yrs) BF100. English guide BF30. **Events:** Night visit of the castle by torch. BF150 & BF70 for compulsory torch.

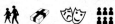

map 261
2

BURG REULAND

4790 Burg Reuland, Belgium
Tel: 00 32 80 32 97 12 Fax: 00 32 80 42 00 46 (Ministère des Travaux Publics)

This solid fortress, the impressive ruins of which dominate the village of the same name, was undoubtedly the work of one of the great heroes of the Middle Ages, John the Blind, count of Luxembourg and King of Bohemia, who died in the Battle of Crécy in 1346, giving his three-feathered crest and motto to the prince of Wales, who bears it to this day. Numerous Rhenish families inherited the property until the local authorities acquired it; it stood in ruins, after it had been damaged in successive wars and had been used as a stone quarry in the 19th century. Today, the castle has regained its former dignity. **Open:** July, Aug and Sept: daily 11–6pm. Open other school holidays and bank holidays 11–5pm. **Admission:** Free.

map 261
3

CHÂTEAU DE CORROY-LE-CHATEAU

Rue du Chateau de Corroy, 5032 Gembloux, Namur
Tel: 00 32 81 63 3232 Fax: 00 32 81 63 33 75 (Marquesses of Trazegnies)

Corry-le-Chateau represents the most impressive 13th century open-country stronghold in Belgium. It was built by the Counts of Vianden to defend the south of the Duchy of Brabant. This fortress has passed down by succession, from the Sponheim, Bavarian and Nassau families, to the Marquesses of Trazegnies who currently live there. The interior has been perfectly restored, and contains a spectacular neo-gothic hall, a chapel dating from 1270, salons featuring canvas paintings and numerous family belongings. **Location:** 5km West of Gembloux, N29. **Open:** Weekends and holidays from 29 Apr–1 Oct, from 10–12pm, and from 2–6pm. **Admission:** Adults 150BF, children (aged 6–10) 80BF, OAPs (groups) 100BF. **Events:** Music festival and summer theatre.

map 261
4

CHÂTEAU FORT ECAUSSINNES LALAING

1, rue de Seneffe–B7191 Ecaussinnes Lalaing, Belgium
Tel & Fax: 00 32 67 44 24 90

From the 11th and 12th century, transformed into a residence in the 15th century, this castle preserves the memory of the family of the counts van der Burch, who lived there from 1624 to 1854. Furnished rooms: grand salon, bedroom, oratory. Medieval part: armoury, ancient kitchen, chapel, dungeon. Collections: portraits of the counts van der Burch; paintings, sculptures, glasses, porcelain, furniture, ancient weapons. **Location:** 7km from exit 20 on E19 (direction Ronquieres). **Open:** 10–12pm, 2–6pm. 1 Apr–1 Nov–weekends and holidays. Jul–Aug, everyday except Tues and Weds. Groups by appointment 1 Apr–2 Nov (guided tours on request).

map 261
5

CHÂTEAU DE HEX

Kasteel Hex, B-3870 Heers-Heks, Belgium
Tel: 00 32 12 74 73 41 Fax: 00 32 12 74 49 87 (Count & Countess G. d'Ursel)

The Château de Hex was built in the 18th century on a beautiful natural site. It was then surrounded by 12 acres of formal gardens set in a 150 acre English-style park. A collection of old and botanical roses - is of particular interest. This collection is the fruit of the never-ending efforts and joy of the late Countess Michel d'Ursel. The vegetable garden, where a wide variety of fruit and vegetables are still grown, includes a vegetable storage-cellar which is still operated using traditional methods. Every year the gardens are open to the public. **Open:** 2nd W/end in June: Festival of Roses 10–5pm (9, 10, 11 June). 3rd W/end in Sept: Festival of Fruit & Vegetables 10–5pm (16–17 Sept). Guided tours, from Apr–Sept, except in Aug, upon written request, weekdays only, min 20 people. **Admission:** BF300. **E-mail:** hex@ping.be **Website:** www.hex.be

map 261
6

CHATEAU DE MODAVE

B-4577 Modave, Belgium
Tel: 00 32 85 411 369 Fax: 00 32 85 412 676

Dating back to 13C, the castle owes its architectural appearance to the restoration by Count de Marchin from 1652–1673. Modave had many distinguished owners, before it was bought in 1941 by the 'Compagnie Intercommunale Bruxelloise des Eaux', in order to protect the impounded water. Twenty richly decorated and furnished rooms are open to the public and include remarkable ceilings, stucco works by Jean-Christian Hansche, sculptures, paintings, Brussels tapestries and 18C furniture. In 1667 Rennequin Sualem built the hydraulic wheel that was used as a pattern for the machine at Marly, bringing the water from the Seine to Versailles Palace. This technical achievement is illustrated in one of the rooms with several documents, plans and an accurate replica of the wheel, made to scale. **Open:** 1 Apr–15 Nov, 9–6pm. 16 Nov–31 Mar, by appointment.

map 261
7

MONCEAU-SUR-SAMBRE

Charleroi, Belgium
Tel: 00 32 71 32 11 23 (Ville de Charleroi)

Although its origins go back a long way, the château of Monceau is essentially the work of two families: the counts of Hamal, who built the main building in the early 17th century and their heirs, the princes of Gavre, who added a wing to it in the late 18th century, during the last years of Austrian rule. It was in 1795 that the prince of Gavre was given the duty of receiving at Bâle the unfortunate Marie-Thérèse of France, the orphan of the Temple, the only member of Louis XVI's family to escape the Terror. During the 19th century, the house passed first to the Eggers, then to the Houtarts, a family of industrialists who redecorated it at the end of the century, before bequeathing it to the local authorities. The town of Charleroi is courageously restoring the house. **Open:** All year from sunrise to sunset. **Admission:** Free.

map 261
8

MONTAIGLE

Falaën (Onhaye), Belgium
Tel: 00 32 82 69 95 85 or 00 32 81 22 37 98 (Patrick et Geoffroy del Marmol)

This impressive fortress, the ruins of which stand at the junction of two wild valleys, was built by Guy of Flanders. He was one of the heroes of the Battle of Courtrai in 1302 when the Flemish militias crushed the army of Philip the Fair, King of France. It became the residence of the dowager countesses of Namur and still harbours the shades of Marguerite of Lorraine and Jeanne d'Harcourt. It was in 1554 that Henri II of France reduced this imposing fortress to ruin once and for all. The Friends of Montaigle have made a tremendous effort to revive the site, which must be one of the most romantic places in the whole of Belgium. **Open:** Easter–30 Nov: Sat, Sun and Bank Hols 11–7pm. 1 July–31 Aug: daily 11–7pm. Other visiting times on request for groups only (min 20 people). **Admission:** Adults BF100, child (0–12) BF40. Groups: adults BF80, child (0–12) BF30.

map 261
9

NATIONAL BOTANIC GARDEN OF BELGIUM

Domein Van Bouchout–B1860 Meise, Belgium
Tel: 00 32 2 260 09 20 Fax: 00 32 2 260 09 45

At only a stones throw from Brussels, the centre of European activity, lies the National Botanic Garden of Belgium in the domain of Bouchout, Meise. The domain is closely interwoven with Belgian history. The earliest remains of the castle date back to the 12th century. In more recent times it was the refuge of the former Empress of Mexico, Charlotte, sister of King Leopold II. She died in 1927. Apart from the castle there are various smaller features. There are ice cellars, small ornamental buildings, an exquisite greenhouse by Alphonse Balat, ancient trees and wide sweeping lawns. The Botanic Garden was located to the site in 1939 and added extensive living collections. The immense Plant-Palace houses the tropical and subtropical collections and covers more than 1 hectare. The temperate collections are grouped in several locations in the park. During summer the old Orangery functions as a restaurant and the castle houses a small shop. **Open:** Every day, closed on 25 Dec and 1 Jan. Closing times vary according to season and weather conditions. Call: +32 (0) 2 260 09 70 for details. **Admission:** Adult BF160, child/student BF120. **Internet:** http//www.BR.fgov.be.

map 261
10

OOIDONK CASTLE

Ooidonkdreef 9, B9800 Deinze, Belgium
Tel: 00 32 9 282 35 70 Fax: 00 32 9 282 52 82 (Count t'Kint de Roodenbeke)

Overlooking one of the bends of the Lys river, the castle proves to be the focal point of the surrounding countryside which sports lush green meadows and centuries old oak trees that shelter a colony of celebrated herons. What an imposing sight - austere and sumptuous as well! Dated from the 14th century, its massive towers and walls bear witness to its past, ravaged by war yet withstanding the fire and destruction that it brings. Although modernised in the 19th century, it stands almost intact as it was in 1595. Several generations can be traced back to its interior decoration, highlighted by its elegant white-stone staircase, its historical architecture, furniture and art collections. **Open:** 1 Apr–15 Sept: Sundays and holidays, 2–5.30pm. Also Saturdays in July and Aug, 2–5.30pm. Groups: Mar–Oct, every day. **Admission:** Castle and garden BF200. Garden only BF30.

map 261
11

POEKE

Poeke, Belgium
Tel: 00 32 51 68 83 00 (Gemeente Aalter)

In former times, a powerful fortress stood on this spot, defending the town of Ghent. It was here that Jacques de Lalaing, known as the Good Knight perished in 1453. Charles-Florent de Preudhomme d'Hailly built a colossal château on the site in the Baroque style, incorporating four towers from the old fortications. The style is a reflection of the wealth of its builders but also of the Flemish style of the 18th century, less concerned with the grace of French influence than with a long tradition of pomp and opulence inspired by Rubens. Poeke later became a Catholic school, but it has lost none of its majesty, standing still in a beautiful park of fifty-three hectares. **Open:** 1 Jan–31 Dec: from sunrise to sunset. **Admission:** Free.

map 261
12

RAEREN

Raeren, Belgium
Tel: 00 32 87 85 09 03 Fax: 00 32 87 85 09 32 (Commune de Raeren)

Built by the Rhineland Schwarzenbergs in the 14th century, this water-castle has retained its medieval and austere appearance despite minor alterations made during the 16th and 17th centuries. However, the crenellated towers at the entrance of the castle have recently been built. The castle house an attractive museum of Raeren stoneware, the success of which dates back to the 16th century. **Open:** Daily 10–5pm (except Mondays). **Admission:** Adults BF80, children Free. Groups (min 10 people)BF50.

map 261
13

PROVINCIAAL MUSEUM STERCKSHOF – SILVER CENTRE

Hooftvunderlei 160–B 2100 Antwerp (Deurne)
Tel: 00 32 3 360 5250   Fax: 00 32 3 360 5253

The Provinciaal Museum Sterckshof –Silver Centre is a museum in a park on the edge of the city of Antwerp. It is a journey of discovery that leads through a picturesque castle to the treasures of Belgian silver production from the 16th to the 20th centuries inclusive. At the end of the 18th century little remained of the castle built in the 16th century. On the basis of the original foundation and iconographic material, a reconstruction emerged during the thirties. The library with public reading room (Internet: www.cipal.be/digibib/home.htm), many exhibitions and the museum workshop throw further light on the art of the silversmith. The garden was relaid in 1994. The Sterckshof Museum is situated in the Provinciaal Domain Rivierenhof (Castle Rivierenhof, now a restaurant). **Location:** Provinciaal Domein Rivierenhof, entrance Cornelissenlaan, Antwerp (Deurne). Antwerp expressway (E 19) exit 3 and motorway Antwerp-Liège (E 313) exit 18. **Stations:** Antwerpen-Centraal and bus 18 (Collegelaan), 41 (Cogelsplein) or tram 10 (Cogelsplein), 24 (Waterbaan). Antwerpen-Berchem and bus 18 (Collegelaan). **Open:** 10–5.30pm. Closed on Mon and 25 Dec–2 Jan. **Admission:** Museum and garden free. Exhibition hall: BF100–150. **Events/Exhibition:** 2000 - Alice in Silverland (Silver Toys and Miniatures), 16 May–23 July. **E-mail:** info@sterckshof.provant.be **Website:** www.provant.be/sterckshof

map 261
14

The Loire Valley

With more than sixty castles, some of which date back as far as the middle ages, the Loire region is one of the most historic and architecturally arresting areas in France. Stretching across the north of France, the region is renowned for its rich alluvial soil and an array of magnificent gardens.

Overlooking the River Cher, the Château de Villandry was commenced in 1536 by Jean Le Breton, a minister at the court of François I, although a large house had occupied the area in the preceding centuries. The castle is constructed around an impressive courtyard and is reflected in the waters of the surrounding moat. It is, however, the breathtaking gardens that have furnished the château with international acclaim. The lowest terrace of the garden comprises a veritable patchwork of intricate beds forming a potager whilst the formal flower gardens on the second terrace explode in a riot of colour. Symbolic shapes, synonymous with Renaissance design, are omnipresent and in the Jardin de l'Amour, the random horn shapes evoke the sense of infidelity and fans scattered throughout signify frivolous love.

Cheverny, one of the most famous Loire châteaux, is an architectural delight. It belongs to descendants of the Hurault family and over the centuries it has welcomed five kings of France including Philippe, Chancellor to Henri III and subsequently Henri IV and the Count of Cheverny, the builder of the castle. An

Top Château de Chenonceau. Middle: Château & Jardins de Villandry.
Bottom: Château de Cheverny

officer of King Louis XIII, Count Henri and his Countess decided to construct the new castle and sought the talents of the best artists of the period. As a result, Cheverny was regarded as one of the forerunners of architectural development and is said to have both inspired and invented French style from 1630 to 1640.

Often considered to be the 'jewel in the Renaissance crown', the Château de Chambord is a magnificent building comprising parkland and waterways. It is truly captivating at night when the castle is illuminated. Throughout the year, various events take place including the equestrian show.

Rebuilt in the late 15th and early 16th century by the Amboise family, the Château de Chaumont is has a defensive yet decorative exterior comprising walkways, a gatehouse and circular towers. Inside, the public rooms are the height of opulence with paintings and tapestries from Brussels and Aubusson adorning the walls.

Often considered to be the 'castle of the women' or 'Château des Dames', Chenonceau is a stunning Renaissance building which has been enhanced and improved by a number of celebrated ladies. A capricious wing in the form of a galleried bridge jutting out across the River Cher was added by Diane de Poitiers. Catherine de Medici also re-designed parts of the building and the garden named after her features a central circular pool and beautiful lawns edged in narrow beds.

France

The contrasting landscapes of France with its lush farmland and breathtaking mountains has been an inspiration to its artists throughout the centuries. Visions of the countryside have been captured in paintings by Monet, Van Gogh and Cézanne and it is these surrounds that visitors seek as they tour the regions of Normandy, Brittany and the South of France.

Priding themselves in a heritage rich in philosophy, the French attach great importance to the works of writers such as Jean-Paul Sartre, Descartes and Voltaire. At every 'lycée', pupils are obliged to study philosophy until the age of 18. Indeed, the theories and stories of Marcel Proust have remained popular and have featured in many adaptations on the silver screen including this year's *Le Temps Rétrouvé* (Time Regained) starring the enigmatic Emmanuelle Béart.

The cinematic world cannot be mentioned without reference to the Cannes Film Festival which attracts a host of celebrities, directors and other members of the glitterati every May. Often associated with romantic yet thought-provoking classics such as *A bout de souffle* and *Un homme et une femme*, the French film industry has recently courted a degree of controversy, initially with the release of Catherine Breillat's erotic *Romance* and now with the new release by Frédéric Fonteyne, *Une liaison pornographique*.

Oenologists from around the globe will be familiar with the regions of Bordeaux, Dordogne, Champagne and The Loire and the wines that may be sampled there. These areas are of particular interest to heritage enthusiasts as the realm of chateaux and vineyards are inexorably linked. A fine accompaniment to these vintages is one of the many cheeses that are produced across the country. In the north, the Camembert de Normandie is a ladle-moulded cheese made with milk whilst further south the Saint-Marcellin is a soft creamy cheese covered in yeast. With its varied countryside and a choice of over 400 cheeses, the words of the capricious Italian fiction writer, Italo Calvino, truly capture the essence of this gastronomic land.

"Each sort of cheese reveals a pasture of a different green, under a different sky".

Les Monuments d'Exception

CHATEAU DES BAUX DE PROVENCE

13520 Les Baux de Provence
Tel: 33 04 90 54 55 56 Fax: 33 04 90 54 55 00

The Baux Château was constructed on one of the most beautiful sites in France, overlooking Provence as far as the sea. The Baux Château, a historic monument, offers various centres of interest in an area of 7 hectares, ensuring a fascinating visit for all the family. The Baux history museum, which retraces the turbulent history of this 1000 yr old town, the imposing remains of the château and the ancient fortified town of Baux, (dungeon, fortified towers, columbarium, hospital, caves). At the foot of the Château, life-size medieval siege machines create a vivid impression of warfare in the middle ages. **Location:** 25km from Avignon, 15km from Arles, 40km from Nice. Off A7 at Avignon Sud/Salon de Provence. On A9 at Nimes exit, towards Arles. **Open:** Daily. Spring 9–7.30pm, Summer 9–8.45pm, Autumn 9–6.30pm. Winter 9–5pm. **Internet:** www.château-baux-provence.com

map 267
1

MUSEE JACQUEMART-ANDRE

158 bd Haussmann, 75008 Paris
Tel: 00 33 1 42 89 04 91 Fax: 00 33 1 42 25 09 23

The Jacquemart-Andre Museum presents collections worthy of the greatest museums in a magnificent private mansion dating from the end of the 19th century, with all the atmosphere of a great residence. This sumptuous palace, property of Institut de France, allows the visitor to discover magnificent, intimate areas which are characteristic of Edouard André and his wife, Nélie Jacquemart: large function rooms, monumental staircase, winter garden, 'Italian Museum', private apartments. United by their passion for art, they created together one of the most beautiful collections in France, particularly for the Italian Renaissance, the Great Flemish Masters and the 18th century French School. **Location:** In the heart of Paris, 5 minutes from the Champs Elysées. **Open:** Every day, throughout the year, 10–6pm. **Internet:** www.musee-jacquemart-andre.com

map 267
2

CHÂTEAU DE VALENCAY

36600 Valencay
Tel: 00 33 2 54 00 15 69 Fax: 00 33 2 54 00 08 79

The Valencay Chateau, one of the most beautiful French Renaissance monuments, was the residence of the Prince of Talleyrand, one of Napoleon Bonaparte's ministers. The castle guarantees a fascinating visit for all the family. The most remarkable architectural feature is undoubtedly the imposing Keep. The Great Function Rooms and furnished private suites retain the memories of Talleyrand and his illustrious guests. The castle is surrounded by magnificent gardens and a park featuring wild animals. Special events. **Location:** 220km from Paris, 50km from Blois, 70km from Tours on the D956 and the D960. **Open:** Every day, throughout the year: 1–31 Mar, 2–5pm. 1 Apr–30 Jun, 9.30–6pm. 1 Jul–31 Aug 9.30–7.30pm. 1 Sept–10 Nov, 9.30–6pm. 1 Nov–28 Feb, Weekends and holidays 2–5pm. **Internet:** www.château-valencay.com

map 267
3

VILLA EPHRUSSI DE ROTHSCHILD

06230 Saint Jean Cap Ferrat
Tel: 00 33 4 93 01 33 09 Fax: 00 33 4 93 01 31 10

Built by Baroness Ephrussi de Rothschild during the Belle Epoque, the villa is surrounded by seven glorious gardens, decorated with ornamental lakes, waterfalls, patios, flower beds, shady paths and rare types of trees. Overlooking the sea and offering a unique view over the French Riveria, this palace has retained all the atmosphere of an inhabited residence. The Villa, inspired by the great residences of the Italian Renaissance, houses private function rooms and apartments with high quality works of art, collected by Beatrice Ephrussi throughout her life. A free English guide book is given to each visitor. In the summer, a series of concerts enlivens the gardens. **Location:** Between Nice & Monaco, on coast road (N 98). **Open:** Everyday throughout the year, 5 Feb–1 Nov, 10–6pm & 2 Nov–14 Feb. Weekends & school hols 10–6pm. Weekdays 2–6pm. **Internet:** www.villa-ephrussi.com

map 267
4

MUSÉE NATIONAL DE L'AUTOMOBILE

192 Avenue de Colmar, 68000 Mulhouse, France
Tel: 00 33 3 89 33 23 23 Fax: 00 33 3 89 32 08 09

The Musee National de l'Automobile, located at Mulhouse, hosts the famous Schlumpf Collection, which numbers 400 outstanding automobiles, including 100 Bugatti. From 26 March 2000, you will discover the museum of the 3rd Millenary, a fully modernised museum, with a new presentation of the vehicles, information cards in front of each item and autoguides, films, interactive terminals, videos, stimulation games, special events, activities available for children. **Location:** 500km from Paris, 100km from Strasbourg, 40km from Bale. On A35 & A36 at Mulhouse west exit. **Open:** Daily, throughout the year. Until 5 Mar, 10–6pm closed on Tues. **6–25 Mar: closed for renovation.** 26 Mar–31 Oct, 9–6pm. 1 Nov–31 Dec, 10–6pm. **Facilities:** guided tours, restaurant, self-service, gift & bookshop, live entertainment/ events, special group rates. **Internet:** www.collection-schlumpf.com

map 267
5

CHÂTEAU DE MALLE

33210 Preignac, France
Tel: 00 33 5 56 62 36 86 Fax: 00 33 5 56 76 82 40 (Comtesse De Bournazel)

Bordeaux area. Magnificent residence surrounded by Italian gardens, in the heart of Sauternes vineyard, Malle built by Jacques de Malle, direct ancestor of the Comte de Bournazel, dates from the early 17 C. The castle is tile-roofed, dominated by a Mansard one-storied slate covered central pavilion with two round towers at each end, topped with slate domes. The chapel is in one of the towers. Ceilings, furniture and paintings have remained as they were. The vineyard encompasses the region of Sauternes (Malle is a great classified vintage under the famous Imperial classification of 1855) and Graves (red & white wines). **Open:** 1 Apr–31 Oct, 10–12 & 2–6.30pm. Every day. Free parking. Groups by appointment. Possibility of tasting. **Location:** 35 m S Bordeaux by R.N. 113 or A62 to Langon. **Internet:** http//www.château–de–malle.fr **E-mail:** chateaudemalle@wanadoo.fr

map 267
6

PARC FLORAL DE HAUTE BRETAGNE

Château de la Foltière, 35133 Le Chatellier, Bretagne, France
Tel: 00 33 2 99 95 48 32 Fax: 00 33 2 99 95 47 74

Not far from the medieval city of Fougères in the direction of the famous Mont Saint-Michel, the Parc Floral de Haute Bretagne unfolds in a romantic landscape These superb grounds were laid out originally in the 19th century, and within them have been planted ten magnificent elegant gardens, an invitation you can't refuse to walk, linger and perhaps ponder a while. This country stroll begins with the Persian garden, followed by the ancient city which plunges us into the Mediterranean world. Then comes Knossos with its camellias. Perhaps the most successful is the Poets' Dell with its pond, its little bridges and its wild groves... It's up to you to discover the rest. Tea rooms in the beautiful castle at the bottom of the garden, and there are small shrubs on sale for you to plant your own echo of what you have seen here.

map 267
7

CHÂTEAU D'ARLAY

39140 Arlay
Tel: 00 33 3 84 85 04 22 Fax: 00 33 3 84 48 17 96 (M et Mme R de Laguiche)

The castle was built in 1774 by the Countess of Lauraguais on the site of a Minime Convent, the only remains of which are the vaulted cellar. It was refurnished during the Restoration (1819–1835). A romantic park laid out inside the medieval ruins of the old fortress of the Princes of Orange, is an illustration of the spirit of playfulness of the late 18th century. The theme of play is also evoked by the garden created in 1996: hoops with roses on croquet lawn, with a central bell-hoop and a box-tree "ball". You can also see the four aces: hearts, spades, diamonds and clubs. Flowers, fruit and vegetables are brought together in harmony. **Open:** From 15 June–15 Sept. **Email:** chateau@arlay.com **Website:** www.arlay.com

map 267
8

ANHOLT CASTLE

Wasserburg Anholt, Postfach 2226, 46417 Isselburg
Tel: 00 49 2874 45353 4 Fax: 00 49 2874 45356

Moated Anholt Castle, set in the Rhine downstream landscape. Residence of the Princes of Salm-Salm. Unique setting with museum, park (35 acres), hotel-restaurant, golf course (18 holes) and rock-garden of 1894 (60 acres). Main castle with 'Broad Tower' from the 12th century. Enlarged into a barrack house in 1700. Since 1966, museum with historic furniture and the Princes' art gallery (700 works of art): Rembrandt, Van Goyen, Murillo, Breughel, Teniers, Terborch. Tapestries, porcelain collection, library, dining rooms, medieval kitchen, coinage, armour and weapons, rooms with fine plasterwork. French gardens with baroque ornaments, maze, tea house, arboretum and rose garden. English landscape gardens by Weyhe (1835) and Edward Milner (1858). The economic building, built in 1700, has been used as a hotel restaurant since 1968.

map 287
1

BENTHEIM CASTLE

Burg Bentheim, D-48455 Bad Bentheim, Niedersachsen, District Osnabruck Germany
Tel/Fax: 0049-5922-5011 (Furst zu Bentheim und Steinfurt)

Situated on a rocky hill, the castle has overlooked the picturesque town and an immense area of 40 miles in each direction for almost 1000 years. Bentheim Castle dates back to the times of the Saxon dukes in the 10th and 11th centuries. At the beginning of the 12th century, the castle became the residence of the counts of Holland. Bentheim Castle offers a medieval keep, the impressive sculpture of the "good lord of Bentheim", one of the most ancient documents of Christian life in northern Germany, the round tower with its dungeons and prisons as well as the tudor style re-erected palace with its magnificent grand

staircase and staterooms built for the late Queen Emma of the Netherlands. The little museum displays unique documents of family history. **Location:** Amsterdam-Osnabruck A30 8km ahead of the Dutch border, exit Bad Bentheim and the motorway Oberhausen-Emden A31 exit Ochtrup 5km. **Open:** 1 Mar–1 Nov. Daily 10–6pm last admission 5.15pm. In Nov, Jan and February. On weekends from 10–sunset. Closed in Dec. **Admission:** Adults DM5, children and groups DM4.

map 287
2

BRANITZ CASTLE

Kastanienallee 11, 03042 Cottbus
Tel: 00 49 355 751 5100 Fax: 00 49 355 751 5230

Branitz Castle stands in a historic English garden. The park (approx. 100 hectares) was laid by Herman Furst of Puckler–Muskau (1785–1871), a landscape gardener of the European circle. With its ponds, small water ways, hills, ornamental trees and bushes, the gardens have a very distinctive character. Rather unique pyramids lie deep within the garden. Inside the late Baroque-style castle and stable are the historically furnished rooms (from 19th century) which contain different exhibitions depicting the life and work of the Princes of Puckler. From June 1998 the Cottbus collection of the romantic painter, Carl Blechen, will be exhibited in the restored castle rooms. **Locations:** Cottbus, around 100km S of Berlin on A15. **Open:** Summer, daily 10–6pm. Winter, daily except for Mons, 10–5pm. Special events include theatre, concerts and readings.

map 287
3

ELTZ CASTLE
Burg Eltz, D-56294 Münstermaifeld
Tel: 00 49 (26 72) 95 05 00 Fax: 00 49 (26 72) 950 50 50

Burg Eltz, perhaps the best known medieval castle in Germany, with its towering buildings reaching up to 10 storeys and its picturesque half-timbering, offers nearly 900 years of history to its visitors. Throughout these centuries it has been formerly, the stronghold, today, the much beloved ancestral home of the Lords and Counts of Eltz. The castle, looking down at the little Elz river from which it took its name, and cradled by the forest that surrounds it, seems very distant from the world today. Still, it is only a few miles away from some of Germany's busiest rivers and highways. It has been the favourite subject to many artists and particularly to William Turner and Edward Lear. Since it has never been destroyed or looted, it contains an interesting display of furniture and armament, reaching back to the 14th century, and some remarkable Old Masters including Lucas Cranach and Michael Pacher.

The treasury holds an impressive collection of gold and silverware, arms and pieces de vertu, all of which were in actual use of the family, some as early as the thirteenth century many bearing the Eltz coat-of-arms. **Location:** Lower Moselle river area, nearby Koblenz/Cochem; **Directions:** Car/coach by motorway A48, exit Polch, or by Federal roads B416/B49, both via Münstermaifeld. Train and boat: stop Moselkern. **Open:** 1 Apr–1 Nov, 9.30–5.30pm. **Admission:** Guided Tour: Adults: DM9 (4,60 Euro), children: DM6 (3,10 Euro), family DM27 (13,80 Euro). Treasury Vault: Adults DM4 (2 Euro), children DM2 (1 Euro). Groups of 20 or more: Adults DM8 (4,10 Euro), children DM5 (2,60 Euro). **E-mail:** kastellanei@burg-eltz.de **Website:** http://www.burg-eltz.de

map 287
4

Germany

CASTLES OF THE PRINCE OF HOHENLOHE – OEHRINGEN

Wald & Schlosshotel – 74639 Friedrichsruhe / Zweiflingen, Germany Tel: 00 49 7941 60870 Fax: 00 49 7941 61468
Schloss Neuenstein – 74632 Neuenstein, Germany Tel: 00 49 7942–2209/49 7941–60990 Fax: 00 49 7941–609920

Wald & Schlosshotel: This graceful hunting castle, once the summer residence of Prince Johann-Friedrich of Hohenlohe-Oehringen, is now part of an elegant hotel in a magnificent park. Visitors will appreciate the handsome reception rooms, with their splendid family portraits and gilt mirrors. The guest rooms are decorated in harmonious colours and extremely comfortable. The Michelin star restaurant, decorated with candles and chandeliers providing attractive lighting, offers a sensational international menu and first-class wines. Leisure facilities include indoor and outdoor pools, tennis, fishing, riding and an 18-hole golf course. **Directions:** BAB 6, Exit Öhringen, follow signs towards Zweiflingen; find signs to the Wald & Schlosshotel at Friedrichsruhe.

Schloss Neuenstein: Schloss Neuenstein, a water castle from the 11th century, was developed 500 years later into a noble residence in the Renaissance style. The castle houses the Hohenlohe Museum which has an extensive historic collection which reflects the art and culture of the Hohenlohe region. One can, amongst other things, visit the splendid Knights Hall, the Kaiser Hall with its rich collection of weapons and the art and rarity cabinet containing finely crafted goldsmiths work and ivory carvings. A special attraction is the fully functioning castle kitchen from 1485, which remains in its original condition. **Location:** BAB 6, exit Neuenstien, B19 Burgenstrasse. **Open:** 1 Apr–30 Nov, daily except Monday (when it is not a Bank Holiday), 9–12am and 1–6pm.

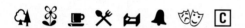

HOHENZOLLERN CASTLE

Burg Hohenzollern–Verwaltung, 72379 Hechingen, Germany
Tel: 00 49 7471 2428 Fax: 00 49 7471 6812

The majestic castle with its fantastic view is the ancestral seat of the Hohenzollern Dynasty, the Prussian Royal Family (Frederick the Great) and the German Emperors. Guided tours, showing a valuable collection of artwork and treasures, including the Prussian King's Crown, offer an insight into 19th century architecture and into Prussian and German history. **Location:** 5km from Hechingen town centre. **Open:** Daily all year except 24 Dec, 16 Mar–15 Oct. 9–5.30pm. 16 Oct–15 Mar, 9–4.30pm. Guided tours every 15 to 30 minutes, English tours on prior arrangement. **Admission:** Castle grounds and house: Adults DM9, groups DM6, children DM3. Castle grounds DM4. **Refreshments:** Snack bar, and restaurant open daily in summertime. **Internet:** www.burg-hohenzollern.com

KRONBURG CASTLE

Burgstrasse 1, 87758 Kronburg, Bavaria
Tel: 00 49 8394/271 Fax: 00 49 8394/1671 Internet: http://www.schloss-kronburg.de

Built on a picturesque hill in the Allgäu, Kronburg Castle has been the property of Baron of Vequel-Westernach for 375 years. This fine four-winged Renaissance style castle is mentioned first in documents from 1227. Part of the building is open to visitors from May–Oct (if booked in advance). The Baron and Baroness guide you personally through some superb rooms. (The German Master Hall, with rich stucco work, the Red drawing room with its original Renaissance ceiling, the Hunting room, Visionary gallery, many rooms with 300 yr old linen wallpaper and the Rococo style chapel).There are chamber and castle-yard concerts during the summer. A newly built guesthouse houses exclusive holiday apartments. **Location:** Nr Memmingen, 5km W on A7 (direction of Konigsschlossern), taking the exit Woringen. **Admission:** Adult DM9, child DM4.50.

LANGENBURG CASTLE

Fürstliche Verwaltung, Schloss Langenburg, 74595 Langenburg
Tel: 00 49 7905 1041 Fax: 00 49 7905 1040 E-mail: schloss.langenburg@t-online.de

With parts of the castle dating back to the 12C it is remarkable that this castle is still home to the noble family Hohenlohe-Langenburg. Offering one of the nicest Renaissance courtyards in Germany, a chapel and a Baroque garden, the former stables also house a classic car museum. In an area almost 2,000m², there are approx. 80 legendary cars from 1899 up to the modern Formula 1 racing car. The castle tour displays the superb Baroque hall, different museum rooms with fine stucco ceilings and the equally splendid furnishings of the Langenburg family. **Castle Tours:** Good Fri–1 Nov, daily, 10–5pm. Tours every hour on the hour. Groups should contact the castle for advance bookings. Groups can also visit at times outside the hours above and tours can also be in English. Castle concerts, stately rooms for weddings and events. Attractive walk, museum shop and cafe situated in rose garden.

map 287
8

LEMBECK CASTLE

46286 Dorsten-Lembeck, Nordrhein–Westfalen, Germany
Tel: 00 49 23697167 Fax: 00 49 236977391 (Ferdinand Graf von Merveldt)

A fine example of an early Baroque Westphalian moated castle built in 1692 on the foundations of a medieval fortress. The northwest wing was re-modelled in 1730 by the eminent architect Johann-Conrad Schlaun who worked extensively on other important houses in the region. The home of Graf Merveldt, whose family and ancestors have owned Lembeck since the Middle Ages, the castle is now a museum and hotel. It contains a substantial collection of Chinese porcelain, Flemish tapestries, Dutch furniture and items of local cultural and historic interest and stands in extensive grounds which include a fine rhododendron park. **Location:** From Autobahn 43 Haltern exit or Autobahn 31 Lembeck exit. Station: Lembeck, **Open:** Daily Mar–Nov from 10–6pm. **Admission:** Adult DM7, child DM4.50.

map 287
9

MARKSBURG CASTLE

56338 Braubach, Germany
Tel: 00 49 26 27 206 Fax: 00 49 26 27 88 66

The imposing Marksburg, known as the jewel of the Rhine Valley, is the only castle on the cliffs of the Rhine that has never been destroyed. Dating back to the 12th century, the castle has maintained its medieval character. The high Keep is surrounded by the Romanesque Palace and the Gothic Hall with the Chapel Tower. Of special interest are the horse steps carved out of the rock, the Great Battery and the medieval Herb Garden with its spectacular view, the Gothic Kitchen, Knights' Hall. Armoury Chamber and collection of torture instruments. The Marksburg is the seat of the German Castles Association. **Location:** Braubach, 12 km south of Koblenz on B42. **Open:** Daily from 10–5pm, Nov–Easter 11–4pm. **Admission:** Adult DM8, families DM24, child DM6. Children under 6 years free. (guided tours also in English). **E-mail:** DBV.Marksburg@deutsche–burgen.org

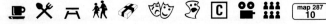

map 287
10

PAPPENHEIM CASTLE

Neues Schloß, 91788 Pappenheim, Germany
Tel: 00 49 9143 83 890   Fax: 00 49 9143 6445 (Gräfliche Verwaltung)

An imposing 12th century castle, extension 300m long, overlooking the picturesque former residence city of the Hereditary Marshals of the Holy Roman Empire, the Marchesses Pappenheim, with important historic buildings, enlarged during the following centuries; partly destroyed since the 30-years-war, an economical building and the arsenal of the 15th century contain a small museum, torture chamber, keep, long fortification walls, falconry, twice a day demonstrations, herb garden, aboretum with collection of trees, shrubs and plants of the area, (more than 100 species). Cafeteria. **Location:** 35 miles W of Eichstaett. **Open:** Easter–5 Nov, Tues–Sun, 10–5pm. **Admission:** Adults DM4,50, children DM3,50. Separate admission for falconry demonstration.

map 287
11

POSTERSTEIN CASTLE

04626 Posterstein/Thuringia Germany
Tel/Fax: 00 49 34496 22595

Going to Saxony's capital Dresden on the busy motorway A4 you will pass Burg Posterstein which is situated halfway between Thuringia's capital Erfurt and Dresden. Burg Posterstein is located in Eastern Thuringia, bordering on the classical Thuringia, marked by Goethe. The first information about the castle dates from 1191. The first owner, Knight Stein, got his landed property from King Friedrich I; Barbarossa. In the 16th and 17th century the old castle was rebuilt and became a little palace. The last restoration work took place from 1984 to 1991. **Museum Open:** Tues–Sat, 10–5pm; Sun 10–6pm. Nov–Feb: Tues–Fri 10–4pm; Sat–Sun 10–5pm. **Admission:** Adults: DM5, pupils, students: DM2, children under 14: free.

QUERFURT CASTLE

06268 Querfurt, Germany
Tel: 00 49 34771/5219 0 Fax: 00 49 34771/5219 99

Gracing the southern slope of the Quernebach Valley, the castle is one of the oldest in Germany. Its first documented mention occurred in the Hersfeld tithe register (866–899). In fact, this is also one of the largest castle compounds in the land, with an area almost seven times as large as that of the Wartburg. Presumably, Querfurt Castle served as a haven for refugees in Carolingian times. Evidence of stone buildings exists from the late 10th century onwards. The most conspicuous features of the castle are its three towers: 'Dicker Heinrich', 'Marterturm' and 'Pariser Turm'. At the centre is the Romanesque church built in the latter half of the 12th century, a crosshoped edifice with three semicircular apses and an octagonal crossing tower. **Open:** Tues–Sun, 9–5pm. Closed Mon. **Admission:** DM5, concessions DM3.

RITTERGUT HAUS LAER

Höfestrasse 45, 44803 Bochum (Ruhrgebiet, Nordrhein–Westfalen), Germany
Tel: 00 49 234 383044 Fax: 00 49 234 385375

Founded in 940, it is the oldest secular building existing in the middle Ruhrgebiet. A picturesque moated castle. The reliefs of the local sovereign Henry the Lion and his spouse Mathilde, who was the daughter of King Henry II and the sister of Richard Lionheart (Robin Hood, Nottinghamshire), are situated in two Suites of Haus Laer that can be rented. In 1704 and 1709 Haus Laer fought under John Churchill, Duke of Marlborough (Blenheim Palace Woodstock), successfully against King Ludwig XIV. Reservations for the suites "Madame Pompadour" and "Prince Soubise" possible. Guest house. Long and short stays in the Apartments/ suites are possible. The Hall of the Knights can be hired. **Location:** 4½km from the main station of Bochum; 2km from exit "Querenburg" of the A43; 1.6km from the Exit "Steinkuhl" of the urban motorway "Nordhausenring".

SAYN CASTLE & BUTTERFLY GARDEN

56170 Bendorf-Sayn Germany
Tel: 00 49 2622 15478 (The Prince & The Princess zu Sayn-Wittgenstein-Sayn)

Burg Sayn, built before 1200 by the Counts of Sayn, was destroyed in 1633 and recently restored. Spectacular view on romanesque Sayn abbey, Rhine Valley and Eifel mountains. A Turmuhrenmuseum contains fine collection of tower clocks. Castellated terraces descend to Schloss Sayn, where a museum for cast iron art will open in 2000. Landscaped park with rare trees, ponds, playgrounds and Garten der Schmetterlinge, an exotic dreamland with hundreds of live tropical butterflies. **Location:** Bendorf-Sayn, 10km NE of Koblenz on A48 and B42. **Open:** Mid Mar–early Nov. Butterfly garden daily from 9–6pm. **Admission:** Butterfly garden: Adult DM8, Child DM5. **Refreshments:** Burgschanke open 11–8pm (closed Mons). Cafeteria at butterfly garden. **Internet:** www.sayn.de

SIGMARINGEN CASTLE

F.H. Schlossverwaltung, 72488 Sigmaringen
Tel: 00 49 7571 729 230   Fax: 00 49 7571 729 255

Sigmaringen Castle is, to this day, the home of the descendants of the Princes of Hohenzollern. The castle majestically overlooks the town of Sigmaringen and its surrounding countryside. There are many fascinating things to see in the castle; the Hubertus hall houses a large collection of hunting trophies and over 3,000 historic weapons of all types (one of the largest private collections of its kind in Europe). Art is indestructible, but it has found a safe hiding place here in Hohenzollern's castle; valuable tapestries and paintings, priceless porcelain pieces, elegant and tasteful furniture, which capture a calm and still ambience, can be found here. **Open:** For guided tours: Nov, Feb–Apr, daily, 9.30–4.30pm; May–Oct, daily, 9–4.45pm; Dec–Jan, only organised tours with prior bookings, until 4pm. **E-mail:** schloss@hohenzollern.com

map 287
16

SONDERSHAUSEN CASTLE

Box 83 99702 Sondershausen (Stiftung Thüringer Schlösser und Gärten)
Tel: 00 49 36 32 6630

The former residence of the Counts (since 1697 Princes) of Schwarzburg-Sonderhausen is the many-sided and in historical and artistical terms, the most interesting building in the north of Thuringia to experience about 600 years of architecture. The castle is situated on a rise above the town, surrounded by a 19C park covering 30 hectares. **Location:** 60km N of Erfurt on B4, parking near castle; railway-line: Intercity to Erfurt, regional-line to Sondershausen. **Open:** Residence-museum Tues–Sun 10–4pm, closed Mon; guided tours 10am & 2pm and by arrangements; special tours by arrangement (contact museum Tel: 00 49 3632 663 120). **Admission:** Adult DM6, seniors/student DM4, child (under 6) free, groups (min 15 pers.) DM3. Restaurants in historical rooms daily 11–12pm. Concerts in historic rooms (symphonic and chamber music, organ recitals) and exhibitions.

map 287
17

STOLPEN CASTLE

Schlossstrasse 10, 01833 Stolpen
Tel: 00 49 35973 23410 Fax: 00 49 35973 23419

30km E of Dresden, this Medieval castle was once the secondary residence of the Bishops of Meissen and the Saxon electoral princes. The building beautifully complements the natural monument the 'Stolpener Basalt'. Stolpen castle with its striking towers dominates the landscape between the 'Lausitz' and the 'Elbsandsteingebirge'. The castle is linked with the tragic fate of Countess Cosel, the most famous of Augustus the Strong's mistresses. He was the electoral prince of Saxony and King of Poland. She was a prisoner in the castle for 49 years (1716–1765) and is buried in the chapel. The medieval character is preserved through prisons, cellars, a torture chamber and the deepest well in the world. The castle museum and events programme make Stolpen one of the liveliest historic places in Saxony. **Open:** Daily, Summer 9–5pm. Winter 10–4pm (weather permitting).

map 287
18

THE PRINCELY CASTLE OF THURN UND TAXIS

Emmeramsplatz 5, 93047 Regensburg, Bavaria
Tel: 00 49 0941 5048133 Fax: 00 49 0941 5048256

Since 1812, this has been the home of the Princes of Thurn und Taxis, who reconstructed parts of the former Benedictine monastery of St. Emmeram as their residence. Besides the palace staterooms, furnished in different styles (rococo, neo-rococo, classic, historic), you can visit the medieval cloister (11–14th centuries) with the mortuary chapel (19th century) and the carriage museum (carriages, sleighs, sedan chairs, harnesses) in the former princely stables and riding hall. **Location:** A93, Exit Regensburg-Konigswiesen, then direction "Regensburg centre" **Open:** Apr–Oct daily 11am, 2, 3, 4pm, on Sats and Suns also 10am, Nov–Mar, Sats, Suns, Bank Hols 10, 11, 2, 3pm (guided tours only), tours for groups by appointment. **Admission:** Adults DM12, reduced fee DM10.

map 287
19

WALLERSTEIN CASTLE

D–86757 Wallerstein, Germany
Tel: +49 (0) 9081 782 300

The 'New Castle' in Wallerstein arose after the thirty year war when the Fortress on the Wallerstein Cliffs was distructed by Swedish troops. In its stately and private rooms (i.e. bedroom chamber, dining room, banquette hall) a fine Porcelain and Glass Collection as well as a unique exhibition of family uniforms of the Princes of Oettingen is on show. The adjacent english stlye park invites you to a relaxing stroll to the Orangerie and the impressive riding school. **Location:** On the Romantic Road (B25) between Dinkelsbühl and Nördlingen. **Open:** mid Mar–Oct, 9–5pm (closed Mons). **Admission:** Adult DM7, child DM4, Group DM6. **Refreshments:** Restaurant of Prince Oettingen–Wallerstein's brewery at the Wallerstein Cliff. **Weddings:** Chapel can be hired for weddings (80 persons). **E-mail:** schloesser@fuerst–wallerstein.de **Internet:** www.fuerst–wallerstein.de

map 287
20

WARTBURG CASTLE

99817 Eisenach, Germany
Tel: 00 49 3691 2500 Fax: 00 49 3691 203342

The Wartburg, situated on a 410m high hill in the heart of Germany, is one of the best preserved German medieval castles. Founded in 1067 and gradually enlarged through the years, it became an enormous castle complex, containing Romanesque, Gothic and 19th century buildings. When the visitor enters the Romanesque Palace, he opens a 900-year old history book: Medieval courtly culture, life and charity work of St. Elizabeth – one of the most remarkable female figures of the Middle Ages – and Martin Luther's translation of the New Testament. The Wartburg Art Collection includes artistic treasures from the Renaissance to the 19th century. **Location:** A4 Frankfurt/Main – Dresden. **Open:** Daily from 8.30–5pm; Nov–Feb 9–3.30pm. (guided tours also in English). **E-mail:** info@wartburg–eisenach.de

WERNIGERODE CASTLE

Schloss Wernigerode GmbH, Am Schloss 1, 38855 Wernigerode
Tel: 00 49 39 43 55 30 30 Fax: 00 49 39 43 55 30 55

The original Romanesque castle dating from the 12th century, extensively altered over the years, was up to 1945 the residential palace of the Earls of Stolberg, who took the name 'von Stolberg-Wernigerode' from their principality, the earldom of Wernigerode. The grand turreted stone and half-timber castle with magnificent views over the medieval town of Wernigerode today ranks as a major example of the North German "Historismus" building style. The remarkable rise to political power of Earl Otto, who became Vice Chancellor of Germany under Bismarck, gave impetus to the sumptuous late 19th century remodelling seen today, including the original staterooms of Europe's highest ranking nobility of that day. Changing exhibits, a variety of events and scientific symposiums fulfil the Schlossmuseum's aim to become a centre of artistic and cultural history of the 19th century. Weddings in the Chapel, banquets in the Dining Hall, receptions, conferences and parties in the grandly appointed staterooms by arrangement. **Location:** Above Wernigerode, 70km south of Brunswick. Transfer service every 20 minutes from the Town Centre. **Open:** May–Oct: daily 10–6pm, last admission 5.30pm, Nov–Apr: closed Mon. Tues–Fri daily 10–4pm, Sat, Sun and on holidays daily 10–6pm. **Admission:** Adults DM8, children DM4. Gardens and panorama terrace free. **Refreshments:** Restaurant and tearoom open daily except Mondays. **Exhibitions/Events:** Open air opera, theatre, concerts and ballet on the central terrace, shop.

WILHELMSBURG CASTLE

Museum Castle Wilhelmsburg, Schlossberg 9, D–98574 Schmalkalden
Tel: 00 49 3683 403186 Fax: 00 49 3683 601682

Castle Wilhelmsburg was built between 1585 and 1590 by Landgrave Wilhelm IV of Hessen–Kassel. This unique monument to art and architecture, a mature example of Renaissance castle building is surrounded by well-preserved grounds and outer buildings. Renaissance ornamentation, wallpaintings and stucco are characteristic of the decor of the apartments and state-rooms. The castle's church provides an example of one of the most mature Protestant church buildings of the 16th centuries. Themes of the exhibitions are Renaissance, Reformation, history of the building and its use as well as contemporary art. **Events:** Recitals on the Renaissance organ (1589), Chamber music recitals. **Location:** A4, Exit Eisenach, 40km S on B19. **Open:** (not Mons) Feb–Oct: 9–5pm, Nov–Jan: 10–4pm. **Admission:** Adults DM6, child DM4, groups DM5. Tours by appointment DM30.

The Netherlands

Girls in clogs dancing under a windmill beside a tulip field. This stereotypical image of The Netherlands, also known as Holland, has been preserved as the country has kept many of its traditional aspects alive. The windmills still turn at the Zaanse Schans, the tulip gardens at Keukenhof explode in a riot of colour every Spring and the beautiful Dutch costumes are still daily wear for some people in the former fishing villages around the Ijsselmer.

However, much as the traditional aspects of the country are cherished, The Netherlands has many other attractive features such as its mixed culture, impressive architecture and art. The land of Rembrandt, Hals and Vermeer has more museums per square foot than any other country in the world. One of the most frequented galleries is the Van Gogh Museum, currently being refurbished. Some of the artist's 206 paintings may be seen at a special exhibition at the Rijksmuseum in Amsterdam.

The capital of The Netherlands, Amsterdam, is a fusion of both the past and present. Since the 16th century, when the diamond trade was first introduced to the city, Amsterdam has remained one of the world's most important diamond centres. The 'Koh-I-Noor' Mountain of Light diamond was cut and polished here for the British Crown Jewels in 1852. The city is striking with architectural masterpieces lining the narrow streets and tall trees forming a canopy along the beautiful canals, filled with houseboats. The beauty of the city contrasts strongly with the more permissive side of Amsterdam and its coffee-shop culture.

Situated further south along the coast is the town of Delft, famous for its Delft blue pottery. The historical walk, which uncovers the birthplace of the painter Vermeer, the old market square and the beautiful convent Het Prinsenhof, is an ideal way in which to explore the town.

Dutch cuisine, although largely influenced by Germanic flavours, incorporates much of its local produce such as the exquisite oysters and mussels from Zeeland. The country's dairy farms are a source of national pride, producing the world-famous Edam cheese. Indeed, such is the country's love of dairy products that the picturesque town of Gouda with its beautiful late Gothic architecture and lively markets gave its name to a cheese.

Nearby Rotterdam, with its impressive skyline, is an international business centre which hosts many trade fairs and conferences. The city on The Meuse combines centuries of architectural splendour with modern properties. This juxtapositioning of the very old with the brand new buildings is represented in the Rotterdam ArchiCentre. The city is currently preparing for the year 2001, when Rotterdam will become the Cultural Capital of Europe.

The Limburg province situated towards Belgium and Luxembourg is the essence of natural beauty with its dramatic landscape and rolling hills. The convivial ambience of the folk dancers and marching bands must be enjoyed from one of the lively pavement cafés. This is considered to be the most continental part of The Netherlands and like the rest of the country, its cultural diversity, rich heritage and traditions are truly quintessential.

CASTLE DE HAAR

Kasteellaan 1, 3455 RR Haarzuilens, The Netherlands
Tel: 00 31 30 677 3804 Fax: 00 31 30 677 5827 (Foundation Kasteel de Haar)

Castle de Haar dates back to the 14th century and got destroyed and rebuilt many times. By the far end of the 17th century it had become a ruin. In 1890 the ruin came into the possession of Baron Etienne van Zuylen van Nijevelt. Castle de Haar was rebuilt by a very famous Dutch architect, namely Pierre Cuypers. Castle de Haar is one of the largest castles in Holland and houses many treasures. Castle de Haar is endowed with an extensive park. **Open:** 2 Jan–12 Mar: Sun, 1–4pm. 14 Mar–28 May: Tues–Sun, 1–4pm. 29 May–1 Oct: Mon–Fri, 11–4pm & W/ends, 1–4pm. 3 Oct–19 Nov: Tues–Sun, 1–4pm. 20–30 Nov: Sun, 1–4pm. Special tours & arrangements for groups can be organised by appointment & can take place outside normal opening hours. **Admission:** Adult FL15, child (5–12) FL10. **E-mail:** informatie@kasteeldehaar.nl **Internet:** www.kasteeldehaar.nl

map 295
1

KEUKENHOF

Stationsweg 166a, 2161 AM Lisse, The Netherlands
Tel: 00 31 252 465 555

Keukenhof is known as the Spring Garden of Europe. In 1949 the area was developed as a permanent showcase for the bulb and flower industry. Today, Keukenhof is the world's largest bulb flower garden, with acres of tulips, daffodils, hyacinths and other flowering bulbs, flowering shrubs, ancient trees and beautiful ponds and fountains. Keukenhof also has changing indoor flower exhibitions or parades, theme gardens and a special 'Bollebozen' route for children. **Open:** 25 Mar–19 May 1999. Also open for a special summer exhibition between 19 Aug–19 Sept. Please call for further details of opening times and admission prices.

map 295
2

MUIDERSLOT

Herengracht 1, 1398 AA Muiden
Tel: 00 31 (0) 294 261325 Fax: 00 31 (0) 294 261056 (Stichting Rijksmuseum Muiderslot)

The history of Muiden castle begins about 1280 when Floris V, Count of Holland, erected a stone fortress at the mouth of the river Vecht. The castle was destroyed in 1296 and rebuilt about 100 years later. The man who made the castle famous is the poet, playwright and historian Pieter Cornelisz Hooft (1581–1647). Hooft was bailiff of Muiden and reeve of Gooiland. For 39 years he summered at the castle, which he endowed with the splendour of Holland's Golden Age. Recently refurbished, the castle has regained its pristine elegance. The herb and kitchen gardens and the plum orchard also recall the sumptuous life of the castle's 17th century residents. During summer there is live falconry.

map 295
3

PALEIS HET LOO NATIONAL MUSEUM

Koninklijk Park 1, NL–7315 JA Apeldoorn, The Netherlands
Tel: 00 31 55 577 2400 Fax: 00 31 55 521 9983

Built around 1686 by William III of Orange, favourite summer residence of the Royal Family until 1975. Palace and gardens restored to their seventeenth century state. Interiors from William & Mary-Wilhelmina (died 1962). Museum of the Chancery of The Netherlands Orders of Knight-hood; Royal stables. **Location:** Follow road signs; Bus 102 and 104 near Railway Station. **Open:** Palace and gardens open all year, Tue–Sun, 10–5pm; closed 1 January & Mon unless Bank Holidays. **Admission:** 6–17 years: Fl 12,50, Adults: FL 15. **Guided Tours:** In English by appointment. **Refreshments:** Tea House, Ballroom. Banquets, Meetings: 00 31 55 577 2408. **E-mail:** paleis.het.loo@wxs.nl **Internet:** www.hetloo.nl

map 295
4

SPAENSWEERD GARDENS

Bronkhorsterweg 18,6971 JA Brummen
Tel: 00 31 575 561104 Fax: 00 31 575 566160 (Diana Hummelen)

Spaensweerd dates back to the 17th century, but was altered in 1835 creating a lovely empire style. It is set in 3 acres of beautiful listed gardens with formal and informal elements. Old topiary, monumental trees and an astonishing number of rare and unusual plants in the herbaceous borders, which provides interest throughout the season. Splendid views from the garden overlooking the countryside. **Location:** 5 km south of Zutphen. **Open:** 2, 3, 4, 17 & 18 June; 8 & 9 July, 11–5pm. Groups by appointment. **Admission:** Adults FL7,50. Children under 12 free. **Refreshments** and accommodation available.

map 295
5

VALKENBURG

Grendelplein 13, Valkenburg, (Limberg), The Netherlands
Tel: 00 31 43 6090110

Visit the only castle in The Netherlands to have been built on a mountain side – these magnificent ruins are situated on the 'Falcon's Mount' – a site occupied by the castle since 1100. The castle once belonged to the ducal house of Cleves and was the setting for the marriage between Beatrice of Valkenburg and Richard of Cornwall (brother of Henry III of England) in 1269. In 1329 the castle was destroyed and rebuilt in its current shape. It was conquered by the Duke of Brabant in 1365 and was subsequently beseiged on a number of occasions until being blown up by the armies of William III in 1672. Today, it is possible to visit the network of secret passages leading to the Velvet Cave. **Open:** Contact for details of opening times. **Admission:** Castle Ruins & Cave Tours: Adult FL10, children 4–12 yrs FL7, OAPs FL9. Family card FL30 (incl 2 adults & children aged 4–16).

map 295
6

Supplementary List of Properties

The list of houses in England, Scotland and Wales printed here are those which are usually open 'by appointment only' with the owner, or open infrequently during the summer months. These are in addition to the Houses and Gardens which are open regularly and are fully classified. Where it is necessary to write for an appointment to view, see code (WA). * denotes owner/address if this is different from the property address. The majority of these properties have received a grant for conservation from the Government given on the advice of the Historic Buildings Councils. Public buildings, almshouses, tithe barn, business premises in receipt of grants are not usually included, neither are properties where the architectural features can be viewed from the street.

ENGLAND

AVON

Birdcombe Court, (Mr & Mrs P. C. Sapsed.) (WA), Wraxall, Bristol

Eastwood Manor Farm, (A. J. Gay), East Harptree

Partis College, (The Bursar.) (WA), Newbridge Hill, Bath, BA1 3QD Tel: 01225 421 532

The Refectory, (Rev. R. Salmon), The Vicarage Tel: 01934 833 126

Woodspring Priory, (WA), Kewstoke, Weston-Super-Mare.*The Landmark Trust.

BEDFORDSHIRE

The Temple, (The Estate Office) (WA), Biggleswade

Warden Abbey, (WA), Nr. Biggleswade
* The Landmark Trust.

BERKSHIRE

High Chimneys, (Mr & Mrs S. Cheetham) (WA), Hurst, Reading Tel: 01734 34517

St. Gabriel's School, (The Headmaster), Sandleford Priory, Newbury Tel: 01635 40663

BUCKINGHAMSHIRE

Bisham Abbey, (The Director), Marlow Tel: 01628 476 911

Brudenell House, (Dr H. Beric Wright) (WA), Quainton, Aylesbury, HP22 4AW

Church of the Assumption, (Friends of Friendless Churches), Harmead, Newport Pagnell Tel: 01234 39257 * For Key: Apply to H. Tranter, Manor Cottage, Hardmead, by letter or phone on 01234 39257.

Iver Grove, (Mr & Mrs T. Stoppard) (WA), Shreding Green, Iver

Repton's Subway Facade, (WA), Digby's Walk, Gayhurst Tel: 01908 551 564* JH Beverly, The Bath House, Gayhurst.

CAMBRIDGESHIRE

The Chantry, (Mrs T. A. N. Bristol) (WA), Ely, Cambridge

The Church of St. John the Baptist, (Friends of Friendless Churches), Papworth St. Agnes * For Key: Apply to Mrs P. Honeybane, Passhouse Cottage, Papworth St. Agnes, by letter or phone on 01480 830 631.

The King's School, Ely, (WA), Bursars Office, The King's School, Ely, CB7 4DB Tel: 01353 662 837, Fax: 01353 662 187

Leverington Hall, (Professor A. Barton) (WA), Wisbech, PE13 5DE

The Lynch Lodge, (WA), Alwalton, Peterborough
* The Landmark Trust

CHESHIRE

Bewsey Old Hall, (The Administrator) (WA), Warrington

Crown Hotel, (Proprietor: P. J. Martin), High Street, Nantwich, CW5 5AS Tel: 01270 625 283, Fax: 01270 628 047

Charles Roe House, (McMillan Group Plc) (WA), Chestergate, Macclesfield, SK11 6DZ

Shotwick Hall, (Tenants: Mr & Mrs G. A. T. Holland), Shotwick Tel: 01244 881 717
* R. B. Gardner, Wychen, 17 St. Mary's Road, Leatherhead, Surrey. By appointment only with the tenants, Mr & Mrs G. A. T. Holland.

Tudor House, Lower Bridge Street, Chester Tel: 01244 20095

Watergate House, (WA), Chester Tel: 01352 713353 * Ferry Homes Ltd, 49 High Street, Holywell, Clwyd, Wales, CH8 9TF.

CLEVELAND

St. Cuthbert's Church & Turner Mausoleum, (Kirkleatham Parochial Church Council), Kirkleatham Tel: Contact Mrs R. S. Ramsdale on 01642 475 198 or Mrs D. Cook, Church Warden on 01642 485 395

CORNWALL

The College, (WA), Week St. Mary
* The Landmark Trust.

Town Hall, (Camelford Town Trust), Camelford

Trecarrel Manor, (N. H. Burden), Trebullett, Launceston Tel: 01566 82286

CUMBRIA

Coop House, (WA), Netherby
* The Landmark Trust.

Preston Patrick Hall, (Mrs J. D. Armitage) (WA), Milnthorpe, LA7 7NY Tel: 01539 567 200, Fax: 01539 567 200

Whitehall, (WA), Mealsgate, Carlisle, CA5 1JS
* Mrs S. Parkin-Moore, 40 Woodsome Road, London, NW5 1RZ.

DERBYSHIRE

Elvaston Castle, (Derbyshire County Council), Nr. Derby, DE72 3EP Tel: 01332 571 342

10 North Street, (WA), Cromford
* The Landmark Trust.

Swarkestone Pavilion, (WA), Ticknall
* The Landmark Trust.

DEVON

Bindon Manor, (Sir John & Lady Loveridge) (WA), Axmouth

Bowringsleigh, (Mr & Mrs M. C. Manisty) (WA), Kingbridge

Endsleigh House, (Endsleigh Fishing Club Ltd), Milton Abbot, Nr. Tavistock Tel: 01822 870 248, Fax: 01822 870 502

Hareston House, (Mrs K. M. Basset), Brixton, PL8 2DL Tel: 01752 880 426

The Library, (WA), Stevenstone, Torrington
* The Landmark Trust.

Sanders, (WA), Lettaford, North Bovey
* The Landmark Trust.

The Shell House, (Endsleigh Fishing Club Ltd), Milton Abbot, Nr. Tavistock Tel: 01822 870 248,
Fax: 01822 870 502

Shute Gatehouse, (WA), Shute Barton, Nr. Axminster
* The Landmark Trust.

Town House, (Tenant: Mr & Mrs R. A. L. Hill), Gittisham, Honiton Tel: 01404 851 041
* Mr & Mrs R. J. T. Marker

Wortham Manor, (WA), Lifton
* The Landmark Trust.

DORSET

Bloxworth House, (Mr T. A. Dulake) (WA), Bloxworth

Clenston Manor, Winterborne, Clenston, Blandford Forum

Higher Melcombe, (M. C. Woodhouse) (WA), Dorchester, DT2 7PB

Moignes Court, (A. M. Cree) (WA), Owermoigne

Smedmore House, Kimmeridge, BH20 5PG

Stafford House, (Mr & Mrs Richard Pavitt), West Stafford, Dorchester Tel: 01305 263 668

Woodsford Castle, (WA), Woodsford, Nr. Dorchester
* The Landmark Trust.

COUNTY DURHAM

The Buildings in the Square, (Lady Gilbertson) (WA), 1 The Square, Greta Bridge, DL12 9SD Tel: 01833 27276

ESSEX

Blake Hall, Battle of Britain Museum & Gardens, (Owner: R. Capel Cure), Chipping Ongar, CM5 0DG Tel: 01277 362 502

Properties by Appointment Only

Church of St. Andrews and Monks Tithe Barn, (Harlow District Council), Harlow Study & Visitors Centre, Netteswellbury Farm, Harlow, CM18 6BW Tel: 01279 446 745, Fax: 01279 421 945

Grange Farm, (J. Kirby), Little Dunmow, CM6 3HY Tel: 01371 820 205

Great Priory Farm, (Miss L. Tabor), Panfield, Braintree, CM7 5BQ Tel: 01376 550 944

The Guildhall, (Dr & Mrs Paul Sauven), Great Waltham Tel: 01245 360 527

Old All Saints, (R. Mill), Old Church Hill, Langdon Hills, SS16 6HZ Tel: 01268 414 146

Rainham Hall, (The National Trust. Tenant: D. Atack), Rainham

Rayne Hall, (Mr & Mrs R. J. Pertwee) (WA), Rayne, Braintree

The Round House, (M. E. W. Heap), Havering-atte-Bower, Romford, RM4 1QH Tel: 01708 728 136

GLOUCESTERSHIRE

Abbey Gatehouse, (WA), Tewksbury
* The Landmark Trust.

Ashleworth Court, (H. J. Chamberlayne), Gloucester Tel: 01452 700 241

Ashleworth Manor, (Dr & Mrs Jeremy Barnes) (WA), Ashleworth, Gloucester, GL19 4LA Tel: 01452 700 350

Bearland House, (The Administrator) (WA), Longsmith Street, Gloucester, GL1 2HL, Fax: 01452 419 312

Castle Godwyn, (Mr & Mrs J. Milne) (WA), Painswick

Chaceley Hall, (W. H. Lane), Tewkesbury Tel: 01452 28205

Cheltenham College, (The Bursar), The College, Bath Road, Cheltenham, GL53 7LD Tel: 01242 513 540

The Cottage, (Mrs S. M. Rolt) (WA), Stanley Pontlarge, Winchcombe, GL54 5HD

East Banqueting House, (WA), Chipping Camden
* The Landmark Trust.

Minchinhampton Market House, (B. E. Lucas), Stroud Tel: 01453 883 241

The Old Vicarage, ('Lord Weymyss' Trust), The Church, Stanway Tel: 01386 584 469
* Apply to Stanway House, Stanway, Cheltenham:

St. Margaret's Church, (The Gloucester Charities Trust), London Road, Gloucester Tel: 01452 23316
By appointment with the Warden on 01831 470 335.

Tyndale Monument, (Tyndale Monument Charity), North Nibley, GL11 4JA Tel: 01453 543 691
For Key: See notice at foot of Wood Lane.

GREATER MANCHESTER

Chetham's Hospital & Library, (The Feoffees of Chetham's Hospital & Library), Manchester, M5 1SB Tel 0161 834 9644, Fax: 0161 839 5797

Slade Hall, (Manchester & District Housing Assn.) (WA), Slade Lane, Manchester, M13 0QP

HAMPSHIRE

Chesil Theatre (formerly 12th century Church of St. Peter Chesil), (Winchester Dramatic Society), Chesil Street, Winchester, SO23 0HU Tel: 01962 867 086

The Deanery, (The Dean & Chapter), The Close, Winchester, SO23 9LS Tel: 01962 853 137, Fax: 01962 841 519

Greywell Hill, near Hook (PR FitzGerald, Wilsons)(WA) Steynings House, Fisherton Street, Salisbury SP2 7RJ

Manor House Farm, (S. B. Mason), Hambledon Tel: 01705 632 433

Moyles Court, (Headmaster, Moyles Court School) (WA), Moyles Court, Ringwood, BH24 3NF Tel: 01425 472 856

HEREFORD & WORCESTER

Britannia House, (The Alice Ottley School), The Tything, Worcester. Apply to the Headmistress.

Church House, (The Trustees), Market Square, Evesham

Grafton Manor, (J. W. Morris, Lord of Grafton), Bromsgrove Tel: 01527 31525

Newhouse Farm, (The Administrator) (WA), Goodrich, Ross-on-Wye

The Old Palace, (The Dean & Chapter of Worcester) (WA), Worcester.

Shelwick Court, (WA), Hereford * The Landmark Trust.

HERTFORDSHIRE

Heath Mount School, (The Abel Smith Trustees), Woodhall Park, Watton-at-Stone, Hertford, SG14 3NG Tel: 01920 830 286, Fax: 01920 830 357

Northaw Place, (The Administrator), Northaw Tel: 01707 44059

KENT

Barming Place, (Mr J. Peter & Dr Rosalind Bearcroft), Maidstone Tel: 01622 727 844

Bedgebury National Pinetum, (Forestry Enterprise), Nr. Goudhurst Tel: 01580 211 044, Fax: 01580 212 523

Foord Almshouses, (The Clerk to the Trustees) (WA), Rochester

Mersham-le-Hatch, (The Hon. M. J. Knatchbull), Nr. Ashford, TN25 5NH Tel: 01233 503 954, Fax: 01233 611 650. Apply to the tenant: The Directors, Caldecott Community.

Nurstead Court, (Mrs S. M. H. Edmeades-Stearns), Meopham Tel: 01474 812 121

Old College of All Saints, Kent Music Centre, Maidstone Tel: 01622 690 404
Apply to the Regional Director.

The Old Pharmacy, (Mrs Peggy Noreen Kerr), 6 Market Place, Faversham, ME13 7EH

Prospect Tower, (WA), Belmont Park, Faversham
* The Landmark Trust.

Yaldham Manor, (Mr & Mrs J. Mourier Lade) (WA), Kemsing, Sevenoaks, TN15 6NN Tel: 01732 761 029

LANCASHIRE

The Music Room, (WA), Lancaster
* The Landmark Trust.

Parrox Hall, (Mr & Mrs H. D. H. Elleston) (WA), Preesall, Nr. Poulton-le-Fylde, FY6 0NW Tel: 01253 810 245, Fax: 01253 811 223

LEICESTERSHIRE

Launde Abbey, (Rev. Graham Johnson), East Norton

The Moat House, (Mrs H. S. Hall), Appleby Magna Tel: 01530 270 301

Old Grammar School, Market Harborough Tel: 01858 462 202

Staunton Harold Hall, (Ryder-Cheshire Foundation), Ashby-de-la-Zouch Tel: 01332 862 798

LINCOLNSHIRE

Bede House, Tattershall

The Chateau, (WA), Gate Burton, Gainsborough
* The Landmark Trust.

East Lighthouse, (Cdr. M. D. Joel R.N.) (WA), Sutton Bridge, Spalding, PE12 9YT

Fulbeck Manor, (J. F. Fane) (WA), Grantham, NG32 3JN Tel: 01400 272 231

Harlaxton Manor, (University of Evansville) (WA), Grantham. *Group Visits by appointment only*

House of Correction, (WA), Folkingham
* The Landmark Trust.

The Norman Manor House, (Lady Netherthorpe) (WA), Boothby Pagnell

Pelham Mausoleum, (The Earl of Yarborough), Limber, Grimsby

Scrivelsby Court, (Lt. Col. J. L. M. Dymoke M.B.E. DL.) (WA), Nr. Horncastle, LN9 6JA Tel: 01507 523 325

LONDON

All Hallows Vicarage, (Rev. R. Pearson), Tottenham, London, N17

69 Brick Lane, (The Administrator) (WA), London, E1

24 The Butts, 192, 194, 196, 198, 202, 204-224 Cable Street, (Mrs Sally Mills) (WA), London

11-13 Cavendish Street, (Heythrop College) (WA), London

Celia & Phillip Blairman Houses, (The Administrator) (WA), Elder Street, London, E1

Charlton House, (London Borough of Greenwich) (WA), Charlton Road, Charlton, London, SE7 8RE Tel: 0181 856 3951

Charterhouse, (The Governors of Sutton Hospital), Charterhouse Square, London, EC1

17-27 Folgate Street, (WA), London, E1

36 Hanbury Street, (WA), London, E1

Heathgate House, (Rev. Mother Prioress, Ursuline Convent), 66 Crooms Hill, Greenwich, London, SE10 8HG Tel: 0181 858 0779

140, 142, 166 168 Homerton High Street, (WA), London, E5

House of St. Barnabas-in-Soho, (The Warden of the House) (WA), 1 Greek Street, Soho, London, W1V 6NQ Tel: 0171 437 1894

Kensal Green Cemetery, (General Cemetery Company), Harrow Road, London, W10 4RA Tel: 0181 969 0152, Fax: 0181 960 9744

69-83 Paragon Road, (WA), London, E5

Red House, (Mr & Mrs Hollamby) (WA), Red House Lane, Bexleyheath

Sunbury Court, (The Salvation Army), Sudbury-on-Thames Tel: 01932 782 196

Vale Mascal Bath House, (Mrs F. Chu), 112 North Cray Road, Bexley, DA5 3NA Tel: 01322 554 894

Wesley's House, (The Trustees of the Methodist Church), 47 City Road, London, EC1Y 1AU Tel: 0171 253 2262, Fax: 0171 608 3825

MERSEYSIDE

The Turner Home, (R. A. Waring RGN., CGN), Dingle Head, Liverpool Tel: 0151 727 4177

NORFOLK

All Saints' Church, (Norfolk Churches Trust) , Barmer Keyholder – No 5, The Cottages.

All Saints' Church, (Norfolk Churches Trust) , Cockthorpe. Keyholder - Mrs Case at farmhouse.

All Saints' Church, (Norfolk Churches Trust) , Dunton Key of Tower at Hall Farm.

All Saints' Church, (Norfolk Churches Trust) , Frenze Keyholder - Mrs Alston at farmhouse.

All Saints' Church, (Norfolk Churches Trust) , Hargham Keyholder – Mrs Clifford, Amost, Station Road, Attleborough.

All Saints' Church, (Rector, Churchwardens and PCC) , Weston Longville, NR9 5JU Keyholder - Rev. J. P. P. Illingworth.

All Saints' Church, (Norfolk Churches Trust) , Snetterton Keyholder - at Hall Farm.

Billingford Mill, (Norfolk County Council), Scole

6 The Close, (The Dean & Chapter of Norwich Cathedral) (WA), Norwich

Fishermen's Hospital, (J. E. C. Lamb F.I.H., Clerk to the Trustees), Great Yarmouth Tel: 01493 856 609

Gowthorpe Manor, (Mrs Watkinson) (WA), Swardeston, NR14 8DS Tel: 01508 570 216

Hales Hall, (Mr & Mrs T. Read) (WA), London, NR14 6QW Tel: 0150 846 395

Hoveton House, (Sir John Blofeld), Wroxham, Norwich, NR12 8JE

Lattice House, (Mr & Mrs T. Duckett) (WA), King's Lynn Tel: 01553 777 292

Little Cressingham Mill, (Norfolk Mills & Pumps Trust), Little Cressingham, Thetford Tel: 01953 850 567

Little Hautbois Hall, (Mrs Duffield) (WA), Nr. Norwich, NR12 7JR Tel: 01603 279 333, Fax: 01603 279 615

The Music House, (The Warden), Wensum Lodge, King Street, Norwich Tel: 01603 666 021/666022, Fax: 01603 765 633

Norwich Cathedral Close, (WA), The Close, Norwich Apply to the Cathedral Steward's Office, Messrs. Percy Howes & Co, 3 The Close, Norwich.

The Old Princes Inn Restaurant, 20 Prince Street, Norwich Tel: 01603 621 043

The Old Vicarage, (Mr & Mrs H. C. Dance), Crown St. Methwold, Thetford, IP25 ANR

St. Andrew's Church, (Norfolk Churches Trust), Frenze Keyholder - Mrs Altston at farmhouse opposite.

St. Celia's Church, West Bilney Keyholder - Mr Curl, Tanglewood, Main Road, West Bilney.

St. Margaret's Church, (Norfolk Churches Trust), Morton-on-the-Hill, NR9 5JS Keyholder - Lady Prince-Smith at the Hall.

St. Mary's Church, (Norfolk Churches Trust), Dunton

St. Peter's Church, (Norfolk Churches Trust), The Lodge, Millgate, Aylsham, NR11 6HX Keyholder - Lord & Lady Romney at Wesnum Farm or Mrs Walker at Pocklethorpe Cottages.

Stracey Arms Mill, (Norfolk County Council), Nr. Acle Tel: 01603 611122 Ext 5224

The Strangers' Club, 22, 24 Elm Hill, Norwich Tel: 01603 623 813

Thoresby College, (King's Lynn Preservation Trust) (WA), Queen Street, King's Lynn, PE30 1HX

Wiveton Hall, (D. MacCarthy) (WA), Holt

NORTHAMPTONSHIRE

Courteenhall, (Sir Hereward Wake Bt. MC) (WA), Northampton

Drayton House, (L. G. Stopford Sackville) (WA), Lowick, Kettering, NN14 3BG Tel: 01832 732 405

The Monastery, (Mr & Mrs R. G. Wigley) (WA), Shutlanger, NN12 7RU Tel: 01604 862 529

Paine's Cottage, (R. O. Barber) (WA), Oundle

Weston Hall, (Mr & Mrs Francis Sitwell) (WA), Towcester

NORTHUMBERLAND

Brinkburn Mill, (WA), Rothbury
* The Landmark Trust.

Capheaton Hall, (J. Browne-Swinburne) (WA), Newcastle-upon-Tyne, NE19 2AB

Causeway House, (WA), Bardon Mill

Craster Tower, (Col. J. M. Craster, Miss M. D. Craster & F. Sharratt) (WA), Alnwick

Netherwitton Hall, (J. C. R. Trevelyon) (WA), Morpeth, NE61 4NW Tel: 01670 772 219 Fax: 01670 772 332

NOTTINGHAMSHIRE

Winkburn Hall, (R. Craven-Smith-Milnes), Newark, NG22 8PQ Tel: 01636 636 465, Fax: 01636 636 717

Worksop Priory Church & Gatehouse, The Vicarage, Cheapside Tel: 01909 472 180

OXFORDSHIRE

26-27 Cornmarket Street & 26 Ship Street, (Home Bursar), Jesus College, Oxford Shop basement by written appointment to: Laura Ashley Ltd, 150 Bath Road, Maidenhead, Berks, SL6 4YS.

Hope House, (Mrs J. Hageman), Woodstock

The Manor, (Mr & Mrs Paul L. Jacques) (WA), Chalgrove, OX44 7SL Tel: 01865 890 836, Fax: 01865 891 810

Monarch's Court House, (R. S. Hine) (WA)Benson

Ripon College, (The Principal) (WA), Cuddesdon

30-43 The Causeway, (Mr & Mrs R. Hornsby), 39-43 The Causeway, Steventon

SHROPSHIRE

Bromfield Priory Gatehouse, (WA), Ludlow Tel: 01628 825 925* The Landmark Trust.

Halston, (Mrs J. L. Harvey) (WA), Oswestry

Hatton Grange, (Mrs P. Afia) (WA), Shifnal

Langley Gatehouse, (WA), Acton Burnell Tel: 01628 825 925 * The Landmark Trust, Shottesbrooke, nr. Maidenhead, Berks, SL6 3SW.

Oakley Manor, (Shrewsbury & Atcham Borough Council), Belle Vue Road, Shrewsbury, SY3 7NW Tel: 01243 231 456, Fax: 01243 271 598

St. Winifred's Well, (WA), Woolston, Oswestry * The Landmark Trust, Shottesbrooke, nr. Maidenhead, Berks, SL6 3SW.

Stanwardine Hall, (P. J. Bridge), Cockshutt, Ellesmere Tel: 01939 270 212

SOMERSET

Cothelstone Manor & Gatehouse, (Mrs J. E. B. Warmington) (WA), Cothelstone, Nr. Taunton, TA4 3DS Tel: 01823 432 200

Fairfield, (Lady Gass), Stogursey, Bridgwater, TA5 1PU Tel: 01278 732 251 Fax: 01278 732277

Gurney Manor, (WA), Cannington Tel: 01628 825 925 * The Landmark Trust, Shottesbrooke, nr. Maidenhead, Berks, SL6 3SW.

The Old Drug Store, (Mr & Mrs E. D. J. Schofield) (WA), Axbridge

The Old Hall, (WA), Croscombe * The Landmark Trust, Shottesbrooke, nr. Maidenhead, Berks, SL6 3SW.

The Priest's Hole, (WA), Holcombe Rogus, Nr. Wellington * The Landmark Trust, Shottesbrooke, nr. Maidenhead, Berks, SL6 3SW.

Stogursey Castle, (WA), Nr. Bridgwater * The Landmark Trust, Shottesbrooke, nr. Maidenhead, Berks, SL6 3SW.

West Coker Manor, (Mr & Mrs Derek Maclaren), West Coker, BA22 9BJ Tel: 01935 862 646

Whitelackington Manor, (E. J. H. Cameron), Dillington Estate Office, Illminster, TA19 9EQ Tel: 01460 54614

Properties by Appointment Only

STAFFORDSHIRE

Broughton Hall, (The Administrator) (WA), Eccleshall

Dunwood Hall, (Dr R. Vincent-Kemp FRSA), Longsdon, Nr. Leek, ST9 9AR Tel: 01538 385 071

The Great Hall in Keele Hall, (The Registrar, University of Keele) (WA), Keele

Ingestre Pavilion, (WA), Nr. Stafford
* The Landmark Trust, Shottesbrooke, nr. Maidenhead, Berks, SL6 3SW.

Old Hall Gatehouse, (R. M. Eades), Mavesyn Ridware Tel: 01543 490 312

The Orangery, (Mrs M Philips), Heath House, Tean, Stoke-on-Trent, ST10 4HA Tel: 01538 722 212

Park Hall, (E. J. Knobbs) (WA), Leigh

Tixall Gatehouse, (WA), Tixall, Nr. Stafford
* The Landmark Trust, Shottesbrooke, Nr. Maidenhead, Berks, SL6 3SW.

SUFFOLK

The Deanery, (The Dean of Bocking), Hadleigh, IP7 5DT Tel: 01473 822 218

Ditchingham Hall, (The Rt. Hon. Earl Ferrers), Ditchingam, Bungay

The Hall, (Mr & Mrs R. B. Cooper) (WA), Great Bricett, Ipswich

Hengrave Hall Centre, (The Warden), Bury St. Edmunds, IP28 6LZ Tel: 01284 701 561

Martello Tower, (WA), Aldeburgh
* The Landmark Trust.

Moat Hall, (J. W. Gray), Woodbridge, IP13 9AE Tel: 01728 746 317

The New Inn, (WA), Peasenhall
* The Landmark Trust.

Newbourne Hall, (John Somerville) (WA), Woodbridge

Worlingham Hall, (Viscount Colville of Culross) (WA), Beccles

SURREY

Crossways Farm, (Tenant: C. T. Hughes) (WA), Abinger Hammer

Great Fosters Hotel, (Manager: J. E. Baumann), Egham, TW20 9UR Tel: 01784 433 822

St. Mary's Home Chapel, Church Lane, Godstone Tel: 01883 742 385

SUSSEX

Ashdown House, (The Headmaster), Ashdown House School, Forest Row, RH18 5JY Tel: 01342 822 574, Fax: 01342 824 380

Chantry Green House, (Mr & Mrs G. H. Recknell), Steyning Tel: 01903 812 239

The Chapel, Bishop's Palace, (Church Commissioners), The Palace, Chichester

Christ's Hospital, (WA), Horsham Tel: 01403 211 293

Laughton Tower, (WA), Lewes * The Landmark Trust.

WARWICKSHIRE

Bath House, (WA), Walton, Stratford-upon-Avon
* The Landmark Trust, Shottesbrooke, nr. Maidenhead, Berks, SL6 3SW.

Binswood Hall, (North Leamington School) (WA), Binswood Avenue, Leamington Spa, CV32 5SF Tel: 01926 423 686

Foxcote, (C. B. Holman) (WA), Shipton-on-Stour

Nicholas Chamberlain's Almshouses, (The Warden), Bedworth Tel: 01203 312 225

Northgate, (R. E. Phllips) (WA), Warwick, CV34 4JL

St. Leonard's Church, (WA), Wroxall
Apply to Mrs J. M. Gowen, Headmistress, Wroxall Abbey School, Warwick, CV35 7NB.

War Memorial Town Hall, (The Secretary, D. R. Young), 27 Henley Street, Alcester, B49 5QX Tel: 01789 765 198

WILTSHIRE

Bradley House, Maiden Bradley, Warminster Tel: 01803 866633 (The Estate Office)

Chinese Summerhouse, Amesbury Abbey, Amesbury Tel: 01980 622 957

Farley Hospital, (The Warden), Church Road, Farley, SP5 1AH Tel: 01722 712 231

Milton Manor, (Mrs Rupert Gentle), The Manor House, Milton Lilbourne, Pewsey, SN9 5LQ Tel: 01672 563 344, Fax: 01672 564 136

Old Bishop's Palace, (The Bursar, Salisbury Cathedral School), 1 The Close, Salisbury Tel: 01722 322 652

The Old Manor House, (J. Teed) (WA), 2 Whitehead Lane, Bradford-upon-Avon

Orpins House, (J. Vernon Burchell) (WA), Church Street, Bradford-upon-Avon

The Porch House, (Tim Vidal-Hall) (WA), 6 High Street, Potterne, Devizes, SN10 5NA

YORKSHIRE

Beamsley Hospital, (WA), Skipton
* The Landmark Trust.

Busby Hall, (G. A. Marwood) (WA), Carlton-in-Cleveland

Calverley Old Hall, (WA), Nr. Leeds
* The Landmark Trust.

Cawood Castle, (WA), Nr. Selby
* The Landmark Trust.

Chapel & Coach House, Aske, Richmond

The Church of Our Lady & St. Everilda, (WA), Everingham Tel: 01430 860 531

The Culloden Tower, (WA), Richmond
* The Landmark Trust.

The Dovecote, (Mrs P. E. Heathcote), Forcett Hall, Forcett, Richmond Tel: 01325 718 226

Home Farm House, (G. T. Reece) (WA), Old Scriven, Knaresborough

Moulton Hall, (The National Trust. Tenant: The Hon. J. D. Eccles) (WA), Richmond

The Old Rectory, (Mrs R. F. Wormald) (WA), Foston, York

The Pigsty, (WA), Robin Hood's Bay
* The Landmark Trust.

Fulneck Boys' School, (I. D. Cleland, BA, M. Phil, Headmaster) (WA), Pudsey

Grand Theatre & Opera House, (General Manager: Warren Smith), 46 New Briggate, Leeds, LS1 6NZ Tel: 0113 245 6014, Fax: 0113 246 5906

Horbury Hall, (D. J. H. Michelmore), Horbury, Wakefield Tel: 01924 277 552

Town Hall, (Leeds City Council), Leeds Tel: 0113 247 7989

Weston Hall, (Lt. Col. H. V. Dawson) (WA), Nr. Otley, LS21 2HP

WALES

CLWYD

Fferm, (Dr M. C. Jones-Mortimer), Pontblyddyn, Mold, CH7 4HN Tel: 01352 770 876

Golden Grove, (N. R. & M. M. J. Steele-Mortimer) (WA), Llanasa, Nr. Holywell, CH8 9NE Tel: 01745 854 452, Fax: 01745 854 547

Halghton Hall, (J. D. Lewis) (WA), Bangor-on-Dee, Wrexham

Lindisfarne College, (The Headmaster) (WA), Wynnstay Hall, Ruabon Tel: 01978 810 407

Pen Isa'r Glascoed, (M. E. Harrop), Bodelwyddan, LL22 9D745 583 501D Tel: 01 45 583501

DYFED

Monkton Old Hall, (WA), Pembroke
* The Landmark Trust.

Taliaris Park, (J. H. Spencer-Williams) (WA), Llandeilo

University of Wales Lampeter, (Prof. Keith Robbins), Lampeter, SA48 7ED Tel: 01570 422 351, Fax: 01570 423 423

West Blockhouse, (WA), Haverfordwest, Dale
* The Landmark Trust.

SOUTH GLAMORGAN

Fonmon Castle, (Sir Brooke Boothby, Bt.), Barry, CF6 9ZN Tel: 01446 710 206, Fax: 01446 711 687

GWENT

Blackbrook Manor, (Mr & Mrs A. C. de Morgan), Skenfrith, Nr. Abergavenny, NP7 8UB Tel: 01600 84453, Fax: 01600 84453

Castle Hill House, (T. Baxter-Wright) (WA), Monmouth

Clytha Castle, (WA), Abergavenny
* The Landmark Trust.

Great Cil-Lwch, (J. F. Ingledew) (WA), Llantilio Crossenny, Abergavenny, NP7 8SR Tel: 01600 780 206

Kemys House, (I. S. Burge) (WA), Keyms Inferior, Caerleon

Llanvihangel Court, (Mrs D. Johnson) (WA), Abergavenny, NP7 8DH

Overmonnow House, (J. R. Pangbourne) (WA), Monmouth

3-4 Priory Street, (H. R. Ludwig), Monmouth

Treowen, (John Wheelock), Wonastow, Monmouth, NP5 4DL Tel: 01600 712 031

GWYNEDD

Cymryd, (Miss D. E. Glynne) (WA), Cymryd, Conwy, LL32 8UA

Dolaugwyn, (Mrs S. Tudor) (WA), Towyn

Nannau, (P. Vernon) (WA), Dolgellau

Penmynydd, (The Rector of Llanfairpwll) (WA), Alms House, Llnafairpwll

Plas Coch, (Mrs N. Donald), Llanedwen, Llanfairpwll Tel: 01248 714272

POWYS

Abercamlais, (Mrs J. C. R. Ballance) (WA), Brecon

Abercynrig, (Mrs W. R. Lloyd) (WA), Brecon

1 Buckingham Place, (Mrs Meeres) (WA), 1 Buckingham Place, Brecon, LD3 7DL Tel: 01874 623 612

3 Buckingham Place, (Mr & Mrs A. Whiley) (WA), 3 Buckingham Place, Brecon, LD3 7DL

Maesmawr Hall Hotel, (Mrs M. Pemberton & Mrs I. Hunt), Caersws Tel: 01686 688 255

Newton Farm, (Mrs Ballance. Tenant: D. L. Evans), Brecon

Pen Y Lan, (J. G. Meade), Meifod, Powys, SY22 6DA Tel: 01938 500 202

Plasdau Duon, (E. S. Breese), Clatter

Poultry House, (WA), Leighton, Welshpool
* The Landmark Trust..

Rhydycarw, (M. Breese-Davies), Trefeglwys, Newton, SY17 5PU Tel: 01686 430 411, Fax: 01686 430 331

Ydderw, (D. P. Eckley) (WA), Llyswen

SCOTLAND

BORDERS

Old Gala House, (Ettrick & Lauderdale District Council), Galashiels Tel: 01750 20096

Sir Walter Scott's Courtroom, (Ettrick & Lauderdale District Council)), Selkirk Tel: 01750 20096

Wedderlie House, (Mrs J. R. L. Campbell) (WA), Gordon, TD3 6NW Tel: 0157 874 0223

DUMFRIES & GALLOWAY

Bonshaw Tower, (Dr J. B. Irving) (WA), Kirtlebridge, Lockerbie, DG11 3LY Tel: 01461 500 256

Carnsalloch House, (The Leonard Cheshire Foundation), Carnsalloch, Kirkton, DG1 1SN Tel: 01387 254 924, Fax: 01387 257 971

Kirkconnell House, (F. Maxwell Witham), New Abbey, Dumfries Tel: 0138 785 276

FIFE

Bath Castle, (Angus Mitchell), Bogside, Oakley, FK10 3RD Tel: 0131 556 7671

The Castle, (J. Bevan) (WA), Elie

Castle of Park, (WA), Glenluce, Galloway
* The Landmark Trust.

Charleton House, (Baron St. Clair Bonde), Colinsburgh Tel: 0133 334

GRAMPIAN

Balbithan House, (J. McMurtie), Kintore Tel: 01467 32282

Balfluig Castle, (Mark Tennant) (WA), Grampian Apply to 30 Abbey Gardens, London, NW8 9AT

Barra Castle, (Dr & Mrs Andrew Bogdan) (WA), Old Meldrum

Castle of Fiddes, (Dr M. Weir), Stonehaven Tel: 01569 740 213

Church of the Holy Rude, St. John Street, Stirling

Corsindae House, (R. Fyffe) (WA), Sauchen by Inverurie, Inverurie, AB51 7PP Tel: 01330 833 295, Fax: 01330 833 629

Drumminor Castle, (A. D. Forbes) (WA), Rhynie

Erskine Marykirk - Stirling Youth Hostel, St. John Street, Stirling

Gargunnock House, (Gargunnock Estate Trust) (WA), Stirling

Gordonstoun School, (The Headmaster) (WA), Elgin Moray

Grandhome House, (D. R. Patton), Aberdeen Tel: 01224 722 202

Guildhall, (Stirling District Council), Municipal Buildings, Stirling Tel: 01786 79000

Old Tolbooth Building, (Stirling District Council), Municipal Buildings, Stirling Tel: 01786 79000

Phesdo House, (J. M. Thomson) (WA), Laurencekirk

The Pineapple, (WA), Dunmore, Airth, Stirling
* The Landmark Trust.

Tolbooth, (Stirling District Council), Broad Street, Stirling Tel: 01786 79400

Touch House, (P. B. Buchanan) (WA), Stirling, FK8 3AQ Tel: 01786 464 278

HIGHLANDS

Embo House, (John G. Mackintosh), Dornoch Tel: Dornoch 810 260

LOTHIAN

Cakemuir, (M. M. Scott) (WA), Parthhead, Tynehead, EH3 5XR

Castle Gogar, (Lady Steel-Maitland), Edinburgh Tel: 0131 339 1234

Ford House, (F. P. Tindall ,OBE) (WA), Ford

Forth Road Bridge, (The Bridgemaster), South Queensferry Tel: 0131 319 1699

Linnhouse, (H. J. Spur(wa)y) (WA), Linnhouse, Livingstone, EH54 9AN Tel: 01506 410 742, Fax: 01506 416 591

Newbattle Abbey College, (The Principal), Dalkeith, EH22 3LL Tel: 0131 663 1921, Fax: 0131 654 0598

Penicuik House, (Sir John Clerk, Bt.), Penicuik

Roseburn House, (M. E. Sturgeon) (WA), Murrayfield

Townhouse, (East Lothian District Council), Haddington Tel: Haddington 4161

SHETLAND ISLES

The Lodberrie, (Thomas Moncrieff), Lerwick

STRATHCLYDE

Ascog House, (WA), Rothea* The Landmark Trust.

Barcaldine Castle, (Roderick Campbell) (WA), Benderloch

Craufurdland Castle, (J. P. Houison Craufurdland), Kilmarnock, KA3 6BS Tel: 01560 600 402

Dunstrune Castle, (Robin Malcolm of Poltallock) (WA), Lochgilphead

Kelburn Castle, (The Earl of Glasgow) (WA), Fairlie, Ayrshire, KA29 0BE Tel: Country Centre: 01475 568 685 Kelburn Castle: 01475 568 204, Fax: Country Centre: 01475 568 121 Kelburn Castle: 01475 568 328

New Lanark, (New Lanark Conservation Trust), New Lanark Mills, Lanark, ML11 9DB Tel: 01555 661 345, Fax: 01555 665 738

The Place of Paisley, (Paisley Abbey Kirk Session), Paisley Abbey, Abbey Close, Paisley, PA1 1JG Tel: 0141 889 7654

Saddell Castle, (WA), Campbeltown, Argyll
* The Landmark Trust.

Tangy Mill, (WA), Campbeltown, Kintyre, Argyll
* The Landmark Trust.

Tannahill Cottage, (Secretary, Paisley Burns Club), Queen Street, Paisley Tel: 0141 887 7500

TAYSIDE

Ardblair Castle, (Laurence P. K. Blair Oliphant), Blairgowrie, PH10 6SA Tel: 01250 873 155

Craig House, (Charles F. R. Hoste), Montrose Tel: 01674 722 239

Kinross House, (Sir David Montgomery, Bt.) (WA), Kinross

Michael Bruce Cottage, (Michael Bruce Trust), Kinnesswood

The Pavilion, Gleneagles, (J. Martin Haldane of Gleneagles) (WA), Gleneagles, Auchterarder, PH3 1PJ

Tulliebole Castle, (The Lord Moncrieff), Crook of Devon

Garden Specialists

If you have been inspired by some of the wonderful gardens contained in this guide, why not recreate some of their beauty in your own garden? Whether you seek to create the traditional elegance of the English Rose Garden, the mass of glorious colour associated with Herbaceous Borders or perhaps are looking for particular varieties, the following specialists offer a range of plants and decorative garden ornaments to enhance gardens everywhere.

ARCHITECTURAL PLANTS

Cooks Farm, Nuthurst, Nr Horsham, West Sussex RH13 6LH
Tel: 01403 891772 Fax: 01403 891056 (Angus White)

Specialising in unusual and hardy exotics from around the world, Architectural Plants is a unique nursery that grows and provides spectacular plants for adventurous gardeners. Set up by owner Angus White in the spring of 1990, the nursery has a well deserved reputation for supplying excellent quality plants, backed up by sound practical help and advice. The range of plants offered concentrate first and foremost on strong shapes, bold outlines and are mostly evergreen. Included amongst the rare and not so rare you will find Bananas, Bamboos, Red-Barked Strawberry Trees, Giant Japanese Pom-Poms, Green Olive Trees, Topiary, Spiky Plants, Chinese Cloud Trees, Hardy Jungle Plants and Lord knows what else.... **Open:** Horsham Nursery open Monday to Saturday 9am to 5pm; Chichester Nursery open from Sunday to Friday 10am to 4pm. Phone for free catalogue.

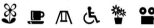

map 4 D6

DEACONS NURSERY (H.H)

Moor View, Godshill, PO38 3HW, Isle of Wight
Tel: 01983 840 750 Fax: 01983 523 575 (G. D. Deacon & B. H. Deacon)

Specialist national fruit tree growers. Trees and bushes sent anywhere so send NOW for a FREE catalogue. Over 300 varieties of apples on various types of root stocks from M27 (4ft), M26 (8ft) to M25 (18ft). Plus Pears, Peaches, Nectarines, Plums, Gages, Cherries, Soft Fruits and an unusual selection of Family Trees. Celebrate the year 2000 with Deacons specially developed millennium apple tree on M26 at £15.95 delivered (will grow to 8ft). Many special offers. Catalogue always available (stamp appreciated). Many varieties of grapes; dessert and wine, plus Hybrid Hops and nuts of all types. **Location:** The picturesque village of Godshill. Deacons Nursery is in Moor View off School Crescent (behind the only school). **Open:** Winter – Mon–Fri, 8–4pm & Sat, 8–1pm. Summer – Mon–Fri, 8–5pm.

map 4 C7

FAMILY TREES

Sandy Lane, Shedfield, Hampshire, SO32 2HQ
Tel: 01329 834 812
(Philip House)

Wide variety of fruit for the connoisseur. Trained tree specialists; standards, espaliers, cordons etc. Other trees, old-fashioned and climbing roses, and evergreens. Free catalogue from Family Trees (as above). **Location:** See map in free catalogue. **Station(s):** Botley (2.5 miles). **Open:** Mid Oct–end Apr, Wed & Sat, 9.30am–12.30. **Admission:** No charge. No minimum order. Courier dispatch for next day delivery.

map 5 V20

HADDONSTONE SHOW GARDEN

The Forge House, Church Lane, East Haddon, Northampton, NN6 8DB
Tel: 01604 770711 Fax: 01604 770027 (Haddonstone Limited)

See Haddonstone's classic garden ornaments in the beautiful setting of the walled manor gardens – including urns, troughs, fountains, statuary, bird baths, sundials, obelisks, columns and balustrading. Featured on BBC Gardeners' World, the garden is on different levels with shrub roses, ground cover plants, conifers, clematis and climbers. In 1998 the new Jubilee Garden opened, complete with temple, pavilion and Gothic Grotto. **Location:** 7 miles NW of Northampton off A428. **Open:** Mon–Fri 9–5.30pm closed weekends, Bank Hols and Christmas period. **Admission:** Free. Groups must apply in writing for permission to visit.

map 4 D1

LANGLEY BOXWOOD NURSERY

Rake, Nr Liss, Hampshire GU33 7JL
Tel: 01730 894467 Fax: 01730 894703 (Elizabeth Braimbridge)

This small nursery, in a beautiful setting, specialises in box-growing, offering a chance to see together a unique range of old and new varieties, hedging, topiary, specimens and rarities. Some taxus also. **National Collection – Buxus.** Descriptive list available (4 x 1st class stamps). **Location:** Off B2070 (old A3) 3 miles south of Liphook. Ring for directions. **Open:** Mon–Fri 9–4.30pm, Sat – enquire by telephone first. **E-mail:** langbox@msn.com **Internet:** www.boxwood.co.uk

map 4 D6

KAYES GARDEN NURSERY

1700 Melton Road, Rearsby, Leicester, Leicestershire LE7 4YR
Tel: 01664 424578 (Mrs Hazel Kaye)

Set in the lovely rural Wreake Valley, this all-year garden houses an extensive collection of interesting and unusual hardy plants. A long pergola leads the visitor into the garden and forms a backdrop to the double herbaceous borders. Mixed beds beyond are filled with a wide range of herbaceous plants, shrubs and shrub roses in subtle colour coordinated groups. A stream dissects the garden and ends in a large wild life pond alive with a myriad of dragonflies. Aromatic herbs surround a much favoured seat which looks out across one of the garden ponds towards flower beds shaded by old fruit trees, where hellebores, ferns and many other shade loving plants abound. **Open:** Mar–Oct incl. Tues–Sat 10–5pm Sun 10am–noon. Nov–Feb incl. Fri & Sat 10–4.30. Closed Dec 25–Jan 31 incl. **Admission:** Entrance to garden £2. Coach parties welcome by appointment.

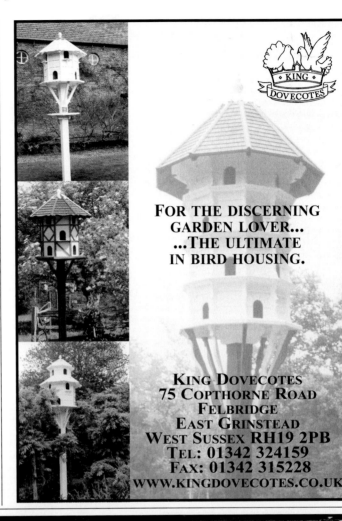

Plants for Sale

ENGLAND

BEDFORDSHIRE

Woburn Abbey, Woburn, MK43 0TP. Tel: 01525 290666 Fax: 01525 290271

BERKSHIRE

Dorney Court, Windsor SL4 6QP. Tel: 01628 604638 Fax: 01628 665772

The Savill Garden, Windsor Great Park. Tel: 01753 847518

BUCKINGHAMSHIRE

Waddesdon Manor, The Dairy, Nr Aylesbury, HP18 0JW. Tel: 01296 651211 Fax: 01296 651142

CAMBRIDGESHIRE

Elton Hall, Elton, Peterborough, PE8 6SH. Tel: 01832 280468
Fax: 01832 280584

The Manor Hemingford Grey PE18 9BN. Tel: 01480 463134 Fax: 01480 465026

CHESHIRE

Arley Hall, nr Great Budworth, Northwich, CW9 6NA. Tel: 01565 777353

Cholmondeley Castle Gardens, Malpas SY14 8AH. Tel: 01829 720383 & Fax

Dunham Massey Hall, Altrincham WA14 4SJ. Tel: 0161 9411025 Fax: 0161 929 7508

Little Moreton Hall, Congleton CW12 4SD. Tel: 01260 272018

Ness Botanic Gardens, Ness, Nesston L64 4AY. Tel: 0151 3530123 Fax: 0151 353 1004

Norton Priory Museum, Tudor Road, Manor Park, Runcorn, WA7 1SX. Tel: 01928 569895

Rode Hall, Church Lane, Scholar Green, ST7 3QP. Tel: 01270 873237 Fax: 01270 882962

Tatton Park, Knutsford, Cheshire WA16 6QN. Tel: 01625 534400

CORNWALL

Bosvigo House, Bosvigo Lane, Truro, TR1 3NH. Tel: 01872 275774 Fax: 01872 275774

Burncoose Nurseries and Garden, Gwennap, Redruth, TR16 6BJ. Tel: 01209 861112

Caerhays Castle And Gardens, Gorran, St Austell PL26 6LY. Tel 01872 501310 Fax: 01872 501870

Godolphin House, Godolphin Cross, Helston, TR13 9RE. Tel: 01736 762409

Lanhydrock House, Bodmin, PL30 5AD. Tel: 01208 73320 Fax: 01208 74084

St. Michael's Mount, The Manor Office, Marazion, nr Penzance, TR17 OEF. Tel: 01736 710507/710265

Pencarrow, Washway, Bodmin, PL30 5AG. Tel: 01208 841369

Tatton Park, Knutsford, WA16 6QN. Tel: 01565 654822 Fax: 01625 534403

Trelowarren House & Chapel, Mawgan-in-Meneage, Helston, TR12 6AD. Tel: 01326 221366

Trevarno Estate & Gardens, Trevarno Manor, Helston, TR13 0RU. Tel: 01326 574274 Fax 01326 574282

COUNTY DURHAM

Raby Castle, Staindrop, Darlington,, DL2 3AH. Tel: 01833 660202 Fax: 01833 660169

CUMBRIA

Acorn Bank Garden, Temple Sowerby, Penrith, CA10 1SP. Tel: 017683 61893

Dalemain, nr Penrith, CA11 0HB. Tel: 017684 86450 Fax: 017684 86223

Holker Hall and Gardens, Cark-in-Cartmel, nr Grange-over-Sands, LA11 7PL. Tel: 015395 58328 Fax: 015395 58776

Levens Hall, Kendal, LA8 0PB. Tel: 015395 60321 Fax: 015395 60669

Muncaster Castle, Ravenglass, CA18 1RQ. Tel: 01229 717614 Fax: 01229 717010

DERBYSHIRE

Chatsworth, Bakewell, DE45 1PP. Tel: 01246 582204 Fax: 01246 583536

Lea Gardens, Lea, Matlock, DE4 5GH. Tel: 01629 534 380 Fax: 01629 534 260

Renishaw Hall, Nr Sheffield, S31 9WB. Tel: 01246 432310

DEVON

Bickleigh Castle, Bickleigh, Tiverton, EX16 8RP. Tel: 01884 855363

Cadhay, Ottery St Mary, EX11 1QT. Tel: 01404 812432

Hartland Abbey, Hartland, Nr Bideford, EX39 6DT. Tel: 01237 441 264/234 Fax: 01884 861134

Killerton House, Broadclyst, nr Exeter, EX5 3LE. Tel: 01392 881345 Fax: 01392 883112

Tiverton Castle, Tiverton, EX16 6RP. Tel: 01884 253200 Fax: 01884 253200

DORSET

Athelhampton House & Gardens, Athelhampton, Dorchester, DT2 7LG. Tel: 01305 848363 Fax: 01305 848185

Chiffchaffs, Chiffeymoor, Bourton, Gillingham, SP8 5BY. Tel: 01747 840841

Compton Acres Gardens, Canford Cliffs, Poole BH13 7ES. Tel: 01202 700778 Fax: 01202 707537

Cranborne Manor Gardens, Cranborne, BH21 5PP. Tel: 01725 517248 Fax: 01725 517862

Deans Court Garden, Deans Court, Wimborne, BH21 1EE.

Forde Abbey and Gardens, nr Chard, TA20 4LU. Tel: 01460 220231 Fax: 01460 220296

Kingston Maurawd, Dorchester DT2 8PY Tel: 01305 215003

Mapperton, Beaminster, DT8 3NR. Tel: 01308 862645

GLOUCESTERSHIRE

Barnsley House Garden, Nr Cirencester GL7 5EE. Tel: 01285 740561 Fax: 01285 740628

Batsford Arboretum, Batsford Estate Office, Moreton-in-Marsh, GL56 9QF. Tel: 01608 650722 Fax: 01608 650290

Berkeley Castle, Berkeley, GL13 9BQ. Tel: 01453 810332

Hodges Barn Gardens, Shipton Moyne, Tetbury, GL8 8PR. Tel: 01666 880202 Fax: 01666 880373

Kiftsgate Court, Mickleton, nr Chipping Campden, GL55 6LW. Tel: 01386 438777 Fax: 01386 438777

Lydney Park Gardens, Estate Office, Lydney GL15 6BU. Tel: 01594 842844 Fax: 01594 842027

Painswick Rococo Garden, The Stables, Painswick House, Painswick, GL6 6TH. Tel: 01452 813204 Fax: 01452 813204

Sudeley Castle, Winchcombe, GL54 5JD. Tel: 01242 602308

HAMPSHIRE

Broadlands, Romsey, SO51 9ZD. Tel: 01794 505010 Fax: 01794 505040

Gilbert White's House & Garden and the Oates , The Wakes, Selborne, GU34 3JH. Tel: 01420 511275

Highclere Castle, Newbury, RG20 9RN. Tel: 01635 253210 Fax: 01635 255315

Houghton Lodge Gardens, Stockbridge, SO20 6LQ. Tel: 01264 810177 Fax: 01794 388072

Langley Boxwood, Rake, Nr Liss, Hampshire GU33 7JL. Tel: 01730 894467 Fax: 01730 894703

Mottisfont Abbey Garden, Mottisfont, Nr Romsey, SO51 0LP. Tel: 01794 340757 Fax: 01794 341492

Sir Harold Hillier Gardens and Arboretum, Ampfield, nr Romsey SO51 0QA. Tel: 01794 368787

Stratfield Saye House, Reading, RG7 2BT. Tel: 01256 882882

The Vyne, Vyne Road, Sherborne St John, Basingstoke Tel:01256 881337

HEREFORD & WORCESTER

Dinmore Manor, nr Hereford, HR4 8EE. Tel: 01432 830332

Eastnor Castle, nr Ledbury, Hereford HR8 1RL. Tel: 01531 633160 Fax: 01531 631776

Harvington Hall, Harvington, Kidderminister, DY10 4LR. Tel: 01562 777846 Fax: 01562 777190

Hergest Croft Gardens, Kington, HR5 3EG. Tel: 01544 230160 Fax: 01544 230160

How Caple Court Gardens, How Caple, HR1 4SX. Tel: 01989 740612 Fax: 01989 740611

Perhill Nurseries, Worcester Road, Great Witley, WR6 6JT. Tel: 01299 896329 Fax: 01299 896 990

HERTFORDSHIRE

Aylett Nurseries Ltd, North Orbital Road, St. Albans. Tel: 01727 822255 Fax: 01727 823024

Knebworth House, Knebworth. Tel: 01438 812661

The Gardens of the Rose, Chiswell Green, St. Albans, AL2 3NR. Tel: 01727 850461 Fax: 01727 850360

St. Pauls Walden Bury, Hitchin, SG4 8BP. Tel: 01438 871218/871229

Hatfield House, Hatfield, AL9 5NQ. Tel: 01707 262823 Fax: 01707 275719

ISLE OF WIGHT

Deacons Nursery H.H. Moor View, Godshill, PO38 3HW. Tel: 01983 840750 Fax: 01983 523575

KENT

Belmont, Throwley, nr Faversham, ME13 0HH. Tel: 01795 890202 Fax: 01795 890042

Doddington Place Gardens, Sittingbourne, ME9 0BB. Tel/Fax: 01795 886101

Finchcocks, Goudhurst, TN17 1HH. Tel: 01580 211702 Fax: 01580 211007

Great Comp Garden, Borough Green, TN15 8QS. Tel: 01732 886154/882 669

Great Maytham Hall, Rolvendon, Cranbrook, TN17 4NE. Tel: 01580 241346 Fax: 01580 241038

Goodnestone Park, Canterbury CT3 IPL Tel:01304 840107

Groombridge Place Gardens, Groombridge, TN3 9QG. Tel: 01892 863999 Fax: 01892 863996

Hall Place, Bourne Road, Bexley DA5 1PQ. Tel: 01322 526574 Fax: 01322 522 921

Hever Castle & Gardens, Hever, nr Edenbridge TN8 7NG. Tel: 01732 865224 Fax: 01732 866796

Ladham House, Ladham Road, Goudhurst. Tel: 01580 211203 Fax: 01580 212596

Leeds Castle, Maidstone ME17 1PL. Tel: 01622 765400 Fax: 01622 735616

Lullingstone Castle, Eynsford, DA14 0JA. Tel: 01322 862114 Fax: 01322 862115

Owl House Gardens, Lamberhurst Tel:01892 890230

Penshurst Place, Penshurst, Tunbridge Wells, TN11 8DG. Tel: 01892 870307 Fax: 01892 870866

Riverhill House Gardens, Riverhill, Sevenoaks Tel:01732 458802

LANCASHIRE

Rufford Old Hall, Rufford, Ormskirk Tel:01704 821254

Towneley Hall Art Gallery, Burnley, BB11 3RQ. Tel: 01282 424213 Fax: 01282 436138

LEICESTERSHIRE

Kayes Garden Nursery, 1700 Melton Rd, Rearsby, Leicester, LE7 4YR. Tel: 01664 424578

LINCOLNSHIRE

Elsham Hall, Brigg DN20 0QZ Tel:01652 688698

Marston Hall, Grantham. Tel: 01400 250225

LONDON

Chelsea Physic Garden, 66 Royal Hospital Road, Chelsea, SW3 4HS. Tel: 0171 352 5646 Fax: 0171 376 3910

Museum of Garden History, Lambeth Palace Road, SE1 7LB. Tel: 0171 401 8865 Fax: 0171 401 8869

Syon Park, Brentford, TW8 8JF. Tel: 0181 560 0881 Fax: 0181 568 0936

NORFOLK

The Fairhaven Garden, 2 The Woodlands, Wymers Lane, South Walsam, Norwich, NR13 6EA. Tel: 01603 270449

Holkham Hall, Holkham Estate Office, Wells-next-the-Sea, NR23 1AB. Tel: 01328 710227 Fax: 01328 711707

Houghton Hall, Kings Lynn, PE31 6UE. Tel: 01485 528569

Hoveton Hall, Norwich NR12 8RJ. Tel: 01603 782798 Fax: 01603 784 564

Mannington Hall, Saxthorpe, Norwich, NR11 7BB. Tel: 01263 584175 Fax: 01263 761214

Sandringham House, Grounds & Museum, The Estate Office, Sandringham PE35 6EN. Tel: 01553 772675 Fax: 01485 541571

NORTHAMPTONSHIRE

Boughton House, Kettering, NN14 1BJ. Tel: 01536 515731 Fax: 01536 417255

Coton Manor Garden, Coton, Nr Guilsborough, NN6 8RQ. Tel: 01604 740219 Fax: 01604 740838

Cottesbrooke Hall and Gardens, nr Northampton, NN6 8PF. Tel: 01604 505808 Fax: 01604 505619

Haddonstone Show Garden, The Forge House, CHurch Lane, East Haddon, NN6 8BD. Tel: 01604 770711 Fax: 01604 770027

Holdenby House Gardens & Falconry Centre, Holdenby, Northampton NN6 8DJ. Tel: 01604 770074 Fax: 01604 770962

The Menagerie - Horton, Horton, Northampton, NN7 2BX. Tel: 01604 870957

NORTHUMBERLAND

Chipchase Castle, Wark on Tyne, Hexham. Tel: 01434 230203 Fax: 01434 230740

OXFORDSHIRE

Blenheim Palace Woodstock OX20 1PX. Tel: 01993 811325 24hr information Fax: 01993 813527

Buscot Park, Buscot, Nr Faringdon, SN7 8BU. Tel: 01367 240786 Fax: 01367 241794

Waterperry Gardens, Waterperry Horticultural Centre, nr Wheatley, OX33 1JZ. Tel: 01844 339226 Fax: 01844 339 883

SHROPSHIRE

Burford House Gardens, Tenbury Wells, WR15 8HQ. Tel: 01584 810777 Fax: 01584 810673

Hodnet Hall Gardens, Hodnet, Nr Market Drayton, TF9 3NN. Tel: 01630 685202 Fax: 01630 685 853

Old Colehurst Manor, Colehurst, Market Drayton TF9 2JB Tel:01630 638833

Walcot Hall, Nr Bishops Castle, Lydbury North SY7 8AZ. Tel: 0171-581 2782 Fax: 0171 589 0195

Wollerton Old Hall, Wollerton, Market Drayton TF9 3NA. Tel: 01630 685760 Fax: 01630 685583

SOMERSET

East Lambrook Manor Garden, South Petherton TA13 5HL. Tel: 01460 240328 Fax: 01460 242 344

Gaulden Manor, Tolland, nr Taunton, TA4 3PN. Tel: 01984 667213

Hestercombe House Gardens, Cheddon Fitzpaine, Taunton, TA2 8LG. Tel: 01823 413923 Fax: 01823 413747

Milton Lodge Gardens, Milton Lodge, Wells BA5 3AQ. Tel: 01749 672168

Orchard Wyndham, Williton, nr Taunton, TA4 4HH. Tel: 01984 632309 Fax: 01984 633526

Sherborne Garden (Pear Tree House), Litton BA3 4PP. Tel: 01761 241220

STAFFORDSHIRE

Dunwood Hall, Longsdon, Nr. Leek ST9 9AR. Tel: 01538 385071

SUFFOLK

Helmingham Hall Gardens, The Estate Office, Helmingham Hall, Stowmarket, IP14 6EF. Tel: 01473 890363 Fax: 01473 890776

Hengrave Hall Centre, Hengrave Hall, Bury St Edmunds, IP28 6LZ. Tel: 01284 701561 Fax: 01284 702950

Somerleyton Hall, nr Lowestoft NR32 5QQ. Tel: 01502 730224 Fax: 01502 732143

Wingfield Old College & Gardens, Wingfield, Nr Stradbroke, IP21 5RA. Tel: 01379 384888 Fax: 01379 384034

Wyken Hall, Stanton, Bury St. Edmunds, IP31 2DW. Tel: 01359 250287 Fax: 01359 252256

SURREY

Clandon Park, West Clandon, Guildford GU4 7RQ. Tel: 01483 222482 Fax: 01483 223479

Loseley Park, Estate Office, Guildford, GU3 1HS. Tel: 01483 304440 Fax: 01483 302036

Painshill Landscape Garden, Portsmouth Road, Cobham Tel:KT11 1JE

Millais Rhododendrons, Crosswater Farm, Churt, Farnham, GU10 2JN. Tel: 01252 792698

RHS Garden Wisley, Woking, GU23 6QB. Tel: 01483 224234

SUSSEX

Borde Hill Garden, Balcombe Road, Haywards Heath, RH16 1XP. Tel: 01444 450326

Charleston Farmhouse, Firle, nr Lewes. Tel: 01323 811626 Fax: 01323 811628

Denmans Garden, Clock House, Denmans, Fontwell BN18 0SU. Tel: 01243 542808 Fax:01243 544064

Fishbourne Roman Palace, Salthill Road, Fishbourne, Chichester, PO19 3QR. Tel: 01243 785859 Fax: 01243 539 266

Glynde Place, Glynde, nr Lewes, BN8 6SX. Tel: 01273 858224 Fax: 01273 858224

Great Dixter House, Northiam, Nr Rye, TN31 6PH. Tel: 01797 252878 Fax: 01797 252879

Leonardslee Gardens, Lower Beeding, Horsham, RH13 6PP. Tel: 01403 891212 Fax: 01403 891305

Michelham Priory, Upper Dicker, Hailsham BN27 3QS. Tel: 01323 844224 Fax: 01323 844030

Merriments Gardens, Hawkhurst Road, Hurst Green TN19 7RA. Tel: 01580 860666 Fax: 01580 860324

Parham House and Gardens, Parham Park Ltd, Pulborough, RH20 4HS. Tel: 01903 742021 Fax: 01903 746557

Pashley Manor Gardens, Ticehurst, Wadhurst, TN5 7HE. Tel: 01580 200692 Fax: 01580 200102

Perryhill Nurseries, Hartfield, TN7 4JP. Tel: 0892 770377

Royal Botanic Gardens, Kew at Wakehurst Place, Ardingly, Haywards Heath RH17 6TN. Tel: 01444 894066 Fax: 01444 894069

The Weald & Downland Open Air Museum, Singleton, Nr Chichester Tel:01243 811348

West Dean Gardens, West Dean Estate, nr Chichester, PO18 0QZ. Tel: 01243 818210 Fax: 01243 811342

WARWICKSHIRE

Coughton Court, Alcester B49 5JA Tel: 01789 400777

Charlecote Park, Warwick CV35 9ER Tel:01789 470277

The Hiller Garden, Dunnington Heath Farm, Alcester, B49 5PD. Tel: 01789 490991

Lord Leycester Hospital, High Street, Warwick, CV34 4BH. Tel: 01926 491422 Fax: 01926 491 422

Shakespearian Properties, Henley Street, Stratford-upon-Avon CV37 6QW. Tel: 01789 204016 Fax: 01789 269083

WEST MIDLANDS

Baddesley Clinton Hall, B93 0DQ. Tel: 01564 783294 Fax: 01564 782706

Birmingham Botanical Gardens and Glasshouses, Westbourne Road, Edgbaston, Birmingham B15 3TR. Tel: 0121 454 1860 Fax: 0121 454 7835

Castle Bromwich Hall Gardens, Chester Road, Castle Bromwich, Birmingham. Tel: 0121 749 4100

WILTSHIRE

Bowood House and Gardens, The Estate Office, Bowood, Calne, SN11 0LZ. Tel: 01249 812102

Longleat, The Estate Office, Warminster, BA12 7NW. Tel: 01985 844400 Fax: 01985 844885

Stourhead, Stourton, nr Mere BA12 6QD. Tel: 01747 841152 Fax: 01747 841 152

YORKSHIRE

Burton Agnes Hall, Burton Agnes, Diffield, YO25 0ND. Tel: 01262 490324 Fax: 01262 490513

Castle Howard, York YO6 7DA. Tel: 01653 648444

Elsham Hall Country and Wildlife Park, The Estate Office, Brigg DN20 0QZ. Tel: 01652 688698 Fax: 01652 688240

Harewood House and Bird Garden, The Estate Office, Harewood, Leeds, LS17 9LQ. Tel: 0113 288 6331 Fax: 0113 288 6467

Harlow Carr Botanical Gardens, Crag Lane, Harrogate, HG3 1QB. Tel: 01423 565418 Fax: 01423 530663

Newby Hall & Gardens, Ripon HG4 5AE. Tel: 01423 322583 Fax: 01423 324 452

Norton Conyers, Ripon HG4 5EQ. Tel: 01765 640333 Fax: 01765 692772.

Nunnington Hall, Nunnington, York YO62 5UY. Tel: 01439 748283 Fax: 01439 748284

Ripley Castle, Ripley HG3 3AY. Tel: 01423 770152 Fax: 01423 771745

Sewerby Hall and Gardens, Church Lane, Sewerby, Bridlington, YO15 1EA. Tel: Estate Office: 01262 673 769 Hall :01262 677874

Shandy Hall, The Laurence Sterne Trust, Coxwold, York, YO6 4AD. Tel: 01347 868465

Skipton Castle, Skipton, BD23 1AQ. Tel: 01756 792442 Fax: 01756 796100

Thorp Perrow Arboretum, Bedale DL8 2PR. Tel: 01677 425323 Fax: 01677 425 323

IRELAND

Bantry House, Bantry, Co. Cork. Tel: 00353 2 750 047 Fax: 00353 2 750 795

Benvarden Gardens, Benvarden Dervock, Co Antrim, N. Ireland. Tel: 012657 41331 Fax: 012657 41955

Birr Castle, Birr Tel:00353 50920336

Hamwood House, Hamwood, Dunboyne. Tel: 00353 1 8255210

Larchill Arcadian Gardens, Kilcock, Kildare. Tel: 00 3511 628 4580 Fax: 003511 628 7354

Powerscourt Gardens & Waterfall, Enniskerry, Co. Wicklow. Tel: 00353 1 204 6000 Fax: 00353 1 286 3561

Seaforde Gardens, Seaforde, Downpatrick BT30 3PG. Tel: +441396 811225 Fax:+441396 811370

Strokestown Park House & Gardens, Strokestown, Co. Roscommon. Tel: 00353 78 33013 Fax: 00353 78 33712

SCOTLAND

Blairquhan Castle and Gardens, Straiton,, Maybole KA19 7LZ. Tel: 016557 70239 Fax: 016557 70278

Bolfracks Garden, Aberfeldy PH15 2EX. Tel: 01887 820207

Bowhill House & Country Park, Bowhill, nr Selkirk TD7 5ET. Tel: 01750 22204 Fax: 01750 22204

Glamis Castle, Estate Office, Glamis DD8 1RT. Tel: 01307 840393 Fax: 01307 840 733

Mount Stuart House and Gardens, Mount Stuart, Isle of Bute PA20 9LR. Tel: 01700 503877 Fax: 01700 505 313

Paxton House & Gardens, Paxton, nr Berwick-upon-Tweed TD15 1SZ. Tel: 01289 386291

Traquair House, Innerleithen EH44 6PW. Tel: 01896 830323 Fax: 01896 830639

WALES

Aberglasney Gardens, East Bailiff's Lodge, Llangathen. Tel: 01558 668998 Fax: 01558 668998

Bodnant Garden, Tal Y Cafn, Colwyn Bay Tel:01492 650460

The Castle House, Usk NP5 1SD. Tel: 01291 672563

Colby Woodland Gardens, Stepaside, Narbeth SA67 8PP. Tel: 01834 811885

Dyffryn Gardens, St Nicholas, Cardiff CF5 6SU. Tel: 01222 593 328 Fax: 01222 591966

Erddig Hall, Gardens & Country Park, Nr Wrexham LL13 0YT. Tel: 01978 355314 Fax: 01978 355314

Picton Castle, Picton Castle Trust, Haverfordwest SA62 4AS. Tel: 01437 751326

Portmerion Village, Portmerion, Gwyned Tel: 01766 770000

305

Universities

CAMBRIDGE

Note: Admission to the Colleges means to the Courts, not to the staircases and students' rooms. All opening times are subject to closing for College functions etc. on occasional days. Halls normally close for lunch (12–2pm) and many are not open during the afternoon. Chapels are closed during services. Libraries are not usually open, special arrangements are noted. Gardens do not usually include the Fellows' garden. Figures denote the date of foundation and existing buildings are often of later date. Daylight hours – some colleges may not open until 9.30am or later and usually close before 6pm – many as early as 4.30pm. All parties exceeding 10 persons wishing to tour the college between Easter and October are required to be escorted by a Cambridge registered Guide. All enquires should be made to the Tourist Information Centre, Wheeler Street, Cambridge CB2 3QB. Terms: Lent: Mid-January to Mid-March. Easter: April to June. Michaelmas: 2nd week October to 1st week December. Examination Period closures which differ from one college to another now begin in early April and extend to late June. Notices are usually displayed. Admission charges vary from college to college. **Visitors and especially guided parties should always call at the Porters' Lodge before entering the College.**

CHRIST'S COLLEGE (1505)
Porter's Lodge, St.Andrew's Street CB2 3BU
Tel:(01223) 334900 Fax: (01223) 334967

CLARE COLLEGE (1326)
Trinity Lane

CORPUS CHRISTI COLLEGE (1352)
Porter's Lodge, Trumpington Street CB2 1RH
Tel: (01223) 338000 Fax: (01223) 338061

DOWNING COLLEGE (1800)
Downing College, Regent Street CB2 1DQ
Tel: (01223) 334800 Fax: (01223) 467934

EMMANUEL COLLEGE (1584)
Porter's Lodge, St. Andrew's Street CB2 3AP
Tel: (01223) 334200 Fax: (01223) 334426

GONVILLE & CAIUS COLLEGE (1348)
Porter's Lodge, Trinity Street CB2 1TA
Tel: (01223) 332400

JESUS COLLEGE (1496)
Porter's Lodge, Jesus Lane CB5 8BL
Tel: (01223) 339339

KING'S COLLEGE (1441)
Porter's Lodge, King's Parade CB2 1ST
Tel: (01223) 331212 Fx:(01223) 331315

MAGDALENE COLLEGE (1542)
Porter's Lodge, Magdalene Street

NEWNHAM COLLEGE (1871)
Sidgewick Avenue

PEMBROKE COLLEGE(1347)
Trumpington Street

PETERHOUSE (1284)
Porter's Lodge, Trumpington Street CB2 1RD
Tel: (01223) 338200 Fax: (01223) 337578

QUEENS' COLLEGE (1448)
Porter's Lodge, Silver Street CB3 9ET
Tel: (01223) 335511 Fax:(01223) 335566

SIDNEY SUSSEX COLLEGE (1596)
Porter's Lodge, Sidney Street CB2 3HU
Tel: (01223) 338800 Fax: (01223) 338884

ST. CATHARINE'S COLLEGE (1473)
Porter's Lodge, Trumpington Street

ST. JOHN'S COLLEGE (1511)
Tourist Liaison Office, St. John Street CB2 1TP

TRINITY COLLEGE (1546)
Porter's Lodge, Trinity Street

TRINITY HALL (1350)
Porter's Lodge, Trinity Lane

Conducted Tours in Cambridge: Qualified badged, local guides may be obtained from: Tourist Information Centre, Wheeler Street, Cambridge CB2 3QB. Tel: (01223) 322640 or Cambridge Guide Service, 2 Montague Road, Cambridge CB4 1BX. We normally obtain the Passes and make all negotiations regarding these with the Tourist Office, so separate application is not needed. We have been providing guides for English, Foreign language and special interest groups since 1950. We supply couriers for coach tours of East Anglia, visiting stately homes etc. As an alternative to the 2 hour walking tour we can now offer half hour panoramic in clients' coach (providing there is an effective public address system) followed by a 1.5 hour tour on foot, or 1 hour panoramic only, special flat rate for up to 55 people.

OXFORD

NOTE: Admission to Colleges means to the Quadrangles, not to the staircases and students' rooms. All opening times are subject to closing for college functions etc., on occasional days. Halls normally close for lunch (12–2pm). Chapel usually closed during services. Libraries are not usually open, special arrangements are noted. Gardens do not usually include the Fellows' garden. Figures denote the date of foundation and existing buildings are often of later date. Terms: Hilary: Mid-January to Mid-March. Trinity: 3rd week April to late June. Michaelmas: Mid October to 1st week December. **Visitors and especially guided parties should always call at the Porter's Lodge before entering the College.**

ALL SOULS COLLEGE (1438)
Porter's Lodge, High Street OX1 4AL
Open: College Weekdays: 2–4.30. (2–4pm Oct–Mar).

BALLIOL COLLEGE (1263)
Porter's Lodge, Broad Street
Open: Hall Chapel & Gardens Daily 2–5. Parties limited to 25.

BRASENOSE COLLEGE (1509)
Radcliffe Square
Open: Hall Chapel & Gardens Tour parties: Daily 10–11.30 2–5 (summer) 10–dusk (winter). Individuals 2–5. College closed 11.30–2.

CHRIST CHURCH (1546)
St. Aldate's , Enter via Meadow Gate OX1 1DP
Tel: (01865) 276499
Open: Cathedral daily 9–4.30 (winter) 9–5.30 (summer). Hall daily 9.30–12,2–5.30. Picture Gallery weekdays 10.30–1, 2–4.30. Meadows daily 7–dusk. Tourist Information-(01865) 276499.

CORPUS CHRISTI COLLEGE (1517)
Porter's Lodge, Merton Street
Open: College, Chapel & Gardens Term and vacations – daily.

EXETER COLLEGE (1314)
Porter's Lodge, Turl Street OX1 3DP
Tel: (01865) 279600 Fax:(01865) 279630
Open: College & Chapel, Fellows' Garden term and vacations daily 2–5. (Except Christmas and Easter).

HERTFORD COLLEGE (1284, 1740 & 1874)
Porter's Lodge, Catte Street OX1 3BW
Tel: (01865) 279400 Fax: (01865) 279437
Open: Quadrangle & Chapel Daily 10–6

JESUS COLLEGE (1571)
Turl Street
Open: College, Hall & Chapel Daily 2.30–4.30.

KEBLE COLLEGE (1868)
Porter's Lodge, Parks Road
Open: College & Chapel Daily 10–7 (or dusk if earlier)

LADY MARGARET HALL (1878)
Porter's Lodge, Norham Gardens
Open: College & Gardens Daily 2–6 (or dusk if earlier). The chapel is also open to the public.

LINCOLN COLLEGE (1427)
Porter's Lodge, Turl Street
Open: College & Hall weekdays 2–5. Suns 11–5. Wesley Room All Saints Library Tues & Thurs 2–4.

MAGDALEN COLLEGE (1458)
High Street OX1 4AU
Tel: (01865) 276000 Fax:(01865) 276103
Open: College Chapel Deer Park & Water Walks daily 2–6 June–Sept 11–6.

MANSFIELD COLLEGE (1886)
Porter's Lodge, Mansfield Road
Open: College, May–July, Mon–Sat, 9–5.

MERTON (1264)
Merton Street OX1 4JD
Tel: (01865) 276310 Fax:(01865) 276361
Open: Chapel & Quadrangle Mon–Fri 2–4 Oct–June: Sat & Sun 10–4. Mon–Fri 2–5. Jul–Sept: Sat & Sun 10–5. Library not open on Sat Nov–Mar.

NEW COLLEGE (1379)
New College Lane
Open: Hall, Chapel, Cloister, Gardens daily. Oct–Easter in Holywell Street Gate 2–4. Easter – Early Oct, in New College Lane Gate (11–5)

NUFFIELD COLLEGE (1937)
Porter's Lodge, New Road
Open: College only, daily 9–5

ORIEL COLLEGE (1326)
Oriel Square OX1 4EW
Tel: (01865) 276555 Fax:(01865) 276532
Open: College daily 2–5.

PEMBROKE COLLEGE (1624)
Porter's Lodge, St.Aldate's
Open: College, Hall & Chapel & Gardens Term – daily on application at the Porter's Lodge.

THE QUEEN'S COLLEGE (1340)
High Street OX1 4AW
Tel: (01865) 279120 Fax:(01865) 790819
Open: Hall Chapel Quadrangles & Garden Open to public by apt.

ST. EDMUNDS HALL (1270)
Queen's Lane OX1 4AR
Tel: (01865) 279000
Open: On application to Porter

ST. JOHN'S COLLEGE (1555)
St. Giles' OX1 3JP
Tel: (01865) 277300 Fax:(01865) 277435
Open: College & Garden, Term & Vacation, daily 1–5. Hall & Chapel summer 2.30–4.30.

TRINITY COLLEGE (1554)
Main Gate, Broad Street OX1 3BH
Tel: (01865) 277300 Fax: (01865) 279898
Open: Hall, Chapel & Gardens daily during daylight hours.

UNIVERSITY COLLEGE (1249)
Porter's Lodge, High Street OX1 4BH
Open: College, Hall & Chapel Term 2–4.

WADHAM COLLEGE (1610)
Parks Road, Oxford

WORCESTER COLLEGE (1714)
Porter's Lodge, Worcester Street OX1 2HB
Tel: (01865) 278300 Fax:(01865) 278387
Open: College & Gardens Term daily, 2–6. Vacation daily 9–12 &2–6. Hall & Chapel Apply Lodge.

GUIDED WALKING TOURS OF THE COLLEGES & CITY OF OXFORD. Tours conducted by the Oxford Guild of Guides. Lectures are offered by The Oxford Information Centre, mornings for much of the year, afternoons, tours daily. For tour times please ring (01865) 726871. Tours are offered for groups in English, French, German, Spanish, Russian, Japanese, Polish and Serbo-Croat. Chinese by appointment. The most popular tour for groups, Oxford Past and Present, can be arranged at any time. The following special interest tours are available in the afternoon only: Alice in Oxford; Literary Figures in Oxford; American Roots in Oxford; Oxford Gardens; Modern Architecture in Oxford; Architecture in Oxford (Medieval, 17th century and Modern); Oxford in the Civil War and 17th century. Further details are available from the Deputy Information Officer.

Properties Used As Film Locations

ENGLAND

BERKSHIRE

Dorney Court, Dorney, Nr. Windsor, Berkshire SL4 6QP. Tel: 01628 604638 Fax: 01628 665772 – *Children of the New Forest / Sliding Doors / The Jump / Vanishing Man / Lock, Stock & Two Smoking Barrels*

BUCKINGHAMSHIRE

Chiltern Open Air Museum, Newland Park, Gorelands Lane, Chalfont St Giles Tel:01494 871117

Claydon House, Middle Claydon, Nr. Buckingham, Bucks MK18 2EY. Tel: 01296 730349 – *Emma / Vanity Fair*

Stowe (Stowe School), Stowe MK18 5EH. Tel: 01280 813650 – *The Avengers*

CAMBRIDGESHIRE

King's College, King's Parade, Cambridge CB2 1ST Tel: 01223 331212

CHESHIRE

Arley Hall and Gardens, Arley, Northwich, Cheshire CW9 6NA. Tel: 01565 777353 Fax: 01565 777465 – *Good Living – Jane Asher / Brookside / Out & About*

Capesthorne Hall, Nr Macclesfield Tel:01625 861221

Little Moreton Hall, Congleton CW12 4SD Tel:01260 272018 – *Moll Flanders / Lady Jane Grey*

Peckforton Castle, Stonehouse Lane, Nr. Tarporley CW6 9TN. Tel: 01829 260930 Fax: 01829 261230. – *Robin Hood*

Tabley House, Knutsford, Cheshire. Tel: 01565 750151 Fax: 01565 653230 – *Some Coronation Street/ Sherlock Homes / Game, Set & Match*

CORNWALL

Caerhays Castle, Gorran, St Austell PL26 6LY Tel: 01872 501310 – *Rebecca, Poldark, Wycliffe, Longitude*

Godolphin House, Godophin Cross, Helston, Cornwall TR13 9RE. Tel: 01736 762409 – *Poldark / Wycliffe / Empty House*

Lanhydrock House, Bodmin, Cornwall. Tel: 01208 73320 Fax: 01208 74084 – *Twelfth Night*

Pencarrow, Washaway, Bodmin PL30 3AG Tel:01208 841369 – *The Red Robe*

CUMBRIA

Holker Hall & Gardens, Cark-in-Cartmel, Nr Grange-over-Sands LA11 7PL. Tel: 015395 58328 Fax: 015395 58776 – *The English Country Garden*

Levens, Kendal LA8 OPD Tel:015395 60321 – *Wives and Daughters (BBC)*

Mirehouse, Keswick CA12 4QE Tel:01768 772287 – *Fell Tiger, Ken Russell's 'Wordsworth'*

DERBYSHIRE

Haddon Hall, Bakewell, Derbyshire DE45 1LA. Tel: 01629 812855 Fax: 01629 814379 – *Jane Eyre / Prince & The Pauper / Moll Flanders / Elizabeth I*

Lea Gardens, Lea, Matlock, Derbyshire ED4 5GH. Tel: 01629 534380 Fax: 01629 534260 – *Gardeners World*

DEVON

Bickleigh Castle, Bickleigh, Nr. Tiverton, Devon EX16 8RP. Tel: 01884 855363 – *One Foot in the Past*

Cadhay, Ottery St Mary, Devon EX11 1QT. Tel: 01404 812432 – *Miss Marple - Sleeping Murder*

Hartland Abbey, Nr Birdeford EX39 6DT Tel:01237441234

DORSET

Athelhampton House, Athelhampton, Dorchester Tel:01305 848363 – *Antiques Roadshow / Time Travellers*

Forde Abbey and Gardens, Forde Abbey, Chard, Somerset TA20 4LU. Tel: 01460 221290 Fax: 01460 220296 – *Restoration*

Lulworth Castle, The Lulworth Estate, East Lulworth, Wareham, Dorset BH20 5QS. Tel: 01929 400352 – *Inspector Morse / Tess of the D'Urbervilles / Red Violin*

Mapperton, Beaminster DT8 3NR Tel:01308 862645 – *Emma / Restoration / Tom Jones*

Parnham House & Gardens, Parnham, Beaminster, Dorset. Tel: 01308 862204 Fax: 01308 863494 – *French Lieutenant's Woman / Jane Austen*

CO DURHAM

Durham Castle, Durham DH1 3RW. Tel: 01913 743863 Fax: 01913 747470 – *Ivanhoe*

Raby Castle, Staindrop, Darlington, Co. Durham DL2 3AY. Tel: 01833 660202 Fax: 01833 660169 – *Elizabeth I*

ESSEX

Hedingham Castle, Halstead CO9 3DJ Tel:01787 460261 – *Ivanhoe / Lovejoy*

Ingatestone Hall, Hall Lane, Ingatestone CM4 9NR Tel:01277 353010 – *Lovejoy*

Layer Marney Tower, Nr Colchester, Essex CO5 9US. Tel/Fax: 01206 330784 – *Canterbury Tales*

The Sir Alfred Munnings Art Museum, Castle House, Dedham CO7 6AZ. Tel/Fax: 01206 322127 – *Liza's Country / Collectors Lot / Treasure Hunt*

GLOUCESTERSHIRE

Barnsley House, Nr Cirencester GL7 5EE Tel:01285 740561 – *Greenfingers*

Chavenage, Tetbury, Gloucestershire GL8 8XP. Tel: 01666 502329 Fax: 01453 836778 – *Cider With Rosie / Berkeley Square*

Frampton Court, Frampton-on-Severn, Gloucester. Tel: 01452 740698 – *Charge of the Light Brigade / Rocking Horse Winner / Animal Ark*

HAMPSHIRE

Avington Park, Winchester, Hampshire SO21 1DB. Tel: 01962 779260 Fax: 01962 779864 – *Jewels / Ruth Rendell*

Breamore House, Nr. Fordingbridge, Hampshire SP6 2DF. Tel: 01725 512468 – *Woodlanders / Florence Nightingale / Children of the New Forest / Barchester Towers*

Houghton Lodge Gardens, Stockbridge, Hampshire SO20 6LQ. Tel: 01264 810177 – *Grass Roots*

HEREFORD & WORCESTER

Eastnor Castle, Ledbury Tel:01531 633160 – *Little Lord Fauntleroy*

Moccas Court, Moccas, HR2 9LH. Tel: 01981 500381

Worcester Cathedral, College Green, Worcester, Worcestershire WR1 2LA. Tel: 01905 28854 Fax: 01905 611139 – *The Choir*

HERTFORDSHIRE

Cathedral & Abbey Church of Saint Alban, St Albans, Herfordshire AL1 1BY. Tel: 01727 860780 Fax: 01727 850944 – *First Knight*

Knebworth House, Knebworth, Hertfordshire. Tel: 01438 812661 – *Batman / Jane Eyre / Canterville Ghost*

KENT

Cobham Hall, Cobham, Nr Gravesend DA12 3BL Tel:01474 823371– *The Mystery of Edwin Drood / Peacock Spring*

Finchcocks, Goudhurst, Kent TN17 1HH. Tel: 01580 211702 Fax: 01580 211007 – *Collectors Lot / French & Saunders / The Making of Pride & Prejudice*

Penshurst Place and Gardens, Penshurst, Nr Tonbridge, Kent TN11 8DG. Tel: 01892 870307 Fax: 01892 870866 – *Love on a Branch Line / Little Lord Fauntleroy / Prince & The Pauper / Young Sherlock Holmes / The Mirror Cracked / Secret Garden*

LANCASHIRE

Dalemain, Nr Penrith, Cumbria Tel: 017684 86450 Fax: 017684 86223 – *Jane Eyre / Border TV Sir Harry Secombe 'Music Is My Life'*

Towneley Hall Art Gallery & Museums, Burnley, Lancashire BB11 3RQ. Tel: 01282 424213 Fax: 01282 436138 – *Whistle Down The Wind*

LEICESTERSHIRE

Belvoir Castle, Nr Grantham NG32 IPD Tel:01476 870262 – *Little Lord Fauntleroy / Young Sherlock Holmes / The Haunting*

Stanford Hall, Lutterworth, Leicestershire LE17 6DH. Tel: 01788 860250 Fax: 01788 860870 – *Lost without Trace / The Deep Concern / The Canal Children*

LINCOLNSHIRE

Elsham Hall, Brigg DN20 0QZ Tel:01652 688698 – *'History of Folk'*

LONDON

Southside House, 3 Woodhayes Road Wimbledon SW19 4RJ Tel:0181 946 7643 – *Dickens Christmas Special*

Dorney Court, Berkshire

Syon Park, Brentford TW8 8JF Tel:0181 560 0883 – *Madness of King George / Avengers / The Wings of the Dove'*

NORFOLK

Mannington Hall, Norwich Tel:01263 584175

Wolterton Park, Erpringham Tel:01263 584175

OXFORDSHIRE

Broughton Castle, Banbury, Oxfordshire OX15 5EB. Tel/Fax: 01295 276070 – *Shakespeare In Lov*

Mapledurham House, Nr Reading RG4 7TR Tel:01189 723350 – *Eagle has Landed / Children of the New Forest*

University of Oxford Botanic Garden, Rose Lane, Oxford Tel:01865 276920 – *Morse / Brideshead Revisited*

SHROPSHIRE

Ironbridge Gorge, Ironbridge, Telford, Shropshire TF8 7AW. Tel: 01952 433522 – *Feast of July / Home & Away / Dr Who / Anna of the Town / Fred Dibnah / Bill Bryson*

Old Colehurst Manor, Colehurst, Market Drayton TF9 2JB Tel:01630 638833 – *BBC Travel / Collectors Lot*

SOMERSET

Museum of Costume & Assembly Rooms, Bennett Street, Bath Tel:01225 477789 – *Persuasion*

STAFFORDSHIRE

Tamworth Castle, The Holloway, Tamworth, Staffordshire. Tel: 01827 63563 Fax: 01827 56567 – *Out & About*

SUFFOLK

Somerleyton Hall & Gardens, Somerleyton, Lowestoft, Suffolk NR32 5QQ. Tel: 01502 730224 Fax: 01502 732143 – *Garden without Borders / Lovejoy / Watercolour Challenge*

SURREY

Albury Park, Albury, Guildford, Surrey GU5 9BB. Tel: 01483 202964 Fax: 01483 205013 – *Four Weddings & A Funeral / Underworld / Unsuitable Job For A Woman*

Clandon Park, West Clandon, Guildford, Surrey, GU4 7RQ. Tel: 01483 222482 Fax: 01483 223479 – *Fashion Shoots (Hello Magazine)*

Loseley Park, Guildford, Surrey GU3 1HS. Tel: 01483 304440 Fax: 01483 302036 – *The Worst Witch / Jonathan Creek / Spice Girls Movie / The Student Prince*

Painshill Landscape Garden, Portsmouth Road, Cobham Tel:KT11 1JE– *101 Dalmations*

SUSSEX

Brickwall House & Gardens, Northiam, Rye, East Sussex TN31 6NL. Tel: 01797 253388 Fax: 01797 252567 – *Cold Comfort Farm*

Firle Place, Nr. Lewes, East Sussex BN8 6LP. Tel/Fax: 01273 858188 – *Return of Soldier / Firelight*

Parham House & Gardens, Parham Park, Nr. Pulborough, West Sussex. Tel: 01903 742021 Fax: 01903 746557 – *Prince & The Pauper / To Be The Best / Haunted*

The Royal Pavilion, Brighton, East Sussex BN1 1EE. Tel: 01273 290900 Fax: 01273 292871 – *Richard III*

WARWICKSHIRE

Arbury Hall, Nuneaton, Warwickshire CV10 7PT. Tel: 01203 382804 Fax: 01203 641147 – *Angels and Insects*

Lord Leycester Hospital, High Street, Warwick, Warwickshire CV34 4BH. Tel: 01926 491422 Fax: 01926 491422 – *Dangerfield / Songs of Praise / Surprise Gardens / Travels with Pevsner / Pride & Prejudice / Tom Jones / Moll Flanders*

WEST MIDLANDS

Baddesley Clinton Hall, Knowle, Solihull, West Midlands B93 0DZ. Tel: 01564 783294 Fax: 01564 782706 – *Sherlock Holmes*

WILTSHIRE

Corsham Court, Corsham SN13 0BZ Tel:01249 701610 – *Remains of the Day / Wives and Daughters*

Longleat, Warminster, Wiltshire BA12 7NW. Tel: 01985 844400 Fax: 01985 844885 – *Barry Lyndon / The Missionary / Adventure of a Lady*

Luckington Court, Luckington, Chippenham, Wilshire SN14 6PQ. Tel: 01666 840205 – *Pride & Prejudice / Wives and Daughters*

Wilton House, The Estate Office, Wilton, Salisbury SP2 0BJ. Tel: 01722 746720 Fax: 01722 744447 – *Madness of King George / Mrs Brown / Sense & Sensibility / Bounty*

YORKSHIRE

Aske Hall, Aske, Richmond, North Yorkshire DL10 5HJ. Tel: 01748 850391 Fax: 01748 823252 – *Collectors Lot*

Bolton Castle, Leyburn, North Yorkshire DL8 4ET. Tel: 10969 623981 Fax: 01969 623332 – *Elizabeth I / Ivanhoe / Heartbeat*

Bramham Park, Wetherby, West Yorkshire LS23 6ND. Tel: 01937 844265 Fax: 01937 845923 – *Life & Crimes of William Palmer*

Castle Howard, Nr York YO60 7DA Tel: 01653 648444 – *Brideshead Revisited / The Buccaneers*

Elsham Hall Country and Wildlife Park and Elsham Hall Barn Theatre, Brigg, East Yorkshire DN20 0Q. Tel: 01652 688698 Fax: 01652 688240 – *History of Folk*

Ripley Castle, Ripley Castle Estate, Harrogate, North Yorkshire. Tel: 01423 770152 Fax: 01423 771745 – *Jane Eyre / The Cater Street Hangman / Duchess of Duke Street / Frankenstein*

WALES

Picton Castle, Haverfordwest SA62 4AS Tel:01437 751326 – *Various Gardening Programs*

Portmerion Village, Portmerion, Gwyned Tel: 01766 770000 – *The Prisoner*

SCOTLAND

Drummond Castle Gardens, Muthill Crieff, Tayside, Scotland PH5 2AA. Tel: 01764 681257/433 Fax: 01764 681550 – *Rob Roy*

Drumlanrig Castle, Thornhill DG3 4AQ Tel:01848 330248

Scone Palace, Scone, Perth PH2 6BD. Tel: 01738 552300 Fax: 01738 552588 – *Antiques Road Show*

IRELAND

Benvarden Gardens, Benvarden, Dervock, Co. Antrim, N Ireland. Tel: 012657 41331 Fax: 012657 41955 – *Beyond The Pale*

The James Joyce Museum, The Joyce Tower, Sandycove, Co. Dublin, Ireland. Tel/Fax: 00 353 1 280 9265 – *My Friend Joe / Ulysses*

Powerscourt Gardens, Enniskerry, Co Wicklow Tel:00353 204 6000 – *BBC All for Love / Aristocrats*

Strokestown Park House & Gardens, Strokestown, Co. Roscommon, Ireland. Tel: 00 353 78 33013 Fax: 00 353 78 33712 – *Ann Devlin*

University College Dublin, Newman House, 85-86 St Stephen's Green, Dublin 2. Tel: +353 1 706 7422 / 706 7419 Fax: +353 1 706 7211 – *Aristocrats / Moll Flanders / Some Mothers Son*

Art Collections

Many properties throughout the guide contain notable works of art. The properties listed here have special collections.

ENGLAND

BEDFORDSHIRE

Woburn Abbey, Woburn, MK43 0TP
Tel: 01525 290666 – *Canaletto, Van Dyck, Reynolds*

BERKSHIRE

Dorney Court, Dorney, Nr Windsor, SL4 6QP
Tel: 01628 604638, Fax: 01628 665772

Eton College, Windsor, SL4 6DW
Tel: 01763 671177, Fax: 01753 671 265 – *Brew House Gallery, Exhibitions change*

Highclere Castle, Nr Newbury, RG20 9RN
Tel: 01635 253210. Old masters including Van Dyck

Taplow Court, Berry Hill, Taplow SL6 OER Tel:01628 591215

BUCKINGHAMSHIRE

Windsor Castle, Windsor, Berkshire SL4 1NJ
Tel: 01753 568286

CAMBRIDGESHIRE

Elton Hall, Elton, Petersborough PE8 6SH Tel:01832 280468

CHESHIRE

Capesthorne Hall, Capesthorne, Siddington, Nr. Macclesfield, SK11 9JY. Tel: 01625 861221. Fax: 01625 861619

Dorfold Hall, Nantwich CW5 8LD Tel:01270 625245

Dunham Massey, Altrincham Tel:0161 941 1025

Norton Priory Museum & Gardens, Tudor Road, Manor Park, Runcorn, WA7 1SX. Tel: 01928 569895 – *Contemporary sculpture*

Tabley House, Knutsford, WA16 0HB
Tel: 01565 750151, Fax: 01565 653230 – *Lely, Lawrence, Opie, Ward, Owen, Devis, Turner*

Tatton Park, Knutsford, WA16 6QN
Tel: 01565 750 250, Fax: 01565 654 822

CORNWALL

Mount Edgcumbe House & Country Park, Cremyll, Torpoint PL10 1HZ Tel: 01752 822236

Pencarrow, Washway, Bodmin PL30 5AG.
Tel: 01208 841369 – *Sir Joshua Reynolds*

COUNTY DURHAM

Auckland Castle, Bishop Auckland DL14 7NR.
Tel: 01388 601627 Fax:01388 609323 – *Zurbaran*

Raby Castle, Staindrop, Darlington, Co Durham DL2 3AY Tel: 01833 660 202

CUMBRIA

Abbot Hall Art Gallery & Museum of Lakeland Life & Industry, Kirkland, Kendal LA9 5AL. Tel: 01539 722464 Fax: 01539 722494

Appleby Castle, Boroughgate, Appleby-In-Westmorland CA16 6XH. Tel: 017683 51402, Fax: 017683 51082 – *Clifford Family Portraits*

Dalemain, nr Penrith CA11 0HB. Tel: 017684 86450 Fax 017684 86223

Hutton-in-the-Forest, Skelton, Penrith CA1 9TH. Tel: 017684 84449 Fax:017684 84571 – *Furniture / Portraits / Ceramics / Tapestry*

DERBYSHIRE

Calke Abbey, Ticknall, Derby DE73 1LE. Tel: 01332 86382 Fax: 01332 865272

Kedleston Hall, Derby, DE22 5JH. Tel: 01332 842191 Fax: 01332 841972 – *17th & 18th century Italian / Dutch collection*

Renishaw Hall, Nr Sheffield S31 9WB.
Tel: 01246 432310

DORSET

Athelhampton House & Gardens, Athelhampton, Dorchester. Tel: 01305 848363 Fax: 01305 848135 – *A.W.Pugin*

Parnham House, Parnham, Beaminster DT8 3NA.
Tel: 01308 862204 Fax 01308 863444

Sandford Orcas Manor House, Sandford Orcas, Sherbourne DT9 4SB Tel:01963 220206

Wolfeton House, Dorchester DT2 9QN.
Tel: 01305 263500

DEVON

Powderham Castle, Kenton, Exeter EX6 8JQ. Tel: 01626 890 243 Fax: 01626 890729 – *Cosway, Hudson, Reynolds*

Torre Abbey, The Kings Drive, Torquay TQ2 5JX
Tel: 01803 293593 Fax: 01803 201154 – *Pre-Raphaelites; 19th century*

ESSEX

Ingatestone Hall, Hall Lane, Ingatestone CM4 9NR
Tel:01277 353010 English Portraits

The Sir Alfred Munnings Art Museum, Castle House, Dedham CO7 6AZ Tel: 01206 322127

GLOUCESTERSHIRE

Berkeley Castle, Gloucestershire GL13 9BQ Tel: 01453 810332

Frampton Court, Frampton-on-Severn GL2 7EU. Tel: Home 01452 740 267 Office 01452 740 698

Owlpen Manor, Owlpen, nr Uley GL11 5BZ. Tel: 01453 860261 Fax 01453 860819

Sudeley Castle, Winchcombe, Gloucs. GL54 5JD
Tel: 01242 602308 – *Van Dyck, Ruben*

HAMPSHIRE

Breamore House, Breamore, nr Fordingbridge SP6 2DF. Tel: 01725 512233 Fax: 01725 512858

Mottisfont Abbey Garden, Mottisfont, Nr Romsey SO51 0LP. Tel: 01794 340757 Fax:01794 341492 – *Derek Hill's 20th Century picture collection*

Stratfield Saye House, Stratfield Saye, Reading, Hampshire RE7 2BT. Tel: 01256 882882

HEREFORD & WORCESTER

Eastnor Castle, Eastnor, Nr Ledbury, HR8 1RL
Tel: 01531 633160 Fax 01531 631776

Hellens, Much Marcle, Ledbury HR8 2LY Tel:01531 660668

HERTFORDSHIRE

Hatfield House, Hatfield, Hertfordshire AL9 5NQ.
Tel: 01707 262823, Fax: 01707 275719

KENT

Cobham Hall, Cobham, Nr Gravesend, Kent DA12 3BL.
Tel: 01474 824319 Fax: 01474 822995

Finchcocks, Goudhurst, Kent TN17 1HH.
Tel: 01580 211702 Fax: 01580 211007 – *18th century, musical theme*

Hever Castle, Nr Edenbridge TN8 7NG Tel:01732 865224

Squerryes Court, Westerham TN16 1SJ. Tel: 01959 562345/563118 Fax:01959 565949 – *Old Masters / Italian / 17th Century Dutch / 18th Century English Schools*

LANCASHIRE

Gawthorpe Hall, Padiham, Nr Burnley BB12 8UA
Tel:01282 771004

Heaton Hall, Heaton Park, Prestwich, Manchester M25 2SW. Tel: 0161 773 1231/236 5244 Fax 0161 236 7369

Towneley Hall Art Gallery & Museum and Museum of Local Crafts & Industries, Burnley BB11 3RQ. Tel: 01282 424213 Fax: 01282 436138 – *18th Century & 19th Century*

LEICESTERSHIRE

Belvoir Castle, Nr Grantham, Lincolnshire. NG32 1PD
Tel: 01476 870262

LINCOLNSHIRE

Elsham Hall, Brigg DN20 0QZ Tel:01652 688698

Grimsthorpe Castle, Grimsthorpe, Bourne.
Tel 01778 591205 – *Family portraits*

LONDON

Apsley House, The Wellington Museum, 149 Piccadilly, Hyde Park Corner, London SW1.
Tel: 0171 499 5676 Fax: 0171 493 6576

Boston Manor House, Boston Manor Road, Brentford TW8 9JX. Tel: 0181 560 5441 Fax: 0181-862-7602

Buckingham Palace, London SW1A 1AA.
Tel: 0171 839 1377

Greenwich Observatory, Queens House, National Maritime Museum, Romney Road, Greenwich SE10 9NF. Tel: 0181-312 6565 Fax:0181 312 6632 – *Maritime / Seascapes / Royal Portraits*

Ham House, Ham Street, Richmond TW10 7RS
Tel:0181 940 1950

Leighton House Museum & Art Gallery, 12 Holland Park Road, London W14 8LZ. Tel: 0171 602 3316 Fax: 0171 371 2467 – *Pre-Raphaelite*

Museum of Garden History, Lambeth Palace Road, Lambeth SE1 7LB. Tel: 0171-261 1891 Fax 0171 401 8869

Orleans House Gallery, Riverside, Twickenham, TW1 3DJ. Tel: 0181-892 0221 Fax: 0181 744 0501

Osterley Park, Jersey Road, Isleworth TW7 4RB.
Tel: 0181 568 7714

St. John's Gate, St John's Lane, Clerkenwell EC1M 4DA. Tel: 0171-253 6644, Fax: 0171 336 0587

Spencer House, 27, St. James's Place SW1A 1NR
Tel:0207 514 1964

Southside House, 3 Woodhayes Road Wimbledon SW19 4RJ Tel:0181 946 7643

Syon Park, Brentford, Middlesex TW8 8JF.
Tel: 0181 560 0881

NORFOLK

Holkham Hall, Wells-next-the-Sea, Norfolk NR23 1AB
Tel: 01328 710227 Fax: 01328 711707 – *Rubens, Van Dyck, Claude, Poussin and Gainsborough*

Norwich Castle Museum, Norwich NR1 3JU.
Tel: 01603 223674

Wolterton Park, Erpingham, Norfolk. Tel: 01263 584175 Fax: 01263 761214

NORTHAMPTONSHIRE

Boughton House, Kettering NN14 1BJ. Tel: 01536 515731 Fax: 01536 417255 – *Van Dyck*

Castle Ashby House, Castle Ashby, Northampton NN7 1LQ. Tel: 01604 696696 Fax: 01604 696516 – *Reynolds, Van Dyck*

Cottesbrooke Hall & Gardens, Nr Northampton, NN6 8PF. Tel: 01604 505808 Fax: 01604 505619 – *Munnings, Gainsborough, Lionel Edwards*

Lamport Hall & Gardens, Northampton, NN6 9HD Tel: 01604 686272 Fax: 01604 686224

NORTHUMBERLAND

Alnwick Castle, Alnwick, Northumberland NE66 1NQ Tel: 01665 510777 Fax: 01665 510876 – *Titian, Van Dyck, Canelleto*

OXFORDSHIRE

Blenheim Palace, Woodstock, Oxon OX20 1PX Tel: 01993 811325 Fax: 01993 813527

Buscot Park, Buscot, Nr Faringdon SN7 8BU. Tel: 01367 240786 Fax:01367 241794

Fawley Court - Marian Fathers Historic House & Museum, Marlow Road, Henley-On-Thames RG9 3AE. Tel: 01491 574917 Fax: 01491 411587

Waterperry Gardens, Nr. Wheatley, Oxon. Tel: 01844 339226/254 – *Art Gallery*

SHROPSHIRE

Burford House Gardens, Tenbury Wells WR15 8HQ. Tel: 01584 810777 Fax 01584 810673 – *Botanical, contemporary*

Ironbridge Gorge Museum, Ironbridge, Telford TF8 7AW. Tel: 01952 433522 Fax:01952 432204 – *History of Industrial Revolution*

Rowleys House Museum, Barker Street, Shrewsbury SY1 1QH. Tel: 01743 361196 Fax: 01743 358411

SOMERSET

Number One, Royal Crescent, Bath Tel:01225 428126 18th Century

STAFFORDSHIRE

Sandon Hall, Sandon, Stafford. Tel: 01889 508004 Fax: 01889 508586

The Shugborough Estate, Milford, Nr. Stafford ST17 Tel: 01889 881388

SUFFOLK

Christchurch Mansion, Christchurch Park, Ipswich Tel: 01473 253246 Fax: 01473 281274

Gainsborough's House, 46 Gainsborough Street, Sudbury, Suffolk CO10 6EU Tel: 01787 372958

Somerleyton Hall & Gardens, Somerleyton, Lowestoft, Suffolk NR32 5QQ. Tel: 01502 730224

Wingfield Old College, Wingfield, Nr Eye, Suffolk IP21 5RA. Tel: 01379 384888 Fax: 01379 384034

SURREY

Clandon Park, West Clandon, Guildford GU4 7RQ Tel: 01483 222 482 – *Gubbay Collection, Porcelain, Needlework & Furniture*

Guildford House Gallery, 155, High Street, Guildford GU1 3AJ. Tel: 01483 444740 Fax 01483 444742 – *John Russell R A / Henry J Sage / Edward Wesson*

SUSSEX

Arundel Castle, Arundel. West Sussex. Tel: 01903 883136

Bentley House & Gardens, Halland, Nr Lewes BN8 5AF. Tel: 01825 840573 – *Philip Rickman*

Charleston Farmhouse, Firle, nr Lewes. Tel: 01323 811265 Fax: 01323 811628

Firle Place, Nr Lewes, East Sussex, BN8 6LP Tel/Fax: 01273 858188. – *Van Dyck, Reynolds, Rubens, Gainsborough, Guardi, Seargeant, Tenniers, Puligo, Larkin plus many others*

Goodwood House, Goodwood, Chichester PO18 0PX. Tel: 01243 755048 Fax 01243 755005

Pallant House, 9 North Pallant, Chichester PO19 1TJ Tel: 01243 774557 – *Modern British*

Parham House and Gardens, Parham Park Ltd, Pulborough RH20 4HS. Tel: 01903 742021/ Info line 01903 744888 Fax: 01903 746557

Preston Manor, Preston Drove, Brighton BN1 6SD Tel:01273 292770

Royal Pavilion, Brighton BN1 1EE. Tel: 01273 290900 Fax 01273 292871 – *Chinoiserie, Regency Silver Gilt*

West Dean Gardens, West Dean Estate, nr Chichester PO18 0QZ. Tel: 01243 818210 Fax: 01243 811342 – *Tapestry studio*

WARWICKSHIRE

Arbury Hall, Nuneaton CV10 7PT. Tel: 01203 382804 Fax 01203 641147

Charlecote Park, Warwick CV35 9ER Tel:01789 470277

Coughton Court, Alcester, B49 5JA. Tel: 01789 400777 Fax: 01789 765544

WEST MIDLANDS

Baddesley Clinton Hall, Rising Lane, Baddesley Clinton Village, Knowle, Solihull, West Midlands. Tel: 01564 783294 Fax: 01564 782706

Birmingham Botanical Gardens & Glasshouse, Westbourne Road, Edgbaston, Birmingham B15 3TR. Tel: 0121 454 1860 Fax: 0121 454 7835

WILTSHIRE

Corsham Court, Corsham, Wilts SN13 0BZ Tel: 01249 701610/701611. – *Van Dyck, Carlo Dolei*

Longleat, The Estate Office, Warminster BA12 7NW. Tel: 01985 844400 Fax: 01985 844885 – *Alexander Thynn / Portraits*

Wilton House, Wilton, Salisbury SP2 0BJ. Tel: 01722 746720 Fax: 01722 744447 – *Van Dyck*

YORKSHIRE

Aske Hall, Aske, Richmond, North Yorkshire DL10 5HJ Tel: 01748 850391 , Fax: 01748 823252

Bramham Park, Wetherby LS23 6ND. Tel: 01937 844265 Fax:01937 845 923

Burton Agnes Hall, Buton Agnes, Driffield, nr Bridlington YO25 0ND. Tel: 01262 490324 – *Impressionists*

Cannon Hall, Cawthorne, Barnsley S75 4AT. Tel: 01226 790 270

Castle Howard, Nr York YO60 7DA Tel: 01653 648444

Elsham Hall Country and Wildlife Park, The Estate Office, Brigg DN20 0QZ. Tel: 01652 688698 Fax 01652 688240

Harewood House and Bird Garden, The Estate Office, Harewood, Leeds LS17 9LQ. Tel: 0113 288 6331 Fax: 0113 288 6467 – *Renaissance / Turner / Reynolds / Contemporary*

Lotherton Hall, Aberford, Yorkshire L25 3EB. Tel: 0113 281 3259 Fax: 0113 281 2100

Newburgh Priory, Coxwold, York YO6 4AS Tel: 01347 868435

Norton Conyers, Ripon HG4 5EQ. Tel: 01765 640333 Fax: 01765 692772 – *17th & 18th Century portraits, 19th Century hunting pictures*

Sewerby Hall & Gardens, Church Lane, Sewerby, Bridlington, East Yorks YOQT 1EA. Tel: Estate Office: 01262 673769

Temple Newsam House, Leeds LS15 0AE. Tel: 0113 264 7321, Fax: 0113 260 2285

WALES

Bodelwyddan Castle, Bodelwyddan, St Asaph, Bodelwyddan LL18 5YA. Tel: 01745 584060 Fax 01745 584563 – *National Portrait Gallery, 19th Century Collection*

Bodrhyddan Hall, Rhuddlan LL18 5SB. Tel: 01745 590414 Fax:01745 590155

Colby Woodland Gardens, Stepaside, Narbeth SA67 8PP. Tel: 01834 811885

Dinefwr Park, Llandeilo, Carmarthenshire. Tel: 01558 823902

Picton Castle, Picton Castle Trust, Haverfordwest SA62 4AS. Tel: 01437 751326

SCOTLAND

Blairquhan Castle, Straiton, Maybole KA19 7LZ Tel:016557 70239

Bowhill House & Country Park, Bowhill, Nr. Selkirk, TD7 5ET Scottish Borders. Tel/Fax: 01750 22204 – *Gainsborough, Canaletto*

Dalmeny House, South Queensferry, Edinburgh, EH30 9TQ. Tel: 0131 331 1888, Fax: 0131 331 1788

Drumlanrig Castle, Thornhill, Dumfrieshire DG3 4AQ Tel: 01848 330248

Fasque, Fettercairn, Laurencekirk AB30 1DN Tel:01561 340202

Glamis Castle, Estate Office, Glamis DD8 1RT. Tel: 01307 840393 Fax: 01307 840 733

Gosford House, Longniddry EH32 0PY. Tel: 01875 870201 Fax:01875 870620

Lennoxlove, Haddington EH41 4NZ. Tel: 01620 823720 Fax:01620 825 112

Mount Stuart House & Gardens, Mount Stuart, Isle of Bute, PA20 9LR. Tel: 01700 503877 Fax: 01700 505 313

Paxton House, Paxton, Nr Berwick upon Tweed TD15 1SZ Tel: 01289 386291

Scone Palace, Perth PH2 6BD. Tel: 01738 552300 Fax:01738 552588 – *Vernis Martin, ivories, porcelain*

Thirlestane Castle, Lauder, Berwickshire TD2 6RU. Tel: 01578 722430 Fax 01578 722761

Traquair House, Innerleithen, Peebleshire EH44 6PW Tel:01896 830323

IRELAND

Bunratty Castle and Folk Park, Bunratty, Co. Clare. Tel: 00353 61 360 788 Fax:00353 61 361 020 – *Medieval*

Glin Castle, Glin. Tel: 00353 68 34173 Fax: 00353 68 34364

Malahide Castle, Malahide, Co. Dublin. Tel: 00353 1 846 2184 Fax:00353 1 846 2537 – *Collection of Irish portrait paintings mainly from the National Gallery*

Strokestown Park House & Gardens, Strokestown, Co. Roscommon. Tel: 00353 78 33013 Fax: 00353 78 33712

Properties Licensed for Civil Marriages

ENGLAND

BEDFORDSHIRE

Woburn Abbey, Woburn, MK43 OTP.
Tel: 01525 290666 Fax: 01525 290271

BUCKINGHAMSHIRE

Stowe Landscape Gardens, Buckingham, MK18 5EH.
Tel: 01280 822850 Fax: 01280 822437

Stowe (Stowe School), Stowe, MK18 5EH.
Tel: 01280 813650

Waddesdon Manor, The Dairy, Nr Aylesbury, HP18
OJW. Tel: 01296 651211 Fax: 01296 651142

CAMBRIDGESHIRE

Kimbolton Castle, Kimbolton School, Kimbolton,
PE18 OAE. Tel: 01480 860505 Fax: 01480 861763

CHESHIRE

Arley Hall, nr Great Budworth, Northwich, CW9 6NA.
Tel: 01565 777353

Bramall Hall, Bramhall Park, Stockport, SK7 3NX.
Tel: 0161 485 3708 Fax: 0161 486 6959

Capesthorne Hall, Siddington, Macclesfield, SK11 9JY.
Tel: 01625 861221 Fax: 01625 861619

Ness Botanic Gardens, Ness, Nesston, L64 4AY.
Tel: 0151 3530123 Fax: 0151 353 1004

Peckforton Castle, Stonehouse Lane, Peckforton,
Tarporley, CW6 9TN. Tel: 01829 260930
Fax: 01829 261230

Tabley House, Knutsford, WA16 OHB. Tel: 01565
750151 Fax: 01565 653230

Tatton Park, Knutsford, WA16 6QN. Tel: 01565 654822
Fax: 01625 534403

CORNWALL

Trevarno Estate & Gardens, Trevarno Manor, Helston
TR13 ORU. Tel: 01326 574274 Fax: 01326 574282

CUMBRIA

Muncaster Castle, Ravenglass CA18 1RQ.
Tel: 01229 717614 Fax: 01229 717010

DERBYSHIRE

Eyam Hall, Hope Valley S32 5QW Tel:01433 631976

Kedleston Hall and Park, Quarndon, Derby DE22 5JH.
Tel: 01332 842191 Fax: 01332 841972

Renishaw Hall, Nr Sheffield S31 9WB. Tel: 01246
432310

DEVON

Bickleigh Castle, Bickleigh, Tiverton EX16 8RP.
Tel: 01884 855363

Buckfast Abbey, Buckfastleigh, TQ11 OEE.
Tel: 01364 642519 Fax: 01364 643891

Kingston House, Staverton, Totnes TQ9 6AR.
Tel: 01803 762235 Fax: 01803 762444

Powderham Castle, Kenton, EX6 8JQ.
Tel: 01626 890243 Fax: 01626 890729

Tiverton Castle, Tiverton, EX16 6RP. Tel: 01884
253200/255200 Fax: 01884 254200

DORSET

Kingston Maurawd, Dorchester DT2 8PY Tel: 01305
215003

ESSEX

Layer Marney Tower, Nr Colchester, CO5 9US.
Tel: 01206 330784

GREATER MANCHESTER

Heaton Hall, Heaton Park, Prestwich, M25 2SW.
Tel: 0161 773 1231/236 5244 Fax: 0161 236 7369

HAMPSHIRE

Avington Park, Winchester, SO21 1DB.
Tel: 01962 779260 Fax: 01962 779864

Highclere Castle, Newbury RG20 9RN.
Tel: 01635 253210 Fax:01635 255315

Mottisfont Abbey Garden Mottisfont, Nr Romsey,
SO51 OLP. Tel: 01794 340757 Fax: 01794 341492

The Vyne, Vyne Road, Sherborne St John, Basingstoke
Tel:01256 881337

HEREFORD & WORCESTER

Avoncroft Museum of Buildings, Stoke Heath,
Bromsgrove, B60 4JR. Tel: 01527 831886 or 831363
Fax: 02527 876934

Eastnor Castle, nr Ledbury, Hereford, HR8 1RL.
Tel: 01531 633160 Fax: 01531 631776

Hopton Court, Cleobury Mortimer, Kidderminster, DY14
OHH. Tel: 01299 270734 Fax: 01299 271132

Worcester Cathedral, College Green, Worcester,
WR1 2LH. Tel: 01905 28854 Fax: 01905 611139

HERTFORDSHIRE

Hatfield House, Hatfield ,AL9 5NQ. Tel: 01707 262823
Fax: 01707 275719

Knebworth House, Knebworth. Tel: 01438 812661

KENT

Cobham Hall, Cobham, nr. Gravesend, DA12 3BL.
Tel: 01474 824319

Down House, Downe, BR6 7JT. Tel: 01689 859119

Finchcocks, Goudhurst, TN17 1HH. Tel: 01580 211702
Fax: 01580 211007

Gad's Hill Place, Gads Hill School, Higham, Rochester
ME3 7PA. Tel: 01474 822366 Fax: 01478 822977

Groombridge Place Gardens, Groombridge, TN3 9QG.
Tel: 01892 863999 Fax: 01892 863996

Mount Ephraim Gardens, Hernhill, nr Faversham,
ME13 9TX. Tel: 01227 751496 Fax: 01227 750940

Owl House, Lamberhurst Tel:01892 890230

Penshurst Place, Penshurst, Tunbridge Wells,
TN11 8DG. Tel: 01892 870307 Fax: 01892 870866

Tonbridge Castle, Tonbridge TN9 1BG.
Tel: 01732 770929 Fax: 01732 770449

LANCASHIRE

Rufford Old Hall, Rufford, Nr Ormskirk L40 1SG
Tel:01704 821254

LINCOLNSHIRE

Elsham Hall, Brigg DN20 0QZ Tel:01652 688698

LONDON

Burgh House, New End Square, Hampstead, NW3 1LT.
Tel: 0171 431 0144 Fax: 0171 435 8817

Chiswick House, Burlington Lane, Chiswick W4.
Tel: 0181 995 0508

Greenwich Observatory, Queens House, National
Maritime Museum, Romney Road, Greenwich, London
SE10 9NF. Tel: 0181 312 6565 Fax: 0181 312 6632

Ham House, Ham Street, Richmond Tel:0181 940 1950

Orleans House Gallery, Riverside, Twickenham,
TW1 3DJ. Tel: 0181 892 0221 Fax: 0181 744 0501

Osterley Park, Jersey Road, Isleworth, TW7 4RB.
Tel: 0181 568 7714

St. John's Gate, St John's Lane, Clerkenwell,
EC1M 4DA. Tel: 0171 253 6644 Fax: 0171 336 0587

Syon Park, Brentford ,TW8 8JF. Tel: 0181 560 0881
Fax: 0181 568 0936

NORTHAMPTONSHIRE

Castle Ashby House, Castle Ashby, Northampton,
NN7 1LQ. Tel: 01604 696696 Fax: 01604 696516

Lamport Hall and Gardens, Northampton, NN6 9HD.
Tel: 01604 686272 Fax: 01604 686 224

NORTHUMBERLAND

Chillingham Castle, Chillingham, Alnwick, NE66 5NJ.
Tel: 01668 215359 Fax: 01668 215643

NOTTINGHAMSHIRE

Norwood Park, Southwell, NG25 OPF.
Tel/Fax: 01636 815649

OXFORDSHIRE

Ardington House, Wantage, OX12 8QA.
Tel: 01235 821566 Fax: 01235 821151

SHROPSHIRE

Burford House Gardens, Tenbury Wells, WR15 8HQ.
Tel: 01584 810777 Fax: 01584 810673

Old Colehurst Manor, Colehurst, Market Drayton, TF9
2JB. Tel: 01630 638833 Fax: 01630 638647

Shrewsbury Castle & Shropshire Regimental Museum,
Castle Street, Shrewsbury, SY1 2AT.
Tel: 01743 358516 Fax: 01743 358411

Walcot Hall, Nr Bishops Castle, Lydbury North,
SY7 8AZ. Tel. 0171-581 2782 Fax: 0171 589 0195

SOMERSET

Museum of Costume & Assembly Rooms, Bennett
Street, Bath Tel:01225 477789

STAFFORDSHIRE

Ford Green Hall, Ford Green Road, Smallthorne, Stoke-
on-Trent, ST6 1NG. Tel: 01782 233195
Fax: 01782 233 194

The Shugborough Estate, Milford, Stafford, ST17 0XB.
Tel: 01889 881388 Fax: 01889 881323

SUFFOLK

Somerleyton Hall, nr Lowestoft, NR32 5QQ.
Tel: 01502 730224 Fax: 01502 732143

SURREY

Clandon Park, West Clandon, Guildford, GU4 7RQ.
Tel: 01483 222482 Fax: 01483 223479

Great Fosters Hotel, Stroude Road, Egham TW20 9UR.
Tel: 0784 433822

Loseley Park, Estate Office, Guildford GU3 1HS.
Tel: 01483 304440 Fax: 01483 302036

SUSSEX

Anne of Cleves House, 52 Southover High Street,
Lewes, BN7 1JA. Tel: 01273 474610 FX 01273 486990

Bentley House & Gardens, Halland, Nr Lewes,
BN8 5AF. Tel: 01825 840573

Brickwall House and Gardens, Northiam, Rye,
TN31 6NL. Tel: 01797 253388 Fax: 01797 252567

Glynde Place, Glynde, nr Lewes, BN8 6SX.
Tel: 01273 858224 Fax: 01273 858224

Goodwood House, Goodwood, Chichester, PO18 0PX.
Tel: 01243 755048 Fax: 01243 755005

Herstmonceux Castle, International Study Centre,
Queens University, Hailsham BN27 1RN.
Tel: 01323 833816 Fax: 01323 834499

Royal Pavilion, Brighton, BN1 1EE. Tel: 01273 290900
Fax: 01273 292871

The Weald & Downland Open Air Museum,
Singleton, Nr Chichester Tel:01243 811348

Eyam Hall, Derbyshire

WARWICKSHIRE

Coughton Court, Alcester B49 5JA Tel: 01789 400777

Ragley Hall, Alcester B49 5NJ. Tel: 01789 762090
Fax: 01789 764791

WEST MIDLANDS

Birmingham Botanical Gardens and Glasshouses,
Westbourne Road, Edgbaston, Birmingham B15 3TR.
Tel: 0121 454 1860 Fax: 0121 454 7835

Hagley Hall, nr Stourbridge DY9 9LG. Tel: 0562 882408

WILTSHIRE

Longleat, The Estate Office, Warminster BA12 7NW.
Tel: 01985 844400 Fax: 01985 844885

YORKSHIRE

Bolton Castle, Leyburn, DL8 4ET. Tel: 01969 623981
Fax:01969 623332

The Bar Convent, 17 Blossom Street, York, YO2 2AH.
Tel: 01904 643238 Fax: 01904 631792

Bolton Abbey Estate, Bolton Abbey, Skipton,
BD23 6EX. Tel: 01756 7110227 Fax: 01756 710535

Duncombe Park, Helmsley, York, YO62 5EB.
Tel: 01439 770213 Fax: 01439 771114

Harewood House and Bird Garden, Harewood, Leeds
LS17 9LQ. Tel: 0113 288 6331 Fax: 0113 288 6467

Newburgh Priory, Coxwold, YO6 4AS.
Tel: 01347 868435

Oakwell Hall, Birstall, WF19 9LG. Tel: 01924 326 240

Ripley Castle, Ripley HG3 3AY. Tel: 01423 770152
Fax: 01423 771745

Sewerby Hall and Gardens, Church Lane, Sewerby,
Bridlington YO15 1EA.
Tel: Estate Office: 01262 673 769 Hall :01262 677874

WALES

Dinefwr Park, Llandeilo Tel:01558 823902

Gwydir Castle, Llanrwst. Tel: 01492 641 687
Fax: 01492 641687

Portmerion Village, Portmerion, Gwyned Tel: 01766
770000

Tredegar House, Newport NP1 9YW. Tel: 01633 815880
Fax: 01633 815895

SCOTLAND

Braemar Castle, Braemar, AB35 5XR.
Tel/Fax: 013397 41219

Dalmeny House, Charisma, South Queensferry,
EH30 9TQ. Tel: 0131-331 1888 Fax: 0131 331 1788

Duff House Country House Gallery, Banff AB45 5SX.
Tel: 01261 818181 Fax: 01261 818900

Fasque, Fettercairn, Laurencekirk AB30 1DN Tel: 01561
340 202

Lennoxlove, Haddington, EH41 4NZ. Tel: 01620 823720
Fax: 01620 825 112

Paxton House & Gardens, Paxton, nr Berwick-upon-
Tweed, TD15 1SZ. Tel: 01289 386291

Rosslyn Chapel, Roslin EH25 9PU. Tel: 0131 448 2948

Scone Palace, Perth PH2 6BD. Tel: 01738 552300
Fax: 01738 552588

Traquair House, Innerleithen, EH44 6PW.
Tel: 01896 830323 Fax: 01896 830639

IRELAND

Antrim Castle Gardens, Antrim.
Tel: 01849 428000 Fax: 01849 460360

Powerscourt Gardens, Enniskerry, Co Wicklow
Tel:00353 204 6000

Strokestown Park House & Gardens, Strokestown, Co.
Roscommon. Tel: 00353 78 33013 Fax: 00353 78
33712

Properties offering Top Teas!

ENGLAND

BEDFORDSHIRE
Woburn Abbey, Woburn MK43 OTP. Tel: 01525 290666

BERKSHIRE
Basildon Park, Lower Basildon, Reading RG8 9NR. Tel: 0118 984 3040
Dorney Court, Windsor SL4 6QP. Tel: 01628 604638
Savill Garden, Crown Estate Office, Windsor Great Park, Windsor SL7 2HT. Tel: 01753 860222
Taplow Court, Berry Hill, Taplow Tel:01628 591215

BUCKINGHAMSHIRE
Claydon House, Middle Claydon, Buckingham MK18 2EY. Tel: 01296 730349
Cliveden, Taplow, Maidenhead SL6 0JA. Tel: 01628 605069
Hughenden Manor, High Wycombe HP14 4LA. Tel: 01494 532580
Stowe Landscape Gardens, Buckingham MK18 5EH. Tel: 01280 822850

CAMBRIDGESHIRE
Ely Cathedral, The Chapter House, The College, Ely CB7 4DL. Tel: 01353 667735

CHESHIRE
Arley Hall and Gardens, Nr Great Budworth, Northwich CW9 6NA. Tel: 01565 777353
Dunham Massey, Altrincham WA14 4SJ. Tel: 0161 9411025
Little Moreton Hall, Congleton CW12 4SD. Tel: 01260 272018
Ness Botanic Gardens, Ness, Nesston L64 4AY. Tel: 0151 3530123
Tabley House Collection, Tabley House, Knutsford WA16 OHB. Tel: 01565 750151
Tatton Park, Knutsford WA16 6QN. Tel: 01565 654822

CORNWALL
Burncoose Nurseries and Garden, Gwennap, Redruth TR16 6BJ. Tel: 01209 861112
Caerhays Castle, Gorran, St Austell PL26 6LY Tel: 01872 501310
Pencarrow Washway, Bodmin PL30 5AG. Tel: 01208 841449
Trevarno Estate & Gardens, Trevarno Manor, Helston TR13 0RU. Tel: 01326 574274
Lanhydrock, Bodmin PL30 5AD. Tel: 01208 73320

CUMBRIA
Dalemain, nr Penrith CA11 0HB. Tel: 017684 86450
Hutton-in-the-Forest, Skelton, Penrith CA1 9TH. Tel: 017684 84449
Muncaster Castle, Ravenglass CA18 1RQ. Tel: 01229 717614

DERBYSHIRE
Haddon Hall, Estate Office, Bakewell DE45 1LA. Tel: 01629 812855
Lea Gardens, Lea, Matlock DE4 5GH. Tel: 01629 534 380
Renishaw Hall, Nr Sheffield, S21 3WB. Tel: 01777 860755

DEVON
Bickleigh Castle, Bickleigh, Tiverton EX16 8RP. Tel: 01884 855363
Buckfast Abbey, Buckfastleigh TQ11 OEE. Tel: 01364 643891
Killerton House, Broadclyst, nr Exeter EX5 3LE. Tel: 01392 881345
Powderham Castle Kenton, Exeter EX6 8JQ. Tel: 01626 890243
Torre Abbey, The Kings Drive, Torquay TQ2 5JX. Tel: 01803 293593

DORSET
Athelhampton House & Gardens, Athelhampton, Dorchester DT2 7LG. Tel: 01305 848363
Compton Acres Gardens, Canford Cliffs, Poole BH13 7ES. Tel: 01202 700778
Deans Court Garden, Wimborne BH21 1EE.
Forde Abbey and Gardens, nr Chard TA20 4LU. Tel: 01460 220231
Kingston Lacy House, Wimborne BH21 4EA Tel:01202 883402
Kingston Maurawd, Dorchester DT2 8PY Tel: 01305 215003
Lulworth Castle, The Lulworth Estate, East Lulworth, Wareham BH20 5QS. Tel: 01929 400352
Parnham House, Parnham, Beaminster Tel:01308 863444
Purse Caundle Manor, Purse Caundle, nr Sherborne DT9 5DY. Tel: 01963 250400
Sherborne Castle, Sherborne DT9 3PY. Tel: 01935 813182
Wolfeton House, Dorchester. Tel: 01305 263500

COUNTY DURHAM
Raby Castle, Staindrop, Darlington DL2 3AH. Tel: 01833 660202

ESSEX
Hedingham Castle, Castle Hedingham, nr Halstead CO9 3DJ. Tel: 01787 460261
Ingatestone Hall, Ingatestone CM4 9NR. Tel: 01277 353010
Layer Marney Tower, Colchester CO5 9US. Tel: 01206 330784

GLOUCESTERSHIRE
Berkeley Castle, Berkeley GL13 9BQ. Tel: 01453 810332
Chavenage, Tetbury GL8 8XP. Tel: 01666 502329
Kiftsgate Court, Mickleton, nr Chipping Campden GL55 6LW. Tel: 01386 438777
Owlpen Manor, Uley, nr Dursley GL11 5BZ. Tel: 01453 860261
Painswick Rococo Garden, The Stables, Painswick House, Painswick GL6 6TH. Tel:01452 813204
Sudeley Castle, Winchcombe GL54 5JD. Tel: 01242 602308

HAMPSHIRE
Avington Park, Winchester SO21 1DD. Tel: 01962 779260
Breamore House, Breamore, nr Fordingbridge SP6 2DF. Tel:01725 512233
Gilbert White's House & Garden and the Oates Museum, The Wakes, Selborne GU34 3JH. Tel: 01420 511275
Mottisfont Abbey Garden, Mottisfont, SO51 0LP. Tel: 011794 341220
Sir Harold Hillier Gardens, Ampfield, Romsey Tel:01794 368787
The Vyne, Vyne Road, Sherborne St John, Basingstoke Tel:01256 881337

HEREFORD & WORCESTER
Burton Court, Eardisland, Leominster HR6 9DN. Tel: 01544 388231
Eastnor Castle, Nr Ledbury, Hereford HR8 1RD. Tel: 01531 633160
Harvington Hall, Harvington, Kidderminister DY10 4LR. Tel: 01562 777846
Hellens, Much Marcle, Ledbury HR8 2LY Tel:01531 660668
Hergest Croft Gardens, Kington. Tel: 01544 230160
How Caple Court Gardens, How Caple HR1 4SX. Tel: 01989 740612
Kentchurch Court, Nr Pontrilias, Hereford. Tel: 01981 240228

HERTFORDSHIRE
Gardens of the Rose, Chiswell Green, St. Albans AL2 3NR. Tel: 01727 850461
Hatfield House, Hatfield AL9 5NQ. Tel: 01707 262823
Knebworth House, Knebworth. Tel: 01438 812661

KENT
Belmont, Throwley, Nr Faversham ME13 OHH. Tel: 01795 890202
Cobham Hall, Cobham, Nr Gravesend DA12 3BL. Tel: 01474 824319/823371
Doddington Place Gardens, Doddington, Sittingbourne ME9 0BB. Tel: 01795 886101
Gad's Hill Place, Gad's Hill School, Rochester ME3 7AA. Tel: 01474 822366
Goodnestone Park, Canterbury CT3 1PL Tel:01304 840107
Groombridge Place Gardens, Groombridge TN3 9QG. Tel: 01892 863999
Ladham House, Goudhurst. Tel: 01580 211203
Lullingstone Castle, Eynsford DA14 0JA. Tel: 01322 862114
Owl House Gardens, Lamberhurst Tel:01892 890230
Penshurst Place, Penshurst, Tunbridge Wells TN11 8DG. Tel: 01892 870307
Squerryes Court, Westerham TN16 1SJ. Tel: 01959 562345

LANCASHIRE
Gawthorpe Hall, Padiham, Nr Burnley BB12 8UA. Tel: 01282 770353
Stonyhurst College, Stonyhurst, Clitheroe BB7 9PZ Tel:01254826345
Towneley Hall Art Gallery, Burnley BD11 3RQ.Tel: 01282 424213

LEICESTERSHIRE
Kayes Garden Nursery, 1700 Melton Rd, Rearsby, Leicester LE7 4YR. Tel: 01664 424578
The Manor House, Donington-le-Heath.
Stanford Hall, Stanford Park, Lutterworth LE17 6DH. Tel: 01788 860250

LINCOLNSHIRE
Elsham Hall, Brigg DN20 0QZ Tel:01652 688698

LONDON
Burgh House, New End Square, Hampstead NW3 1LT. Tel: 0171 431 0144
Chelsea Physic Garden, 66 Royal Hospital Road, Chelsea SW3 4HS. Tel: 0171 352 5646
Museum of Garden History, Lambeth Palace Road, Lambeth SE1 7LB. Tel: 0171 261 1891
Osterley Park, Jersey Road, Isleworth TW7 4RB. Tel: 0181 568 7714

NORFOLK
Hoveton Hall Gardens, Wroxham NR11 7BB.

NORTHAMPTONSHIRE
Boughton House, Kettering Tel:01536 515731
Coton Manor Garden, Coton, Nr Guilsborough NN6 8RQ. Tel: 01604 740219
Lamport Hall and Gardens, Northampton NN6 9HD. Tel: 01604 686272

NOTTINGHAMSHIRE
Norwood Park, Norwood Park, Southwell, NG25 0PF.

OXFORDSHIRE
Buscot Park, Buscot, Nr Faringdon SN7 8BU. Tel: 01367 240786
Kelmscott Manor, Kelmscott, Lechlade GL7 3HJ Tel:01367 252486
Mapledurham House, Nr Reading RG4 7TR Tel:01189 723350
Waterperry Gardens, Waterperry Horticultural Centre, Nr Wheatley OX9 1SZ. Tel: 01844 339226/339254

SHROPSHIRE
Burford House Gardens, Tenbury Wells WR15 8HQ. Tel: 01584 810777
Hodnet Hall Gardens, Nr Market Drayton TF9 3NN. Tel: 01630 685202
Ironbridge Gorge Museum, Ironbridge, Telford TF8 7AW. Tel: 01952 433522
Old Colehurst Manor, Colehurst, Market Drayton TF9 2JB Tel:01630 638833
Walcot Hall, Nr Bishops Castle, Lydbury North SY7 8AZ. Tel: 0171-581 2782
Wollerton Old Hall, Wollerton, Market Drayton TF9 3NA. Tel: 01630 685760

SOMERSET
Gaulden Manor, Tolland, Nr Taunton TA4 3PN. Tel: 019847 213
Hestercombe House Gardens, Cheddon Fitzpaine, Taunton TA2 8LQ. Tel: 01823 413923

STAFFORDSHIRE
Dunwood Hall, Longsdon, Nr. Leek ST9 9AR. Tel: 01538 385071
Sandon Hall, Sandon ST18 0BZ. Tel: 01889 508004

SUFFOLK
Helmingham Hall Gardens, The Estate Office, Helmingham Hall, Stowmarket IP14 6EF. Tel: 01473 890363
Kentwell Hall. Long Melford, Nr. Sudbury CO10 9BA. Tel: 01787 310207
Somerleyton Hall, nr Lowestoft. Tel: 01502 730224
Wingfield Old College, Wingfield, Eye IP21 5RA. Tel: 01379 384888

SURREY
Clandon Park, West Clandon, Guildford GU4 7RQ. Tel: 01483 222482
Claremont Landscape Garden, Portsmouth Road, Esher KT10 9JG. Tel: 01372 469421
Guildford House Gallery, 155 High Street, Guildford GU1 3AJ Tel:01483 444740
Hatchlands Park, West Clandon, Guildford GU4 7RT. Tel: 01483 222482
Loseley House, Estate Office, Guildford GU3 1HS. Tel: 01483 304440
RHS Garden Wisley, Woking GU23 6QB. Tel: 01483 224234

SUSSEX
Bentley House & Gardens, Halland, Nr Lewes BN8 5AF. Tel: 01825 840573
Borde Hill Garden, Haywards Heath RH16 1XP. Tel: 01444 450326
Denmans Garden, Clock House, Denmans, Fontwell BN18 0SU. Tel: 01243 542808
Firle Place, Nr Lewes BN8 6LP. Tel: 01273 858188
Fishbourne Roman Palace, Salthill Road, Fishbourne, Chichester PO19 3QR. Tel: 01243 785859
Glynde Place, Nr Lewes BN8 6SX. Tel: 01273 858224
Goodwood House, Goodwood, Chichester PO18 0PX. Tel: 01243 755048
Hammerwood Park, East Grinstead RH19 3QE. Tel: 01342 850594
Leonardslee Gardens, Lower Beeding, Horsham RH13 6PP. Tel: 01403 891212
Merriments Gardens, Hawkhurst Road, Hurst Green TN19 7RA. Tel: 01580 860666
Michelham Priory, Upper Dicker, Hailsham BN27 3QS. Tel: 01323 844224 FX- 844030
Parham House and Gardens, Parham Park Ltd, Pulborough RH20 4HS. Tel: 01903 742021
Pashley Manor Gardens, Ticehurst, Wadhurst TN5 7HE. Tel: 01580 200692
Royal Pavilion, Brighton BN1 1EE. Tel: 01273 290900
Sheffield Park Garden, TN22 3QX Tel:01825 790231
The Weald & Downland Open Air Museum, Singleton, nr Chichester PO18 OEL. Tel: 01243 811363
West Dean Gardens, West Dean Estate, Nr Chichester PO18 0QZ. Tel: 01243 818210

WARWICKSHIRE
Arbury Hall, Nuneaton CV10 7PT. Tel: 01203 382804
Charlecote Park, Warwick CV35 9ER Tel:01789 470277
Coughton Court, Alcester B49 5JA Tel: 01789 400777
The Hiller Garden, Dunnington Heath Farm, Nr Alcester Tel:01789 490439
Lord Leycester Hospital, High Street, Warwick CV34 4BH. Tel: 01926 492797

WEST MIDLANDS
Baddesley Clinton Hall, B93 0DQ. Tel: 01564 783294
Castle Bromwich Hall, Chester Road, Castle Bromwich Tel:0121 7494100

WILTSHIRE
Longleat, The Estate Office, Warminster BA12 7NW. } Tel: 01985 844400

YORKSHIRE
Aske Hall, Aske, Rickmond DL10 5HJ. Tel: 01748 823222
The Bar Convent, 17 Blossom Street, York Y02 2AH. Tel: 01904 643238
Bolton Castle, Leyburn DL8 4ET. Tel: 01969 623981
Brodsworth Hall, Brodsworth. Tel: 01302 722598
Oakwell Hall, Birstall WF19 9LG. Tel: 01924 474926
Sewerby Hall and Gardens, Church Lane, Sewerby, Bridlington YO15 1EA. Tel: Estate Office: 01262 673 769

WALES
Colby Woodland Garden, Amroth, Narbeth SA67 8PP. Tel: 01558 822800/01834 811885
Dinefwr Park, Llandeilo SA19 6RT. Tel: 011558 823902
Picton Castle, Picton Castle Trust, Haverfordwest SA62 4AS. Tel: 01437 751326
Tredegar House, Newport, Newport NP1 9YW. Tel: 01633 815880

SCOTLAND
Cawdor Castle, Nairn, Inverness IV12 5RD. Tel: 01667 404615
Dalmeny House, Charisma, South Queensferry EH30 9TQ. Tel: 0131-331 1888
Manderston, Duns, Berwickshire TD11 3PP. Tel: 01361 882636
Paxton House, Paxton, Nr Berwick upon Tweed TD15 1SZ Tel: 01289 386291

IRELAND
Bantry House, Bantry, Co. Cork. Tel: 00353 2750047
Benvarden Garden, Dervock, Ballymoney, CO. Antrim. Tel: 012657 41331
Dublin Writer's Museum, 18 Parnell Square, Dublin 1. Tel: 00353 1 872 2077
Kylemore Abbey, Kylemore, Connemara. Tel: 0195 41146
Malahide Castle, Malahide, Co. Dublin. Tel: 00353 1 846 2184
Mount Usher Gardens, Ashford. Tel: 00353 404 40205 /40116
Newbridge House, Donabate, Co. Dubin. Tel: 00353 1 8436534
Powerscourt Gardens & Waterfall, Enniskerry, Co. Wicklow. Tel: 00353 1 204 6000
Seaforde Gardens, Seaforde, Downpatrick BT30 3PG. Tel: +441396 811225
Strokestown Park House & Gardens, Strokestown, Co. Roscommon. Tel: 00353 78 33013
Tullynally Castle, Castlepollard, Co. Westmeath. Tel: 00353 44 61159

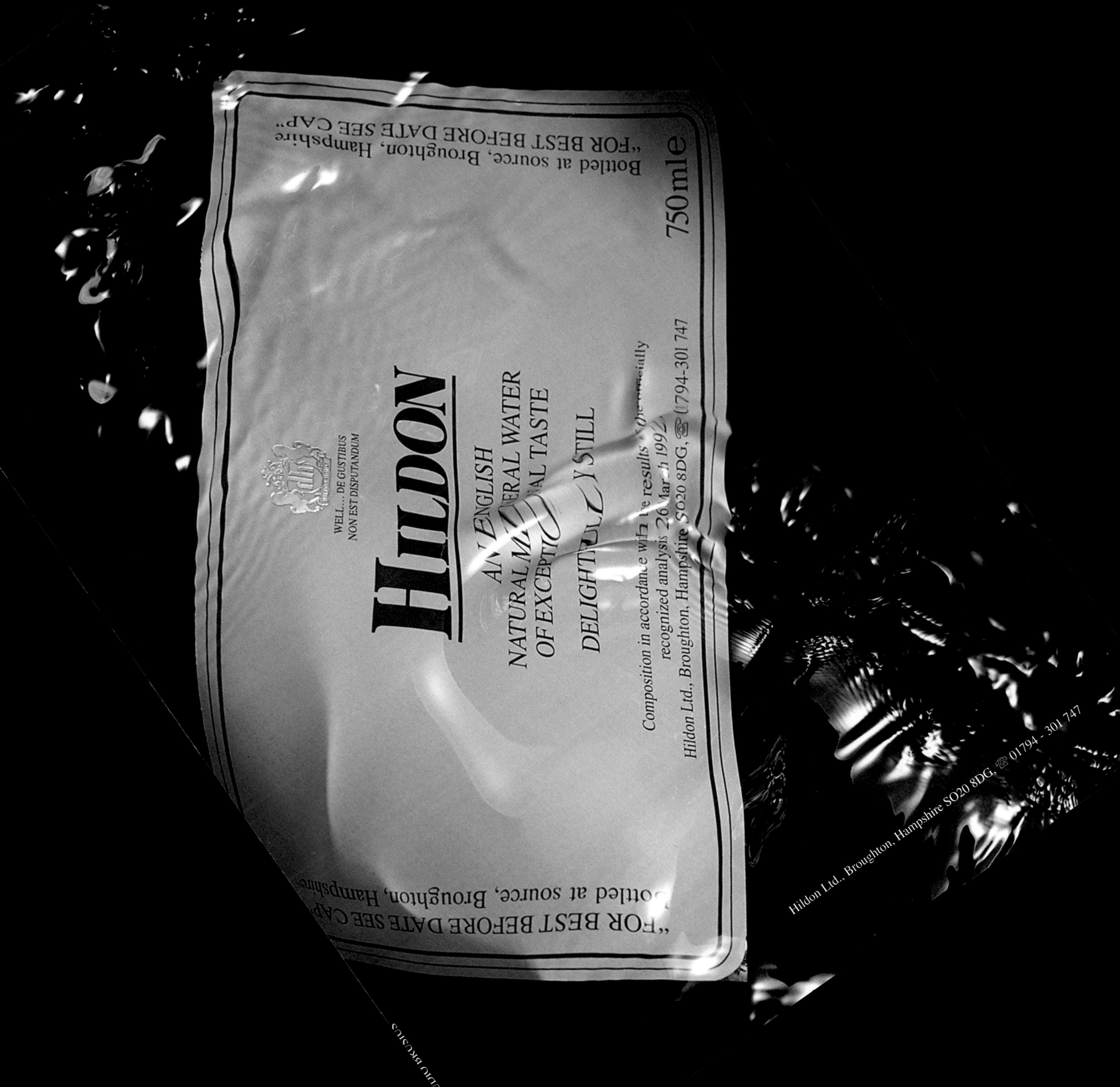
HILDON
WELL... DE GUSTIBUS NON EST DISPUTANDUM
750mle
Bottled at source, Broughton, Hampshire
"FOR BEST BEFORE DATE SEE CAP"
Hildon Ltd., Broughton, Hampshire SO20 8DG, 01794-301 747
Hildon Ltd., Broughton, Hampshire SO20 8DG, ☎ 01794 - 301 747

Properties Open All Year

ENGLAND

BERKSHIRE

Dorney Court, Windsor SL4 6QP. Tel: 01628 604638 Fax: 01628 665772
The Savill Garden, Windsor Great Park, Tel: 01753 860222 Crown Property.
Windsor Castle, Windsor, SL4 INJ Tel: 01753 868286

BUCKINGHAMSHIRE

Cliveden, Taplow, Maidenhead SL6 OJA. Tel: 01628 605069 Fax: 01628 669461
Stowe Landscape Garden, Buckingham, Buckinghamshire MK18 5EH Tel: 01280 822850

CAMBRIDGESHIRE

Ely Cathedral, The Chapter House, The College, Ely CB7 4DL.
  Tel: 01353 667735 Fax: 01353 665658
King's College, Cambridge CB2 1ST. Tel: 01223 331212
  Fax: 01223 331315
The Manor, Hemingford Grey PE18 9BN. Tel: 01480 463134
  Fax: 01480 465026
Oliver Cromwell's House, 29 Mary Street, Ely CB7 4DF
  Tel: 01353 665555 ext.294 Fax: 01353 668518

CHESHIRE

Adlington Hall, Macclesfield SK10 4LF Tel: 01625 820875
  Fax: 01625 828756
Bramall Hall, Bramhall, Stockport SK7 3NX Tel:0161 485 3706
Ness Botanic Gardens, Ness, Nesston L64 4AY.
  Tel: 0151 3530123 Fax: 0151 353 1004
Norton Priory Museum, Tudor Road, Manor Park, Runcorn WA7 1SX. Tel: 01928 569895
Tatton Park, Knutsford WA16 6QN Tel:01625 534400

CORNWALL

Burncoose Nurseries & Garden, Gwennap, Redruth
  TR16 6BJ Tel: 01209 861112
Trevarno Estate & Gardens, Trevarno Manor, Helston TR13 0RU. Tel: 01326 574274 Fax: 01326 574282

CUMBRIA

Hutton-In-The-Forest, Penrith Tel: 017684 84449
Muncaster Castle, Ravenglass CA18 1RQ. Tel: 01229 717614
  Fax: 01229 717010. Gardens Only

DEVON

Buckfast Abbey, Buckfastleigh TQ11 OEE. Tel: 01364 642519
  Fax: 01364 643891
Killerton House, Broadclyst, nr Exeter EX5 3LE. Tel: 01392 881345 Fax: 01392 883112. Gardens Only

DORSET

Athelhampton House & Gardens, Athelhampton, Dorchester
  Tel: 01305 848363 Fax: 01305 848135
Christchurch Priory, Quay Road, Christchurch, BH23 1BU.
  Tel: 01202 485804 Fax: 01202 488645
Forde Abbey, Chard Tel: 01460 220231
Lulworth Castle, The Lulworth Estate, East Lulworth, Wareham BH20 5QS. Tel: 01929 400352
Wolfeton House, Dorchester, DT2 9QN Tel:01305 263500 By Apointment

GLOUCESTERSHIRE

Barnsley House Garden, The Close, Barnsley,
  Nr Cirencester GL7 5EE.
Frampton Court, Frampton-on-Severn
  Gloucester GL2 7EU Tel: 01452 740267

HAMPSHIRE

Beaulieu, Brockenhurst, SO42 7ZN Tel: 01590 612345
Langley Boxwood Nursery, Rake, Nr. Liss, GU33 7JL
  Tel: 01730 894467 Fax: 01730 894703
Gilbert White's House & Garden & The Oates Museum, 'The Wakes' Selborne, Nr
  Alton, GU34 3JH
Sir Harold Hillier Gardens and Arboretum, Ampfield, nr Romsey SO51 0QA. Tel: 01794 368787

HERTFORDSHIRE

Cathedral & Abbey Church Of St. Alban, St. Albans, Hertfordshire AL1 1BY.

HEREFORD & WORCESTER

Burford House Gardens, Tenbury Wells, WR15 8HQ.
  Tel 01584 810777 Fax: 01584 810673
Dinmore Manor, nr Hereford HR4 8EE. Tel: 01432 830332
How Caple Court Gardens, How Caple HR1 4SX.
  Tel: 01989 740612 Fax: 01989 740611
Hopton Court, Cleobury Mortimer DY14 OEF Tel:01299 270734
Worcester Cathedral, College Green, Worcester WR1 2LH.
  Tel: 01905 28854 Fax: 01905 611139

KENT

Hall Place, Bourne Road, Bexley, DA5 1PQ.
  Tel: 01322 526574 Fax: 01322 522921
Ladham House, Gouldhurst, Tel: 01580 212674
Leeds Castle, Maidstone. Tel: 01622 765400
Lullingstone Castle, Eynsford, Kent DA14 OJA.
  Tel: 01322 862114
The New College Of Cobham, Cobham, Nr Gravesend, DA12 3BX Tel: 01474 812503
Owl House Gardens, Lamberhurst, Tel: 01892 890962
Pattyndenne Manor, Goudhurst TN17 2QU. Tel: 01580 211361
The Theatre Royal, 102 High Street, Chatham, ME4 4BY
  Tel: 01634 831028
Tonbridge Castle, Tonbridge TN9 1BG. Tel: 01732 770929
  Fax: 01732 770449

LANCASHIRE

Towneley Hall Art Gallery & Museums, Burnely, BB11 3RQ
  Tel: 01282 424213

LINCOLNSHIRE

Elsham Hall, Brigg DN20 0QZ Tel:01652 688698

LONDON

Apsley House, The Wellington Museum, Hyde Park Corner W1 Tel:0171 499 5676
Buckingham Palace, The Queens Gallery, SW1A 1AA
  Tel: 0171 839 1377
Burgh House, New End Square, Hampstead,
  Tel: 0171 431 0144
College Of Arms, Queen Victoria Stret Tel: 0171 248 2762
Greenwich – Observatory, National Maritime Museum,
  Romney Road, Greenwich SE10 9NF. Tel:0181 858 4422
Kew Gardens, Royal Botanic Gardens, Kew, Richmond
  Tel: 0181 940 1171
Orleans House Gallery, Riverside, Twickenham, TW1 3DJ.
  Tel: 0181-892 0221 Fax: 0181 744 0501
Osterley Park, Jersey Road, Isleworth TW7 4RB. Tel: 0181 568 7714
Pitshanger Manor Museum, Percival House, Mattock Lane, Ealing W5 5EQ. Tel: 0181-567 1227 Fax: 0181-567 0595
Syon Park, Brentford TW8 8JF. Tel: 0181 560 0881
St. John's Gate, St John's Lane, Clerkenwell EC1M 4DA.
  Tel: 0171-253 6644 Fax: 0171 336 0587
Tower of London, Tower Hill Tel: 0171 709 0765
Wallace Collection, Hertford House, Manchester Square
  Tel: 0171 935 0687 Fax: 0171 224 2155

NORFOLK

Mannington Hall, Saxthorpe, Norwich NR11 7BB. Tel: 01263 584175 Fax: 01263 761214
Norwich Castle Museum, Norwich NR1 3JU
  Tel: 01603 223624
Walsingham Abbey Grounds, Walsingham, NR22 6BP.
  Tel: 01328 820 259
Wolterton Park, Erpingham Tel: 01263 584175

NORTHAMPTONSHIRE

Castle Ashby House, Castle Ashby, Northampton NN7 1LQ.
  Tel: 01604 696696 Fax: 01604 696516

NOTTINGHAMSHIRE

Norwood Park, Southwell, Nottingham NG25 OP
  Tel: 01636 815649 Fax: 01636 815649

OXFORDSHIRE

Broughton Castle, Banbury, OX15 5EB Tel: 01295 262624
Rousham House, Rousham, Steeple Aston, OX6 3QX.
  Tel: 01869 347110
University of Oxford Botanic Gardens, Rose Lane, Oxford OX1 4AX.
Wallingford Castle Gardens, Castle Street, Wallingford
  Tel: 01491 835373
Waterperry Gardens Ltd, Nr Wheatley, Oxfordshire
  Tel: 01844 339226/254

SHROPSHIRE

Burford House Gardens, Tenbury Wells WR15 8HQ.
  Tel: 01584 810777 Fax: 01584 810673
Ironbridge Gorge Museum, Ironbridge, Telford TF8 7AW.
  Tel: 01952 433522 Fax: 01952 432204
Ludlow Castle, Castle Square, Ludlow
  Tel – Custodian: 01584 873947.
Shipton Hall, Much Wenlock TE13 6JZ. Tel: 01746 785 225
Walcot Hall, Lydbury North, Nr. Bishops Castle, SY7 8AZ
  Tel: 0171 581 2782

SOMERSET

Hestercombe Gardens, Cheddon Fitzpain, Taunton,
  TA2 8LG Tel: 01823 423923

STAFFORDSHIRE

Ancient High House, Greengate Street, Stafford ST16 2HS Tel:01785 619619
Dunwood Hall, Longsdon, Nr. Leek ST9 9AR
  Tel: 01538 385071
Ford Green Hall, Ford Green Road Smallthorne,
  Stoke-on-Trent. Tel: 01782 233195
Sandon Hall, Sandon, Stafford Tel: 01889 508004
Stafford Castle, Newport Road, Stafford ST16 1DJ. Tel: 01785 257 698
Tamworth Castle, The Holloway, Tamworth B79 7LR. Tel: 01827 709626 Fax: 01827 709630

SUFFOLK

Christchurch Mansion, Christchurch Park, Ipswich
  Tel: 01473 253246 Fax: 01473 281274
Gainsborough's House, 46 Gainsborough Street, Sudbury CO10 6EU Tel: 01787 372958 Fax: 01787 376991
Hengrave Hall, Bury St Edmunds Tel:01284 701561
Ipswich Museum, Ipswich IP1 3QH Tel: 01473 213761

SURREY

Claremont Landscape Garden, Portsmouth Road, Esher
  Tel: 01372 467842
Great Fosters Hotel, Stroude Road, Egham TW20 9UR.
  Tel: 0784 433822
Guildford House Gallery, 155, High Street, Guildford GU1 3AJ.
  Tel: 01483 444740 Fax: 01483 444742

Painshill Landscape Gardens, Portsmouth Road, Cobham KT11 1JE. Tel: 01932 868113 Fax: 01932 868001
RHS Garden Wisley, Woking GU23 6QB. Tel: 01483 224234

SUSSEX

Anne Of Cleves House, 52 Southover High Street, Lewes BN7 1JA. Tel: 01273 474610 Fax: 01273 486990
Borde Hill, Balcombe Road, Haywards Heath S16 1XP.
  Tel: 01444 450326
Chichester Cathedral, West Street, Chichester PO19 1PX.
  Tel: 01243 782595 Fax: 01243 536190
Lewes Castle, Barbican House, 169 High Street, Lewes
  BN7 1YE. Tel: 01273 486290 Fax: 01273 486990
Pallant House, 9 North Pallant, Chichester PO19 1TJ
  Tel: 01243 774557
Preston Manor, Preston Drove, Brighton BN1 6SD
  Tel: 01273 290900 Fax: 01273 292871
Royal Botanic Gardens, Kew At Wakehurst Place, Ardingly, Nr Haywards Heath
  RH17 6TN Tel: 01444 894066
The Royal Pavilion, Brighton, East Sussex BN1 1EE
  Tel: 01273 290900 Fax: 01273 292871
Saint Hill Manor, Sant Hill Road, East Grinstead
  RH19 4JY Tel: 01342 326711
Sheffield Park Garden, TN22 3QX Tel:01825 790231
The Weald & Downland Open Air Museum, Singleton, Nr Chichester Tel:01243 811348

WARWICKSHIRE

Lord Leycester Hospital, High Street, Warwick, CV34 4BH.
The Hiller Garden, Dunnington Heath Farm, Nr Alcester Tel:01789 490439
Shakespeare Birthplace Trust, 38/39 Henley Street, Stratford upon Avon, Tel: 01789 204016
Warwick Castle, Warwick, CV34 4QU. Tel: 01976 406600

WEST MIDLANDS

Birmingham Botanical Gardens & Glasshouses, Westbourne Road, Edgbaston,
  Birmingham, B15 3TR. Tel: 0121 454 1860
  Fax: 0121 454 7835
Soho House, Soho Avenue, Handsworth, Birmingham
  B18 5LB Tel: 0121 554 9122

WILTSHIRE

Longleat, The Estate Office, Warminster BA12 7NW.
  Tel: 01985 844400 Fax: 01985 844885
Luckington Court, Luckington, Chippenham SN14 6PQ Tel:01666 840205
Stourhead, Stourton, Mere BA12 6QH Tel: 01747 841152

YORKSHIRE

Aske Hall, Aske, Richmond DL10 5HJ. Tel: 01748 850391
Bolton Abbey, Skipton, North Yorkshire BD23 6EX.
  Tel: 01756 710227 Fax: 01756 710535
Harlow Carr Botanical Gardens, Crag Lane, Harrogate HG3 1QB.
  Tel: 01423 565418 Fax: 01423 530663
Oakwell Hall, Nutter Lane, Birstall, Batley
  Tel: 01924 326240
Red House, Oxford Road, Gomersal, Cleckheaton
  Tel: 01274 335100
Sewerby Hall & Gardens, Church Lane, Sewerby, Bridlington, YO15 1EA. Tel: 01262 673769
Skipton Castle, Skipton, North Yorkshire BD23 1AQ.
  Tel: 01756 792442 Fax: 01756 796100
Thorp Perrow Arboretum, Bedale DL8 2PR Tel:01677 425 323
Wilberforce House, 25 High Street, Kingston-upon-Hull, HU1 1EP. Tel: 01482 613902

IRELAND

Antrim Castle Gardens, Antrim Tel: 01849 428000
Birr Castle, Birr Tel:00353 50920336
Dublin Writers Museum, 18 Parnell Square, Dublin 1.
  Tel: 00 353 1 872 2077 Fax: 00 353 1 872 2231
Kylemore Abbey, Conemara, Co. Galway.
  Tel: 00 353 95 41146 Fax: 00 353 95 41123
Malahide Castle, Malahide, Co. Dublin.
  Tel: 00 353 1 846 2184 Fax: 00 353 1 846 2537
Newbridge House, Donabate, Co Dublin.
  Tel: 00 353 1 8436534 Fax: 00 353 1 8462537
Powerscourt Gardens & Waterfall, Enniskerry, Co. Wicklow. Tel: 00 353 204 6000
  Fax: 00 353 28 63561

SCOTLAND

Ayton Castle, Eyemouth, Berwickshire TD14 5RD.
  Tel: 018907 81212 Fax: 018907 81550
Blairquhan Castle, Straiton, Maybole KA19 7LZ Tel:016557 70239
Dalmeny House, South Queensferry, Edinburgh EH30 9TQ Tel: 0131 331 1888 Fax:
  0131 331 1788
The Doune of Rothiemurchus, Rothiemurchus Estate Office, Aviemore PH22 1QH.
  Tel: 01479 810858 Fax: 01479 811778
Duff House Country House Gallery, Banff AB45 5SX. Tel: 01261 818181 Fax: 01261 818900
Mirehouse, Keswick CA12 4QE Tel:01768 772287
Palace Of Holyroodhouse, Edinburgh, EH8 8DY
  Tel: 0131 556 7371.

WALES

Bodelwyddan Castle, Bodelwyddan, St Asaph, Bodelwyddan LL18 5YA. Tel: 01745 584060 Fax: 01745 584563
Penhow Castle, Nr Newport NP6 3AD. Tel: 01633 400800 fax: 01633 400990
Portmerion Village, Portmerion, Gwyned Tel: 01766 770000
St. Davids Cathedral, The Deanery, The Close, St. Davids, Pembrokeshire. Tel: 01437 720202 Fax: 01437 721 885

316

Properties with Conference Facilities

ENGLAND

BEDFORDSHIRE

Woburn Abbey, Woburn MK43 OTP. Tel: 01525 290666 Fax: 01525 290271

BERKSHIRE

Dorney Court, Windsor SL4 6QP. Tel: 01628 604638 Fax: 01628 665772

Eton College, The Visits Office, WIndsor SL4 6DW. Tel: 01753 671177 Fax: 01753 671265

Highclere Castle, Nr Newbury, RG20 9RN. Tel: 01635 253210 Fax: 01635 255315

BUCKINGHAMSHIRE

Stowe Stowe School, Stowe MK18 5EH. Tel: 01280 813650

Waddesdon Manor, The Dairy, Nr Aylesbury HP18 OJW. Tel: 01296 651211 Fax: 01296 651142

CAMBRIDGESHIRE

Elton Hall, Elton, Peterborough PE8 6SH. Tel: 01832 280468 Fax: 01832 280584

Kimbolton Castle, Kimbolton School, Kimbolton PE18 OAE. Tel: 01480 860505 Fax: 01480 861763

King's College, Cambridge CB2 1ST. Tel: 01223 331212 Fax: 01223 331315

CHESHIRE

Adlington Hall, Macclesfield SK10 4LF. Tel: 01625 820875 Fax: 01625 828756

Arley Hall, nr Great Budworth, Northwich CW9 6NA. Tel: 01565 777353

Bramall Hall, Bramhall Park, Stockport SK7 3NX. Tel: 0161 485 3708 Fax: 0161 486 6959

Capesthorne Hall, Siddington, Macclesfield SK11 9JY. Tel: 01625 861221 Fax: 01625 861619

Ness Botanic Gardens, Ness, Nesston L64 4AY. Tel: 0151 3530123 Fax: 0151 353 1004

Peckforton Castle, Stonehouse Lane, Nr. Taporley CW6 9TN. Tel: 01829 260930 Fax: 01829 261230

Tabley House Stately Home, Tabley House, Knutsford WA16 OHB. Tel: 01565 750151 Fax: 01565 653230

Tatton Park, Knutsford, Cheshire, WA16 6QN. Tel: 01625 534400 fax: 01625 534402

CUMBRIA

Dalemain, nr Penrith CA11 0HB. Tel: 017684 86450 Fax: 017684 86223

Muncaster Castle, Ravenglass CA18 1RQ. Tel: 01229 717614 Fax: 01229 717010

DERBYSHIRE

Chatsworth, Bakewell DE45 1PP. Tel: 01246 582204 Fax: 01246 583536

Renishaw Hall, Nr Sheffield S21 3WB Tel:01246 632310

DEVON

Bickleigh Castle, Bickleigh, Tiverton EX16 8RP. Tel: 01884 855363

Buckfast Abbey, Buckfastleigh, TQ11 0EE. Tel: 01364 642519 Fax: 01364 643891

Hartland Abbey, Hartland, Nr Bideford EX39 6DT. Tel: 01237 441 264/234 Fax: 01884 861134

Kingston House, Staverton, Totnes TQ9 6AR. Tel: 01803 762235 Fax: 01803 762444

Powderham Castle, Kenton, Exeter EX6 8JQ. Tel: 01626 890243 Fax: 01626 890729

Tiverton Castle, Tiverton EX16 6RP. Tel/Fax: 01884 253200

Torre Abbey, The Kings Drive, Torquay TQ2 5JX. Tel: 01803 293593 Fax: 01803 215948

Ugbrooke House, Chudleigh TQ13 OAD. Tel: 01626 852179 Fax: 01626 853322

DORSET

Athelhampton House & Gardens, Athelhampton, Dorchester DT2 7LG. Tel: 01305 848363 Fax: 01305 848135

Forde Abbey, Chard, TA20 4LU. Tel: 01460 221290 Fax: 01460 220296

Castle Asbhy, Norhants

Kingston Maurawd, Dorchester DT2 8PY Tel: 01305 215003

Lulworth Castle, The Lulworth Estate, East Lulworth, Wareham BH20 5QS. Tel: 01929 400352

Parnham House, Parnham, Beaminster DT8 3NA. Tel: 01308 862204 Fax: 01308 863444

Sherborne Castle, Sherborne DT9 3PY. Tel: 01935 813182 Fax: 01935 816727

Wolfeton House, Dorchester, DT2 9QN Tel:01305 263500

COUNTY DURHAM

Auckland Castle, Bishop Auckland DL14 7NR. Tel: 01388 601627 Fax: 01388 609323

ESSEX

Gosfield Hall, Halstead, CO9 1SF. Tel: 01787 472914 Fax: 01787 479551

Hylands House, Park & Gardens, Writtle, Chelmsford CM1 3HW. Tel: 01245 606812

Layer Marney Tower, Nr Colchester CO5 9US. Tel: 01206 330784

GLOUCESTERSHIRE

Chavenage, Tetbury GL8 8XP. Tel: 01666 502329 Fax: 01453 836778

Owlpen Manor, Owlpen, nr Uley GL11 5BZ. Tel: 01453 860261 Fax: 01453 860819

Sudeley Castle, Winchcombe GL54 5JD. Tel: 01242 602308

HAMPSHIRE

Avington Park, Winchester SO21 1DB. Tel: 01962 779260 Fax: 01962 779864

Beaulieu, Brockenhurst, SO42 7ZN. Tel: 01590 612345 Fax: 01590 612624

Gilbert White's House & Garden and the Oates Museum, The Wakes, Selborne GU34 3JH. Tel: 01420 511275

Mottisfont Abbey Garden, Mottisfont, Nr Romsey SO51 0LP. Tel: 01794 340757 Fax: 01794 341492

St Agatha's Church, 9 East Street, Fareham PO16 OBW. Tel: 01329 230330 Fax: 01329 230330

Sir Harold Hillier Gardens and Arboretum, Ampfield, nr Romsey SO51 0QA. Tel: 01794 368787

Somerley, Ringwood BH24 3PL. Tel: 01425 480819

HEREFORD & WORCESTER

Avoncroft, Stoke Heath, Bromsgrove, B60 4JR. Tel 01527 831363 Fax: 01527 876934

Burton Court, Eardisland, Leominster HR6 9DN. Tel: 01544 388231

Dinmore Manor, nr Hereford HR4 8EE. Tel: 01432 830332

Eastnor Castle, nr Ledbury, Hereford HR8 1RL. Tel: 01531 633160 Fax: 01531 631776

Harvington Hall, Harvington, Kidderminister DY10 4LR. Tel: 01562 777846 Fax: 01562 777190

Hopton Court, Cleobury Mortimer, Kidderminster DY14 0HH. Tel: 01299 270734

Worcester Cathedral, Worcester WR1 2LA Tel:01905 28854

HERTFORDSHIRE

The Gardens of the Rose, Chiswell Green, St. Albans AL2 3NR. Tel: 01727 850461 Fax: 01727 850360

Hatfield House, Hatfield AL9 5NQ. Tel: 01707 262823 Fax: 01707 275719

Knebworth House, Knebworth. Tel: 01438 812661

KENT

Cobham Hall, Cobham, nr. Gravesend DA12 3BL. Tel: 01474 824319

Finchcocks, Goudhurst TN17 1HH. Tel: 01580 211702 Fax: 01580 211007

Hever Castle & Gardens, Hever, nr Edenbridge TN8 7NG. Tel: 01732 865224 Fax: 01732 866796

Ladham House, Goudhurst. Tel: 01580 211203 Fax: 01580 212596

Leeds Castle, Maidstone ME17 1PL. Tel: 01622 765400 Fax: 735616

Mount Ephraim Gardens, Hernhill, nr Faversham ME13 9TX. Tel: 01227 751496 Fax: 01227 750940

Penshurst Place, Penshurst, Tunbridge Wells TN11 8DG. Tel: 01892 870307 Fax: 01892 870866

Riverhill House Gardens, Riverhill, Sevenoaks TN15 ORR. Tel: 01732 458802/452557

Squerryes Court, Westerham TN16 1SJ. Tel: 01959 562345/563118 Fax: 01959 565949

LANCASHIRE

Gawthorpe Hall, Padiham, Nr Burnley BB12 8UA Tel:01282 771004

Towneley Hall, Burnley, BB11 3RQ. Tel: 01282 424213 Fax: 01282 436138

LEICESTERSHIRE

Belvoir Castle, Nr Grantham, NG32 1PD. Tel: 01476 870262

Stanford Hall, Stanford Park, Lutterworth LE17 6DH. Tel: 01788 860250 Fax: 01788 860870

LINCOLNSHIRE

Elsham Hall, Brigg DN20 0QZ Tel:01652 688698

LONDON

Banqueting House, Whitehall Palace. Tel 0171 930 4179

Boston Manor House, Boston Manor Road, Brentford TW8 9JX. Tel: 0181 560 5441 Fax: 0181 862 7602

Chelsea Physic Garden, 66 Royal Hospital Road, Chelsea SW3 4HS. Tel: 0171 352 5646 Fax: 0171 376 3910

Greenwich Observatory, Queens House, National Maritime Museum, Romney Road, Greenwich SE10 9NF. Tel: 0181 312 6565 Fax: 0181 312 6632

Kenwood House, Hampstead. Tel: 0181 348 1286

Museum of Garden History, Lambeth Palace Road, SE1 7LB. Tel: 0171 401 8865 Fax: 0171 401 8869

Orleans House Gallery, Riverside, Twickenham, TW1 3DJ. Tel: 0181 892 0221 Fax: 0181 744 0501

Pitshanger Manor & Gallery, Mattock Lane, Ealing, W5 5EQ. Tel: 0181 567 1227 Fax: 0181 567 0595

St. John's Gate, Clerkenwell, EC1M 4DA. Tel: 0171 253 6644 Fax: 0171 336 0587

Strawberry Hill House, Waldegrave Road, Strawberry Hill, Twickenham. Tel: 0181 240 4114 Fax: 0181 255 6174

Syon Park, Syon House & Gardens, Brentford, TW8 8JF. Tel: 0181 560 0883 Fax: 0181 568 0936

NORFOLK

Mannington Hall, Norwich Tel:01263 584175

Wolterton Park, Erpingham NR11 7BB. Tel: 01263 584175 Fax: 01263 761214

NORTHAMPTONSHIRE

Castle Ashby House, Castle Ashby, Northampton NN7 1LQ. Tel: 01604 696696 Fax: 01604 696516

Cottesbrooke Hall, Nr Northampton NN6 8PF Tel:01604 505808

Holdenby House Gardens & Falconry Centre, Holdenby, Northampton NN6 8DJ. Tel: 01604 770074 Fax: 01604 770962

Lamport Hall and Gardens, Northampton NN6 9HD. Tel: 01604 686272 Fax: 01604 686 224

NORTHUMBERLAND

Alnwick Castle, Estate Office, Alnwick NE66 1NQ. Tel: 01665 510777 Fax: 01665 510876

Chillingham Castle, Chillingham, Alnwick NE66 5NJ. Tel: 01668 215359 Fax: 01668 215643

NOTTINGHAMSHIRE

Norwood Park, Southwell NG25 0PF. Tel: 01636 815649

Papplewick Hall, Nr Nottingham, NG15 8FE. Tel: 0115 963 3491 Fax: 0115 964 2767

OXFORDSHIRE

Ardington House, Wantage OX12 8QA. Tel: 01235 821566 Fax: 01235 821151

Blenheim Palace, Woodstock, OX20 1PX. Tel: 01993 811325 Fax: 01993 813527

Ditchley Park, Enstone, Chipping Norton OX7 4ER Tel:01608 677346

Fawley Court - Marian Fathers Historic House & Museum Marlow Road, Henley-On-Thames RG9 3AE. Tel: 01491 574917 Fax: 01491 411587

Kelmscott Manor, Kelmscott, nr Lechlade GL7 3HJ. Tel: 01367 252486 Fax: 01367 253 754

SHROPSHIRE

Burford House Gardens, Tenbury Wells, Worcestershire WR15 8HQ. Tel: 01584 810777 Fax: 01584 810673

Hawkstone Historic Park & Follies, Weston-under-Redcastle, Shrewsbury SY4 5UY. Tel: 01939 200611 Fax: 01939 200 311

Ironbridge Gorge Museum, Ironbridge, Telford TF8 7AW. Tel: 01952 433522 Fax: 01952 432204

Old Colehurst Manor, Colehurst, Market Drayton TF9 2JB. Tel: 01630 638833 Fax: 01630 638647

Walcot Hall, Nr Bishops Castle, Lydbury North SY7 8AZ. Tel: 0171-581 2782 Fax: 0171 589 0195

SOMERSET

Maunsel House, North Newton, nr Bridgwater TA7 O8U. Tel: 01278 663413/661076

Museum of Costume & Assembly Rooms, Bennett Street, Bath Tel:01225 477789

The Bishop's Palace, Wells BA5 2PD. Tel: 01749 678691

STAFFORDSHIRE

Sandon Hall, Sandon ST18 0BZ. Tel: 01889 508004 Fax: 01889 508586

The Shugborough Estate, Milford, Stafford ST17 0XB. Tel: 01889 881388 Fax: 01889 881323

SUFFOLK

Hengrave Hall Centre, Hengrave Hall, Bury St Edmunds IP28 6LZ. Tel: 01284 701561 Fax: 01284 702950

Haughley Park, Nr Stowmarket IP14 3JY Tel:01359 240701

Kentwell Hall, Long Melford, nr. Sudbury CO10 9BA. Tel: 01787 310207 Fax: 01787 379318

Otley Hall, Otley, nr Ipswich IP6 9PA. Tel: 01473 890264 Fax: 01473 890803

Somerleyton Hall, nr Lowestoft NR32 5QQ. Tel: 01502 730224 Fax: 01502 732143

Wingfield Old College & Gardens, Wingfield, Nr Stradbroke IP21 5RA. Tel: 01379 384888 Fax: 01379 384034

SURREY

Clandon Park, West Clandon, Guildford GU4 7RQ. Tel: 01483 222482 Fax: 01483 223479

Farnham Castle, Farnham GU7 0AG. Tel: 01252 721194 Fax: 01252 711283

Great Fosters Hotel, Stroude Road, Egham TW20 9UR. Tel: 0784 433822

Guildford House Gallery, 155 High Street, Guildford GU1 3AJ Tel:01483 444740

Loseley Park, Estate Office, Guildford GU3 1HS. Tel: 01483 304440 Fax: 01483 302036

Painshill Landscape Garden, Portsmouth Road, Cobham KT11 1JE. Tel: 01932 868113 Fax: 01932 868001

SUSSEX

Borde Hill Garden, Balcombe Road, Haywards Heath, RH16 1XP. Tel: 01444 450326 Fax: 01444 440427

Brickwall House and Gardens, Northiam, Rye TN31 6NL. Tel: 01797 253388 Fax: 01797 252567

Chichester Cathedral, Cathedral Cloisters, West Street, Chichester PO19 1PX. Tel: 01243 782595 Fax: 01243 536190

Firle Place, Nr Lewes BN8 6LP. Tel: 01273 858188

Goodwood House, Goodwood, Chichester PO18 0PX. Tel: 01243 755048 Fax: 01243 755005

Herstmonceux Castle, International Study Centre, Queens University, Hailsham BN27 1RN. Tel: 01323 833816 Fax: 01323 834499

Pallant House, 9 North Pallant, Chichester PO19 1TY. Tel: 01243 774557

Preston Manor, Preston Drove, Brighton BN1 6SD. Tel: 01273 292770 Fax: 01273 292871

Royal Pavilion, Brighton, East Sussex BN1 1EE. Tel: 01273 290900 Fax: 01273 292871

Saint Hill Manor, Saint hill Road, East Grinstead, RH19 4JY. Tel: 01342 325711

The Weald & Downland Open Air Museum, Singleton, Nr Chichester Tel:01243 811348

West Dean Gardens, West Dean Estate, nr Chichester PO18 0QZ. Tel: 01243 818210 Fax: 01243 811342

WARWICKSHIRE

Arbury Hall, Nuneaton CV10 7PT. Tel: 01203 382804 Fax: 01203 641147

Coughton Court, Alcester B49 5JA. Tel: 01789 400777

Lord Leycester Hospital, High Street, Warwick CV34 4BH. Tel: 01926 491422 Fax: 01926 491 422

Ragley Hall, Alcester B49 5NJ. Tel: 01789 762090 Fax: 01789 764791

Warwick Castle, Warwick CV34 4QU. Tel: 01926 406600 Fax: 01926 401692

WEST MIDLANDS

Birmingham Botanical Gardens and Glasshouses, Westbourne Road, Edgbaston, Birmingham B15 3TR. Tel: 0121 454 1860 Fax: 0121 454 7835

Hagley Hall, nr Stourbridge DY9 9LG. Tel: 0562 882408

WILTSHIRE

Longleat, The Estate Office, Warminster BA12 7NW. Tel: 01985 844400 Fax: 01985 844885

Wilton House, Wilton, Salisbury SP2 0BJ. Tel: 01722 746720 Fax: 01722 744447

YORKSHIRE

Aske Hall, Aske, Richmond DL10 5HJ. Tel: 01748 850391 Fax: 01748 823252

The Bar Convent, 17 Blossom Street, York Y02 2AH. Tel: 01904 643238 Fax: 01904 631792

Bolton Abbey Estate, Bolton Abbey, Skipton BD23 6EX. Tel: 01756 7110227 Fax: 01756 710535

Bolton Castle, Leyburn, DL8 4ET. Tel: 01969 623981. Fax: 01969 623332

Duncombe Park, Helmsley, York YO62 5EB. Tel: 01439 770213 Fax: 01439 771114

Elsham Hall Country and Wildlife Park, The Estate Office, Brigg DN20 0QZ. Tel: 01652 688698 Fax: 01652 688240

Harewood House and Bird Garden, The Estate Office, Harewood, Leeds LS17 9LQ. Tel: 0113 288 6331 Fax: 0113 288 6467

Hovingham Hall, Hovingham, York YO6 4LU. Tel: 01653 628206 Fax: 01653 628668

Newby Hall, Ripon, HG4 5AE. Tel: 01423 322583. Fax: 01423 324452

Ripley Castle, Ripley HG3 3AY. Tel: 01423 770152 Fax: 01423 771745

Sewerby Hall and Gardens, Church Lane, Sewerby, Bridlington YO15 1EA. Tel: Estate Office: 01262 673 769 Hall :01262 677874

WALES

Cresselly, Cresselly, Kilgetty SA68 0SP. Tel: 01646 651992

Dinefwr Park, Llandeilo SA19 6RT. Tel: 01558 823902 Fax: 01558 822036

Picton Castle, Picton Castle Trust, Haverfordwest SA62 4AS. Tel: 01437 751326

Portmerion Village, Portmerion, Gwyned Tel: 01766 770000

Tredegar House, Newport NP1 9YW. Tel: 01633 815880 Fax: 01633 815895

SCOTLAND

Ayton Castle, Estate Office, Eyemouth TD14 5RD. Tel: 0189 07 81212 Fax: 018907 81550

Blairquhan Castle and Gardens, Straiton,, Maybole KA19 7LZ. Tel: 016557 70239 Fax: 016557 70278

Bowhill House & Country Park, Bowhill, nr Selkirk TD7 5ET. Tel: 01750 22204 Fax: 01750 22204

Dalmeny House, Charisma, South Queensferry EH30 9TQ. Tel: 0131-331 1888 Fax: 0131 331 1788

Doune of Rothiemurchus, By Aviemore, Inverness-shire, PH22 1QH. Tel: 01479 812345 Fax: 01479 811778

Drumlanrig Castle, Thornhill, Dumfrieshire DG3 4AQ Tel: 01848 330248

Drummond Castle Gardens, Muthill, Crieff PH5 2AA. Tel: 01764 681257/433 Fax: 01764 681 550

Duff House Country House Gallery, Banff AB45 5SX. Tel: 01261 818181 Fax: 01261 818900

Dunrobin Castle, Golspie, Sutherland KW10 6SF. Tel: 01408 633177 Fax: 01408 634081

Lennoxlove House, Haddington, East Lothian, EH41 4NZ. Tel: 01620 823720 Fax: 01620 825112

Manderston, Duns, Berwickshire TD11 3PP. Tel: 01361 883450 Fax: 01361 882010

Mount Stuart House, Isle of Bute PA20 9LR Tel:01700 503877

Paxton House & Gardens, Paxton, nr Berwick-upon-Tweed TD15 1SZ. Tel: 01289 386291

Scone Palace, Scone, Perth PH2 6BD Tel:01738 552300

Traquair House, Innerleithen EH44 6PW. Tel: 01896 830323 Fax: 01896 830639

IRELAND

Antrim Castle Gardensm, Antrim. Tel: 01849 428000 Fax: 01849 460360

Bantry Housem, Bantry, Co. Cork. Tel: 00353 2 750 047 Fax: 00353 2 750 795

Dublin Writer's Museum, 18 Parnell Square, Dublin 1. Tel: 00353 1 872 2077 Fax: 00353 1 872 2231

Glin Castlem, Glin. Tel: 00353 68 34173 Fax: 00353 68 34364

Newman House, 85/86 St. Stephens Green, Dublin 2. Tel: +353 7067422 Fax: +353 7067211

Powerscourt Gardens, Enniskerry, Co Wicklow Tel:00353 204 6000

Shannon Heritage, Bunratty Castle & Folk Park, Bunratty, Co. Clare, Ireland. Tel 00 353 61 360788 Fax: 00 353 61 361020

Strokestown Park House & Gardens, Strokestown, Co. Roscommon. Tel: 00353 78 33013 Fax: 00353 78 33712

Tullynally Castle, Castlepollard, Co. Westmeath. Tel: 00353 44 61159/ 61289 Fax: 00353 44 61856

INSURANCE FOR YOUR LIFESTYLE

In the important areas of insurance and risk management, you want a company who can deliver tailored, personal insurance solutions, not merely off-the-shelf policies. When that company is a Johansens Preferred Partner, you expect an additional level of expertise and quality.

Marsh Private Client Services have built a loyal client base over many decades of serving discerning individuals who like the way we do business.

Backed by the globally respected broking strength of the world's leading insurance broking and risk management group, our clients know they can rely on us to provide the right products at the right price, tailored to their own special requirements.

Global reach with a personal touch

- Motor
- Home
- Travel
- Fine Art
- Estates
- Farms

- Personal Accident
- Healthcare
- Dental
- Legal Protection
- Pets and equestrian

Telephone today:
01462 428000

Marsh Private Client Services, Garden House, 42 Bancroft, Hitchin, Herts SG5 1DD Tel: 01462 428000 Fax: 01462 428008

Specialist areas:

- **Buildings and Contents**
  Including larger, distinctive homes through to weekend retreats and overseas properties. Personal valuables, antiques, collections, fine art and jewellery.

- **Motor**
  For all vehicles including private, commercial and agricultural, including prestige and performance cars.

- **Countryside**
  Farms, estates and country properties, plus risks associated with all country pursuits including fishing, shooting and equestrian.

- **Horses and Pets**
  Vets fees and liabilities for dogs, cats and horses.

MARSH
An MMC Company

Properties Offering Accommodation

ENGLAND

BERKSHIRE
Swallowfield Park, Swallowfield, RG7 1TG. Tel: 01734 883815
Welford Park, Newbury RG20 8HU. Tel: 01488 608203 Fax: 01488 608853

BUCKINGHAMSHIRE
Waddesdon Manor, Nr. Aylesbury, HP18 OJW. Tel: 01296 651236, Fax: 01296 651 142

CAMBRIDGESHIRE
The Manor, Hemingford Grey PE18 9BN. Tel: 01480 463134 Fax: 01480 465026

CHESHIRE
Adlington Hall, Macclesfield SK10 4LF. Tel: 01625 820875 Fax: 01625 828756

CORNWALL
Tregrehan, Par, PL24 25J Tel: 01726 814 389/812 438.
    Accommodation: Self-catering cottages available

CUMBRIA
Acorn Bank Garden & Watermill, Temple Sowerby, Nr Penrith Tel:017683 61893
Castletown House, Rockcliffe, Carlisle CA6 4BN. Tel: 01228 74792 Fax: 01228 74464
Dalemain, Nr. Penrith, CA11 0HB Tel: 017684 86450
    Accommodation: B&B, Parkhouse Farm, Dalemain. Tel: 017684 86212

DEVON
Buckfast Abbey, Buckfastleigh TQ11 OEE
    Tel: 01364 642519, Fax: 01364 643891
Yarde, Marlborough, Nr Salcombe TQ7 3BY
    Tel: 01548 842367

DORSET
Mapperton, Beaminster DT8 3NR. Tel: 01308 862645
Wolfeton House, Dorchester, DT2 9QN Tel:01305 263500 By Apointment

ESSEX
Gosfield Hall, Halstead, CO9 1SF Tel: 01787 472 914

GLOUCESTERSHIRE
Frampton Court, Frampton-on-Severn GL2 7EU. Tel: Home 01452 740 267
Owlpen Manor, Uley, nr Dursley GL11 5BZ
    Tel: 01453 860261 Accommodation: Nine period cottages available, including listed buildings.
Sudeley Castle and Gardens, Winchcombe, GL54 5JD
    Tel: 01242 603197/602308 Accommodation: 14 romantic Cotswold Cottages on Castle Estate. Private guided tours of Castle Apartments and Gardens by prior arrangement. Schools educational pack available.

HAMPSHIRE
Gilbert White's House & Garden and the Oates Museum, The Wakes, Selborne GU34 3JH. Tel: 01420 511275
Hall Farm House, Bentworth, Alton GU34 5JU. Tel: 01420 564010
Houghton Lodge Gardens, Stockbridge SO20 6LQ. Tel: 01264 810177 Fax: 01794 388072

HEREFORD & WORCESTER
Bernithan Court, Llangarron
    Accommodation: On application.
Brobury House & Garden, Borbury, Nr Hereford, HR3 6BS Tel: 01981 500 229
Burton Court, Eardisland HR6 9DN Tel: 01544 388231
    Accommodation: Holiday flat, self contained – sleeps 7.
Eastnor Castle, Nr Ledbury, HR8 1RD
    Tel: 01531 633160/632362, Fax: 01531 631766
    Luxury accommodation for select groups.
Hergest Croft Gardens, Kington Tel: 01544 230160
    Accommodation: Self-catering house – nursery sleeps 7.
Kentchurch Court, Hereford Tel: 01981 240228
    Accommodation by appointment.
Moccas Court, Moccas HR2 9LH Tel: 01981 500381
    Accommodation: Available at The Red Lion Hotel, Bredwardine.

KENT
Cobham Hall, Cobham, nr. Gravesend, DA12 3BL
    Tel: 01474 824319/823371 Accommodation: The house, grounds, accommodation 250 beds and sports facilities are available for private hire, wedding receptions, business conferences, residential and non-residential courses and film and photographic location.
Down House, Downe BR6 7JT. Tel: 01689 859119

Great Maytham Hall, Rolvenden, Cranbrook, TN17 4NE. Tel: 01580 241 346, Fax: 01580 241 038
Goodnestone Park, Goodnestone, Canterbury CT3 1PL. Tel: 01304 840107
Ladham House, Ladham Road, Goudhurst. Tel: 01580 211203 Fax: 01580 212596
Pattyndenne Manor, Goudhurst TN17 2QU. Tel: 01580 211361

LONDON
De Morgan Foundation, Old Battersea House, 30 Vicarage Crescent, Battersea SW11 3LD.
Linley Sambourne House, 18 Stafford Terrace W8 7BH. Tel: 0171 937 0663 Fax: 0181 995 4895
Museum of Garden History, Lambeth Palace Road, Lambeth SE1 7LB. Tel: 0171 261 1891 Fax 0171 401 8869
The Traveller's Club, Pall Mall SW1Y 5EP. Tel: 0171-930 8688 Fax: 0171 930 2019

NORFOLK
Mannington Hall, Saxthorpe, Norwich NR11 7BB. Tel: 01263 584175 Fax: 01263 761214
Walsingham Abbey, Estate Office, Walsingham, NR22 6BP Tel: 01328 820259 Accommodation: Also available in the village Hotel, B&B etc..

NORTHAMPTONSHIRE
Castle Ashby House, Castle Ashby, Northampton NN7 1LQ Tel: 01604 696696
    Accommodation: Holiday cottages.
The Menagerie, Horton, Horton, Northampton NN7 2BX. Tel: 01604 870957

NORTHUMBERLAND
Alnwick Castle, Alnwick, Northumberland NE66 1NQ
    Tel: 01665 510777 Accommodation: Holiday cottages.
Chillingham Castle and Gardens, Alnwick
    Tel: 01668 215359 Accommodation: Private family suites of rooms available.
Norwood Park, Southwell NG25 0PF. Tel: Tel/Fax: 01636 815649

NOTTINGHAMSHIRE
Carlton Hall, Carlton-On-Trent, Newark NG23 6NW
    Tel: 01636 821421 Accommodation: Self-catering by appointment.
Norwood Park, Southwell, Nottingham NG25 OPF
    Tel: 01636 815649
Papplewick Hall, Near Nottingham NG15 8FE
    Tel: 0115 9633491 Accommodation: Country House hospitality, full breakfast and dinner, prices on request.

OXFORDSHIRE
Ardington House, Wantage OX12 8QA. Tel: 01235 821566 Fax: 01235 821151
Aynhoe Park, Suite 10, Aynho, Banbury, Oxfordshire, OX17 3BQ
    Tel: 01869 810 636
Ditchley Park, Ditchley Foundation, Enstone OX7 4ER. Tel: 01608 677346 Fax: 01608 677399
Mapledurham House and Watermill, Mapledurham RG4 7TR Tel: 01734 723350 Accommodation: Eleven self catering holiday cottages.

SHROPSHIRE
Fairfield, Stogursey, Bridgwater TA5 1PU. Tel: 01278 732251 Fax: 01278 732277
Hawkstone Historic Park & Follies, Weston-under-Redcastle, Shrewsbury SY4 5UY. Tel: 01939 200611 Fax: 01939 200 311
Ironbridge Gorge Museum, Ironbridge, Telford TF8 7AW. Tel: 01952 433522 Fax:01952 432204
Ludford House, Ludlow SY8 1PJ. Tel: 01584 872542 Fax: 01584 875662
Old Colehurst Manor, Colehurst, Market Drayton TF9 2JB. Tel: 01630 638833 Fax: 01630 638647
Walcot Hall, Lydbury North, Nr Bishops Castle SY7 8AZ
    Tel: 0171 581 2782 Accommodation: 3 flats and Ground Floor wing available all year.

SOMERSET
Barstaple House Trinity Almshouses, Old Market Street, Bristol BS2 OEU. Tel: 01179 265777 Warden
Maunsel House, North Newton, nr Bridgwater TA7 O8U. Tel: 01278 663413/661076

STAFFORDSHIRE
Dunwood Hall, Longsdon, Nr Leek, Staffordshire, ST9 9AR Tel: 01538 385071
Sandon Hall, Sandon ST18 0BZ. Tel: 01889 508004 Fax: 01889 508586
Shugborough, Stafford ST17 OXB Tel: 01889 881388
    Accommodation: Details of group accommodation can be obtained from the booking office

SUFFOLK
Haughley Park, nr Stowmarket IP14 3JY. Tel: 01359 240701
Hengrave Hall Centre, Hengrave Hall, Bury St Edmunds IP28 6LZ. Tel: 01284 701561 Fax: 01284 702950

SURREY
Albury Park, Albury, Guildford GU5 9BB
    Tel: 01483 202 964, Fax: 01483 205 013
Goddards, Abinger Common, Dorking RH5 6TH. Tel: 01628 825920
Great Fosters Hotel, Stroude Road, Egham TW20 9UR. Tel: 0784 433822
Greathed Manor, Dormansland, Lingfield, RH7 6PA
    Tel: 01342 832 577, Fax: 01342 836 207

SUSSEX
Goddards, Abinger Common, Dorking RH5 6TH. Tel: 01628 825920
Goodwood House, Chichester PO18 OPX
    Tel: 01243 774107 Accommodation: Goodwood Park Hotel, Golf and Country Club- reservations 01345 123333/01243 775537
Hammerwood Park, nr East Grinstead RH19 3QE
    Tel: 01342 850594, Fax: 01342 850864
    Accommodation: B&B with a difference in an idyllically peaceful location only 20 minutes from Gatwick.

WILTSHIRE
Malmesbury House, The Close, Salisbury SP1 2EB. Tel: 01722 327027 Fax: 01722 334 414
Pythouse, Tisbury, Salisbury SP3 6PB Tel: 01747 870 210, Fax: 01747 871 786

WILTSHIRE
Hopton Court, Cleobury Mortimer, Kidderminster DY14 0HH. Tel: 01299 270734

YORKSHIRE
Aske Hall, Aske, Richmond DL10 5HJ. Tel: 01748 850391 Fax: 01748 823252
The Bar Convent, 17 Blossom Street, York YO2 2AH
    Tel: 01904 643238
Bolton Abbey, Skipton, North Yorkshire, BD23 6EX
    Tel: 01756 710 535
Broughton Hall, Skipton BD23 3AE. Tel: 01756 792267 Fax: 01756 792362
Hovingham Hall, Hovingham, York YO6 4LU. Tel: 01653 628206 Fax: 01653 628668
Elsham Hall Country and Wildlife Park, The Estate Office, Brigg DN20 0QZ. Tel: 01652 688698 Fax 01652 688240
Lindley Murray Summerhouse, The Mount School, Dalton Terrace YO24 4DD. Tel: 01904 667500 Fax: 01904 667524
The Orangery at Settrington, Settrington, Malton YO17 8NP. Tel: 01944 768345 / 768440out of hours Fax: 01944 768484
Ripley Castle, Ripley HG3 3AY Tel: 01423 770152
    Accommodation: 25 deluxe bedrooms at the Estate owned Boar's Head Hotel, 100 yards from the Castle in Ripley village. The hotel is rated RAC****.
Sutton Park, Sutton-on-the-Forest, York YO61 1DP Tel:01347 81024

IRELAND
Bunratty Castle and Folk Park, Bunratty, Co. Clare. Tel: 00353 61 360 788. Knappogue Castle appartment – sleeps up to 10 people.
Bantry House, Bantry, Co. Cork. Tel: 027 50047
    Accommodation: Bed & Breakfast and dinner. Nine rooms en suite.
Benvarden Gardens, Dervock, Ballymoney, CO. Antrim . Tel: 012657 41331 Fax: 012657 41955
Glin Castle, Glin Tel: 068 34173/34112
    Accommodation: Overnight stays arranged. Castle can be rented.
Powerscourt Gardens & Waterfall, Enniskerry, Co. Wicklow . Tel: 00353 1 204 6000

SCOTLAND
Ayton Castle, Eyemouth, Berwickshire TD14 5RD
    Tel: 018907 812812
Balcarres, Leven, Colinsburgh KY9 1HL. Tel: 01333 340206
Blairquhan Castle, Straiton, Maybole KA19 7LZ Tel:016557 70239
Dalmeny House, Charisma, South Queensferry EH30 9TQ. Tel: 0131-331 1888 Fax: 0131 331 1788
The Doune of Rothiemurchus, Rothiemurchus Estate Office, Aviemore PH22 1QH. Tel: 01479 810858 Fax: 01479 811778
Dunvegan Castle, Isle Of Skye Tel: 01470 521206
    Accommodation: Self catering cottages within grounds.
Manderston, Duns, Berwickshire TD11 3PP
    Tel: 01361 883450 Accommodation: By arrangement.
Sorn Castle, Sorn, Mauchline Tel: 01505 612124
    Accommodation: Available - contact Cluttons.
Traquair, Innerleithan EH44 6PW Tel: 01896 830323,
    Accommodation: 2 rooms B&B and Holiday flat to rent.

WALES
Cresselly, Cresselly, Kilgetty SA68 OSP. Tel: 01646 651992
Gwydir Castle, Llanrwst, Gwynedd Tel: 01492 641 687
Llanvihangel Court, Abergavenny NP7 8DH. Tel: 01873 890217
Portmerion Village, Portmerion, Gwyned Tel: 01766 770000

Museums & Galleries

Alphabetical list of Museums & Galleries in Great Britain

ENGLAND

AVON

American Museum In Britain	Bath	01225 460503
Arnolfini	Bristol	0117 929 9191
Bristol City Museums & Art Gallery	Bristol	0117 922 3571
Number 1 Royal Crescent	Bath	01225 428126
RPS Octagon Galleries	Bath	01225 462841
The Holburne Museums of Art	Bath	01225 466669
Victoria Art Gallery	Bath	01225 477772

BEDFORDSHIRE

Cecil Higgins Art Gallery	Bedford	01234 211222

BERKSHIRE

Reading Museum Service	Reading	0118 9390029

BUCKINGHAMSHIRE

Buckinghamshire County Museum	Aylesbury	01296 331441
Chiltern Open Air Museum	Chalfont St Giles	01494 872163

CAMBRIDGESHIRE

Cromwell Museum	Shire Hall	01223 718136
Fitzwilliam Museum	Cambridge	01223 332900
Peterborough Museum & Art Gallery	Peterborough	01733 343329

CHESHIRE

Chester Museums	Chester	01244 402008
Opto International Ltd	Dukinfield	0161 330 9136

CLEVELAND

Kirkleatham Old Hall Museum	Redcar	01642 479500

CORNWALL

Jamaica Inn & Musuems	Bolventor	01566 86250
Tate Gallery St. Ives	St. Ives	01736 796226
Trevarno Estate Gardening Museum	Helston	01326 574274

CUMBRIA

Abbot Hall Art Gallery	Kendal	01539 722464
Cars of the Stars Museum	Keswick	01768 73757
Cumbria's Western Lakes & Coast Museums	Workington	01900 735408
The Dock Museum	Barrow	01229 894444
Windermere Steamboat Museum	Windermere	015394 45565

DERBYSHIRE

Arkwright's Mill	Nr. Matlock	01629 824297
Donington Grand Prix Collection	Derby	01332 811027

DEVON

Plymouth City Museum	Plymouth	01752 304774

DORSET

Waterfront Museum	Poole	01202 683138

EAST SUSSEX

Brighton Museum and Art Gallery	Brighton	01273 603005
Rye Castle Museum	Rye	01797 226728

GLOUCESTERSHIRE

Cheltenham Art Gallery	Cheltenham	01242 237431
Cotswold Museums	Cirencester	01285 655611
Gloucester City Museums	Gloucester	01452 526467
Jet Age Museum	Cheltenham	01452 330761
Nature in Art Museum	Gloucester	01452 731422

GREATER MANCHESTER

Bury Art Gallery & Museum	Bury	0161 253 5879
Oldham Museum & Art Gallery	Oldham	0161 911 4651
Salford Museum and Art Gallery	Salford	0161 736 2649
Wigan Pier	Wigan	01942 323666

HAMPSHIRE

Hampshire County Council Museums Service	Winchester	01962 846304
Museum of Army Flying	Stockbridge	01980 674421
The Goss & Crested China Centre	Waterlooville	01705 597440
Winchester City Museum	Winchester	01962 848269

HEREFORDSHIRE

Hereford City Museums & Art Galleries	Hereford	01432 260000l

HERTFORDSHIRE

Mill Green Museum & Mill	Hatfield	01707 271362
Verulamium Museum	St. Albans	01727 819339
Walter Rothschild Zoological Museum	Tring	01442 824181
Welwyn Roman Baths	Hatfield	01707 271362

KENT

Bexley Museum	Bexley	01332 526574
Bromley Museum	Orpington	01689 873826
Canterbury Museums	Canterbury	01227 455047
Dickens House Museum	Broadstairs	01863 862852
Finchcock's Living Museum of Music	Cranbrook	01580 211702
Powell-Cotton Museum	Birchington	01843 842168

LANCASHIRE

Blackburn Museum & Art Gallery	Blackburn	01254 667130
Haworth Art Gallery	Accrington	01254 233782

LEICESTERSHIRE

Leicestershire City Museums	Leicester	0116 255 4100
Bosworth Battlefield Visitor Centre	Market Bosworth	01445 290429
Snibston Discovery Park	Coalville	01530 510851

LINCOLNSHIRE

Boston Guildhall Museum	Boston	01205 365954
Normanby Hall Country Park	Scunthorpe	01724 720588
Spalding Museums	Spalding	01775 725468

LONDON

Age Exchange Reminiscence	London	020 8318 9105
Bankside Gallery	London	020 7928 7521
Bramah Tea and Coffee Museum	London	020 7378 0222
British Library	London	020 7412 7000
Christies Education	London	020 7581 3933
Christopher Wood Gallery	London	020 7839 3963
De Morgan Foundation	London	01344 625142
Design Museum	London	020 7403 6933
Dulwich Picture Gallery	London	020 8693 5254
Fan Museum	London	020 8858 7879
Fine Art Commissions Ltd	London	020 7589 4111
Freud Museum	London	020 7435 2002
Geffrye Museum	London	020 7739 9893
Gunnersbury Park Museum	London	020 8922 1612
Hayward Gallery	London	020 7928 3144
Hogarth's House	London	020 8994 6757
Horniman Museum & Gardens	London	020 8699 1872
Imperial War Museum	London	020 7416 5321
Jewish Museum - Camden	London	020 7284 1997
Leighton House Museum & Art Gallery	London	020 7602 3316
Markfield Beam Engine & Museum	London	01763 287331
Medici Galleries	London	020 7837 7099
Museum of Garden History	London	020 7261 1891
National Portrait Gallery	London	020 7306 0055
Natural History Museum	London	020 7938 9123
New Academy Gallery & Business Art Galleries	London	020 7323 4700
Newham Museum Service	London	020 8472 1430
Order of St. John	London	020 7253 6644
Shakespeare's Globe Exhibition	London	020 7902 1500
South London Gallery	London	020 7703 6120
The Tate Gallery	London	020 7887 8734
The Wallace Collection	London	020 7935 0687
Victoria & Albert Museum	London	020 7499 5676
Westminster Abbey	London	020 7233 6019

MERSEYSIDE

National Museums & Galleries on Merseyside	Liverpool	0151 207 0001
Tate Gallery Liverpool	Liverpool	0151 709 3223

MIDDLESEX

DAR Colourskills	Hatch End	0181 428 1055
Forty Hall Museum	Enfield	0181 363 8196
Musical Museum	Brentford	0181 560 8108
Orleans House Gallery	Twickenham	0181 892 0221
RFU Museum (Rugby Football Museum)	Twickenham	0181 892 8161

NORFOLK

Norwich Castle Museum	Norwich	01603 4936

NORTH YORKSHIRE

Jorvik Viking Centre	York	01904 643211
York City Art Gallery	York	01904 551861

NORTHAMPTONSHIRE

Northampton Museums & Art Gallery	Northampton	01604 639415
The National Dragonfly Museum	Ashton	01832 272427

OXFORDSHIRE

Museum of Modern Art	Oxford	01865 722733
Oxford Story	Oxford	01865 790055
The Oxfordshire Museum	Woodstock	01993 811456
River & Rowing Museum	Henley-on -Thames	01491 415610
University of Oxford	Oxford	01865 278009

SHROPSHIRE

Ironbridge Gorge Museum Trust	Telford	01952 433522
Royal Airforce Museum	Shifnal	01902 374872

SOMERSET

Museum of East Asian Art	Bath	01225 464640

SOUTH YORKSHIRE

Rotherham Museum	Clifton Park	01709 823633

STAFFORDSHIRE

Bass Museum	Burton-upon-Trent	01283 511000
Potteries Museum & Art Gallery	Stoke on Trent	0161 236 5244
Stafford Castle & Visitor Centre	Stafford	01785 57698
Tamworth Castle Museum	Tamworth	01827 63563

SUFFOLK

Christchurch Mansion	Ipswich	01473 253246
Gainsborough House	Sudbury	01787 372958
National Horseracing Museum	Newmarket	01638 667333
St. Edmunsbury Borough Council	Bury St. Edmonds	01284 757093
Sue Ryder Foundation	Sudbury	0178 728 0252

SURREY

Elmbridge Museum	Weybridge	01932 843573
Guildford House Gallery	Guildford	01483 444740
Kensington Palace		0181 781 9786
Merton Heritage Centre	Mitcham	0181 640 9387

TYNE AND WEAR

Bede's World	Jarrow	0191 489 2106

WARWICKSHIRE

Shakespeare Birth Place Trust	Stratford-upon-Avon	01789 204016

WEST MIDLANDS

Barber Institute of Fine Arts	Birmingham	0121 414 7333
Birmingham Museum and Art Gallery	Birmingham	0121 235 2834
Walsall Museum & Art Gallery	Walsall	01922 653116

WEST SUSSEX

Amberley Museum	Arundel	01798 831370
Henfield Museum	Henfield	01273 492546
Weald & Downland Open Air Museum	Chichester	01243 811348

WEST YORKSHIRE

Eureka! The Children's Museum	Halifax	01422 330069
Leeds Museums & Galleries	"Armley, Leeds"	0113 263 7861
Wakefield Museum Service	Wakefield	01924 305796

WILTSHIRE

Devizes Museum	Devizes	01380 727369

WORCESTERSHIRE

Bewdley Museum	Bewdley	01299 403573
Worcester City Museums	Worcester	01905 722349

SCOTLAND

Blair Castle	Pitlochry	01796 481207
City of Edinburgh Council	Edinburgh	0131 200 2000
Glasgow Museums	Glasgow	0141 331 1854
Gracefield Arts Centre	Dumfries	01387 262084
Manchester Jewish Museum	Manchester	0161 834 9879
Manchester Museum	Manchester	0161 275 2634
National Galleries Of Scotland	Edinburgh	0131 624 6200
National Museum of Scotland	Edinburgh	0131 225 7534
New Lanark Conservation Trust	Lanark	01555 661345
North Ayrshire Musuems Service	Irvine	01294 324100
Rozelle House Galleries	Ayr	01292 445447

WALES

"The National Museum & Gallery, Cardiff"	Cardiff	01222 397951
Newport Museum and Art Gallery	Newport	01633 840064
Ruthin Craft Centre	Denbighshire	01824 704774
W H SMITH	Powys	01686 626280

N IRELAND

The Tower Museum	County Londonderry	01504 377331
Ulster-American Folk Park	County Tyrone	016662 243292

MINI LISTINGS
Johansens Recommended Traditional Inns, Restaurants & Hotels 2000

Here in brief are the entries that appear in full in Johansens Recommended Traditional Inns, Restaurants & Hotels 2000 – Great Britain.
They are listed in order by country and location. To order Johansens guides turn to the order forms on p343 & 345.

ALDBURY (ASHRIDGE N.T ESTATE)

The Greyhound Inn
Stocks Road, Aldbury, Near Tring,
Hertfordshire HP23 5RT
Tel: 01442 851228
Fax: 01442 851495

ALDEBURGH

The Dolphin Inn
Thorpeness, Aldeburgh, Suffolk IP16 4NA
Tel: 01728 454994
Fax: 01728 454300

ALFRISTON

Deans Place Hotel
Seaford Road, Alfriston, East Sussex BN26
5TW
Tel: 01323 870248
Fax: 01323 870918

AMBERLEY (NEAR ARUNDEL)

The Boathouse Brasserie
Houghton Bridge, Amberley, Nr Arundel,
West Sussex BN18 9LR
Tel: 01798 831059
Fax: 01798 831063

AMBLESIDE (GREAT LANGDALE)

The New Dungeon Ghyll Hotel
Great Langdale, Ambleside, Cumbria
LA22 9JY
Tel: 015394 37213
Fax: 015394 37666

APPLEBY-IN-WESTMORLAND

The Royal Oak Inn
Bongate, Appleby-In-Westmorland ,
Cumbria CA16 6UN
Tel: 017683 51463
Fax: 017683 52300

ASHBOURNE (HOGNASTON)

Red Lion Inn
Main Street, Hognaston, Ashbourne,
Derbyshire DE6 1PR
Tel: 01335 370396
Fax: 01335 370961

ASHBOURNE (WALDLEY)

Beeches Country Restaurant
Waldley, Doveridge, Nr Ashbourne,
Derbyshire DE6 5LR
Tel: 01889 590288
Fax: 01889 590559

BADBY NR DAVENTRY

The Windmill At Badby
Main Street, Badby, Nr Daventry,
Northamptonshire NN11 6AN
Tel: 01327 702363
Fax: 01327 311521

BAMBURGH

The Victoria Hotel
Front Street, Bamburgh, Northumberland
NE69 7BP
Tel: 01668 214431
Fax: 01668 214404

BASSENTHWAITE LAKE

The Pheasant
Bassenthwaite Lake, Nr Cockermouth,
Cumbria CA13 9YE
Tel: 017687 76234
Fax: 017687 76002

BECKINGTON NR BATH

The Woolpack Inn
Beckington, Nr Bath, Somerset BA3 6SP
Tel: 01373 831244
Fax: 01373 831223

BELFORD

The Blue Bell Hotel
Market Place, Belford, Northumberland
NE70 7NE
Tel: 01668 213543
Fax: 01668 213787

BIBURY

The Catherine Wheel
Bibury, Nr Cirencester, Gloucestershire GL7
5ND
Tel: 01285 740250
Fax: 01285 740779

BICKLEIGH (NR TIVERTON)

The Fisherman's Cot
Bickleigh, Nr Tiverton, Devon EX16 8RW
Tel: 01884 855237 / 855289
Fax: 01884 855241

BINFIELD

Stag & Hounds
Forest Road, Binfield, Berkshire RG12 9HA
Tel: 01344 483553
Fax: 01344 423620

BLAKENEY

White Horse Hotel
4 High Street, Blakeney, Holt, Norfolk
NR25 7AL
Tel: 01263 740574
Fax: 01263 741303

BOURTON-ON-THE-WATER

Dial House Hotel
The Chestnuts, High Street, Bourton-On-
The-Water , Gloucestershire GL54 2AN
Tel: 01451 822244
Fax: 01451 810126

BRIDPORT (WEST BEXINGTON)

The Manor Hotel

West Bexington, Dorchester, Dorset DT2 9DF

Tel: 01308 897616
Fax: 01308 897035

BRISTOL

The New Inn

Badminton Road, Mayshill, Nr Frampton Cottrell, Bristol BS36 2NT

Tel: 01454 773161
Fax: 01454 774341

BRISTOL (AUST)

The Boars Head

Main Road, Aust, Bristol BS12 3AX

Tel: 01454 632581
Fax: 01454 632278

BROADWAY

The Broadway Hotel

The Green, Broadway, Worcestershire WR12 7AA

Tel: 01386 852401
Fax: 01386 853879

BROCKENHURST

The Snakecatcher

Lyndhurst, Brockenhurst, Hampshire SO42 7RL

Tel: 01590 622348
Fax: 01590 624155

BURFORD

Cotswold Gateway Hotel

Cheltenham Road, Burford, Oxfordshire OX18 4HX

Tel: 01993 822695
Fax: 01993 823600

BURFORD

The Golden Pheasant Hotel & Restaurant

The High Street, Burford, Oxford OX18 4QA

Tel: 01993 823417
Fax: 01993 822621

BURFORD

The Lamb Inn

Sheep Street, Burford, Oxfordshire OX18 4LR

Tel: 01993 823155
Fax: 01993 822228

BURFORD (THE BARRINGTONS)

The Inn For All Seasons

The Barringtons, Burford, Oxfordshire OX18 4TN

Tel: 01451 844324
Fax: 01451 844375

BURNHAM MARKET

The Hoste Arms Hotel

The Green, Burnham Market, Norfolk PE31 8HD

Tel: 01328 738777
Fax: 01328 730103

BURNLEY (FENCE)

Fence Gate Inn

Wheatley Lane Road, Fence, Nr Burnley, Lancashire BB12 9EE

Tel: 01282 618101
Fax: 01282 615432

BURNSALL (SKIPTON)

The Red Lion

By the bridge at Burnsall, Near Skipton, North Yorkshire BD23 6BU

Tel: 01756 720204
Fax: 01756 720292

BURTON UPON TRENT

Ye Olde Dog & Partridge

High Street, Tutbury, Burton upon Trent, Staffordshire DE13 9LS

Tel: 01283 813030
Fax: 01283 813178

BURTON UPON TRENT (SUDBURY)

Boar's Head Hotel

Lichfield Road, Sudbury, Derbyshire DE6 5GX

Tel: 01283 820344
Fax: 01283 820075

CALVER (NEAR BAKEWELL)

The Chequers Inn

Froggatt Edge, Nr Calver, Derbyshire S30 1ZB

Tel: 01433 630231
Fax: 01433 631072

CAMBORNE

Tyacks Hotel

27 Commercial Street, Camborne, Cornwall TR14 8LD

Tel: 01209 612424
Fax: 01209 612435

CAMBRIDGE (WITHERSFIELD)

The White Horse Inn

Hollow Hill, Withersfield, Haverhill, Suffolk CB9 7SH

Tel: 01440 706081
Fax:

CARLISLE (TALKIN TARN)

The Tarn End House Hotel

Talkin Tarn, Brampton, Cumbria CA8 1LS

Tel: 016977 2340
Fax: 016977 2089

CASTLE ASHBY

The Falcon Hotel

Castle Ashby, Northampton, Northamptonshire NN7 1LF

Tel: 01604 696200
Fax: 01604 696673

CHIPPENHAM

The Crown Inn

Giddea Hall, Yatton Keynell, Chippenham, Wiltshire SN14 7ER

Tel: 01249 782229
Fax: 01249 782337

CHIPPING SODBURY
The Codrington Arms
Wapley Road, Codrington, Nr Chipping Sodbury, Bristol BS37 6RY
Tel: 01454 313145
Fax:

CHRISTCHURCH (HIGHCLIFFE ON SEA)
The Lord Bute
181 / 185 Lymington Road, Highcliffe on Sea, Christchurch , Dorset BH23 4JS
Tel: 01425 278884
Fax: 01425 279258

CIRENCESTER (COLN ST-ALDWYNS)
The New Inn at Coln
Coln St-Aldwyns, Nr Cirencester, Gloucestershire GL7 5AN
Tel: 01285 750651
Fax: 01285 750657

CIRENCESTER (SOUTH CERNEY)
The Eliot Arms Hotel
Clarks Hay, South Cerney, Cirencester, Gloucestershire GL7 2UA
Tel: 01285 860215
Fax: 01285 861121

CLARE (HUNDON)
The Plough Inn
Brockley Green, Sudbury, Nr Hundon, Suffolk CO10 8DT
Tel: 01440 786789
Fax: 01440 786710

CLAVERING (STANSTED)
The Cricketers
Clavering, Nr Saffron Walden, Essex CB11 4QT
Tel: 01799 550442
Fax: 01799 550882

CLEOBURY MORTIMER
Crown At Hopton
Hopton Wafers, Cleobury Mortimer, Shropshire DY14 0NB
Tel: 01299 270372
Fax: 01299 271127

CLEOBURY MORTIMER
The Redfern Hotel
Cleobury Mortimer, Shropshire DY14 8AA
Tel: 01299 270 395
Fax: 01299 271 011

COLCHESTER (COGGESHALL)
The White Hart Hotel & Restaurant
Market End, Coggeshall, Essex CO6 1NH
Tel: 01376 561654
Fax: 01376 561789

COLEFORD
The New Inn
Coleford, Crediton, Devon EX17 5B
zTel: 01363 84242
Fax: 01363 85044

DARTMOUTH
The Little Admiral Hotel
Victoria Road, Dartmouth, Devon TQ6 9RT
Tel: 01803 832572
Fax: 01803 835815

DITCHEAT (NR WELLS)
The Manor House Inn
Ditcheat, Somerset BA4 6RB
Tel: 01749 860276
Fax:

DONCASTER
Hamilton's Restaurant & Hotel
Carr House Road, Doncaster, South Yorkshire DN4 5HP
Tel: 01302 760770
Fax: 01302 768101

DORCHESTER-ON-THAMES
The George Hotel
High Street, Dorchester-On-Thames, Oxford OX10 7HH
Tel: 01865 340404
Fax: 01865 341620

EAST WITTON (WENSLEYDALE)
The Blue Lion
East Witton, Nr Leyburn, North Yorkshire DL8 4SN
Tel: 01969 624273
Fax: 01969 624189

ECCLESHALL
The George Inn
Eccleshall, Staffordshire ST21 6DF
Tel: 01785 850300
Fax: 01785 851452

EDENBRIDGE
Ye Old Crown
High Street, Edenbridge, Kent TN8 5AR
Tel: 01732 867896
Fax: 01732 868316

EGTON (NR WHITBY)
The Wheatsheaf Inn
Egton, Nr Whitby, North Yorkshire YO21 1T
zTel: 01947 895271
Fax: 01947 895391

ETON (WINDSOR)
The Christopher Hotel
High Street, Eton, Windsor, Berkshire SL4 6AN
Tel: 01753 811677 / 852359
Fax: 01753 830914

EVERSHOT
The Acorn Inn Hotel
Fore Street, Evershot, Nr Dorchester, Dorset DT2 0JW
Tel: 01935 83228
Fax:

EVESHAM
The Northwick Hotel
Waterside, Evesham, Worcestershire WR11 6BT
Tel: 01386 40322
Fax: 01386 41070

EVESHAM (OFFENHAM)
Riverside Restaurant And Hotel
The Parks, Offenham Road, Nr Evesham, Worcestershire WR11 5JP
Tel: 01386 446200
Fax: 01386 40021

EXMOOR
The Royal Oak Inn
Winsford, Exmoor National Park, Somerset TA24 7JE
Tel: 01643 851455
Fax: 01643 851009

FALMOUTH (CONSTANTINE)
Trengilly Wartha Country Inn & Restaurant
Nancenoy, Constantine, Falmouth, Cornwall TR11 5RP
Tel: 01326 340332
Fax: 01326 340332

FIFIELD (NR BURFORD)
The Merrymouth Inn
Stow Road, Fifield, Nr Burford, Oxford OX7 6HR
Tel: 01993 831652
Fax: 01993 830840

FORD, NR BATH
The White Hart
Ford, Chippenham, Wiltshire SN14 8RP
Tel: 01249 782213
Fax: 01249 783075

FORDINGBRIDGE (NEW FOREST)
The Woodfalls Inn
The Ridge, Woodfalls, Fordingbridge, Hampshire SP5 2LN
Tel: 01725 513222
Fax: 01725 513220

GORING-ON-THAMES
The Leatherne Bottel Riverside Inn & Restaurant
The Bridleway, Goring-On-Thames, Berkshire RG8 0HS
Tel: 01491 872667
Fax: 01491 875308

GRIMSTHORPE (BOURNE)
The Black Horse Inn
Grimsthorpe, Bourne, Lincolnshire PE10 0LY
Tel: 01778 591247
Fax: 01778 591373

GRINDLEFORD
The Maynard Arms
Main Road, Grindleford, Derbyshire S32 2HE
Tel: 01433 630321
Fax: 01433 630445

HALIFAX/HUDDERSFIELD
The Rock Inn Hotel
Holywell Green, Halifax, West Yorkshire HX4 9BS
Tel: 01422 379721
Fax: 01422 379110

HANDCROSS (SLAUGHAM)
The Chequers At Slaugham
Slaugham, Nr Handcross, West Sussex RH17 6AQ
Tel: 01444 400239/400996
Fax: 01444 400400

HARROGATE
The George & Olive's Restaurant
Wormald Green, Nr Harrogate, North Yorkshire HG3 3PR
Tel: 01765 677214
Fax: 01765 676201

HARROGATE (KILLINGHALL)
The Low Hall Hotel
Ripon Road, Killinghall, Harrogate, North Yorkshire HG3 2AY
Tel: 01423 508598
Fax: 01423 560848

HARROGATE (KNARESBOROUGH)
The Dower House
Bond End, Knaresborough, Nr Harrogate, North Yorkshire HG5 9AL
Tel: 01423 863302
Fax: 01423 867665

HARROGATE (RIPLEY CASTLE)
The Boar's Head Hotel
Ripley, Harrogate, North Yorkshire HG3 3AY
Tel: 01423 771888
Fax: 01423 771509

HARTLEY WINTNEY (BRAMSHILL)
The Hatchgate
Bramshill, Nr Hook, Hampshire RG27 0JX
Tel: 01189 32666
Fax: 01189 326608

HATHERSAGE
The Plough Inn
Leadmill Bridge, Hathersage, Derbyshire S30 1BA
Tel: 01433 650319
Fax: 01433 651049

HAY-ON-WYE
Rhydspence Inn
Whitney-On-Wye, Nr Hay-On-Wye, Herefordshire HR3 6EU
Tel: 01497 831262
Fax: 01497 831751

HAYFIELD (HIGH PEAK)
The Waltzing Weasel
New Mills Road, Birch Vale, High Peak, Derbyshire SK22 1BT
Tel: 01663 743402
Fax: 01663 743402

HELMSLEY

The Feathers Hotel

Market Place, Helmsley, North Yorkshire
YO6 5BH
Tel: 01439 770275
Fax: 01439 771101

HELMSLEY (NEAR YORK)

The Feversham Arms Hotel

Helmsley , North Yorkshire YO6 5AG
Tel: 01439 770766
Fax: 01439 770346

HINDON (NR SALISBURY)

The Grosvenor Arms

Hindon, Salisbury, Wiltshire SP3 6DJ
Tel: 01747 820696
Fax: 01747 820869

HINDON, NR SALISBURY

The Lamb at Hindon

High Street, Hindon, Salisbury, Wiltshire
SP3 6DP
Tel: 01747 820573
Fax: 01747 820605

HONITON (WILMINGTON)

Home Farm Hotel

Wilmington, Nr Honiton, Devon EX14 9JR
Tel: 01404 831278
Fax: 01404 831411

HUDDERSFIELD (GOLCAR)

The Weavers Shed Restaurant with Rooms

Knowl Road, Golcar, Huddersfield, West
Yorkshire HD7 4AN
Tel: 01484 654284
Fax: 01484 654284

ILCHESTER

Northover Manor

Ilchester, Somerset BA22 8LD
Tel: 01935 840447
Fax: 01935 840006

KENILWORTH

Clarendon House Bar Brasserie Hotel

High Street, Kenilworth, Warwickshire CV8
1L
zTel: 01926 857668
Fax: 01926 850669

KINGSKERSWELL (NR TORQUAY)

The Barn Owl Inn

Aller Mills, Kingskerswell, Devon TQ12
5AN
Tel: 01803 872130
Fax: 01803 875279

KNUTSFORD

Longview Hotel And Restaurant

51/55 Manchester Road, Knutsford,
Cheshire WA16 0LX
Tel: 01565 632119
Fax: 01565 652402

LEDBURY

Feathers Hotel

High Street, Ledbury, Herefordshire HR8
1DS
Tel: 01531 635266
Fax: 01531 638955

LEEK (BLACKSHAW MOOR)

The Three Horseshoes Inn & Kirk's Restaurant

Buxton Road, Blackshaw Moor, Nr Leek,
Staffordshire ST13 8TW
Tel: 01538 300296
Fax: 01538 300320

LONG MELFORD

The Countrymen

The Green, Long Melford, Suffolk CO10
9DN
Tel: 01787 312356
Fax: 01787 374557

LONGLEAT (HORNINGSHAM)

The Bath Arms

Horningsham, Warminster, Wiltshire BA12
7LY
Tel: 01985 844308
Fax: 01985 844150

LYMINGTON

The Angel Inn

High Street, New Forest, Hampshire SO41
9AP
Tel: 01590 672050
Fax: 01590 671661

LYNMOUTH

The Rising Sun

Harbourside, Lynmouth, Devon EX35 6EQ
Tel: 01598 753223
Fax: 01598 753480

MAIDSTONE (RINGLESTONE)

Ringlestone Inn

'Twixt Harrietsham and Wormshill, Nr
Maidstone, Kent ME17 1NX
Tel: 01622 859900
Fax: 01622 859966

MALMESBURY

The Horse And Groom Inn

Charlton, Near Malmesbury, Wiltshire SN16
9DL
Tel: 01666 823904
Fax: 01666 823390

MELLS (NR BATH)

The Talbot Inn at Mells

Selwood Street, Mells, Nr Bath, Somerset
BA11 3PN
Tel: 01373 812254
Fax: 01373 813599

NEWBURY (GT SHEFFORD)

The Swan Inn

Newbury Road, Great Shefford, Newbury,
Berkshire RG17 7DS
Tel: 01488 648271
Fax:

NEWBY BRIDGE

The Swan Hotel

Newby Bridge, Nr Ulverston, Cumbria
LA12 8NB
Tel: 015395 31681
Fax: 015395 31917

NORTH WALSHAM

Elderton Lodge

Gunton Park, Thorpe Market, Nr North
Walsham, Norfolk NR11 8T
zTel: 01263 833547
Fax: 01263 834673

NOTTINGHAM

Hotel Des Clos

Old Lenton Lane, Nottingham,
Nottinghamshire NG7 2SA
Tel: 01159 866566
Fax: 01159 860343

OLD HUNSTANTON

The Lodge Hotel & Restaurant

Old Hunstanton, Norfolk PE36 6HX
Tel: 01485 532896
Fax: 01485 535007

OXFORD (BANBURY)

Holcombe Hotel

High Street, Deddington, Nr Woodstock,
Oxfordshire OX15 0SL
Tel: 01869 338274
Fax: 01869 337167

OXFORD (MIDDLETON STONEY)

The Jersey Arms

Middleton Stoney, Oxfordshire OX6 8SE
Tel: 01869 343234
Fax: 01869 343565

OXFORD (MINSTER LOVELL)

The Mill & Old Swan

Minster Lovell, Nr Burford, Oxfordshire
OX8 5RN
Tel: 01993 774441
Fax: 01993 702002

PELYNT,NR LOOE

Jubilee Inn

Pelynt, Nr Looe, Cornwall PL13 2J
zTel: 01503 220312
Fax: 01503 220920

PENISTONE (INGBIRCHWORTH)

The Fountain Inn & Rooms

Wellthorne Lane, Ingbirchworth, Nr
Penistone, South Yorkshire S36 7GJ
Tel: 01226 763125
Fax: 01226 761336

PETWORTH

The Stonemason's Inn

North Street, Petworth, West Sussex GU28
9NL
Tel: 01798 342510
Fax: 01798 342510

PETWORTH (COULTERSHAW BRIDGE)

Badgers

Coultershaw Bridge, Petworth, West Sussex
GU28 0JF
Tel: 01798 342651
Fax: 01798 343649

PETWORTH (FITTLEWORTH)

The Swan Inn

Lower Street, Fittleworth, Nr Petworth,
West Sussex RH20 1EN
Tel: 01798 865429
Fax: 01798 865721

PETWORTH (SUTTON)

White Horse Inn

Sutton, Nr Pulborough, West Sussex RH20
1PS
Tel: 01798 869 221
Fax: 01798 869 291

PORT GAVERNE

The Port Gaverne Inn

Nr Port Isaac, North Cornwall PL29 3SQ
Tel: 01208 880244
Fax: 01208 880151

PRESTON (GOOSNARGH)

Ye Horn's Inn

Horn's Lane, Goosnargh, Nr Preston,
Lancashire PR3 2FJ
Tel: 01772 865230
Fax: 01772 864299

READING (STREATLEY)

The Bull at Streatley

Reading Road, Reading, Berkshire RG8 9TJ
Tel: 01491 875231
Fax: 01491 875231

ROMSEY (GREATBRIDGE)

Duke's Head

Greatbridge, Nr Romsey, Hampshire SO51
0HB
Tel: 01794 514450
Fax: 01794 830192

RUGBY (EASENHALL)

The Golden Lion Inn of Easenhall

Easenhall, Nr Rugby, Warwickshire CV23
0JA
Tel: 01788 832265
Fax: 01788 832878

RYE

The George Hotel

High Street, Rye, East Sussex TN31 7JP
Tel: 01797 222114
Fax: 01797 224065

SADDLEWORTH (DELPH)

The Old Bell Inn Hotel

Huddersfield Road, Delph, Saddleworth, Nr
Oldham, Greater Manchester OL3 5EG
Tel: 01457 870130
Fax: 01457 876597

SALISBURY (DOWNTON)

The White Horse

Downton, Salisbury, Wiltshire SP5 3LY
Tel: 01725 510408
Fax: 01725 511954

SHEFFIELD (DRONFIELD)

Manor House Hotel & Restaurant

High Street, Old Dronfield, Derbyshire S18 1PY
Tel: 01246 413971
Fax: 01246 412104

SHERBORNE

The Half Moon Inn

Half Moon Street, Sherborne, Dorset DT9 3LN
Tel: 01935 812017
Fax: 01935 815295

SHERBORNE (OBORNE)

The Grange Hotel & Restaurant

Oborne, Nr Sherborne, Dorset DT9 4LA
Tel: 01935 813463
Fax: 01935 817464

SHERBORNE (WEST CAMEL)

The Walnut Tree

West Camel, Nr Sherborne, Somerset BA22 7QW
Tel: 01935 851292
Fax: 01935 851292

SHIFNAL (TELFORD)

Naughty Nell's

1 Park Street, Shifnal, Shropshire TF11 9BA
Tel: 01952 411412
Fax: 01952 463336

SHIPTON UNDER WYCHWOOD

The Shaven Crown Hotel

High Street, Shipton Under Wychwood, Oxfordshire OX7 6BA
Tel: 01993 830330
Fax: 01993 832136

SNETTISHAM (NR KING'S LYNN)

The Rose & Crown

Old Church Road, Snettisham, King's Lynn, Norfolk PE31 7LX
Tel: 01485 541382
Fax: 01485 543172

SOUTHPORT (FORMBY)

Tree Tops Country House Restaurant & Hotel

Southport Old Road, Formby, Nr Southport, Lancashire L37 0AB
Tel: 01704 572430
Fax: 01704 572430

STAFFORD (INGESTRE)

The Dower House

Ingestre Park, Great Haywood, Staffordshire ST18 0RE
Tel: 01889 270707
Fax: 01889 270707

STAMFORD

The Crown Hotel

All Saints Place, Stamford, Lincolnshire PE9 2AG
Tel: 01780 763136
Fax: 01780 756111

STAMFORD (NR GRANTHAM)

Black Bull Inn

Lobthorpe, Nr Grantham, Lincolnshire NG33 5LL
Tel: 01476 860086
Fax: 01476 860796

STOW-ON-THE-WOLD

The Unicorn Hotel

Sheep Street, Stow-on-the-Wold, Gloucestershire GL54 1HQ
Tel: 01451 830257
Fax: 01451 831090

STOW-ON-THE-WOLD (BLEDINGTON)

The Kings Head Inn & Restaurant

The Green, Bledington, Oxfordshire OX7 6XQ
Tel: 01608 658365
Fax: 01608 658902

STRATFORD-UPON-AVON

The Coach House Hotel & Cellar Restaurant

16/17 Warwick Road, Stratford-upon-Avon, Warwickshire CV37 6YW
Tel: 01789 204109 / 299468
Fax: 01789 415916

STROUD (FRAMPTON MANSELL)

The Crown Inn

Frampton Mansell, Stroud, Gloucestershire GL6 8JG
Tel: 01285 760601
Fax: 01285 760681

SUDBURY (LONG MELFORD)

The Bull Hotel

Hall Street, Long Melford, Suffolk CO10 9JG
Tel: 01787 378494
Fax: 01787 880307

TAUNTON (STAPLE FITZPAINE)

Greyhound Inn

Staple Fitzpaine, Nr Taunton, Somerset TA3 5SP
Tel: 01823 480227
Fax: 01823 481117

TELFORD (HADLEY PARK)

Hadley Park House Hotel

Hadley Park, Telford, Shropshire TF1 4UL
Tel: 01952 677269
Fax: 01952 676938

TELFORD (NORTON)

The Hundred House Hotel

Bridgnorth Road, Norton, Nr Shifnal, Telford, Shropshire TF11 9EE
Tel: 01952 730353
Fax: 01952 730355

TENTERDEN
The White Lion Hotel
The High Street, Tenterden, Kent TN30 6BD
Tel: 01580 765077
Fax: 01580 764157

THAXTED
Recorders House Restaurant (With Rooms)
17 Town Street, Thaxted, Essex CM6 2LD
Tel: 01371 830438
Fax: 01371 831645

THIRSK
Crab & Lobster
Asenby, North Yorkshire YO7 3QL
Tel: 01845 577286
Fax: 01845 577109

THORNHAM
The Lifeboat Inn
Ship Lane, Thornham, Norfolk PE36 6LT
Tel: 01485 512236
Fax: 01485 512323

THORPE MARKET
Green Farm Restaurant And Hotel
North Walsham Road, Thorpe Market, Norfolk NR11 8TH
Tel: 01263 833602
Fax: 01263 833163

TINTAGEL (TREBARWITH STRAND)
The Port William
Trebarwith Strand, Nr Tintagel, Cornwall PL34 0HB
Tel: 01840 770230
Fax: 01840 770936

TOTNES (BOW BRIDGE, ASHPRINGTON)
The Watermans Arms
Bow Bridge, Ashprington, Nr Totnes, Devon TQ9 7EG
Tel: 01803 732214
Fax: 01803 732314

TOTNES (STAVERTON)
The Sea Trout Inn
Staverton, Nr Totnes, Devon TQ9 6PA
Tel: 01803 762274
Fax: 01803 762506

TROUTBECK (NEAR WINDERMERE)
The Mortal Man Hotel
Troutbeck, Nr Windermere, Cumbria LA23 1PL
Tel: 015394 33193
Fax: 015394 31261

UPTON-UPON-SEVERN, NR MALVERN
The White Lion Hotel
High Street, Upton-Upon-Severn, Nr Malvern, Worcestershire WR8 0HJ
Tel: 01684 592551
Fax: 01684 593333

WARMINSTER (UPTON SCUDAMORE)
The Angel Inn
Upton Scudamore, Warminster, Wiltshire BA12 0AG
Tel: 01985 213225
Fax: 01985 218182

WELLS
The Market Place Hotel
Wells, Somerset BA5 2RW
Tel: 01749 672616
Fax: 01749 679670

WEOBLEY
The Salutation Inn
Market Pitch, Weobley, Herefordshire HR4 8SJ
Tel: 01544 318443
Fax: 01544 318216

WEST AUCKLAND
The Manor House Hotel & Country Club
The Green, West Auckland, County Durham DL14 9HW
Tel: 01388 834834
Fax: 01388 833566

WEST WITTON (WENSLEYDALE)
The Wensleydale Heifer Inn
West Witton, Wensleydale, North Yorkshire DL8 4LS
Tel: 01969 622322
Fax: 01969 624183

WHITEWELL
The Inn At Whitewell
Forest Of Bowland, Clitheroe, Lancashire BB7 3AT
Tel: 01200 448222
Fax: 01200 448298

WITNEY (HAILEY)
The Bird in Hand
Hailey, Witney, Oxfordshire OX8 5XP
Tel: 01993 868321
Fax: 01993 868702

WOOLER
The Tankerville Arms Hotel
Wooler, Northumberland NE71 6AD
Tel: 01668 281581
Fax: 01668 281387

WORTHING (BRAMBER)
The Old Tollgate Restaurant And Hotel
The Street, Bramber, Steyning, West Sussex BN44 3WE
Tel: 01903 879494
Fax: 01903 813399

WROXHAM
The Barton Angler Country Inn
Irstead Road, Neatishead, Nr Wroxham, Norfolk NR12 8XP
Tel: 01692 630740
Fax: 01692 631122

YORK (EASINGWOLD)

The George at Easingwold

Market Place, Easingwold, York, North
Yorkshire YO6 3AD
Tel: 01347 821698
Fax: 01347 823448

CHEPSTOW

The Castle View Hotel

16 Bridge Street, Chepstow, Monmouthshire
NP6 5E
zTel: 01291 620349
Fax: 01291 627397

LLANARMON DYFFRYN CEIRIOG

The West Arms Hotel

Llanarmon D C, Nr Llangollen,
Denbighshire LL20 7LD
Tel: 01691 600665
Fax: 01691 600622

LLANDEILO (RHOSMAEN)

The Plough Inn

Rhosmaen, Llandeilo, Carmarthenshire
SA19 6NP
Tel: 01558 823431
Fax: 01558 823969

MACHYNLLETH

The Wynnstay

Maengwyn Street, Machynlleth, Powys
SY20 8AE
Tel: 01654 702941
Fax: 01654 703884

PRESTEIGNE

The Radnorshire Arms

High Street, Presteigne, Powys
Tel: 01544 267406
Fax: 01544 260418

GLENDEVON (SOUTH PERTHSHIRE)

Tormaukin Hotel

Glendevon, By Dollar, Perthshire FK14 7JY
Tel: 01259 781252
Fax: 01259 781526

INVERNESS (FARR)

Grouse & Trout

Flichity, By Farr, Inverness, IV2 6X5
Tel: 01808 521314
Fax: 01808 521314

ISLE OF SKYE (EILEAN IARMAIN)

Hotel Eilean Iarmain

Sleat, Isle Of Skye IV43 8QR
Tel: 01471 833332
Fax: 01471 833275

ISLE OF SKYE (UIG)

Uig Hotel

Uig, Isle Of Skye, Isle Of Skye IV51 9YE
Tel: 01470 542205
Fax: 01470 542308

KYLESKU (SUTHERLAND)

Kylesku Hotel

Kylesku, Via Lairg, Sutherland IV27 4HW
Tel. 01971 502231/502200
Fax: 01971 502313

LOCH EARN (PERTHSHIRE)

Achray House on Loch Earn

Loch Earn, St Fillan, Perthshire PH6 2NF
Tel: 01764 685231
Fax: 01764 685320

MOFFAT

Annandale Arms Hotel

High Street, Moffat, Dumfriesshire DG10
9HF
Tel: 01683 220013
Fax: 01683 221395

PITLOCHRY

The Moulin Hotel

Moulin, By Pitlochry, Perthshire PH16 5EW
Tel: 01796 472196
Fax: 01796 474098

PLOCKTON (BY KYLE OF LOCHALSH)

The Plockton Hotel & Garden Restaurant

Harbour Street, Plockton, Wester Ross IV52
8TN
Tel: 01599 544274
Fax: 01599 544475

POOLEWE (WESTER ROSS)

Pool House Hotel

Poolewe, Achnasheen, Wester Ross IV22
2LD
Tel: 01445 781272
Fax: 01445 781403

GUERNSEY (ST PETER PORT)

Les Rocquettes Hotel

Les Gravees, St Peter Port, GY1 1RN
Tel: 01481 722176
Fax: 01481 714543

Johansens Recommendations

Alphabetical list of Johansens Recommendations in Great Britain & Ireland

HOTELS

ENGLAND

BEDFORDSHIRE

The Bedford Arms	Woburn	01525 290441
Flitwick Manor	Woburn	01525 712242
Moore Place Hotel	Milton Keynes	01908 282000
Woodlands Manor	Bedford	01234 363281

BERKSHIRE

Chauntry House Hotel & Restaurant	Bray-on-Thames	01628 673991
Cliveden	Maidenhead	01628 668561
Donnington Valley Hotel & Golf Course	Newbury	01635 551199
Fredrick's Hotel & Restaurant	Maidenhead	01628 581000
The French Horn	Sonning-On-Thames	01189 692204
Hollington House Hotel	Newbury	01635 255100
Monkey Island Hotel	Bray-on-Thames	01628 623400
Oakley Court	Windsor	01753 609988
Royal Berkshire	Ascot	01344 623322
Sir Christopher Wren's Hotel	Windsor	01753 861354
The Swan Diplomat	Streatley-On-Thames	01491 873737
Taplow House Hotel	Maidenhead	01628 670056
The Vineyard At Stockcross	Newbury	01635 528770

BRISTOL

Hotel Du Vin & Bistro	Bristol	0117 925 5577
Swallow Royal Hotel	Bristol	0117 9255100/200

BUCKINGHAMSHIRE

Danesfield House	Marlow-On-Thames	01628 891010
Hartwell House	Aylesbury	01296 747444
The Priory Hotel	Aylesbury	01296 641239
Stoke Park	Heathrow	01753 717171

CAMBRIDGESHIRE

The Haycock	Peterborough	01780 782223

CHESHIRE

The Alderley Edge Hotel	Alderley Edge	01625 583033
The Bridge Hotel	Prestbury	01625 829326
Broxton Hall Country House Hotel	Chester	01829 782321
Carden Park	Chester	01829 731000
The Chester Grosvenor	Chester	01244 324024
Crabwall Manor	Chester	01244 851666
Mere Court Hotel	Knutsford	01565 831000
Nunsmere Hall	Chester	01606 889100
Rookery Hall	Nantwich	01270 610016
Rowton Hall Hotel	Chester	01244 335262
Shrigley Hall Hotel Golf & Country Club	Macclesfield	01625 575757
The Stanneylands Hotel	Manchester	01625 525225
Woodland Park Hotel	Altrincham	0161 928 8631

CLEVELAND

Grinkle Park Hotel	Easington	01287 640515

CORNWALL

Budock Vean Golf & Country House Hotel	Falmouth	01326 250288
Fowey Hall Hotel & Restaurant	Fowey	01726 833866
The Garrack Hotel & Restaurant	St. Ives	01736 796199
Meudon Hotel	Falmouth	01326 250541
The Nare Hotel	Veryan	01872 501279
Penmere Manor	Falmouth	01326 211411
Rose-in-Vale Country House Hotel	St Agnes	01872 552202
The Rosevine Hotel	St.Mawes	01872 580206
Talland Bay Hotel	Polperro	01503 272667
The Well House	St Keyne	01579 342001

COUNTY DURHAM

Headlam Hall	Darlington	01325 730238
Lumley Castle Hotel	Durham	0191 389 1111
Redworth Hall Hotel & Country Club	Newton Aycliffe	01388 772442

CUMBRIA

Appleby Manor Country House Hotel	Appleby-in-Westmorland	017683 51571
The Borrowdale Gates Country House Hotel	Keswick	017687 77204
Farlam Hall Hotel	Brampton	016977 46234
Gilpin Lodge	Windermere	015394 88818
Graythwaite Manor	Grange-Over-Sands	015395 32001
Holbeck Ghyll Country House Hotel	Ambleside	015394 32375
Lakeside Hotel On Lake Windermere	Windermere	0541 541586
Langdale Chase	Windermere	015394 32201
Langdale Hotel & Country Club	Ambleside	015394 37302
Linthwaite House Hotel	Windermere	015394 88600
Lovelady Shield Country House Hotel	Alston	01434 381203
Michaels Nook	Grasmere	015394 35496
Miller Howe	Windermere	015394 42536
Nanny Brow Country House Hotel	Ambleside	015394 32036
Rampsbeck Country House Hotel	Lake Ullswater	017684 86442
Rothay Manor	Ambleside	015394 33605
Sharrow Bay Country House Hotel	Lake Ullswater	017684 86301
Storrs Hall	Windermere	015394 47111
Tufton Arms Hotel	Appleby-In-Westmorland	017683 51593
The Wordsworth Hotel	Grasmere	015394 35592

DERBYSHIRE

Callow Hall	Ashbourne	01335 343403
The Cavendish Hotel	Baslow	01246 582311
Fischer's	Baslow	01246 583259
George Hotel	Hathersage	01433 650436
Hassop Hall	Bakewell	01629 640488
The Izaak Walton Hotel	Ashbourne	01335 350555
The Lee Wood Hotel & Restaurant	Buxton	01298 23002
Makeney Hall Country House Hotel	Derby	01332 842999
Mickleover Court	Derby	01332 521234
The Palace Hotel	Buxton	01298 22001
The Priest House On the River	Derby	01332 810649
Riber Hall	Matlock	01629 582795
Risley Hall Country House Hotel	Derby	0115 939 9000
Riverside House	Ashford-In-The-Water	01629 814275
The Wind In The Willows	Glossop	01457 868001

DEVON

The Arundell Arms	Lifton	01566 784666
Bel Alp House	Dartmoor	01364 661217
Bolt Head Hotel	Salcombe	01548 843751
Buckland-Tout-Saints	Kingsbridge Estuary	01548 853055
Combe House at Gittisham	Exeter	01404 540400
The Edgemoor	Bovey Tracey	01626 832466
Gidleigh Park	Chagford	01647 432367
Holne Chase Hotel & Restaurant	Ashburton	01364 631471
The Horn Of Plenty	Tavistock	01822 832528
Hotel Riviera	Sidmouth	01395 515201
Ilsington Country Hotel	Ilsington	01364 661452
Lewtrenchard Manor	Lewdown	01566 783 256
Northcote Manor Country House Hotel	Burrington	01769 560501
The Osborne Hotel & Langtry's Restaurant	Torquay	01803 213311
The Palace Hotel	Torquay	01803 200200
Soar Mill Cove Hotel	Salcombe	01548 561566
St Olaves Court Hotel	Exeter	01392 217736
The Tides Reach Hotel	Salcombe	01548 843466
Watersmeet Hotel	Woolacombe	01271 870333
Whitechapel Manor	South Molton	01769 573377
Woolacombe Bay Hotel	Woolacombe	01271 870388

DORSET

Bridge House Hotel	Beaminster	01308 862200
The Dormy	Bournemouth	01202 872121
Langtry Manor	Bournemouth	01202 553887
Moonfleet Manor	Weymouth	01305 786948
The Norfolk Royale Hotel	Bournemouth	01202 551521
Plumber Manor	Sturminster Newton	01258 472507
The Priory	Wareham	01929 551666
Summer Lodge	Evershot	01935 83424

EAST SUSSEX

Ashdown Park Hotel & Country Club	Forest Row	01342 824988
Broomhill Lodge	Rye	01797 280421
Buxted Park Country House Hotel	Buxted	01825 732711
Dale Hill	Ticehurst	01580 200112
The Grand Hotel	Eastbourne	01323 412345
Horsted Place Hotel	Uckfield	01825 750581
Netherfield Place Hotel & Country Club	Battle	01424 774455
Newick Park	Lewes	01825 723633
The Old Ship Hotel	Brighton	01273 329001
PowderMills Hotel	Battle	01424 775511
White Lodge Country House Hotel	Alfriston	01323 870265

EAST YORKSHIRE

Willerby Manor Hotel	Hull	01482 652616

ESSEX

Five Lakes Hotel Golf & Country Club	Colchester	01621 868888
Maison Talbooth	Dedham	01206 322367
Pontlands Park Country Hotel	Chelmsford	01245 476444
Whitehall	Stansted	01279 850603

GLOUCESTERSHIRE

The Bear of Rodborough Hotel	Cirencester	01453 878522
Calcot Manor	Tetbury	01666 890391
Charingworth Manor	Chipping Campden	01386 593555
The Cheltenham Park Hotel	Cheltenham	01242 222021
The Close Hotel	Tetbury	01666 502272
Corse Lawn House Hotel	Tewkesbury	01452 780479 / 771
The Cotswold House	Chipping Campden	01386 840330
The Grapevine Hotel	Stow-On-The-Wold	01451 830344
The Greenway	Cheltenham	01242 862352
Hotel On The Park	Cheltenham	01242 518898
Lords Of The Manor Hotel	Stow-on-the-Wold	01451 820243
The Manor House Hotel	Moreton-In-Marsh	01608 650501
Noel Arms Hotel	Chipping Campden	01386 840317
The Painswick Hotel	Painswick	01452 812160
Stonehouse Court	Stonehouse	01453 825155
The Swan Hotel At Bibury	Bibury	01285 740695
Washbourne Court Hotel	Lower Slaughter	01451 822143
Wyck Hill House	Stow-On-The-Wold	01451 831936

GREATER MANCHESTER

Etrop Grange	Manchester Airport	0161 499 0500

HAMPSHIRE

The Balmer Lawn	Brockenhurst	01590 623116
Careys Manor Hotel	Brockenhurst	01590 623551
Esseborne Manor	Andover	01264 736444
Fifehead Manor	Andover	01264 781565
Hotel Du Vin & Bistro	Winchester	01962 841414
Lainston House Hotel	Winchester	01962 863588
The Master Builder's House	Beaulieu	01590 616253
The Montagu Arms Hotel	Beaulieu	01590 612324
New Park Manor	Brockenhurst	01590 623467
Parkhill Country House Hotel	Lyndhurst	023 80282944
Passford House Hotel	Lymington	01590 682398
Rhinefield House Hotel	Brockenhurst	01590 622922
Stanwell House	Lymington	01590 677123
Tylney Hall	Basingstoke	01256 764881

HEREFORDSHIRE

The Chase Hotel	Ross-On-Wye	01989 763161
Pengethley Manor	Ross-On-Wye	01989 730211

HERTFORDSHIRE

Down Hall Country House Hotel	Bishop's Stortford	01279 731441
Hanbury Manor	Ware	01920 487722
Pendley Manor Hotel & Conference Centre	Tring	01442 891891
Sopwell House Hotel Country Club & Spa	St Albans	01727 864477
West Lodge Park	Hadley Wood	020 8216 3900

ISLE OF WIGHT

The George Hotel	Yarmouth	01983 760331
The Priory Bay Hotel	Seaview	01983 613146

KENT

Chilston Park	Maidstone	01622 859803
Eastwell Manor	Ashford	01233 213000
Hotel Du Vin & Bistro	Tunbridge Wells	01892 526455
Howfield Manor	Canterbury	01227 738294
Rowhill Grange	Dartford	01322 615136
The Spa Hotel	Tunbridge Wells	01892 520331

LANCASHIRE

Astley Bank Hotel & Conference Centre	Blackburn	01254 777700
The Gibbon Bridge Country House Hotel	Preston	01995 61456
Barnsdale Lodge	Rutland Water	01572 724678
Quorn Country Hotel	Loughborough	01509 415050

LEICESTERSHIRE

Sketchley Grange Hotel	Leicester	01455 251133
Stapleford Park, An Outpost of The Carnegie Club	Melton Mowbray	01572 787522

LINCOLNSHIRE

The George Of Stamford	Stamford	01780 750750
Kenwick Park Hotel & Leisure Club	Louth	01507 608806
The Olde Barn Hotel	Marston	01400 250909

LONDON

The Ascott Mayfair	London	020 7499 6868
Basil Street Hotel	London	020 7581 3311
The Beaufort	London	020 7584 5252
Beaufort House Apartments	London	020 7584 2600
Blakes Hotel	London	020 7370 6701
Brown's Hotel	London	020 7493 6020
The Cadogan	London	020 7235 7141
Cannizaro House	London	020 8879 1464
Chelsea Green Hotel	London	020 7225 7500
Chequers of Kensington	London	020 7969 3555
Claridge's	London	020 7629 8860
The Cliveden Town House	London	020 7730 6466
The Colonnade Town House	London	020 7286 1052
The Dorchester	London	020 7629 8888
Draycott House Apartments	London	020 7584 4659
Fountains	London	020 7706 7070
Harrington Hall	London	020 7396 9696
The Hempel	London	020 7298 9000
Hendon Hall	London	020 8203 3341
The Leonard	London	020 7935 2010
The Lexham Apartments	London	020 7559 4444
London Bridge Hotel & Apartments	London	020 7855 2200
The Milestone Hotel	London	020 7917 1000
No 5 Maddox Street	London	020 7647 0200
Number Eleven Cadogan Gardens	London	020 7730 7000
Number Sixteen	London	020 7589 5232
One Aldwych	London	020 7300 1000
Pembridge Court Hotel	London	020 7229 9977

The Royal Horseguards ....London 020 7839 3400
Sandringham Hotel ....Hampstead Village 020 7435 1569
Swan Hellenic Minerva ....London 020 7800 2227
Twenty Nevern Square ....London 020 7565 9555
Westbury Hotel ....London 020 7629 7755

NORFOLK
Congham Hall ....King's Lynn 01485 600250
The Hoste Arms Hotel ....Burnham Market 01328 738777
Park Farm Hotel & Leisure ....Norwich 01603 810264
Petersfield House Hotel ....Norwich 01692 630741
Swallow Sprowston Manor Hotel ....Norwich 01603 789409

NORTH YORKSHIRE
The Balmoral Hotel ....Harrogate 01423 508208
The Boar's Head Hotel ....Harrogate 01423 771888
Crab Manor ....Thirsk 01845 577286
Crathorne Hall Hotel ....Crathorne 01642 700398
The Devonshire Arms Country House Hotel ....Bolton Abbey 01756 710441
The Grange Hotel ....York 01904 644744
Grants Hotel ....Harrogate 01423 560666
Hackness Grange ....Scarborough 01723 882345
Hazlewood Castle Hotel ....Hazlewood 01937 535353
Hob Green Hotel & Restaurant ....Harrogate 01423 770031
Middlethorpe Hall ....York 01904 641241
Monk Fryston Hall ....York 01977 682369
Mount Royale Hotel ....York 01904 628856
The Pheasant ....Helmsley ..01439 771241 /770416
Rudding Park House & Hotel ....Harrogate 01423 871350
The Worsley Arms Hotel ....Hovingham 01653 628234
Wrea Head Country Hotel ....Scarborough 01723 378211
Simonstone Hall ....Hawes 01969 667255

NORTHAMPTONSHIRE
Fawsley Hall Hotel ....Daventry 01327 892000
Kettering Park Hotel ....Kettering 01536 416666

NORTHUMBERLAND
Linden Hall Hotel, Health Spa & Golf Course ....Newcastle-Upon-Tyne 01670 516611
Marshall Meadow Country House Hotel ....Berwick-Upon-Tweed ..01289 331133
Tillmouth Park ....Berwick-Upon-Tweed ..01890 882255
Linden Hall Hotel, Health Spa & Golf Course ..Newcastle-Upon-Tyne 01670 516611

NOTTINGHAMSHIRE
Langar Hall ....Nottingham 01949 860559

OXFORDSHIRE
The Bay Tree Hotel & Restaurant ....Burford 01993 822791
Fallowfields ....Oxford 01865 820416
The Feathers Hotel ....Woodstock 01993 812291
Le Manoir aux Quat' Saisons ....Oxford 01844 278881
Mill House Hotel ....Kingham 01608 658188
Phyllis Court Club ....Henley-On-Thames 01491 570500
The Plough at Clanfield ....Clanfield 01367 810222
The Spread Eagle Hotel ....Thame 01844 213661
The Springs Hotel & Golf Club ....Wallingford 01491 836687
Studley Priory ....Oxford 01865 351203
Weston Manor ....Oxford 01869 350621
Wroxton House Hotel ....Banbury 01295 730777

RUTLAND
Hambleton Hall ....Oakham 01572 756991
The Lake Isle ....Uppingham 01572 822951

SHROPSHIRE
Albrighton Hall Hotel & Restaurant ....Shrewsbury 01939 291000
Dinham Hall ....Ludlow 01584 876464
Hawkstone Park Hotel ....Shrewsbury 01939 200611
Madeley Court ....Telford 01952 680068
The Old Vicarage Hotel ....Wolverhampton 01746 716497
Rowton Castle ....Shrewsbury 01743 884044

SOMERSET
The Bath Priory Hotel and Restaurant ....Bath 01225 331922
Bindon Country House Hotel & Restaurant ....Taunton 01823 400070
The Castle At Taunton ....Taunton 01823 272671
Charlton House and The Mulberry Restaurant....Shepton Mallet 01749 342008
Combe Grove Manor & Country Club ....Bath 01225 834644
Daneswood House Hotel ....Bristol South 01934 843145
Homewood Park ....Bath 01225 723731
Hunstrete House ....Bath 01761 490490
The Mount Somerset Country House Hotel ....Taunton 01823 442500
Periton Park Hotel ....Middlecombe 01643 706885
The Queensberry ....Bath 01225 447928
The Royal Crescent Hotel ....Bath 01225 823333
Ston Easton Park ....Bath 01761 241631

SOUTH YORKSHIRE
Charnwood Hotel ....Sheffield 0114 258 9411
Hellaby Hall Hotel ....Sheffield 01709 702701
Whitley Hall Hotel ....Sheffield 0114 245 4444

STAFFORDSHIRE
Hoar Cross Hall Health Spa Resort ....Lichfield 01283 575671
The Moat House ....Acton Trussell 01785 712217

SUFFOLK
The Angel Hotel ....Bury St Edmunds 01284 753926
Hintlesham Hall ....Ipswich 01473 652268
The Marlborough Hotel ....Ipswich 01473 257677

Ravenwood Hall ....Bury St Edmunds....01359 270345
Seckford Hall ....Woodbridge 01394 385678
Swallow Belstead Brook Hotel ....Ipswich 01473 682891
The Swan Hotel ....Southwold 01502 722186
Swynford Paddocks Hotel & Restaurant ....Newmarket 01638 570234
Wentworth Hotel ....Aldeburgh 01728 452312

SURREY
The Angel Posting House And Livery ....Guildford 01483 564555
The Carlton Mitre Hotel ....Hampton Court 020 8979 9988
Foxhills ....Ottershaw 01932 704500
Grayshott Hall Health Fitness Retreat ....Grayshott 01428 602000
Great Fosters ....Egham 01784 433822
Langshott Manor ....Gatwick 01293 786680
Lythe Hill Hotel ....Haslemere 01428 651251
Nutfield Priory ....Redhill 01737 824400
Oatlands Park Hotel ....Weybridge 01932 847242
Pennyhill Park Hotel And Country Club ....Bagshot 01276 471774
The Richmond Gate Hotel And Restaurant ......Richmond-Upon-Thames..020 8940 0061
Woodlands Park Hotel ....Cobham 01372 843933

WARWICKSHIRE
Billesley Manor Stratford-Upon-Avon01789 279955
Coombe Abbey ....Coventry 024 76450450
Ettington Park Stratford-Upon-Avon01789 450123
The Glebe At Barford ....Warwick 01926 624218
Mallory Court ....Leamington Spa ..01926 330214
Nailcote Hall ....Coventry 024 76466174
Nuthurst Grange ....Hockley Heath 01564 783972
Welcombe Hotel & Golf Course Stratford-Upon-Avon01789 295252

WEST MIDLANDS
The Burlington Hotel ....Birmingham 0121 643 9191
The Mill House Hotel & Lombard Room Restaurant....Birmingham 0121 459 5800
New Hall ....Birmingham 0121 378 2442
The Swallow Hotel ....Birmingham 0121 455 7073

WEST SUSSEX
Alexander House ....Gatwick 01342 714914
Amberley Castle ....Amberley 01798 831992
The Angel Hotel ....Midhurst 01730 812421
Bailiffscourt ....Arundel 01903 723511
Ghyll Manor Country Hotel ....Rusper 01293 871571
The Millstream Hotel ....Chichester 01243 573234
Ockenden Manor ....Cuckfield 01444 416111
South Lodge Hotel ....Horsham 01403 891711
The Spread Eagle Hotel & Health Spa ....Midhurst 01730 816911

WEST YORKSHIRE
42 The Calls ....Leeds 0113 244 0099
Bagden Hall Hotel & Golf Course ....Huddersfield 01484 865330
Chevin Lodge Country Park Hotel ....Otley 01943 467818
Haley's Hotel and Restaurant ....Leeds 0113 278 4446
Holdsworth House ....Halifax 01422 240024
Oulton Hall ....Leeds 0113 282 1000
Rombalds Hotel ....Ilkley 01943 603201
Wood Hall ....Wetherby 01937 587271

WILTSHIRE
Beechfield House ....Lacock 01225 703700
Bishopstrow House ....Warminster 01985 212312
Crudwell Court Hotel ....Malmesbury 01666 577194
Howard's House ....Salisbury 01722 716392
Ivy House Hotel ....Marlborough 01672 515333
Lucknam Park ....Bath 01225 742777
The Manor House Hotel & Golf Club ....Castle Combe ..01249 782206
The Old Bell ....Malmesbury 01666 822344
The Pear Tree at Purton ....Swindon 01793 772100
Whatley Manor ....Malmesbury 01666 822888
Woolley Grange ....Bradford-On-Avon ..01225 864705

WORCESTERSHIRE
Brockencote Hall ....Chaddesley Corbett 01562 777876
The Colwall Park Hotel ....Malvern 01684 540206
The Cottage In The Wood ....Malvern Wells 01684 575859
Dormy House ....Broadway 01386 852711
The Elms ....Abberley 01299 896666
The Evesham Hotel ....Evesham 01386 765566
Grafton Manor Country House Hotel ....Bromsgrove 01527 579007
The Lygon Arms ....Broadway 01386 852255
Salford Hall Hotel ....Stratford-Upon-Avon 01386 871300
Stone Manor Hotel ....Kidderminster 01562 777555
Wood Norton Hall ....Evesham 01386 420007

WALES

CEREDIGION
Conrah Country House Hotel ....Aberystwyth 01970 617941
Ynyshir Hall ....Machynlleth 01654 781209

CLWYD
Llyndir Hall Hotel ....Wrexham 01244 571648

DENBIGHSHIRE
Bodidris Hall ....Llandegla 01978 790434
Tyddyn Llan Country House Hotel ....Corwen 01490 440264

FLINTSHIRE
St. David's Park Hotel ....Chester 01244 520800

GWYNEDD
Bodysgallen Hall ....Llandudno 01492 584466

GWYNEDD
Bontddu Hall ....Barmouth 01341 430661
Bron Eifion Country House Hotel ....Criccieth 01766 522385
Hotel Maes-Y-Neuadd ....Harlech 01766 780200
The Hotel Portmeirion ....Portmeirion Village ..01766 770000
Palé Hall ....Bala 01678 530285
Penmaenuchaf Hall ....Dolgellau 01341 422129
Porth Tocyn Country House Hotel ....Abersoch 01758 713303
St Tudno Hotel ....Llandudno 01492 874411
Trearddur Bay Hotel ....Anglesey 01407 860301
Ye Olde Bull's Head ....Beaumaris 01248 810329

HEREFORDSHIRE
Allt-Yr-Ynys Hotel ....Abergavenny 01873 890307

MID-GLAMORGAN
Miskin Manor ....Cardiff 01443 224204
Ty Newydd Country Hotel ....Aberdare 01685 813433

MONMOUTHSHIRE
The Cwrt Bleddyn Hotel ....Usk 01633 450521
Llansantffraed Court Hotel ....Abergavenny 01873 840678

MONTGOMERYSHIRE
Lake Vyrnwy Hotel ....Lake Vyrnwy 01691 870 692

PEMBROKESHIRE
The Court Hotel & Restaurant ....Pembroke 01646 672273
Penally Abbey ....Tenby 01834 843033
Warpool Court Hotel ....St David's 01437 720300

POWYS
Gliffaes Country House Hotel ....Crickhowell 01874 730371
The Lake Country House ....Llangammarch Wells01591 620202
Llangoed Hall ....Brecon 01874 754525

VALE OF GLAMORGAN
Coed-Y-Mwstwr Hotel ....Bridgend 01656 860621

SCOTLAND

ABERDEENSHIRE
Ardoe House Hotel & Restaurant ....Aberdeen 01224 867355
Darroch Learg Hotel ....Ballater 013397 55443
Kildrummy Castle Hotel ....Kildrummy 019755 71288
Pittodrie House ....Inverurie 01467 681444
Raemoir House Hotel ....Banchory 01330 824884
Thainstone House Hotel & Country Club ....Aberdeen 01467 621643

ANGUS
Letham Grange Resort ....Angus 01241 890373

ARGYLL
Ardanaiseig ....Kilchrenan by Taynuilt 01866 833333
Enmore Hotel ....Dunoon 01369 702230
Knipoch Hotel ....Oban 01852 316251

AYRSHIRE
Glenapp Castle ....Ballantrae 01465 831212
Piersland House Hotel ....Troon 01292 314747
Marine Highland Hotel ....Troon 01292 314444

BANFFSHIRE
Craigellachie Hotel ....Craigellachie 01340 881204

BORDERS
Dryburgh Abbey Hotel ....St Boswells 01835 822261

DUMFRIES & GALLOWAY
Balcary Bay Hotel ....Auchencairn 01556 640217
Cally Palace Hotel ....Gatehouse Of Fleet ..01557 814341
Corsewall Lighthouse Hotel ....Stranraer 01776 853220

EAST LOTHIAN
Greywalls ....Gullane 01620 842144

`FIFE
St. Andrews Golf Hotel ....St. Andrews....01334 472611

GLASGOW
Carlton George Hotel ....Glasgow 0141 353 6373

INVERNESS-SHIRE
Arisaig House ....Beasdale By Arisaig ..01687 450622
Bunchrew House Hotel ....Inverness 01463 234917
Culloden House Hotel ....Inverness 01463 790461
Glenspean Lodge Hotel ....Fort William 01397 712223
Loch Torridon Hotel ....Torridon 01445 791242
Mansion House Hotel ....Elgin 01343 548811
Swallow Kingsmills Hotel ....Inverness 01463 237166

Johansens Recommendations

ISLE OF SKYE

Flodigarry Country House Hotel	Isle Of Skye	01470 552203

LANARKSHIRE

Shieldhil	Biggar	01899 220035

MID LOTHIAN

The Bonham	Edinburgh	0131 226 6050
Borthwick Castle	Edinburgh	01875 820514
Channings	Edinburgh	0131 315 2226
Dalhousie Castle	Edinburgh	01875 820153
The Howard	Edinburgh	0131 557 3500
The Norton House Hotel	Edinburgh	0131 333 1275
Prestonfield House	Edinburgh	0131 668 3346
The Scotsman	Edinburgh	0113 244 0099

MORAYSHIRE

Muckrach Lodge Hotel & Restaurant	Grantown-on-Spey	01479 851257

PEEBLESHIRE

Cringletie House Hotel	Peebles	01721 730233

PERTHSHIRE

Auchterarder House	Auchterarder	01764 663646
Ballathie House Hotel	Perth	01250 883268
Cromlix House	Kinbuck	01786 822125
Dalmunzie House	Glenshee	01250 885224
Huntingtower Hotel	Perth	01738 583771
Kinfauns Castle	Perth	01738 620777
Kinloch House Hotel	Blairgowrie	01250 884237
Kinnaird	Dunkeld	01796 482 440
Roman Camp Hotel	Callander	01877 330003

RENFREWSHIRE

Gleddoch House	Glasgow	01475 540711

ROSS-SHIRE

Coul House Hotel	Strathpeffer	01997 421487
Mansfield House Hotel	Tain	01862 892052

ROXBURGHSHIRE

Ednam House Hotel	Kelso	01573 224168
The Roxburghe Hotel & Golf Course	Kelso	01573 450331

STRATHCLYDE

Macdonald Crutherland House Hotel	East Kilbride	01355 577000

STIRLINGSHIRE

Forest Hills	Aberfoyle	01877 387277
Stirling Highland Hotel	Stirling	01786 272727

SUTHERLAND

Inver Lodge Hotel	Lochinver	01571 844496

TAYSIDE

Pine Trees Hotel	Pitlochry	01796 472121

WEST LOTHIAN

Houstoun House	Uphall	01506 853831

WIGTOWNSHIRE

Fernhill Hotel	Portpatrick	01776 810220
Kirroughtree House	Newton Stewart	01671 402141

IRELAND

BELFAST (N. IRELAND)

The McCausland Hotel	Belfast	028 9022 0200

CO. CLARE

Dromoland Castle	Newmarket-On-Fergus	00 353 61 368144

CO CORK

Hayfield Manor Hotel	Cork	00 353 21 315600
The Lodge & Spa at Inchydoney Island	Clonakilty	00 353 23 33143
Longueville House & Presidents' Restaurant	Mallow	00 353 22 47156

CO DONEGAL

The Sand House Hotel	Rossnowlagh	00 353 72 51777

CO DUBLIN

The Fitzwilliam Hotel	Dublin	00 353 1 478 7000
The Merrion Hotel	Dublin	00 353 1 603 0600
Portmarnock Hotel & Golf Links	Dublin	00 353 1 846 0611

CO GALWAY

Renvyle House Hotel	Connemara	00 353 95 43511

CO KERRY

Aghadoe Heights Hotel	Killarney	00 353 64 31766
Muckross Park Hotel	Killarney	00 353 64 31938
The Park Hotel Kenmare	Kenmare	00 353 64 41200
Parknasilla Hotel	Parknasilla	00 353 64 45122
Randles Court Hotel	Killarney	00 353 64 35333
Sheen Falls Lodge	Kenmare	00 353 64 41600

CO KILDARE

Kildare Hotel & Country Club	Dublin	00 353 1 601 7200

CO LIMERICK

Adare Manor	Adare	00 353 61 396566

CO. MAYO

Ashford Castle	Cong	00353 92 46003

CO MONAGHAN

Nuremore Hotel & Country Club	Carrickmacross	00 353 429 661438

CO WEXFORD

Kelly's Resort Hotel	Rosslare	00 353 53 32114
Marlfield House	Gorey	00 353 55 21124

CO WICKLOW

Humewood Castle	Kiltegan	00 353 508 73215
Hunter's Hotel	Rathnew	00 353 404 40106

DUBLIN

Brooks Hotel	Dublin	00 353 1 670 4000
The Hibernian	Dublin	00 353 1 668 7666

GALWAY

Connemara Coast Hotel	Galway	00 353 91 592108

CHANNEL ISLANDS

GUERNSEY

St Pierre Park Hotel	Guernsey	01481 728282

JERSEY

The Atlantic Hotel	Jersey	01534 744101
Château La Chaire	Jersey	01534 863354
Hotel L'Horizon	Jersey	01534 43101
Longueville Manor	Jersey	01534 725501

COUNTRY HOUSES

ENGLAND

CAMBRIDGESHIRE

Abbey House & Coach House	Maxey	01778 344642
Melbourn Bury	Cambridge	01763 261151

CHESHIRE

Green Bough Hotel	Chester	01244 326241
Willington Hall Hotel	Tarporley	01829 752321

CO.DURHAM

Grove House	Hamsterley Forest	01388 488203
Horsley Hall	Stanhope	01388 517239

CORNWALL

Coombe Farm	Looe	01503 240223
The Cormorant Hotel	Golant by Fowey	01726 833426
The Countryman At Trink Hotel	St Ives	01736 797571
Cross House Hotel	Padstow	01841 532391
The Hundred House Hotel	St Mawes	01872 501336
Nansloe Manor	Helston	01326 574691
The Summer House	Penzance	01736 363744
Trebrea Lodge	Tintagel	01840 770410
Trehellas House & Memories of Malaya Restaurant	Wadebridge	01208 72700
Trelawne Hotel-The Hutches Restaurant	Falmouth	01326 250226
Tye Rock Country House Hotel	Porthleven	01326 572695

CUMBRIA

Aynsome Manor Hotel	Cartmel	015395 36653
Crosby Lodge Country House Hotel	Carlisle	01228 573618
Dale Head Hall Lakeside Hotel	Keswick	017687 72478
Fayrer Garden House Hotel	Windermere	015394 88195
Hipping Hall	Kirkby Lonsdale	015242 71187
Nanny Brow Country House Hotel	Ambleside	015394 32036
New House Farm	Buttermere	01900 85404
The Old Vicarage Country House Hotel	Witherslack	015395 52381
Quarry Garth Country House Hotel	Windermere	015394 88282
Sawrey House Country Hotel	Hawkshead	015394 36387
Swinside Lodge Hotel	Keswick	017687 72948
Temple Sowerby House Hotel	Penrith	017683 61578
White Moss House	Grasmere	015394 35295
Winder Hall	Lorton	01900 85107

DERBYSHIRE

Biggin Hall	Biggin-By-Hartington	01298 84451
Dannah Farm Country Guest House	Belper	01773 550273 / 630
East Lodge Country House Hotel	Bakewell	01629 734474
The Peacock Hotel at Rowsley	Bakewell	01629 733518

DEVON

Ashelford	Combe Martin	01271 850469
Bel Alp House	Dartmoor	01364 661217
Coombe House Country Hotel	Crediton	01363 84487
Downrew House Hotel	Barnstaple	01271 342497
Easton Court Hotel	Chagford	01647 433469
Foxdown Manor	Clovelly	01237 451325
Heron House Hotel	Thurlestone Sands	01548 561308
Hewitt's Hotel	Lynton	01598 752293
Ilsington Country Hotel	Ilsington	01364 661452
Kingston House	Staverton	01803 762 235
Mill End Hotel	Chagford	01647 432282
Moor View House	Lydford	01822 820220
Preston House Hotel	Saunton	01271 890472
The Thatched Cottage Country Hotel	Lifton	01566 784224
Wigham	Morchard Bishop	01363 877350
Yeoldon House Hotel	Bideford	01237 474400
Beechleas	Wimborne Minster	01202 841684
The Eastbury Hotel	Sherborne	01935 813131
Kemps Country House Hotel & Restaurant	Wareham	01929 462563
Rectory House	Evershot	0193583 273
Thatch Lodge Hotel	Lyme Regis	01297 560407
Yalbury Cottage Hotel	Dorchester	01305 262382

EAST SUSSEX

The Granville	Brighton	01273 326302
Hooke Hall	Uckfield	01825 761578
White Vine House	Rye	01797 224748

EAST YORKSHIRE

The Manor House	Beverley	01482 881645

GLOUCESTERSHIRE

Bibury Court	Bibury	01285 740337
Burleigh Court	Minchinhampton	01453 883804
Charlton Kings Hotel	Cheltenham	01242 231061
Halewell	Cheltenham	01242 890238
Lower Brook House	Blockley	01386 700286
The Malt House	Chipping Campden	01386 840295
The Old Rectory	Broadway	01386 853729
Owlpen Manor	Owlpen	01453 860261
Tudor Farmhouse Hotel & Restaurant	Clearwell	01594 833046
The Unicorn Hotel	Stow-on-the-Wold	01451 830257
Upper Court	Tewkesbury	01386 725351

HAMPSHIRE

The Beaufort Hotel	Portsmouth	023 92823707
Hotel Gordleton Mill	Lymington	01590 682219
Langrish House	Petersfield	01730 266941
Moortown Lodge	Ringwood	01425 471404
The Nurse's Cottage	Sway	01590 683402
Rosefield House	Lymington	01590 671526
Thatched Cottage Hotel & Restaurant	Brockenhurst	01590 623090
Whitley Ridge & Country House Hotel	Brockenhurst	01590 622354

HEREFORDSHIRE

The Bowens Country House	Hereford	01432 860430
Glewstone Court	Ross-On-Wye	01989 770367
Lower Bache House	Leominster	01568 750304
The Steppes	Hereford	01432 820424

HERTFORDSHIRE

Little Offley	Luton	01462 768243
Redcoats Farmhouse Hotel & Restaurant	Stevenage	01438 729500

ISLE OF WIGHT

Rylstone Manor	Isle of Wight	01983 862806

KENT

Romney Bay House	New Romney	01797 364747
Tanyard	Maidstone	01622 744705
Wallett's Court	Dover	01304 852424
The Woodville Hall	Dover	01304 825256

LANCASHIRE

Pelton Fold Farm	Bolton	01204 852207
Pickering Park Country House	Preston	01995 600999
Quarlton Manor Farm	Bolton	01204 852277

LEICESTERSHIRE

Abbots Oak	Coalville	01530 832 328
The Old Manor Hotel	Loughborough	01509 211228
White Wings	Fenny Drayton	01827 716100

LINCOLNSHIRE

Washingborough Hall	Lincoln	01522 790340

MIDDLESEX

Oak Lodge Hotel	Enfield	020 8360 7082
Stanwell Hall	Stanwell	01784 252292

NORFOLK

The Beeches Hotel & Victorian Gardens	Norwich	01603 621167
Beechwood Hotel	North Walsham	01692 403231
Broom Hall	Saham Toney	01953 882125
Catton Old Hall	Norwich	01603 419379
Felbrigg Lodge	Holt	01263 837588
Norfolk Mead Hotel	Norwich	01603 737531
The Old Rectory	Great Snoring	01328 820597
The Old Rectory	Norwich	01603 700772
Starston Hall	Diss	01379 854252
The Stower Grange	Norwich	01603 860210

NORTH YORKSHIRE

Appleton Hall	Appleton-Le-Moors	01751 417227
Millers House Hotel	Middleham	01969 622630
Newstead Grange	Malton	01653 692502
The Parsonage Country House Hotel	York	01904 728111
Rookhurst Country House Hotel	Hawes	01969 667454
Shallowdale House	Ampleforth	01439 788325
Waterford House	Middleham	01969 622090
The White House	Harrogate	01423 501388

NORTHUMBERLAND

The Tower	Otterburn	01830 520620
Waren House Hotel	Bamburgh	01668 214581

NOTTINGHAMSHIRE

Cockliffe Country House Hotel	Nottingham	01159 680179
The Cottage Country House Hotel	Nottingham	01159 846882
L'Auberge	Nottingham	01949 843086
Langar Hall	Nottingham	01949 860559

OXFORDSHIRE

Bignell Park Hotel	Bicester	01869 241444
The George Hotel	Dorchester-On-Thames	01865 340404
Fallowfields	Oxford	01865 820416
The Shaven Crown Hotel	Shipton-Under-Wychwood	01993 830330
The Stonor Arms Hotel	Stonor	01491 638866
The Tollgate Inn	Stow-On-The-Wold	01608 658389

SHROPSHIRE

Cross Lane House Hotel	Bridgnorth	01746 764887
Delbury Hall	Ludlow	01584 841267
Mynd House Hotel & Restaurant	Church Stretton	01694 722212
Overton Grange Hotel	Ludlow	01584 873500
Pen-y-Dyffryn Country Hotel	Oswestry	01691 653700
Soulton Hall	Wem	01939 232786
Upper Brompton Farm	Shrewsbury	01743 761629

SOMERSET

Apsley House	Bath	01225 336966
Ashwick Country House Hotel	Dulverton	01398 323868
Bath Lodge Hotel	Bath	01225 723040
The Beacon Country House Hotel	Exmoor	01643 703476
Beryl	Wells	01749 678738
Bloomfield House	Bath	01225 420105
Bond's - Bistro with Rooms	Castle Cary	01963 350464
The Cottage Hotel	Porlock Weir	01643 863300
Coxley Vineyard	Wells	01749 670285
The Crown Hotel	Exford	01643 831554/5
Duke's Hotel	Bath	01225 463512
Eagle House	Bath	01225 859946
Glencot House	Wells	01749 677160
Holbrook House Hotel	Wincanton	01963 32377
The Old Priory Hotel	Bath	01761 416784
The Old Rectory	Ilminster	01460 54364
Oldfields	Bath	01225 317984
Paradise House	Bath	01225 317723
Periton Park Hotel	Middlecombe	01643 706885
The Pheasant Hotel	Seavington St Mary	01460 240502
Porlock Vale House	Porlock Weir	01643 862338
Simonsbath House Hotel	Simonsbath	01643 831259
Villa Magdala	Bath	01225 466329
Woolverton House	Bath	01373 830415

SOUTH YORKSHIRE

Hamilton's Restaurant & Hotel	Doncaster	01302 760770

SUFFOLK

Butley Priory	Snape	01394 450046
Chippenhall Hall	Diss	01379 588180 / 586733
Hope House	Yoxford	01728 668281
Lavenham Priory	Lavenham	01787 247404
Wood Hall Country House Hotel	Woodbridge	01394 411283

SURREY

Chalk Lane Hotel	Epsom	01372 721179
Chase Lodge	Hampton Court	020 8943 1862
The Hautboy	Ockham	01483 225355
Stanhill Court Hotel	Gatwick	01293 862166

WARWICKSHIRE

The Ardencote Manor Hotel & Country Club	Warwick	01926 843111
Arrow Mill Hotel And Restaurant	Alcester	01789 762419
Chapel House	Atherstone	01827 718949
Glebe Farm House	Stratford-upon-Avon	01789 842501

WEST SUSSEX

Burpham Country House Hotel	Arundel	01903 882160
Chequers Hotel	Pulborough	01798 872486
Crouchers Bottom Country Hotel	Chichester	01243 784995
The Old Railway Station	Petworth	01798 342346
Woodstock House Hotel	Chichester	01243 811666

WILTSHIRE

Stanton Manor	Chippenham	01666 837552
Widbrook Grange	Bath	01225 864750 / 863173

WORCESTERSHIRE

The Broadway Hotel	Broadway	01386 852401
Collin House Hotel	Broadway	01386 858354
The Mill At Harvington	Evesham	01386 870688

WALES

CONWY

The Old Rectory	Conwy	01492 580611
Tan-y-Foel	Betws-y-Coed	01690 710507

DYFED

Stone Hall	Fishguard	01348 840212

GWYNEDD

Plas Bodegroes	Pwllheli	01758 612363
Plas Dolmelynllyn	Dolgellau	01341 440273
Plas Penhelig Country House Hotel	Aberdovey	01654 767676
Ty'n Rhos Country Hotel	Caernarfon	01248 670489

MONMOUTHSHIRE

The Crown At Whitebrook	Monmouth	01600 860254
Llanwenarth House	Abergavenny	01873 830289
Parva Farmhouse and Restaurant	Tintern	01291 689411

PEMBROKESHIRE

Waterwynch House Hotel	Tenby	01834 842464

POWYS

Glangrwyney Court	Abergavenny	01873 811288
Old Gwernyfed Country Manor	Brecon	01497 847376

WEST GLAMORGAN

Norton House Hotel & Restaurant	Swansea	01792 404891

YNYS YUON

Tre-Ysgawen Hall	Anglesey	01245 750750

SCOTLAND

ABERDEENSHIRE

Balgonie Country House	Ballater,Royal Deeside	013397 55482
The Old Manse of Marnoch	By Huntly	01466 780873

ARGYLLSHIRE

Ardsheal House	Kentallen Of Appin	01631 740227
Highland Cottage	Isle of Mull	01688 302030
Dungallan House Hotel	Oban	01631 563799
Killiechronan	Isle Of Mull	01680 300403
The Manor House Hotel	Oban	01631 562087

AYRSHIRE

Culzean Castle	Maybole	01655 760274

DUMFRIES & GALLOWAY

Longacre Manor	Castle Douglas	01556 503576

DUMFRIESSHIRE

The Dryfesdale Hotel	Lockerbie	01576 202427
Well View Hotel	Moffat	01683 220184
Trigony House Hotel	Dunfries	01848 331211

FIFE

The Argyle House Hotel	St. Andrews	01334 473387
Balgeddie House Hotel	Leslie	01592 742511
Garvock House Hotel	Edinburgh	01383 621067

GLASGOW

Nairns	Glasgow	0141 353 0707

INVERNESS-SHIRE

Boath House	Nairn	01667 454896
Corriegour Lodge Hotel	The Great Glen	01397 712685
Corrour House Hotel	Rothiemurchus	01479 810220
Culduthel Lodge	Inverness	01463 240089
Maple Court & Chandlery Restaurant	Inverness	01463 230330
Mullardoch House Hotel	Glen Cannich	01456 415460
Polmaily House Hotel	Loch Ness	01456 450343

ISLE OF SKYE

Bosville Hotel & Chandlery Seafood Restaurant	Isle of Skye	01478 612846

PERTHSHIRE

The Four Seasons Hotel	St Fillans	01764 685333
The Killiecrankie Hotel	Killiecrankie,By Pitlochry	01796 473220
Knockendarroch House	Pitlochry	01796 473473
The Lake Hotel	Port Of Menteith	01877 385258
The Pend	Dunkeld	01350 727586
Queen's View Hotel	Strathtummel	01796 473291
The Royal Hotel	Comrie	01764 679200

ROSS-SHIRE

Glenmorangie House at Cadbol	Tain	01862 871671

ROXBURGHSHIRE

Clint Lodge	St. Boswell	01835 822027

STIRLING & TROSSACHS

Culcreuch Castle Hotel & Country Park	Fintry	01360 860555

SUTHERLAND

The Kinlochbervie Hotel	Kinlochbervie	01971 521275
Navidale House Hotel	Helmsdale	01431 821 258

WESTERN ISLES

Ardvourlie Castle	Isle Of Harris	01859 502307

IRELAND

CO CLARE

Halpins Hotel & Vittles Restaurant	Kilkee	00 353 65 9056032

CO DONEGAL

Castle Grove Country House	Letterkenny	00 353 745 1118

CO DUBLIN

Aberdeen Lodge	Dublin	00 353 1 2838155
Fitzwilliam Park	Dublin	00 353 1 6628 280

CO GALWAY

Ross Lake House Hotel	Connemara	00 353 91 550109
St. Clerans	Craughwell	00 353 91 846 555

CO KERRY

Caragh Lodge	Caragh Lake	00 353 66 9769115
Earls Court House	Killarney	00 353 64 34009

CO SLIGO

Coopershill House	Riverstown,	00 353 71 65108
Markree Castle	Sligo	00 353 71 67800

CO TIPPERARY

Cashel Palace Hotel	Cashel	00 353 62 62707

CO WATERFORD

The Old Rectory - Kilmeaden House	Kilmeaden	00 353 51 384254

CO WICKLOW

The Old Rectory	Wicklow	00 353 404 67048

CHANNEL ISLANDS

Bella Luce Hotel & Restaurant	Guernsey	01481 38764
Hotel La Tour	Jersey	01534 743770
The White House	Herm Island	01481 722159
La Favorita Hotel	Guernsey	01481 35666
La Sablonnerie	Sark Island	01481 832061

EUROPE & THE MEDITERRANEAN

BELGIUM

Art Hotel Siru	Brussels	32 2 203 35 80
Château d'Hassonville	Marche-en-Famenne	32 84 31 10 25
Chateau de Palogne	Vieuxville	32 86 21 38 74
Chateau Du Lac	Genval	32 2 655 71 11
Die Swaene	Bruges	32-50- 34 27 98
Firean Hotel	Antwerp	32 3237 02 60
Hostellerie Le Prieuré De Conques	Florenville	32 61 41 14 17
Hostellerie Sparrenhof	De Panne	30-58- 41 13 28
Hostellerie Trôs Marets	Malmedy	32-80- 33 79 17
Hotel Acacia	Bruges	32 50 34 44 11
Hotel de Orangerie	Bruges	32 50 34 16 49
Hotel De Tuilerieen	Bruges	32-50- 34 36 91
Hotel Hansa	Bruges	32 50 33 84 44
Hotel Jan Brito	Bruges	32 50 33 06 01
Hotel Manoir Du Dragon	Knokke-Heist	32 50 63 05 80
Hotel Montanus	Bruges	32 50 33 11 76
Hotel Prinsenhof	Bruges	32-50- 34 26 90
Hotel Rubens	Antwerp	32 3 22 48 48
L'Amigo	Brussels	32 2 547 47 47
La Butte Aux Bois	Lanaken	32 89 72 12 86
Les Ardilliéres Du Pont D'Oye	Habay-La-Neuve	32 63 42 22 43
Relais Oud Huis Amsterdam	Bruges	32-50- 34 18 10
Romantik Pandhotel	Bruges	32 50 34 06 66
Scholteshof	Stervoort	32 11 25 02 02
The Stanhope	Brussels	32 2 506 91 11

FRANCE

Auberge de Cassagne	Avignon-Le Pontet	33 4 90 31 04 18
Auberge De Noves	Noves	33 4 90 94 19 21
Château d'Aiguefonde	Castres	33 563 98 1370
Château de Bellinglise	Elincourt-Sainte-Marguerite	00 33 3 44 96 00 33
Chateau de Bonaban	La Gouesniere/St Malo	33 299 58 24 50
Château de Candie	Chambéry-le-Vieux	33 47 99 66 300
Château de Coudrée	Scier sur Leman	33 4 50 72 62 33
Château de Courcelles	Courcelles-sur-Vesle	33 3 23 74 13 53
Château de Danzay	Chinon	33 2 47 58 46 86
Château de la Bourdaisière	Montlouis-sur-Loire	33 2 47 45 16 31
Château de Madières	Madieres-Ganges	33 4 67 73 84 03
Chateau de Pray	Amboise	33 2 47 57 23 67

Château de Rochecotte	Langeais	33 2 47 96 16 16
Chateau de Saint Paterne	St Paterne	33 2 3327 5471
Château de Vault de Lugny	Avallon	33 3 86 34 07 86
Château des Alpilles	Saint-Rémy-de-Provence	33 4 90 92 03 33
Château des Briottières	Champigné	33 2 41 42 00 02
Château des Vigiers	Monestier	33 5 53 61 50 00
Chateau Du Tertre	Normandy	33 31 90 01 04
Château Eza	Eze Village	33 4 93 41 12 24
Château Hôtel André Ziltener	Chambolle-Musigny	33 3 80 62 41 62
Chenevière La	Port-en-Bessin	33 31 21 47 96
Domaine de Beauvois	Luynes	33 2 4755 5011
Domaine de Belesbat	Boutigny Nr Barbizon	33 1 69 23 19 00
Domaine de Rochebois	Sarlat-Vitrac	33 5 53 31 52 52
Domaine de Valmouriane	St Remy	33 4 90 92 44 62
Ermitage de Corton	Beaune	33 3 80 22 05 28
Grand Hotel De La Reine	France Nanc	33 83 35 03 01
Grand Hotel Miramar	Propriano/Corsica	33 4 95 76 06 13
Grand Hôtel Vista Palace	Roquebrune Cap-Martin	33 4 92 10 40 00
Hostellerie de la Poste	Avallon	33 3 86 34 16 16
Hostellerie Du Vallon De Valrugues	St Remy-de-Provence	33 4 90 92 04 40
Hostellerie La Briqueterie	Épernay	33 3 26 59 99 99
Hostellerie Le Castellas	Collias Nr Uzes/Nimes	33 66 22 88 88
Hostellerie Le Phebus	Joucas	33 4 90 05 78 83
Hostellerie Les Bas Rupts	Gérardmer	33 3 29 63 09 25
Hôtel Annapurna	Courchevel	33 4 79 08 04 60
Hôtel Buci Latin	Paris	33 1 4329 0720
Hôtel Byblos	Saint Tropez	33 4 94 56 68 00
Hotel Château Grand Barrail	Saint-Emilion	33 5 57 55 37 00
Hôtel de Crillon	Paris	33 1 4471 1500
Hôtel de L'Arcade	Paris	331 533 0 60 00
Hotel De La Corderie Royale	Rochefort-sur-Mer	33 5 46 99 35 35
Hôtel de Mougins	Mougins	33 4 92 92 17 07
Hôtel Des Trois Vallées	Courchevel	33 4 79 08 00 12
Hôtel du Louvre	Paris	33 1 4458 3838
Hôtel du Palais	Biarritz	33 5 59 41 64 00
Hotel Du Roy	Paris	33 42 89 59 59
Hotel Franklin D. Roosevelt	Paris	33 1 53 57 49 50
Hotel L'Horset Opera	Paris	33 1 44 71 87 00
Hotel La Pérouse	Nice	33 93 62 34 63
Hotel Lancaster	Paris	33 1 4076 4076
Hotel Le Beauvallon	Sainte-Maxime	33 4 94 55 78 88
Hotel Le Lana	Courchevel	33 4 79 08 01 10
Hotel Le Maquis	Corsica-Porticcio	33 4 95 25 05 55
Hôtel Le Parc	Paris	33 1 44 05 66 66
Hôtel le Saint-Grégoire	Paris	33 1 45 48 23 23
Hôtel Le Tourville	Paris	33 1 47 05 62 62
Hôtel Les Têtes	Colmar	33 3 89 24 43 43
Hotel Majestic	Cannes	33 4 92 98 77 00
Hotel Majestic	Paris	33 1 45 00 83 70
Hôtel Mont-Blanc	Megève	33 4 50 21 20 02
Hotel Raphael	Paris	33 01 44 28 00 28
Hôtel Regent Petite France	Strasbourg	33 3 88 76 43 43
Hotel Regina	Paris	33 1 42 60 31 10
Hôtel Royal	Deauville	33 2 31 98 66 33
Hotel Royal Saint-Honoré	Paris	33-142 60 32 79
Hôtel Savoy	Cannes	33 4 92 99 72 00
Hôtel Square	Paris	33 1 44 14 91 90
Hôtel Sube	Saint Tropez	334 94973004
Hotel Vernet	Paris	331 44 31 98 00
Hôtel Villa Belrose	Saint Tropez	33 4 94 55 97 97
Hotel Westminster	Nice	33 4 92 14 86 86
Hôtel Westminster	Paris	33 1 4261 5746
L'Antarès	Méribel	33 4 79 23 28 23
L'Auberge du Choucas	Serre-Chevalier	33 4 92 24 42 73
L'Hôtel	Paris	33 1 43 25 27 22
L'Hotel Des Neiges	France Courcheve	33 4 79 08 03 77
L'Hôtel Pergolese	Paris	33 1 53 64 04 04
L'Imperial Palace	Annecy	33 4 5009 3000
La Cardinale et sa Residence	Baix	33 4 75 85 80 40
La Chaumière	Honfleur	33 2 31 81 63 20
La Domaine de Rochevilaine	Billiers	33 2 97 41 61 61
La Ferme Saint Siméon	Honfleur	33 2 31 89 23 61
La Réserve de Beaulieu	Beaulieu-sur-Mer	33 4 93 01 00 01
La Résidence de la Pinède	Saint Tropez	33 4 94 55 91 00
La Tour Du Roy	Vervins	33 3 23 98 00 11
La Tour Rose	Lyon	33 4 78 37 25 90
La Villa Maillot	Paris	33 1 53 64 52 52
Le Byblos des Neiges	Courchevel	33 4 79 00 98 00
Le Castel Marie-Louise	La Baule	33 40 11 48 38
Le Château	Faverges de La Tour	33 4 74 97 42 52
Le Domaine de Divonne	Divonne-les-Bains	33 4 50 40 3434
Le Hameau Albert 1st	France Chamoni	33 4 50 53 05 09
Le Lavoisier	Paris	33 1 53 30 06 06
Le Manoir de Gressy	Gressy-en-France/Chantilly	33 1 60 26 68 00
Le Manoir de Vaumadeuc	Pleven	33 2 96 84 46 17
Le Manoir du Butin	Honfleur	33 2 31 81 63 00
Le Moulin de Connelles	Connelles	33 2 32 59 53 33
Le Prieure	Chenehutte-Les-Tuffeau	33 2 41 67 90 14
Le Relais Saint-Germain	Paris	33 1 43 29 12 05
Les Bruyéres	Saint-Félix	33 4 5060 9653
Les Sources de Caudalie	Martillac	33 5 57 83 83 83
Lodge Park Hôtel	Megève	33 4 50 93 05 03
Manoir de la Roseraie	Grignan	33 4 75 46 58 15
Mas d'Artigny	Saint Paul	33 4 93 32 84 54
Mas De Peint Le	Le Sambuc	33 90 4 97 20 62
Montalembert	France Pari	33 1 45 49 68 68
Monte Carlo Beach Hotel	Monte Carlo	33 4 93 28 66 66
Pavillon De La Reine	Paris	33 1 42 77 96 40
Relais Brenner	Paimpol	33 96 20 11 05
Relais Christine	Paris	33 1 43 26 71 80
Romantik Hostellerie Le Maréchal	Colmar	33 3 89 41 60 32
Royal Hôtel	Paris	331 43 59 08 14
Saint James-Paris	Paris	33 144 05 81 81
Saint-Paul Le	Saint-Paul-De-Vence	33 93 32 65 25
Suites Saint Honoré Les	France Pari	33 1 44 51 16 35
Villa Saint Elme	Les Issambres	33 4 94 49 52 52

GERMANY

Alpenhof Murnau	Murnau	49 8841 4910
Bülow Residenz	Dresden	49 351 80030
Burghotel Auf Schönburg	Oberwesel/Rhein	49 67 44 93 93 0
Burghotel Hardenberg	Göttingen	49 5503 9810
Der Kleine Prinz	Baden Baden	49 7221 3464
Grand Hotel Esplanade Berlin	Berlin	00 49 30261011
Hotel Alexandra	Germany Plaue	49 37 41 22 14 14
Hotel Arminius	Bad Salzuflen	49 052 22 5 30 70
Hotel Brandenburger Hof	Berlin	49 30 214050
Hotel Burg Wassenberg	Wassenberg	49 2432 9490
Hotel Burg Wernberg	Wernberg-Köblitz	49 9604 9390
Hotel Cristall	Cologne	49 221 163 00
Hôtel Eisenhut	Rothenburg ob der Tauber	49 9861 70 50
Hotel im Wasserturm	Cologne	49 221 20080
Hotel Königshof	Munich	49 89 551 360
Hotel Römerbad	Badenweiler	49 76 32 70 0
Hotel Schloss Waldeck	Waldeck	49 5623 5890
Hôtel Stadt Hamburg	Westerland/Sylt	49 46 51 85 80
Hotel Töpferhaus	Alt Duvenstedt Nr Rendsburg	49 43 38 333
Jagdschloss Neiderwald	Rüdesheim am Rhein	49 67 22 1004
Kempinski Hotel Atlantic Hamburg	Germany Hambur	49 40 28 880
Kempinski Hotel Bristol	Germany Berli	49 30 8 84 340
Mönchs Posthotel	Bad Herrenalb	49 70 83 74 40
Parkhotel Schlangenbad	Schlangenbad	49 61 29 420
Pflaums Posthotel Pegnitz	Pegnitz	49 92 41 72 50
Posthotel Garmisch Partenkirchen	Garmisch-Partenkirchen	49 8821 510 67
Reindl's Partenkirchner Hof	Garmisch Partenkirchen	49 8821 58025
Residenz Heinz Winkler	Aschau	49 8052 17990
Romantik Hotel Goldene Traube	Coburg	49 9561 8760
Romantik Parkhotel Wehrle	Triberg	49 7722 86020
RR Binshof Resort	Speyer	49 6232 6470
Schlosshotel Buhlerhöhe	Baden Baden	49 7226 55-0
Schlosshotel Hugenport	Kettwig	49 20 54 12 040
Schlosshotel Oberstotzingen	Niederstotzingen	49 7325 1030
Schweizer Stuben	Wertheim-Bettingen	49 9342 3070
Seehotel Siber	Konstanz	49 7531 63044
Wald & Schlosshotel	Friedrichsruhe	49 7941 60870

THE NETHERLANDS

Ambassade Hotel	Amsterdam	31 20 5550222
De Hoefslag	Bosch en Duin	31 30 225 1051
Hotel De Arendshoeve	Bergambacht	31 182 35 1000
Hotel De Duinrand	Drunen	31 416 372 498
Hotel de Wiemsel	Ootmarsum	31 541 292 155
Hotel Restaurant de Swaen	Oisterwijk	31 135 23 3233
Manoir Restaurant Inter Scaldes	Kruiningen	31 11338 1753
Restaurant-Hotel Savelberg	Voorburg	31 70 387 2081
Bilderberg Landgoed Lauswolt	Beetsterzwaag	31 512 38 12 45
The Canal House Hotel	Amsterdam	31 20 622 5182
Hotel De Holtwenjde	Lattrop	31 541 229 234
Seven One Seven	Amsterdam	31 20 42 70 717

HOLIDAY COTTAGES

ENGLAND

BERKSHIRE

Dower House	Bray - On - Thames	01628 673991

CORNWALL

Broomhill Manor	Poughill	01288 352940
Cant Cove	Rock	01208 862841
Treworgey Cottages	Looe	01503 262730

CUMBRIA

Bridge End Farm Cottages	Eskdale	01242 679900
Derwent Manor	Keswick	017687 72211
Staffield Hall	Penrith	01768 898656

DERBYSHIRE

The Chapel	Alport	01629 636190
Hopton Hall	Matlock	01629 540458
Slade House Farm	Ashbourne	01538 308 123

DEVON

Ashelford	Combe Martin	01271 850469
Corffe	Barnstaple	01271 342588
Downe Cottages	Hartland	01237 441881
Higher Bowden	Dartmouth	01803 770745
Kingston Estate	Staverton	01803 762235
Old Bridwell Holiday Cottages	Uffculme	01884 841464
Valley Springs	Sherford	01548 531574

DORSET

Champernhayes	Lyme Regis	01297 560853

ESSEX

The Pump House Apartment	Billericay	01277 656579
Whitensmere Farm Cottages	Cambridge	01799 584544

GLOUCESTERSHIRE

Folly Farm Cottages	Tetbury	01666 502475
Old Mill Farm	Cirencester	01285 821255
Owlpen Manor	Owlpen	01453 860261
Rural Retreats		01386 701177
Upper Court Courtyard Cottages	Tewkesbury	01386 725351

HAMPSHIRE

Culverley Old Farm Cottage	Beaulieu	01590 612260

ISLE OF WIGHT

Plantation House	Isle of Wight *(contact Rural Retreats)*	01386 701177

KENT

Eastwell Mews	Ashford	01233 213000

LINCOLNSHIRE

Woodthorpe Hall Country Cottages	Alford	01507 450294

LONDON

Draycott House Apartments	London	020 7584 4659
The Lexham Apartments	London	020 7559 4444
The Preston Suite	London	07071 885555

NORFOLK

Countryside Cottages	Blakeney	07041 564005
The Great Escape Holiday Co Ltd	North Norfolk Coast	01485 518717
Vere Lodge	Fakenham	01328 838261
Wiveton Hall	Wiveton	01263 740525
The Priory	Wiggenhall *(Contact Rural Retreats)*	01386 701177

NORTH DEVON

Barkham	Exmoor	01643 831370

NORTH YORKSHIRE

Rudding Holiday Park	Harrogate	01423 870439
Wrea Head Cottage Holidays	Scarborough	01723 375844

NORTHUMBERLAND

Beacon Hill Farm	Morpeth	01670 788372
Outchester Manor Cottages	Bamburgh	01668 213336

SHROPSHIRE

The Netley Hall Estate	Dorrington	01743 318339

SOMERSET

Grange Barn	Cannington	01278 652216
Highercombe Cottage & Wing	Dulverton	01398 323451

SUFFOLK

Gladwins Farm	Colchester	01206 262261

WILTSHIRE

Queenwood Golf Lodge	Bowood	01249 822228

SCOTLAND

ABERDEENSHIRE

Blairmore	Huntly	01466 700200
Mar Lodge	Braemar	0131 243 9331

ARGYLL

Burnknowe House & Cottage	Lochgoilhead	01555 893592

FIFE

Cobwebs	St. Andrews	01334 650000

INVERNESS-SHIRE

Achneim Cottage	Highlands *(contact Rural Retreats)*	01667 404666

ISLE OF SKYE

Duntulm Coastguard Cottages	Isle of Skye	01470 552213

MORAYSHIRE

The Old Steading	Elgin	01343 850222

PERTHSHIRE

Camusericht Estate	Loch Rannoch	01882 633207
Kinnaird Estate	Dunkeld	01796 482440

STIRLINGSHIRE

Forest Hills Hotel	Aberfoyle	01877 387277
Stucan-T-iobairt Cottage	Loch Lomond	0141 339 2774

SUTHERLAND

Navidale Lodges	Helmsdale	01431 821258

Calendar of Events

Leeds Castle, Kent

Pashley Manor, Sussex

Lulworth Castle, Dorset

JANUARY

Jan–26 Mar Exhibition Gallery- 'Looking Back at Vaisakhi 1999' ....Soho House Museum, Birmingham 0121 554 9122

FEBRUARY

19–27th All the King's Creatures ....Hampton Court Palace, 0181 781 9500
26–4th June Eat, Drink & Be Merry – Exhibition ....Fairfax House, York 01904 655543

MARCH

3–14th Garden Crafts ....RHS Wisley, Surrey 01483 224234
4th Winston Churchill Memorial Concert ....Blenheim Palace, Oxon 01869 350049
10–12th Cheshire County Antiques Fair ....Arley Hall, Cheshire 01565 777353
18–19th Spring Lambing ....Kingston Maurward, Dorset 01305 215000
19–26th Art Exhibition ....Sausmarez Manor, Guernsey 01481 235571
25–26th Rare Plants Sale ....Hatfield House, Hertforshire 01707 260228
25–26th Spring Craft Fair ....Ragley Hall, Warks 01789 762090

APRIL

2nd The Stowe Wedding Affaire ....Stowe House, Bucks 01280 813650
8–9th Crafts ....Stanford Hall, Leics 01788 860250
8–16th Meet the Gardeners ....Warwick Castle, Warks 01926 495421
8–9th Living History Weekend ....Harvington Hall, H & W 01562 777846
14–16th Galloway Antiques Fair ....Ripley Castle, Yorkshire 01423 770152
15th Bournemouth Bach Choir ....Christchurch Priory 01202 485804
15–16th The Fine Art Fair ....Cecil Higgins Art Gallery, Bedfordshire 01234 211222
16th Special Plant Fair ....Spetchley Park Garden, H & W 01905 345224
19th & 24th Concert ....St Davids Cathedral, Wales 01437 720202
21–24th The Medway Craft Show ....Cobham Hall, Kent 01474 824319
22–23rd Rufus 2000– A celebration of the New Forest ....Beaulieu, Hampshire 01590 612345
22–30th Royal Sport at Hampton Court ....Hampton Court Palace, 0181 781 9500
22–24th Great Easter Egg Hunt ....Kingston Maurward, Dorset 01305 215000
22–24th Celebration of Easter ....Leeds Castle, Kent 01622 765400
23rd Easter Egg & Hat Parade, 2pm–5pm ....Castle Bromwich Gardens, Birmingham 0121-749 4100
23–24th Easter Extravaganza & The Tales of the Ugly Duckling ....Groombridge Place, Kent 01892 861444
23–24th Victorian Easter ....Holdenby House, Nothants 01604 770074
23–24th Antique Fair ....Lamport Hall, Northamptonshire 01604 686272
23–24th Easter Egg Hunts ....Sudeley Castle, Glos 01242 602308
23rd Easter Egg Trail ....The Vyne, Hampshire 01256 881337
23–24th Easter Egg Trail ....Rievaulx Terrace & Temples, Yorkshire 01439 748283
23–24th Easter Egg Hunt ....Burton Agnes Hall, Yorkshire 01262 490324
23–24th Easter Fun ....Penshurst Place, Kent 01892 870307
23–24th Traditional Food Fair ....Weald & Downland Open Air Museum, Sussex 01243 811363
24th Annual Diocesan Youth Pilgrimage ....Cathedral & Abbey Church of St Alban, Herts 01707 332321
24th Mapperton Rare Plant Fair 10–4pm ....Mapperton, Dorset 01308 862645
27–30th Symposium to mark the Bi–Centenary of the death of William Cowper ....Cowper & Newton Museum, Bucks 01234 711516
27–1st May Tulip Festival ....Pashley Manor, Sussex 01580 200692
29–1st May Living Heritage Oxfordshire Craft Fair ....Blenheim Palace, Oxon 01283 820548
29–1st May May Day Music & Dance ....Hever Castle, Kent 01732 865224
30–1st May Tulip Festival ....Constable Burton Hall Gardens, Yorkshire 01677 450428
30–1st May Their Finest hour – Dover & Dunkirk ....Dover Castle, Kent 01304 840107
30–1st May Magical May Puppet Festival ....Elsham Hall, Lincs 01652 688698
30–1st May Jousting Tournament ....Hedingham Castle, Essex 01787 460261

MAY

1st May Day Festival ....Avoncroft Museum of Historic Buildings, H & W 01527 831886
1st Bluebell Time ....High Beeches Gardens, Sussex 01444 400589
1st Spring Plant Sale ....Ness Botanic Gardens, Cheshire 0151 353 0123
4–7th Living Crafts ....Hatfield House, Hertfordshire 023 9242 6523
5–7th Home Design & Interiors Exhibition ....Elton Hall, Cambridgeshire 01705 677200
6th Plant Fair ....Savill Garden, Berks 01753 847518
6–7th Bonsai Weekend & Demonstrations ....Leonardslee Gardens, Sussex 01403 891212
6–7th Angling Fair ....Chatsworth, Derbys 01246 582204
7th Plant Sale ....Birmingham Botanical Gardens & Glasshouses 0121 454 1860
7th Plant Fair in the Riding School ....Hovingham Hall, Yorkshire 01653 628206
7th Family Nature Day ....Mannington Hall, Norfolk 01263 584175
11–13th Homes and Gardens, Spring Grand Sale ....Sudeley Castle, Glos 01242 602308
11th Thyme & Tiffin – 10.30am Tour & Lunch ....Baddesley Clinton, Warks 01564 783294
13–14th Garden Show ....Firle Place, Sussex 01273 858567
13–14th Knebworth Garden Show ....Knebworth, Hertfordshire 01438 812661

Calendar of Events

Warwick Castle, Warwickshire

Holkner Hall, Cumbria

Hatfield House, Hertfordshire

13–14th	Country Gardening & Food Fair	Lulworth Castle, Dorset 01929 400352
13–19th	Sculpture Week	Pashley Manor, Sussex 01580 200692
13th	An Evening with Fanny Burney	Wolteron Hall, Norfolk 01263 584175
13–14th	Woodland Fair – An Activity Weekend	Brantwood, Cumbria 015394 41396
13–14th	Festival of English Food & Wine	Leeds Castle, Kent 01622 765400
13–14th	Horse Trials	Chatsworth, Derbys 01246 582204
14–25th June	Pendle Potters	Towneley Hall Art Gallery, Lancashire 01282 424213
17th	Spring Flower Walk – Booking Essential	Rievaulx Terrace & Temples, Yorks 01439 748283
20th	Spring Plant Sale	Picton Castle, Wales 01437 751326
20th–29 Oct	Alfred Wallis & James Dixon Exhibition	Tate St.Ives, Cornwall 01736 796543
21st	Cheshire Kit Car Show	Capesthorne Hall, Cheshire 01625 861221
25–26th	BBC Music for the Millennium	Sausmarez Manor, Guernsey 01481 235571
25–28th	Craft Fair	Loseley Park, Surrey 01483 304440
27–29th	Crafts at Arley	Arley Hall, Cheshire 01565 777353
27–29th	Crafts at Arley	Arley Hall, Cheshire 01565 777353
27–29th	Craft Festival	Harewood House, Yorks 0113 218 1024
27–28th	Oak Apple Day Celebrations	The Commandery, Hereford & Worcs 01905 361821
27–29th	Jousting	Warwick Castle, Warks 01926 495421
28–29th	Medieval Entertainment	Charlecote Park, Warks 01789 470277
28th	Music in the Gardens	Cholmondeley Castle, Cheshire 01829 720383
28–29th	The Imperial Roman Army	Dover Castle, Kent 01304 840107
28–29th	Spring Fair & Flower Festival	Finchcocks, Kent 01580 211702
28–29th	Plant Fair	Holdenby House, Nothants 01604 770074
28–29th	Medieval Festival	Hedingham Castle, Essex 01787 460261
28th	Atholl Gathering & Highland Games	Blair Castle, Scotland 01796 481 355
28–29th	Medieval Falconry Display	Bolton Castle, Yorkshire 01969 623981
29th	Steam Fair & Country Show	Eastnor Castle, H & W 01531 633160
29th	Country Fair	Duncombe Park, Yorkshire 01439 788517
30th	Rare Giant Plant Sale	Sausmarez Manor, Guernsey 01481 235571
30th	Out of this World' – A Space Odyssey	The Priest's House Museum, Dorset 01202 882533
30–31st	Classic Car Show	Penshurst Place, Kent 01892 870307

JUNE

All Month	Michael Elsden Exhibition	Ayscoughfee Hall Museum, Lincs 01775 725468
3rd	Kingston Maurward Show	Kingston Maurward, Dorset 01305 215000
3–4th	Raby Festival, Concert on the 3rd	Raby Castle, Co Durham 01833 660207
4–6th	The Holker Garden Festival	Holker Hall, Cumbria 015395 58838
4th	Heavy Horse Spectacular	Weald & Downland Open Air Museum, Sussex 01243 811363
4th	VW Car Rally	Stonor Park, Oxfordshire 01491 638587
4th	Band Concert in Gardens	Wallingford Castle, Oxon 01491 836972
7th	Gardens of County Wicklow', Tour 7.30pm	Mount Usher, Ireland 00353 404 40205
8–11th	Grand Summer Sale	Ripley Castle, Yorkshire 01423 770152
9–11th	Garden Festival	Ness Botanic Gardens, Cheshire 0151 353 0123
10–11th	Carlisle through the Ages	Carlisle Abbey, Cumbria 01228 548151
10th	Romeo & Juliet	Uppark, Hampshire 01730 825415
10–11th	Gardeners' Fair	Burton Agnes Hall, Yorkshire 01262 490324
14–15th	Shakespeare's The Tempest	Painswick Rococo Garden, Glos 01452 813204
15th–18th	Summer Flower Festival	Pashley Manor, Sussex 01580 200692
16–18th	Craft Show	Firle Place, Sussex 01273 858567
17–30th	Rose & Craft Days	Borde Hill Garden, Sussex 01444 412151
17th	Picnic to 'Jazz in June'	Gilbert White's House, Hampshire 01420 511275
17th	Pure Puccini – Open Air Opera	Harewood House, Yorks 0113 218 1024
18th	British Red Cross Charity Garden Opening Day	Norton Conyers Hall, Yorks 01765 640333
18th	Wind in the Willows, Production	Penshurst Place, Kent 01892 870307
18th–9th July	Great Annual Re–Creation of Tudor Life	Kentwell Hall, Suffolk 01787 310207
21st	A Midsummer Night's Dream'	Torre Abbey, Devon 01803 293593
23rd	Open Air Brass Band Concert in the Park	Bramall Hall, Cheshire 0161 485 3708
23rd–26th	FLORA 2000 – Festival of Flowers	Christchurch Priory 01202 485804
23rd–25th	Goodwood Festival of Speed	Goodwood House, Sussex 01243 755055
23rd	Open Air Opera	Loseley Park, Surrey 01483 304440
23–25th	Stonor Garden Show	Stonor Park, Oxfordhire 01491 638587
24–25th	Arley Garden Festival	Arley Hall, Cheshire 01565 777353
24–25th	Festival of Gardening	Hatfield House, Hertfordshire 0707 262823
24–24th	Garden Event	West Dean, Sussex 01243 811205
24–25th	Rose Festival	Hever Castle, Kent 01732 865224
24–25th	West Sussex Country Craft Fair	Leonardslee Gardens, Sussex 01403 891212
24–25th	Warwickshire Country Home, Leisure & Garden Show	Arbury Hall, Warks 01203 382804
24th–30th	Flower Festival	Haddon Hall, Derbys 01629 812855
25th	Picnic in the Park – Concert	Firle Place, Sussex 01273 858567
25th	Lulworth Classic Car Event	Lulworth Castle, Dorset 01929 400352
25th	Specialist Plant Fair	Nunnington Hall, Yorks 01439 748283
30th	The European Chamber Opera	Mottisfont Abbey, Hampshire 01794 451596

JULY

All Month	Privy Garden Celebration	Hampton Court Palace, 0181 781 9500
1st	Francis House Charity Concert	Arley Hall, Cheshire 01565 777353
1st	Glastonbury Pilgrimage	Glastonbury Abbey, Somerset 01458 832267
1st	Battle Proms Concert	Ragley Hall, Warks 01789 762090

Leeds Castle, Kent

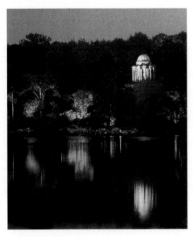

Stourhead, Wiltshire

Norton Conyers, Yorkshire

1st	The Emperor's New Clothes	Uppark, Hampshire 01730 825415
1st–2nd	Grand Summer Fireworks Concert	Warwick Castle, Warks 01926 495421
1st	'Mid–Summer Nights Dream' by Oddsocks Productions	Nunnington Hall, Yorks 01439 748283
1–2nd	Tonbridge – Millenium Festival	Tonbridge Castle, Kent 01580 201471
1st	Open Air Concert	Leeds Castle, Kent 01622 880008
2–16th	Pembrokeshire Craft Makers Selling Fair	Picton Castle, Wales 01437 751326
6th	Pelargoniums, Plant Pots & Pastries, Tour & Talk	Stourhead, Wiltshire 01747 841152
7–8th	Open Air Shakespeare in the Park	Bramall Hall, Cheshire 0161 485 3708
7th	Concert by Devon Youth Jazz Orchestra	Torre Abbey, Devon 01803 293593
7–8th	Harvington Festival	Harvington Hall, H & W 01562 777846
8–9th	Animal Magic!	Avoncroft Museum of Historic Buildings, H & W 01527 831886
8–9th	Tonbridge Castle Arts Festival	Tonbridge Castle, Kent 01732 876169
9th	Amnesty International Charity Garden Opening Day	Norton Conyers Hall, Yorks 01765 640333
9th	Bygones Day	Wolteron Hall, Norfolk 01263 584175
9th	A Midsummer Night's Dream – Open Air	Ingatestone Hall, Essex 01277 353010
9th	Partake Elizabethan Dancers	Haddon Hall, Derbys 01629 812855
13th	Choristers in Concert	Worcester Cathedral, H & W, 01905 726311
14–16th	Sevenoaks Flower Club 'Festival of Flowers 2000'	Squerryes Court, Kent 01959 562345
15–16th	Garden Festival	Coughton Court, Warks 01789 762435
15–16th	Dalemain Rainbow Craft Fair	Dalemain, Cumbria 017684 86450
15–16th	Garden Weekend	Parham Park, Sussex 01903 742021
15th	Charity Concert	Ingatestone Hall, Essex 01277 353010
16th	Mowbray Singers 2–4pm	Rievaulx Terrace & Temples, Yorkshire 01439 748283
18–Jan 2001	The House Beautiful– Oscar Wilde and the Aesthetic Style	Geffrye Museum, London 0171 739 9893
18–31st	Kent Costume Trust Exhibition in the House	Goodnestone Park, Kent 01304 840107
18–22nd	Shakespeare's Twelfth Night	Painswick Rococo Garden, Glos 01452 813204
20–22nd	Stourhead– A Journey Through Time– Picnic, Concert, Fireworks	Stourhead, Wiltshire 01747 841152
21–23rd	Craft Fair	The Vyne, Hampshire 01256 881337
21–23rd	Centenary Weekend	Brantwood, Cumbria 015394 41396
22–23rd	Motorcycle World	Beaulieu, Hampshire 01590 612345
22nd	Camerata	Cholmondeley Castle, Cheshire BO 0161 907 9040
22–10th Sept	Summer Exhibition	Doddington Hall, Lincs 01522 694308
22/29 & Aug	Jousting Tournaments	Hever Castle, Kent 01732 865224
22–23rd	Craft Fair	Haddon Hall, Derbys 01629 812855
23rd	St.John's Ambulance Charity Garden Opening Day	Norton Conyers Hall, Yorks 01765 640333
23rd	Vintage Motorcycle Club Founders Day Rally	Stanford Hall, Leics 01788 860250
27–30, 3–5 Aug	The Importance of being Earnest	Smallhythe Place, Kent 01580 762334
28–30th	Craft Fayre	Broadlands, Hampshire – 01283 820548
28–30th	Game Fair	Blenheim Palace, Oxon 01256 389767
28–29th	Jazz in the Park	Stonor Park, Oxfordhire 01491 638587
29th	Palace House Proms	Beaulieu, Hampshire 01590 612345
29–30th	Homes & Gardens Weekend	Castle Bromwich Gardens, Birmingham 0121 749 4100
29th	Midsummer Concert, 7pm	Charlecote Park, Warks 01789 470277
29–30th	Food Festival	Coughton Court, Warks 01789 762435
29–12th Aug	Quinart Group of Watercolours	East Lambrook Manor , Glos 01460 240328
29th	Gilbert & Sullivan's Ruddigore	Ingatestone Hall, Essex 01277 353010
29th	Glen Miller Concert	Kentwell Hall, Suffolk 01787 310207

AUGUST

1st–5th	Festival Week, Horseracing	Goodwood House, Sussex 01243 755048
4–6th	Art in Clay	Hatfield House, Hertfordshire 0115 9873966
5th	Shakespeare's 'As You Like It' in the Gardens	Lamport Hall, Northamptonshire 01604 686272
5th	A Midsummer Night's Dream	Stourhead, Wiltshire 01747 841152
5th	Gloucestershire Youth Jazz – Open Air evening Concert	Sudeley Castle, Glos 01242 602308
5–6th	Medieval Heritage Society Weekend	Bolton Castle, Yorkshire 01969 623981
6–1st Oct	Annual Summer Opening	Buckingham Palace State Rooms 020 7839 1377
9th	Darnley Dickens Day	Cobham Hall, Kent 01474 824319
11th	Garden Opera	Goodnestone Park, Kent 01304 840107
11th	Jazz on a Summers Evening	Penshurst Place, Kent 01892 870307
12–13th	Craft Fair	Coughton Court, Warks 01789 762435
12/13/19/20	Pirate Party	Mottisfont Abbey, Hampshire 01794 340758
12th	Ripley Show	Ripley Castle, Yorkshire 01423 770152
13th	Summer Plant Fair	Pashley Manor, Sussex 01580 200692
13–14th	Illyria Outdoor Theatre – Romeo & Juliet	The Vyne, Hampshire 01256 881337
13th	Open Air Concert & Fireworks	Loseley Park, Surrey 01483 304440
13th	Band Concert in Gardens	Wallingford Castle, Oxon 01491 836972
15–29th	Fine Art & Craft Exhibition	St Davids Cathedral, Wales 01437 720202
18–20th	Live Crafts in the Park	Parham Park, Sussex 01494 450504
18th	Pirate Party, 2–5pm	Smallhythe Place, Kent 01580 762334
19th	Classical Extravaganza with the Royal Philarmonic Orchestra	Glastonbury Abbey, Somerset 01458 832267
19–20th	Hertfordshire Craft Fair	Knebworth, Hertfordshire 01438 812661
19th	Mapperton Courtyard Fair 2–5pm	Mapperton, Dorset 01308 862645
19–20th	Feudal Archers re–enactment	Skipton Castle, Yorks 01756 792442
19–20th	Motor Transport Spectacular	Arbury Hall, Warks 01203 382804
20th	The Rivals' Play in Gardens	Hergest Croft Gardens 01544 230160
20th	Living History in the 16th Century	Eastnor Castle, H & W 01531 633160
24th	Beatrix Potter & Friends	The Priest's House Museum, Dorset 01202 882533
24–27th	Bowmore Blair Castle International Horse Trials & Country Fair	Blair Castle, Scotland 01796 481 543
24–29th	Rural History Re–enactment	Weald & Downland Open Air Museum, Sussex 01243 811363
25–28th	Chilterns Craft Show	Stonor Park, Oxfordhire 01491 638587

Calendar of Events

Avoncoroft Museum, Hereford & Worcester

Norton Priory, Cheshire

Hampton Court Palace, London

27–28th	Living History Event	Avoncroft Museum of Historic Buildings, H & W 01527 831886
27th	Cumbrian Classic Car Show	Dalemain, Cumbria 017684 86450
27–30th	Folk Dance & Puppet Festival	Elsham Hall, Lincs 01652 688698
27–28th	Medieval Weekend	Holdenby House, Nothants 01604 770074
27th	MG Rally	Holker Hall, Cumbria 015395 58838
27–28th	Knebworth '99 – The Classic Car Show	Knebworth, Hertfordshire 01438 812661
27–28th	Living History Weekend	Harvington Hall, H & W 01562 777846
28th	Medieval Combat by the Lake	Ragley Hall, Warks 01789 762090

SEPTEMBER

2nd–3rd	Autumn Garden Festival	Sudeley Castle, Glos 01242 602308
2nd	Firework Festival in the Park	Arbury Hall, Warks 01203 382804
2–3rd	Country Fair	Chatsworth, Derbys 01246 582204
3rd	Rare Plants Fair	Borde Hill Garden, Sussex 01444 412151
3rd	Classic Car Rally	Cholmondeley Castle, Cheshire 01829 720383
3rd	King Henry V & The Battle of Agincourt	Groombridge Place, Kent 01892 861444
3rd	Charities Day in the Gardens	Mannington Hall, Norfolk 01263 584175
3rd	York Concert Band – Music afternoon	Rievaulx Terrace & Temples, Yorkshire 01439 748283
7–10th	The Blenheim International Horse Trials	Blenheim Palace, Oxon 01993 813335
8–10th	Country Homes & Gardens Show	Hatfield House, Hertfordshire 01628 631131
8–11th	Torre Abbey Flower Festival 'On the Silver Screen'	Torre Abbey, Devon 01803 293593
8–10th	Weald of Kent Craft Show	Penshurst Place, Kent 01892 870307
9th	Romsey Show	Broadlands, Hampshire –01794 517521
9–10th	Country Show in the Park	Parham Park, Sussex 01306 741302
9th	Autumn Plant Sale	Picton Castle, Wales 01437 751326
9–10th	The Medieval Pageant	The Commandery, Hereford & Worcs 01905 361821
9–10th	Totally Tomato Show	West Dean, Sussex 01243 811205
9–5thNov	Glassblown Art'	Wycombe Museum, Bucks 01494 421895
10th	Mini Owners Club National Rally	Stanford Hall, Leics 01788 860250
16–17th	Rainbow Craft Fair	Capesthorne Hall, Cheshire 01625 861221
16–17th	Heritage Open Days	Soho House Museum, Birmingham 0121 554 9122
17th	Arley Bridal Fair	Arley Hall, Cheshire 01565 777353
17th	Horticultural Show	Norton Priory, Cheshire 01928 569895
22–24th	International Floral Design Show	Lulworth Castle, Dorset 01929 400352
29–1st Oct	International Early Music Showcase	Wingfield College, Suffolk 01379 384505

OCTOBER

1st	East Midlands Doll Fair	Lamport Hall, Northamptonshire 01604 686272
3rd–12th	Alban 2000 – Sound & Light	Cathedral & Abbey Church of St Alban, Herts 01707 860780
7th	Woodland Den Building, a Family Event	Stourhead, Wiltshire 01747 841152
7–8th	Festival of Fine Food & Drink	Eastnor Castle, H & W 01531 633160
13–15th	Finchcocks Autumn Fair	Finchcocks, Kent 01580 211703
14–15th	The Battle of Hastings	Battle Abbey, Sussex 01424 773792
14–15th	Craft Fair	Ragley Hall, Warks 01789 762090
14–15th	Craft Fair	Hedingham Castle, Essex 01787 460261
15th	Autumn Splendour	High Beeches Gardens, Sussex 01444 400589
15th	Apple Day	West Dean, Sussex 01243 811205
19–22nd	Apple Days	RHS Wisley, Surrey 01483 224234
20th	Autumn Designer Clothes Sale	Uppark, Hampshire 01730 825415
21–22nd	The Medway Flower Festival & Craft Show	Cobham Hall, Kent 01474 824319
21–22nd	Gifts & Craft Fair	Lamport Hall, Northamptonshire 01604 686272
21st	Apple Day Event	Norton Priory, Cheshire 01928 569895
22nd	Costume Family Day	Cecil Higgins Art Gallery, Bedfordshire 01234 211222
24th	Autumn into Winter	Mottisfont Abbey, Hampshire 01794 340758
28th	Fireworks Fair/ Spooks & Sparks	Beaulieu, Hampshire 01590 612345
28–29th	The Stowe Christmas Fayre	Stowe House, Bucks 01280 813650

NOVEMBER

3–5th	Antiques Fair	Duncombe Park, Yorkshire 01423 522122
4th	Fireworks Spectacular	Cathedral & Abbey Church of St Alban, Herts 01707 860780
4th	Bijou Circus of Fire, 6pm	Charlecote Park, Warks 01789 470277
4th	Firework Spectacular	Groombridge Place, Kent 01892 861444
11–12th	Christmas Craft Fayre	Broadlands, Hampshire 01794 505020
18–19th	Craftmakers Fair	Brantwood, Cumbria 015394 41396
24–26th	Christmas Craft Festival	Harewood House, Yorks 0113 218 1024
25–26th	Annual Craft Show	Avoncroft Museum of Historic Buildings, H & W 01527 831886

DECEMBER

All Month	A Tudor Christmas	Hampton Court Palace, 0181 781 9500
5–10th	Aston Hall by Candlelight	Aston Hall, Birmingham 0121 327 0062
9th	Christmas Concert, in the Library	Stourhead, Wiltshire 01747 841152
9th	Christmas Medieval Banquet– 7.30pm	Baddesley Clinton, Warks 01564 783294

RAINBOW FAIR *presents*

CRAFTS
4 DAYS

at

GATCOMBE PARK

(Minchinhampton near Stroud)

FOLLOW SIGNPOSTED ROUTE

Held in the Grounds by kind permission of H.R.H The Princess Royal

Hand made goods on sale to the public - buy direct from the makers at bargain prices!

VISITING CRAFTSPEOPLE
FROM ALL OVER THE COUNTRY WITH
DISPLAYS, DEMONSTRATION3 AND
GOODS FOR SALE

A WIDE VARIETY OF WORK INCLUDES . . .
FISHING FLIES ○ JIGSAWS ○ CROCHET ○ CHEESES
PAINTINGS ○ POTTERY ○ KNITWEAR ○ PRINTS
CHOCOLATES ○ CERAMICS ○ SOFT TOYS ○ WOOD TOYS
WATER COLOURS ○ JEWELLERY ○ LIQUEURS
WOOD TURNING ○ DOUGH CRAFT ○ MIRRORS
RESIN FIGURES ○ STAINED GLASS ○ COIN JEWELLERY
WAISTCOATS ○ PHOTOGRAPHY ○ CHILDREN'S CLOTHES
COSMETICS ○ FURNITURE ○ CARDS
and MUCH, MUCH MORE!!

PUBLIC ADMISSION TO
THE CRAFT MARQUEES
(no access to the House)

**ADULTS £3.50 OAP £2.50
ACCOMPANIED CHILDREN £1.00**

Refreshments

FREE PARKING

CRAFTS OPEN TO THE PUBLIC 10.00 am. to 5.30 pm.

**Friday, Saturday, Sunday & Monday
April 28th, 29th, 30th & May 1st**

Rainbow Fair
Telephone: 01529 414793

☆ AROUND 300 STANDS ☆

☆ *NOW IN OUR FIFTEENTH YEAR . . . NOW OVER FOUR DAYS* ☆

© 2000 Original artwork & design copyright Rainbow Fair

RAINBOW FAIR

promoting the work of Britsh craft workers at high quality venues throughout the Country.

All exhibitors are vetted to ensure a high standard of work and originality of design.

Demonstrations are encouraged to add to an interesting visit, and all goods are for sale to the public.

Beautiful settings, interesting venues and **BRITISH** crafts (no bought in goods) have made Rainbow the Country's leading promoters of events of this kind.

THE SANDRINGHAM SPRING CRAFT FAIR

NEAR KINGS LYNN, NORFOLK
(follow RAC Signs)

By Gracious Permission of Her Majesty The Queen

NOW IN ITS 7th YEAR ON A SLIGHTLY SMALLER SCALE THAN
THE FAMOUS 'CRAFTS AT SANDRINGHAM' IN AUGUST

VISITING CRAFTSPEOPLE
FROM ALL OVER THE COUNTRY WITH
DISPLAYS, DEMONSTRATIONS AND
GOODS FOR SALE

A WIDE VARIETY OF WORK INCLUDES . . .
PAINTINGS ○ POTTERY ○ WOOD TURNING ○ JEWELLERY
WAISTCOATS ○ LEATHER ○ CHILDREN'S CLOTHES
EMBROIDERED PICTURES ○ FLY TYING ○ KNITWEAR
WOODEN TOYS ○ DIPS ○ LIQUEURS ○ TOYS ○ FABRIC CRAFTS
RESIN FIGURES ○ COSMETICS ○ DRIED FLOWERS ○ CHEESES
STAINED GLASS ○ CROCHET ○ FURNITURE ○ DOUGH CRAFT
JIGSAWS ○ COIN JEWELLERY ○ WOOD CARVING
3-D PICTURES ○ HANDMADE SOAP and MUCH, MUCH MORE!!

A Major Professional
Craft Fair

PUBLIC ADMISSION TO THE
HUGE CRAFT MARQUEES

Something for all the Family

**ADULTS £3.50 OAP £2.50
ACCOMPANIED CHILDREN £1.00**

Refreshments

*SANDRINGHAM HOUSE AND GARDENS WILL BE OPEN
TO THE PUBLIC AT A SEPARATE CHARGE*

CRAFTS OPEN TO THE PUBLIC 10.00 am. to 5.30 pm.

**Friday, Saturday & Sunday
April 14th, 15th & 16th**

Rainbow Fair
Telephone: 01529 414793

© 2000 Original artwork & design copyright Rainbow Fair

★ A SPLENDID EVENT WITH OVER 200 EXHIBITORS ★

**Rainbow Fair, Navigation Wharfe, Carre Street, Sleaford, Lincolnshire NG34 7TW
Telephone: (01529) 414793 Fax: (01529) 414985**

TALISKER.
A PLACE WHERE THE THUNDER ROLLS OVER YOUR TONGUE.

Of all the islands that defend Scotland's west coast from the Atlantic, Skye is the most dramatic. How fitting then that this is the home of the fiery Talisker. Standing on Skye's western shore, the distillery lies in the shadow of The Cuillins. Jagged mountains that rise out of the sea to skewer the clouds for a thunderous retort. In the shadow of these peaks, next to a fearsome sea, Talisker takes its first breath and draws it all in. Skye's explosive fervour captured forever in its only single malt. That Talisker is not a whisky for the faint-hearted is beyond dispute. Indeed even when one seasoned whisky taster once went as far as calling it "The lava of The Cuillins", no one disagreed.

ORDER FORM

Call our 24hr credit card hotline UK FREEPHONE 0800 269 397

Simply indicate which title(s) you require by putting the quantity in the boxes provided. Choose your preferred method of payment and mail to Johansens, FREEPOST (CB 264), 43 Millharbour, London E14 9BR, England (no stamp needed). Your FREE gifts will automatically be dispatched with your order. Fax orders welcome on 0171 537 3594

CHOOSE FROM 7 SPECIAL GUIDE COLLECTIONS – SAVE UP TO £56

TITLE	Normal Price	PRICE	SAVE	QTY	TOTAL
OFFER ONE – The Basic Collection					
3 Johansens Guides A+B+C	£42.85	£36.00	£6.85		
OFFER TWO – The extended Collection					
4 Johansens Guides A+B+C+G	£58.80	£46.00	£12.80		
OFFER THREE – The Full Selection					
5 Johansens Guides A+B+C+G+K PLUS Southern Africa Guide **FREE**	£71.75	£56.00	£15.75		
OFFER FOUR - The Executive Collection					
Business Meeting Venues Guide & CD-ROM M+R	£40.00	£30.00	£10.00		
OFFER FIVE - The Holiday Pack					
3 Johansens Guides D+E+F	£18.93	£9.99	£8.94		
OFFER SIX - The Digital Collection					
3 Johansens CD-ROMs N+O+P PLUS Southern Africa CD-ROM Q **FREE**	£69.85	£59.85	£10.00		
OFFER SEVEN - The Chairman's Collection					
Business Meeting Venues Guide & CD-ROMs M+R **PLUS** 5 Johansens Boxed Guides A+B+C+G+K, **PLUS** D+E+F **PLUS** 3 CD-ROMs N+O+P **FREE** Southern Africa Guide L + CD ROM Q + Mystery Gift	£205.53	£149.00	£56.53		
Privilege Card	£20.00	FREE	£20.00		
1 Presentation box for offers 1, 2 and 3		£5.00			
TOTAL 1					

JOHANSENS PRINTED GUIDES 2000

CODE	TITLE	PRICE	QTY	TOTAL
A	Recommended Hotels – Great Britain & Ireland 2000	£19.95		
B	Recommended Country Houses & Small Hotels – Great Britain & Ireland 2000	£11.95		
C	Recommended Traditional Inns, Hotels & Restaurants – Great Britain 2000	£10.95		
NEW D	Recommended Holiday Cottages – Great Britain & Ireland 2000	£4.99		
E	Historic Houses, Castles & Gardens 2000	£4.99		
F	Museums & Galleries 2000	£8.95		
G	Recommended Hotels – Europe & The Mediterranean 2000	£15.95		
NEW H	Recommended Hotels – Europe & The Mediterranean 2000 (French Language)	£15.95		
NEW J	Recommended Hotels – Europe & The Mediterranean 2000 (German Language)	£15.95		
K	Recommended Hotels & Inns – North America, Bermuda & The Caribbean 2000	£12.95		
NEW L	Recommended Hotels & Game Lodges – Southern Africa, Mauritius & The Seychelles 2000	£9.95		
M	Recommended Business Meeting Venues 2000	£20.00		

JOHANSENS CD ROMs DIGITAL COLLECTION 2000

CODE	TITLE	PRICE	QTY	TOTAL
N	The Guide 2000 – Great Britain & Ireland	£29.95		
O	The Guide 2000 – Europe & The Mediterranean (English, French, German Language)	£22.95		
P	The Guide 2000 – North America, Bermuda & The Caribbean	£16.95		
NEW Q	The Guide 2000 – Southern Africa, Mauritius & The Seychelles	£16.95		
R	Business Meeting Venues 2000	£20.00		
S	Privilege Card 2000 (Free with your order. Additional Cards £20 each)	£20.00		

Postage & Packing (UK) £4.50 or £2.50 for orders of 1 book and CD-ROMs

Outside UK add £5 or £3 for orders of 1 book and CD-ROMs

TOTAL 2

GRAND TOTAL 1+2+P&P

Name	(Mr/Mrs/Miss)						
Address							
			Postcode				
Card No			Exp Date				
Signature							

I have chosen my Johansens Guides/CD-ROMs and

☐ **I enclose a cheque for £** _____ **payable to Johansens**

☐ **I enclose my order on company letterheading, please invoice (UK only)**

☐ **Please debit my credit/charge card account (please tick).**

☐ **MasterCard** ☐ **Diners** ☐ **Amex**

☐ **Visa** ☐ **Switch** (Issue Number) _____

A25

ORDER FORM

Call our 24hr credit card hotline UK FREEPHONE 0800 269 397

Simply indicate which title(s) you require by putting the quantity in the boxes provided. Choose your preferred method of payment and mail to Johansens, FREEPOST (CB 264), 43 Millharbour, London E14 9BR, England (no stamp needed). Your FREE gifts will automatically be dispatched with your order. Fax orders welcome on 0171 537 3594

CHOOSE FROM 7 SPECIAL GUIDE COLLECTIONS – SAVE UP TO £56

TITLE	Normal Price	PRICE	SAVE	QTY	TOTAL
OFFER ONE – The Basic Collection					
3 Johansens Guides A+B+C	£42.85	£36.00	£6.85		
OFFER TWO – The extended Collection					
4 Johansens Guides A+B+C+G	£58.80	£46.00	£12.80		
OFFER THREE – The Full Selection					
5 Johansens Guides A+B+C+G+K PLUS Southern Africa Guide FREE	£71.75	£56.00	£15.75		
OFFER FOUR - The Executive Collection					
Business Meeting Venues Guide & CD-ROM M+R	£40.00	£30.00	£10.00		
OFFER FIVE - The Holiday Pack					
3 Johansens Guides D+E+F	£18.93	£9.99	£8.94		
OFFER SIX - The Digital Collection					
3 Johansens CD-ROMs N+O+P PLUS Southern Africa CD-ROM Q FREE	£69.85	£59.85	£10.00		
OFFER SEVEN - The Chairman's Collection					
Business Meeting Venues Guide & CD-ROMs M+R **PLUS** 5 Johansens Boxed Guides A+B+C+G+K, **PLUS** D+E+F **PLUS** 3 CD-ROMs N+O+P **FREE** Southern Africa Guide L + CD ROM Q + Mystery Gift	£205.53	£149.00	£56.53		
Privilege Card	£20.00	FREE	£20.00		
1 Presentation box for offers 1, 2 and 3		£5.00			
			TOTAL 1		

JOHANSENS PRINTED GUIDES 2000

CODE	TITLE	PRICE	QTY	TOTAL
A	Recommended Hotels – Great Britain & Ireland 2000	£19.95		
B	Recommended Country Houses & Small Hotels – Great Britain & Ireland 2000	£11.95		
C	Recommended Traditional Inns, Hotels & Restaurants – Great Britain 2000	£10.95		
NEW D	Recommended Holiday Cottages – Great Britain & Ireland 2000	£4.99		
E	Historic Houses, Castles & Gardens 2000	£4.99		
F	Museums & Galleries 2000	£8.95		
G	Recommended Hotels – Europe & The Mediterranean 2000	£15.95		
NEW H	Recommended Hotels – Europe & The Mediterranean 2000 (French Language)	£15.95		
NEW J	Recommended Hotels – Europe & The Mediterranean 2000 (German Language)	£15.95		
K	Recommended Hotels & Inns – North America, Bermuda & The Caribbean 2000	£12.95		
NEW L	Recommended Hotels & Game Lodges – Southern Africa, Mauritius & The Seychelles 2000	£9.95		
M	Recommended Business Meeting Venues 2000	£20.00		

JOHANSENS CD ROMs DIGITAL COLLECTION 2000

CODE	TITLE	PRICE	QTY	TOTAL
N	The Guide 2000 – Great Britain & Ireland	£29.95		
O	The Guide 2000 – Europe & The Mediterranean (English, French, German Language)	£22.95		
P	The Guide 2000 – North America, Bermuda & The Caribbean	£16.95		
NEW Q	The Guide 2000 – Southern Africa, Mauritius & The Seychelles	£16.95		
R	Business Meeting Venues 2000	£20.00		
S	Privilege Card 2000 (Free with your order. Additional Cards £20 each)	£20.00		

Postage & Packing (UK) £4.50 or £2.50 for orders of 1 book and CD-ROMs

Outside UK add £5 or £3 for orders of 1 book and CD-ROMs

TOTAL 2

GRAND TOTAL 1+2+P&P

Name (Mr/Mrs/Miss)

Address

Postcode

Card No

Exp Date

Signature

I have chosen my Johansens Guides/CD-ROMs and

☐ I enclose a cheque for £ _____ payable to Johansens

☐ I enclose my order on company letterheading, please invoice (UK only)

☐ Please debit my credit/charge card account (please tick).

☐ MasterCard ☐ Diners ☐ Amex

☐ Visa ☐ Switch (Issue Number) _____

A25

As recommended

Dorlux Beds, Keighley Road, Ovenden, Halifax HX2 8DD
Telephone (+44) 1422 254555 Fax: (+44) 1422 345025
email: beds@dorlux.co.uk www.dorlux.co.uk

DREAM on

HANDCRAFTED BEDS FOR OVER 80 YEAR

Index to Properties

Indexes

Indexes

Indexes

Key to Map Pages

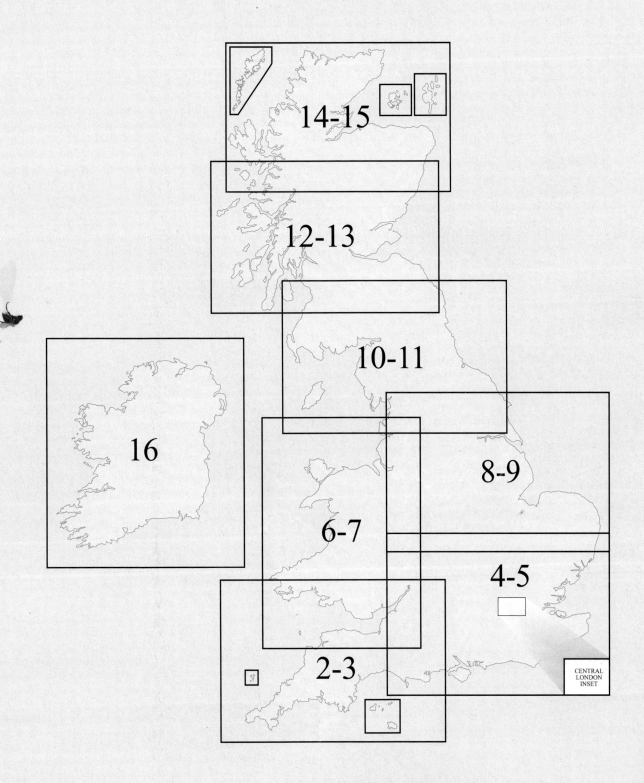

14-15

12-13

10-11

16

8-9

6-7

4-5

2-3

CENTRAL
LONDON
INSET

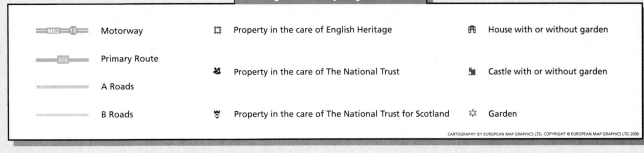

Key to Map Symbols

══M62══12══ Motorway	⌂ Property in the care of English Heritage	🏠 House with or without garden
═══A55═══ Primary Route		
──────── A Roads	♣ Property in the care of The National Trust	🏰 Castle with or without garden
──────── B Roads	♣ Property in the care of The National Trust for Scotland	✾ Garden

CARTOGRAPHY BY EUROPEAN MAP GRAPHICS LTD, COPYRIGHT © EUROPEAN MAP GRAPHICS LTD 2000

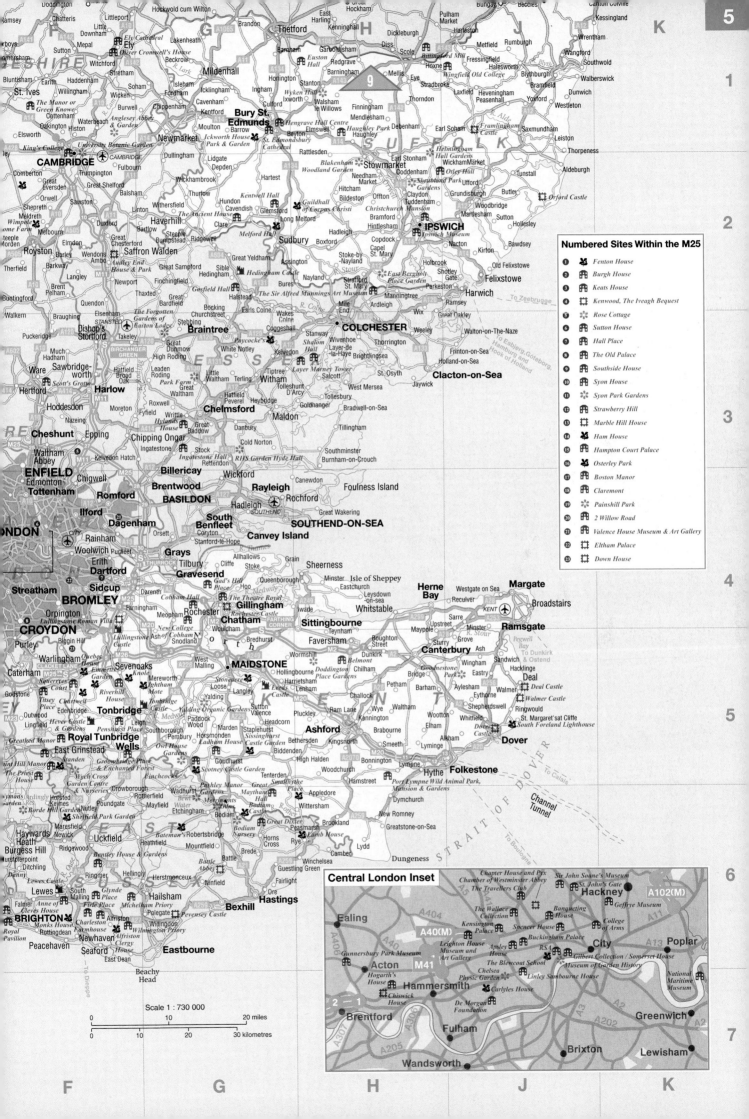

5

Numbered Sites Within the M25

1. Fenton House
2. Burgh House
3. Keats House
4. Kenwood, The Iveagh Bequest
5. Rose Cottage
6. Sutton House
7. Hall Place
8. The Old Palace
9. Southside House
10. Syon House
11. Syon Park Gardens
12. Strawberry Hill
13. Marble Hill House
14. Ham House
15. Hampton Court Palace
16. Osterley Park
17. Boston Manor
18. Claremont
19. Painshill Park
20. 2 Willow Road
21. Valence House Museum & Art Gallery
22. Eltham Palace
23. Down House

Scale 1 : 730 000

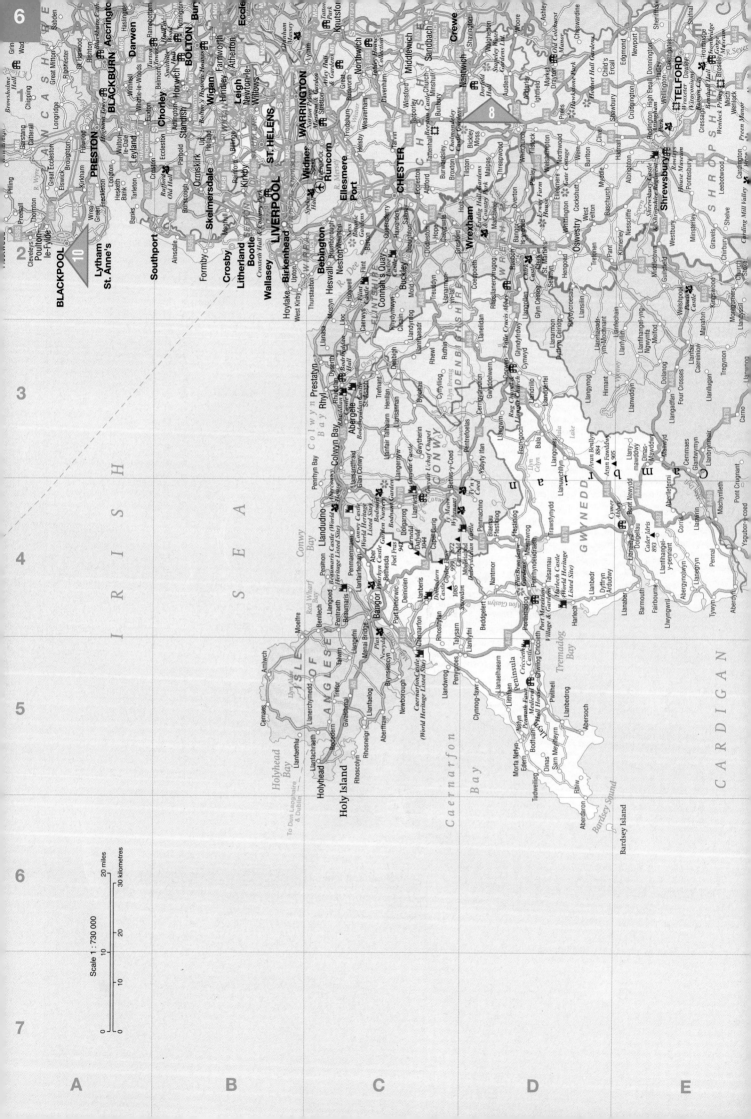

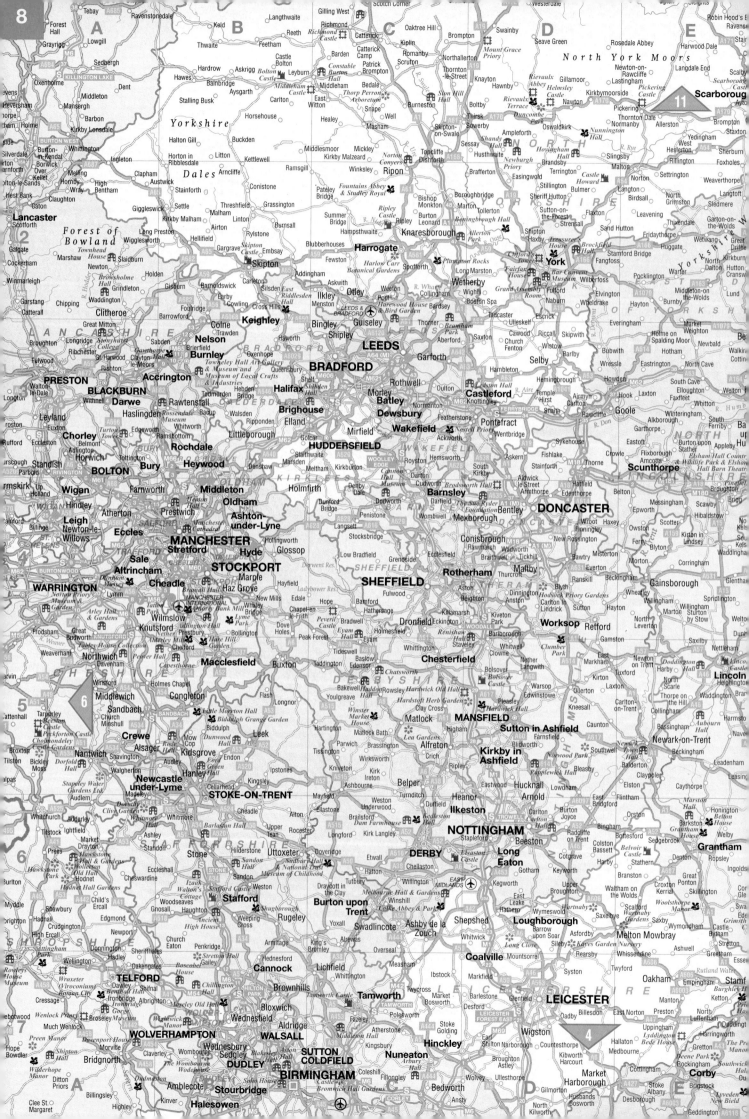

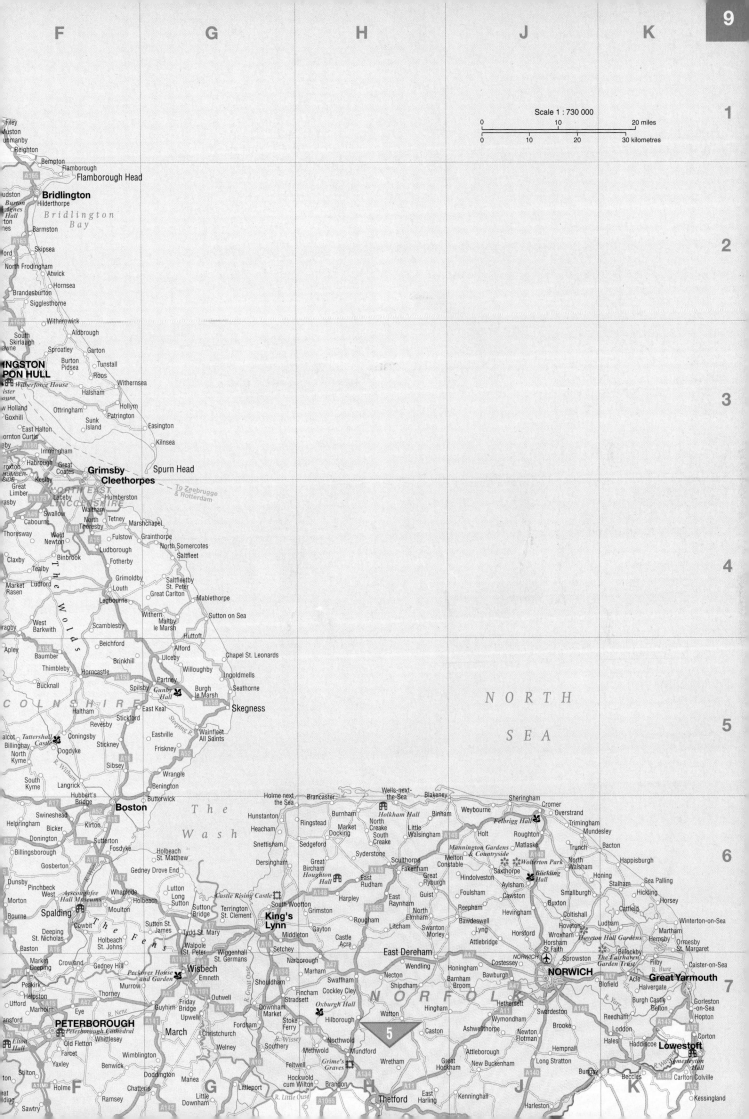

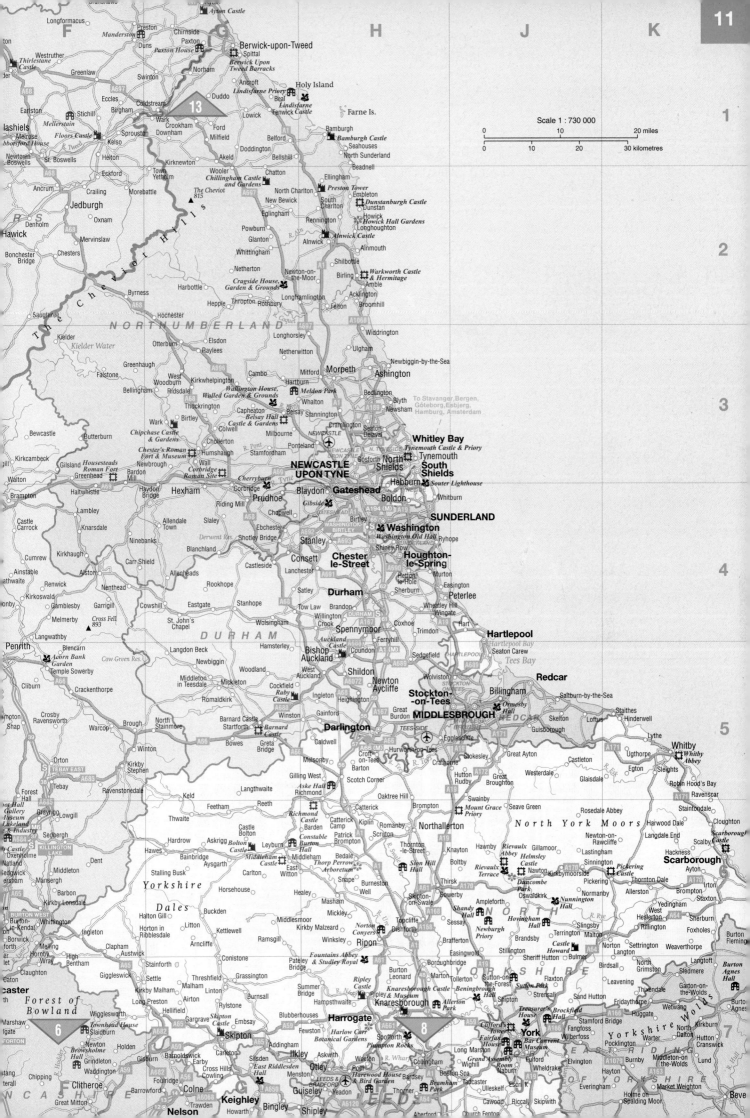

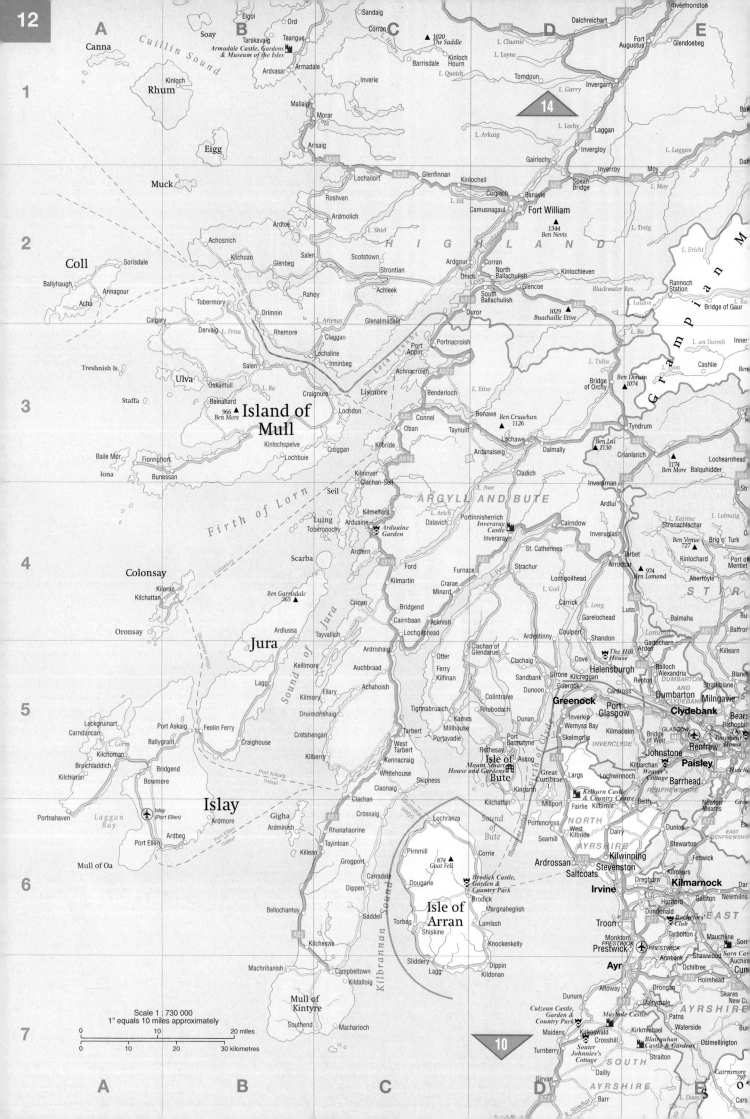

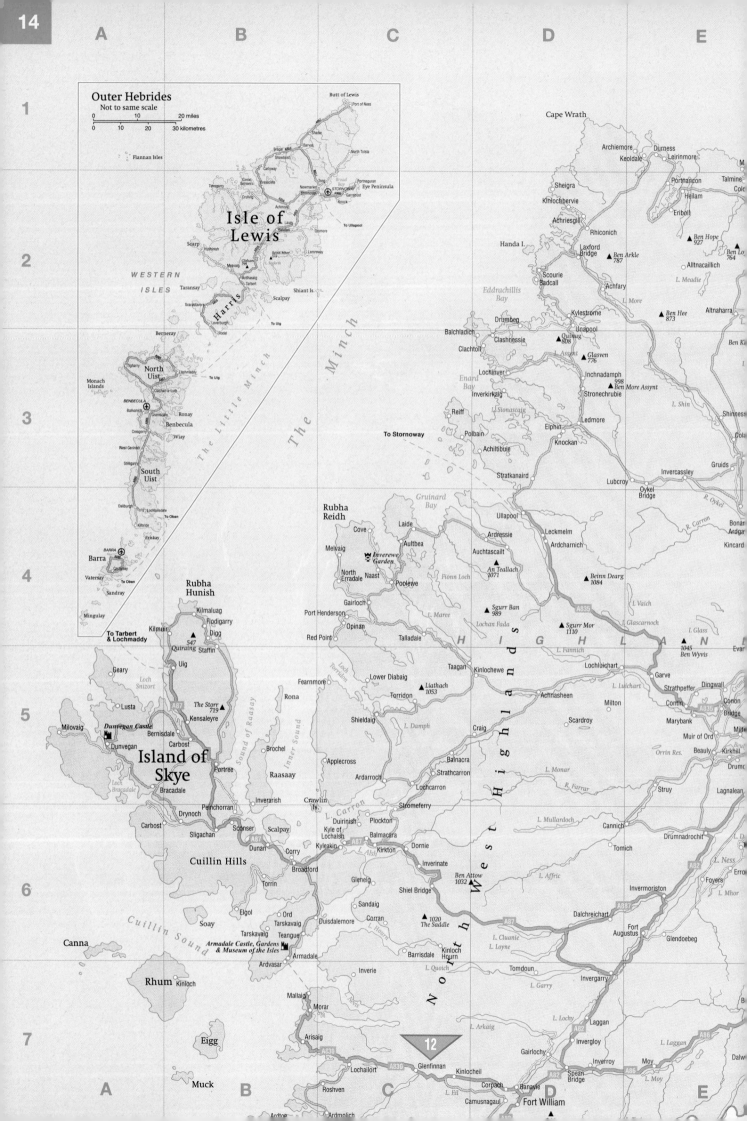

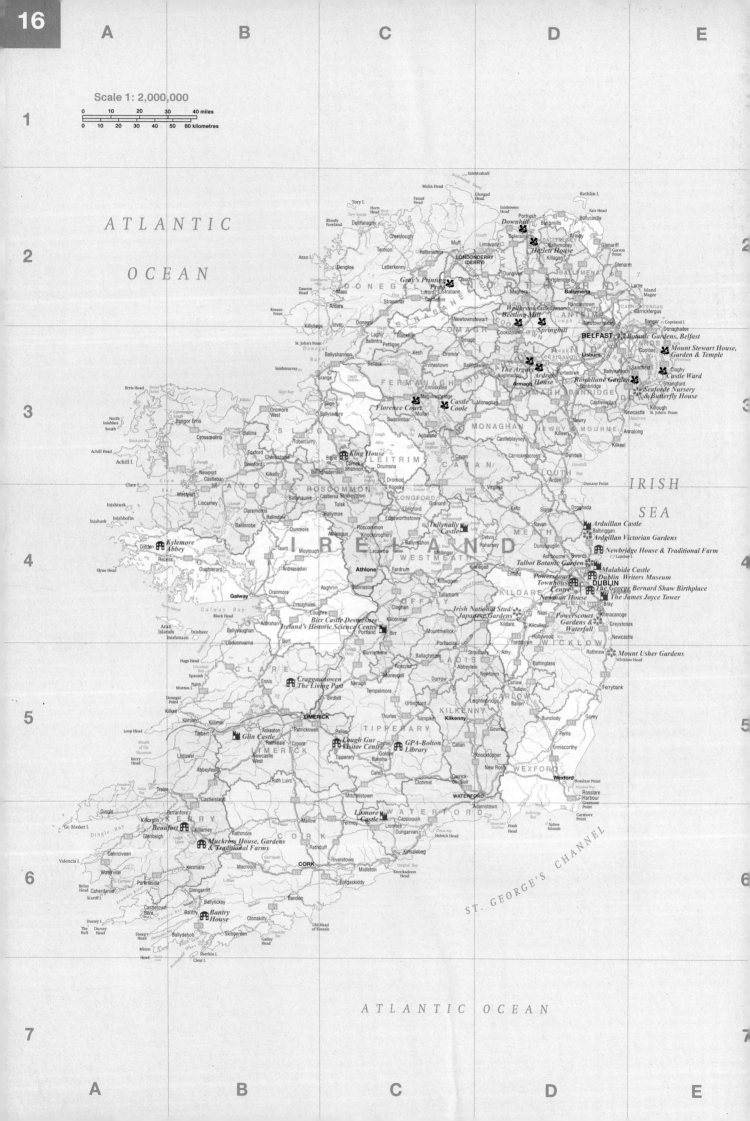